OCA Oracle Database 11*g*: Database Administration I: A Real-World Certification Guide

Learn how to become an Oracle-certified Database Administrator

Steve Ries

[PACKT] PUBLISHING enterprise
professional expertise distilled

BIRMINGHAM - MUMBAI

OCA Oracle Database 11*g*: Database Administration I: A Real-World Certification Guide

First published: February 2013

Production Reference: 1150213

Published by Packt Publishing Ltd.
Livery Place
35 Livery Street
Birmingham B3 2PB, UK.

ISBN 978-1-84968-730-0

`www.packtpub.com`

Cover Image by Artie Ng (`artherng@yahoo.com.au`)

Credits

Author
Steve Ries

Reviewer
Saurabh K. Gupta

Acquisition Editor
Erol Staveley

Lead Technical Editor
Shreerang Deshpande

Technical Editors
Vrinda Amberkar
Dennis John
Dominic Pereira

Copy Editors
Brandt D'Mello
Insiya Morbiwala
Alfida Paiva
Laxmi Subramanian
Ruta Waghmare

Project Coordinator
Arshad Sopariwala

Proofreaders
Lawrence Herman
Clyde Jenkins
Kevin McGowan

Indexer
Rekha Nair

Graphics
Aditi Gajjar
Valentina D'silva

Production Coordinators
Manu Joseph
Shantanu Zagade

Cover Work
Manu Joseph

Foreword

There's never been a time in the Information Technology industry where professional certifications have been more important. Because of the specialized nature of technological careers today, certifications are considered by some to be nearly as important as technological degrees. This focus on certifications has led to the rise of an entire industry around books that assist readers in preparing for various certification tests. In the author's opinion, many, if not most, of these books make a lot of assumptions as to the prior knowledge of the reader and serve more as reference material than a cohesive learning experience.

In my role as an instructor of Oracle technologies, I have noticed a shift in the types of people seeking to learn Oracle. In the past several years, more and more students with little or no experience have been seeking to "break in" to an Oracle career path. Whether they come from backgrounds in business analysis, project management, or other non-database technical areas, these students need to be able to learn Oracle from the ground up. When instructing these types of students, I cannot make assumptions as to the knowledge they bring with them. We must start at the beginning and work our way to "certification level" knowledge. To accomplish this goal in class, the accompanying textbook must be designed in the same way.

Similarly, many certification books today serve only as "exam cram" books that neglect application to real-world scenarios. Readers of these types of books may find themselves with a certification, yet possess no way to apply the knowledge in their first job.

My goal in writing this book has been to address both of these problems. This book attempts to begin at the foundation and continue with the knowledge of the subject required for the certification exam, using real-world examples and tips along the way. This book is heavily example oriented and is intended to serve more as a step-by-step instruction than simply reference material. In essence, I attempt to bring the classroom experience to the reader, using examples, real-world tips, and end-of-the-chapter reviews. This book has been written to be read cover to cover, with the reader completing the examples and questions as they go. Using this process, it is my hope that readers can truly "begin at the beginning", regardless of previous experience, and learn Oracle database administration in a relevant way that will serve them in their pursuit of an Oracle certification as well as an Oracle career path.

About the Author

Steve Ries has been an Oracle DBA for 16 years, specializing in all aspects of database administration, including security, performance tuning and backup and recovery. He is a specialist in Oracle Real Application Clusters (RAC) and has administered Oracle clustered environments in every version of Oracle since the creation of Oracle Parallel Server. Steve is the author of *OCA Oracle Database 11g: SQL Fundamentals I: A Real-World Certification Guide, Packt Publishing*. He holds five Oracle certifications as well as a Security+ certification. He currently consults for the Dept. of Defense, US Marine Corps, and holds a high-level security clearance. Additionally, Steve has been an adjunct instructor of Oracle technologies at Johnson County Community College for 9 years, where he teaches classes that prepare students for the Oracle certification exams. He was also a speaker at the 2011 and 2012 Oracle Open World conferences. Steve is a two-time, award-winning technical paper writer and the creator of the `alt.oracle` blog.

I would like to thank my wife Dee and daughter Faith for their love, personal support, and patience. I would also like to thank Bear McCreary, whose music inspired me as I wrote. A special thanks goes to Adam vonNieda for getting me started in the world of Oracle.

About the Reviewer

Saurabh K. Gupta works as Principal Technologist at Oracle. He is the author of *Oracle Advanced PL/SQL Developer Professional Guide, Packt Publishing*.

He has been synchronizing his on-job and off-job interests with Oracle databases for the last 6 years. His areas of expertise are database architecture, PL/SQL development, Performance Tuning, and High Availability.

He has the OCP 11*g* Advanced PL/SQL certification under his belt. He has been an active Oracle blogger and OTN forum member. He has published more than 70 articles on online forums and journals. His work can be seen in the RMOUG journal, PSOUG, dbanotes, Exforsys, and Club Oracle. He shares his technical experience through his blog at `www.sbhoracle.wordpress.com`. He is a member of the All India Oracle Users Group (AIOUG) and loves to attend technical meets and conferences.

Reach out to him through his blog to get in touch with him.

Table of Contents

Preface

The *Oracle 11g: Database Administration I* exam is the final step to achieving the Oracle Certified Associate (OCA) certification for Oracle Database 11*g*. To pass the exam, an extensive knowledge of Oracle Database administration topics is required.

This book gives you the essential real-world skills to master relational database administration with Oracle 11*g* and prepares you to become an Oracle Certified Associate. Beginners are introduced to concepts in a logical manner while practitioners can use it as a reference to jump to relevant concepts directly.

In the first section of the book, we cover the essential topics of the Oracle 11*g* architecture, including installation and configuration of both the Oracle 11*g* software and database as well as an in-depth examination of the instance and storage architectures of the Oracle database. In the second section, we use this information to explore the types of administrative tasks that a real-world DBA encounters every day, including instance management, security, concurrence, networking, and performance management. In our final section, we examine the very important topic of database recoverability, including backup concepts, hands-on backups, and recoveries.

This book prepares you to master the fundamentals of database administration using an example-driven method that is easy to understand.

This definitive certification guide provides a disciplined approach for successfully clearing the *1Z0-052 Oracle Database 11g Administration I* exam, which is the second and final test needed to attain the OCA on Oracle Database 11*g* certification. This exam is also the second requirement for the Oracle Certified Professional (OCP) certification.

Each chapter contains ample practice questions at the end. A full-blown mock test is included for practice so you can test your knowledge and get a feel of the actual exam.

What this book covers

Chapter 1, Introducing the Oracle Relational Database System, introduces the concept of the relational database management system as well as explores the Oracle product family.

Chapter 2, Installing the Oracle Database Software, takes a hands-on, step-by-step approach to installing the heart of the Oracle database—the database software.

Chapter 3, Creating the Oracle Database, examines the process of creating a database in Oracle using the Database Configuration Assistant tool, as well as examines the scripted approach to database creation.

Chapter 4, Examining the Oracle Architecture, gives us a deeper look at Oracle "under the hood", including a thorough examination of how Oracle uses CPU and memory to perform database operations.

Chapter 5, Managing Oracle Storage Structures, examines the ways in which Oracle stores its data on disk, including a look at tablespaces and datafiles.

Chapter 6, Managing the Oracle Instance, introduces a number of subjects at the core of Oracle instance management, including database parameters, the data dictionary, and database startup and shutdown procedures.

Chapter 7, Managing Security, covers one of the most important and relevant topics in database administration—database security. We examine the important and foundational topics of Oracle security, including the management of object and system-level privileges.

Chapter 8, Managing Concurrency, examines the process by which Oracle manages the life cycle of a transaction and the architectural structures that support this process.

Chapter 9, Configuring an Oracle Network, examines the fundamental ways in which Oracle operates over a network, including the types of name resolution and the differences between dedicated-server and shared-server operations.

Chapter 10, Managing Database Performance, takes us through one of the most demanding tasks of an Oracle DBA—performance tuning. We examine the basic tools available to the DBA for detecting and resolving performance issues.

Chapter 11, Understanding Backup and Recovery Concepts, is the first of a three-chapter look at one of the most fundamentally important concepts in database administration—backup and recovery. This chapter explores the ways in which the Oracle architecture provides options for complete and incomplete recovery.

Chapter 12, Performing Database Backups, explores the process of backing up Oracle databases using a hands-on approach. It shows us how to perform several types of backups, including user-managed, RMAN-managed, full, incremental, offline, and hot backups.

Chapter 13, Performing Database Recovery, takes what we learned in the previous chapter and uses it to perform a number of different types of database recoveries, including recoveries from cold and hot backups. We also examine the new feature of Oracle 11*g*, the Data Recovery Advisor.

Chapter 14, Migrating Data, explores the numerous methods in Oracle that we can use to migrate data between databases, including SQL*Loader and Data Pump.

Appendix, Preparing for the Certification Exam, examines some useful tips and techniques for preparing for the 1ZO-052 exam.

Online Chapter 1, Managing Oracle Tables, examines types and structures of database tables, including datatypes and partitioned tables, as well as database constraints.

Online Chapter 2, Managing Other Database Objects, examines several other common database objects, including indexes, index-organized tables, views, sequences, and synonyms.

What you need for this book

This book is heavily example oriented. As such, it will be beneficial for the reader to download and install the Oracle database software as outlined in *Chapter 2, Installing the Oracle Database Software*, and create the database as outlined in *Chapter 3, Creating the Oracle Database*. An example set of database tables is available on the Packt support website; you can use them by downloading and running the example code. A working knowledge of the SQL language is also required. The subject of SQL is covered in the first book in this series—*OCA Oracle Database 11g: SQL Fundamentals I: A Real-World Certification Guide (1ZO-051), Packt Publishing*.

Who this book is for

This book is for anyone who requires the essential skills to pass the Oracle Database 11*g* Database Administration I exam and use those skills in daily life as an Oracle database administrator.

Conventions

In this book, you will find a number of styles of text that distinguish between different kinds of information. Here are some examples of these styles, and an explanation of their meaning.

Code words in text are shown as follows: "This file is generally found within the `stage` directory in your installation media."

A block of code is set as follows:

```
db_create_file_dest = E:\APP\ORACLE\ORADATA\ORCL
db_create_online_log_dest_1 = E:\APP\ORACLE\ORADATA\ORCL\REDOLOG1
db_create_online_log_dest_2 = F:\APP\ORACLE\ORADATA\ORCL\REDOLOG2
db_recovery_file_dest = G:\APP\ORACLE\ORADATA\ORCL\RECOVERY
```

Any command-line input or output is written as follows:

```
E:\app\oracle\product\11.2.0\db_home1\bin\oradim.exe -edit -sid ORCL -
startmode auto -srvcstart system
```

New terms and **important words** are shown in bold. Words that you see on the screen, in menus or dialog boxes for example, appear in the text like this: "The **Connection Mode** tab refers to the type of paradigm used to establish database connections, either dedicated server or shared server."

> Warnings or important notes appear in a box like this.

> Tips and tricks appear like this.

Reader feedback

Feedback from our readers is always welcome. Let us know what you think about this book—what you liked or may have disliked. Reader feedback is important for us to develop titles that you really get the most out of.

To send us general feedback, simply send an e-mail to `feedback@packtpub.com`, and mention the book title via the subject of your message.

If there is a topic that you have expertise in and you are interested in either writing or contributing to a book, see our author guide on `www.packtpub.com/authors`.

Customer support

Now that you are the proud owner of a Packt book, we have a number of things to help you to get the most from your purchase.

Downloading the example code

You can download the example code files for all Packt books you have purchased from your account at `http://www.packtpub.com`. If you purchased this book elsewhere, you can visit `http://www.packtpub.com/support` and register to have the files e-mailed directly to you.

Errata

Although we have taken every care to ensure the accuracy of our content, mistakes do happen. If you find a mistake in one of our books—maybe a mistake in the text or the code—we would be grateful if you would report this to us. By doing so, you can save other readers from frustration and help us improve subsequent versions of this book. If you find any errata, please report them by visiting `http://www.packtpub.com/submit-errata`, selecting your book, clicking on the **errata submission form** link, and entering the details of your errata. Once your errata are verified, your submission will be accepted and the errata will be uploaded on our website, or added to any list of existing errata, under the Errata section of that title. Any existing errata can be viewed by selecting your title from `http://www.packtpub.com/support`.

Piracy

Piracy of copyright material on the Internet is an ongoing problem across all media. At Packt, we take the protection of our copyright and licenses very seriously. If you come across any illegal copies of our works, in any form, on the Internet, please provide us with the location address or website name immediately so that we can pursue a remedy.

Please contact us at `copyright@packtpub.com` with a link to the suspected pirated material.

We appreciate your help in protecting our authors, and our ability to bring you valuable content.

Questions

You can contact us at `questions@packtpub.com` if you are having a problem with any aspect of the book, and we will do our best to address it.

1

Introducing the Oracle Relational Database System

We truly live in the Information age. Think for a moment about all the data that exists about you in computers around the world:

- Your name
- Your birth date and information
- Your hobbies
- Purchases you've made
- The identities of your friends
- Your place of employment

Whether it's a hospital's record system, your employer's payroll system, the invoicing records of an online store, or your financial accounts, the examples are endless. Next, multiply that amount of data by the number of people in the world. The result is a truly staggering amount of information. How is it possible that all this data can be organized and retrieved? How is it possible that you can search an online bookstore and find exactly the book you're looking for within seconds? How is all of this sensitive data protected and kept secure? In today's data-centric world, by and large, it is the **Relational Database Management System** (**RDBMS**) that makes this possible. The RDBMS is the cornerstone of the information technology world. While user interfaces, web servers, and application servers are all important parts of the way we save and obtain information, it is the RDBMS that serves as the massive storehouse for the data itself. Additionally, this massive amount of data is growing exponentially. New systems and strategies are constantly being devised in order to store and retrieve this information in a way that is useful to companies. In this book, we examine every aspect of the Oracle RDBMS, the most widely-used commercial database in the world. We will look at its architecture, the way it stores data, its security configuration, and its high degree of configurability.

This book takes a from-the-ground-up approach to Oracle database administration. The first chapter will cover topics that are not specifically covered on *exam 1Z0-052, Oracle Database 11g: Administration I*. Rather, it serves as a foundational knowledge for readers who are new to Oracle and a refresher for those already familiar with it. However, even experienced DBAs will likely discover new information in these chapters. Because of the amount of information we cover, we place a strong emphasis on learning by example. In addition, we will focus on comprehending the information needed for the Oracle Certification with special attention on how the information pertains to the life of a real-world Oracle DBA. At the end of each chapter, we'll highlight the exact certification topics that come directly from the Oracle Certification syllabus.

In this chapter we shall:

- Understand the purpose of relational database management systems
- Outline the Oracle family of products
- Interpret Oracle naming and versioning
- Examine the role of the Database Administrator (DBA)
- Identify the common tools for DBAs

Understanding the RDBMS

To better prepare ourselves to understand the Oracle database, we should first familiarize ourselves with the history of databases and how the RDBMS became such an important part of today's IT infrastructure. We'll follow this with a look at the Oracle product family.

The importance of databases

Imagine, for a moment, that you have telephone books for the twenty largest cities in the United States, and I ask you to find all the phone numbers for all individuals named "Rick Clark" in the greater Chicago area. In order to satisfy the request, you simply do the following:

1. Open the Chicago phone book.
2. Scan to the "C" section of names.
3. Find all individuals that match with "Clark" and"Rick".
4. Report back their phone numbers.

Now imagine that I take each phone book, tear out all of the pages and throw them into the air. I then proceed to shuffle the thousands of pages on the ground into a completely disorganized mess. Now I repeat the same request to find all the phone numbers for individuals named "Rick Clark" in the greater Chicago area. How do you think you would do it? It would be nearly impossible. The data is all there, but is completely disorganized. Finding the individuals named "Rick Clark" of Chicago would involve individually examining each page to see if it satisfied the request—a very frustrating task, to say the least.

This example underscores the importance of an RDBMS. Today's RDBMS is the system that enables the storage, modification, and retrieval of massive amounts of data.

Flat file databases

When the devices that we know as computers first came into existence, they were primarily used for one thing—computation. Computers became useful entities because they were able to do numeric computation on an unprecedented scale. For example, one of the first computers, ENIAC, was designed (although not used) for the US Army to calculate artillery trajectories, a task made simpler through the use of complex sequences of mathematical calculations. As such, originally, computers were primarily a tool for mathematical and scientific research. Eventually, the use of computers began to penetrate the business market, where the company's data itself became as important as computational speed. As the importance of this data grew, the need for data storage and management grew as well, and the concept of a database was born.

The earliest databases were simple to envision. Most of them were simply large files that were similar in concept to a spreadsheet or a **comma-separated values** (**CSV**) file. Data were stored as fields. A portion of these databases might look something like the following:

```
Susan, Bates, 123 State St, Somewhere, VA
Fred, Hartman, 234 Banner Rd, Anywhere, CA
Bill, Franklin, 345 Downtown Rd, Somewhere, MO
Emily, Thompson, 456 Uptown Rd, Somewhere, NY
```

In this example, the first field is determined by reading from left to right until a delimiter, in this case a comma, is reached. This first field refers to the first name of the individual. The next field is determined by reading from the first delimiter to the next. That second field refers to the last name of the individual. It continues in this manner until we have five fields: first name, last name, street address, city, and state. Each individual line or **record** in the file refers to the information for a distinct individual. Because this data is stored in a file, it is often referred to as a flat file database. To retrieve a certain piece of information, programs could be written that would scan through the records for the requested information. In this way, large amounts of data could be stored and retrieved in an ordered, structured way.

Limitations of the flat file paradigm

The flat file database system served well for many years. However, as time passed and the demands of businesses to retain more data increased, the flat file paradigm began to show some flaws.

In our previous example, the amount of information in the flat file is quite limited. It contains only five fields representing five distinct pieces of information. If this flat file database contained the data for a real company, five distinct pieces of information would not even begin to suffice. A complete set of customer data might include addresses, phone numbers, order information, the date of the order, the delivery date of the order, and so on. In short, as the need to retain more data increases, the number of fields grows. As the number of fields grows, our flat file database gets wider and wider. We should also consider the amount of data being stored. Our first example had four distinct records, not a very realistic amount for storing customer data. The number of records could actually be in the thousands or even millions. Eventually, it is completely plausible that we could have a single flat file that is hundreds of fields wide and millions of records long. We could easily find that the speed with which our original data retrieval programs can retrieve the required data is decreasing at a rapid rate and is insufficient for our needs. It is clear that this flat file paradigm needs to be revised in order to meet the growing demands for our database.

A new paradigm

The world of databases changed in the early 1970s due in large part to the work done by Dr. Edgar "Ted" Codd. In his paper *A Relational Model of Data for Large Shared Data Banks*, Dr. Codd presented a new paradigm—the **relational paradigm**. The relational paradigm seeks to resolve the limitations of the flat file architecture by organizing our data in such a way that the data and its inter-relationships can be clearly identified. When we design a database, we begin by asking two questions: "What data do I have ?" and "How do the pieces of data relate to each other?" During this process, the data is identified and organized into entities. An **entity** is any person, place, or thing. An entity also has **attributes**, or characteristics that pertain to it.

These entities represent distinct pieces of information. We could have an Employee entity that represents information about employees, an Email entity that represents information about e-mail addresses, and so on. These entities, and any others we choose to add, make up our data model. We can also look a little closer at the attributes of a particular entity, as shown in the following diagram:

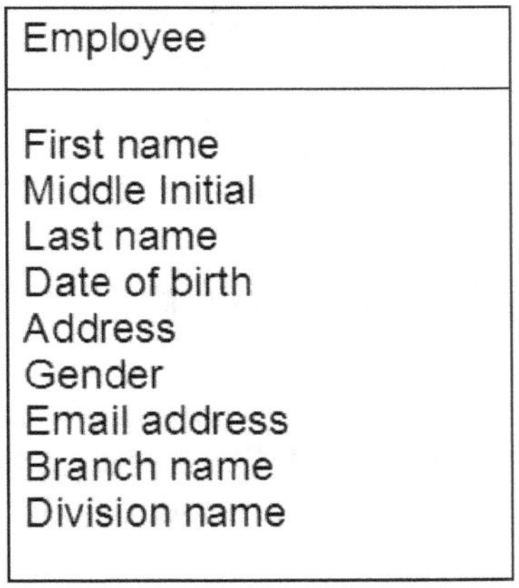
Employee
First name
Middle Initial
Last name
Date of birth
Address
Gender
Email address
Branch name
Division name

In our example, data such as **First name, Last name**, **Address**, and **Branch name** are the attributes of the **Employee** entity—they provide information about the employee. We can extend this idea to any other entities that represent a group of related information.

The true strength of the relational paradigm, however, is its ability to structure these entities in a way that forms relationships between them based on data that is common to both. Following is a simple diagram of this:

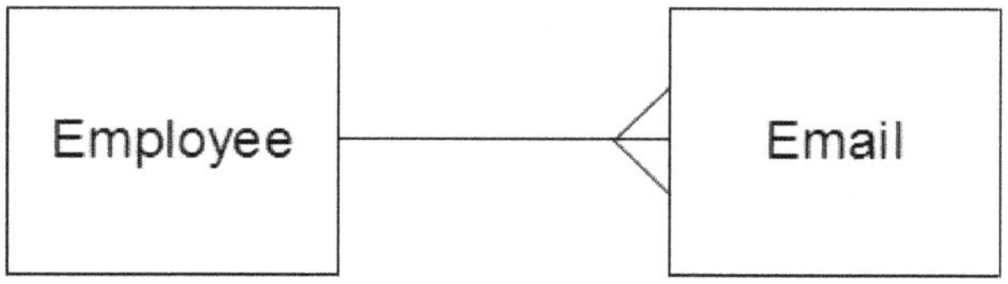
Employee
Email

Here, we have two entities, **Employee** and **Email**, that form a relationship. The **Employee** entity contains information about the various employees in `Companylink`. The **Email** entity contains the e-mail addresses of these employees. Since any given employee can have one or more e-mail addresses, we say that there is a one-to-many relationship between **Employee** and **Email**, designated by the **crowsfoot** symbol between them. This relationship is the heart of the relational model that allows us to separate data into different entities. In the RDBMS world, we call these entities **tables**, while their attributes are known as **columns**. We will look much more closely at tables and their characteristics in future chapters. An entire data model can be visually displayed using an **Entity Relationship Diagram** (**ERD**). An ERD makes it easier to view the inter-relationships between entities.

Introducing the Oracle product family

When someone says, "I work with Oracle" what does he or she mean? The name Oracle (not to be confused with ORACLE, an early computer built by the Oak Ridge National Laboratory) can be used to refer to several different aspects of Oracle Corporation and its products. Oracle is a company, a database, and a family of products.

Exploring the history of Oracle

Oracle Corporation as we know it, began in 1977 as a company called Software Development Laboratories (SDL), founded by Larry Ellison, Bob Miner, and Ed Oates. These men, inspired by the relational theory set forth by Dr. Ted Codd and the work done on an IBM project known as System R, set out to develop the relational idea into a commercial product. In 1979, the company, renamed Relational Software Inc. (RSI), sold the first version of their relational database software, called Oracle, to Wright-Patterson Air Force Base. Although it was the first version of the Oracle database, it was designated as Version 2 because Larry Ellison didn't believe that customers would buy a Version 1 product. In 1982, RSI was renamed Oracle Corporation to more closely align the company with its flagship database.

For many years, the Oracle database software was primarily available on mainframe and minicomputer systems, the primary computing platforms of that time. In 1983, in a move that would bode well for Oracle's future, Version 3 was rewritten in the C programming language, making it portable to many other platforms. It was ported to the PC architecture with Version 4. The modern history of Oracle Corporation can be traced to the release of Oracle Version 7 in 1992. Version 7 released many new enhancements, including new security and performance features. It is at this point that the Oracle database software began its rise to become the most widely used commercial RDBMS in the world.

Understanding the Oracle Database product

Since Oracle's inception, the **Oracle Database Server** has been and remains Oracle's flagship product. It has maintained its position as the world's most widely used database for many years and stands essentially unchallenged in the market today. The Oracle database is designed to be high performing, highly available, and highly secure. It can run on a variety of hardware and operating system platforms. One of the Oracle Database Server's strengths is its ability to run on a range of system types, from small departmental servers to massive symmetric multiprocessing servers to enormous highly available clustered systems. Many of the largest companies in the world run their database systems on Oracle software. Oracle currently holds a larger revenue share of the worldwide RDBMS market than its five closest competitors *combined*.

The primary language used to access Oracle databases is **Structured Query Language**, (**SQL**). SQL (pronounced either "S-Q-L" or "sequel") is the language most commonly used to address relational databases today, and likely will be for some time to come. The structure and syntax of SQL are governed by the American National Standards Institute (ANSI) and the International Organization for Standardization (ISO). It is these organizations that decide, albeit with input from other companies such as Oracle, what comprises the accepted standard for SQL. The current revision is SQL 2008. Although most commercial RDBMS products generally conform to the ANSI standard, they can differ in their implementations. This means that not every RDBMS uses the exact same SQL syntax. Oracle database also supports the use of two other programming languages within the database: PL/SQL and Java. PL/SQL is Oracle's proprietary third-generation programming language. It allows programmers to write structured code that integrates easily with SQL and stores that code as objects within the database. Java is an industry standard object-oriented language used in many types of applications today. Oracle also supports the storage of Java code within the database.

Understanding the different editions of Oracle Database

Apart from the different versions of Oracle available, Oracle also offers a number of different editions of their database software. These editions primarily differ by cost and availability of features. They are as follows:

- **Enterprise Edition (EE)**:The **EE** has no maximum as to the number of server central processing unit (CPU) sockets allowed, as well as no limits on memory accessibility or database size. It contains a number of database options not found in any of the other editions. It is available for Linux, Unix, and Windows, and supports both 32-bit and 64-bit versions.
- **Standard Edition (SE)**: The **SE** is only available for servers with four or fewer CPU sockets, although, like the EE, it has no limits on memory or database size. It includes many database options, though generally fewer than the EE. It is also available for Linux, Unix, and Windows, and supports both 32-bit and 64-bit versions. The SE and the SE1 can also be licensed on a per user basis, rather than the standard per CPU core basis.
- **Standard Edition (SE1):** The SE1, although similar in many respects to the SE, only supports servers with two or fewer CPU sockets. SE1 is available for Linux, Unix, and Windows. For smaller IT organizations that don't require large database servers, SE1 can provide a low-cost, high-performance database solution.
- **Express Edition (XE)**: The XE is a somewhat different product, an entry-level, free version of the Oracle database that lacks many of the capabilities of higher editions. It can only support one CPU and has a 1 GB limit for usable random access memory (RAM) and a maximum database size of 4 GB. It is only available for Linux and Windows, and lacks the 64-bit support. The XE is primarily targeted for developers working on applications that will eventually be deployed in larger environments.

Oracle also offers Oracle **Personal Edition** (**PE**), a low-cost, full-featured version of the Oracle database. PE is restricted to only one user per database, but provides access to all the features of the EE. Throughout the course of the book, we will use and focus on the Enterprise Edition so as to have access to the widest range of features.

> **The real-world DBA**
>
> Although the Enterprise Edition of Oracle is the most commonly found one in the IT world, a DBA shouldn't completely discount other editions. Often, significant cost savings can be achieved for companies that don't require "all the bells and whistles." Also, although uncommon, Oracle may separately negotiate the licensing of the EE at a lower cost, provided that the license being purchased is large enough. In these situations, companies may negotiate the purchase of the EE without a license for some of the included options. This can result in a DBA being required to administer an EE database that lacks the expected features. Always check your licensing agreement.

Understanding Oracle Database options

In addition to the various editions of the Oracle RDBMS, Oracle offers a number of **options**, depending on your chosen edition. These options function primarily as "add-ons," and are available at an additional cost. Some of the more commonly used options are listed here:

- **Advanced Security**: This is an option, sometimes known as ASO for Advanced Security Option, that provides encryption for both data at rest and data in transit over a network. It can also integrate with services such as Kerberos and RADIUS to provide strong authentication.
- **Active Data Guard**: This is an enhancement to the standard Data Guard feature that provides the ability to create a standby copy of the database that can also be used for read-only business reporting.
- **Advanced Compression**: This allows the use of internal compression routines within the database that facilitate reduction of disk use. It is especially useful in databases that store large amounts of binary data.
- **Total Recall**: This is an add-on that simplifies the long-term storage of large amounts of historical data. This can be important for environments that are subject to compliance and accounting audits, such as the health insurance and legal industries.
- **Partitioning**: This is a feature that allows a DBA to take a very large table, with perhaps many millions of rows, and convert it into a partitioned table. A partitioned table is one that actually exists as a number of smaller tables that can be seen as one. Under certain circumstances, this can dramatically improve the performance of queries, particularly in data warehousing environments.

- **Database Vault**: This is an option that extends Oracle's auditing capabilities and allows for extremely fine-grained access control over the database environment.
- **Real Application Clusters**: This is a popular enhancement, usually referred to as RAC, which allows database servers to be clustered together and appear as one large database. RAC can be an essential component for a high-availability database environment.

Examining the Oracle product family

Although the Oracle Database Server is the cornerstone of their product offerings, Oracle has offered additional types of software products for many years. Recently, however, Oracle has acquired an enormous number of software companies to add to their product family. In 2009, Oracle acquired Sun Microsystems, signaling an important shift in the direction of the company. With the acquisition, Oracle acquired Sun's well-respected line of hardware, as well as the Solaris operating system, the MySQL open source RDBMS, and the Java programming language. Although many in the industry believed that this move would signal the end of Sun's software product line, Oracle has continued to offer, promote, and support many of these products. As a result, Oracle now offers a staggering amount of hardware and software solutions that span every layer of enterprise IT, including hardware, operating systems, databases, application servers, and enterprise administration. An exhaustive discussion of the complete line of Oracle products is beyond the scope of this book; however, we mention some of the most important ones here.

Understanding Oracle's hardware solutions

With the purchase of Sun Microsystems, Oracle achieved its long standing desire to offer complete hardware solutions bundled with Oracle software. These hardware products come pre-installed with Oracle software and are ready to operate after a quick installation and configuration. They represent an attractive offering for customers that require new solutions that can be up and running in a short period of time. The flagship of Oracle's product line is the **Exadata Database Machine**. Exadata is a complete hardware/storage/database solution that provides a highly available, high performance database platform out of the box. Exadata can provide superior performance for most types of database operations, since the hardware itself is tailored to the requirements of the database. Oracle also offers the **Database Appliance**, a smaller, less expensive platform tailored for the Oracle Database that lacks some of the high-performance features of Exadata. For the application server side of IT, Oracle offers **Exalogic** and **Exalytics**, two hardware platforms that can be used to support application operations and data analysis, respectively.

Examining Oracle virtualization solutions

Server virtualization has become extremely important to enterprise IT in recent years. The concept of allowing one server or a group of servers to appear as many *virtual* servers provides IT organizations with a way to make more effective use of expensive hardware resources. Say for instance that a company's database servers, on average, use less than 50 percent of their available memory, and run at 20 percent CPU usage. With virtualization, these servers could serve as hosts for virtualized servers and make more effective use of these resources. When users connect to these virtual servers, they *see* what appears to be a physical machine, when in reality they are connected to a virtual machine. For enterprises, Oracle offers **Oracle VM**, a complete virtualization solution that allows servers to host virtual machines. Oracle VM is based on the Xen Hypervisor technology and actually runs from a Linux kernel. For desktop-level virtualization, Oracle offers **VirtualBox**, which it acquired from Sun. With VirtualBox, users can create their own virtual machines on a desktop system, such as a personal computer. To do this, we simply install the VirtualBox software on a PC and create a new virtual machine. Then we install the operating system, as well as any other software we desire, on this empty virtual machine.

> **The real-world DBA**
>
> It is interesting to note that the author runs VirtualBox on a Linux desktop and can use it to run many different operating systems, including DOS, Windows 95, and several distributions of Linux. In fact, all of the screenshots in this book were taken using Oracle databases and tools running in virtual machines from a desktop. VirtualBox can be a great way to experience and learn about different operating systems without trying to maintain multiple computers at home!

Exploring Oracle operating systems

The choice of an operating system for any platform running the Oracle database is a crucial one. The operating system stands between the database and the hardware that services the needs of the database. An operating system that makes efficient use of hardware resources to serve the database can have a positive impact on the performance of the database. Although many Oracle products are supported on various operating systems, Oracle offers two different operating systems of their own.

In 2006, Oracle began offering **Oracle Enterprise Linux** (now simply known as **Oracle Linux**), a repackaged version of the Red Hat Linux operating system. Oracle Linux, like all distributions of Linux under the GNU General Public License, can be downloaded and used for free, even for enterprise production-level systems. Oracle, like many other companies that offer Linux, also offers paid support contracts for the use of Oracle Linux. Oracle Linux is distributed with two separate kernels. The **Red Hat Compatible Kernel** is identical to the one shipped with Red Hat Linux. In 2010, Oracle announced the second kernel, the **Unbreakable Enterprise Kernel**, which includes enhancements designed to increase performance for the Oracle database.

In addition to its Linux product, Oracle offers the Solaris operating system, now known as **Oracle Solaris**. While Solaris is commonly associated with the SPARC chip architecture found in Sun hardware, it is also available for x86 and x86-64 chip architectures, such as the ones found in personal computers. Solaris is a true POSIX-compliant version of the Unix operating system.

> **The real-world DBA**
>
> Since both Oracle Linux and Oracle Solaris can run on the x86 platform, you can download either of them and install them at home if you have a spare computer with sufficient resources. Additionally, both operating systems can run the Oracle Database. This can be a great way to learn about administering Oracle on a Unix-like environment.

Examining Oracle Application Servers

Application servers provide an environment that facilitates the development, deployment, and execution of the various software applications that a company utilizes. This can include anything from simple web servers to more advanced middleware architectures that use Java and clustering for high availability. In this domain, Oracle has historically offered the Oracle Application Server, which was later incorporated into Oracle Fusion Middleware, a package of software products that facilitate business intelligence, SOA, and content management operations. In 2008, Oracle acquired BEA Systems and their WebLogic application server product. It has, since then, essentially replaced Oracle Application Server as Oracle's de facto standard.

Oracle also has a significant presence in the **Customer Relationship Management** (**CRM**) market. In 2005, Oracle purchased PeopleSoft, which had previously acquired JD Edwards. Adding these two products to their own CRM product, Oracle Applications, Oracle became a major player in the CRM market.

Interpreting Oracle Database versioning

People who are new to the world of Oracle are often curious about the different versions available and what their letter suffixes (the "g" in 11*g*, for instance) actually mean. As we mentioned previously, the first release of Oracle Database was Oracle 2. Oracle continued the standard approach of numbering subsequent major releases of the Oracle database with increasing number values until Version 8. With Version 8*i*, Oracle began suffixing their version numbers with abbreviations to align their products with their marketing focus. The "i" in 8*i* stands for "internet" as that version contains many features that facilitate the use of the Oracle database as the backend for Internet applications. The ninth major version of Oracle was similarly named Oracle 9*i*. With the release of the tenth version of Oracle in 2004, Oracle suffixed the letter "g" (short for "grid") to the version, naming the release "10*g*", to align their product with the grid computing market. Version 11*g* followed this pattern as well. With the current focus on cloud computing, it is speculated that Oracle Database Version 12 will be named, "12*c*", for "cloud."

Apart from the common release name, since Version 8*i*, Oracle Database products have been versioned in an extended form as well. While the database may be "11*g*," its proper version name may be 11.2.0.2.0. The following table shows what this long version number of Version 11.2.0.2.0 describes:

Version number	Description
11	Major version (release) number
.2	Database maintenance release number
.0	Application server release number
.2	Component-specific release number (akin to "patch level")
.0	Platform-specific release number

The Application server release number (the third decimal digit) is used only for application server releases and doesn't apply to the database version. Rather, it's a way for Oracle to standardize release naming across its product family. The platform-specific release number (the last decimal digit) applies only when a certain platform requires a release that only applies to that platform and not others. Additionally, Oracle database versions are often referred to by the information in the first two decimal digits of their version. So, if our database is Version 11.2.0.2.0, we might say that we're running Oracle 11*g* Release 2. If our version is 10.1.0.3.0, we could refer to it as Oracle 10*g* Release 1. Moving to a later major release of the database is usually referred to as an *upgrade* while a later release of any other components (the other digits) is referred to as a *patch*.

Understanding the role of the DBA

Despite all of the industry talk about "zero administration systems," DBAs are as necessary today as they have ever been, and likely more so. The basic function of an Oracle DBA is to safeguard the integrity and availability of the data in the database. However, defining the precise role of a DBA can be difficult in today's world. In the past, the DBA would be responsible for every aspect of the database, often including the operation of the hardware and operating system. In such a role, the morning of the DBA's day might be spent writing SQL statements to create new tables within the database, while the afternoon would find him or her troubleshooting issues with the disks in a storage unit. Relatively speaking, the systems of the past were less complicated and less demanding in terms of time and resources, allowing (or perhaps burdening) the DBA to be involved in all operations even tangentially related to the database. At times, the DBA was also the system administrator, the network administrator, or the programmer. While these types of DBA positions still exist, today, because of the demands of modern IT, the role of the DBA is often highly specialized. Rather than a single DBA, IT organizations today often have teams that are responsible for database administration. The responsibilities of these teams are sometimes divided based on the lines of business. For instance, one part of the DBA team might be responsible for all databases that support the finance department of a company, while another group would administer any databases related to the HR department. Each member of the team is a DBA, but different parts of the team focus on certain lines of business to provide better support.

Because of the complex nature of technology, it is not uncommon to differentiate DBAs based on their skillsets or functional roles. In the spectrum of technologists, the role of the DBA stands between system administrators on one side and developers on the other. Because of the vast difference between those two roles, it can be difficult to find DBAs who have all of the skillsets required to span that gap. In some IT organizations, DBAs are roughly divided into Physical DBAs and Logical DBAs. A **Physical DBA** (sometimes called an Environmental DBA) has a role that generally tracks closer to the hardware and system side of database operations, while the **Logical DBA** (sometimes referred to as an Application DBA) tends to work more with developers in the creation and support of the database objects required for the application to function. This delineation can be somewhat subjective, but we list a general division of responsibilities as follows:

- The role of the Physical DBA:
    - Oracle database installation and configuration
    - Backup and recovery

    - Database tuning, as it relates to the overall system performance
    - Administration of the overall database physical architecture, such as server configuration, memory usage, and disk layout
    - Configuration of database parameters
    - Works more closely with system administrators

- The role of the Logical DBA is as follows:
    - Creation and maintenance of database objects, such as tables and indexes
    - Closely involved in software deployments
    - Database tuning as it relates to the performance of SQL statements
    - Responsible for internal database security
    - Data modeling and supervision of the application data model
    - Works more closely with developers

Naturally, the role of any individual DBA may overlap these categories, but these are some of the divisions that have developed over time in many IT organizations.

> **The real-world DBA**
> In today's IT world, it is very easy for a DBA to allow oneself to become "stuck" in a certain job role. It is always safer to stick with what you already know than to branch out into new areas. However, having a skillset that spans both categories of a DBA can be very satisfying and rewarding, since such DBAs are highly sought after. Always press yourself to learn and expand your knowledge.

What makes a good DBA? What types of characteristics are needed for the job? Being an Oracle DBA is one of the most demanding and rewarding jobs in all technologies. A DBA is afforded the opportunity to work with many diverse types of technologies, but that opportunity can require an extremely broad knowledge base. It's been said that, in IT, "everyone wants to be a DBA." However, not everyone is capable of being one. Here are a few of the traits commonly found in successful DBAs:

- *A logical thinker with exceptional problem solving skills*: The core of database administration is the ability to solve problems, both big and small. A good DBA operates based on factual information and observation and is highly detail-oriented.

- *Self-confident in the face of challenges*: A DBA meets challenges on a daily basis. A good one is confident in his or her knowledge, accepts his or her limitations, and moves to solve the problem, rather than folding under pressure.
- *Professionalism*: Good DBAs are professional in every aspect of their work, from their dealings with users, to their daily interaction with other IT specialists. They value the quality of their work and their reputation as capable and trustworthy.
- *Effective communicator*: You can't be a DBA by simply sitting in your cube with the phone off the hook. DBAs must be able to explain and communicate complex ideas, both verbally and in writing, to users, customers, and the management in a way that they can understand.
- *Lifelong learner*: Technology is complex and is always moving forward at a rapid pace. Good DBAs are always looking forward and educating themselves for what's to come.

Examining the tools of the Oracle DBA

Although the greatest asset of any DBA is his or her own mind, it doesn't hurt to have the right tools. As a DBA in today's world, there is an abundance of administration tools from which to choose. There are benefits and drawbacks to each, but the choice of a tool is generally about one's comfort level with the tool as well as its feature set. Some tools are free, some are open source, and some require paid licenses; however, each tool uses the same syntax for SQL when it connects to an Oracle database. The following are some commonly used DBA tools:

The real-world DBA

While your choice of SQL tool is an important one, in the industry it is one that is sometimes dictated by the toolset standards of your employer. It's important that you don't completely dedicate yourself to one tool. If you become an expert at one and then transfer to a different employer whose standards don't allow for the use of your tool, you may find yourself with an initial learning curve.

SQL*Plus

For years, **SQL*Plus** has been the de facto standard tool for connecting to Oracle databases. Since the early versions of Oracle, it has been included as a part of any Oracle RDBMS installation. SQL*Plus is a command-line tool and is launched on all Oracle platforms using the command, `sqlplus`. This command-line tool has been a staple of Oracle DBAs for many years and has a powerful, interactive command interface that can be used to issue SQL statements, create database objects, launch scripts, and start up databases. For some beginners, that power comes at a price, in the form of SQL*Plus's somewhat steep learning curve. However, although SQL*Plus can be challenging to use as a SQL and PL/SQL development tool, it is an extremely useful tool for DBAs, since most of the commands we will execute are fairly straightforward. Until Version 11*g*, the Windows installation of Oracle included a version of SQL*Plus that could be executed from the desktop. That tool, invoked using the `SQLPLUSW.exe` program, was deprecated starting with Version 11*g*. Throughout the course of this book, we will learn to use SQL*Plus to execute basic administration commands such as startup and shutdown. The following is a screenshot of the command-line SQL*Plus tool from a DOS command line in Windows:

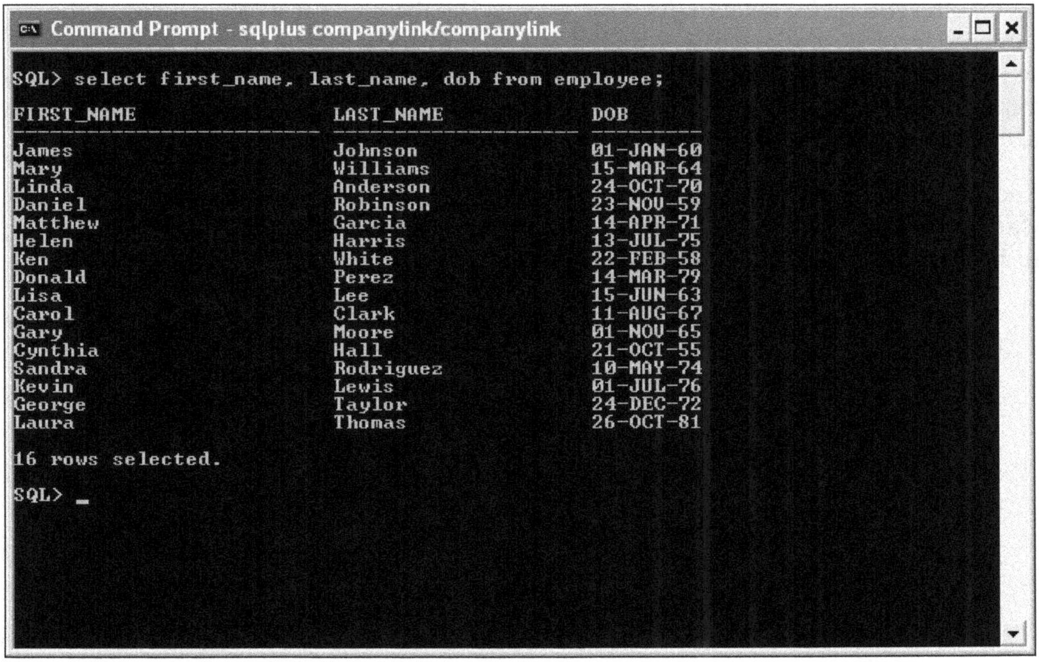
Command Prompt - sqlplus companylink/companylink
SQL> select first_name, last_name, dob from employee;
FIRST_NAME LAST_NAME DOB
James Johnson 01-JAN-60
Mary Williams 15-MAR-64
Linda Anderson 24-OCT-70
Daniel Robinson 23-NOV-59
Matthew Garcia 14-APR-71
Helen Harris 13-JUL-75
Ken White 22-FEB-58
Donald Perez 14-MAR-79
Lisa Lee 15-JUN-63
Carol Clark 11-AUG-67
Gary Moore 01-NOV-65
Cynthia Hall 21-OCT-55
Sandra Rodriguez 10-MAY-74
Kevin Lewis 01-JUL-76
George Taylor 24-DEC-72
Laura Thomas 26-OCT-81
16 rows selected.
SQL>

Oracle Enterprise Manager

Oracle Enterprise Manager (**OEM**) is an interesting and useful tool that has been available since Oracle Database Server Version 8.0. With Version 8*i*, Oracle moved to a Java-capable browser console that could be run standalone or with a management server. The management server served as a central repository for database information, and would communicate with various agents on the database servers. These agents acted to gather information from all the databases in the enterprise and relayed it to the management server, giving the DBA a centralized single point of administration. Enterprise Manager followed this architecture through Version 9*i*.

Beginning with Version 10*g*, Enterprise Manager experienced a graphical and architectural overhaul. OEM 10*g* featured a completely integrated browser interface that offered complete control of nearly every aspect of database administration, including storage allocation, schema object manipulation, backup and recovery, database parameter configuration, and performance monitoring. OEM 10*g* and 11*g* can be used in either of the two configurations, **Database Control** or **Grid Control**. Database Control runs on a database server and gives the DBA full administrative control of all aspects of a single database running on that server. Grid Control can be used at the enterprise level in the same way as Database Control can be used at the database level. Grid Control is installed as a centralized server with agents deployed on individual database servers. Like the earlier versions of OEM, these agents communicate with the Grid Control server, allowing the DBA direct control over every administrative aspect of these databases.

Another makeover for OEM comes with the latest version, Oracle Enterprise Manager 12*c*, Cloud Control. OEM 12*c* features a cleaner graphical interface and a number of new features, a few of which are listed here:

- Integration with Oracle Support for easier creation and resolution of service requests
- A compliance framework for easier monitoring and reporting in environments where compliance auditing and oversight is crucial

- Improved web interface security
- Enhancements providing better control over backup and recovery operations
- Automatic discovery of databases

The following screenshot shows the UI of OEM 11*g*:

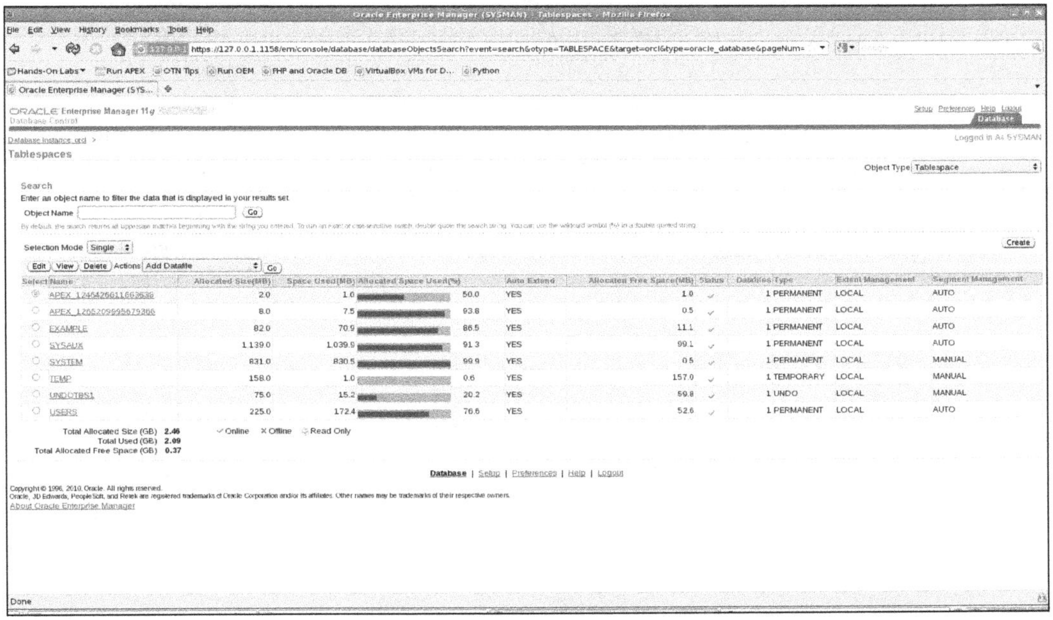
Oracle Enterprise Manager (SYSMAN) - Tablespaces - Mozilla Firefox
Tablespaces
Search
Object Name
Selection Mode
Create
Total Allocated Size (GB) 2.46
Total Used (GB) 2.09
Total Allocated Free Space (GB) 0.37
Done

TOAD

The **Tool for Oracle Application Developers** (**TOAD**) is a full-featured development and administration tool for Oracle as well as other relational database systems, including Microsoft SQL Server, Sybase, and IBM's DB2. It was originally created by Jim McDaniel for his own use; he later released it as freeware for the Oracle community at large. Eventually, Quest Software acquired the rights to TOAD and began distributing a licensed version, while greatly expanding on the original functionality. TOAD is immensely popular among both DBAs and developers, due to its large feature set. For DBAs, it is a complete administration tool, allowing the user to control every major aspect of the database, including storage manipulation, object creation, and security control. For developers, TOAD offers a robust coding interface, including advanced debugging facilities. TOAD is available for download in both freeware and trial licensed versions. A screenshot of the TOAD UI is shown as follows:

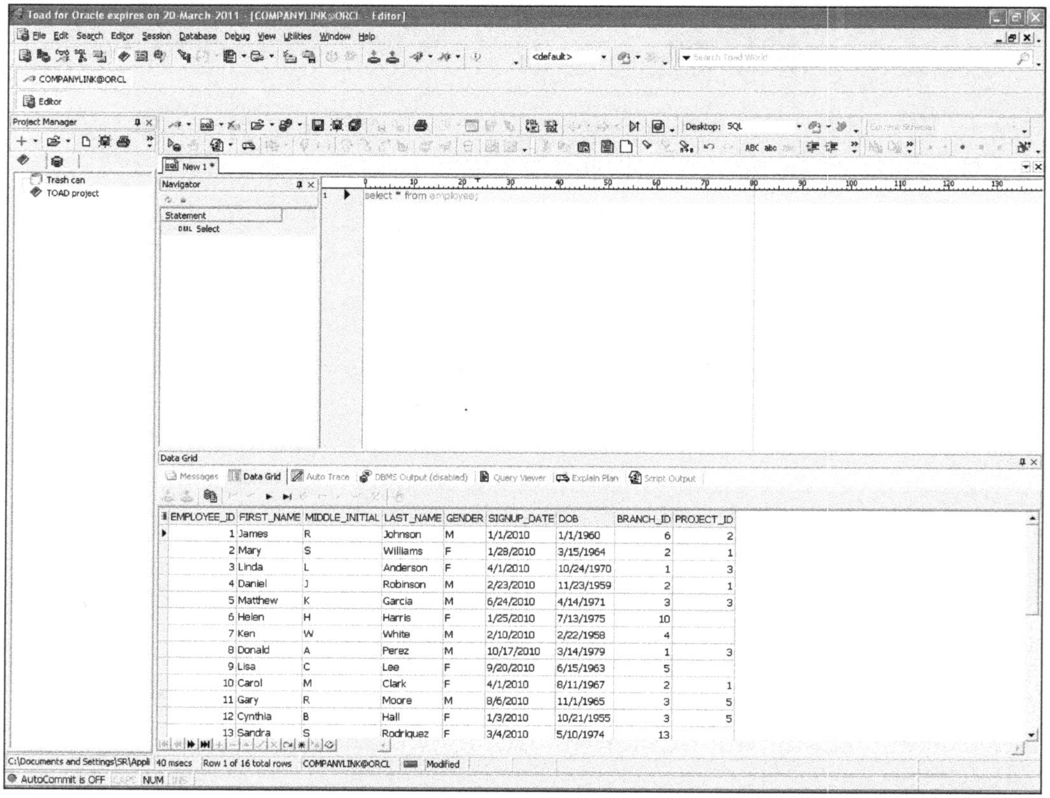
Toad for Oracle expires on 20 March 2011 - [COMPANYLINK@ORCL - Editor]
File Edit Search Editor Session Database Debug View Utilities Window Help
COMPANYLINK@ORCL
Editor
Project Manager
Trash can
TOAD project
New 1 *
Navigator
Statement
DML Select
select * from employee;
Data Grid
Messages
Data Grid
Auto Trace
DBMS Output (disabled)
Query Viewer
Explain Plan
Script Output
EMPLOYEE_ID FIRST_NAME MIDDLE_INITIAL LAST_NAME GENDER SIGNUP_DATE DOB BRANCH_ID PROJECT_ID
1 James R Johnson M 1/1/2010 1/1/1960 6 2
2 Mary S Williams F 1/28/2010 3/15/1964 2 1
3 Linda L Anderson F 4/1/2010 10/24/1970 1 3
4 Daniel J Robinson M 2/23/2010 11/23/1959 2 1
5 Matthew K Garcia M 6/24/2010 4/14/1971 3 3
6 Helen H Harris F 1/25/2010 7/13/1975 10
7 Ken W White M 2/10/2010 2/22/1958 4
8 Donald A Perez M 10/17/2010 3/14/1979 1 3
9 Lisa C Lee F 9/20/2010 6/15/1963 5
10 Carol M Clark F 4/1/2010 8/11/1967 2 1
11 Gary R Moore M 8/6/2010 11/1/1965 3 5
12 Cynthia B Hall F 1/3/2010 10/21/1955 3 5
13 Sandra S Rodriquez F 3/4/2010 5/10/1974 13
C:\Documents and Settings\SR\Appl
40 msecs
Row 1 of 16 total rows
COMPANYLINK@ORCL
Modified
AutoCommit is OFF
NUM

DBArtisan

DBArtisan (now called DBArtisanXE), by Embarcadero Technologies, is another complete suite of database management tools that operate across multiple platforms. DBArtisan is only available as a licensed product, but has extensive administration capabilities, including the ability to do advanced capacity and performance management, all packaged in an attractive and user-friendly GUI front end. A trial version is available for download from Embarcadero's website.

Oracle SQL Developer

Oracle SQL Developer, originally called Raptor, is a GUI database interface that takes a somewhat different approach from its competitors. While many of the major licensable GUI administration products have continued to expand their product offerings through more and more add-on components, SQL Developer is a much more dedicated tool. Although it lacks a full set of administration features, it serves well as a streamlined SQL interface to the Oracle database. You can create and manipulate database objects in the GUI interface, as well as write and execute SQL statements from a command line. Administration-oriented activities such as storage control are left to other tools. SQL Developer aims to be a strong SQL and PL/SQL editor with some GUI functionalities. SQL Developer has gained popularity in recent years, in large part owing to several benefits, which are listed as follows:

- It is completely free with no mandatory licensable components, although third-party add-ons are available for purchase.
- It is a true cross-platform client-side tool written primarily in Java. While a majority of the commonly used SQL tools are available only on the Windows platform, SQL Developer runs on Windows, Linux, and even the Mac.
- SQL Developer supports read-only connections to many popular databases, including SQL Server, Sybase, MySQL, Microsoft Access, DB2, and Teradata.
- Because it is written in Java, it allows for the creation and addition of third-party extensions. If you want a capability that SQL Developer does not have, you can write your own!

- It is provided by Oracle and is now included with any installation of Oracle database. It has essentially replaced SQL*Plus as Oracle's default SQL interface, although SQL*Plus is still available from the command line.

The UI of SQL Developer is as shown in the following screenshot:

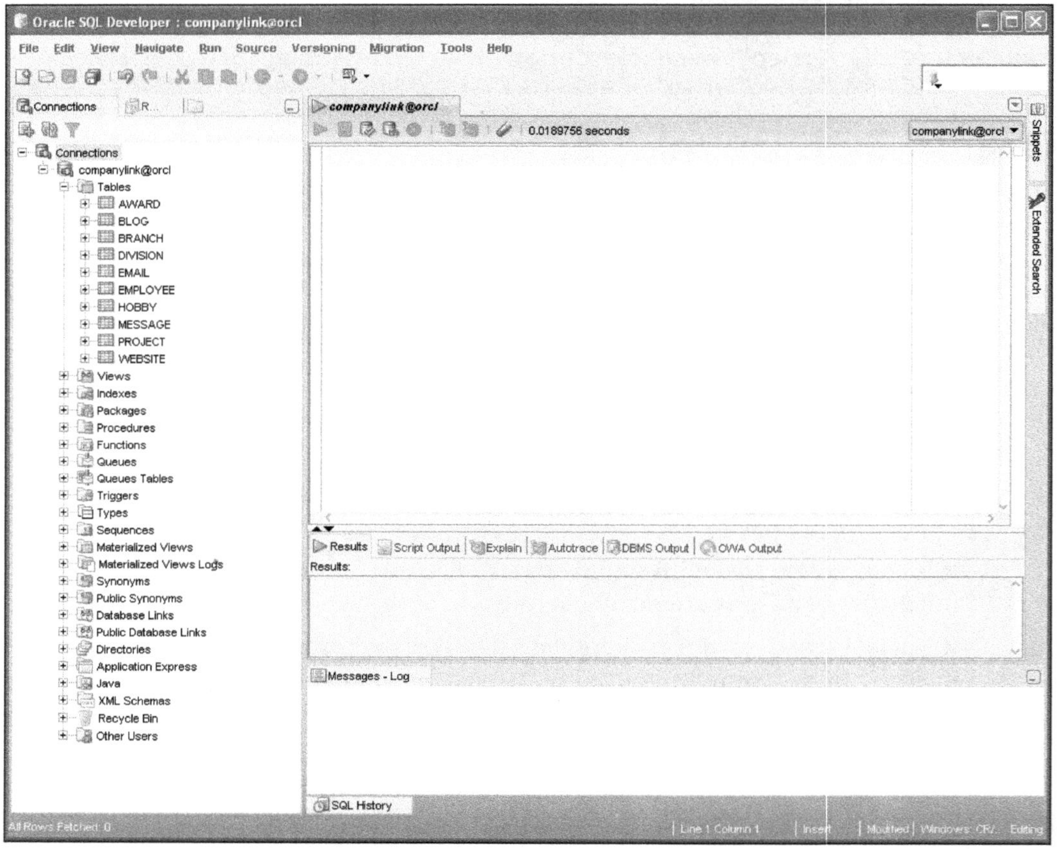
Oracle SQL Developer : companylink@orcl
File Edit View Navigate Run Source Versioning Migration Tools Help
Connections
Connections
companylink@orcl
Tables
AWARD
BLOG
BRANCH
DIVISION
EMAIL
EMPLOYEE
HOBBY
MESSAGE
PROJECT
WEBSITE
Views
Indexes
Packages
Procedures
Functions
Queues
Queues Tables
Triggers
Types
Sequences
Materialized Views
Materialized Views Logs
Synonyms
Public Synonyms
Database Links
Public Database Links
Directories
Application Express
Java
XML Schemas
Recycle Bin
Other Users
companylink@orcl
0.0189756 seconds
companylink@orcl
Snippets
Extended Search
Results
Script Output
Explain
Autotrace
DBMS Output
OWA Output
Results:
Messages - Log
SQL History

For these reasons, the tools we use in this book for the purposes of demonstration will primarily be SQL Developer and SQL*Plus. From time to time, we'll also look at managing database operations with Enterprise Manager. But before we get ahead of ourselves, let's find out a little about the data we'll be using, and look at the `Companylink` database.

Introducing the Companylink database

This book focuses on two objectives: first, to prepare you for the *Oracle Database 11g: Administration I* exam, number *1Z0-052,* and second, to present the knowledge needed for the exam in such a way that you can use it in a real-world setting. To that end, rather than using the default tables included in Oracle, we will be working with simulated real-world data. The database we will use throughout this book is for the fictional company Companylink. Although most people are aware of the impact of social networking in our private lives, companies are realizing the importance of using it in their industries as well. Our fictional Companylink is a business that focuses on social networking in the corporate setting. The data model that we will use is a small but realistic set of working data that could support a social networking website. The following tables are included in the `Companylink` database, which can be downloaded from the support site at `http://www.packtpub.com/support`.

- `Employee`: Information about employees that use the Companylink site.
- `Address`: Information about the street address, city, and state of each employee.
- `Branch`: The corporate branch to which each employee belongs. Each employee belongs to one branch.
- `Division`: The corporate division to which each branch belongs. Each division is associated with multiple branches.
- `E-mail`: An employee can store multiple e-mail addresses.
- `Message`: The fictional Companylink social networking site allows you to send messages to fellow employees. That information is stored here.
- `Website`: Companylink allows users to create their own personal web pages. The URL of these pages are contained in this table.
- `Blog`: In addition to a website, users can optionally create their own blogs. This information is stored in the `Blog` table.
- `Project`: Each employee is assigned to a single primary project, which is contained here.
- `Award`: Employees can win corporate awards. The list of possible awards is stored here. Employees can win more than one award.
- `Employee_award`: This table is used to relate employees with their awards. Since multiple employees can win the same award and multiple awards can be won by the same employee, this creates a many-to-many table relationship, which, in the relational paradigm, must be avoided. The `Employee_award` table divides this many-to-many relationship into two distinct one-to-many relationships.

Once we've installed the Oracle software and created our database, these tables will form the backbone of the data that we'll use as examples throughout this book.

> **Downloading the example code**
> You can download the example code files for all Packt books you have purchased from your account at `http://www.packtpub.com`. If you purchased this book elsewhere, you can visit `http://www.packtpub.com/support` and register to have the files e-mailed directly to you.

Summary

In this chapter, we've introduced the Oracle RDBMS. We've learned about the importance of the RDBMS in today's world and described the way Oracle's product line supports RDBMS operations. We've looked at the standards for naming and versioning in Oracle. We've outlined the job role of today's Oracle DBA and described some of the characteristics required to become a DBA. Lastly, we've presented several of the common tools used by DBAs and introduced the table structures of the `Companylink` database. In our next chapter, we'll perform a step-by-step installation of the Oracle software that will provide the software framework for our database.

Test your knowledge

Q 1. Which of the following database paradigms can organize our data in such a way that the data and its inter-relationships can be clearly identified?

a. Hierarchical
b. Flat-file
c. Relational
d. Network

Q 2. Which of the following languages is not supported directly within an Oracle database?

a. SQL
b. Perl
c. Java
d. PL/SQL

Q 3. Which of the following types of products are offered in the current Oracle product line?

a. Application servers
b. Server hardware
c. Virtualization solutions
d. All of the above

Q 4. Given that your database is running Oracle database Version 11.2.0.1.0, which of the following statements is false?

a. The major software release level is 11.
b. The database could be referred to a Oracle 11*g* Release 2.
c. The patch level is 0.
d. None of these statements is false

Q 5. Which of the following Oracle database tools only runs as a command-line interface?

a. SQL*Plus
b. Oracle Enterprise Manager 12*c*
c. SQL Developer
d. TOAD

2

Installing the Oracle Database Software

Before we can venture very far into the world of Oracle database administration, we're going to need to install the software required to actually run the database. In this chapter, we'll take a step-by-step look at various methods of installing Oracle on a server machine. Additionally, we'll look at the steps and requirements for an Oracle installation on both Windows and Linux to establish a broader outlook for database administration as a whole. In fact, throughout this book, rather than dedicating all of our examples to one particular OS, we'll take a broader approach and examine Oracle administration on two different operating systems: Windows and Linux. Note that it will not be necessary for you to do three different installations. Primarily, Oracle installation and administration can be done with tools that are cross-platform and have the same look and feel. Where they differ, we'll be sure to make note of the differences.

In this chapter we will:

- Plan an installation of Oracle
- Examine the prerequisites for an install on different operating systems
- Look at the Oracle Universal Installer
- Run a complete Oracle installation

Planning an Oracle installation

As we begin an Oracle installation, it's important to understand exactly what an installation of the Oracle Database Server will provide us. In this section, we examine the concepts behind an Oracle installation and look at what will actually be installed on the machine when we're finished.

Understanding Oracle installation concepts

When installing Oracle, we should first note that an Oracle software installation is not the same as creating a database, although it is possible to accomplish both with certain installation procedures. When we speak of an Oracle database installation, we're referring to the process of loading the necessary software on a server that can support the creation and operation of an Oracle Database. Thus, we can say that an Oracle database cannot be created on a server unless an Oracle installation has occurred first. Once the installation is complete, our server will contain the Oracle kernel and the various tools needed to administer the database. While an in-depth look into the Oracle kernel is beyond our scope here, we can essentially refer to it as the "heart" of the services that Oracle provides. The kernel facilitates the low-level interaction between the server hardware and operating system and the services that the Oracle software provides. In that sense, it is similar in some ways to an operating system. As such, it is difficult to "see" the kernel in any meaningful way. Rather, we're more interested in the concept itself and the knowledge that it forms the basis for database processing. Aside from the kernel, an Oracle installation lays down many of the basic tools used in database operation and administration. We'll take a closer look at these later in the chapter. Once the installation is complete, we are free to proceed through the process of creating a database, the subject of the next chapter.

Acquiring the Oracle software

In order to install the Oracle software, we must first obtain the software installation package. Generally, the Oracle software is made available in one of two ways: an installation DVD-ROM or a set of ZIP files downloaded from Oracle's website. If you are already a DBA working in a company that has purchased Oracle licenses, you may have access to an installation DVD-ROM, sometimes referred to as a **media pack**. A media pack provides a full installation of Oracle on physical media in accordance with your company's license agreement.

If not, Oracle provides its software in the form of ZIP files that can be freely downloaded from its Oracle Technology Network website. These files form the complete package necessary to install a fully functional version of Oracle, just as you would use in a commercial setting. However, it is crucial to note that Oracle provides this software under the strict terms that it cannot be installed for commercial use in any way. Rather, it is provided free of cost to those who use it only for self-educational purposes. Once it enters the commercial realm, it is necessary to purchase a license. However, for readers of this book who will only use the software for non-commercial, learning purposes, this provides an outstanding opportunity to install and learn the very same Oracle software used in data centers around the world. To download the software, follow these instructions:

1. Navigate your browser to the Oracle Technology Network at `http://www.oracle.com/technetwork/index.html`.
2. Click **Software Downloads** from the **Essential Links** section.
3. Here you'll find the download categories. Scroll down to **Database** and click **Database 11g Enterprise/Standard Editions**.
4. Near the top, click the radio button for **Accept License Agreement**.
5. Choose the operating system that is appropriate to the machine you intend to use as your Oracle database server. For instance, if you intend to install Oracle on a home machine running Windows, scroll down to the first occurrence (for the latest version) of **Microsoft Windows** and click each link for **File 1** and **File 2**. Remember to download both the files and make sure you choose the bit level that matches your machine, either **32-bit** or **x64** for 64-bit.
6. At this point, you will be prompted for your Oracle sign-in. If you do not have an account, click **Sign up** to create a free account. Otherwise, enter your username and password.
7. When the download initiates, select an appropriate place on your hard drive to save the files. Make sure you have sufficient space (approximately 2 GB for Oracle 11*g*).
8. Once your downloads complete, unzip each file separately. The first file you unzip will create a directory called `database` and the second will extract its files into that same directory as well. This unzips the necessary files for installing the Oracle database software. We will revisit this directory shortly.

Note that these directions apply to downloading the Oracle software at the time of this writing. It is possible that the site could change over time, but the process should be very similar, regardless.

> **The real-world DBA**
>
> The extent to which Oracle makes its software available for self-educational use is unparalleled in the IT industry. Through the Oracle Technology Network, not only can you download and install many different versions of the Oracle database software for non-commercial use, you can download almost any of Oracle's software products under the same agreement. That includes virtualization, application server, and operating system software. And as if that wasn't enough, the documentation for these products is available as a free download as well. With a sufficient computer and a willingness to learn, you can educate yourself in every major level of the IT stack—from operating systems to applications and everything in between.

Reviewing the installation prerequisites

Now that we've looked at the concepts behind an Oracle installation and acquired our installation media, either DVD-ROM or a ZIP file, it's time to examine some of the prerequisites our system will need to meet prior to installation. We'll look at both hardware and software requirements as we prepare our installation.

Reviewing hardware prerequisites for an installation

The hardware requirements for an Oracle system boil down to the three basic resources used by any software application: CPU, memory, and disk space. It might be surprising that, although Oracle Database Server is the pre-eminent RDBMS in the world, its minimum hardware requirements aren't as vast as one might think. Of course, we must take into account that the minimum requirements won't support a large-scale production environment, but a minimum installation is sufficient for learning purposes and executing the examples in this book. Although the hardware installation requirements are similar for most operating systems, we'll look at them individually here and note the differences.

Meeting the minimum hardware requirements for an installation

For an Oracle Database 11*g* system, the minimum hardware requirements are as follows:

- **Processor**: Intel (x86), AMD64, or Intel EM64T
- **Physical memory**: 1 GB
- **Virtual memory**: Between 1.5 times the size of physical RAM and 16 GB of RAM, depending on the operating system
- **Installation disk space**: 4 GB

In terms of the processor speed, Oracle documentation doesn't list any required minimum. The processor speed of your system will impact performance more than any perceived minimums required to run the system. Most modern processors possess a sufficient amount of power to run a base Oracle system.

Likewise, Oracle will operate on a system running any of the major chip platforms, including both Intel and AMD. Take special care to note the bit-level of your system, either 32- or 64-bit. This will have a bearing on the download package or DVD media you select. 1 GB of physical memory is the base amount required, although a database of any significant size will require more. The base disk space requirement for an Oracle installation is approximately 4 GB, but this does not include the size of the database itself, which will require more.

> **Beyond the exam**
>
> Apart from the basic knowledge of hardware requirements needed for the exam, the real-world DBA must take a number of factors into account when designing a system. Today's multi-core CPUs add a complexity beyond the simple question of "How many CPUs do I need?" Large Linux and Unix systems can possess extremely large amounts of memory as well. Certain considerations are required to make the most of these large memory areas. Furthermore, one of the most important factors a DBA must consider is not simply, "how much disk do I need?", but how the disk is laid out. Large, real-world production systems use **Storage Area Networks** (**SAN**), **Network Attached Storage** (**NAS**), and **Internet Small Computer System Interface** (**iSCSI**) storage systems. Storage systems such as these require the DBA to be familiar with the issues surrounding fiber-optic connections and storage network bandwidth speeds as well.

Reviewing software prerequisites for an installation

Traditionally, the Oracle Database Server has been ported to an extremely large number of operating systems and platforms, from mainframe systems to Macintosh OS X. Recently, however, Oracle has narrowed their offerings to more widely used systems. Oracle is supported on the majority of the major versions of Windows, as well as various distributions of Linux, including Red Hat, SUSE Linux, and Oracle Linux. Oracle also is used for enterprise-class database servers on major Unix platforms, such as Oracle Solaris, HP-UX, and IBM's AIX operating system. Generally, each of these platforms has its own patch level and package requirements.

> **The real-world DBA**
>
> The question often raised is whether or not the Oracle database can run on other popular Linux distributions, such as Ubuntu and Fedora. In many cases these distributions can in fact run the Oracle database with certain tweaks and package installations prior to the software installation. Keep in mind, however, that only the ones previously listed are supported by Oracle. The use of non-supported platforms for Oracle is best left to systems that are used for practice and educational purposes, rather than real-world commercial systems.

Using the Oracle Universal Installer

Installing enterprise-level server software can be significantly different than installing your favorite word processor or video game. There are many factors that must be considered—hardware platform, operating system differences, and performance, just to name a few. There are few examples of this kind of software that are simple and straightforward to install. Fortunately for us, the Oracle Database Server is one of them. In the past, Oracle was just as difficult to install as any other enterprise RDBMS, and perhaps more so. Additionally, the installation procedure was significantly different on every platform. That changed with the introduction of the **Oracle Universal Installer**, or **OUI**.

Understanding how OUI works

The Oracle Universal Installer is a fully graphical, Java-based installation program that aims to "universalize" the process of installing the Oracle Database software across multiple platforms. Thus, once you learn the installation process on one operating system, your knowledge should serve you well in an installation on another. Say, for instance, that we learn the screens and process for an Oracle installation on Windows. When we start up the OUI on Linux, we see basically the same set of screens, with a few exceptions. The Java-based nature of OUI allows it to run on any platform that can run Java. In the past, because the OUI ran on Java, it was necessary to have certain versions of Java pre-installed before running the Oracle installation. The Oracle installation software itself now contains the necessary Java software to run the OUI.

Although the OUI is a graphical, wizard-oriented program, at its heart are command-line operations that simply execute the installation as we direct within the GUI. As we will see shortly, the OUI reads the product manifest—a list of products available for installation—from an XML file named `product.xml`. This file is generally found within the `stage` directory in your installation media. While it's not necessary for us to have an in-depth knowledge of this file, it is interesting to look at it to see the kind of information it contains. A short sample is shown here:


```
- <DEP_GRP_PRPS NAME="OptionalDecideNow" OPEN="T" ASK="F">
    <DEP_GRP_CMP NAME="oracle.swd.oui" VER="11.2.0.1.0" PLAT="ALL_PLATFORMS" INST_TYPE="Custom" SEL="T" />
    <DEP_GRP_CMP NAME="oracle.swd.opatch" VER="11.2.0.0.2" PLAT="ALL_PLATFORMS" INST_TYPE="Custom" SEL="T" />
    <DEP_GRP_CMP NAME="oracle.dbjava.jdbc" VER="11.2.0.1.0" PLAT="ALL_PLATFORMS" INST_TYPE="Typical" SEL="T" />
  </DEP_GRP_PRPS>
</INST_TYPE>
- <INST_TYPE NAME="Custom" NAME_ID="Custom" DESC_ID="Custom_DESC">
- <DEP_GRP_PRPS NAME="Optional" OPEN="T" ASK="T">
    <DEP_GRP_CMP NAME="oracle.rdbms" VER="11.2.0.1.0" PLAT="Solaris Intel_Solaris SINIX_Y ReliantUNIX_M UNIX_Alpha IBM_AIX Dynix UnixWare DG_UX HP_UX NEC Hitachi_UX Iris NCOS OpenVMS
      IBM_MVS Linux Linux_S390 HP_IA64 MACOSX Linux_IA64 Linux_PPC NT_X86 NT_IA64 NT_AMD64 NT_Alpha NetWare_411 NetWare_500" INST_TYPE="Custom" SEL="F" />
    <DEP_GRP_CMP NAME="oracle.options" VER="11.2.0.1.0" PLAT="ALL_PLATFORMS" INST_TYPE="Custom" SEL="T" />
    <DEP_GRP_CMP NAME="oracle.network" VER="11.2.0.1.0" PLAT="ALL_PLATFORMS" INST_TYPE="ServerCustom" SEL="T" />
    <DEP_GRP_CMP NAME="oracle.rdbms.oci" VER="11.2.0.1.0" PLAT="ALL_PLATFORMS" INST_TYPE="Custom" SEL="T" />
    <DEP_GRP_CMP NAME="oracle.precomp" VER="11.2.0.1.0" PLAT="ALL_PLATFORMS" INST_TYPE="ServerCustom" SEL="T" />
    <DEP_GRP_CMP NAME="oracle.xdk" VER="11.2.0.1.0" PLAT="ALL_PLATFORMS" INST_TYPE="Custom" SEL="T" />
    <DEP_GRP_CMP NAME="oracle.winprod" VER="11.2.0.1.0" PLAT="NT_X86 NT_IA64 NT_AMD64 W95 W98 NT_Alpha" INST_TYPE="Custom" SEL="F" />
    <DEP_GRP_CMP NAME="oracle.rdbms.lsm_dummy" VER="11.2.0.1.0" PLAT="Solaris Intel_Solaris SINIX_Y ReliantUNIX_M UNIX_Alpha IBM_AIX Dynix UnixWare DG_UX HP_UX NEC Hitachi_UX Iris NCOS
      OpenVMS IBM_MVS Linux Linux_S390 HP_IA64 MACOSX Linux_IA64 Linux_PPC" INST_TYPE="Custom" SEL="F" />
    <DEP_GRP_CMP NAME="oracle.sysman.ccr" VER="10.2.4.0.0" PLAT="ALL_PLATFORMS" INST_TYPE="Typical" SEL="T" />
  </DEP_GRP_PRPS>
- <DEP_GRP_PRPS NAME="Required" OPEN="T" ASK="F">
    <DEP_GRP_CMP NAME="oracle.rdbms.install.common" VER="11.2.0.1.0" PLAT="ALL_PLATFORMS" INST_TYPE="Custom" SEL="T" />
    <DEP_GRP_CMP NAME="oracle.install.deinstalltool" VER="11.2.0.1.0" PLAT="ALL_PLATFORMS" INST_TYPE="Custom" SEL="T" />
  </DEP_GRP_PRPS>
```


This small section (of a very large file) contains information about a subject we've already discussed—the types of platforms on which the Oracle software can run. We never edit this file in any way. It comes with the installation package, either in the ZIP files or on disc, and contains a manifest of the packages available for installation.

One of the first operations completed by the OUI is to establish the **OUI Inventory**, a set of files that serve as an inventory of the Oracle software installed on the host machine. Although we're concerned primarily with database software, the inventory can store information about many of the Oracle products available, including the **Oracle Fusion Middleware**. Thus, an inventory is created the first time an Oracle product is installed on a host machine. When we attempt to install another product, or perhaps a different version of the same product, the inventory is read and the OUI knows what products already exist on the machine.

An interesting note is that the OUI can be run in silent mode. This mode allows the DBA to install Oracle without using the GUI interface at all. If we're required to complete an installation of Oracle Database Server on one or two machines, the GUI interface of OUI can be an easy and efficient way to do this. However, what if we're tasked with installing identical configurations of Oracle on two hundred machines? Stepping through the OUI graphical interface 200 times would be an extraordinarily time-consuming task (usually reserved for the junior DBA on the team). A better solution might be to run scripted, command-line installations using silent mode. To run an installation in silent mode, we must first configure a response file. This is simply a text file, formatted in a certain way that is readable by the OUI, which contains all of the responses we would have entered had we completed the installation using the GUI. An excerpt from an example response file is shown in the following screenshot:

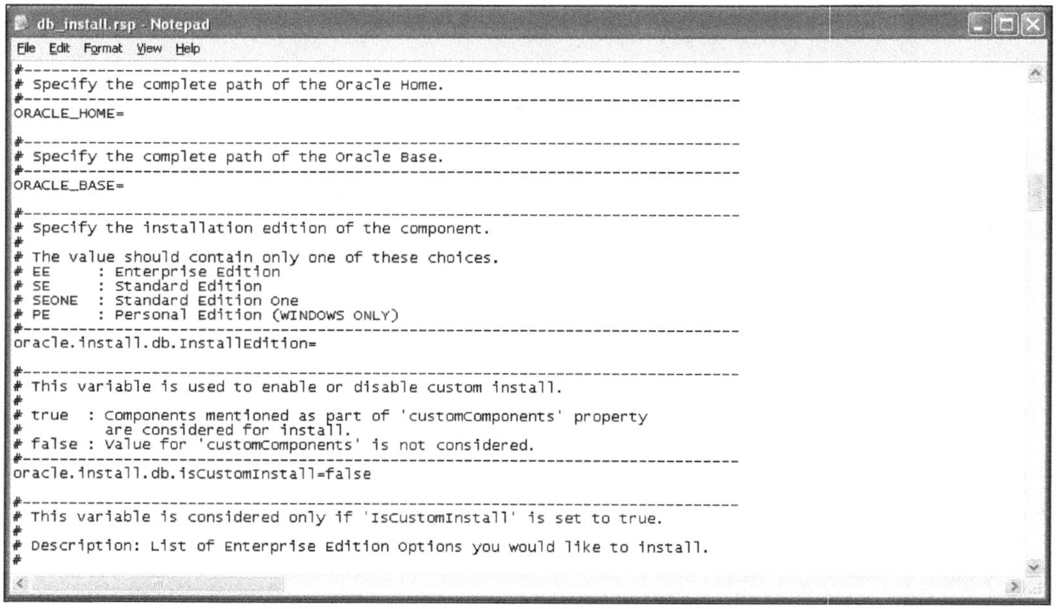
db_install.rsp - Notepad
File Edit Format View Help

```
#------------------------------------------------------------------------------
# Specify the complete path of the Oracle Home.
#------------------------------------------------------------------------------
ORACLE_HOME=

#------------------------------------------------------------------------------
# Specify the complete path of the Oracle Base.
#------------------------------------------------------------------------------
ORACLE_BASE=

#------------------------------------------------------------------------------
# Specify the installation edition of the component.
#
# The value should contain only one of these choices.
# EE     : Enterprise Edition
# SE     : Standard Edition
# SEONE  : Standard Edition One
# PE     : Personal Edition (WINDOWS ONLY)
#------------------------------------------------------------------------------
oracle.install.db.InstallEdition=

#------------------------------------------------------------------------------
# This variable is used to enable or disable custom install.
#
# true  : Components mentioned as part of 'customComponents' property
#         are considered for install.
# false : Value for 'customComponents' is not considered.
#------------------------------------------------------------------------------
oracle.install.db.isCustomInstall=false

#------------------------------------------------------------------------------
# This variable is considered only if 'IsCustomInstall' is set to true.
#
# Description: List of Enterprise Edition Options you would like to install.
#
```

Writing your own response file from scratch could be as time consuming as doing 200 GUI Oracle installations, so Oracle provides a few examples response files on the database media. The `response` directory within our Oracle installation package contains a file called `db_install.rsp`. This file is essentially a blank slate containing the necessary variables that must be defined in order for a silent install to run. This example response file is fully commented and describes the possible values for the variable responses required. It is important to remember that before performing a silent installation, you must also manually create a file called `oraInst.loc` that specifies the location of the Oracle Inventory.

Although a silent install is not for novice DBAs, it is an interesting example of how flexible the Oracle Universal Installer can be.

> **The real-world DBA**
>
> Although the DBA is usually responsible for installing the Oracle Database software, this is not always the case. Sometimes system administrators are tasked with this job. Some very large companies have their own dedicated installation group that is responsible for installing all server software, including Oracle. Even if you work in such a situation, it is always important to understand the concepts and process of completing an Oracle installation. This knowledge can be invaluable when trying to debug problems.

Completing final preparations to install the Oracle software

We're almost ready to step through an Oracle installation. Before we do, however, there are a few more concepts we need to introduce. These include Oracle user accounts, directory structures, and environment variables.

Creating Oracle user accounts and groups

In order to install the Oracle Database software, it must be installed under an operating system user. Our choice of user is important, since the installation process will be run while logged in as that user. Once completed, the software that has been installed will be owned by that user. This can affect user access to the software, so we must ensure that we choose the user correctly. Generally, we want this user to be a dedicated operating system user, rather than a personal user account, such as `ssarah` or `frankross`.

In Windows, our choice is fairly straightforward. We simply create a dedicated user account with administrator-level privileges. To create a new user, we will need to be logged in as a user with the operating system privileges. To stay consistent with the Linux and Unix standards, a user named `oracle` would be a good choice, but that is up to the person doing the installation. The individual standards of your company may differ. Once the user is created, log in as that user before you begin the installation.

In Linux and other Unix-based operating systems, the process is similar, with one significant difference. As with Windows, we need to choose or create a user to own the installation. The well-established standard in this case is to create a user called `oracle` for our installation. However, in Unix-based systems, we also need to create an **operating system group** to which this user belongs. Here, due to the established standards, we create an OS group called `dba`. The choice of this group name will become significant during the installation process. The creation of users and groups in Unix-based systems requires the root user or privileges. We must remember to log in as the `oracle` user before running the OUI under Linux and Unix.

> **The real-world DBA**
> For security reasons, it is generally a bad idea to use the administrator user on Windows or the root user on Unix-based system as your Oracle installation user. The Oracle software owner should be a dedicated user with the proper permissions.

Establishing Oracle directory structures

Before we run the OUI, we need to decide where our software will reside. Our choice will depend on several factors, including the amount of available disk space on our hard drives, how the drives are laid out, and what operating system we use. When we say "drives" (plural), we're referring to the fact that systems often have more than one drive or set of drives attached to them. The simplest layout (and one that you may be using if you're installing on a PC) would be a Windows system with one hard drive, labeled `C:`. In this case, many of our decisions are made for us. However, say that we have a small, commercial server running the Windows OS on one hard drive, a CD-ROM drive, and a second hard drive, labeled `C:`, `D:`, and `E:`, respectively. In this case, we have a choice as to where we install our software. But let's keep a few factors in mind. First, in a true server environment, `C:` is often reserved for the operating system alone. Second, we need to keep in mind that we will also eventually need space to store our actual database. Where possible, we'll often want to separate our Oracle installation from our database files for performance and recoverability reasons. This leaves us with some choices to make in our fictional three-drive system.

If we were to take a look at installing on Linux, we would see a different directory structure paradigm. Aside from directories that are separated by a / instead of a `\`, as in Windows, Linux does not use letter-labeled drives in the way that Windows does. Instead, Linux and Unix-based systems make use of **mount points**. All directories in Unix-based systems run from the root directory, or `/`. All other directories flow from that root directory.

A physical drive or partition can be attached to a particular directory, creating a mount point for that drive. Thus, instead of deciding that we will install Oracle on `E:`, we might say that our installation will be located on a mount point called `/app` or `/oracle` or any other mount point we wish to use.

Understanding the Optimal Flexible Architecture

In order to reduce some of this complexity, Oracle has defined the **Optimal Flexible Architecture**, or **OFA**. The OFA was originally designed as a directory structure standard for optimizing performance. With the OFA, you could structure your drives and mount points to spread processing across multiple disks, ensuring recoverability and reducing I/O bottlenecks. Today, the OFA is also promoted as a way to manage multiple installations of Oracle software on a single machine. From the database perspective, a DBA could use the OFA standard to install and run multiple versions of the Oracle Database software. The two primary directory structures for the OFA are known as the `ORACLE_BASE` and the `ORACLE_HOME`. These two locations are important even if you don't build an OFA-compliant system.

The `ORACLE_BASE` is the high-level root directory for the Oracle software "tree." All Oracle software installations, whether database, application server, or any other software that conforms to the OFA standard, are based in the directory defined by `ORACLE_BASE`. The recommended directory to be used as the `ORACLE_BASE` directory has changed over time with different versions of the Oracle software, and is different depending on your choice of operating system.

As of 11*g* Release 2, the recommended Windows directory for `ORACLE_BASE` is `C:\app\username`.

Where `username` is the name of the user under which the Oracle software is installed. The `ORACLE_BASE` directory on Linux is commonly defined as `/u01/app/oracle/` or `/app/oracle/`.

In the case of the Linux standard, `oracle` actually refers to the name of the user installing the software, not the product itself. As we mentioned, in Linux, this user is normally named `oracle`. Although it is necessary to define the `ORACLE_BASE` directory, the directory that most concerns the DBA is the `ORACLE_HOME`. The `ORACLE_HOME` directory is the base directory for any given installation of an Oracle product. Thus, when we install the Oracle Database software, we must specify an `ORACLE_HOME` directory as the location for the software. Like `ORACLE_BASE`, the `ORACLE_HOME` directory is operating-system dependent.

As of 11*g* Release 2, the recommended Windows directory for `ORACLE_HOME` is `C:\app\username\product\11.2.0\dbhome_1`.

Where `username` is the name of the user under which the Oracle software is installed. `11.2.0` designates the software version, and could differ depending on the version of the software installed. The `dbhome_1` directory allows for the flexibility of adding additional directories to host other versions of the software, for instance, `dbhome_2` and `dbhome_3`. In Linux, the `ORACLE_HOME` directory is usually located at `/u01/app/oracle/product/11.2.0/dbhome_1`.

Optionally, `u01` can be omitted, since the `/app` filesystem is often a standard on Linux machines.

Note that the OFA is not necessarily a hard-and-fast rule. It can be flexible enough to accommodate different disk drive letters on Windows and can also work with different mount points in Linux and Unix-based systems.

> **The real-world DBA**
>
> The OFA has another benefit; namely, it aims to be a common directory standard used by all DBAs. Ideally, a DBA could leave one place of employment and go to another without needing to learn an entirely different standard. This, however, is not always the case. Not every DBA organization follows the OFA to the letter or even at all. Even so, most standards that a DBA will encounter are derived in some way from the OFA. The fact that you have a standard is generally more important than which standard you use.

Using environment variables in Oracle

One of the most important reasons we cover `ORACLE_BASE` and `ORACLE_HOME` is that they take us into the subject of environment variables. An **environment variable** is an assigned value that contains information about the operating system or affects the way it behaves. Environment variables are common to operating systems, but they are not always expressed the same way. For instance, in Linux, an environment variable called `$PWD` for the present working directory contains the value of the user's current directory. It is referenced with the `echo` command, as shown here:

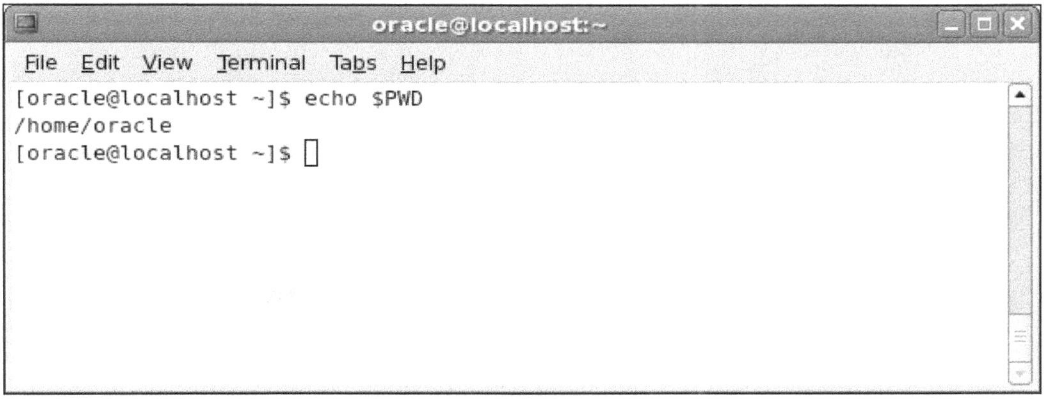
oracle@localhost:~
File Edit View Terminal Tabs Help
[oracle@localhost ~]$ echo $PWD
/home/oracle
[oracle@localhost ~]$

In Windows, we can also reference certain environment variables at the command line, albeit slightly differently. This example shows how to reference the environment variable that stores the name of the computer:

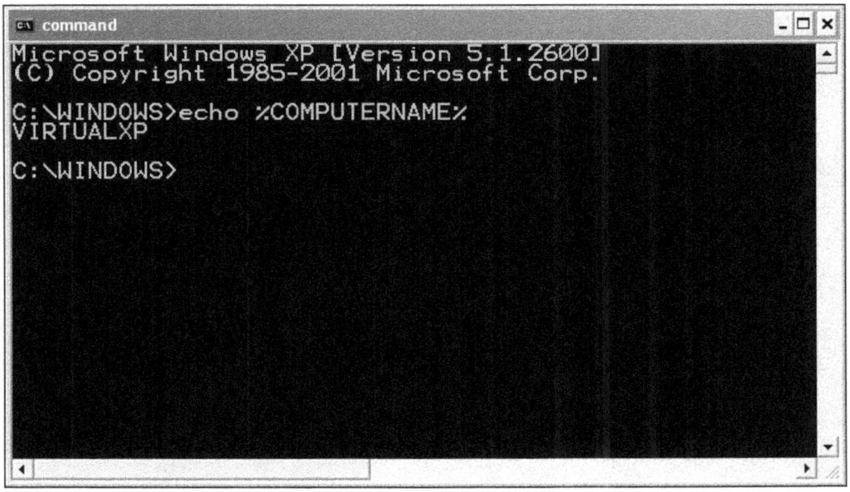
command
Microsoft Windows XP [Version 5.1.2600]
(C) Copyright 1985-2001 Microsoft Corp.
C:\WINDOWS>echo %COMPUTERNAME%
VIRTUALXP
C:\WINDOWS>

Remember that Windows and Unix-based systems have different rules about case sensitivity. Both the commands and variable names are case sensitive in Linux and Unix, but not in Windows. Also note that the environment variables are also stored in the registry in Windows. The Windows registry is a hierarchical database that contains a vast amount of system configuration information. We will revisit this topic once our Oracle installation is complete.

While environment variables are an important part of any operating system, they have a special relevance to DBAs. On a system with Oracle installed, there are several environment variables that directly relate to the Oracle software, in this case, the database software. In fact, both the `ORACLE_BASE` and `ORACLE_HOME` directories are stored as environment variables on systems running Oracle. In Unix-based systems, such as Solaris and Linux, they are referenced with the `$ORACLE_BASE` and `$ORACLE_HOME` variables. We can display the value of these variables using the command shown in the following screenshot:

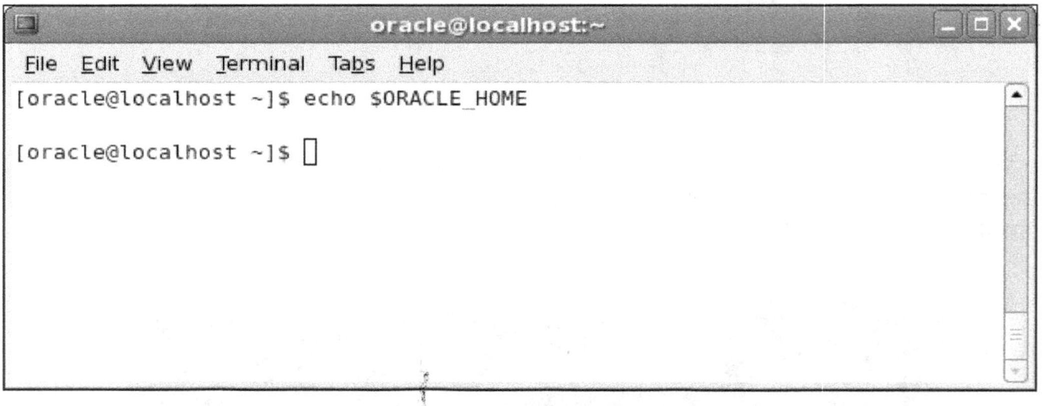
oracle@localhost:~
File Edit View Terminal Tabs Help
[oracle@localhost ~]$ echo $ORACLE_HOME
[oracle@localhost ~]$

As we can see, no value is currently displayed for `$ORACLE_HOME`, owing to the fact that we have not yet installed the software. The definition of Oracle environment variables is generally done as a part of the installation process. We can, however, define them beforehand if we wish. An example of this in Linux is shown here:

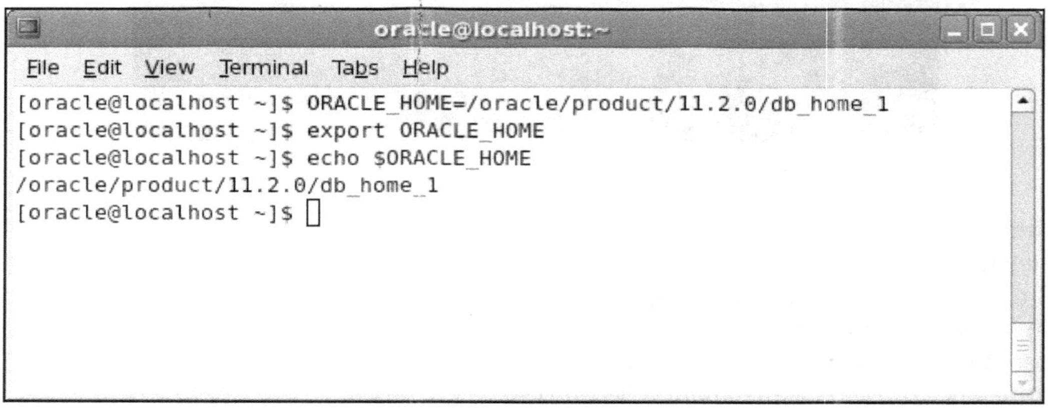
oracle@localhost:~
File Edit View Terminal Tabs Help
[oracle@localhost ~]$ ORACLE_HOME=/oracle/product/11.2.0/db_home_1
[oracle@localhost ~]$ export ORACLE_HOME
[oracle@localhost ~]$ echo $ORACLE_HOME
/oracle/product/11.2.0/db_home_1
[oracle@localhost ~]$

Once our Windows installation is complete, we will have no need to manually define the relevant Oracle environment variables, since they'll be permanently stored in the Windows registry. A table summarizing some of the more common Oracle-related environment variables is shown here:

Environment Variable	Description
ORACLE_BASE	The base directory for Oracle software
ORACLE_HOME	The directory for the Oracle database installation
PATH	Identifies directories to search for executables
DISPLAY	Identifies the display location for graphical windowing
LD_LIBRARY_PATH	Defines the path to use when searching for shared libraries
ORACLE_SID	Specifies the name of the Oracle database

Installing the Oracle Database software

Having reviewed the prerequisite considerations for an Oracle Database installation, we're now ready to step through the process. We've already noted that the Oracle Universal Installer attempts to make the installation process as similar as possible between different operating systems. However, there are key differences, and we will note them as we move ahead in the chapter. Most of the screens we'll present are done from an installation of Oracle 11*g* Release 2, v11.2.0.1, on the Red Hat Linux operating system. If you're installing on Windows or another Unix-based OS, you should see very similar screens for the most part. In situations that are distinct for certain operating systems, we'll note that fact and show screens from that operating system to highlight the differences.

Running the Oracle Universal Installer

Although there are not many differences between running the OUI on the different operating systems supported by Oracle, we begin our installation procedure with a significant one—the installation executable itself. Assuming we've downloaded the installation package from Oracle in the form of ZIP files and unzipped them, we see that on both Windows and Unix-based systems, a directory called `database` is created. If we're using the DVD installation media, we see that same directory on the disc itself. If we look inside that directory on a Windows system, we notice an executable named `setup.exe`. This is the file that starts the OUI on Windows. A screenshot showing the contents of the `database` directory from within Windows Explorer is shown here:

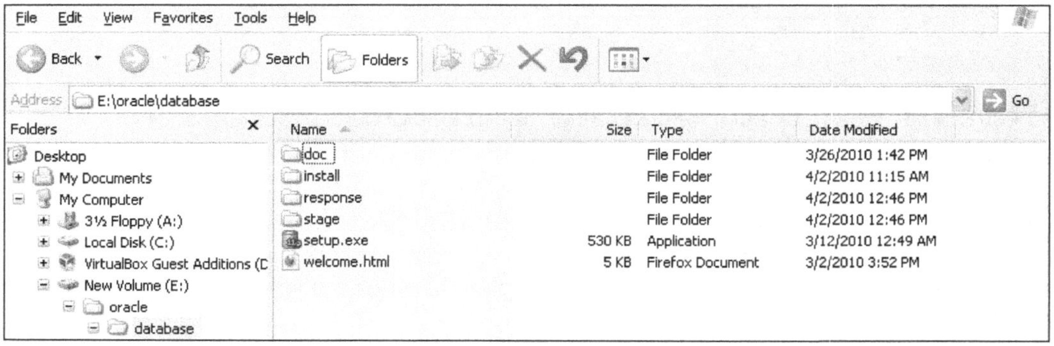
File Edit View Favorites Tools Help
Back
Search
Folders
Address E:\oracle\database
Go
Folders
Desktop
My Documents
My Computer
3½ Floppy (A:)
Local Disk (C:)
VirtualBox Guest Additions (C
New Volume (E:)
oracle
database
Name
Size
Type
Date Modified
doc File Folder 3/26/2010 1:42 PM
install File Folder 4/2/2010 11:15 AM
response File Folder 4/2/2010 12:46 PM
stage File Folder 4/2/2010 12:46 PM
setup.exe 530 KB Application 3/12/2010 12:49 AM
welcome.html 5 KB Firefox Document 3/2/2010 3:52 PM

To begin the installation, we simply double-click the `setup.exe` executable. The first screen we see is a command-line window that invokes the installer, as shown in the following screenshot. Simply wait for the GUI installer to begin:

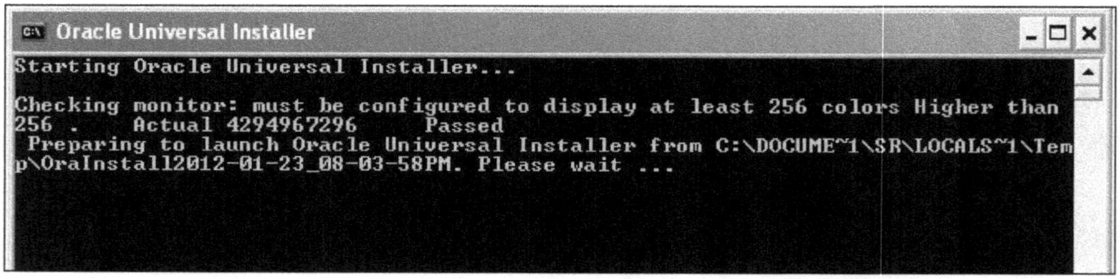
Oracle Universal Installer
Starting Oracle Universal Installer...
Checking monitor: must be configured to display at least 256 colors Higher than 256 . Actual 4294967296 Passed
Preparing to launch Oracle Universal Installer from C:\DOCUME~1\SR\LOCALS~1\Temp\OraInstall2012-01-23_08-03-58PM. Please wait ...

In Linux, our start-up executable is completely different. Instead, within the `database` directory we find several files, one of which is named `runInstaller`:

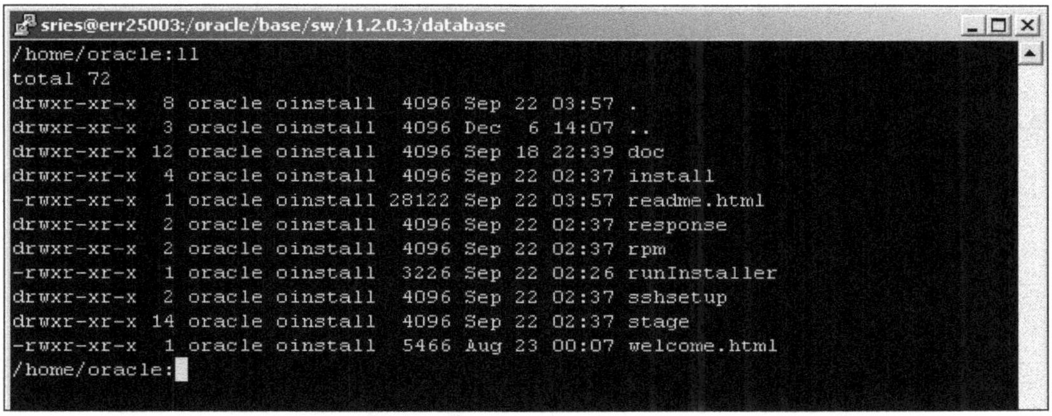
sries@err25003:/oracle/base/sw/11.2.0.3/database
/home/oracle:ll
total 72
drwxr-xr-x 8 oracle oinstall 4096 Sep 22 03:57 .
drwxr-xr-x 3 oracle oinstall 4096 Dec 6 14:07 ..
drwxr-xr-x 12 oracle oinstall 4096 Sep 18 22:39 doc
drwxr-xr-x 4 oracle oinstall 4096 Sep 22 02:37 install
-rwxr-xr-x 1 oracle oinstall 28122 Sep 22 03:57 readme.html
drwxr-xr-x 2 oracle oinstall 4096 Sep 22 02:37 response
drwxr-xr-x 2 oracle oinstall 4096 Sep 22 02:37 rpm
-rwxr-xr-x 1 oracle oinstall 3226 Sep 22 02:26 runInstaller
drwxr-xr-x 2 oracle oinstall 4096 Sep 22 02:37 sshsetup
drwxr-xr-x 14 oracle oinstall 4096 Sep 22 02:37 stage
-rwxr-xr-x 1 oracle oinstall 5466 Aug 23 00:07 welcome.html
/home/oracle:

To begin the installation in Linux, we type `./runInstaller`. This begins the installation procedure in a similar fashion to the Windows installer we saw previously. This portion of the install is loading the necessary Java libraries to invoke the GUI installer, which is written in Java. The remainder of the screens shown will be from an install in Linux. For those that differ from a Windows install, we'll note this as we move ahead in the chapter.

The first GUI screen we're presented with allows us to configure the ability to receive security update notifications from Oracle. The first option allows us to enter an e-mail address to receive notification alerts from Oracle when a security patch is released. The second allows us to receive notifications directly to a **My Oracle Support** account. These accounts are associated with the license support agreements between Oracle and the customers who have paid for support. For our purposes, we will skip these features by deselecting any checkboxes and clicking **Next**:

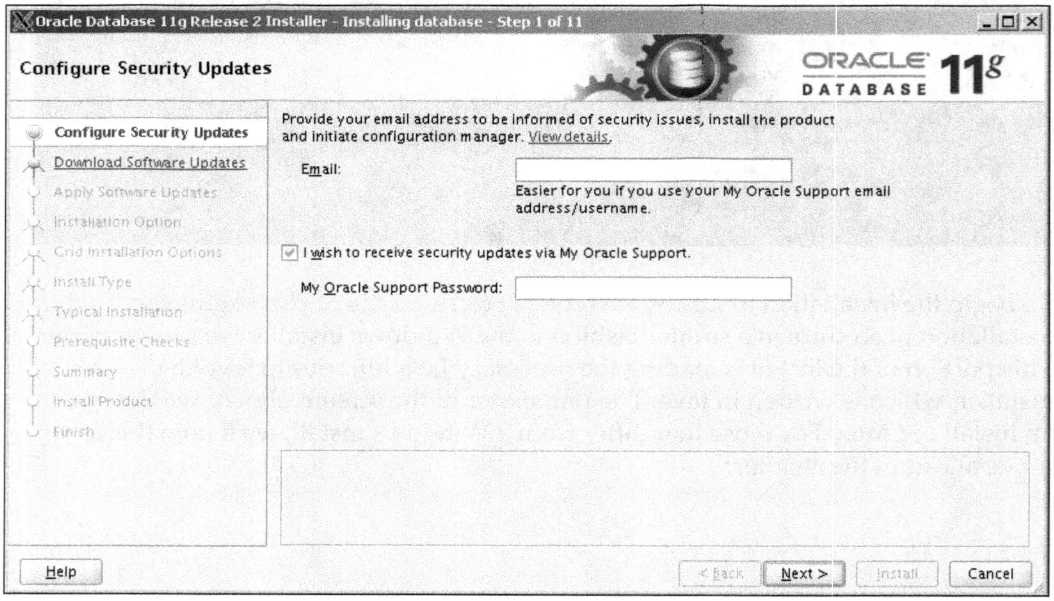
Oracle Database 11g Release 2 Installer - Installing database - Step 1 of 11
Configure Security Updates
ORACLE DATABASE 11g
Configure Security Updates
Download Software Updates
Apply Software Updates
Installation Option
Grid Installation Options
Install Type
Typical Installation
Prerequisite Checks
Summary
Install Product
Finish
Provide your email address to be informed of security issues, install the product and initiate configuration manager. View details.
Email:
Easier for you if you use your My Oracle Support email address/username.
I wish to receive security updates via My Oracle Support.
My Oracle Support Password:
Help
< Back
Next >
Install
Cancel

When we deselect the checkboxes and don't include an e-mail address, we're prompted with the following dialog box asking us to be sure that these selections are correct; simply choose **Yes**:

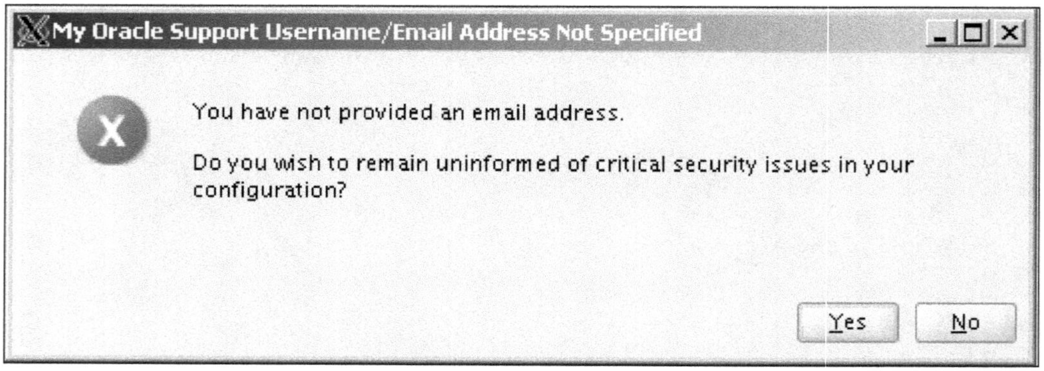
My Oracle Support Username/Email Address Not Specified
You have not provided an email address.
Do you wish to remain uninformed of critical security issues in your configuration?
Yes
No

The second screen of the installation wizard allows us to configure our software to easily apply any current patches for the Oracle software. These include security patches and **Patch Set Updates** (or **PSUs**). We have three choices here. First, if our software installation is covered under an Oracle license agreement, we can enter our **My Oracle Support** credentials for an easy download. Second, if we've pre-downloaded the patches from Oracle, we can browse to the directory where they're stored. Lastly, we can skip software updating. For our purposes, we'll select this option, as shown in the following screenshot, and continue by clicking **Next**:

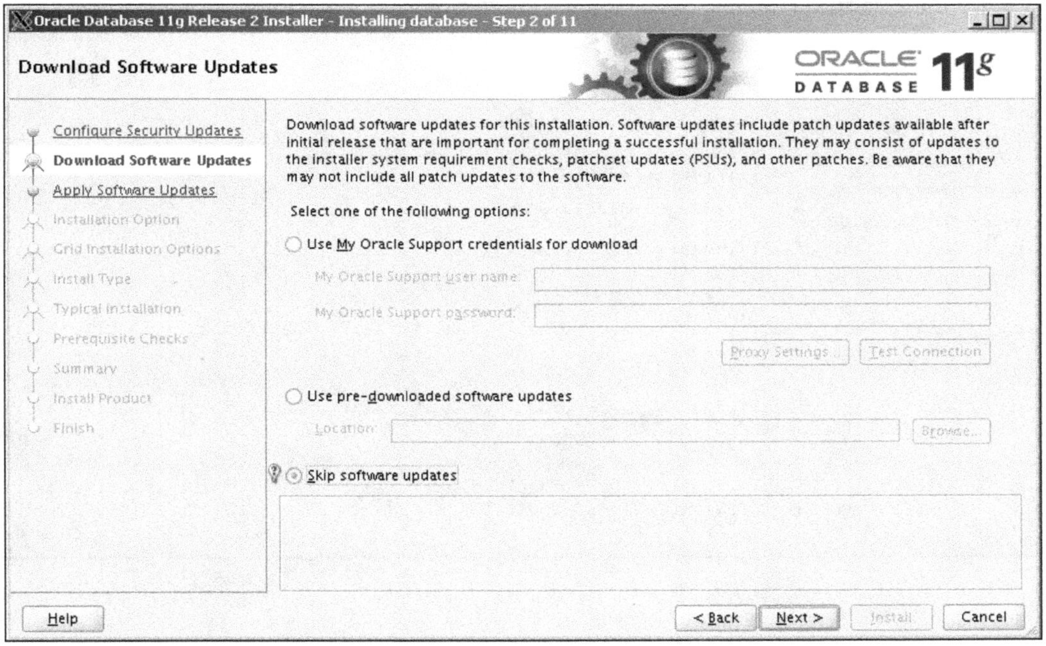

Oracle Database 11g Release 2 Installer - Installing database - Step 2 of 11
Download Software Updates
ORACLE DATABASE 11g
Configure Security Updates
Download Software Updates
Apply Software Updates
Installation Option
Grid Installation Options
Install Type
Typical Installation
Prerequisite Checks
Summary
Install Product
Finish
Download software updates for this installation. Software updates include patch updates available after initial release that are important for completing a successful installation. They may consist of updates to the installer system requirement checks, patchset updates (PSUs), and other patches. Be aware that they may not include all patch updates to the software.
Select one of the following options:
Use My Oracle Support credentials for download
My Oracle Support user name:
My Oracle Support password:
Proxy Settings...
Test Connection
Use pre-downloaded software updates
Location:
Browse...
Skip software updates
Help
< Back
Next >
Install
Cancel

Our next screen (labeled **Installing database - Step 3 of 10**, in the following title window) allows us to choose the type of installation we wish to run. Our first option actually allows us to run the installation and then immediately run the wizard to create a database—all in one series of steps. Although we would still need to work through all of the steps involved, this option doesn't require us to separately run the configuration of the database. The third option allows us to upgrade an existing installation. Since this is a new installation and we'll cover database creation in the next chapter, we choose the second option, **Install database software only**, and click **Next**:

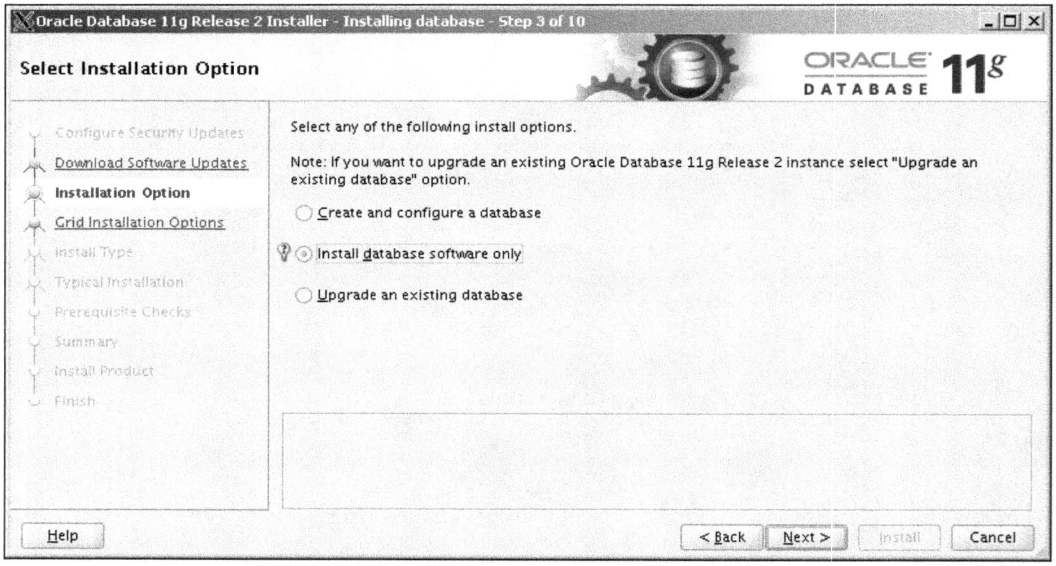
Oracle Database 11g Release 2 Installer - Installing database - Step 3 of 10
Select Installation Option
ORACLE DATABASE 11g
Configure Security Updates
Download Software Updates
Installation Option
Grid Installation Options
Install Type
Typical Installation
Prerequisite Checks
Summary
Install Product
Finish
Select any of the following install options.
Note: If you want to upgrade an existing Oracle Database 11g Release 2 instance select "Upgrade an existing database" option.
Create and configure a database
Install database software only
Upgrade an existing database
Help
< Back
Next >
Install
Cancel

The next screen presents us with **Grid Installation Options**. These are advanced options that we will touch on briefly when we discuss database architecture. We choose **Single instance database installation** and click **Next**:

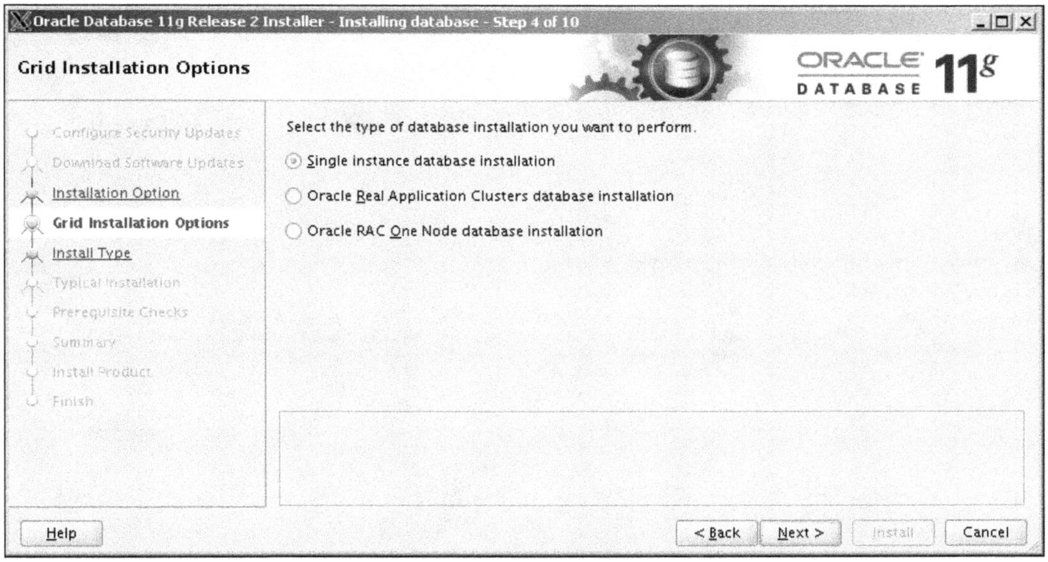
Oracle Database 11g Release 2 Installer - Installing database - Step 4 of 10
Grid Installation Options
ORACLE DATABASE 11g
Configure Security Updates
Download Software Updates
Installation Option
Grid Installation Options
Install Type
Typical Installation
Prerequisite Checks
Summary
Install Product
Finish
Select the type of database installation you want to perform.
Single instance database installation
Oracle Real Application Clusters database installation
Oracle RAC One Node database installation
Help
< Back
Next >
Install
Cancel

We're next given the opportunity to select the type of language support we need for our database. By default, English is selected in the right-hand side pane. If you wish to add support for another language, choose it from the left pane and add it to the right pane with the single arrow button. Otherwise, click **Next**.

As we mentioned previously in the chapter, the Oracle installation package allows us to install different editions of the Oracle Database software. In this screen, we see selections for the **Enterprise Edition**, **Standard Edition**, and **Standard Edition One**. On a Windows installation, we would also see the **Personal Edition** as well:

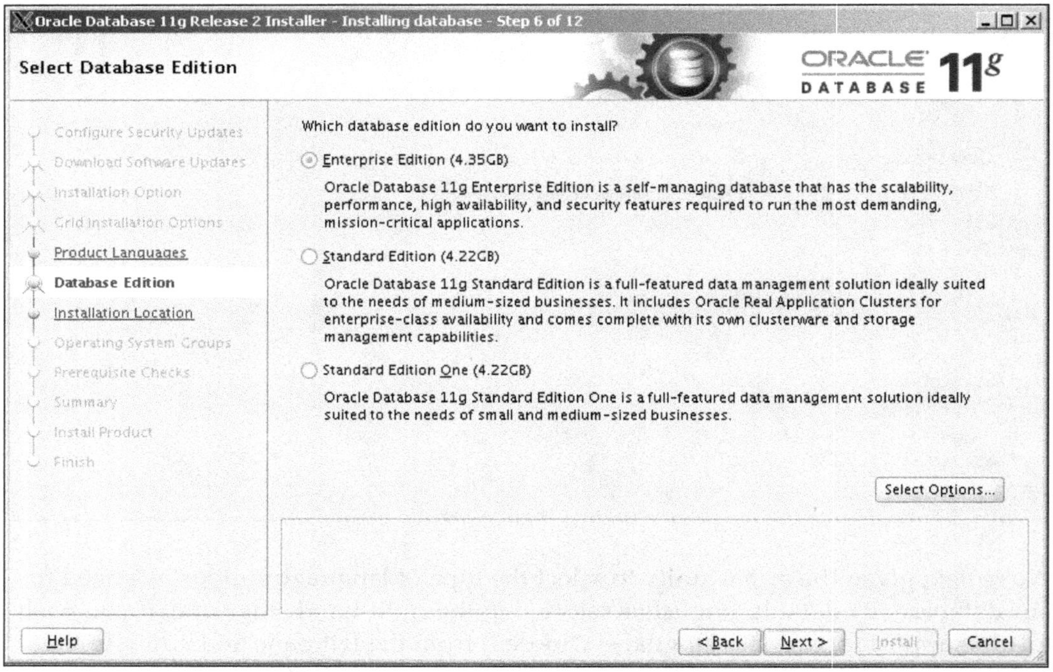
Oracle Database 11g Release 2 Installer - Installing database - Step 6 of 12
Select Database Edition
ORACLE DATABASE 11g
Configure Security Updates
Download Software Updates
Installation Option
Grid Installation Options
Product Languages
Database Edition
Installation Location
Operating System Groups
Prerequisite Checks
Summary
Install Product
Finish
Which database edition do you want to install?
Enterprise Edition (4.35GB)
Oracle Database 11g Enterprise Edition is a self-managing database that has the scalability, performance, high availability, and security features required to run the most demanding, mission-critical applications.
Standard Edition (4.22GB)
Oracle Database 11g Standard Edition is a full-featured data management solution ideally suited to the needs of medium-sized businesses. It includes Oracle Real Application Clusters for enterprise-class availability and comes complete with its own clusterware and storage management capabilities.
Standard Edition One (4.22GB)
Oracle Database 11g Standard Edition One is a full-featured data management solution ideally suited to the needs of small and medium-sized businesses.
Select Options...
Help
< Back
Next >
Install
Cancel

We can also see some of the database options that we mentioned earlier. By clicking the **Select Options...** button, we're presented with the following screen:

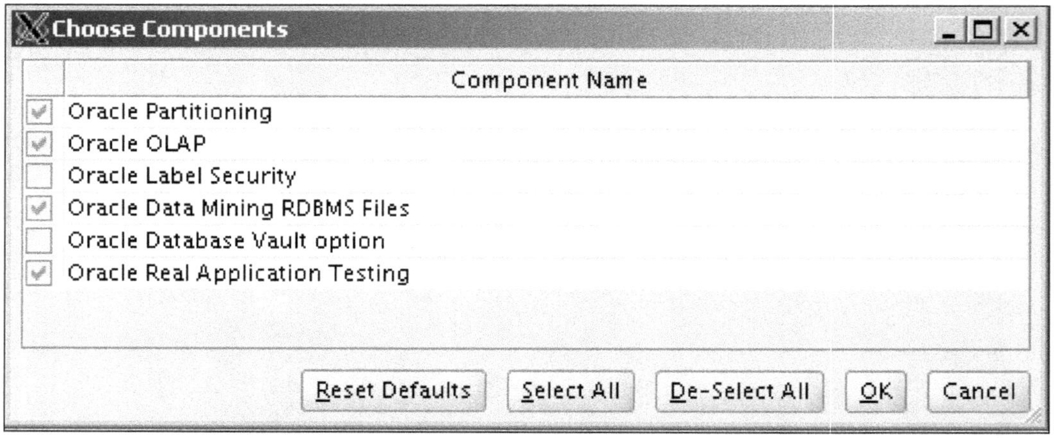
Choose Components
Component Name
Oracle Partitioning
Oracle OLAP
Oracle Label Security
Oracle Data Mining RDBMS Files
Oracle Database Vault option
Oracle Real Application Testing
Reset Defaults
Select All
De-Select All
OK
Cancel

This window allows us to choose from the options available to us in this installation package. For our purposes, we'll leave the default options selected and click **OK**. This returns us to the **Select Database Edition** screen. We ensure that the **Enterprise Edition** radio button is selected and click **Next**.

> **Beyond the exam**
>
> Some database options, such as **Real Application Clusters**, are not shown in the list of database options in the previous screenshot. These options require installation using separate packages, which are also available from the Oracle Technology Network.

The next screen allows us to choose our installation location. Recall from earlier in the chapter that we discussed `ORACLE_BASE` and `ORACLE_HOME`. For the purposes of the installation, we define these in this screen. The first box, labeled **Oracle Base**, will contain our selection for the `ORACLE_BASE` directory. The second, labeled **Software Location**, is actually our `ORACLE_HOME` directory. Because this screen requires us to enter operating system directories, these screens will differ slightly in Linux and Windows. First, we display an example of the installation location screen in Linux in the following screenshot:

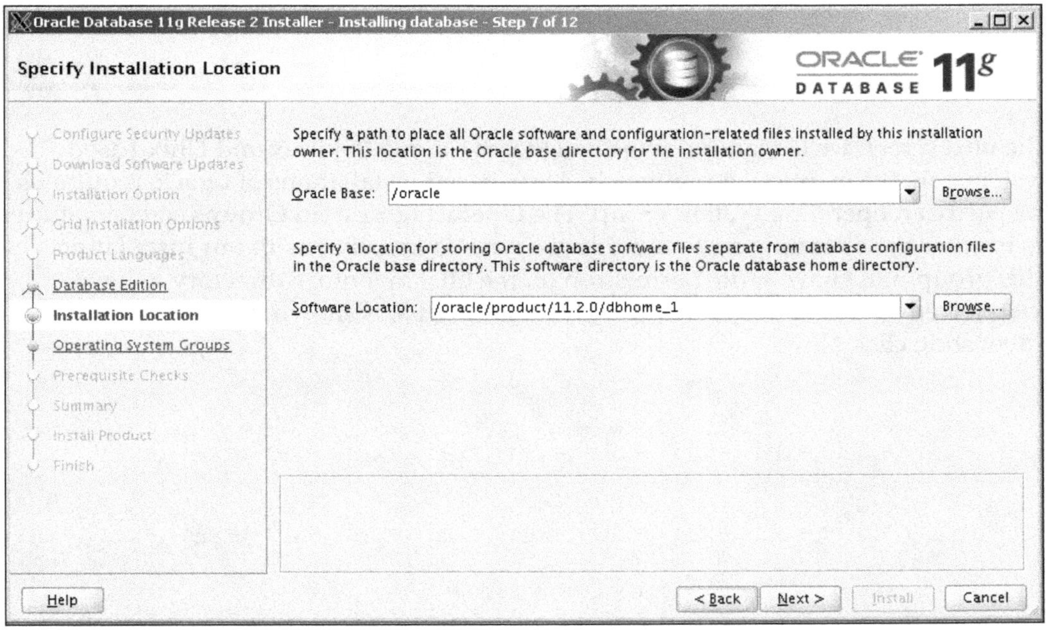
Oracle Database 11g Release 2 Installer - Installing database - Step 7 of 12
Specify Installation Location
ORACLE DATABASE 11g
Configure Security Updates
Download Software Updates
Installation Option
Grid Installation Options
Product Languages
Database Edition
Installation Location
Operating System Groups
Prerequisite Checks
Summary
Install Product
Finish
Specify a path to place all Oracle software and configuration-related files installed by this installation owner. This location is the Oracle base directory for the installation owner.
Oracle Base: /oracle
Browse...
Specify a location for storing Oracle database software files separate from database configuration files in the Oracle base directory. This software directory is the Oracle database home directory.
Software Location: /oracle/product/11.2.0/dbhome_1
Browse...
Help
< Back
Next >
Install
Cancel

Next, we see the same screen in Windows. Notice that the screens themselves are very similar. The only real difference is the directories we choose. In any operating system, we either manually enter the directories for `ORACLE_BASE` and `ORACLE_HOME` or browse to them. Once this is complete, we choose **Next**.

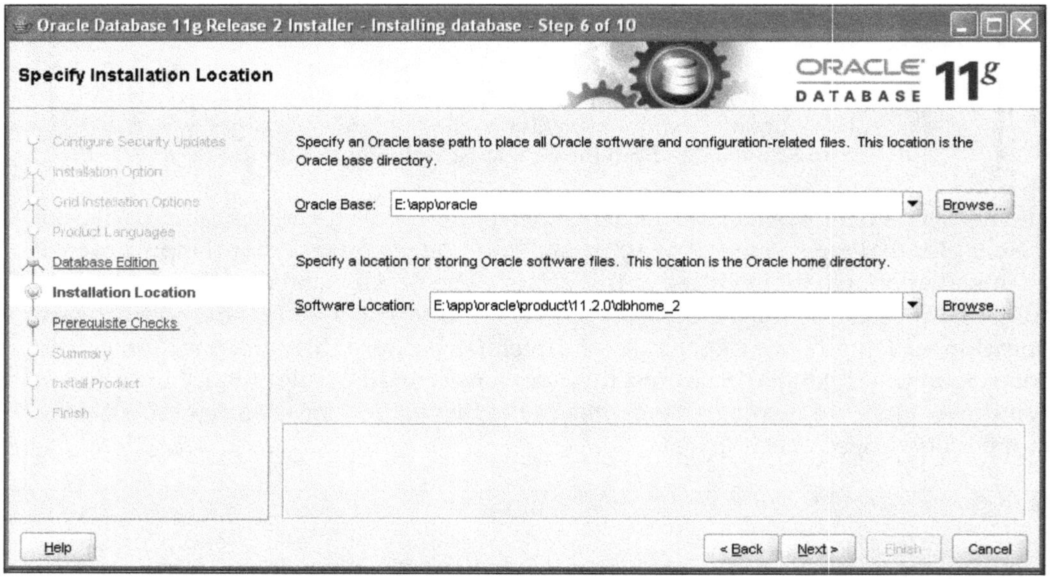
Oracle Database 11g Release 2 Installer - Installing database - Step 6 of 10
Specify Installation Location
ORACLE DATABASE 11g
Configure Security Updates
Installation Option
Grid Installation Options
Product Languages
Database Edition
Installation Location
Prerequisite Checks
Summary
Install Product
Finish
Specify an Oracle base path to place all Oracle software and configuration-related files. This location is the Oracle base directory.
Oracle Base: E:\app\oracle
Browse...
Specify a location for storing Oracle software files. This location is the Oracle home directory.
Software Location: E:\app\oracle\product\11.2.0\dbhome_2
Browse...
Help
< Back
Next >
Finish
Cancel

The next screen we'll examine is the one that is unique to Linux and Unix-based systems. As we mentioned previously, Unix-based installations of Oracle require us to specify an operating system group. The **Operating System Groups** screen requires us to enter the operating system group we wish to associate with our installation. This group must have write permission on the OUI inventory directory, which we referred to earlier in the chapter. The default, **dba**, is shown in the following screenshot; click **Next**:

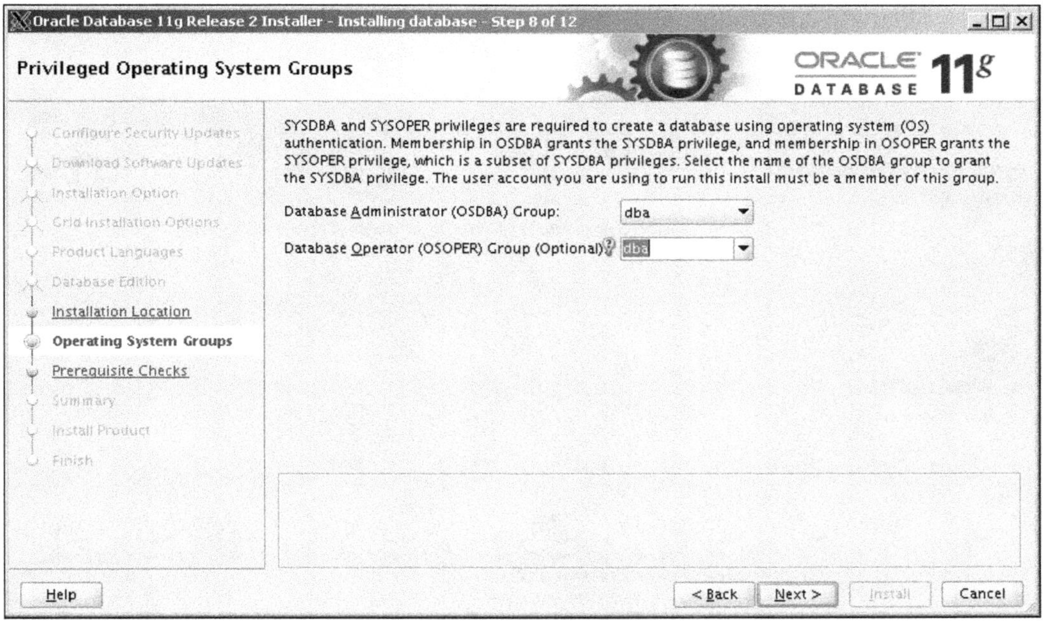
Oracle Database 11g Release 2 Installer - Installing database - Step 8 of 12
Privileged Operating System Groups
ORACLE DATABASE 11g
Configure Security Updates
Download Software Updates
Installation Option
Grid Installation Options
Product Languages
Database Edition
Installation Location
Operating System Groups
Prerequisite Checks
Summary
Install Product
Finish
SYSDBA and SYSOPER privileges are required to create a database using operating system (OS) authentication. Membership in OSDBA grants the SYSDBA privilege, and membership in OSOPER grants the SYSOPER privilege, which is a subset of SYSDBA privileges. Select the name of the OSDBA group to grant the SYSDBA privilege. The user account you are using to run this install must be a member of this group.
Database Administrator (OSDBA) Group:
dba
Database Operator (OSOPER) Group (Optional):
dba
Help
< Back
Next >
Install
Cancel

Following this selection, we return to a screen that is common to both Windows and Linux—the prerequisites screen. Here, the OUI checks the system for the various OS characteristics necessary to complete the installation. An example from our Linux installation is shown in the next screenshot.

It is possible that some checks will fail during the course of the prerequisite check, as shown in the following screenshot for an Oracle install on Windows:

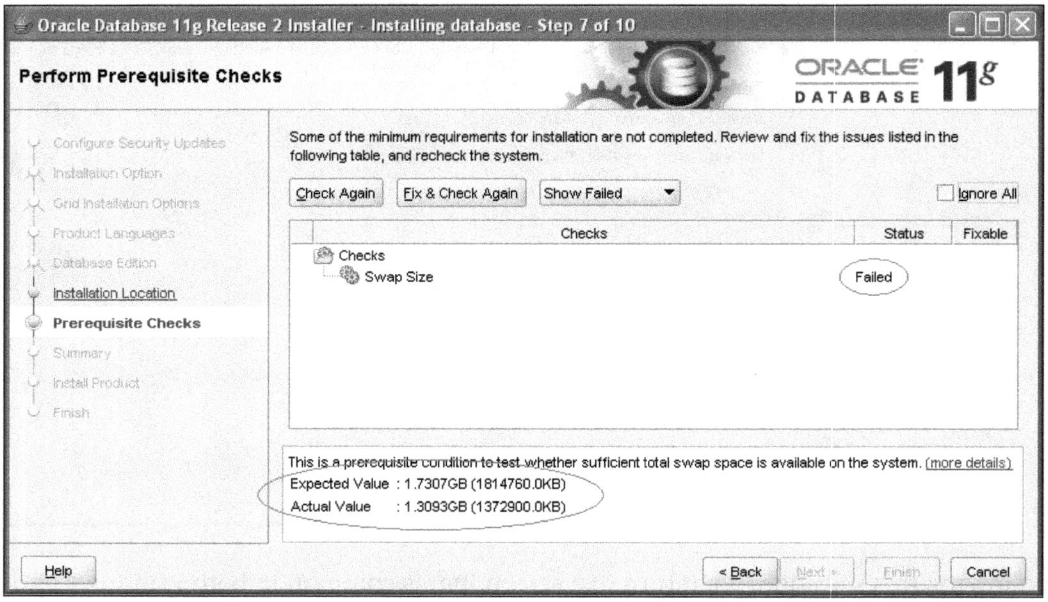
Oracle Database 11g Release 2 Installer - Installing database - Step 7 of 10
Perform Prerequisite Checks
ORACLE DATABASE 11g
Configure Security Updates
Installation Option
Grid Installation Options
Product Languages
Database Edition
Installation Location
Prerequisite Checks
Summary
Install Product
Finish
Some of the minimum requirements for installation are not completed. Review and fix the issues listed in the following table, and recheck the system.
Check Again
Fix & Check Again
Show Failed
Ignore All
Checks
Status
Fixable
Checks
Swap Size
Failed
This is a prerequisite condition to test whether sufficient total swap space is available on the system. (more details)
Expected Value : 1.7307GB (1814760.0KB)
Actual Value : 1.3093GB (1372900.0KB)
Help
< Back
Next >
Finish
Cancel

Here, the check for swap size has failed, indicating that our operating system swap size, **1.3093 GB**, is less than the recommended value of **1.7307 GB**. The prudent course of action at this point is to fix the failed prerequisites and click the **Check Again** button. Once we have cleared our prerequisites, we click **Next** to continue.

The real-world DBA

It's worth noting that some checks, including the swap size check, can be safely ignored in some cases. In view of the fact that our swap size, while less than the expected value, is fairly close, we can click the **Ignore All** checkbox and continue. If our swap size were significantly lower than expected, we may encounter problems during the installation. Ignoring some checks, such as package requirements on Linux, can cause the installation to fail. Understanding the situations where certain checks can be ignored comes with testing and experience.

As we near the end of the interactive part of the installation, we're presented with a summary screen. At this point, we should check the information shown to ensure that we've correctly entered the correct settings and click **Install**. If we intend to use this installation as the basis for a silent mode install, we can click the **Save Response File...** button to save a response file that contains all of the configuration details that we have entered from the GUI:

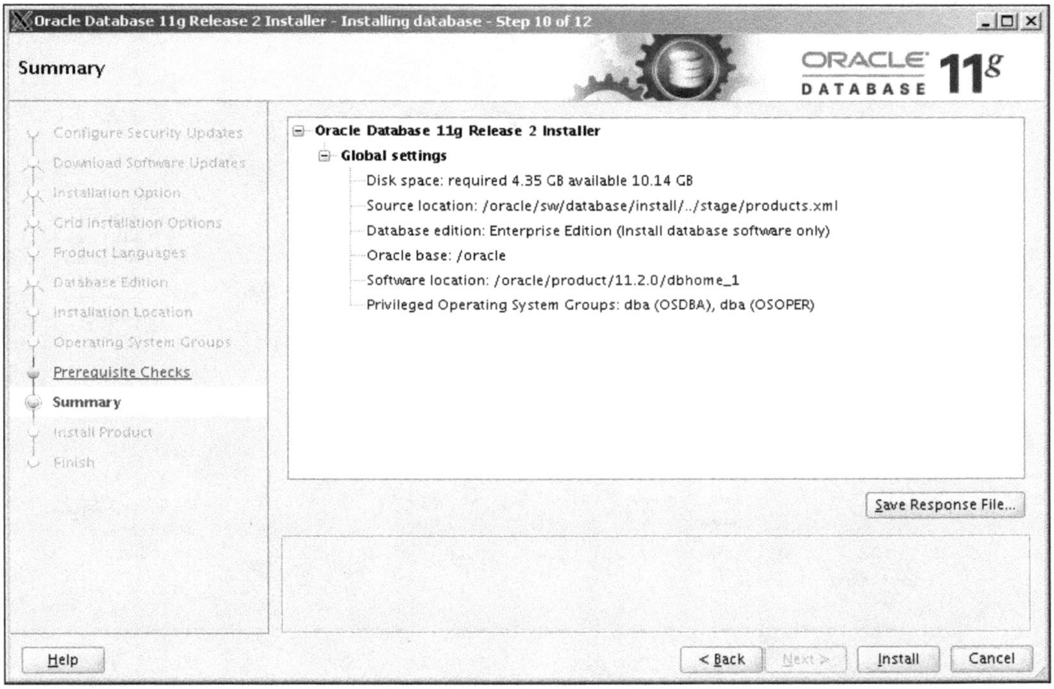
Oracle Database 11g Release 2 Installer - Installing database - Step 10 of 12
Summary
ORACLE DATABASE 11g
Configure Security Updates
Download Software Updates
Installation Option
Grid Installation Options
Product Languages
Database Edition
Installation Location
Operating System Groups
Prerequisite Checks
Summary
Install Product
Finish
Oracle Database 11g Release 2 Installer
Global settings
Disk space: required 4.35 GB available 10.14 GB
Source location: /oracle/sw/database/install/../stage/products.xml
Database edition: Enterprise Edition (Install database software only)
Oracle base: /oracle
Software location: /oracle/product/11.2.0/dbhome_1
Privileged Operating System Groups: dba (OSDBA), dba (OSOPER)
Save Response File...
Help
< Back
Next >
Install
Cancel

While the software is being installed, we're shown a screen that indicates our progress. As shown in the next screenshot, the steps are **Prepare**, **Copy files**, **Link binaries**, and **Setup files**. These steps take varying amounts of time depending on the options selected and resources of the host machine itself:

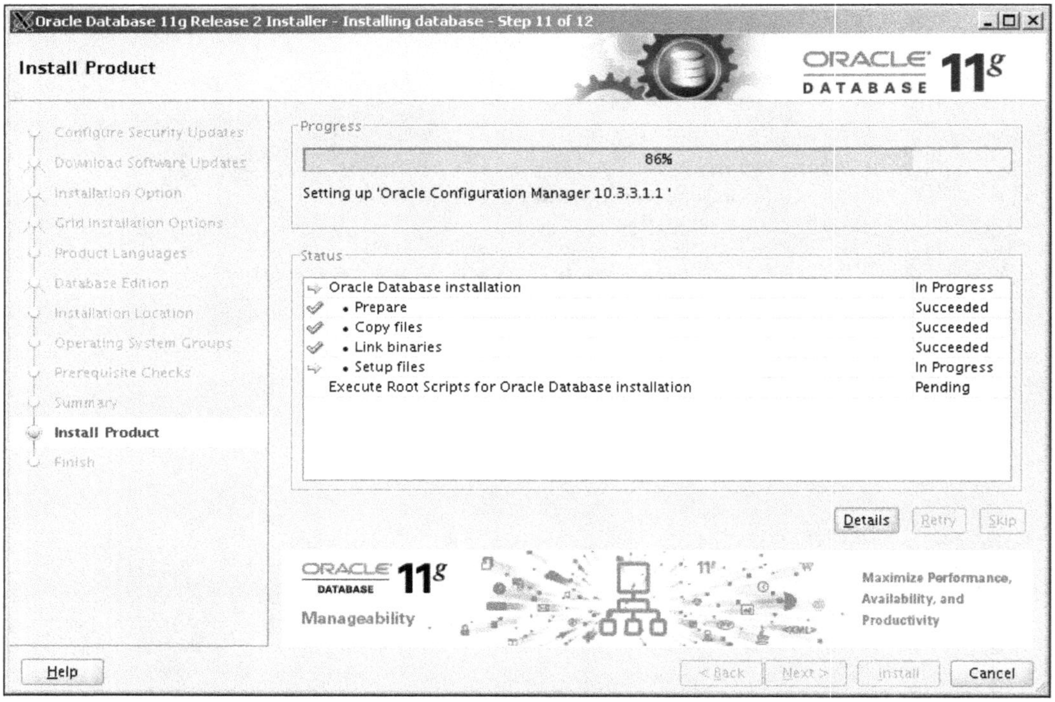
Oracle Database 11g Release 2 Installer - Installing database - Step 11 of 12
Install Product
ORACLE DATABASE 11g
Configure Security Updates
Download Software Updates
Installation Option
Grid Installation Options
Product Languages
Database Edition
Installation Location
Operating System Groups
Prerequisite Checks
Summary
Install Product
Finish
Progress
86%
Setting up 'Oracle Configuration Manager 10.3.3.1.1 '
Status
Oracle Database installation In Progress
• Prepare Succeeded
• Copy files Succeeded
• Link binaries Succeeded
• Setup files In Progress
Execute Root Scripts for Oracle Database installation Pending
Details
Retry
Skip
ORACLE DATABASE 11g
Manageability
Maximize Performance, Availability, and Productivity
Help
< Back
Next >
Install
Cancel

If our software is being installed on a Unix-based system, as in our Linux example, we have one additional step required to complete the install. A final configuration script, the `root.sh` script, is required. To complete this, open a separate terminal window and run the script as indicated. This script must be run as the `root` user because of this user's elevated system permissions. Do not run this script as the `oracle` user. This step is not present in Windows-based installs. If we've never installed an Oracle product on this machine before, we may also see a script called `orainstroot.sh`, which must also be run as `root`. If this is the case, run the scripts in the order indicated by the installer window:

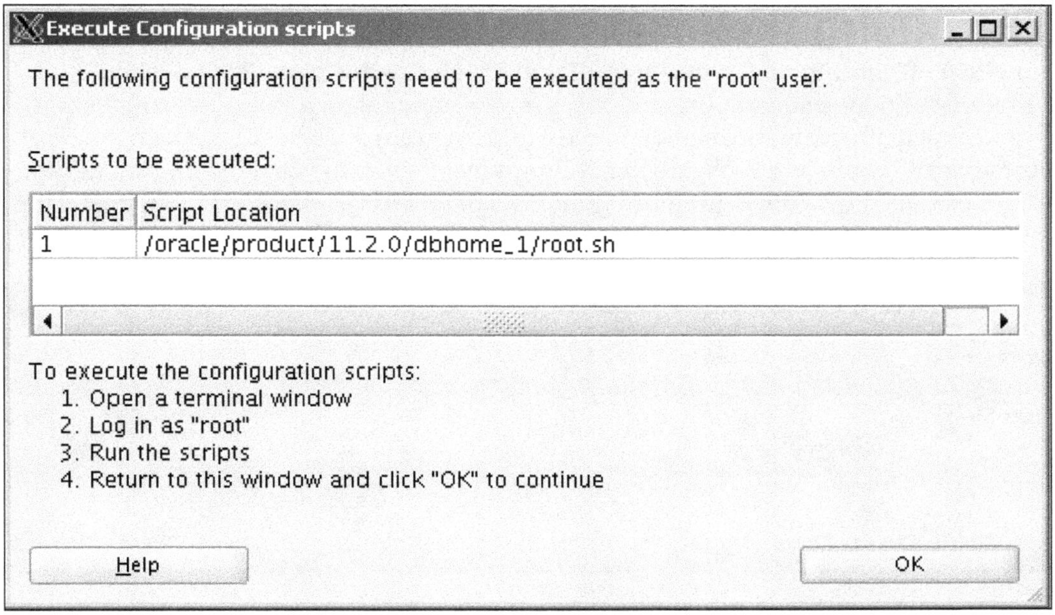
Execute Configuration scripts
The following configuration scripts need to be executed as the "root" user.
Scripts to be executed:
Number
Script Location
1
/oracle/product/11.2.0/dbhome_1/root.sh
To execute the configuration scripts:
1. Open a terminal window
2. Log in as "root"
3. Run the scripts
4. Return to this window and click "OK" to continue
Help
OK

Provided that the installation completes without error, we're presented with the **Finish** screen, indicating that our installation was successful. We then click **Close** to end the installation. We now have a fully functional installation of the software necessary to run the Oracle Database Server. At this point, we may consider removing the installation package itself to free up disk space, since the installer and its packages take up over 2 GB of space.

Examining the installation

Now that our installation of the Oracle Database software is complete, we should take a moment and look at what we have. This is most evident on a Windows installation, where Oracle programs are shown in the program groups. To begin, click on the **Start** button in Windows and navigate to **All Programs**, then to the Oracle program group. In this example, the Oracle program group is named **Oracle - OraDb11g_home2**. The following example shows the program groups in Windows Explorer:

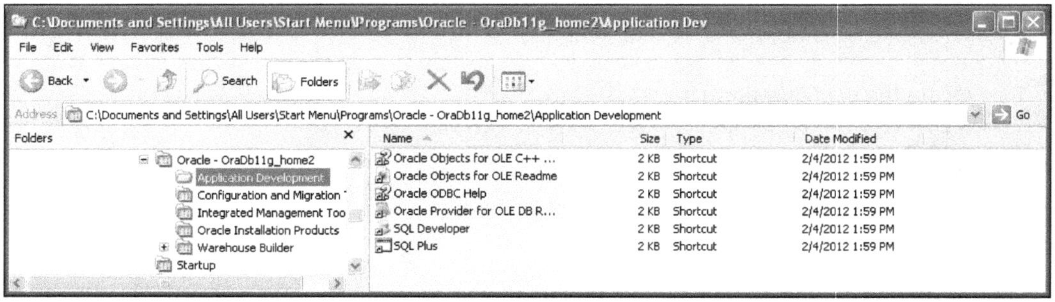
C:\Documents and Settings\All Users\Start Menu\Programs\Oracle - OraDb11g_home2\Application Dev
File
Edit
View
Favorites
Tools
Help
Back
Search
Folders
Address
C:\Documents and Settings\All Users\Start Menu\Programs\Oracle - OraDb11g_home2\Application Development
Go
Folders
Oracle - OraDb11g_home2
Application Development
Configuration and Migration
Integrated Management Too
Oracle Installation Products
Warehouse Builder
Startup
Name
Size
Type
Date Modified
Oracle Objects for OLE C++ ...
Oracle Objects for OLE Readme
Oracle ODBC Help
Oracle Provider for OLE DB R...
SQL Developer
SQL Plus
2 KB
Shortcut
2/4/2012 1:59 PM

The program groups you see under the **Start** menu should be similar. Although the majority of these tools will not concern us, two that we should take note of are in the **Application Development** program group. As we mentioned in *Chapter 1, Introducing the Oracle Relational Database System*, we will primarily use the SQL*Plus and SQL Developer tools located in that program group. Take note of these two programs, as we will use them frequently throughout the book.

We looked at the subject of environment variables earlier in this chapter and demonstrated how to view their values using the `echo` command in Linux. While we have a somewhat limited capacity to control environment variables from the command line in Windows, we can see them more readily in the Windows registry. Even though we will examine Oracle's registry entries here, it is not recommended that you attempt to change the registry or its values in any way unless you're expertly familiar with the registry and have a backup. Corrupting the Windows registry can, in some cases, cause your system to become unstable. If you are not familiar with the registry, it's recommended that you follow the examples in the reading and not attempt them yourself.

To examine the Oracle environment variables, we must first invoke the registry editor. This can be done from the Windows command line with the `regedit.exe` command. From `regedit`, we navigate using the following path:

My Computer | **HKEY_LOCAL_MACHINE** | **Software** | **ORACLE**

Within the `Oracle` folder, there will be a folder named `KEY_` followed by the name of the Oracle Home. Remember that the name of the Oracle Home is not the same as the directory value of `ORACLE_HOME`. The Oracle registry keys that represent environment variables are located within this `KEY_` folder. An example set of keys is shown in the following screenshot:

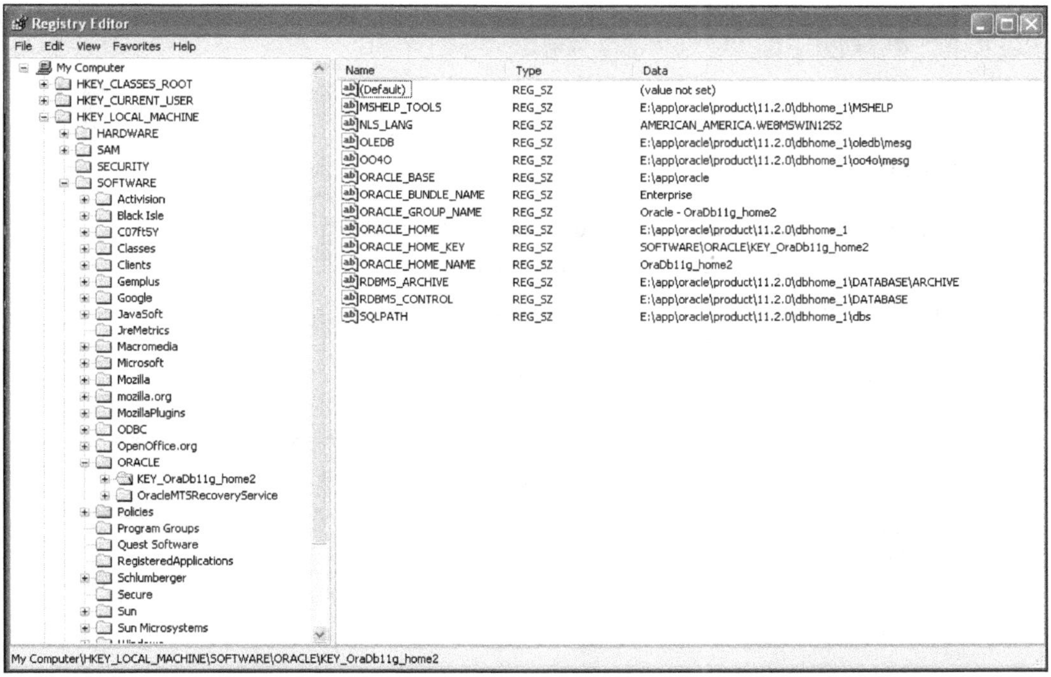
Registry Editor
File Edit View Favorites Help
My Computer
HKEY_CLASSES_ROOT
HKEY_CURRENT_USER
HKEY_LOCAL_MACHINE
HARDWARE
SAM
SECURITY
SOFTWARE
Activision
Black Isle
C07ft5Y
Classes
Clients
Gemplus
Google
JavaSoft
JreMetrics
Macromedia
Microsoft
Mozilla
mozilla.org
MozillaPlugins
ODBC
OpenOffice.org
ORACLE
KEY_OraDb11g_home2
OracleMTSRecoveryService
Policies
Program Groups
Quest Software
RegisteredApplications
Schlumberger
Secure
Sun
Sun Microsystems
Name
Type
Data
(Default) REG_SZ (value not set)
MSHELP_TOOLS REG_SZ E:\app\oracle\product\11.2.0\dbhome_1\MSHELP
NLS_LANG REG_SZ AMERICAN_AMERICA.WE8MSWIN1252
OLEDB REG_SZ E:\app\oracle\product\11.2.0\dbhome_1\oledb\mesg
OO4O REG_SZ E:\app\oracle\product\11.2.0\dbhome_1\oo4o\mesg
ORACLE_BASE REG_SZ E:\app\oracle
ORACLE_BUNDLE_NAME REG_SZ Enterprise
ORACLE_GROUP_NAME REG_SZ Oracle - OraDb11g_home2
ORACLE_HOME REG_SZ E:\app\oracle\product\11.2.0\dbhome_1
ORACLE_HOME_KEY REG_SZ SOFTWARE\ORACLE\KEY_OraDb11g_home2
ORACLE_HOME_NAME REG_SZ OraDb11g_home2
RDBMS_ARCHIVE REG_SZ E:\app\oracle\product\11.2.0\dbhome_1\DATABASE\ARCHIVE
RDBMS_CONTROL REG_SZ E:\app\oracle\product\11.2.0\dbhome_1\DATABASE
SQLPATH REG_SZ E:\app\oracle\product\11.2.0\dbhome_1\dbs
My Computer\HKEY_LOCAL_MACHINE\SOFTWARE\ORACLE\KEY_OraDb11g_home2

In this example, we can see a few environment variables that we're already familiar with, such as `ORACLE_BASE` and `ORACLE_HOME`. When necessary, we can double-click these values and change them.

Understanding the de-installation process – advanced topic

While it is not covered on the certification exam, we close this chapter with a look at an advanced topic—de-installing the Oracle software. We touch on this for two reasons. First, in real-world situations, it is always possible that a DBA would need to uninstall the Oracle software, perhaps from a failed installation or a server that is being decommissioned. Second, the process in Oracle 11*g* R2 is somewhat different from previous versions.

After an installation of Oracle, the Oracle Universal Installer can be invoked at any time. On the Windows platform, we can start the OUI from the Oracle program group by navigating to **Start** | **All Programs** | **Oracle Program Group** | **Oracle Installation Products** | **Oracle Universal Installer**.

Invoking the OUI in this manner presents us with the following screen:

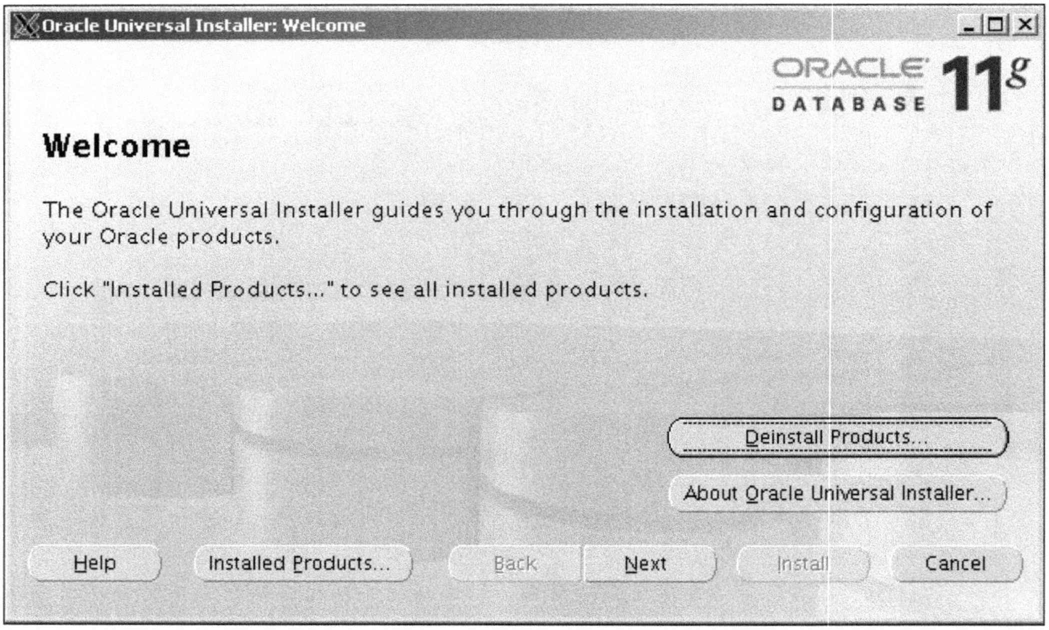
Oracle Universal Installer: Welcome
ORACLE DATABASE 11g
Welcome
The Oracle Universal Installer guides you through the installation and configuration of your Oracle products.
Click "Installed Products..." to see all installed products.
Deinstall Products...
About Oracle Universal Installer...
Help
Installed Products...
Back
Next
Install
Cancel

From here, we can click the **Deinstall Products** button. We're then shown a list of Oracle Homes that we can remove:

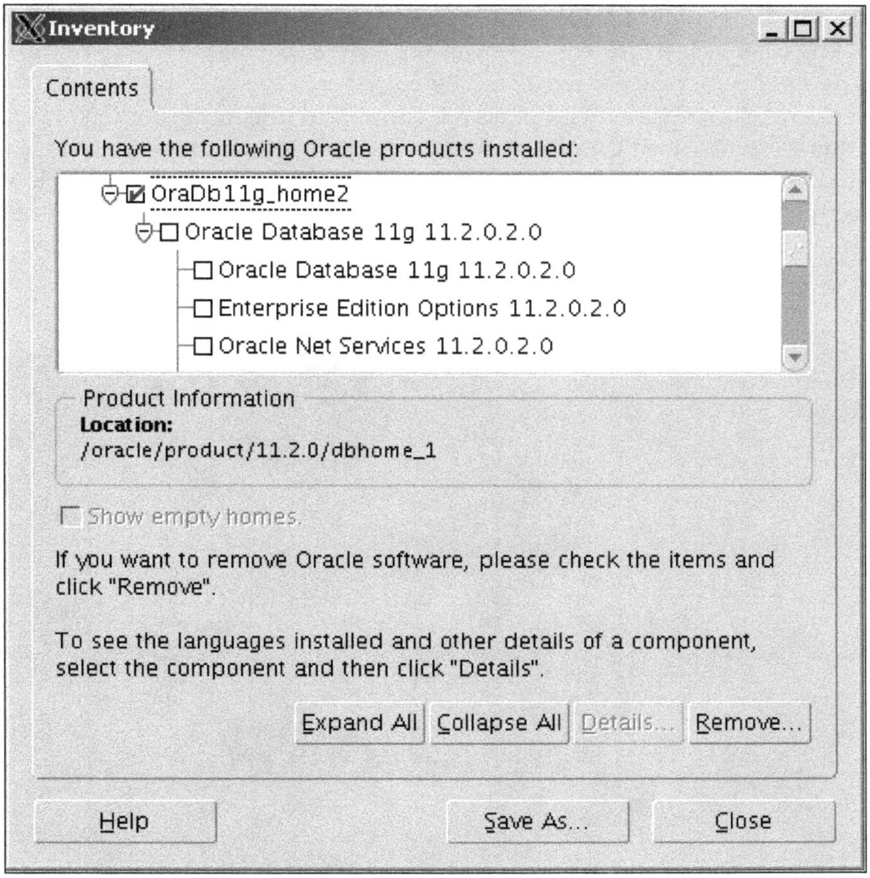
Inventory
Contents
You have the following Oracle products installed:
OraDb11g_home2
Oracle Database 11g 11.2.0.2.0
Oracle Database 11g 11.2.0.2.0
Enterprise Edition Options 11.2.0.2.0
Oracle Net Services 11.2.0.2.0
Product Information
Location:
/oracle/product/11.2.0/dbhome_1
Show empty homes.
If you want to remove Oracle software, please check the items and click "Remove".
To see the languages installed and other details of a component, select the component and then click "Details".
Expand All
Collapse All
Details...
Remove...
Help
Save As...
Close

Selecting one and clicking **Remove...** will display the following screen, which directs us to run a command. This differs from previous installation versions, which would begin the removal process without the need to invoke a command:

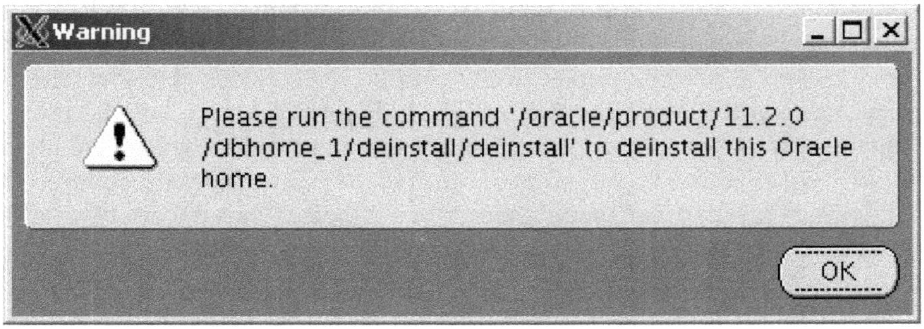
Warning
Please run the command '/oracle/product/11.2.0/dbhome_1/deinstall/deinstall' to deinstall this Oracle home.
OK

The process is the same in Linux, except that we invoke the OUI differently. From within the `ORACLE_HOME` directory, we can see a directory named `oui`. Within that directory is a subdirectory named `bin`. The `runInstaller` script is located within that directory and can be invoked from the command line in the same way as our initial installation. As with Windows, when we attempt to remove an Oracle Home, we are directed to run the `deinstall` script. When we do, the output will look similar to the following screenshot. During execution of the script, we will be asked several questions, most of which can be answered with the default responses. Once completed, the Oracle software will be removed:

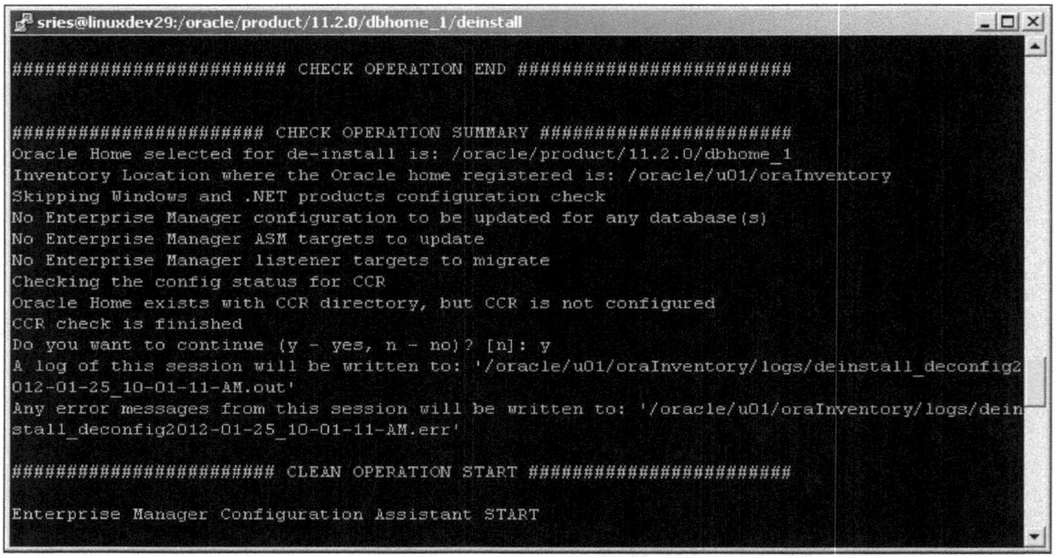
sries@linuxdev29:/oracle/product/11.2.0/dbhome_1/deinstall
######################### CHECK OPERATION END #########################
####################### CHECK OPERATION SUMMARY #######################
Oracle Home selected for de-install is: /oracle/product/11.2.0/dbhome_1
Inventory Location where the Oracle home registered is: /oracle/u01/oraInventory
Skipping Windows and .NET products configuration check
No Enterprise Manager configuration to be updated for any database(s)
No Enterprise Manager ASM targets to update
No Enterprise Manager listener targets to migrate
Checking the config status for CCR
Oracle Home exists with CCR directory, but CCR is not configured
CCR check is finished
Do you want to continue (y - yes, n - no)? [n]: y
A log of this session will be written to: '/oracle/u01/oraInventory/logs/deinstall_deconfig2012-01-25_10-01-11-AM.out'
Any error messages from this session will be written to: '/oracle/u01/oraInventory/logs/deinstall_deconfig2012-01-25_10-01-11-AM.err'
######################## CLEAN OPERATION START ########################
Enterprise Manager Configuration Assistant START

Summary

In this chapter, we installed the Oracle software needed to run an Oracle database. We looked at the hardware requirements for various systems, including Windows and Linux, as well as the operating system prerequisites. We explored the Oracle Universal Installer and looked at its capabilities. We examined the concept of environment variables in Oracle and viewed them in both Windows and Linux. We then stepped through the installation process, noting operating system differences as we moved ahead. Finally, we examined the results of our installation and briefly covered the process of de-installation. In our next chapter, we'll look at the concept of database creation and step through the process of creating our own database.

Test your knowledge

Q 1. Which of these hardware specifications would be insufficient to install an Oracle Database system on any platform?

a. 5 GB of disk
b. 500 M of physical memory
c. Virtual memory that is triple the size of the physical memory
d. Intel (x86) processor

Q 2. Which of the following Windows versions is *not* a supported platform for Oracle 11*g*R2?

a. Windows XP Professional
b. Windows Server 2008 Standard
c. Windows Vista
d. Windows ME

Q 3. Which of the following Linux distributions is *not* a supported platform for Oracle 11*g*R2?

a. Red Hat Enterprise Linux 5
b. SUSE Linux Enterprise Server 11
c. Ubuntu Linux 11
d. Asianux Server 3 SP2

Q 4. What type of file contains the product manifest information that lists all products available in a particular installation package?

a. Unicode Text file
b. XML file
c. HTML file
d. SQL file

Q 5. What is the name given to the type of Oracle installation that does not require interaction with the graphical interface?

a. GUI mode
b. Hierarchical mode
c. Silent mode
d. Root mode

Q 6. On Unix-based systems, which username is commonly used for the installer and owner of the database software?

a. root
b. dba
c. anonymous
d. oracle

Q 7. On Unix-based systems, which OS group name is commonly used for the installer and owner of the database software?

a. root
b. dba
c. administrator
d. oracle

Q 8. What is the name given to the standard directory structure used to manage multiple installations of Oracle?

a. Optimal Flexible Architecture
b. Hierarchical Installation Architecture
c. Oracle Clustered Filesystem
d. ORACLE_HOME

Q 9. Which of these environment variable names denotes the base directory for any given installation of an Oracle product?

a. `ORACLE_BASE`
b. `ORACLE_HOME`
c. `PATH`
d. `LD_LIBRARY_PATH`

Q 10. Which of the following executable is used to start the OUI on the Windows platform?

a. `runInstaller.exe`
b. `cmd.exe`
c. `services.msc`
d. `setup.exe`

Q 11. Which of the following executable is used to start the OUI on the Linux platform?

a. `setup`
b. `runInstaller`
c. `runinstaller`
d. `java.exe`

Q 12. Which of the following directories would *not* be acceptable for an `ORACLE_HOME` on the Linux platform?

a. `/oracle/product/11.2.0/dbhome`
b. `/app/oracle/product/11.2.0/dbhome_2`
c. `C:\oracle\product\11.2.0\dbhome`
d. `/home/oracle/product/11.2.0/dbhome_15`

Q 13. Which of the following operating systems that support Oracle would *not* require the execution of the `root.sh` script?

a. Red Hat Linux
b. Oracle Linux
c. Oracle Solaris
d. Windows Server 2008

3

Creating the Oracle Database

Now that we've installed the necessary software, we're ready to take on the task of creating an Oracle database. Once we've completed this chapter, we'll be free to operate on a database that, though small, will have the same essential architecture as any Oracle database being used in production systems around the world. It's important to note that we'll be introducing a number of unfamiliar concepts and terms in this chapter. Although we will briefly introduce them, the focus of this chapter is on building the database itself. Don't be overwhelmed—we'll take an in-depth look at how these concepts work in the next chapter.

In this chapter we shall:

- Plan a database creation
- Create a database using the Database Configuration Assistant
- Examine the steps needed for a manual database creation
- Understand how Oracle makes use of Windows Services

Planning for a database creation

Although fewer in number than those needed for an installation, there are certain system prerequisites that should be considered before creating a database. These generally center on the need for adequate amounts of memory and disk.

Understanding the memory requirements of a database

System RAM is an extremely important consideration in running an Oracle database. The Oracle Database architecture is highly dependent on the use of **memory caches** to perform basic operations. The concept of a memory cache is one of the most fundamental principles in computer science. Basically, we make use of volatile memory such as system RAM because its I/O access speeds, for both reading and writing, are considerably higher than non-volatile memory, such as hard disk. Simply put, we might say that in Oracle, *storage* occurs on disk, while *work* occurs in RAM. While every computer application—from spreadsheets to web servers—uses RAM, the Oracle database makes use of highly specialized memory caches. This places a crucial significance on the amount and speed of the RAM we choose for our database.

In the previous chapter, we listed the minimum memory requirements as 1 GB for installations on both Windows and Unix-based systems. While this is sufficient for the installer itself, it would probably not be enough to run a database of any significant size or activity level. It would, however, be sufficient to run a small learning or prototyping database that is accessed by a very limited number of users. For true commercial production systems, it is likely that the amount of RAM allocated to Oracle must be considerably greater. For our use, we will specify the minimum amount of RAM needed for our database to be not less than 1 GB. The system you use may have more. In fact, there is no hard-and-fast rule about the amount of RAM your database environment will require. It is highly dependent on the size of the database and the number of users utilizing it.

To determine the amount of available memory on a Windows system, we have several options. However, for our purposes, let's use a command-line approach. Using the `systeminfo` command, we can display the total memory in a Windows system.

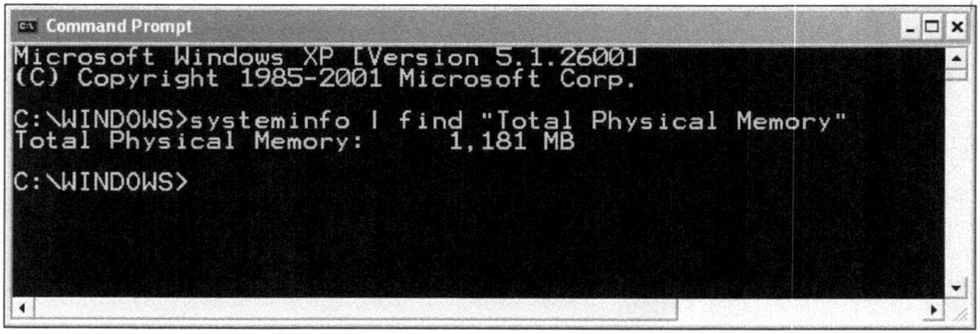
Command Prompt
Microsoft Windows XP [Version 5.1.2600]
(C) Copyright 1985-2001 Microsoft Corp.
C:\WINDOWS>systeminfo | find "Total Physical Memory"
Total Physical Memory: 1,181 MB
C:\WINDOWS>

On Linux systems, we can make use of a number of different commands to discover the amount of physical RAM on a system. One of the simplest is the `free` command, shown in the following screenshot. Using the `free -k` command displays free memory in kilobytes, while `free -m` shows it in megabytes.

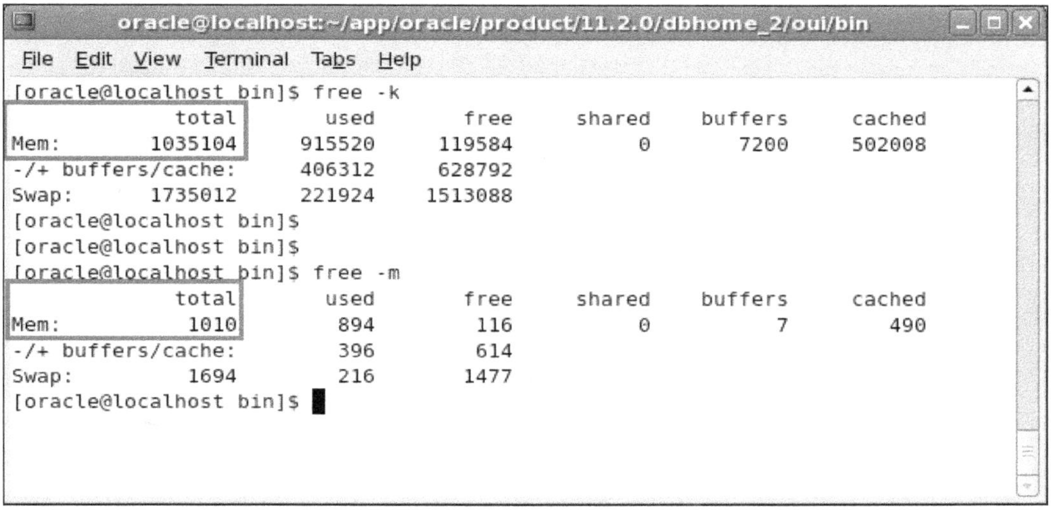
oracle@localhost:~/app/oracle/product/11.2.0/dbhome_2/oui/bin
File Edit View Terminal Tabs Help
[oracle@localhost bin]$ free -k
total used free shared buffers cached
Mem: 1035104 915520 119584 0 7200 502008
-/+ buffers/cache: 406312 628792
Swap: 1735012 221924 1513088
[oracle@localhost bin]$
[oracle@localhost bin]$
[oracle@localhost bin]$ free -m
total used free shared buffers cached
Mem: 1010 894 116 0 7 490
-/+ buffers/cache: 396 614
Swap: 1694 216 1477
[oracle@localhost bin]$

Understanding the disk requirements of a database

Determining the amount of disk space necessary for our database requires even more consideration. The amount of non-volatile disk space our hard drive or drives require is solely dependent on the size of the database itself. This includes all of the tables and framework overhead needed to run the database.

We can view the available disks and disk space on the Windows platform from the **Computer** or **My Computer** window. The following screenshot from a Windows 7 machine displays disk usage:

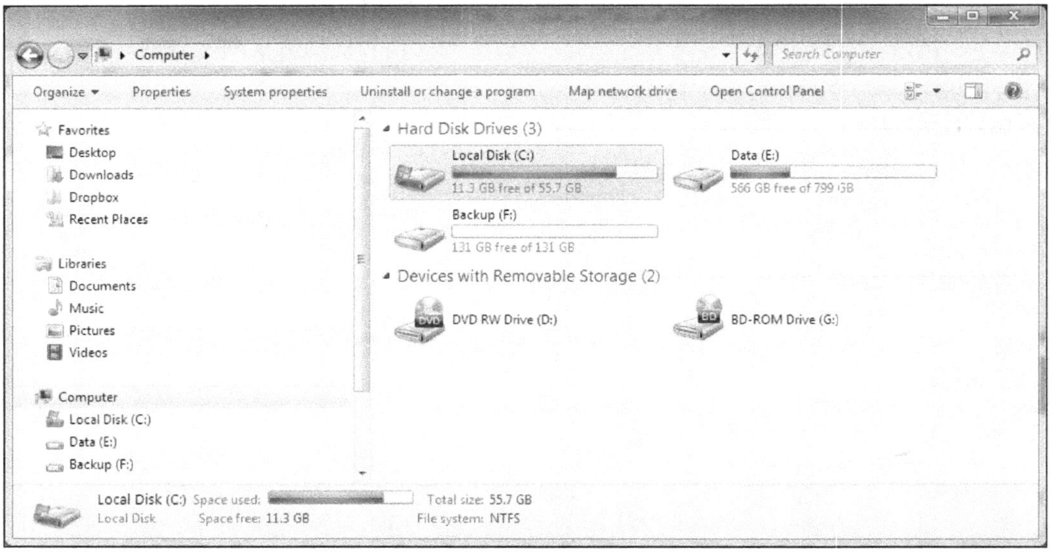
Computer
Organize
Properties
System properties
Uninstall or change a program
Map network drive
Open Control Panel
Favorites
Desktop
Downloads
Dropbox
Recent Places
Libraries
Documents
Music
Pictures
Videos
Computer
Local Disk (C:)
Data (E:)
Backup (F:)
Hard Disk Drives (3)
Local Disk (C:)
11.3 GB free of 55.7 GB
Data (E:)
566 GB free of 799 GB
Backup (F:)
131 GB free of 131 GB
Devices with Removable Storage (2)
DVD RW Drive (D:)
BD-ROM Drive (G:)
Local Disk (C:) Space used:
Total size: 55.7 GB
Local Disk
Space free: 11.3 GB
File system: NTFS

There are several commands we can use on a Linux machine to discover available disk space and mount points. One commonly used command is the `df` command, as shown in the following screenshot:

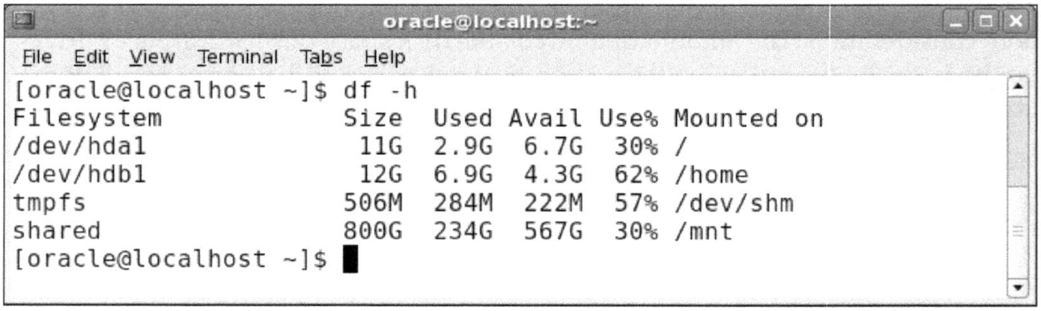
oracle@localhost:~
File Edit View Terminal Tabs Help
[oracle@localhost ~]$ df -h
Filesystem Size Used Avail Use% Mounted on
/dev/hda1 11G 2.9G 6.7G 30% /
/dev/hdb1 12G 6.9G 4.3G 62% /home
tmpfs 506M 284M 222M 57% /dev/shm
shared 800G 234G 567G 30% /mnt
[oracle@localhost ~]$

Let's examine the available disk space on these two machines and assess whether they are appropriate to host an Oracle database. In the Windows example, we see a `C:` location which hosts the operating system. We also have `E:` with over half of a terabyte of available space. This should be adequate to host a medium-sized database. Additionally, we have an `F:` of 131 GB, called **Backup**, which could be used to hold a relatively small amount of backup data.

Our Linux example, on the other hand, seems less suitable. We see several mount points, but the only one of significant size is mounted on **/mnt**. We can see from its description on the left-hand side that it is a shared filesystem, which may not be appropriate for our purposes. Keep in mind that if we're building a small database, the 4.3 GB of space available in **/home** may be adequate. If this is a database of significantly larger size, we may need to add drives and mount them on new mount points, such as `/oracle` or `/oradata`. The database we will create will be approximately 2.5 GB in size, so we ensure that the available disk on our host system is sufficient.

> **The real-world DBA**
>
> In real-world production situations, the question of disk and disk layout can be extremely complex. Large commercial environments can make use of **Storage Area Networks** (**SAN**) and **Network Attached Storage** (**NAS**). Disk systems such as these are important for databases requiring high availability owing to their use of redundant disks and power supplies. Often, for performance reasons, multiple drives or mount points are created to separate disk I/O, preventing contention in the disk subsystem. Thus, our database data may exist on many drives instead of just one.

Once we've determined that we have sufficient space for our database, we should also consider the directory structure that will contain the database files. Recall from the previous chapter that we explored the OFA, or Optimal Flexible Architecture, for our software installation. The rules of the OFA can be applied to database file directories as well, but there is no true rule of thumb that covers every possible database size or configuration. Generally, small databases may use a simple directory structure with one or two directories to contain the database. Larger systems may employ more complex structures that separate various types of data from other data.

Running the Network Configuration Assistant

Our last step before we begin the database creation process is an optional one. During the installation, we will configure a tool for database administration that requires certain network components to be configured. We'll dive into the subject of Oracle networking in greater detail in a later chapter. For now, however, we'll use a tool called **NETCA**, or the **Network Configuration Assistant**, to configure the necessary networking components. Later, we'll look at the manual configuration for these components. Note that, while these steps are not required to build a database, they are required to use certain tools we will explore throughout this book.

We have two options when invoking NETCA. To run NETCA from a Windows installation of Oracle, we can access it from the program groups, where it is listed as **Net Configuration Assistant**, as shown in the following screenshot:

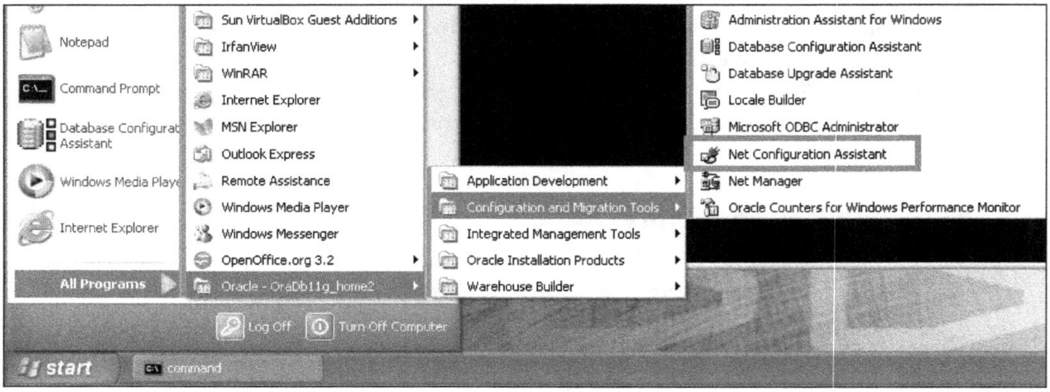
Notepad
Command Prompt
Database Configuration Assistant
Windows Media Player
Internet Explorer
All Programs
Sun VirtualBox Guest Additions
IrfanView
WinRAR
Internet Explorer
MSN Explorer
Outlook Express
Remote Assistance
Windows Media Player
Windows Messenger
OpenOffice.org 3.2
Oracle - OraDb11g_home2
Application Development
Configuration and Migration Tools
Integrated Management Tools
Oracle Installation Products
Warehouse Builder
Administration Assistant for Windows
Database Configuration Assistant
Database Upgrade Assistant
Locale Builder
Microsoft ODBC Administrator
Net Configuration Assistant
Net Manager
Oracle Counters for Windows Performance Monitor
Log Off
Turn Off Computer
start
command

Alternatively, in both Windows and Linux, we can start NETCA using the command `netca` from the command line. When we invoke NETCA, we're presented with an introductory screen as shown in the following screenshot. This lists the configuration operations at our disposal. For now, we only need to concern ourselves with the first option, **Listener configuration**. The listener is the Oracle process that accepts incoming network connections to the database. This is the default selection, so we choose **Next**.

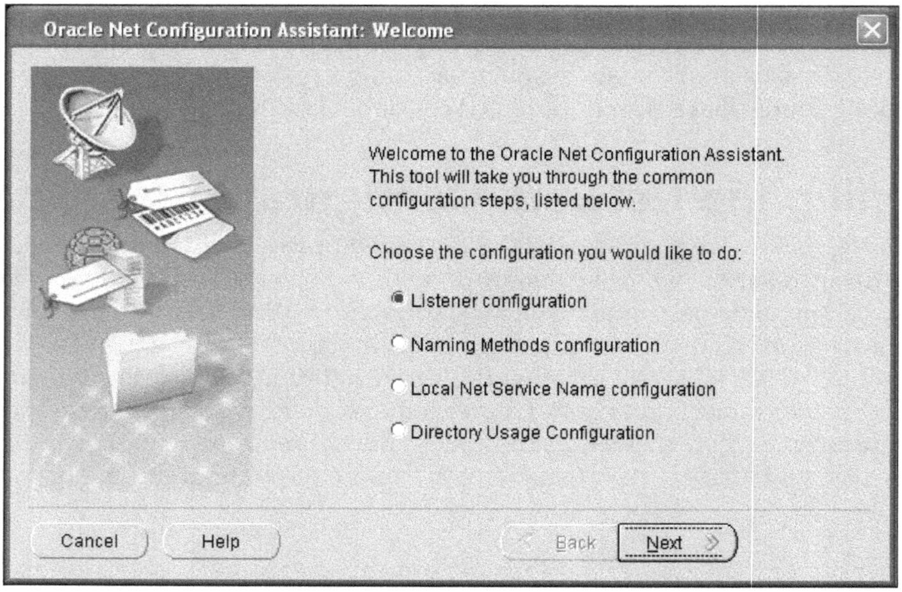
Oracle Net Configuration Assistant: Welcome
Welcome to the Oracle Net Configuration Assistant.
This tool will take you through the common configuration steps, listed below.
Choose the configuration you would like to do:
Listener configuration
Naming Methods configuration
Local Net Service Name configuration
Directory Usage Configuration
Cancel
Help
Back
Next

The next screen asks which type of listener configuration we wish to run. For a new installation, **Add** is the only option available, so we choose **Next**.

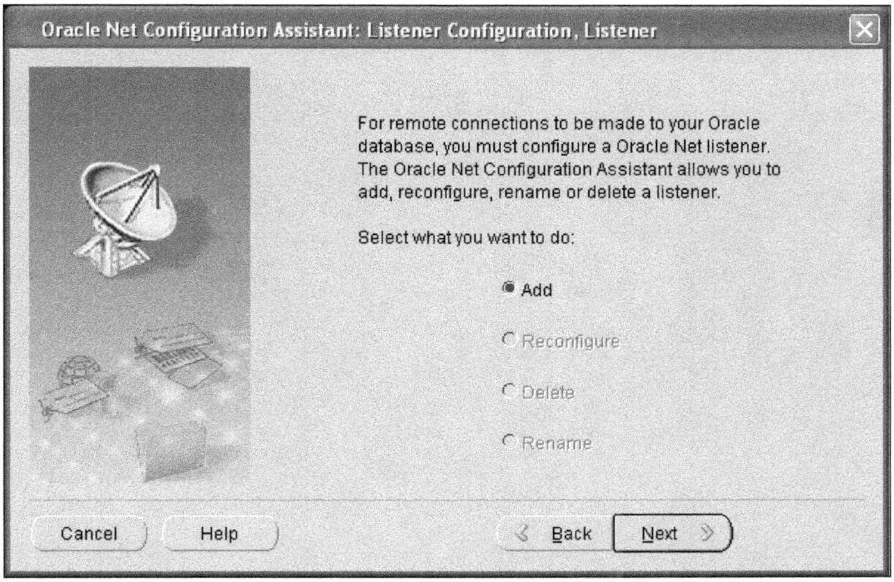
Oracle Net Configuration Assistant: Listener Configuration, Listener
For remote connections to be made to your Oracle database, you must configure a Oracle Net listener. The Oracle Net Configuration Assistant allows you to add, reconfigure, rename or delete a listener.
Select what you want to do:
Add
Reconfigure
Delete
Rename
Cancel
Help
Back
Next

A listener requires a name that can be referenced, so we choose the default, **LISTENER**, and select **Next**.

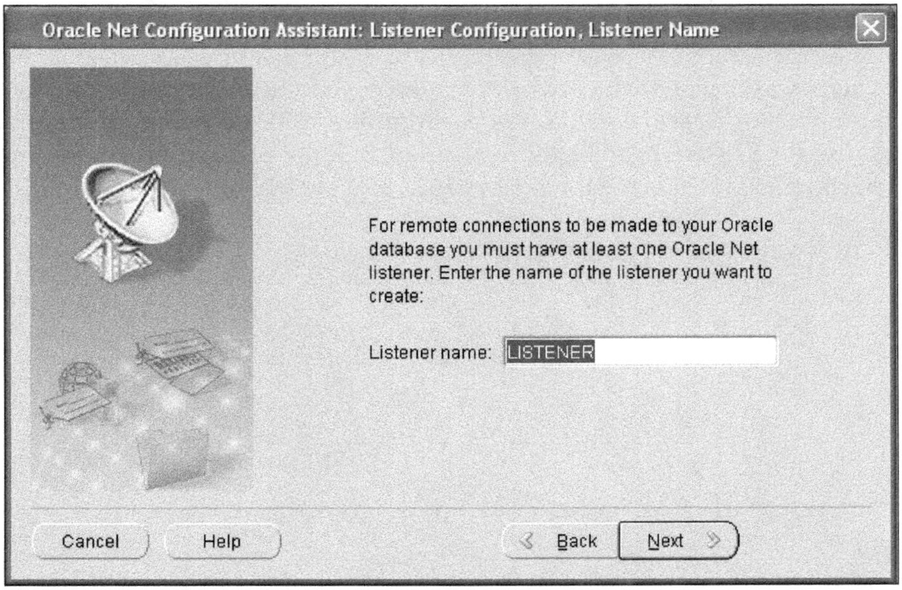
Oracle Net Configuration Assistant: Listener Configuration, Listener Name
For remote connections to be made to your Oracle database you must have at least one Oracle Net listener. Enter the name of the listener you want to create:
Listener name: LISTENER
Cancel
Help
Back
Next

The next screen in NETCA asks us which network protocols we wish to configure. The default, **TCP**, stands for the TCP/IP set of network protocols, which is the standard protocol for most operating systems. This is already selected, so we click **Next**.

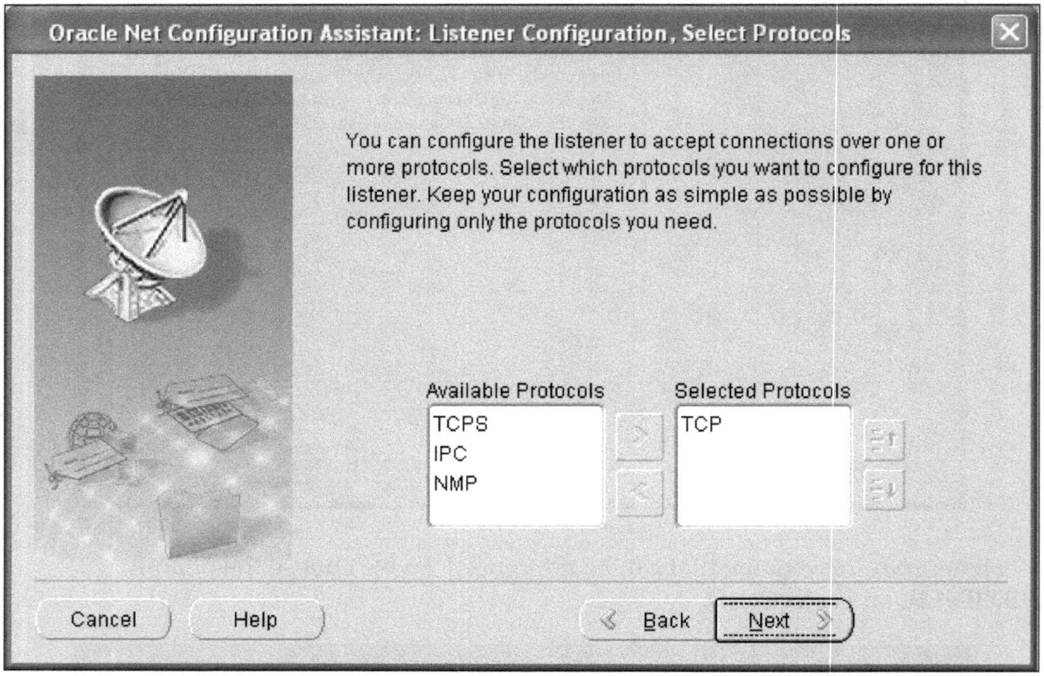
Oracle Net Configuration Assistant: Listener Configuration, Select Protocols
You can configure the listener to accept connections over one or more protocols. Select which protocols you want to configure for this listener. Keep your configuration as simple as possible by configuring only the protocols you need.
Available Protocols
TCPS
IPC
NMP
Selected Protocols
TCP
Cancel
Help
Back
Next

The next screen asks us which network port we wish to use for our listener. The default port for Oracle databases is port number 1521. Although the selection of port to use for a listener can be more complex in large production environments, for our purposes we will leave the port as **1521** and click **Next**.

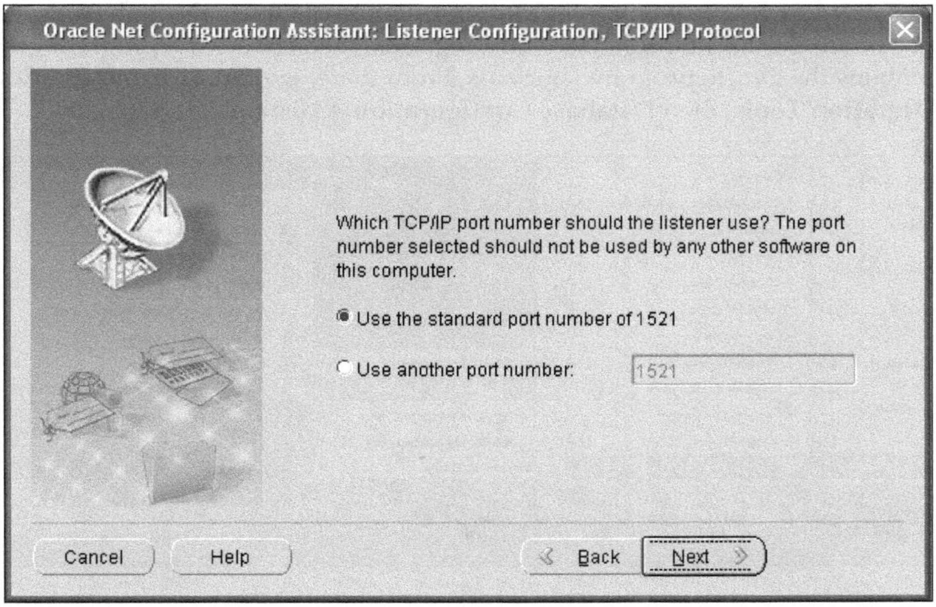
Oracle Net Configuration Assistant: Listener Configuration, TCP/IP Protocol
Which TCP/IP port number should the listener use? The port number selected should not be used by any other software on this computer.
Use the standard port number of 1521
Use another port number:
1521
Cancel
Help
Back
Next

At this point, we're asked whether we want to configure another listener. We leave the default, **No**, selected and click **Next**. At the final screen we click **Next** to exit the tool.

Creating an Oracle database using DBCA

With these operations complete, we're ready to begin the creation process. We'll first look at the tool we'll be using and then go through each step of the process, pausing to describe the significance of each step.

Introducing the Database Configuration Assistant

Many experienced DBAs are most familiar with the manual process of creating a database. Although building a database manually allows the DBA the greatest amount of freedom in configuring a database to exact specifications, it has many steps and requires a fairly advanced knowledge of the Oracle architecture. We will examine the steps involved in a manual creation, but first we'll create a database using a simpler approach—the **Database Configuration Assistant** (**DBCA**). The DBCA is Oracle's standard GUI tool for building and configuring Oracle databases. The DBCA uses a step-by-step, wizard-like approach that takes the administrator through the entire process of building a database.

The DBCA can be invoked on a Windows installation of Oracle through its program group. Choose the **start** button, then **All Programs**, then choose the program group that contains the Oracle program shortcuts. From there, we choose **Configuration and Migration Tools**, then **Database Configuration Assistant**, as shown here:

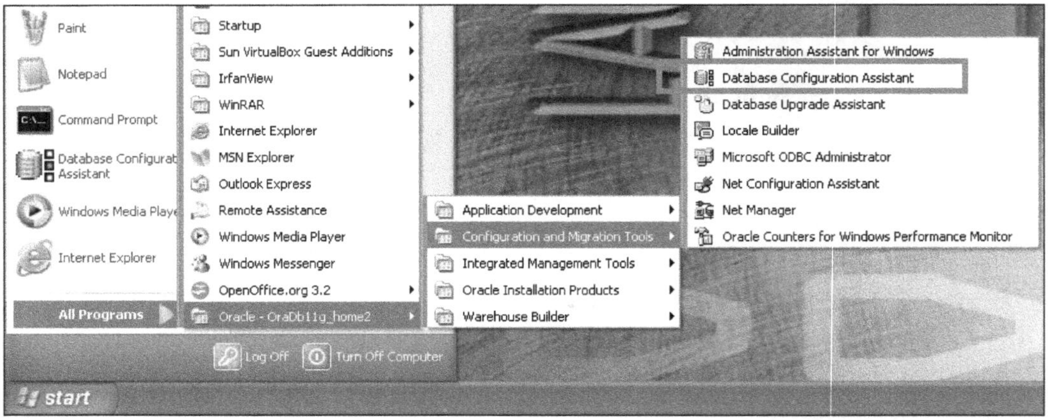
Paint
Notepad
Command Prompt
Database Configurat Assistant
Windows Media Playe
Internet Explorer
All Programs
Startup
Sun VirtualBox Guest Additions
IrfanView
WinRAR
Internet Explorer
MSN Explorer
Outlook Express
Remote Assistance
Windows Media Player
Windows Messenger
OpenOffice.org 3.2
Oracle - OraDb11g_home2
Application Development
Configuration and Migration Tools
Integrated Management Tools
Oracle Installation Products
Warehouse Builder
Administration Assistant for Windows
Database Configuration Assistant
Database Upgrade Assistant
Locale Builder
Microsoft ODBC Administrator
Net Configuration Assistant
Net Manager
Oracle Counters for Windows Performance Monitor
Log Off
Turn Off Computer
start

Alternatively, we can invoke DBCA by simply typing `dbca` from the command line. Keep in mind that in Linux, this requires the `$ORACLE_HOME/bin` directory to be defined in `$PATH`. When the DBCA is executed, we're presented with a splash screen, as shown in the following screenshot:

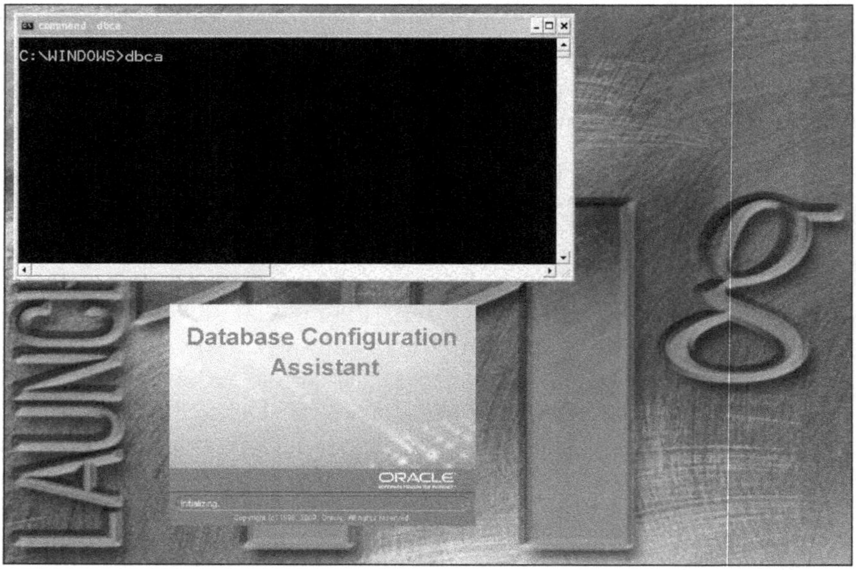
C:\WINDOWS>dbca
Database Configuration Assistant
ORACLE

The process of creating a database using DBCA begins with an opening screen that welcomes us to the DBCA and highlights a few of its features. Although the remainder of our example screen will be shown from a database creation on Windows, running the DBCA on other platforms will present the same screens. We click **Next**.

Our first interactive screen, labeled in the title bar as **Step 1 of 12: Operations**, presents us with several options. Step 1 allows us to choose between database creation, configuration, or deletion options, and the management of templates. The configuration options mentioned here refer primarily to initialization of parameters that we will discuss shortly. The **Delete a Database** selection is available when a database has already been created on the host machine. This allows us to conveniently remove a database. The **Manage Templates** selection allows us to manage database templates on the host. Database templates are files that store all of the configuration options for a particular database. Thus, we will see that the last page of the DBCA will allow us to save all of our configuration responses into a single database template. In a sense, database templates are analogous to the response files for an Oracle software installation. The **Manage Templates** selection allows us to create database templates from either an existing template or an existing database, or to delete database templates. Our concern here is the creation of a database, so we ensure that **Create a Database** is selected and click **Next**.

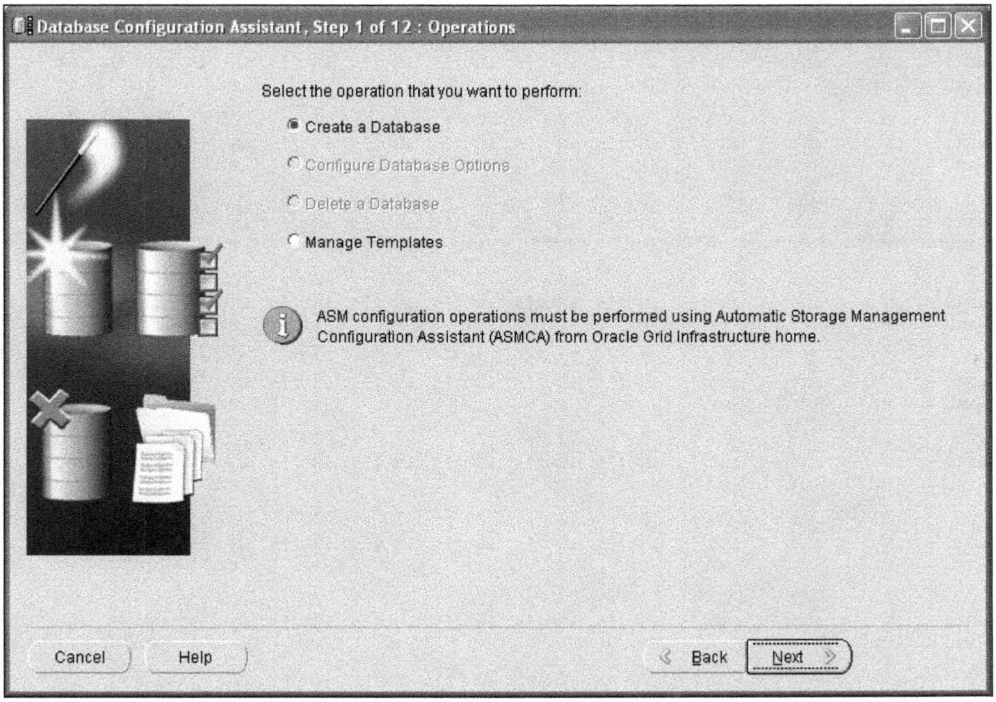
Database Configuration Assistant, Step 1 of 12 : Operations
Select the operation that you want to perform:
Create a Database
Configure Database Options
Delete a Database
Manage Templates
ASM configuration operations must be performed using Automatic Storage Management Configuration Assistant (ASMCA) from Oracle Grid Infrastructure home.
Cancel
Help
Back
Next

Having chosen to create a database, the next screen gives us the option to create it from an existing template of database options. Aside from **Custom Database**, which is our selection, we can also choose the Oracle recommended structure for either an **Online Transaction Processing** (**OLTP**) database, or a data warehouse. We will refer to these types of databases at a later point, but we note for now that these two types of database serve two very different functions and user communities.

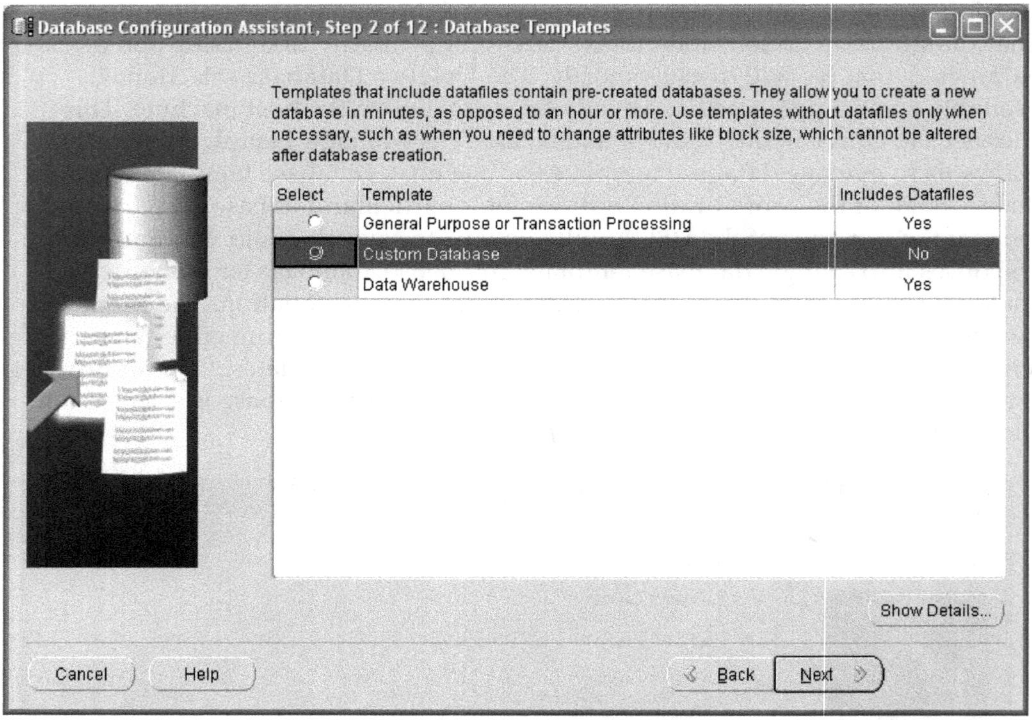
Database Configuration Assistant, Step 2 of 12 : Database Templates
Templates that include datafiles contain pre-created databases. They allow you to create a new database in minutes, as opposed to an hour or more. Use templates without datafiles only when necessary, such as when you need to change attributes like block size, which cannot be altered after database creation.
Select
Template
Includes Datafiles
General Purpose or Transaction Processing
Yes
Custom Database
No
Data Warehouse
Yes
Show Details...
Cancel
Help
Back
Next

Our next screen, the **Database Identification** screen, allows us to choose a name for our new database. Note that there are two fields for database name, one listed as **Global Database Name** and another listed as **SID**. In Oracle, the global database name refers to the name of the database in a networked context. Usually, this means that the name of the database is suffixed with the network domain in which the database resides. Thus, we might have a database that is globally named `orcl.companylink.com`. The second field is the database **SID** or System Identifier. The database SID is the name that uniquely identifies a database on a particular server. Having two databases with the same SID on the same physical host is not allowed. Although the choice of name is up to us, there are a few rules by which Oracle database names, or SIDs, must abide. They are as follows:

- The SID must be a string of alphanumeric characters, no more than eight characters in length
- The SID can contain alphabetic and numeric characters or the special characters, such as dollar sign ($), pound sign (#), or underscore (_)
- The SID cannot begin with a number or special character. It must begin with an alphabetic character
- The SID is case-sensitive on Unix-based systems, but not on Windows
- The SID is defined by the `ORACLE_SID` environment variable

The real-world DBA

In real-world situations, it is often preferable to choose a name that somewhat meaningfully describes the database. If our database is used for testing or hosts financial data, we may wish to reflect that in the name. In fact, many DBA organizations have standards that define the rules by which all databases must be named. Also, from a security perspective, it is generally considered unacceptable to identify the database version in the database name. If a database is found to be named "ora11g", attackers can assume that they only need to attempt vulnerability exploits that apply to Oracle Version 11*g*.

In our case, we will name our database with the commonly used SID, `orcl`, and refer to the **Global Database Name** without a domain, as shown in the following screenshot. Click **Next**.

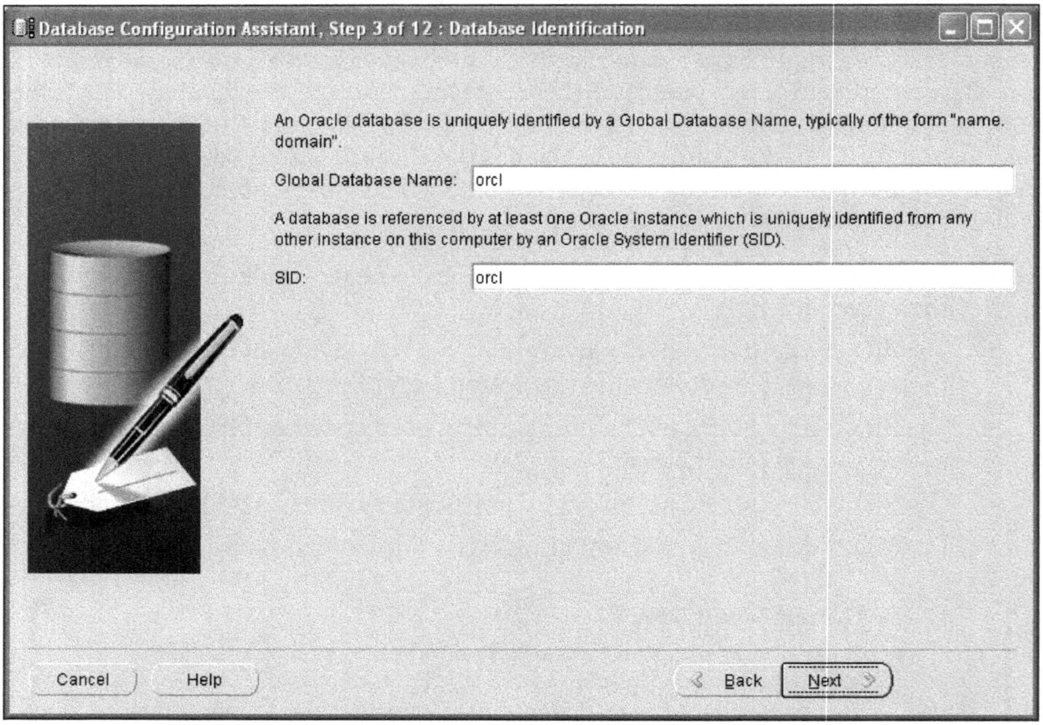
Database Configuration Assistant, Step 3 of 12 : Database Identification
An Oracle database is uniquely identified by a Global Database Name, typically of the form "name. domain".
Global Database Name:
orcl
A database is referenced by at least one Oracle instance which is uniquely identified from any other instance on this computer by an Oracle System Identifier (SID).
SID:
orcl
Cancel
Help
Back
Next

Our next screen allows us to define the options as to how we will manage the database. Our first choice is whether to use Enterprise Manager to administer our database. Recall from *Chapter 1, Introducing the Oracle Relational Database System,* that OEM is a tool used to perform a multitude of database administration tasks. We indicated that OEM can be used in two configurations: Database Control and Grid Control. Database Control can be used to administer a single database on a single server, while Grid Control can be used to administer any database within our enterprise, provided that an **OEM Agent** is installed on the host.

Since no agents have been installed on this server, we note that the option **Register with Grid Control for centralized management** is grayed out. Thus, we leave the box checked for the **Configure Enterprise Manager** option, along with the radio button labeled **Configure Database Control for local management**. This will install and configure the necessary components for us to run Database Control.

The second section also gives us the ability to enable alert notifications. This feature allows for notifications of certain events to be sent to an e-mail server, which, if checked, has to be specified here. This allows alert notifications to be sent directly to a DBA through SMTP e-mail, which can also be redirected to pagers and cell phones. We can also schedule a daily backup job to run. For our purposes, we will check the options listed in the following screenshot and click **Next**.

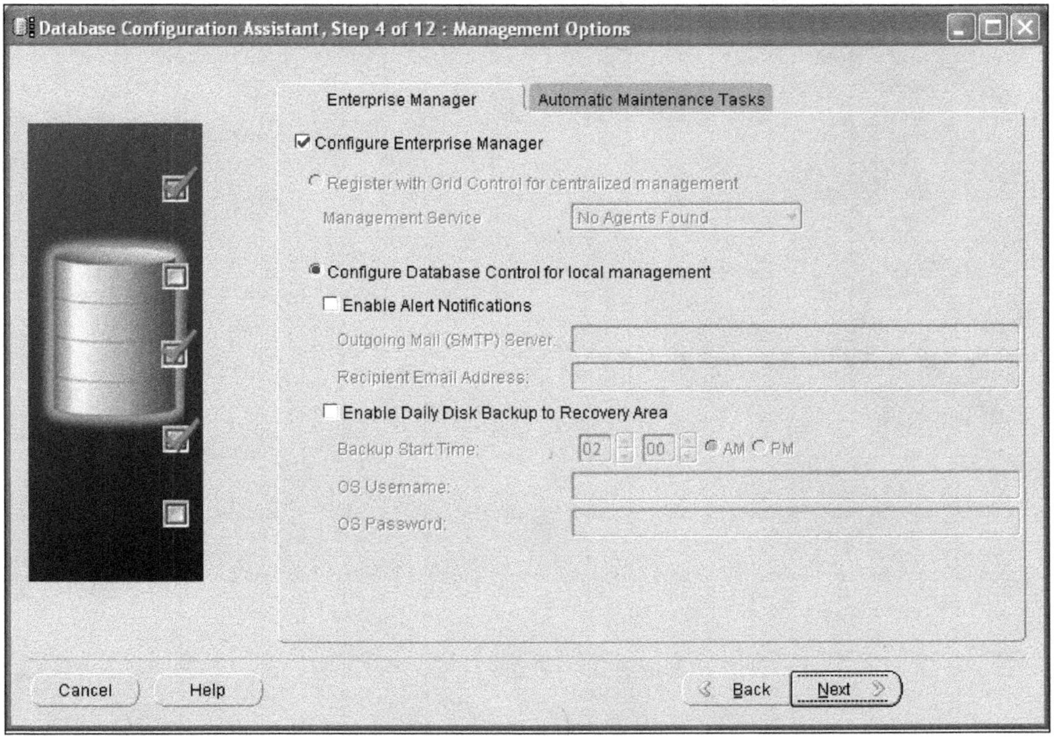
Database Configuration Assistant, Step 4 of 12 : Management Options
Enterprise Manager
Automatic Maintenance Tasks
Configure Enterprise Manager
Register with Grid Control for centralized management
Management Service
No Agents Found
Configure Database Control for local management
Enable Alert Notifications
Outgoing Mail (SMTP) Server:
Recipient Email Address:
Enable Daily Disk Backup to Recovery Area
Backup Start Time:
02
00
AM
PM
OS Username:
OS Password:
Cancel
Help
Back
Next

The page labeled **Step 5 of 12: Database Credentials** allows us to enter the passwords for critical system accounts. We will explore these accounts in greater detail in the chapters to come, but they need to have a password assigned during the creation of the database. We have the option of defining them separately, a prudent choice in real-world scenarios, or to use the same administrative password for all accounts, as shown here. In this case the password, although hidden, is `oracle`. We can choose any password we wish, but we need to ensure that we don't forget it.

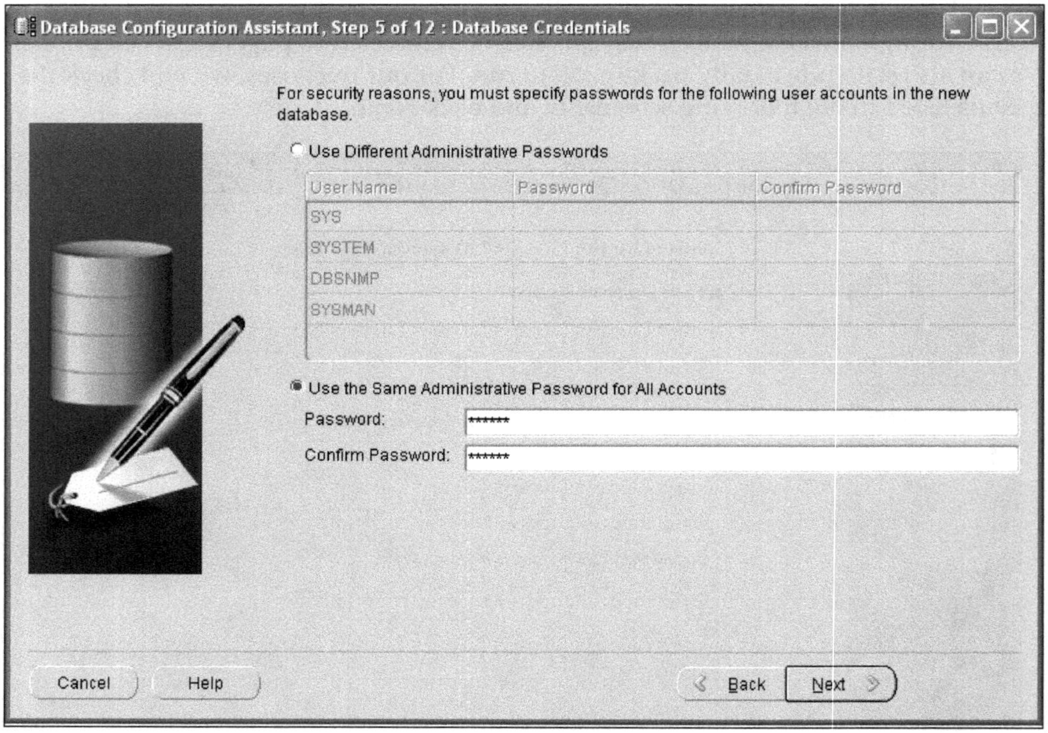
Database Configuration Assistant, Step 5 of 12 : Database Credentials
For security reasons, you must specify passwords for the following user accounts in the new database.
Use Different Administrative Passwords
User Name
Password
Confirm Password
SYS
SYSTEM
DBSNMP
SYSMAN
Use the Same Administrative Password for All Accounts
Password:
Confirm Password:
Cancel
Help
Back
Next

Because we entered the simple and easily cracked password `oracle`, notice that the DBCA has detected this and now recommends that we change the password. It also includes some basic guidelines for choosing sufficiently complex passwords. At this point, we can choose not to continue and return to the previous page to enter a password that meets the minimum requirements, or choose **Yes** to continue with the simple password.

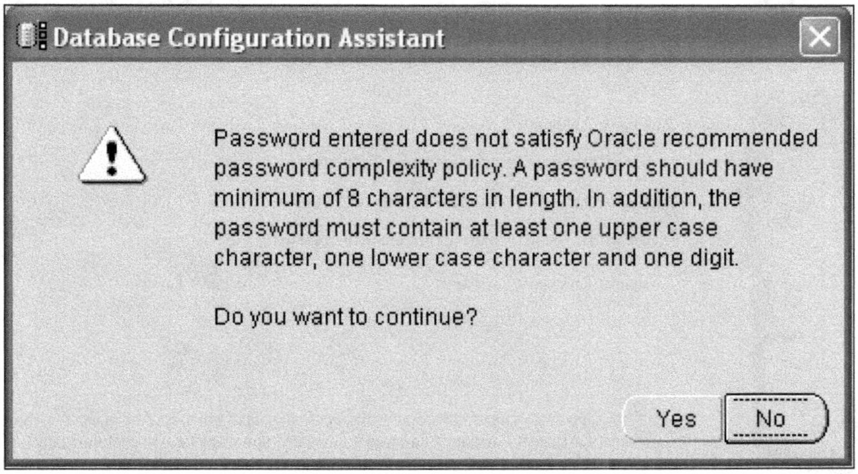
Database Configuration Assistant
Password entered does not satisfy Oracle recommended password complexity policy. A password should have minimum of 8 characters in length. In addition, the password must contain at least one upper case character, one lower case character and one digit.
Do you want to continue?
Yes
No

The next window enables us to choose the location where our database will actually be stored. A database consists, in part, of physical files residing on or attached to the host machine. We need to specify a location for these files and we have several options for doing so. If we click the drop-down menu for **Storage Type**, we see choices for File System and **Automatic Storage Management** (**ASM**). ASM is a high-performance, high-redundancy filesystem designed especially for Oracle databases that requires additional setup; it is beyond our scope for now. For our purposes, we'll choose to store our files on the operating system itself and select **File System**, as it is by default. The second section of the window specifies the storage location options. We can read our file directory locations from a template or make use of **Oracle Managed Files** (**OMF**). OMF is a special directory naming feature that we will examine a little later.

For now, we'll click the selection **Use Common Location for All Database Files**, and choose a directory by clicking the **Browse** button. The example shown here uses a directory called **oradata** that is located within the **ORACLE_BASE** directory, **E:\app\oracle**. If you choose a directory that does not exist, DBCA will present a prompt to create it for you. Click **Next**.

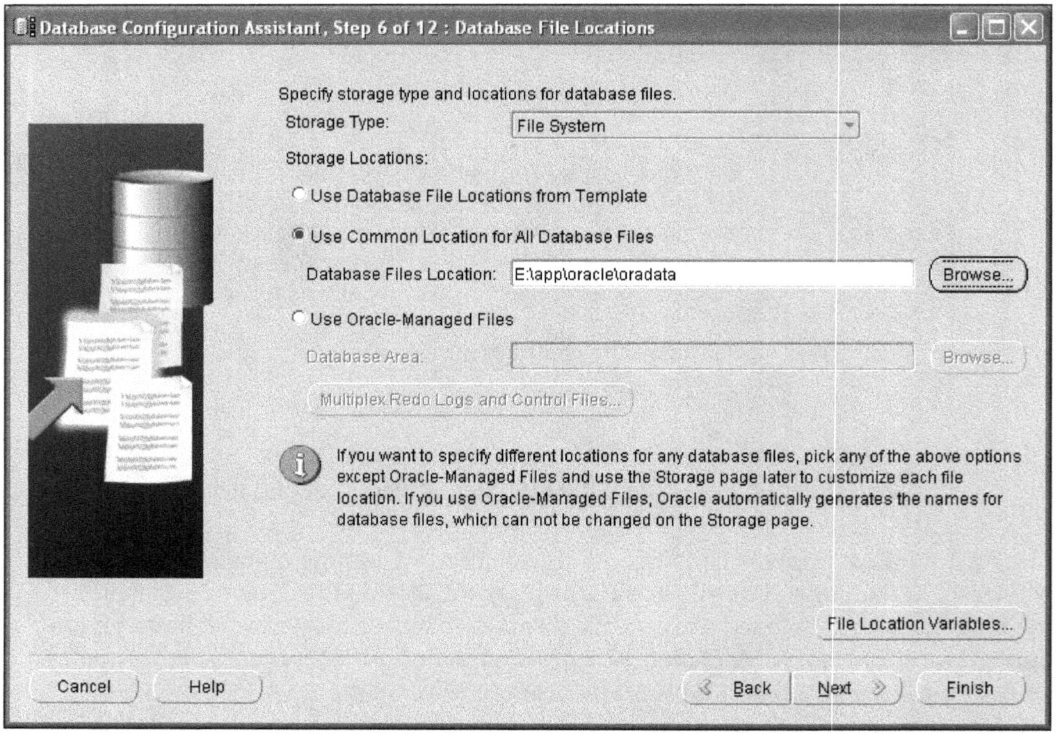
Database Configuration Assistant, Step 6 of 12 : Database File Locations
Specify storage type and locations for database files.
Storage Type:
File System
Storage Locations:
Use Database File Locations from Template
Use Common Location for All Database Files
Database Files Location:
E:\app\oracle\oradata
Browse...
Use Oracle-Managed Files
Database Area:
Browse...
Multiplex Redo Logs and Control Files...
If you want to specify different locations for any database files, pick any of the above options except Oracle-Managed Files and use the Storage page later to customize each file location. If you use Oracle-Managed Files, Oracle automatically generates the names for database files, which can not be changed on the Storage page.
File Location Variables...
Cancel
Help
Back
Next
Finish

The next window gives us the opportunity to configure options related to recoverability. Backup and recovery is one of the most important aspects of database administration, and we'll examine it at great length later in this book. The first checkbox of the window shown here allows us to configure a Flash Recovery Area, a backup location that manages the files needed for recovery. The second checkbox enables the archiving of changes that occur in the database, which is used in recovery scenarios. For now we'll leave both of these options unchecked and click **Next**.

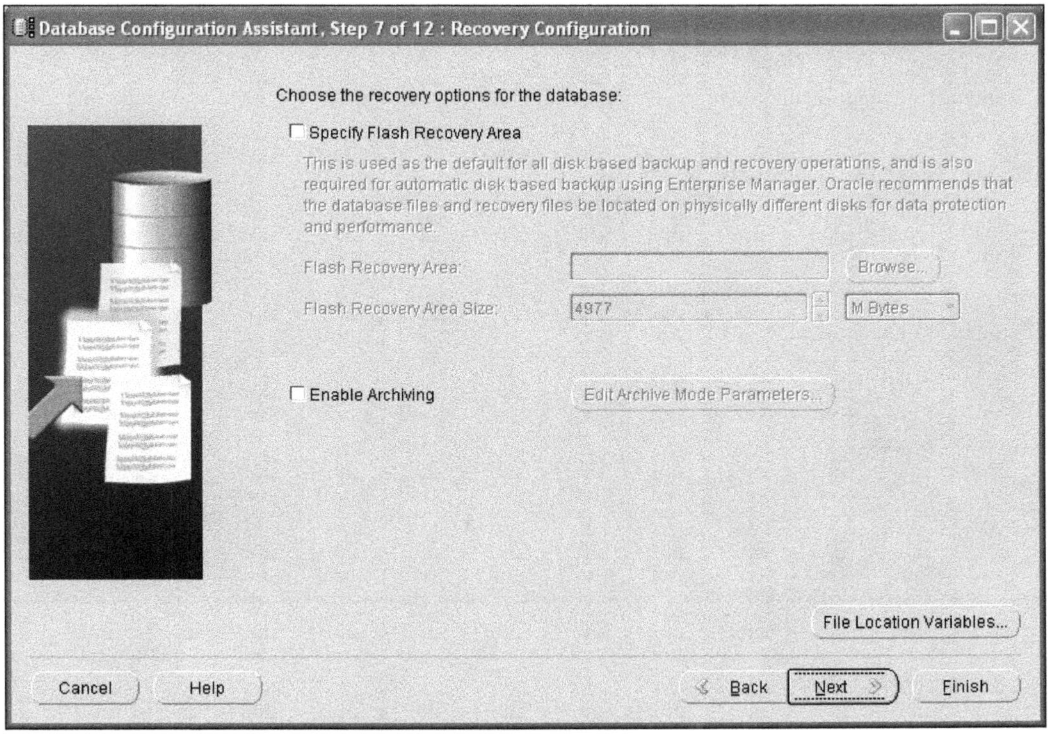
Database Configuration Assistant, Step 7 of 12 : Recovery Configuration
Choose the recovery options for the database:
Specify Flash Recovery Area
This is used as the default for all disk based backup and recovery operations, and is also required for automatic disk based backup using Enterprise Manager. Oracle recommends that the database files and recovery files be located on physically different disks for data protection and performance.
Flash Recovery Area:
Browse...
Flash Recovery Area Size:
4977
M Bytes
Enable Archiving
Edit Archive Mode Parameters...
File Location Variables...
Cancel
Help
Back
Next
Finish

Step 8 of 12 presents us with the ability to configure various options within the database. In a real-world situation, our choices are determined by the licenses that have been purchased for the corresponding database options. Some are greyed out due to the fact that a particular option has not been installed.

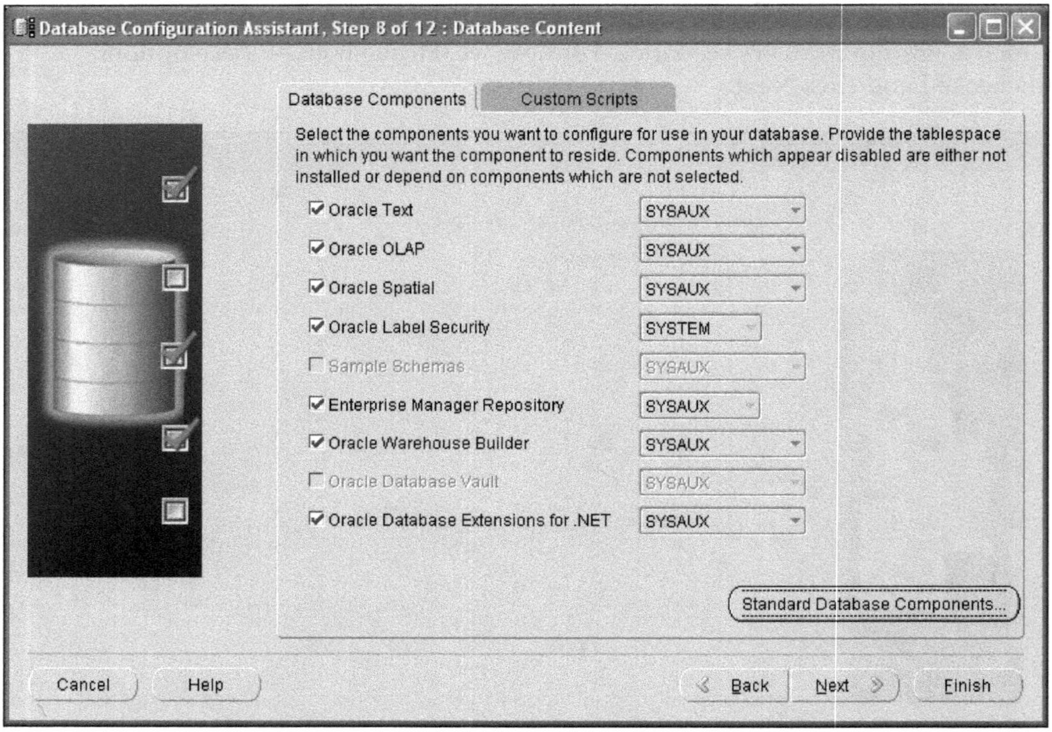
Database Configuration Assistant, Step 8 of 12 : Database Content
Database Components
Custom Scripts
Select the components you want to configure for use in your database. Provide the tablespace in which you want the component to reside. Components which appear disabled are either not installed or depend on components which are not selected.
Oracle Text
SYSAUX
Oracle OLAP
SYSAUX
Oracle Spatial
SYSAUX
Oracle Label Security
SYSTEM
Sample Schemas
SYSAUX
Enterprise Manager Repository
SYSAUX
Oracle Warehouse Builder
SYSAUX
Oracle Database Vault
SYSAUX
Oracle Database Extensions for .NET
SYSAUX
Standard Database Components...
Cancel
Help
Back
Next
Finish

If we click the **Standard Database Components...** button, we see the base components that are added during a database creation. We can select or deselect these as well. When we're finished, we click **OK** to return to the previous screen.

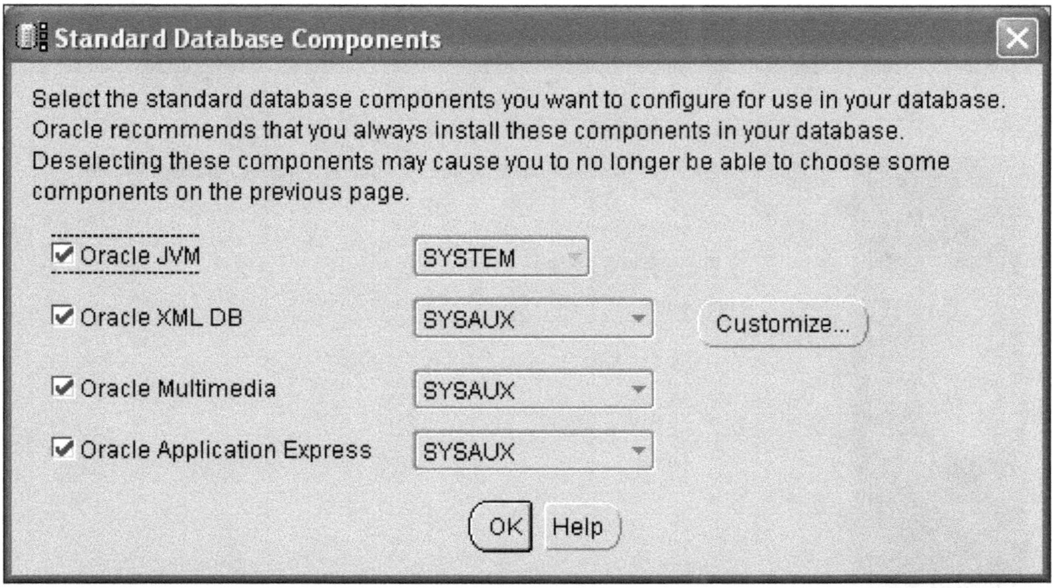
Standard Database Components
Select the standard database components you want to configure for use in your database. Oracle recommends that you always install these components in your database. Deselecting these components may cause you to no longer be able to choose some components on the previous page.
Oracle JVM
SYSTEM
Oracle XML DB
SYSAUX
Customize...
Oracle Multimedia
SYSAUX
Oracle Application Express
SYSAUX
OK
Help

On the **Database Content** screen, we also have a tab called **Custom Scripts** available to us, as shown in the following screenshot. This useful tab allows us to add any specialized scripts to the creation process. The scripts that we add will be run following the successful creation of the database.

For example, we may have written a custom script that creates a set of users and permissions for our database. We could add the script here and those users and permissions would be automatically created, following the creation of the database. In our case, we don't wish to add any custom scripts, so we click **Next**.

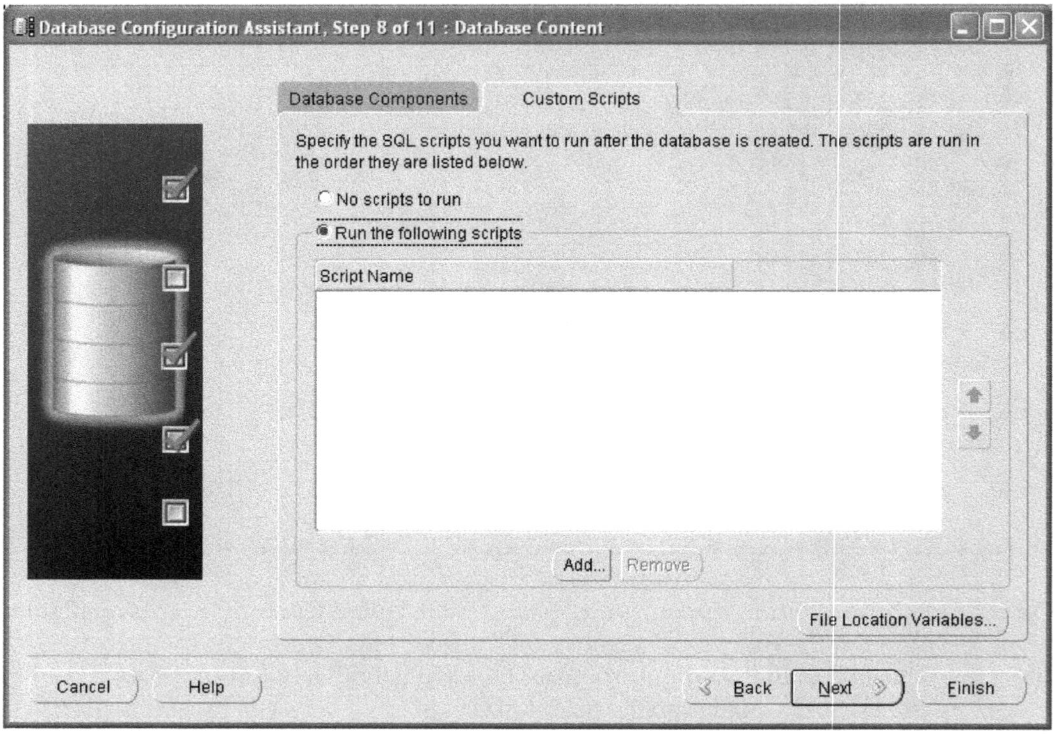
Database Configuration Assistant, Step 8 of 11 : Database Content
Database Components
Custom Scripts
Specify the SQL scripts you want to run after the database is created. The scripts are run in the order they are listed below.
No scripts to run
Run the following scripts
Script Name
Add...
Remove
File Location Variables...
Cancel
Help
Back
Next
Finish

The real-world DBA

When installing components in the database, it's generally preferred to take a "less is best" approach. While we must ensure that we do not install unlicensed components from a liability standpoint, installing unnecessary components can lead to holes in your database security posture as well.

Our next screen, **Initialization Parameters**, contains a vast amount of configuration possibilities for our database. This screen allows us to set the database's initialization parameters, the settings that let us fully control the way our database operates. These parameters give us extremely fine-grained control of database behavior. As such, the subject of initialization parameters is extremely complex and will be covered in detail in the later chapters. However, this DBCA screen simplifies the subject considerably. It allows us to set some of the most important initialization parameters—those that affect memory usage—very easily. DBCA determines the total amount of memory available on the host machine, in this case **1181 MB**, as shown on the far end of the slider. DBCA will then suggest an amount of memory—40 percent of the total by default—to use for the database. If we wish to use more, we can either adjust the slider to the preferred amount or enter it manually. Oracle will then automatically allocate that amount of memory to the database. However, for our purposes, we will use the **Custom** option.

In Oracle, we have three general methods of allocating memory. We can configure our memory allocations manually or choose from two different automatic algorithms. The automatic methods, Automatic Memory Management and Automatic Shared Memory Management, will give Oracle control of how various database memory caches are sized. For now, we want to maintain that control, so we want our memory allocations to be set manually, as shown in the following screenshot. To do this, we choose the radio button labeled **Custom**. Next, we select **Manual Shared Memory Management** from the drop-down menu labeled **Memory Management**. Notice that when we select this option, the screen changes to list the individual sizes of various memory caches. Thus, Oracle has taken 40 percent of total memory available on the host machine and divided it into appropriate sizes. We will learn how to change these parameter values a little later; for now, we'll stick with what we're given. The values we see would be different if the amount of available system memory were different, as you may experience yourself. If we were using DBCA on a system with considerably more memory, it may be wise to reduce the slider below 40 percent to begin with, since it is unlikely that our test database will require a substantial amount of memory.

The amount of memory that we choose to allocate to Oracle is dependent on a number of factors, such as the size and activity of the database, the number of instances present on the server, and the performance requirements. This choice is usually at the discretion of the DBA. If the server is only hosting one database and no other applications, we may choose a larger percentage, for example, 75 percent, since the operating system won't necessarily require a substantial percentage of the memory in order to operate.

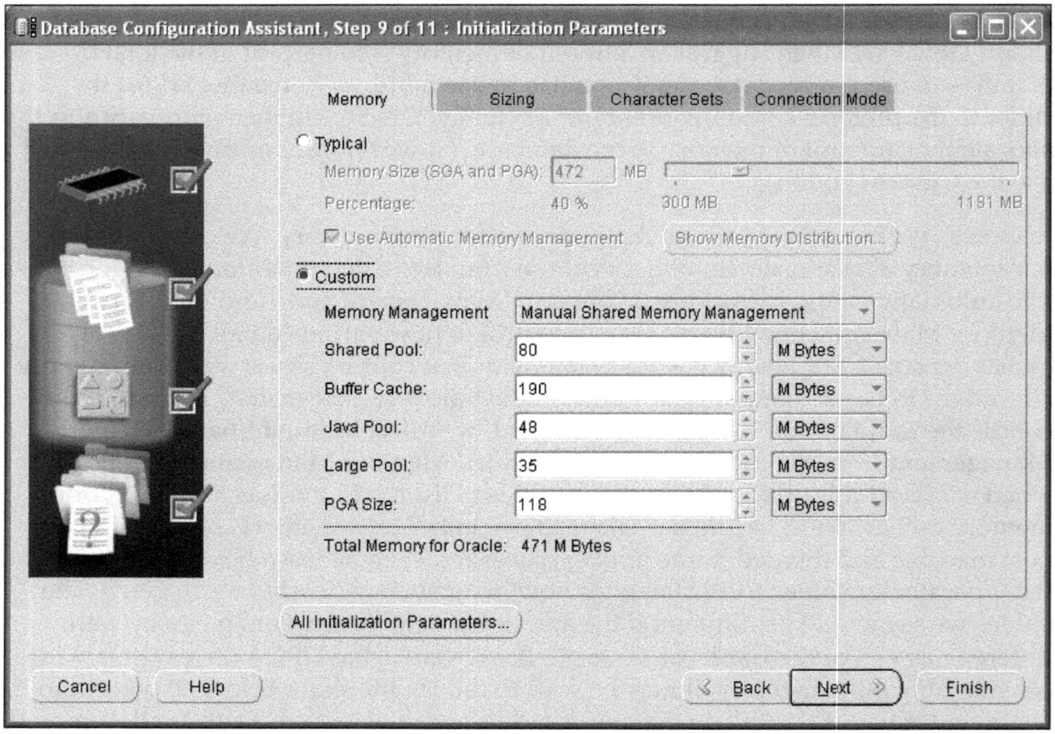
Database Configuration Assistant, Step 9 of 11 : Initialization Parameters
Memory
Sizing
Character Sets
Connection Mode
Typical
Memory Size (SGA and PGA): 472 MB
Percentage: 40 % 300 MB 1181 MB
Use Automatic Memory Management
Show Memory Distribution...
Custom
Memory Management
Manual Shared Memory Management
Shared Pool: 80 M Bytes
Buffer Cache: 190 M Bytes
Java Pool: 48 M Bytes
Large Pool: 35 M Bytes
PGA Size: 118 M Bytes
Total Memory for Oracle: 471 M Bytes
All Initialization Parameters...
Cancel
Help
Back
Next
Finish

Once this is complete, we can optionally click on the **All Initialization Parameters...** button to see a list of database parameters. Notice that clicking the **Show Description** button will display a short description of any parameter we select. Our purpose at this point is to simply create a database on which we can work rather than an exhaustive description of every database parameter. The next screenshot gives an example of the types of configuration parameters that are available to us. When we're finished, we click **Close**, returning us to the **Initialization Parameters** screen.

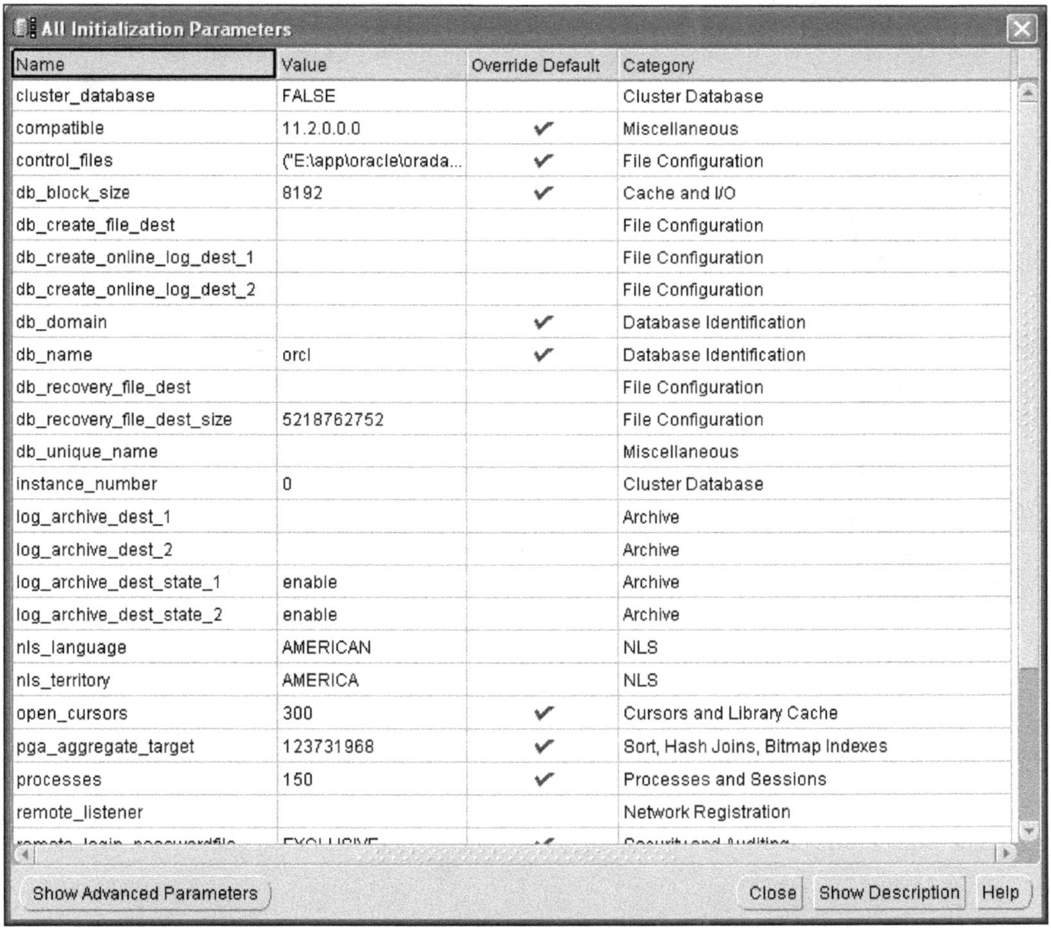

All Initialization Parameters

Name	Value	Override Default	Category
cluster_database	FALSE		Cluster Database
compatible	11.2.0.0.0	✓	Miscellaneous
control_files	("E:\app\oracle\orada...	✓	File Configuration
db_block_size	8192	✓	Cache and I/O
db_create_file_dest			File Configuration
db_create_online_log_dest_1			File Configuration
db_create_online_log_dest_2			File Configuration
db_domain		✓	Database Identification
db_name	orcl	✓	Database Identification
db_recovery_file_dest			File Configuration
db_recovery_file_dest_size	5218762752		File Configuration
db_unique_name			Miscellaneous
instance_number	0		Cluster Database
log_archive_dest_1			Archive
log_archive_dest_2			Archive
log_archive_dest_state_1	enable		Archive
log_archive_dest_state_2	enable		Archive
nls_language	AMERICAN		NLS
nls_territory	AMERICA		NLS
open_cursors	300	✓	Cursors and Library Cache
pga_aggregate_target	123731968	✓	Sort, Hash Joins, Bitmap Indexes
processes	150	✓	Processes and Sessions
remote_listener			Network Registration

Show Advanced Parameters — Close — Show Description — Help

From the main screen of this step, we also have several tabs to explore. If we click the **Sizing** tab, we're presented with two sizing options. The first, **Block Size**, allows us to change the size of the base unit of disk space allocation—the database block. The second option allows us to specify the number of processes that can run within the database. Since, in most cases, a process will be allocated for any user that connects to the database, we should be mindful of the number of expected user connections when setting this value. In our case, both of these values will be sufficient, so we click the next tab to explore, **Character Sets**.

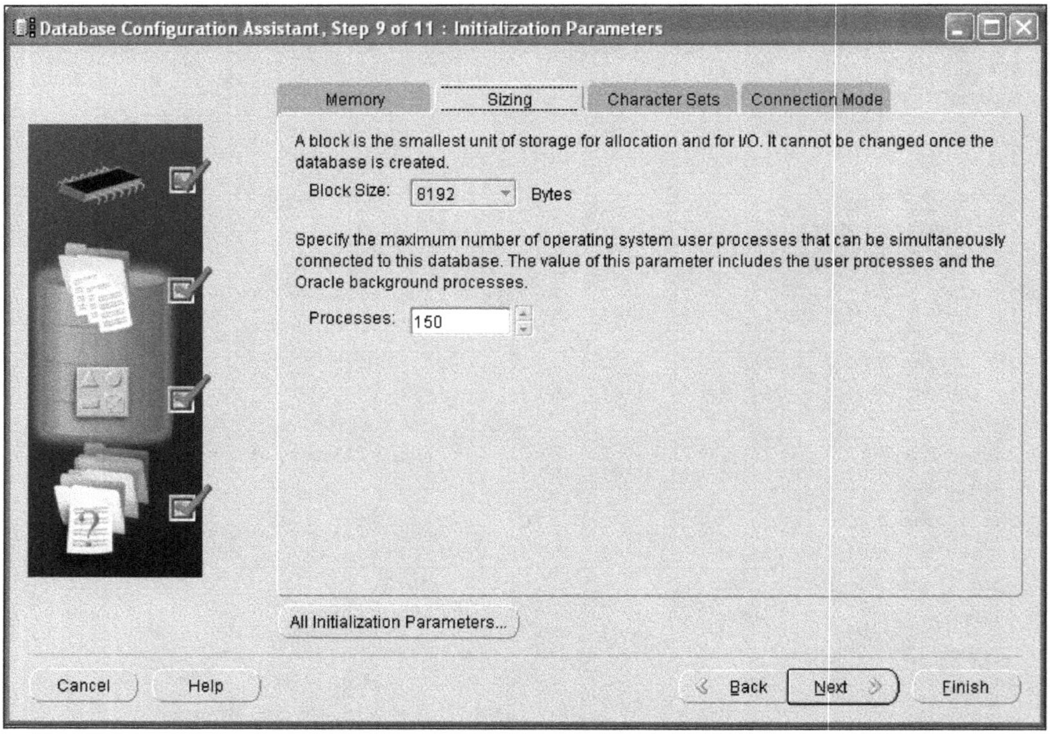
Database Configuration Assistant, Step 9 of 11 : Initialization Parameters
Memory
Sizing
Character Sets
Connection Mode
A block is the smallest unit of storage for allocation and for I/O. It cannot be changed once the database is created.
Block Size:
8192
Bytes
Specify the maximum number of operating system user processes that can be simultaneously connected to this database. The value of this parameter includes the user processes and the Oracle background processes.
Processes:
150
All Initialization Parameters...
Cancel
Help
Back
Next
Finish

The **Character Sets** tab allows the database administrator to change the character set of the database. In database terms, the character set refers to the characters available for storage and retrieval within the database, and the way those characters are encoded. In the simplest terms, we could think of this as the set of all alphanumeric characters (both upper and lower case) combined with all special characters. However, this simple example doesn't take non-western languages, such as Chinese or Japanese, into account. Some languages do not correlate to the letters in the English alphabet and require a different set of characters. For our purpose, we will leave **Use the default** as selected and click the **Connection Mode** tab. Note that the default character set used is not always the same for different operating systems.

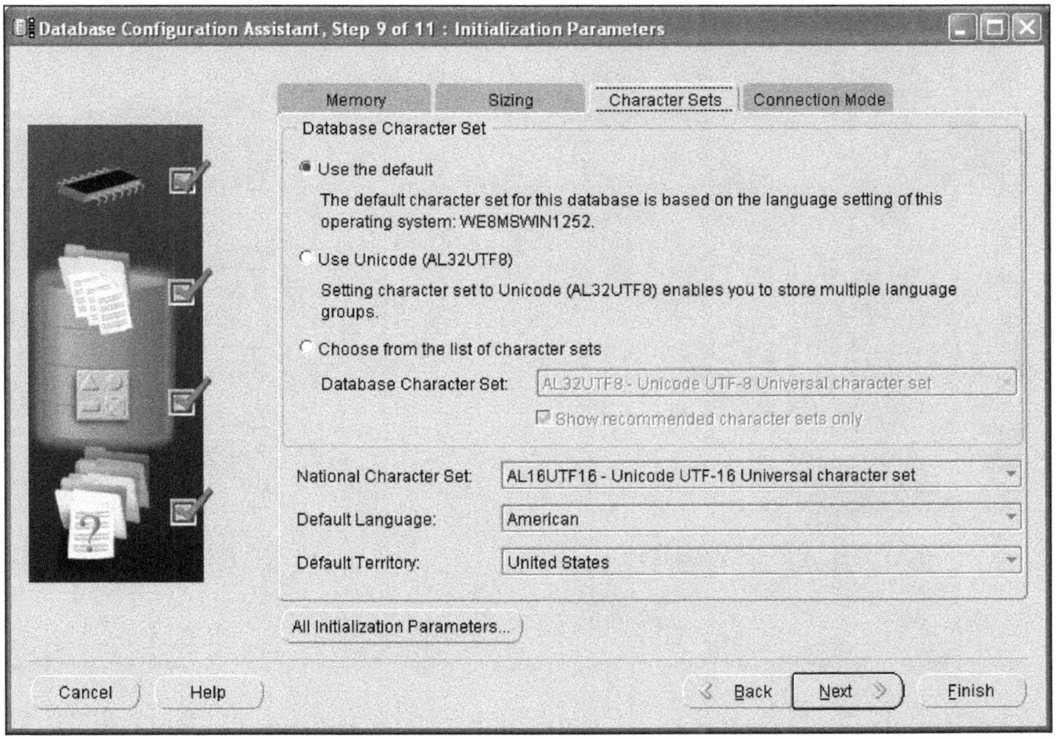
Database Configuration Assistant, Step 9 of 11 : Initialization Parameters
Memory
Sizing
Character Sets
Connection Mode
Database Character Set
Use the default
The default character set for this database is based on the language setting of this operating system: WE8MSWIN1252.
Use Unicode (AL32UTF8)
Setting character set to Unicode (AL32UTF8) enables you to store multiple language groups.
Choose from the list of character sets
Database Character Set:
AL32UTF8 - Unicode UTF-8 Universal character set
Show recommended character sets only
National Character Set:
AL16UTF16 - Unicode UTF-16 Universal character set
Default Language:
American
Default Territory:
United States
All Initialization Parameters...
Cancel
Help
Back
Next
Finish

The **Connection Mode** tab refers to the type of paradigm used to establish database connections, either dedicated server or shared server. The **Dedicated Server Mode** allocates dedicated server resources to service each client connection into the database. The **Shared Server Mode** allocates connection resources from a pool of available resources, particularly the number of processes used. Dedicated server mode suits our purposes, so we leave this screen by clicking **Next**. Reviewing our interaction with the **Initialization Parameters** screen in this step, we only changed the settings on the **Memory** tab at the beginning and left all other tabs unchanged.

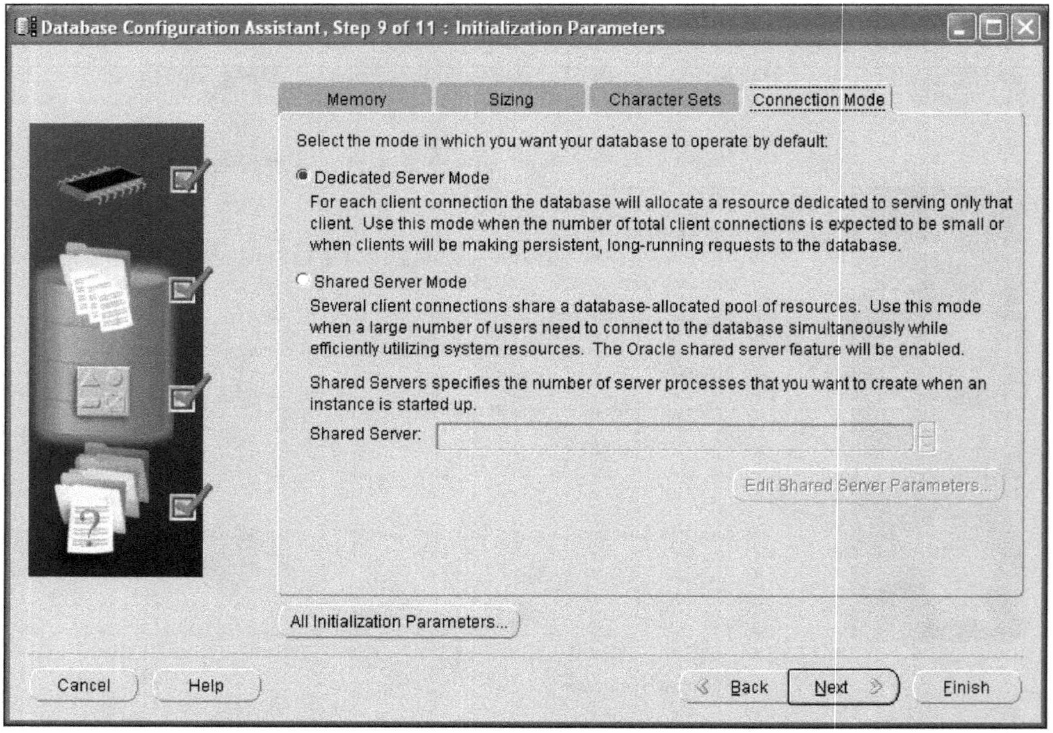

Database Configuration Assistant, Step 9 of 11 : Initialization Parameters
Memory
Sizing
Character Sets
Connection Mode
Select the mode in which you want your database to operate by default:
Dedicated Server Mode
For each client connection the database will allocate a resource dedicated to serving only that client. Use this mode when the number of total client connections is expected to be small or when clients will be making persistent, long-running requests to the database.
Shared Server Mode
Several client connections share a database-allocated pool of resources. Use this mode when a large number of users need to connect to the database simultaneously while efficiently utilizing system resources. The Oracle shared server feature will be enabled.
Shared Servers specifies the number of server processes that you want to create when an instance is started up.
Shared Server:
Edit Shared Server Parameters...
All Initialization Parameters...
Cancel
Help
Back
Next
Finish

As we near the end of our interaction with the DBCA, we're presented with the **Database Storage** screen. Recall that earlier in the chapter, we mentioned that a database consists of various physical files residing on or attached to the host machine. Although we specified their general location in an earlier step, here we can adjust the sizing and naming of individual files. Under the **Datafiles** section, each file is listed individually with its full directory path. Notice the directory structure that DBCA uses. It begins with the directory we chose while accessing the **Database File Locations** screen and creates a subdirectory within it labeled `{DB_UNIQUE_NAME}`.

This identifier will take on the value given earlier as the database name. Thus, in our example, the path used for the individual datafiles will be `E:\app\oracle\oradata\orcl`. We will look at each of these files at a later point and adjust their characteristics then; for now we'll accept these default settings and click **Next**.

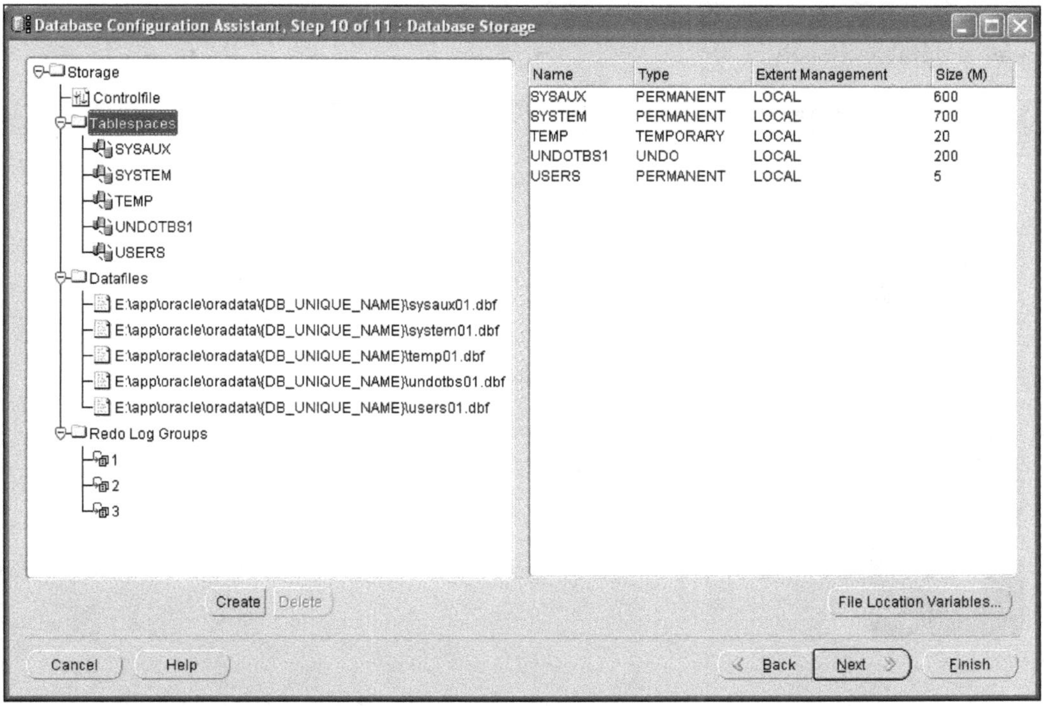
Database Configuration Assistant, Step 10 of 11 : Database Storage
Storage
Controlfile
Tablespaces
SYSAUX
SYSTEM
TEMP
UNDOTBS1
USERS
Datafiles
E:\app\oracle\oradata\{DB_UNIQUE_NAME}\sysaux01.dbf
E:\app\oracle\oradata\{DB_UNIQUE_NAME}\system01.dbf
E:\app\oracle\oradata\{DB_UNIQUE_NAME}\temp01.dbf
E:\app\oracle\oradata\{DB_UNIQUE_NAME}\undotbs01.dbf
E:\app\oracle\oradata\{DB_UNIQUE_NAME}\users01.dbf
Redo Log Groups
1
2
3
Name Type Extent Management Size (M)
SYSAUX PERMANENT LOCAL 600
SYSTEM PERMANENT LOCAL 700
TEMP TEMPORARY LOCAL 20
UNDOTBS1 UNDO LOCAL 200
USERS PERMANENT LOCAL 5
Create
Delete
File Location Variables...
Cancel
Help
Back
Next
Finish

Our last step in the DBCA is an important one. Here, we're given three creation options before DBCA begins creating the database. We can choose any combination of these three options before we proceed. In our case, we certainly want to select the **Create Database** option, which will allow DBCA to run through the necessary process to build the database using the configuration we've entered in the previous steps. We also have the option to take this configuration and save it as a database template, as discussed earlier in the chapter. Finally, we can select the **Generate Database Creation Scripts** checkbox, which will take our configuration and create the necessary scripts to manually create the database. This is, in essence, a different kind of template, and can be useful for creating multiple databases that use the same configuration without using DBCA. For our purposes, we will use this to examine the inner workings of the database creation itself, so we ensure that this option is checked.

The location of these scripts is displayed and we can choose another location if we wish. We also need to make a note of this location, as we will be returning to it shortly. When the options are checked as indicated in the following example, we click **Finish** to begin the database creation. Notice that although we've taken a great deal of time stepping through the DBCA for learning purposes, the number of actual changes we made was relatively small. With practice, you can move quickly through the DBCA to create a database easily.

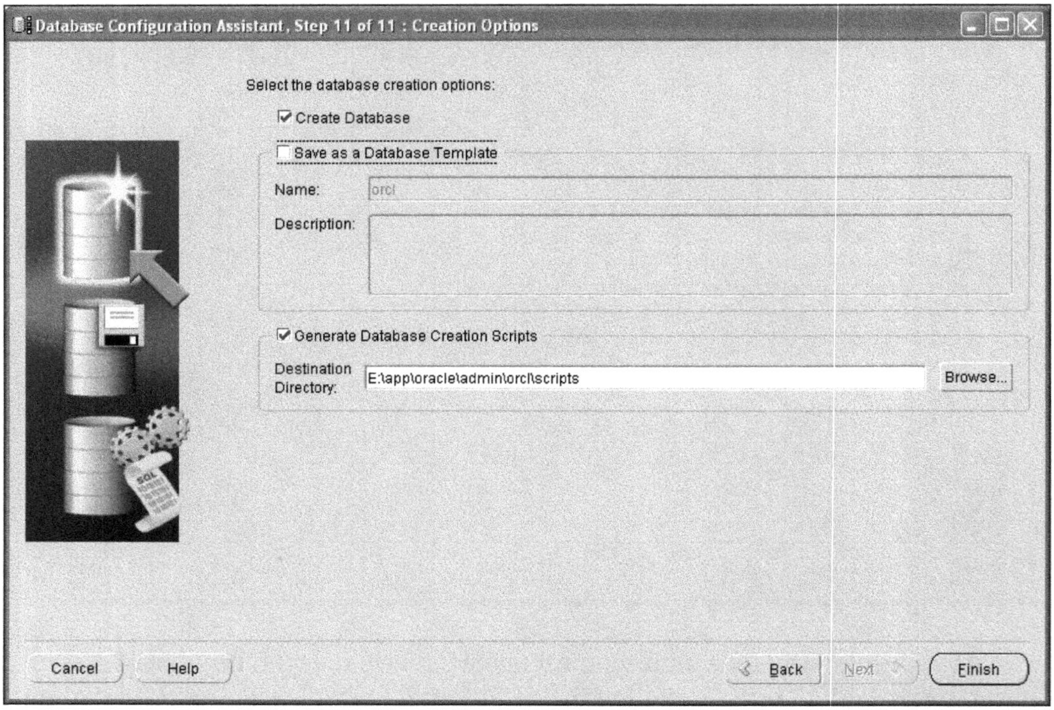
Database Configuration Assistant, Step 11 of 11 : Creation Options
Select the database creation options:
Create Database
Save as a Database Template
Name:
orcl
Description:
Generate Database Creation Scripts
Destination Directory:
E:\app\oracle\admin\orcl\scripts
Browse...
Cancel
Help
Back
Next
Finish

Before the creation process begins, we're presented with a summary screen, as shown in the next screenshot. We can scroll down the screen to see more if we wish. We click **OK** to close the screen.

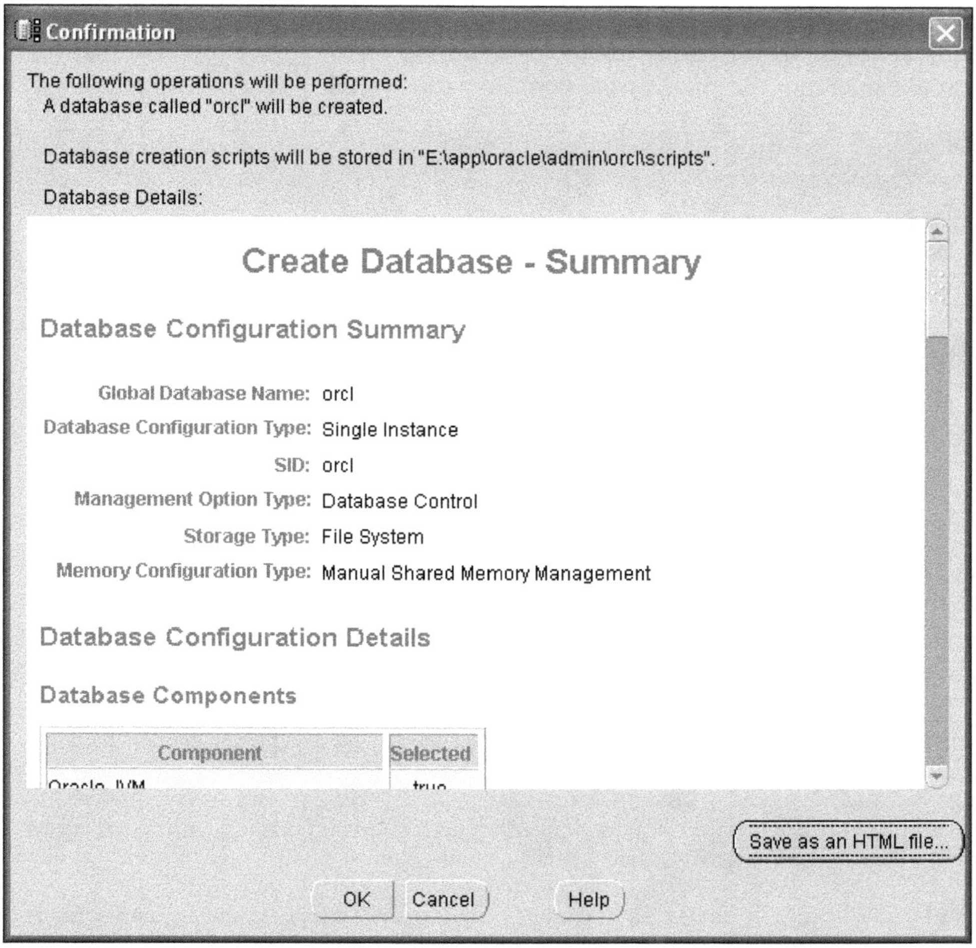
Confirmation
The following operations will be performed:
A database called "orcl" will be created.
Database creation scripts will be stored in "E:\app\oracle\admin\orcl\scripts".
Database Details:
Create Database - Summary
Database Configuration Summary
Global Database Name: orcl
Database Configuration Type: Single Instance
SID: orcl
Management Option Type: Database Control
Storage Type: File System
Memory Configuration Type: Manual Shared Memory Management
Database Configuration Details
Database Components
Component
Selected
Save as an HTML file...
OK
Cancel
Help

Assuming that we've chosen to generate creation scripts, a screen confirming this will be shown, followed by a dialog box indicating that the script generation is complete. Click **OK** to continue.

Following this, the actual creation of the database begins. We will break down exactly what is happening during this process in the next section, but for now we'll sum it up. The DBCA is allocating memory and operating system processes, creating physical files for the database and adding the essential metadata that supports the database. Next, DBCA adds each of the components we selected and then finishes the database creation. This can take a considerable amount of time depending on the number of components selected.

Once the database has been created, we are presented with the following verification screen. It contains information about the database that has been created, including the database name. We click **Exit** to complete our DBCA session.

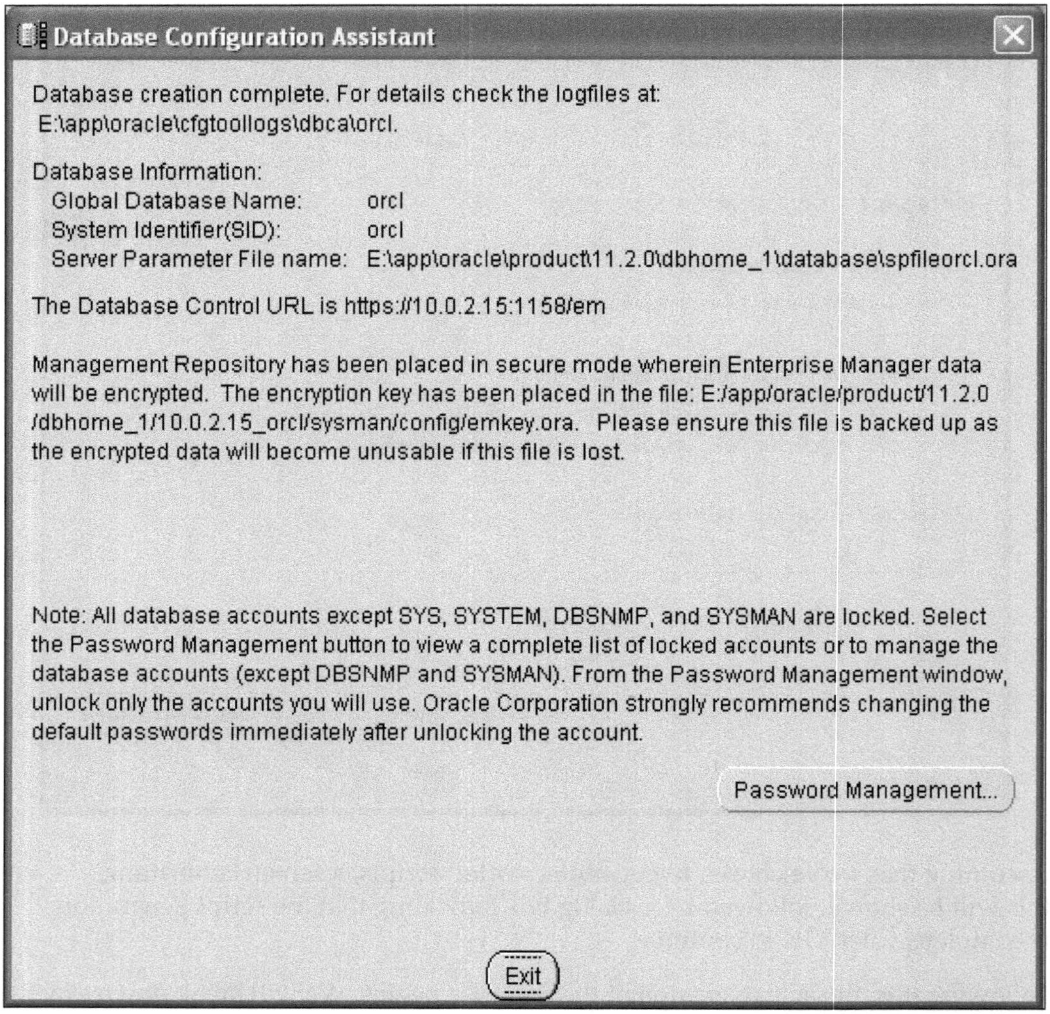
Database Configuration Assistant
Database creation complete. For details check the logfiles at:
E:\app\oracle\cfgtoollogs\dbca\orcl.
Database Information:
Global Database Name: orcl
System Identifier(SID): orcl
Server Parameter File name: E:\app\oracle\product\11.2.0\dbhome_1\database\spfileorcl.ora
The Database Control URL is https://10.0.2.15:1158/em
Management Repository has been placed in secure mode wherein Enterprise Manager data will be encrypted. The encryption key has been placed in the file: E:/app/oracle/product/11.2.0/dbhome_1/10.0.2.15_orcl/sysman/config/emkey.ora. Please ensure this file is backed up as the encrypted data will become unusable if this file is lost.
Note: All database accounts except SYS, SYSTEM, DBSNMP, and SYSMAN are locked. Select the Password Management button to view a complete list of locked accounts or to manage the database accounts (except DBSNMP and SYSMAN). From the Password Management window, unlock only the accounts you will use. Oracle Corporation strongly recommends changing the default passwords immediately after unlocking the account.
Password Management...
Exit

Examining a manual database creation

There's no doubt that the DBCA can make the creation of a database significantly simpler. However, for our purposes as DBAs, there is a downside to using it. Although we've walked through the individual configuration steps, we don't know how DBCA actually did it. For instance, we mentioned earlier that DBCA created the physical files needed to store the database. However, we don't know the commands that were actually used.

Since it is important for us to understand steps like these, we need to dig deeper into the actual process. In truth, DBCA is only a frontend application that builds a set of scripts—the same ones we generated at the end of our DBCA session. Those scripts are then run, and the database is created. To see how DBCA created the database, we need to look at the scripts it generated.

The scripts themselves are located in the directory specified on the last step before the database creation runs. The default for this location is `$ORACLE_BASE/admin/<SID>/scripts` where `SID` is the database system identifier name. In this example, the location is **E:\app\oracle\admin\orcl\scripts**. We see the list of scripts in the following Windows Explorer screenshot:

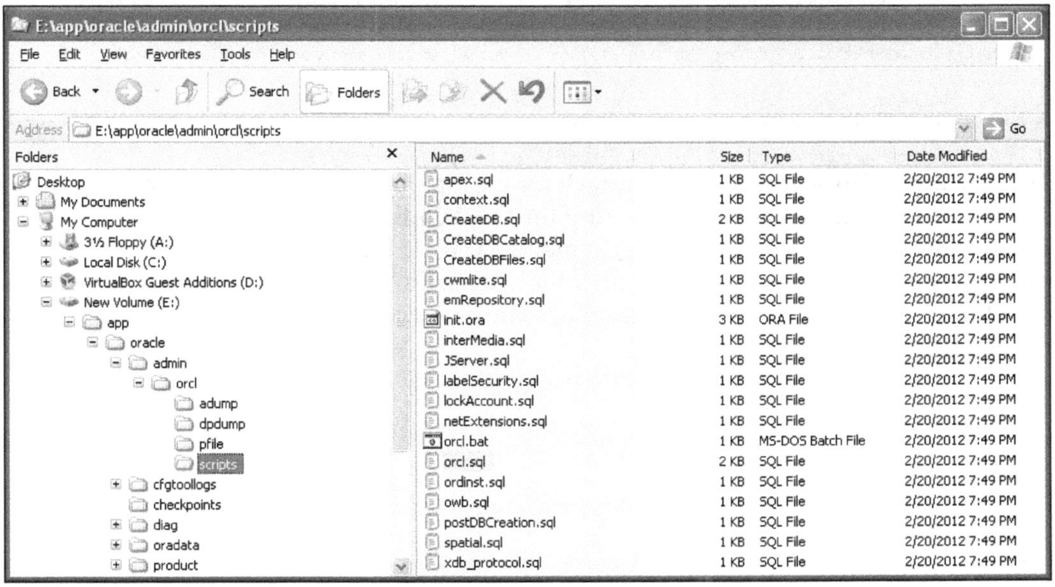
E:\app\oracle\admin\orcl\scripts
File Edit View Favorites Tools Help
Back Search Folders
Address E:\app\oracle\admin\orcl\scripts Go
Folders
Desktop
My Documents
My Computer
3½ Floppy (A:)
Local Disk (C:)
VirtualBox Guest Additions (D:)
New Volume (E:)
app
oracle
admin
orcl
adump
dpdump
pfile
scripts
cfgtoollogs
checkpoints
diag
oradata
product
Name Size Type Date Modified
apex.sql 1 KB SQL File 2/20/2012 7:49 PM
context.sql 1 KB SQL File 2/20/2012 7:49 PM
CreateDB.sql 2 KB SQL File 2/20/2012 7:49 PM
CreateDBCatalog.sql 1 KB SQL File 2/20/2012 7:49 PM
CreateDBFiles.sql 1 KB SQL File 2/20/2012 7:49 PM
cwmlite.sql 1 KB SQL File 2/20/2012 7:49 PM
emRepository.sql 1 KB SQL File 2/20/2012 7:49 PM
init.ora 3 KB ORA File 2/20/2012 7:49 PM
interMedia.sql 1 KB SQL File 2/20/2012 7:49 PM
JServer.sql 1 KB SQL File 2/20/2012 7:49 PM
labelSecurity.sql 1 KB SQL File 2/20/2012 7:49 PM
lockAccount.sql 1 KB SQL File 2/20/2012 7:49 PM
netExtensions.sql 1 KB SQL File 2/20/2012 7:49 PM
orcl.bat 1 KB MS-DOS Batch File 2/20/2012 7:49 PM
orcl.sql 2 KB SQL File 2/20/2012 7:49 PM
ordinst.sql 1 KB SQL File 2/20/2012 7:49 PM
owb.sql 1 KB SQL File 2/20/2012 7:49 PM
postDBCreation.sql 1 KB SQL File 2/20/2012 7:49 PM
spatial.sql 1 KB SQL File 2/20/2012 7:49 PM
xdb_protocol.sql 1 KB SQL File 2/20/2012 7:49 PM

There are several scripts here, and not all of them are equally important, so we'll examine the crucial scripts one at a time. These scripts are actually run in a set sequence that is started by the `orcl.bat` batch file. The `orcl` in the batch file name refers to the name of our database. Had we named our database something different, the batch file name would reflect that. In Unix-based systems, this file will be named `orcl.sh`, as `.bat` files are native to Windows. While we will examine this script, it is vitally important that you do not execute it. This will attempt to restart the creation of the database that we have just completed. It is this script that starts the entire chain of events. Instead of double-clicking it, we simply right-click on `orcl.bat` and select **Edit** (not **Open**). In Linux, just edit the `.sh` script with a text editor, such as `vi`. We've shown the batch file here with white space separation for clarity.

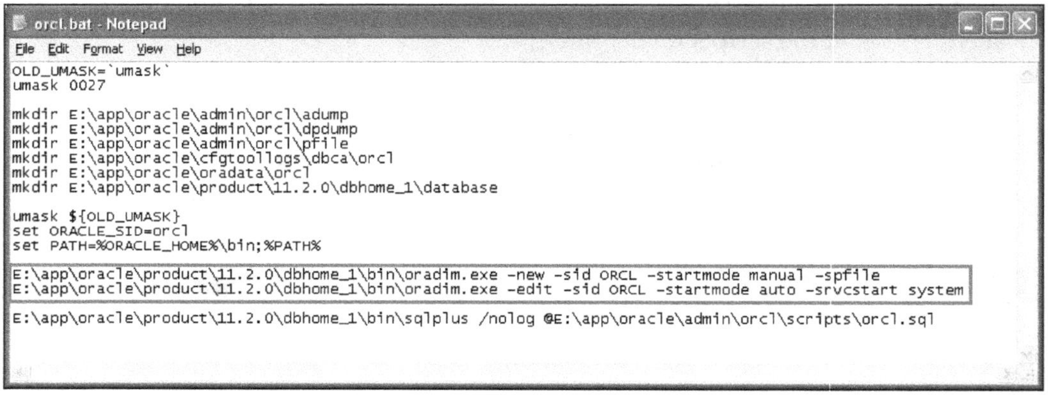
orcl.bat - Notepad
File Edit Format View Help

```
OLD_UMASK=`umask`
umask 0027

mkdir E:\app\oracle\admin\orcl\adump
mkdir E:\app\oracle\admin\orcl\dpdump
mkdir E:\app\oracle\admin\orcl\pfile
mkdir E:\app\oracle\cfgtoollogs\dbca\orcl
mkdir E:\app\oracle\oradata\orcl
mkdir E:\app\oracle\product\11.2.0\dbhome_1\database

umask ${OLD_UMASK}
set ORACLE_SID=orcl
set PATH=%ORACLE_HOME%\bin;%PATH%

E:\app\oracle\product\11.2.0\dbhome_1\bin\oradim.exe -new -sid ORCL -startmode manual -spfile
E:\app\oracle\product\11.2.0\dbhome_1\bin\oradim.exe -edit -sid ORCL -startmode auto -srvcstart system

E:\app\oracle\product\11.2.0\dbhome_1\bin\sqlplus /nolog @E:\app\oracle\admin\orcl\scripts\orcl.sql
```

The first and third sections define **umask** for permissions and set two other environment variables, including setting the **ORACLE_SID** variable to **orcl**. The second section uses the **mkdir** command to create the various directories needed for the database. Note that all of these directories stem from the `ORACLE_BASE` directory, in this case, **E:\app\oracle**. These three sections set up the environment necessary to proceed.

The highlighted section contains commands that are not necessary on Linux and Unix platforms. These two lines use a specialized command, **oradim.exe**, which is only found on Oracle installations for Windows. This command creates the Windows services that are necessary to run the Oracle database. A **Windows service** is a low-level program that can start when the Windows operating system boots without requiring user intervention. On the Windows platform, Oracle runs as a Windows Service that requires us to create these services ourselves during a manual database creation. It is important to reiterate that services such as these are not used in Linux and Unix systems.

The first line of the following command executes the `oradim.exe` command and creates a new service, signified by the `-new` value:

```
E:\app\oracle\product\11.2.0\db_home1\bin\oradim.exe -new -sid ORCL -
startmode manual -spfile
```

It specifies the new SID for this service as `ORCL` and that it has a `startmode` of `manual`, meaning that the database will not start automatically when the service starts. Note that this command creates the service needed to run the database, not the database itself.

The second line of the following command indicates that that we are editing this service, signified by the SID `ORCL`, to run with a `startmode` of `auto` and a `srvcstart` of `system`:

```
E:\app\oracle\product\11.2.0\db_home1\bin\oradim.exe -edit -sid ORCL -
startmode auto -srvcstart system
```

This means that the database will automatically start when the database service starts, and the `srvcstart` value indicates that the service will start automatically when the system is booted. Oracle also creates several other services during database creation. We will examine these in the next section.

The last line of `orcl.bat` calls the SQL*Plus program (`sqlplus`) and instructs it to run a script called `orcl.sql`. We need to examine this script next, so we right-click on the script, choose **Open With**, and choose **Notepad**. The `orcl.sql` script is displayed:

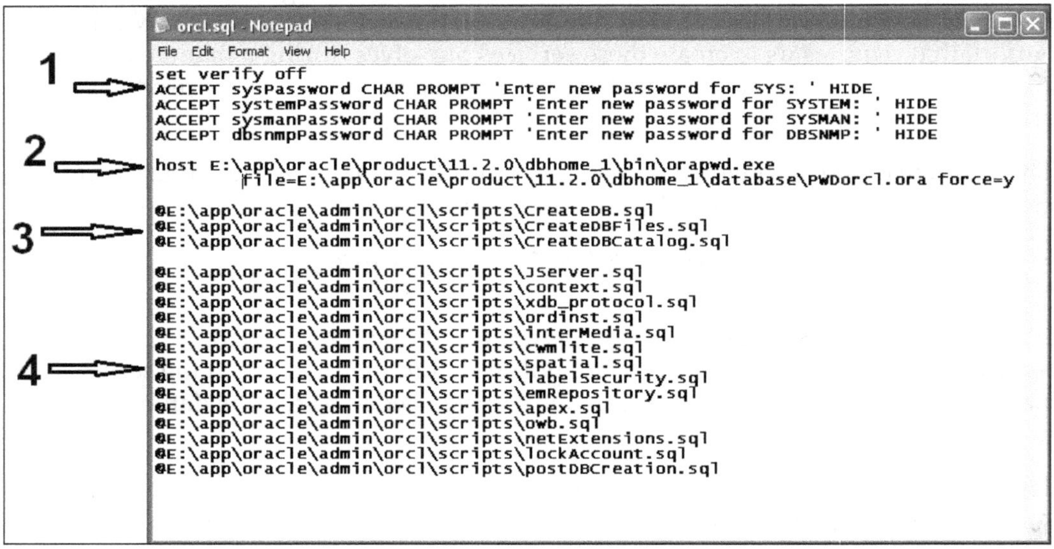
orcl.sql - Notepad
File Edit Format View Help
1
2
3
4
set verify off
ACCEPT sysPassword CHAR PROMPT 'Enter new password for SYS: ' HIDE
ACCEPT systemPassword CHAR PROMPT 'Enter new password for SYSTEM: ' HIDE
ACCEPT sysmanPassword CHAR PROMPT 'Enter new password for SYSMAN: ' HIDE
ACCEPT dbsnmpPassword CHAR PROMPT 'Enter new password for DBSNMP: ' HIDE
host E:\app\oracle\product\11.2.0\dbhome_1\bin\orapwd.exe
file=E:\app\oracle\product\11.2.0\dbhome_1\database\PWDorcl.ora force=y
@E:\app\oracle\admin\orcl\scripts\CreateDB.sql
@E:\app\oracle\admin\orcl\scripts\CreateDBFiles.sql
@E:\app\oracle\admin\orcl\scripts\CreateDBCatalog.sql
@E:\app\oracle\admin\orcl\scripts\JServer.sql
@E:\app\oracle\admin\orcl\scripts\context.sql
@E:\app\oracle\admin\orcl\scripts\xdb_protocol.sql
@E:\app\oracle\admin\orcl\scripts\ordinst.sql
@E:\app\oracle\admin\orcl\scripts\interMedia.sql
@E:\app\oracle\admin\orcl\scripts\cwmlite.sql
@E:\app\oracle\admin\orcl\scripts\spatial.sql
@E:\app\oracle\admin\orcl\scripts\labelSecurity.sql
@E:\app\oracle\admin\orcl\scripts\emRepository.sql
@E:\app\oracle\admin\orcl\scripts\apex.sql
@E:\app\oracle\admin\orcl\scripts\owb.sql
@E:\app\oracle\admin\orcl\scripts\netExtensions.sql
@E:\app\oracle\admin\orcl\scripts\lockAccount.sql
@E:\app\oracle\admin\orcl\scripts\postDBCreation.sql

This is the primary SQL script that continues the creation of the database. We've labeled several sections of it for clarity. Section **1** displays four different prompts that ask us to enter passwords for the four database user accounts: **SYS**, **SYSTEM**, **SYSMAN**, and **DBSNMP**. These password values are stored using the **ACCEPT** command and used later in one of the secondary scripts. Section **2** uses the **orapwd.exe** program to create a password file that can store the passwords of certain privileged database accounts in an encrypted format. Password files in Oracle, running under Windows, follow the `PWD<SID>.ora` format, where `SID` is the database SID name. The password file in our example is **PWDorcl.ora**. In Linux, the Oracle password files follow the `orapw<SID>` format. Both serve the same purpose. Skipping section **3** for a moment, section **4** contains a list of SQL scripts that are run after the database is created. These scripts create the tables and data needed to support the various options that we selected in DBCA. For instance, we selected the InterMedia option, so a script called **interMedia.sql** is in the list of scripts to run. Each of the scripts is run individually. The first script is run, as designated by the @ sign, the SQL symbol used to run a script. After the first script finishes, the second runs, and so on. Once these scripts are finished, all of the supporting data for our database options are in place.

So, to review, section **1** prompts for passwords, section **2** creates a password file, and section **4** builds the tables that support our database options. However, as DBAs, it is section **3** that is of most concern to us. Section **3** contains the scripts that are most fundamental to actually building the database. We'll look at them one at a time, starting with **CreateDB.sql**.

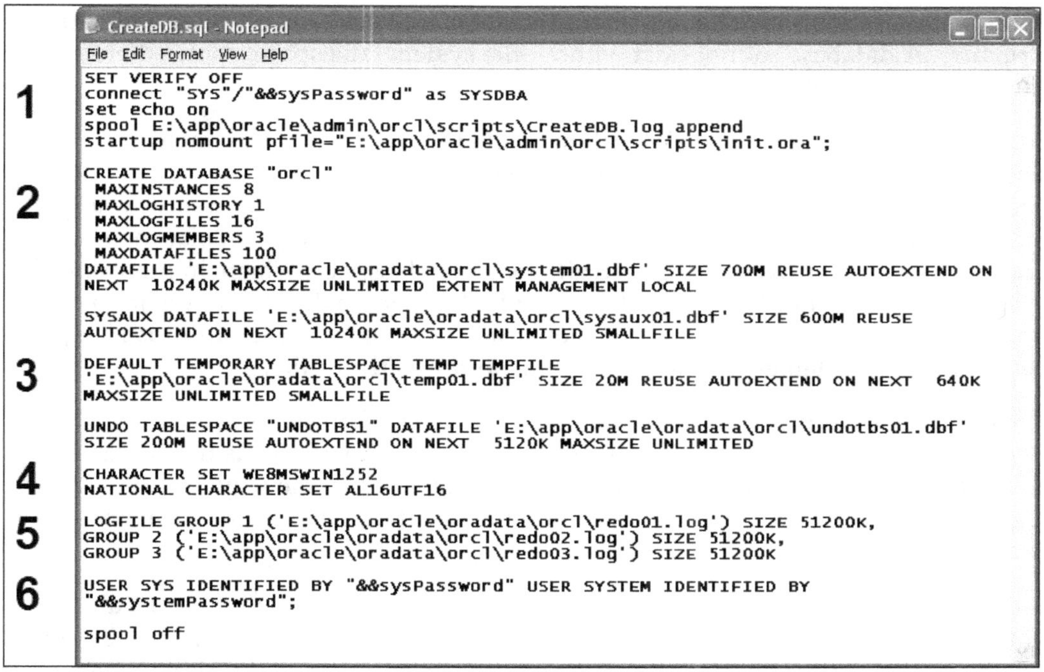
CreateDB.sql - Notepad
File Edit Format View Help
1
2
3
4
5
6

```
SET VERIFY OFF
connect "SYS"/"&&sysPassword" as SYSDBA
set echo on
spool E:\app\oracle\admin\orcl\scripts\CreateDB.log append
startup nomount pfile="E:\app\oracle\admin\orcl\scripts\init.ora";

CREATE DATABASE "orcl"
 MAXINSTANCES 8
 MAXLOGHISTORY 1
 MAXLOGFILES 16
 MAXLOGMEMBERS 3
 MAXDATAFILES 100
DATAFILE 'E:\app\oracle\oradata\orcl\system01.dbf' SIZE 700M REUSE AUTOEXTEND ON
NEXT  10240K MAXSIZE UNLIMITED EXTENT MANAGEMENT LOCAL

SYSAUX DATAFILE 'E:\app\oracle\oradata\orcl\sysaux01.dbf' SIZE 600M REUSE
AUTOEXTEND ON NEXT  10240K MAXSIZE UNLIMITED SMALLFILE

DEFAULT TEMPORARY TABLESPACE TEMP TEMPFILE
'E:\app\oracle\oradata\orcl\temp01.dbf' SIZE 20M REUSE AUTOEXTEND ON NEXT  640K
MAXSIZE UNLIMITED SMALLFILE

UNDO TABLESPACE "UNDOTBS1" DATAFILE 'E:\app\oracle\oradata\orcl\undotbs01.dbf'
SIZE 200M REUSE AUTOEXTEND ON NEXT  5120K MAXSIZE UNLIMITED

CHARACTER SET WE8MSWIN1252
NATIONAL CHARACTER SET AL16UTF16

LOGFILE GROUP 1 ('E:\app\oracle\oradata\orcl\redo01.log') SIZE 51200K,
GROUP 2 ('E:\app\oracle\oradata\orcl\redo02.log') SIZE 51200K,
GROUP 3 ('E:\app\oracle\oradata\orcl\redo03.log') SIZE 51200K

USER SYS IDENTIFIED BY "&&sysPassword" USER SYSTEM IDENTIFIED BY
"&&systemPassword";

spool off
```

There's a lot to take in here, so we'll take it one section at a time. This script, `CreateDB.sql`, is the SQL script that actually creates the framework of the database. Keep in mind that our goal at this point is to become familiar with the manual creation process, not to examine every keyword within this script. We will briefly touch on the major points here, and examine them in greater detail as the book progresses. Section **1** connects to the database as a privileged user, **SYS**, and begins a logfile of the creation process using the **spool** command. Finally, we start the database with the **startup** command.

Sections **2** through **6** are actually one single SQL statement, although we've separated various portions with whitespace for clarity. Section **2** begins the **CREATE DATABASE** command to initiate the creation of the database called **orcl**. The last two lines of this section use the **DATAFILE** keyword to specify a physical database file, **system01.dbf**, for the system tablespace. In Oracle, the **system tablespace** is the location that holds all of the database's internal metadata, referred to as the **data dictionary**. This is metadata about the database itself—its physical and logical structure. A database cannot exist without the system tablespace, so it is defined early within the statement.

Section **3** lists several more disk locations that are infrastructure-oriented. The **SYSAUX** tablespace stored in the **sysaux01.dbf** file contains Oracle internal performance information. The **temp01.dbf** file is designed to be an overflow area for certain operations that are performed in memory. When a particular memory cache is full, it spills over into the **TEMPORARY** tablespace, which, in our example, is located in the **temp01.dbf** file. The **UNDO** tablespace is the location that holds undo data—data that is required to reconstruct a transaction if it fails or is rolled back. The **UNDO** tablespace is stored in the **undotbs01.dbf** file.

Recall from earlier in the chapter that one of the choices presented by DBCA referred to the database character set. We defined a character set as the characters available for storage and retrieval within the database, and the way those characters are encoded. Section **4** lists the lines within the script that define our database character set.

Section **5** defines the database redo logs. **Redo logs** are the files that record all of the changes in the database, in what we might describe as a circular disk buffer. Changes are written to each of the files in sequence and then overwritten when they are full. The redo logs are crucial to enabling database recovery from a backup. In our example, there are three redo log groups stored in **redo01.log, redo02.log,** and **redo03.log**.

Section **6** assigns passwords to the two most privileged users in the database—**SYS** and **SYSTEM**. These two users own and control every aspect of database access, with **SYSTEM** having slightly fewer privileges than **SYS**. From a database perspective, the **SYS** user is analogous to the root user in Unix or the Administrator user in Windows. The script ends by closing the logfile using the **SPOOL OFF** command. Again, there is a great deal of information in this script. The terms will become more familiar as we examine the Oracle Database in greater detail.

> **The real-world DBA**
>
> Many experienced DBAs prefer to build a script for the creation of databases in a fashion similar to that of the previous script. Doing so can be a tremendous learning experience and one that should be attempted by every aspiring DBA at some point. However, the complex nature of the `CREATE DATABASE` command makes it easy to do it incorrectly. Test your script thoroughly in a practice environment before attempting to use it to build a crucial system.

Referring back to the `orcl.sql` script, the next script executed is `CreateDBFiles.sql`. This script, which is considerably less complex than the previous one, is shown in the following screenshot:

CreateDBFiles.sql - Notepad

File Edit Format View Help

```
SET VERIFY OFF
connect "SYS"/"&&sysPassword" as SYSDBA
set echo on
spool E:\app\oracle\admin\orcl\scripts\CreateDBFiles.log append

CREATE SMALLFILE TABLESPACE "USERS" LOGGING DATAFILE
'E:\app\oracle\oradata\orcl\users01.dbf' SIZE 5M REUSE AUTOEXTEND ON NEXT
1280K MAXSIZE UNLIMITED EXTENT MANAGEMENT LOCAL SEGMENT SPACE MANAGEMENT  AUTO;

ALTER DATABASE DEFAULT TABLESPACE "USERS";
spool off
```

The first four lines perform similar functions to those done in section **1** of the previous **CreateDB.sql** script. We connect to the database using the password provided to the original script, the variable referred to a **&&sysPassword**, and begin a logfile with the **spool** command. The heart of this script, however, is the **CREATE TABLESPACE "USERS"** statement, along with the optional keyword, **SMALLFILE**. This command creates a tablespace that can hold non-system related data. A tablespace is simply the logical name given to a physical database file. This allows us to refer database files by a logical name, **USERS**, instead of their physical location, **E:\app\oracle\oradata\orcl\users01.dbf**. This command also specifies a number of storage characteristics that we will examine in detail later. For now, notice the **SIZE** keyword that follows the physical database file location. Here, **SIZE 5M** indicates that the **users01.dbf** datafile will be 5 megabytes in size.

The third script listed in section **3** of the `orcl.sql` script is **CreateDBCatalog.sql**. A highlighted version of this script is shown in the following screenshot:

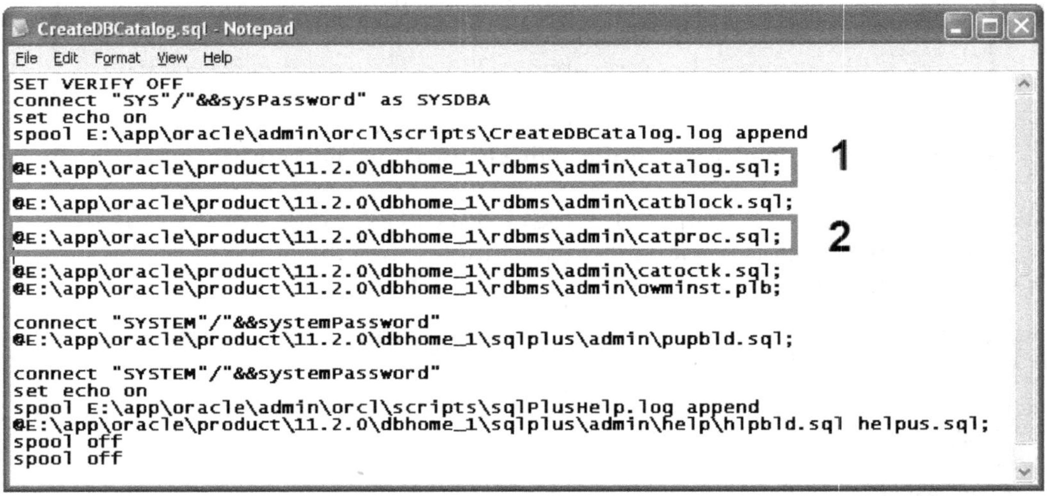
CreateDBCatalog.sql - Notepad
File Edit Format View Help
1
2

```
SET VERIFY OFF
connect "SYS"/"&&sysPassword" as SYSDBA
set echo on
spool E:\app\oracle\admin\orcl\scripts\CreateDBCatalog.log append
@E:\app\oracle\product\11.2.0\dbhome_1\rdbms\admin\catalog.sql;
@E:\app\oracle\product\11.2.0\dbhome_1\rdbms\admin\catblock.sql;
@E:\app\oracle\product\11.2.0\dbhome_1\rdbms\admin\catproc.sql;
@E:\app\oracle\product\11.2.0\dbhome_1\rdbms\admin\catoctk.sql;
@E:\app\oracle\product\11.2.0\dbhome_1\rdbms\admin\owminst.plb;

connect "SYSTEM"/"&&systemPassword"
@E:\app\oracle\product\11.2.0\dbhome_1\sqlplus\admin\pupbld.sql;

connect "SYSTEM"/"&&systemPassword"
set echo on
spool E:\app\oracle\admin\orcl\scripts\sqlPlusHelp.log append
@E:\app\oracle\product\11.2.0\dbhome_1\sqlplus\admin\help\hlpbld.sql helpus.sql;
spool off
spool off
```

Recall from earlier in this section that we discussed the database data dictionary. We said that the data dictionary was the storehouse of database metadata. Simply put, metadata is "data about data." It defines the structure of the data within the database. The data dictionary can be an extraordinary tool in the hands of an experienced DBA. It contains information on every facet of database functionality. It is also vast, ever-changing with new versions, and initially difficult to grasp. Because of its importance, we will refer to various data dictionary views throughout this book in order to gain a greater familiarity with how to leverage them to learn about the database. There are several sub-scripts run in the `CreateDBCatalog.sql` script. These are used to set up various functionalities in the database, including the help system and product user profile for the SQL*Plus tool. For our purposes, we're most concerned with the two scripts we've highlighted. These two scripts create the greater part of the data dictionary. Understand that, up to this point in the manual creation, we have a database that is truly empty. It has a physical structure, with datafiles and redo logfiles, but no logical structure. When we refer to the term logical structure, we mean the tables, indexes, and other database objects that we use within the database. The first script, **catalog.sql**, creates the base tables and views that Oracle uses to store internal metadata. We could refer to these as the system tables and data dictionary views. The script itself runs various other scripts in the same directory, and chasing them all down can be both educational and time-consuming. For our purposes, we want to understand the importance of **catalog.sql** and its part in creating the data dictionary.

The second script, **catproc.sql**, creates the PL/SQL procedures, functions, and packages that are used to enable various functionalities within the database, including backup and recovery, space management, and performance tuning. These two scripts create the core of the database metadata used by the system itself as well as DBAs to determine the state of the database at any given time.

Examining Windows Services in Oracle

Recall from the previous section that we examined the `orcl.bat` batch file from a manual database creation procedure. We noted two commands in that script that created and modified Windows Services related to the Oracle database. We said that a Windows Service is a low-level program that can start when the operating system boots without requiring user intervention. In Windows (and only in Windows), the core Oracle kernel operates within these Services. To close this chapter, we look at the Services that were created for Oracle during our database creation using DBCA.

There are several ways to invoke the services window that vary between the versions of Windows, so we'll choose a standard way that should suffice for each of them. This will also give us a desktop shortcut that will be useful as we go forward. The example shown here is for Windows XP, although other versions of Windows will be similar. We want to create a shortcut on the desktop for the command prompt in Windows. We begin by right-clicking on the Windows desktop and choosing **New**, then **Shortcut**. The **Create Shortcut** window is displayed. In the location box, we type `cmd.exe` and click **Next**.

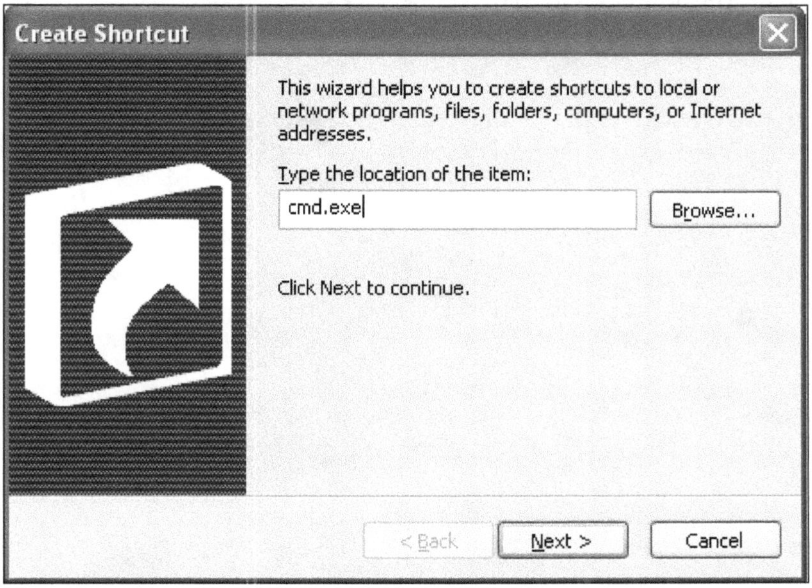
Create Shortcut
This wizard helps you to create shortcuts to local or network programs, files, folders, computers, or Internet addresses.
Type the location of the item:
cmd.exe
Browse...
Click Next to continue.
< Back
Next >
Cancel

The **Select a Title for the Program** window is displayed next. Here, we simply enter a name for our command prompt shortcut. We enter `Command Prompt` and click **Finish**.

We now have a desktop shortcut to the Windows command prompt. We double-click this shortcut and are presented with the command prompt window. To invoke the Windows Services program, we type `services.msc` and hit the *Enter* key, as shown in the following screenshot:

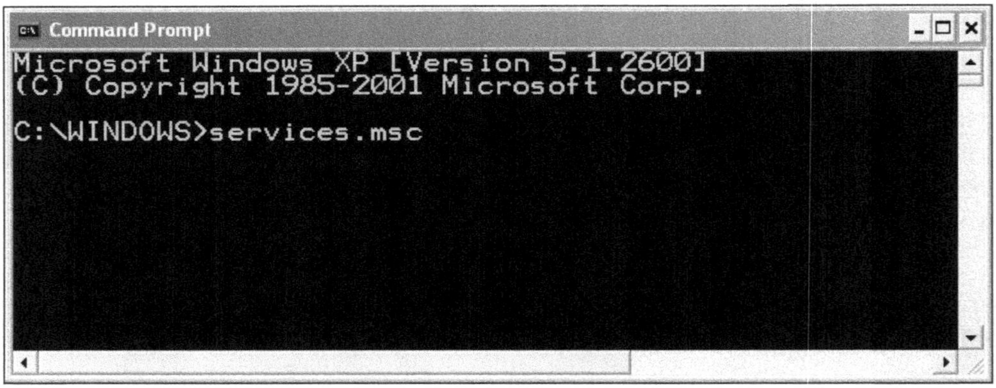
Command Prompt
Microsoft Windows XP [Version 5.1.2600]
(C) Copyright 1985-2001 Microsoft Corp.
C:\WINDOWS>services.msc

Next, we see the **Services** window shown here in the Standard view. There are many types of services shown here, and the ones we see will vary based on the version of Windows and the software that has been installed. Just to give us an idea about the types of non-Oracle services that can run on Windows, we might see software auto-updaters, video driver services, and anti-virus programs in the list.

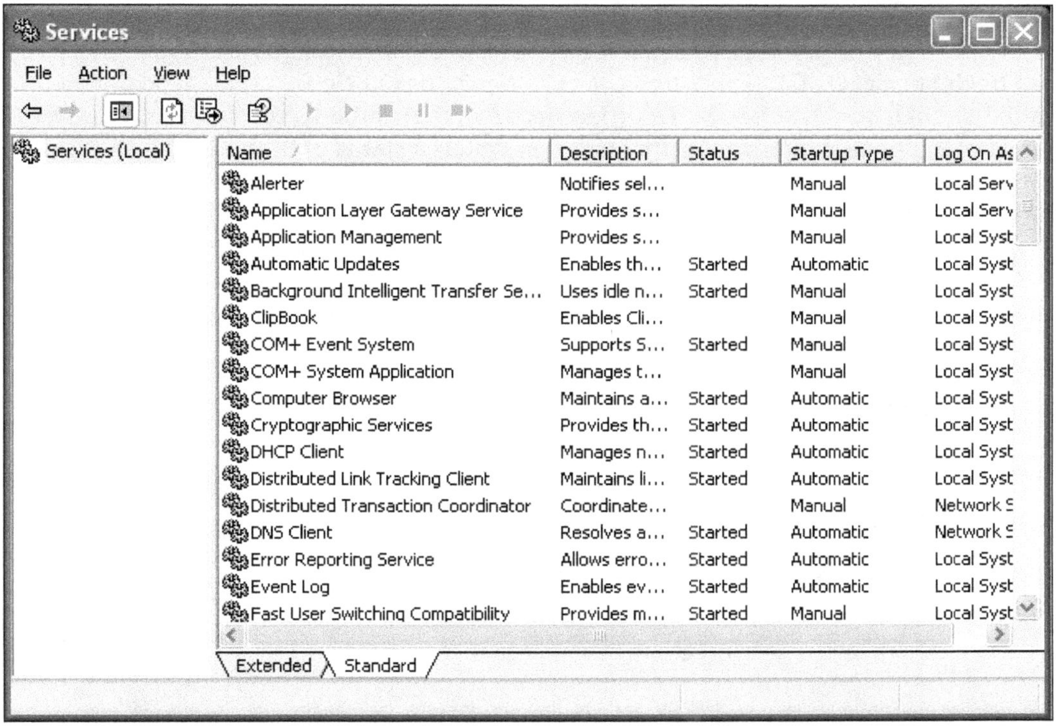
Services
File
Action
View
Help
Services (Local)
Name
Description
Status
Startup Type
Log On As
Alerter Notifies sel... Manual Local Serv
Application Layer Gateway Service Provides s... Manual Local Serv
Application Management Provides s... Manual Local Syst
Automatic Updates Enables th... Started Automatic Local Syst
Background Intelligent Transfer Se... Uses idle n... Started Manual Local Syst
ClipBook Enables Cli... Manual Local Syst
COM+ Event System Supports S... Started Manual Local Syst
COM+ System Application Manages t... Manual Local Syst
Computer Browser Maintains a... Started Automatic Local Syst
Cryptographic Services Provides th... Started Automatic Local Syst
DHCP Client Manages n... Started Automatic Local Syst
Distributed Link Tracking Client Maintains li... Started Automatic Local Syst
Distributed Transaction Coordinator Coordinate... Manual Network S
DNS Client Resolves a... Started Automatic Network S
Error Reporting Service Allows erro... Started Automatic Local Syst
Event Log Enables ev... Started Automatic Local Syst
Fast User Switching Compatibility Provides m... Started Manual Local Syst
Extended
Standard

For our purposes, we're concerned with the services that were created during the creation of our database with DBCA. To see these, we scroll down to the services that begin with the word "Oracle", as seen here:

OracleDBConsoleorcl Started Automatic
OracleJobSchedulerORCL Disabled
OracleOraDb11g_home2ClrAgent Manual
OracleOraDb11g_home2TNSListener Started Automatic
OracleRemExecService Started Disabled
OracleServiceORCL Started Automatic

There are six Oracle-related services shown here, but we're primarily concerned with only three of them. The primary service for the Oracle database is shown here as **OracleServiceORCL**. This service encapsulates the Oracle kernel and the database called `ORCL`. If our database had a different name, that name would be reflected in the name of the service. It is crucial that this service has a status of **Started** before we can start the database. If it does not, we will receive an error when attempting to run the database. However, while starting the service is necessary, it does not guarantee that the database itself is running. The service may be set with a **Startup type** of **Automatic**, but the database does not have to be configured to start when the service starts, requiring us to start the database manually. DBCA configures Windows database services to automatically start both the service and the database when the host machine is started. We can configure the properties of a service, including its startup behavior, by right-clicking on the name of the service and choosing **Properties**, as shown in the following screenshot:

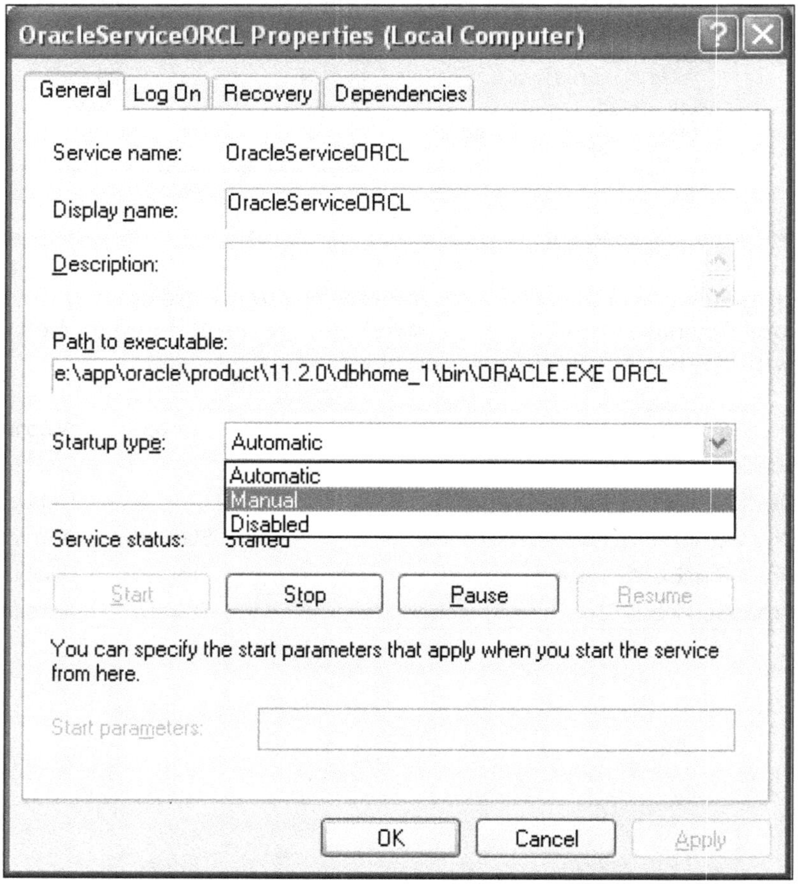
OracleServiceORCL Properties (Local Computer)
General
Log On
Recovery
Dependencies
Service name:
OracleServiceORCL
Display name:
OracleServiceORCL
Description:
Path to executable:
e:\app\oracle\product\11.2.0\dbhome_1\bin\ORACLE.EXE ORCL
Startup type:
Automatic
Automatic
Manual
Disabled
Service status:
Start
Stop
Pause
Resume
You can specify the start parameters that apply when you start the service from here.
Start parameters:
OK
Cancel
Apply

Here, we can start and stop the service, as well as change the type of startup the service uses. To set the service to a manual startup, we click the drop-down list for **Startup type** and choose **Manual**. Generally, it is simplest for us to leave the service settings the same way as DBCA created them. We click **Cancel**.

The other two services we'll concern ourselves with are the **Listener** and **Console** services. Recall from earlier in the chapter that we used the NETCA, or Network Configuration Assistant, to create a listener—a process that listens for incoming database connections. In Windows, the listener runs on the operating system as a service, named here as **OracleOra11gDB_home2TNSListener**. In order for the database to receive incoming network connections, this service must be started. We also mentioned a tool called Database Control in *Chapter 1, Introducing the Oracle Relational Database System*. In Windows, this tool runs as a Windows Service as well, called **OracleDBConsoleorcl**. Note that if we were to create another database on this host using DBCA, additional services for the database and Database Control would be created, but not for the listener. In standard configurations, one listener is configured for each host and will service every database on it. For now, we will leave these services configured as we have in the example's screenshots. However, keep in mind that this means that both the database service and database itself will automatically start when the host machine starts, possibly consuming a significant amount of your machine's resources. Because these services only apply to Oracle on Windows, we will not refer to them often. Instead, we'll take the broader approach of administering Oracle using cross-platform tools and commands that don't rely on a particular operating system. However, if you administer Oracle on the Windows platform, an understanding of the Oracle services on Windows is crucial.

Certification objectives covered

- Use DBCA to create a database
- Understand the manual database creation method

Summary

In this chapter, we've covered a lot of ground. We've examined the hardware requirements for the Oracle Database on a number of different operating systems. We've configured a listener for our database using NETCA. We then used the DBCA to step through the creation of the database that we'll use throughout the course of this book. Along the way, we've gained an introductory understanding of some of the architectural features of the Oracle database, including datafiles, redo logs, initialization parameters, and memory caches. We then looked deeper into the concept of database creation, examining the steps behind a manual database creation with scripts. Lastly, we examined the concept of Windows Services on Oracle and looked at how we can manipulate them. In our next chapter, we'll take what we've learned about the Oracle architecture so far and expand it, covering the full breadth of how Oracle works "under the hood."

Test your knowledge

Q 1. Which of these terms is relevant to the way that Oracle uses RAM to facilitate the faster access of data?

a. Datafiles
b. Database Configuration Assistant
c. Memory caches
d. x86 chip processing power

Q 2. Which of the following Linux commands can be used to determine the amount of available disk space for an Oracle Database creation?

a. `Windows services`
b. `vi`
c. `df`
d. `free`

Q 3. Which of these operations can be accomplished using the NETCA tool?

a. Database creation
b. Database template administration
c. Initialization parameter configuration
d. Listener creation

Q 4. Which of these is the standard port number for an Oracle listener?

a. `22`
b. `1024`
c. `1521`
d. `3306`

Q 5. Which of the following is a syntactically correct name for an Oracle SID?

a. MYPRACTICEDATABASE
b. 1ORCL
c. FINANCE
d. ORACLE!

Q 6. Using DBCA, which of the following is *not* an option for specifying the location of database files?

a. Using a local filesystem directory
b. Using Oracle Managed Files (OMF)
c. Using locations from a database template
d. Using a filesystem directory on a remote machine

Q 7. Which of the following is *not* a way that DBCA allows us to configure memory allocation?

a. Dynamic Operating System Memory Management
b. Automatic Shared Memory Management
c. Automatic Memory Management
d. Manual Shared Memory Management

Q 8. What term is given to the base unit of disk space allocation in an Oracle database?

a. Database memory cache
b. Database block
c. Initialization parameter
d. Database character set

Q 9. Which of the following database connection modes allocates connection resources from a pool of available resources?

a. Dynamic allocation protocol
b. Dedicated server mode
c. Shared server mode
d. Memory pool mode

Q 10. During the final step of the DBCA, we are given three database creation options. Which of the following is *not* one of those options?

a. Generate database creation scripts
b. Create a database template
c. Create a database
d. Delete a database

Q 11. What is the purpose of the following command:

```
E:\app\oracle\oradim.exe -new -sid DEVL -startmode manual -spfile
```

a. Create a database named `DEVL`
b. Create a Windows Service named `DEVL`
c. Create a Windows Service for a database named `DEVL`
d. Create a Linux kernel module for a database named `DEVL`

Q 12. On a Windows installation of the Oracle database software, what is the name of the Oracle executable used to create an encrypted password file?

a. `oradim.exe`
b. `orapwd.exe`
c. `pwdfile.exe`
d. `dbsnmp.exe`

Q 13. In a manual database creation, the `CREATE DATABASE` command is used to create a database from the command line or from a script. Which of the following is *not* defined in the `CREATE DATABASE` command?

a. Size and location of the system tablespace datafile
b. Size and location of the redo logs

c. Size and location of the encrypted password file

d. Database character set

Q 14. Which of the following Oracle-provided scripts creates the base tables and views that Oracle uses to store internal metadata, known as the data dictionary?

a. `catalog.sql`

b. `catblock.sql`

c. `CreateDataDictionary.sql`

d. `system01.dbf`

Q 15. Given a database named `TEST`, which of the following is *not* an example of a Windows Service that would be associated with the database?

a. `OracleDBConsoletest`

b. `OracleOra11gDB_homeTNSListener`

c. `OracleTNSServiceTEST`

d. `OracleServiceTEST`

4
Examining the Oracle Architecture

Now that we have both the software and a database in place, we can begin to really explore what Oracle has to offer. This chapter covers the Oracle architecture and how it operates to provide data integrity and high performance in an Oracle system. We can think of this chapter as Oracle "behind the curtain." We will examine the part of the Oracle database that users and developers don't see. There are a great deal of terms in this chapter, but many of them will not be completely unfamiliar. We will find that many of them were introduced in the previous chapter.

In this chapter we will:

- Understand the distinction between a database and an instance
- Explore the Oracle instance
- Understand Oracle's process architecture
- Examine the Oracle memory cache architecture
- Explore the Oracle database
- Investigate Oracle's datafile structure

Understanding the Oracle RDBMS

In the previous chapters, we made a reference to the term RDBMS, or Relational Database Management System. This term can be used in many ways and, more often than not, simply refers to a commercial database management product. However, the true meaning of the term RDBMS refers to the way the product operates internally to store and retrieve data. There are many commercial and open source database management systems available today. While they all attempt to interface with the user in a manner that is generally compliant with international standards, they all operate differently internally. We will explore the characteristics that make the Oracle RDBMS unique and, in doing so, understand how it works.

Distinguishing between an instance and a database

To define the Oracle database architecture, we must first define two terms and make a distinction between them. An **instance** is the set of background processes and memory structures that enable the Oracle kernel to operate. A **database** is the set of files that stores the data contained in the RDBMS. These two entities account for the three basic resources available to computers, namely the CPU, RAM, and disk. The instance represents the usage of the CPU and RAM, while the database represents the usage of the disk. These definitions are architecturally oriented, and the distinction between the two isn't always fully recognized. In fact, the two are often used interchangeably. In most database configurations, it is reasonable to do so since, on a single server, the instance and database operate together. However, it's important to draw a distinction at this point, for three reasons. First, the terms themselves are used differently with other RDBMS products, such as Microsoft SQL Server. Secondly, when investigating the Oracle architecture, it is simpler to see the relationship between the various architectural components if we divide them accordingly. Lastly, although an instance and a database generally operate together on a single server, other database configurations are possible. In Oracle's **Real Application Clusters**, or **RAC**, the instance and database are both logically and physically separated. We will examine the subject of RAC later in the chapter.

The following diagram gives us a broad look of the Oracle architecture as a whole. We will refer back to portions of it throughout the chapter:

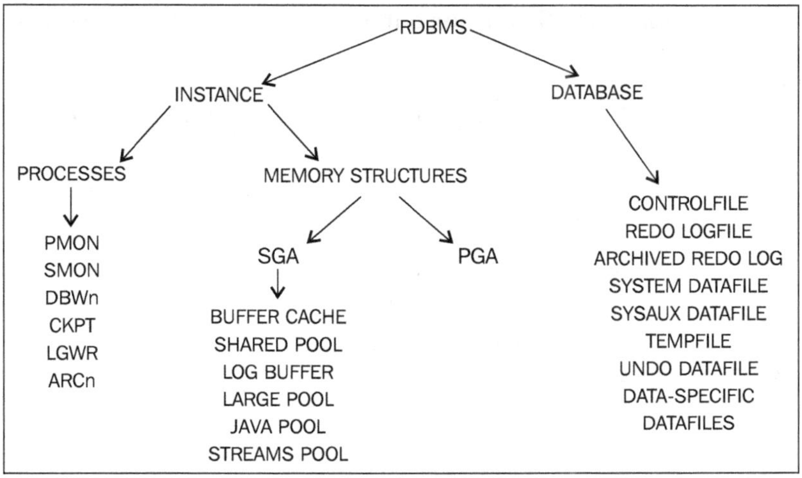
RDBMS
INSTANCE
DATABASE
PROCESSES
MEMORY STRUCTURES
PMON
SMON
DBWn
CKPT
LGWR
ARCn
SGA
PGA
BUFFER CACHE
SHARED POOL
LOG BUFFER
LARGE POOL
JAVA POOL
STREAMS POOL
CONTROLFILE
REDO LOGFILE
ARCHIVED REDO LOG
SYSTEM DATAFILE
SYSAUX DATAFILE
TEMPFILE
UNDO DATAFILE
DATA-SPECIFIC
DATAFILES

Note that this is a logical diagram that groups similar functions together. We display this as a reverse tree diagram. The top of the tree is the RDBMS itself. From there, it branches into the instance and the database, the terms we have just defined. We will look at each branch of this diagram and examine the individual components, as well as how they operate and contribute to the inner working of the Oracle RDBMS.

Examining the Oracle instance

As we mentioned before, the Oracle instance is composed of the necessary processes and memory structures required to operate the Oracle kernel. The instance is the first thing invoked when the database is started.

Recognizing the primary Oracle processes

The first components of the Oracle instance that we will examine are the **Oracle background processes**. These processes run in the background of the operating system and are not interacted with directly. Each process is highly specialized and has a specific function in the overall operation of the Oracle kernel. While these processes accomplish the same functions regardless of the host operating system, their implementation is significantly different. On Unix-based systems, owing to Unix's multiprocess architecture, each Oracle process runs as a separate operating system process. Thus, we can actually see the processes themselves from within the operating system.

For instance, we can use the `ps` command on Linux to see these processes, as shown in the following screenshot. We've highlighted a few of them that we will examine in depth. Note that our background processes are named in the format `ora_processtype_SID`. Since the SID for our database is `ORCL`, that name forms a part of the full process name:

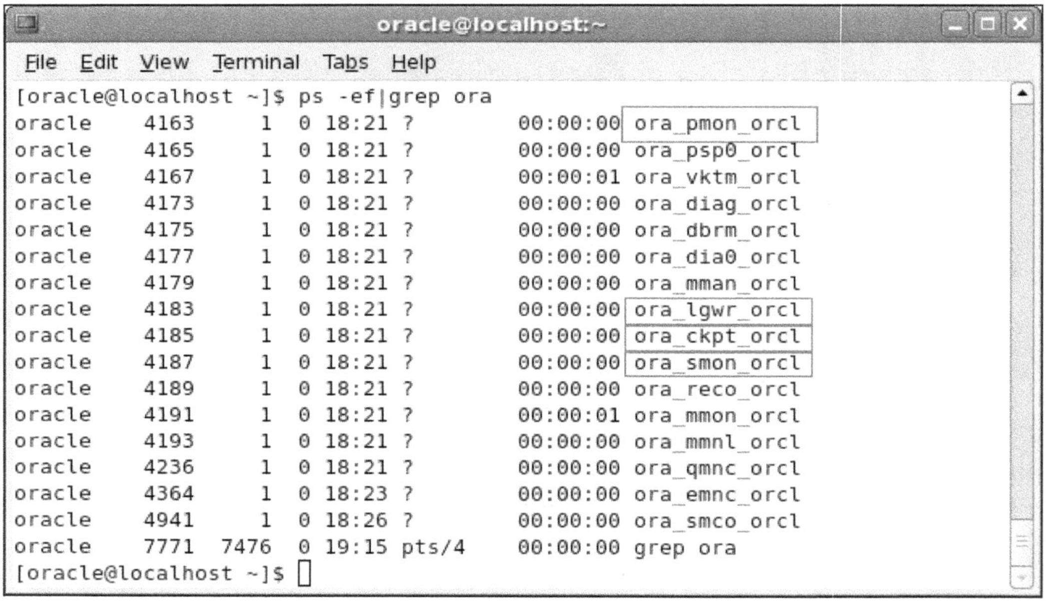
oracle@localhost:~
File Edit View Terminal Tabs Help
[oracle@localhost ~]$ ps -ef|grep ora
oracle 4163 1 0 18:21 ? 00:00:00 ora_pmon_orcl
oracle 4165 1 0 18:21 ? 00:00:00 ora_psp0_orcl
oracle 4167 1 0 18:21 ? 00:00:01 ora_vktm_orcl
oracle 4173 1 0 18:21 ? 00:00:00 ora_diag_orcl
oracle 4175 1 0 18:21 ? 00:00:00 ora_dbrm_orcl
oracle 4177 1 0 18:21 ? 00:00:00 ora_dia0_orcl
oracle 4179 1 0 18:21 ? 00:00:00 ora_mman_orcl
oracle 4183 1 0 18:21 ? 00:00:00 ora_lgwr_orcl
oracle 4185 1 0 18:21 ? 00:00:00 ora_ckpt_orcl
oracle 4187 1 0 18:21 ? 00:00:00 ora_smon_orcl
oracle 4189 1 0 18:21 ? 00:00:00 ora_reco_orcl
oracle 4191 1 0 18:21 ? 00:00:01 ora_mmon_orcl
oracle 4193 1 0 18:21 ? 00:00:00 ora_mmnl_orcl
oracle 4236 1 0 18:21 ? 00:00:00 ora_qmnc_orcl
oracle 4364 1 0 18:23 ? 00:00:00 ora_emnc_orcl
oracle 4941 1 0 18:26 ? 00:00:00 ora_smco_orcl
oracle 7771 7476 0 19:15 pts/4 00:00:00 grep ora
[oracle@localhost ~]$

On Windows, rather than implementing each Oracle process as a separate OS process, the Oracle processes are implemented as threads since Windows is a multithreaded operating system. As a result, the Oracle kernel runs under a single executable called **Oracle.exe**. The background processes then run as threads under that single process. So, if we attempt to see the Oracle background processes using Windows's **Task Manager**, we only see the **Oracle.exe** executable, as shown in the next screenshot. The threads representing the Oracle processes are masked to us, at least at the operating system level:

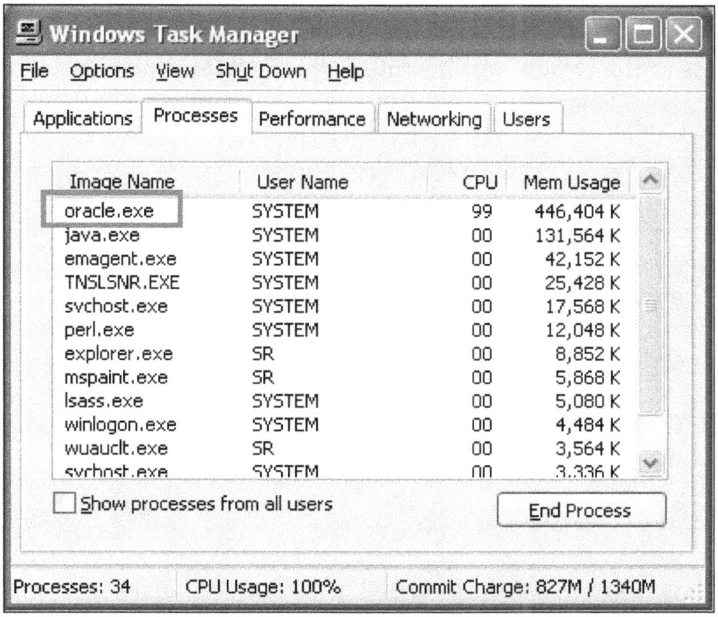
Windows Task Manager
File Options View Shut Down Help
Applications Processes Performance Networking Users
Image Name User Name CPU Mem Usage
oracle.exe SYSTEM 99 446,404 K
java.exe SYSTEM 00 131,564 K
emagent.exe SYSTEM 00 42,152 K
TNSLSNR.EXE SYSTEM 00 25,428 K
svchost.exe SYSTEM 00 17,568 K
perl.exe SYSTEM 00 12,048 K
explorer.exe SR 00 8,852 K
mspaint.exe SR 00 5,868 K
lsass.exe SYSTEM 00 5,080 K
winlogon.exe SYSTEM 00 4,484 K
wuauclt.exe SR 00 3,564 K
Show processes from all users
End Process
Processes: 34 CPU Usage: 100% Commit Charge: 827M / 1340M

We can also display this information from the Windows command line by running the **tasklist** command:

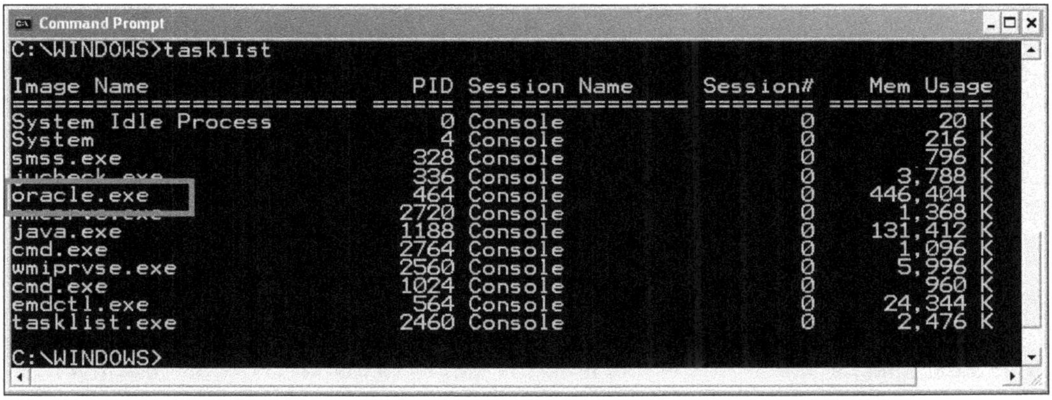
Command Prompt
C:\WINDOWS>tasklist
Image Name PID Session Name Session# Mem Usage
System Idle Process 0 Console 0 20 K
System 4 Console 0 216 K
smss.exe 328 Console 0 796 K
336 Console 0 3,788 K
oracle.exe 464 Console 0 446,404 K
2720 Console 0 1,368 K
java.exe 1188 Console 0 131,412 K
cmd.exe 2764 Console 0 1,096 K
wmiprvse.exe 2560 Console 0 5,996 K
cmd.exe 1024 Console 0 960 K
emdctl.exe 564 Console 0 24,344 K
tasklist.exe 2460 Console 0 2,476 K
C:\WINDOWS>

Regardless of whether we can see each process directly from the operating system, once the instance starts, they are present. Each has a specific job and all run in concert to service the needs of the database.

PMON – the Process Monitor

The core process of the Oracle architecture is the **PMON** process—the **Process Monitor**. The PMON is tasked with monitoring and regulating all other Oracle-related processes. This includes not only background processes but server processes as well. As we discussed briefly in the previous chapter, most databases run in a dedicated server mode. In this mode, any user that connects to the database is granted a server process with which to do work. In Linux systems, this process can actually be viewed at the server level with the `ps -ef` command. When the user connects over the network, the process will be labeled with **LOCAL=NO** in the process description. Privileged users such as database administrators can also make an internal connection to the database, provided that we are logging in from the server that hosts the database. When an internal connection is made, the process is labeled with **LOCAL=YES**. We see an example of each in the following screenshot of the `ps -ef` command on a Linux machine hosting Oracle:

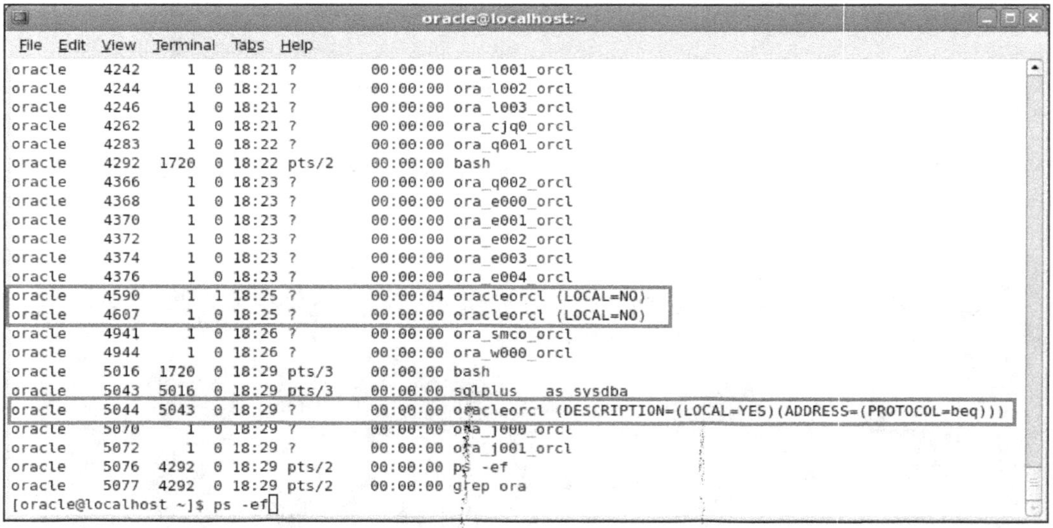
oracle@localhost:~
File Edit View Terminal Tabs Help
oracle 4242 1 0 18:21 ? 00:00:00 ora_l001_orcl
oracle 4244 1 0 18:21 ? 00:00:00 ora_l002_orcl
oracle 4246 1 0 18:21 ? 00:00:00 ora_l003_orcl
oracle 4262 1 0 18:21 ? 00:00:00 ora_cjq0_orcl
oracle 4283 1 0 18:22 ? 00:00:00 ora_q001_orcl
oracle 4292 1720 0 18:22 pts/2 00:00:00 bash
oracle 4366 1 0 18:23 ? 00:00:00 ora_q002_orcl
oracle 4368 1 0 18:23 ? 00:00:00 ora_e000_orcl
oracle 4370 1 0 18:23 ? 00:00:00 ora_e001_orcl
oracle 4372 1 0 18:23 ? 00:00:00 ora_e002_orcl
oracle 4374 1 0 18:23 ? 00:00:00 ora_e003_orcl
oracle 4376 1 0 18:23 ? 00:00:00 ora_e004_orcl
oracle 4590 1 1 18:25 ? 00:00:04 oracleorcl (LOCAL=NO)
oracle 4607 1 0 18:25 ? 00:00:00 oracleorcl (LOCAL=NO)
oracle 4941 1 0 18:26 ? 00:00:00 ora_smco_orcl
oracle 4944 1 0 18:26 ? 00:00:00 ora_w000_orcl
oracle 5016 1720 0 18:29 pts/3 00:00:00 bash
oracle 5043 5016 0 18:29 pts/3 00:00:00 sqlplus as sysdba
oracle 5044 5043 0 18:29 ? 00:00:00 oracleorcl (DESCRIPTION=(LOCAL=YES)(ADDRESS=(PROTOCOL=beq)))
oracle 5070 1 0 18:29 ? 00:00:00 ora_j000_orcl
oracle 5072 1 0 18:29 ? 00:00:00 ora_j001_orcl
oracle 5076 4292 0 18:29 pts/2 00:00:00 ps -ef
oracle 5077 4292 0 18:29 pts/2 00:00:00 grep ora
[oracle@localhost ~]$ ps -ef

Under ordinary circumstances, when a user properly disconnects his or her session from the database by exiting the tool used to connect to it, the server process given to that user terminates cleanly. However, what if instead of disconnecting the connection properly, the machine that the user was connected to was rebooted? In situations like these, the server process on the database is left running since it hasn't received the proper instructions to terminate. When this occurs, it is the job of PMON to monitor sessions and clean up orphaned processes. The PMON normally "wakes up" every 3 seconds to check these processes and clean them up. In addition to this primary function, PMON is also responsible for registering databases with network listeners.

> **The real-world DBA**
>
> Since the instance cannot run unless PMON is running, DBAs sometimes check for it using the `ps` command as a way of determining whether the instance is down, because, on Unix-based systems, we can actually see the processes at the server level using the command `ps -ef | grep pmon`. If a process is not returned, we know the instance is down.

SMON – the System Monitor

The **SMON**, or **System Monitor** process, has several very important duties. Chiefly SMON is responsible for instance recovery. Under normal circumstances, databases are shut down using the proper commands to do so. When this occurs, all of the various components, mainly the datafiles, are properly recorded and synchronized so that the database is left in a consistent state. However, if the database crashes for some reason (the database's host machine loses power, for instance), this synchronization cannot occur. When the database is restarted, it will begin from an inconsistent state. Every time the instance is started, SMON will check for these marks of synchronization. In a situation where the database is in an inconsistent state, SMON will perform instance recovery to resynchronize these inconsistencies. Once this is complete, the instance and database can open correctly. Unlike database recovery, where some data loss has occurred, instance recovery occurs without intervention from the DBA. It is an automatic process that is handled by SMON.

The SMON process is also responsible for various cleanup operations within the datafiles themselves. In the previous chapter we mentioned tempfiles, the files that hold the temporary data that is written when an overflow from certain memory caches occurs. This temporary data is written in the form of temporary segments within the tempfile. When this data is no longer needed, SMON is tasked with removing them. The SMON process can also coalesce data within datafiles, removing gaps, which allows the data to be stored more efficiently.

DBWn – the Database Writer process

For all of the overhead duties of processes such as PMON and SMON, we can probably intuit that there must be a process that actually reads and writes data from the datafiles. Until later versions, that process was named **DBWR** - the **Database Writer** process. The DBWR is responsible for reading and writing the data that services user operations, but it doesn't do it in the way that we might expect.

In Oracle, *almost no operation is executed directly on the disk*. The Oracle processing paradigm is to read data into memory, complete a given operation while the data is still in memory, and write it back to the disk. We will cover the reason for this in greater depth when we discuss memory caches, but for now let's simply say it is for performance reasons. Thus, the DBWR process will read a unit of data from the disk, called a **database block**, and place it into a specialized memory cache. If data is changed using an `UPDATE` statement, for instance, it is changed in memory. After some time, it is written back to the disk in its new state.

If we think about it, it should be obvious that the amount of reading and writing in a database would constitute a great deal of work for one single process. It is certainly possible that a single DBWR process would become overloaded and begin to affect performance. That's why, in more recent versions of Oracle, we have the ability to instantiate multiple database writer processes. So we can refer to DBWR as DBWn, where "n" is a given instantiation of a database writer process. If our instance is configured to spawn three database writers, they would be `dbw0`, `dbw1`, and `dbw2`. The number of the DBWn processes that are spawned is governed by one of our initialization parameters, namely, `db_writer_processes`.

Let's take a closer look at how the value for `db_writer_processes` affects the database writer processes that we can see in the Linux operating system. We won't go into great depth with the commands that we'll be using at this point, but we can still see how the spawning of multiple DBWn processes works. We will become very familiar with commands such as these as we revisit them frequently throughout many of the examples in this book. First, let's examine the number of DBWn processes on our system using the `ps` command, with which we're familiar:

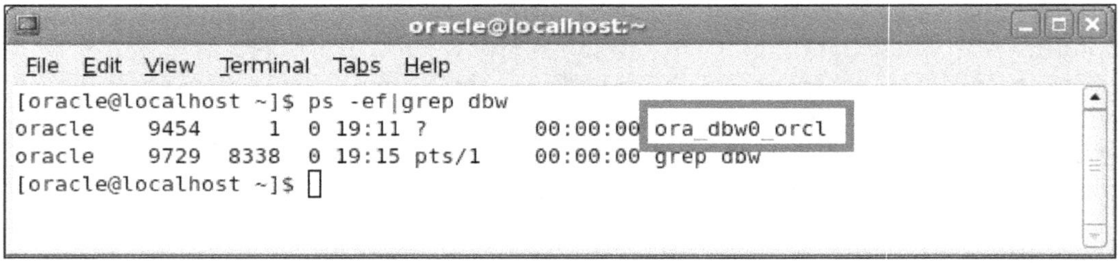
oracle@localhost:~
File Edit View Terminal Tabs Help
[oracle@localhost ~]$ ps -ef|grep dbw
oracle 9454 1 0 19:11 ? 00:00:00 ora_dbw0_orcl
oracle 9729 8338 0 19:15 pts/1 00:00:00 grep dbw
[oracle@localhost ~]$

From the Linux command line, we use the **ps -ef** command along with the **grep** command that searches through the processes in the system with the string **dbw** in their names. This restricts our output to only those processes that contain **dbw**, which will be the database writer processes. As we can see in the preceding screenshot, there is only one database writer process named **ora_dbw0_orcl**.

As mentioned, the number of the database writer processes is determined by an initialization parameter. The name of that parameter is **db_writer_processes**. We can determine the value of this parameter by logging into the database using SQL*Plus (the command `sqlplus / as sysdba`) and showing its value using the **show parameter** command, as in the following screenshot:

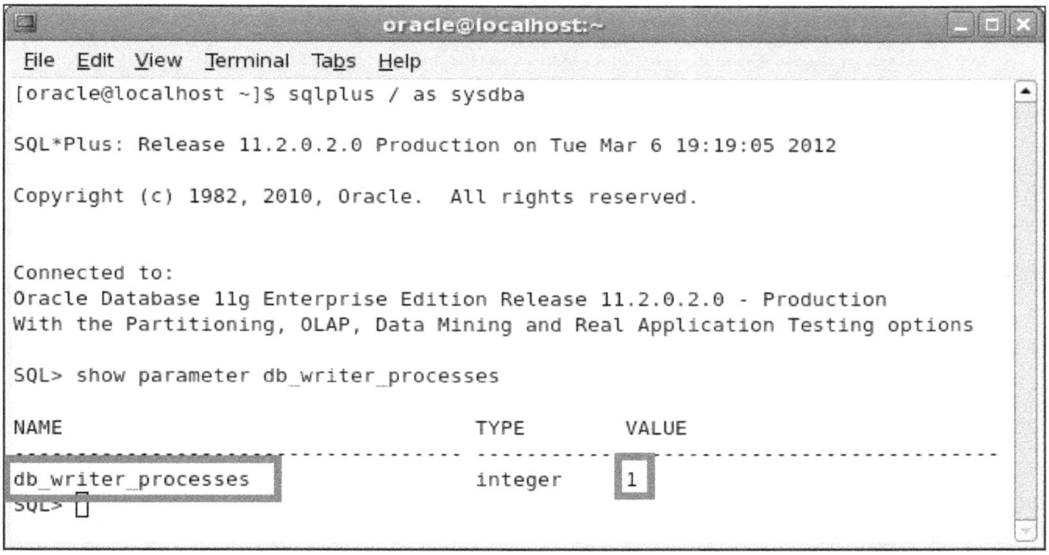
oracle@localhost:~
File Edit View Terminal Tabs Help
[oracle@localhost ~]$ sqlplus / as sysdba
SQL*Plus: Release 11.2.0.2.0 Production on Tue Mar 6 19:19:05 2012
Copyright (c) 1982, 2010, Oracle. All rights reserved.
Connected to:
Oracle Database 11g Enterprise Edition Release 11.2.0.2.0 - Production
With the Partitioning, OLAP, Data Mining and Real Application Testing options
SQL> show parameter db_writer_processes
NAME TYPE VALUE
db_writer_processes integer 1
SQL>

Since we've already determined that we only have a single `dbw0` process, it should come as no surprise that the value for our parameter is **1**. However, if we wish to add more database writers, it is simple to do so. From the SQL*Plus command line, we issue the following command, followed by the **shutdown immediate** and **startup** commands to shut down and start up the database:

```
oracle@localhost:~
File  Edit  View  Terminal  Tabs  Help
SQL> show parameter db_writer_processes

NAME                                 TYPE        VALUE
------------------------------------ ----------- ------------------------------
db_writer_processes                  integer     1
SQL> alter system set db_writer_processes=4 scope=spfile;

System altered.

SQL> shutdown immediate
Database closed.
Database dismounted.
ORACLE instance shut down.
SQL> startup
ORACLE instance started.

Total System Global Area  456146944 bytes
Fixed Size                  1344840 bytes
Variable Size             381684408 bytes
Database Buffers           67108864 bytes
Redo Buffers                6008832 bytes
Database mounted.
Database opened.
SQL> 
```

The **alter system** command instructs Oracle to set the **db_writer_processes** parameter to **4**. The change is recognized when the database is restarted. From here, we type `exit` to leave SQL*Plus and return to the Linux command line. We then issue our **ps** command again and view the results:

```
oracle@localhost:~
File  Edit  View  Terminal  Tabs  Help
[oracle@localhost ~]$ ps -ef|grep dbw
oracle   10113     1  0 19:20 ?        00:00:00 ora_dbw0_orcl
oracle   10115     1  0 19:20 ?        00:00:00 ora_dbw1_orcl
oracle   10117     1  0 19:20 ?        00:00:00 ora_dbw2_orcl
oracle   10119     1  0 19:20 ?        00:00:00 ora_dbw3_orcl
oracle   10322  8338  0 19:21 pts/1    00:00:00 grep dbw
[oracle@localhost ~]$ 
```

As we can see in the preceding screenshot, there are four database writer processes, called **ora_dbw0_orcl**, **ora_dbw1_orcl**, **ora_dbw2_orcl**, and **ora_dbw3_orcl**, that align with our value for `db_writer_processes`. We now have four database writer processes with which to read and write data.

> **The real-world DBA**
>
> What's the optimal number of database writers? The answer is that, as with many aspects of database administration, it depends. The parameter has a maximum value of `20`, so does that mean more is better? Not necessarily. The simplest answer is that the default value, either `1` or the integer value resulting from the number of CPUs divided by 8 (whichever is greater), will generally provide the best performance. Most opinions regarding best practices vary greatly and are usually based on the number of CPUs in the host box. Generally, the default value will serve you well unless your server is very large or heavy tuning is needed.

CKPT – the Checkpoint process

We mentioned in the preceding section that the purpose of the DBWn process is to move data in and out of memory. Once a block of data is moved into memory, it is referred to as a **buffer**. When a buffer in memory is changed using an `UPDATE` statement, for instance, it is called a **dirty buffer**. Dirty buffers can remain in memory for a time and are not automatically flushed to disk. The event that signals the writing of dirty buffers to disk is known as a **checkpoint**. The checkpoint ensures that memory is kept available for other new buffers and establishes a point for recovery. In earlier versions of Oracle, the type of checkpoint that occurred was known as a **full checkpoint**. This checkpoint will flush all dirty buffers back to the datafiles on the disk. While full checkpoints represent a complete flush of the dirty buffers, they are expensive in terms of performance. Since Version 8*i*, the Oracle kernel makes use of an incremental checkpoint that intelligently flushes only part of the available dirty buffers when needed. Full checkpoints only occur now during a shutdown of the database or on demand, using a command.

The process in the instance that orchestrates checkpointing is the **CKPT** process. The CKPT process uses incremental checkpoints at regular intervals to ensure that dirty buffers are written out and any changes recorded in the redo logs are kept consistent for recovery purposes. Unlike the DBWn process, there is only one CKPT process. Although the incremental checkpoint method is used by CKPT, we can also force a full checkpoint using the command shown in the following screenshot:

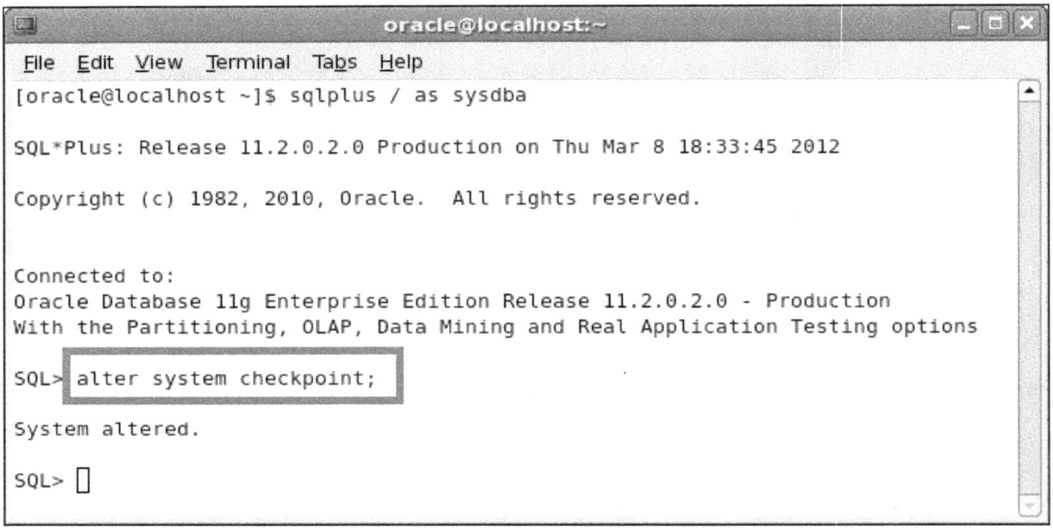
oracle@localhost:~
File Edit View Terminal Tabs Help
[oracle@localhost ~]$ sqlplus / as sysdba
SQL*Plus: Release 11.2.0.2.0 Production on Thu Mar 8 18:33:45 2012
Copyright (c) 1982, 2010, Oracle. All rights reserved.
Connected to:
Oracle Database 11g Enterprise Edition Release 11.2.0.2.0 - Production
With the Partitioning, OLAP, Data Mining and Real Application Testing options
SQL> alter system checkpoint;
System altered.
SQL>

LGWR – the Log Writer process

During our database creation in the previous chapter, we mentioned the concept of a redo log. **Redo logs** are files that serially store the changes that occur in the database. These changes can be anything from `INSERT`, `DELETE`, or `UPDATE` statements executed against the database to the creation of new tables. Note, however, that queries against the database using `SELECT` statements do not constitute changes and are not recorded in the redo logs. The primary function of redo logs is to act during database recovery, where database changes can be "rolled forward" from a backup.

When a change occurs in the database, that change is first written into a memory buffer called the **log buffer** that is specifically tasked with handling database changes. It is then written into the redo logs. The process that writes changes from memory to disk is the **LGWR** process. There is only one LGWR process, so it is important that it moves data as efficiently as possible. There are three conditions that can occur to cause LGWR to move changes from memory into the redo logfiles:

- When a `COMMIT` command is issued
- When the log buffer fills to one-third of its capacity
- Every three seconds

The last of these conditions, "every three seconds," is actually caused by the DBWn process. The database writer has a three-second timeout before it must write a limited number of dirty buffers to disk. When this occurs, the LGWR process also flushes its changes just before DBWn does its work. This ensures that uncommitted transactions can always be rolled back.

ARCn – the Archiver process

The **ARCH**, or the **Archiver** process, is an optional but very important process. Let's continue describing the life cycle of a change in Oracle. To review, as sessions change data, those changes are written into the log buffer. At periodic intervals, those changes are written out serially to the redo logs by the LGWR process. The number and size of the redo logs can vary, but there are always a limited number of them. When one redo log becomes full, LGWR switches to the next one. Since there are a finite number of redo logs, LGWR eventually fills them all. When that happens, LGWR switches back to the original redo log and overwrites the changes that exist in the log. This effectively destroys those changes and invalidates the purpose of storing the changes at all. When the database operates in this manner, overwriting changes that were stored in the redo logs, we say that we're operating in **NOARCHIVELOG** mode. In order to prevent changes from being overwritten, we must operate using a different mode—**ARCHIVELOG** mode. When the database is in ARCHIVELOG mode, the contents of the redo logs are written out to a different type of file called **archive logs**. Archive logs simply contain the data that was in the redo log and serve as its static copy. However, archive logs never overwrite each other. Thus, the history of changes stored in the archive logs and redo logs constitute all the changes that have occurred from a given point in time. The process that enables ARCHIVELOG mode is the **Archiver** process, or **ARCH**. The ARCH copies data from the redo logs to the archive logs and does so before the data in the redo logs can be overwritten.

Like DBWn, the Archiver process can run as multiple processes, albeit with a different purpose. In previous versions of Oracle, the Archiver process ran as a single process—ARCH. In recent versions, it is more accurate to call the Archiver process by its proper name, **ARCn**, where "n" is the number for one of multiple Archiver processes. When ARCn runs as multiple processes, it does so in order to write to multiple locations, rather than using multiple processes to write to a single location.

Since, along with the redo logs, the archive logs contain all of the changes that have occurred in the database, they are critical to database recovery. As such, we can configure our database to write out archive log copies to more than one location. For instance, we may want to configure the Archiver process to write archive logs to two different locations on disk or write a copy of them out to a tape drive to mitigate the risk of data loss.

Recognizing the secondary Oracle processes

We've seen what we referred to as the primary Oracle processes. These are the instance processes that are the foundations of how the Oracle architecture functions. While there is no official definition distinguishing between primary and secondary processes, we use the distinction here as a way of separating those processes that function as an integral component of the architecture and those that make other, secondary operations possible.

MMON – the Manageability Monitor

Prior to Oracle Version 10*g*, database performance tuning was accomplished primarily using data dictionary views. Oracle's extensive data dictionary provided a great deal of insight into the inner workings of the database. However, these views had limitations as to how much internal data was stored and how often it was updated. In short, the performance tuning needs of today's databases required a more extensive interface into Oracle. With Version 10*g*, the Oracle database included what amounts to a second data dictionary, the **Automatic Workload Repository** (**AWR**), that focuses solely on performance tuning metrics. The **MMON** process, the **Manageability Monitor**, extracts these metrics from the Oracle memory caches and writes them to the AWR. MMON essentially takes point-in-time snapshots of performance data, allowing the data to be used in trend analysis. MMON also invokes the **ADDM**, the **Automatic Database Diagnostic Monitor**, which analyses these metrics and can offer performance optimization suggestions in the form of a report. MMON is assisted by another process, **MMNL**, the **Manageability Monitor Light**, to gather these statistics. The following screenshot displays some of these secondary processes:

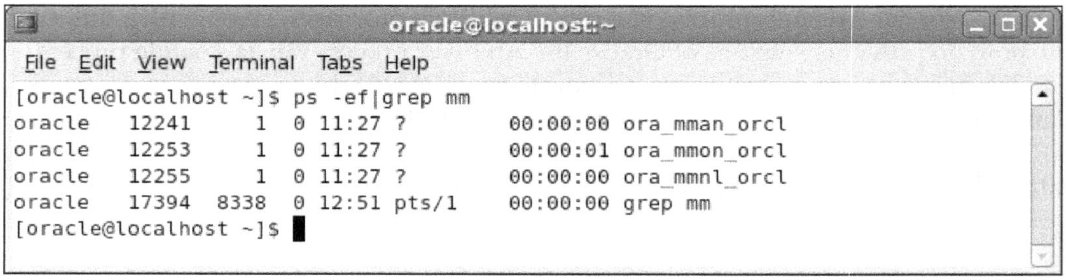
oracle@localhost:~
File Edit View Terminal Tabs Help
[oracle@localhost ~]$ ps -ef|grep mm
oracle 12241 1 0 11:27 ? 00:00:00 ora_mman_orcl
oracle 12253 1 0 11:27 ? 00:00:01 ora_mmon_orcl
oracle 12255 1 0 11:27 ? 00:00:00 ora_mmnl_orcl
oracle 17394 8338 0 12:51 pts/1 00:00:00 grep mm
[oracle@localhost ~]$

MMAN – Memory Manager

If you recall from the previous chapter, during our database creation we were given the opportunity to configure our database's memory in one of three ways. We chose to configure the memory caches manually, but we were also offered **Automatic Memory Management** (**AMM**) and **Automatic Shared Memory Management** (**ASMM**) as options. These two options allow us to turn over the sizing of instance memory caches to Oracle's automatic management algorithm. In environments that run in either of these two configurations, it is the **MMAN** process, or **Memory Manager**, that controls the allocation and deallocation of memory between the various memory caches.

RECO – the Recoverer process

The Oracle database can be run in many different configurations. While we normally think of database operations as running on a centralized server, we can also configure them to run in a distributed fashion. For instance, we may have a system with three databases, one in London, one in Berlin, and one in Miami, that are required to always contain and present the same data, regardless of which location is used. In such a distributed configuration, a transaction that runs on one database must also replicate to another database or databases. We refer to these operations as **distributed transactions**. Because of the complexity of maintaining operations such as these, the Oracle instance uses a separate process called **RECO**, the **Recoverer** process, to ensure that distributed transactions commit properly at all distributed sites. Failing that, RECO rolls back the transaction at each location to ensure data integrity.

Recognizing other database processes

The Oracle instance contains several other processes that are less commonly referred to. A DBA does not typically need to be concerned with the operation of these processes, but we include them here for the sake of curiosity and completeness. There are also other processes that are particular to an Oracle installation on any given operating system:

- **Dnnn**: The dispatcher process that is responsible for distributing SQL calls to shared server processes **Snnn**. These processes are only used in a shared server configuration.
- **DBRM**: The database resource manager that controls resource allocations in databases that use the **Resource Manager** feature.
- **DIAG**: The diagnosability process that performs diagnostic resource dumps in the event of certain error conditions.

- **FBAR**: The flashback archiver process that controls the operation of Oracle's flashback data archive feature, which allows a user to query data as it was during a time in the past.
- **CJQn**: The job queue coordinator that controls the job queue and routes various jobs to slave processes, the **Jnnn** processes, for execution.
- **SMCn**: The space management coordinator that controls database space related tasks involving allocation and cleanup. It uses the **Wnnn** subprocesses to accomplish these operations.
- **VKTM**: The virtual timekeeper process that keeps track of time. This is especially important in distributed or clustered environments.

So, by way of review, let's look at the section of our RDBMS diagram that deals specifically with the background processes and note how it relates to the rest of the instance and database components:

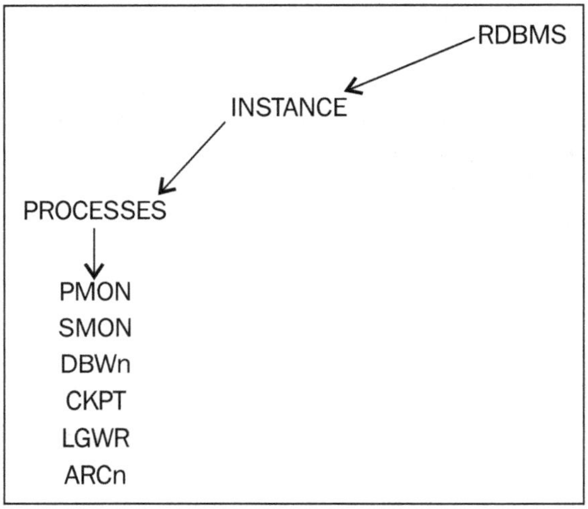
RDBMS
INSTANCE
PROCESSES
PMON
SMON
DBWn
CKPT
LGWR
ARCn

Identifying Oracle's memory caches

In the previous chapter, we briefly discussed the topic of memory space. We said that one of the most basic tenets of the computer's architecture is the concept of using volatile memory as a work area. Processing can be accomplished more quickly in a volatile storage area, such as RAM, than it can in non-volatile storage, such as disk. As we continue to look into the Oracle instance, we turn our attention to its second major component, the Oracle memory caches.

Throughout our review of Oracle's process structure, we've mentioned some of them in passing. The complex specialization of Oracle's memory caches is impressive. Every opportunity is taken to separate different types of data into different caches for the most optimized approach to high performance. At this point, we'll identify these caches and their purpose in the Oracle instance.

Understanding the SGA

The most well-known of Oracle's caches is the SGA. The **SGA**, or **System Global Area**, is a set of memory caches that generally pertain to memory that must be shared between users. As such, it might be better referred to as the **Shared Global Area**. The concept of sharing memory between users is unique to systems that function as servers. In simpler systems, such as a desktop computing environment, resources such as files may be shared, but the idea of actually sharing the RAM of different personal computers is relatively foreign. In such systems, RAM acts as a volatile work area of higher speed that can be used for processing. So if you open a word processing document on your desktop, its contents are read into memory for faster manipulation. You don't, at the same time, "share" your memory with another user down the hall who can manipulate your document. In such situations, memory is more of a private resource than a shared one.

In shared resources such as database systems, processing is more efficient if some amount of information can be shared or even re-used between users. So, an enterprise-level RDBMS makes use of memory that is defined at the server level and presents it in a manner in which it can be accessed by multiple users. When one considers that Oracle databases can service thousands or even hundreds of thousands of users simultaneously, it's impressive to grasp that memory can be shared between each of them.

While the SGA is a collection of other caches, its overall size is determined by an initialization parameter, `sga_max_size`, at the discretion of the DBA. We noted during our database creation with DBCA that memory can be managed automatically by defining other parameters, but it can also be sized manually. When we manage the SGA manually, the value for `sga_max_size` represents the sum total of each of the caches within it. Prior to Oracle Version 9*i*, it was not possible to resize the individual caches without shutting down the database, changing the appropriate parameter, and restarting (much to the chagrin of many DBAs). From Version 9*i* onwards, it has been possible to resize individual caches dynamically without restarting the database, provided that their sum total does not exceed the value established by `sga_max_size`. We can think of this parameter as an outer boundary for all of the caches within the SGA. While individual caches can be changed dynamically, the value of `sga_max_size` cannot.

Examining the database buffer cache

Let's review the job of the DBWn process that we covered earlier. We learned that the DBWn process reads data from the disk and places it into a specialized memory cache. We also learned that the smallest unit of data that can be read in Oracle is called the database block. When DBWn reads a block of data, it places it in memory in the form of a database buffer. The area of the SGA in which the buffer is placed is known as the **database buffer cache**. Why is it important that Oracle operates in this way? We learned earlier that it was for performance reasons. To be more specific, Oracle operates under the assumption that if one user is requesting a certain block of data, other users may request it as well. When data is read into a database buffer, it remains in the database buffer cache so that other users may access it without the need to do a relatively expensive read from disk. Doing so creates a mechanism by which "hot" data, data accessed by many users, remains in memory for as long as possible, without re-reading from disk. The Oracle kernel uses an algorithm to define this mechanism known as the **Least Recently Used** algorithm, or **LRU**. Note that the use of the LRU algorithm doesn't mean that the oldest data is written back to disk. It means that the data that has been accessed most recently is retained, while data that has not been accessed recently is aged out of the cache. In this way, the number of disk reads is efficiently reduced.

When manually sizing the database buffer cache, its size is determined by the initialization parameter `db_cache_size`. As we've mentioned, it is possible to dynamically resize this value within the bounds of `sga_max_size`. The process of doing this is shown, in the following screenshot, using an Oracle database on Windows as an example. First, we log in to the database from the command prompt and determine the current value using the **show parameter** command:

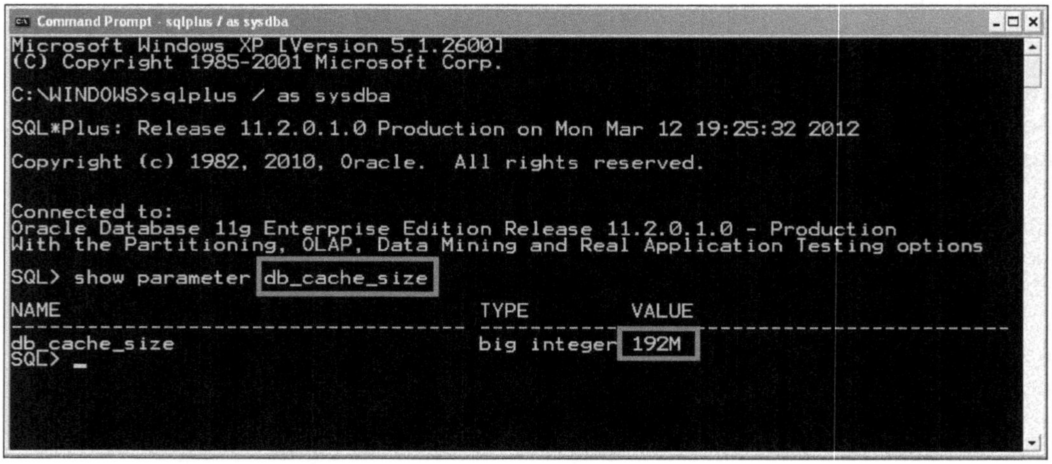
Command Prompt - sqlplus / as sysdba
Microsoft Windows XP [Version 5.1.2600]
(C) Copyright 1985-2001 Microsoft Corp.
C:\WINDOWS>sqlplus / as sysdba
SQL*Plus: Release 11.2.0.1.0 Production on Mon Mar 12 19:25:32 2012
Copyright (c) 1982, 2010, Oracle. All rights reserved.
Connected to:
Oracle Database 11g Enterprise Edition Release 11.2.0.1.0 - Production
With the Partitioning, OLAP, Data Mining and Real Application Testing options
SQL> show parameter db_cache_size
NAME TYPE VALUE
db_cache_size big integer 192M
SQL> _

We can see from our results in this example that the value for **db_cache_size** is **192M**. We can change this value dynamically using the `alter system` command:

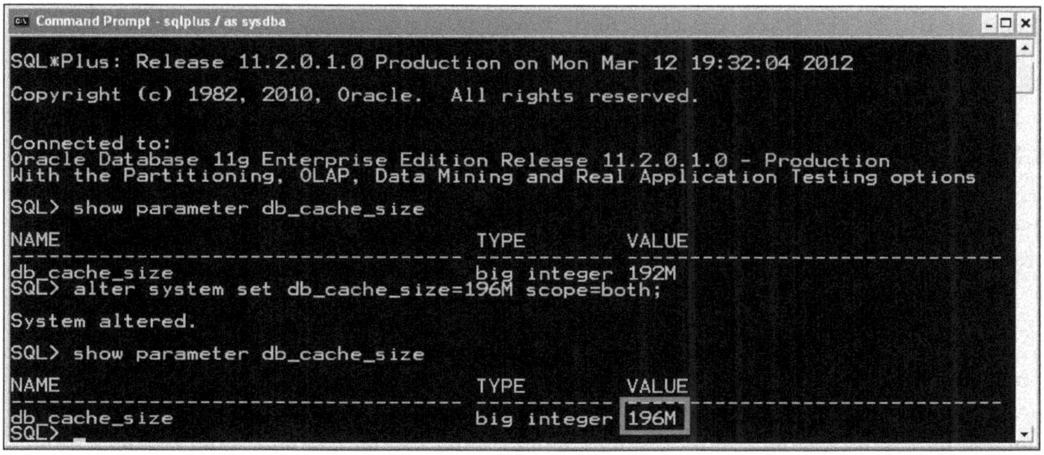

Command Prompt - sqlplus / as sysdba
SQL*Plus: Release 11.2.0.1.0 Production on Mon Mar 12 19:32:04 2012
Copyright (c) 1982, 2010, Oracle. All rights reserved.
Connected to:
Oracle Database 11g Enterprise Edition Release 11.2.0.1.0 - Production
With the Partitioning, OLAP, Data Mining and Real Application Testing options
SQL> show parameter db_cache_size
NAME TYPE VALUE
db_cache_size big integer 192M
SQL> alter system set db_cache_size=196M scope=both;
System altered.
SQL> show parameter db_cache_size
NAME TYPE VALUE
db_cache_size big integer 196M
SQL>

As we can see in the preceding screenshot, we use the **alter system** command, specifying the new value **196M** (M for megabytes) for **db_cache_size**. We also indicate that we wish to make this change in both the current memory and in the parameter file itself using **scope=both**. This will ensure that our change will remain in effect after a database restart. In the event that we attempt to increase the size of the cache to a value that causes the sum total of SGA caches to exceed that of **sga_max_size**, we will receive the following **ORA-00384** error:

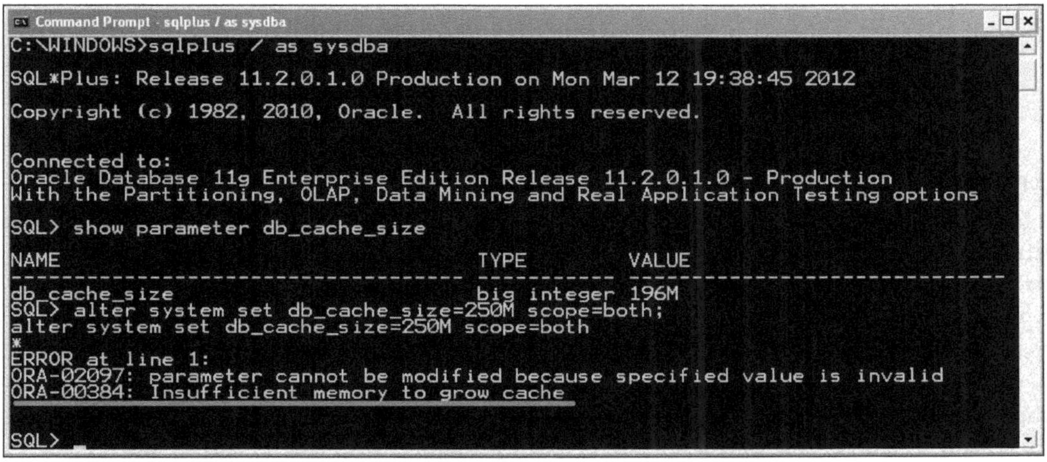

Command Prompt - sqlplus / as sysdba
C:\WINDOWS>sqlplus / as sysdba
SQL*Plus: Release 11.2.0.1.0 Production on Mon Mar 12 19:38:45 2012
Copyright (c) 1982, 2010, Oracle. All rights reserved.
Connected to:
Oracle Database 11g Enterprise Edition Release 11.2.0.1.0 - Production
With the Partitioning, OLAP, Data Mining and Real Application Testing options
SQL> show parameter db_cache_size
NAME TYPE VALUE
db_cache_size big integer 196M
SQL> alter system set db_cache_size=250M scope=both;
alter system set db_cache_size=250M scope=both
*
ERROR at line 1:
ORA-02097: parameter cannot be modified because specified value is invalid
ORA-00384: Insufficient memory to grow cache
SQL>

Ensuring that the various caches are properly sized is vital for system performance, and doubly so for the database buffer cache. If our cache is too large, our database will allocate unneeded memory that could be used for other operations. If the cache is too small, our database won't be able to keep the necessary buffers in memory and will, instead, age them out too frequently and provoke an inordinate amount of disk activity.

Examining the shared pool

Our second cache within the SGA manages memory using a philosophy similar to the buffer cache, but in an entirely different way. The shared pool is used to cache objects in memory, but not database blocks. The **shared pool** is a cache composed of four areas, namely the library cache, the data dictionary cache, the PL/SQL area, and the new result cache.

Consider for a moment the following SQL statement:

```
select first_name, last_name from employee where employee_id = 5;
```

While we normally don't think about all of the steps necessary in order to run this query, there are many. The Oracle kernel must answer several questions like the following before executing even a simple statement such as the preceding one:

1. Is this statement syntactically correct in every respect?
2. Does the `employee` table exist in the database?
3. Do the `first_name` and `last_name` columns exist and are they a part of the `employee` table?
4. Does the user executing the statement have permission to query from the `employee` table?
5. What is the most efficient way to retrieve the rows? Should every row in the table be scanned for matching values or should an index be used?

All of these steps and more must occur every time any SQL statement is executed against the database. In addition, the SQL code must be translated into machine code that can be efficiently understood and executed by Oracle. These steps are referred to as **parsing**. All the steps required for a database parse can make it an expensive operation in terms of resources. While our statement is being parsed, it's not being executed. Obviously, there is no way to avoid parsing a statement the *first* time it is used, but what about subsequent requests? Often, in applications such as those that deal with reporting, the same or similar statements are executed many times by different users. Without a way to retain the parsed statements, every statement requested must be reparsed.

To avoid this, Oracle employs the **library cache**, a memory area within the shared pool that stores parsed statements. Thanks to the library cache, similar statements are not required to be reparsed every time they are requested. The specific location in the library cache that contains this information is referred to as the shared SQL area. Oracle makes this distinction because another area called the **private SQL area** exists in the **Program Global Area (PGA)**, which we discuss later in the chapter.

How does Oracle decide if a statement is "similar" enough to be read directly from the library cache instead of being re-parsed? The library cache utilizes a unique hashing algorithm that takes the statement and breaks down each character in the statement into its corresponding ASCII value. It then sums those values and determines a value that represents that statement. When a matching value is found, it is checked against the statement in the library cache. The parsed statement components of that match are used instead of reparsing, improving overall application performance. This algorithm is efficient, but results in a crucial fact that must be considered. Since the basis for the hashing algorithm is the ASCII values of the characters in the statement, the slightest deviation between two statements that are intended to be matching will result in a re-parse. For instance, because ASCII values vary according to the character's case, either upper or lowercase, the clause `SELECT` is not the same as `select`. Each will result in a different ASCII value total and cause the hashed statement values to differ. If the hashed values differ, the second statement will not be seen as a match and a re-parse will occur.

The real-world DBA

The fact that differences in case and syntax will "throw off" Oracle's hashing algorithm is an excellent example of why coding standards are important. If application developers are to write SQL code in a way that it can be re-used, taking care to use standardized syntax, the performance of the application can be improved greatly. While it may seem like a small point, there is no reason to perform two parses when one is sufficient. In certain systems, you may save on not just a few but perhaps thousands of re-parses.

We mentioned earlier that one of the "questions" that must be answered during the parsing phase dealt with the existence of tables or columns within tables. In Oracle, the structure of tables, columns, and indeed all database objects is stored within the data dictionary. If you recall during our manual database creation, the data dictionary is created after the base database structure is created by running the `catalog.sql` script. Since the data dictionary is queried to answer these questions during a parse, it would be advantageous to avoid rereading them repeatedly. The shared pool provides an area where this can be accomplished.

The data dictionary cache resides in the shared pool and provides a memory area to store database object definitions, such as table and column structures. Using this cache, the parser can read frequently accessed object definitions from the cache instead of from the dictionary tables on disk.

SQL statements are not the only type of code that is executed within the database. There are actually three programming languages that can be natively run within Oracle, namely SQL, PL/SQL, and Java. Just as SQL statements can benefit from storing parsed code in memory, so can these languages as well. We normally think of PL/SQL (Procedural Language/SQL) as the most common of these, so the PL/SQL area provides a cache where PL/SQL code, such as procedures, packages, functions, and triggers, can be stored after being read from the data dictionary. Applications that make extensive use of PL/SQL can greatly benefit from the operation of the PL/SQL area. Incidentally, Java's stored procedures also make use of this cache.

Our final area within the shared pool is new in Version 11*g*. As we've noted, some applications execute similar statements repeatedly. It is also true that these statements may return the same set of results, for instance, from a query that is repeatedly executed. In such situations, it would be beneficial to actually cache these results so that they might be available to other sessions. Within the shared pool, it is the job of the result cache to perform this operation. The result cache caches the results of SQL queries and PL/SQL functions, making them available to other sessions. Note that since not all applications require this level of caches, the result cache is not enabled by default. It must be enabled programmatically in one of several ways.

Note that, although the size of the shared pool itself can be sized either automatically or manually, the sizes of the various areas within the shared pool are automatically controlled by the Oracle kernel. This underscores the importance of properly sizing the shared pool since an undersized shared pool can lead to performance problems in all of its respective memory areas. The shared pool is sized manually by adjusting the `shared_pool_size` parameter.

Utilizing the log buffer

Our next SGA memory component is one that we've already mentioned. Recall from our discussion of the LGWR process that the log buffer is used to store database changes as they occur. They are then written out of memory in batches by the LGWR process. Remember the three conditions that can occur to cause LGWR to move changes from memory into the redo logfiles:

- When a `COMMIT` command is issued
- When the log buffer fills to one-third of its capacity
- Every three seconds

The statements that create these changes, such as DML and DDL statements, benefit from a memory cache that can be read from and written to in a quicker fashion. The log buffer provides this cache. The log buffer is unique among the caches in the SGA in that it is the only cache that cannot be dynamically resized. The size of the log buffer is determined by the `log_buffer` parameter and can only be altered with a restart of the database. The speed at which changes can be read and written from the buffer is crucial to overall database performance, and an improperly sized log buffer can impact the efficiency of these operations. That being said, the default size of the `log_buffer` parameter is sufficient for most databases.

Understanding the large pool

Owing to the fact that so many database operations can benefit from intelligent caching, Oracle added a versatile cache in Version 9*i* that is slightly less specialized. The **large pool** is a cache within the SGA that can be utilized for certain operations, freeing up the memory use of the shared pool. The large pool is particularly useful in environments that use the shared server architecture. In a shared server architecture, a finite number of server processes address the needs of every session, rather than giving each session a dedicated server process. Memory from the large pool can be allocated to sessions that use the shared server processes. The large pool can also be used to cache data involved in backup and recovery operations, greatly improving the performance of these long-running operations.

Examining the streams pool

Oracle Streams is a product that allows data to be dynamically replicated between databases. We can think of Streams as the successor to Oracle's **Advanced Replication** option, with some significant improvements. Oracle Streams propagates data between databases by mining the redo logs for changes, queuing them, and then pushing them to corresponding databases. The process of mining the redo logs in Streams benefits from having its own memory cache, and that cache is the **streams pool**. The streams pool is not utilized unless Oracle Streams is in use and can be ignored in cases where it's not. The streams pool is sized manually using the `streams_pool_size` parameter. Note that although Oracle Streams is outside the scope of the exam, the concept of the streams pool itself as one of the memory caches may be covered.

Understanding the Java pool

The Java programming language is one of the most important languages in use today. Oracle was quick to capitalize on its growing importance in the IT industry by adding a great deal of support for Java within its flagship database. We mentioned earlier in the chapter that the Oracle database supports the use of Java stored procedures. These units allow for Java programming code to be stored as objects within the database. If an IT organization uses Java stored procedures, the Java pool can be extremely beneficial. The **Java pool** is a specialized memory cache within the SGA that is used to instantiate Java objects. It is generally best for a DBA to consult with Java application developers to determine the optimal size for the Java pool. The Java pool size is determined by the `java_pool_size` initialization parameter.

To summarize the structure of the SGA and how it fits within the architecture of the Oracle instance, we revisit our overall architecture diagram:

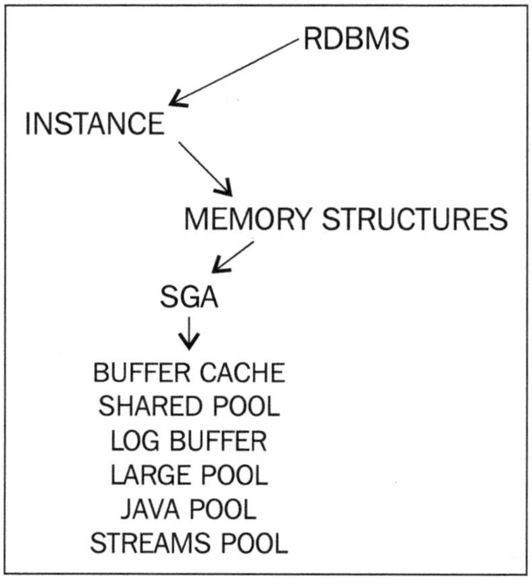
RDBMS
INSTANCE
MEMORY STRUCTURES
SGA
BUFFER CACHE
SHARED POOL
LOG BUFFER
LARGE POOL
JAVA POOL
STREAMS POOL

Beyond the exam

In Unix-based systems, there are operating system-level parameters dealing with shared memory that must be considered beyond just the Oracle parameters. These OS parameters provide a great deal of flexibility for configuring the shared memory on a server. These parameters must be configured properly to ensure optimal system performance, usually in coordination with the system administrator:

- `shmmax` or shared memory max refers to the maximum size of a shared memory segment. This should be sized to contain the entire SGA.
- `shmmin` or shared memory min refers to the minimum size of a shared memory segment.
- `shmseg` or shared memory segment refers to the maximum number of shared memory segments that can be attached to a process.
- `shmmni` or shared memory identifiers refers to the number of shared memory identifiers in the system.

Understanding the PGA

The second major memory component of the Oracle instance is the **PGA** or **Program Global Area**. We will find that the PGA "side" of the Oracle instance is somewhat less complex than the SGA. It might be more accurate to refer to the PGA as the Private Global Area. So how can a memory area be both private and global at the same time?

The principle behind a memory area such as the SGA is that there are portions of data that should be available to be shared between user sessions. It is equally true that not all operations include data that should be shareable. Take a sorting operation, for instance. During a sort operation, such as a `SELECT` query involving an `ORDER BY` clause, it is advantageous to use memory to do the sort, since using disk would be a much slower process. However, sorts can be notoriously large and demanding in terms of resources. It wouldn't be efficient to sort in a memory area such as the SGA, since the sort operations may rob memory from other important areas, such as the database buffer cache. Ideally, such operations should run in memory where possible and write to disk in situations where the memory overflows.

Historically, Oracle accomplished this by allocating "slices" of memory to each user session. An initialization parameter defined a sorting area in memory, outside of the SGA, and allocated that area to a user when the user connected. That slice of memory could be used for sort operations. If the sort required more memory than the slice provided, the data would be written out to a temporary area on disk. The results were then returned to the user as an ordered set of rows. Similar portions of memory were granted to users for actions that required hashing algorithms and other related operations. While this paradigm accomplishes the goal of providing users with a private memory area for such operations, it is somewhat inefficient. Using this method, every user is given the same amount of memory for private operations whether it is needed or not. Additionally, because the total amount of memory used by these slices is determined by the number of users that access the database at a given time, the total system memory has to be taken into account. For instance, if we estimate that a database has a maximum of 1000 users connected at any given moment and each is given 1 M of memory for sorting, we must allow for 1000 M of memory for these users. However, the number of users that access databases isn't always consistent. At certain times of the day, for instance, only 100 users may be connected. These users are only allocated a total of 100 M, but since we must account for the maximum number of users, we can't allocate the other 900 M in any other way. This leads us to a situation where, at any given time, our database may be overallocated in terms of memory and the users that have the allocations may not even be using them.

To combat this problem, Oracle introduced the concept of the PGA, or Program Global Area, in Version 9*i*. The PGA is a single cache that provides the private memory needed for user sessions. Rather than allocating individual work areas in memory, the PGA allows us to set a parameter value, `pga_aggregate_target` that defines the total amount of memory to be allocated for user sessions. Within the PGA, memory allocation is managed by Oracle, giving more to sessions that require it. As a result, user sessions that require more memory receive it, making operations such as sorting much more efficient, since having more memory available requires less use of temporary space on disk. Additionally, the private SQL area within the PGA contains pointers that refer back to the shared SQL area within the SGA, facilitating the efficient sharing of SQL statements. The PGA stores several types of user-session information after sorting operations are performed:

- Data in sorting operations
- Session variable information
- Bind variables
- Query execution work areas
- Cursor information and state

Starting with Oracle 11*g*, the PGA and SGA can be sized together using a feature called **Automatic Memory Management** (**AMM**). This simplifies the administration tasks involved in determining memory structure sizing and is discussed extensively in a later chapter. To review the position of the PGA within the Oracle architecture, we refer to our architecture diagram:

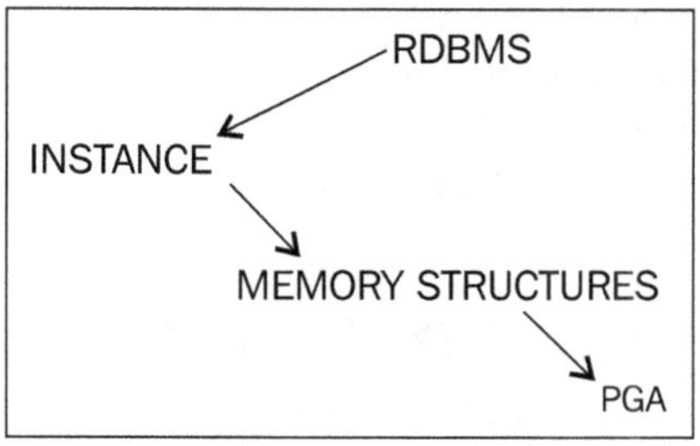
RDBMS
INSTANCE
MEMORY STRUCTURES
PGA

This completes our examination of the Oracle instance architecture. As a full review of all instance components, we refer back to our architecture diagram, where we can see the greater context of how these individual components relate:

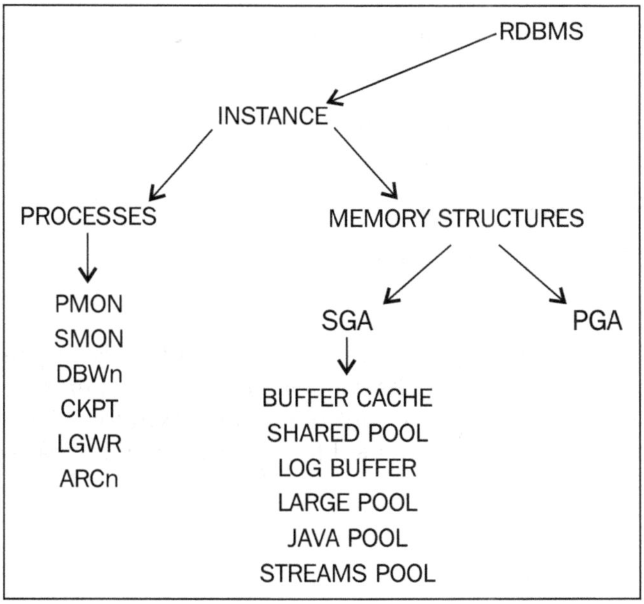
RDBMS
INSTANCE
PROCESSES
MEMORY STRUCTURES
PMON
SMON
DBWn
CKPT
LGWR
ARCn
SGA
PGA
BUFFER CACHE
SHARED POOL
LOG BUFFER
LARGE POOL
JAVA POOL
STREAMS POOL

Examining the Oracle database components

Although we typically use the term "database" to refer to an RDBMS in general, in this chapter we're examining it in its most literal sense. We've made the distinction between an instance and a database and have seen the components of the instance that are the background processes and memory caches. In the most literal sense, the term "database" refers to the set of files that make up the Oracle RDBMS. Each type of file serves a different function within the infrastructure of the RDBMS.

Understanding the control file

Each component of the Oracle RDBMS is highly specialized, from processes that serve a certain function to caches that contain a certain type of data. However, there must be a central place, a "brain" of sorts, that stores information about the database at any given moment. In Oracle, that central storage file is called the **control file**. The control file contains a multitude of time-sensitive information dealing with the state of the database. Some of this information includes, but is not limited to, the following:

- The names and locations of all the database files
- The name of the database
- The current redo log sequence number
- The time and date when the database was created
- Recent archive log names and locations
- The current **SCN** (**System Change Number**)
- Backup and recovery information

Despite the wealth of information stored in the control file, it is surprisingly small. We can see this by actually viewing the control file from the operating system. In the following screenshot, we examine the control files on a Windows installation of Oracle within the directory structure we provided to DBCA during database creation:

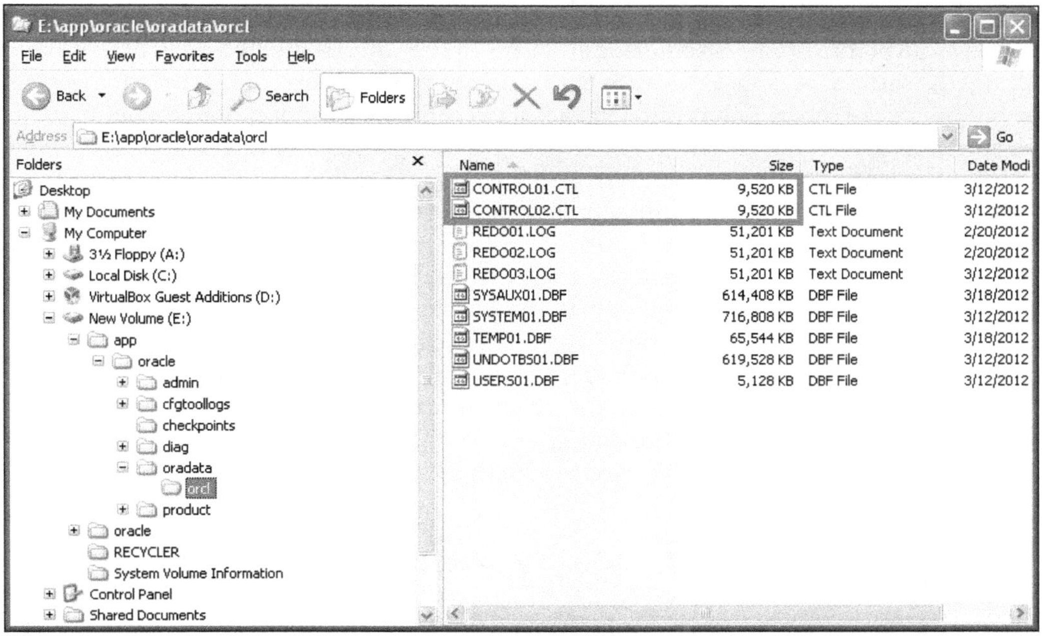
E:\app\oracle\oradata\orcl
File Edit View Favorites Tools Help
Back Search Folders
Address E:\app\oracle\oradata\orcl
Go
Folders
Desktop
My Documents
My Computer
3½ Floppy (A:)
Local Disk (C:)
VirtualBox Guest Additions (D:)
New Volume (E:)
app
oracle
admin
cfgtoollogs
checkpoints
diag
oradata
orcl
product
oracle
RECYCLER
System Volume Information
Control Panel
Shared Documents
Name Size Type Date Modi
CONTROL01.CTL 9,520 KB CTL File 3/12/2012
CONTROL02.CTL 9,520 KB CTL File 3/12/2012
REDO01.LOG 51,201 KB Text Document 2/20/2012
REDO02.LOG 51,201 KB Text Document 2/20/2012
REDO03.LOG 51,201 KB Text Document 3/12/2012
SYSAUX01.DBF 614,408 KB DBF File 3/18/2012
SYSTEM01.DBF 716,808 KB DBF File 3/12/2012
TEMP01.DBF 65,544 KB DBF File 3/18/2012
UNDOTBS01.DBF 619,528 KB DBF File 3/12/2012
USERS01.DBF 5,128 KB DBF File 3/12/2012

Note that the two control files shown here are less than 10 M in size. The control file is very efficient in the manner in which it stores critical database information. It is both read from and written to very frequently in order to be kept informed of the state of the database. Here, the two control files are named **CONTROL01.CTL** and **CONTROL02.CTL**. This is the standard way of naming control files, with a number that distinguishes it and the `.CTL` suffix. Here, we show a similar example of a control file on the Linux platform:

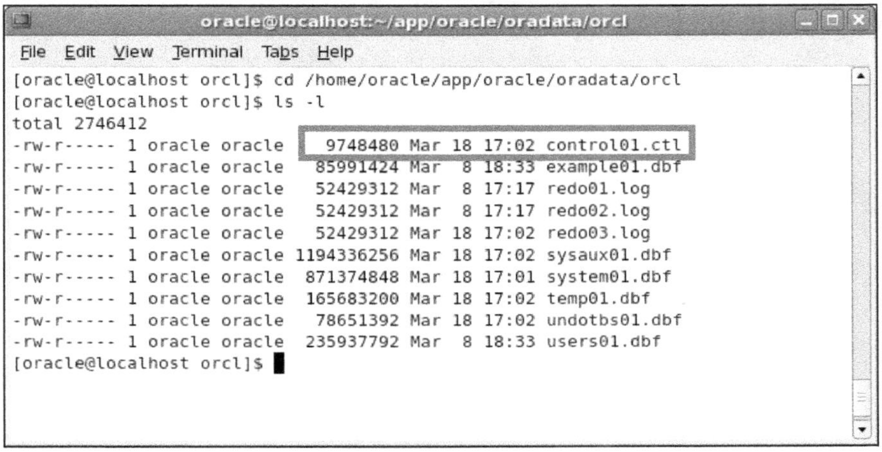
oracle@localhost:~/app/oracle/oradata/orcl
File Edit View Terminal Tabs Help
[oracle@localhost orcl]$ cd /home/oracle/app/oracle/oradata/orcl
[oracle@localhost orcl]$ ls -l
total 2746412
-rw-r----- 1 oracle oracle 9748480 Mar 18 17:02 control01.ctl
-rw-r----- 1 oracle oracle 85991424 Mar 8 18:33 example01.dbf
-rw-r----- 1 oracle oracle 52429312 Mar 8 17:17 redo01.log
-rw-r----- 1 oracle oracle 52429312 Mar 8 17:17 redo02.log
-rw-r----- 1 oracle oracle 52429312 Mar 18 17:02 redo03.log
-rw-r----- 1 oracle oracle 1194336256 Mar 18 17:02 sysaux01.dbf
-rw-r----- 1 oracle oracle 871374848 Mar 18 17:01 system01.dbf
-rw-r----- 1 oracle oracle 165683200 Mar 18 17:02 temp01.dbf
-rw-r----- 1 oracle oracle 78651392 Mar 18 17:02 undotbs01.dbf
-rw-r----- 1 oracle oracle 235937792 Mar 8 18:33 users01.dbf
[oracle@localhost orcl]$

Notice how in our first example our system displayed two control files while the second showed only one. Also note that, in the first example, the two control files have exactly the same size. This is because, when using multiple control files, each one is an exact copy of the other. They contain exactly the same information. Then what would the benefit be of having more than one? Because of the crucial nature of the control file, it is highly recommended to multiplex it. **Multiplexing** is the act of making more than one copy of the control file for protection against file corruption or loss. The loss of a control file can be a catastrophic event. It is generally recommended that your database have no less than two control files, preferably three. It is also highly recommended that your control files exist on more than one physical disk. In a disk-failure situation, having three control files on the same failed disk will not save our system. The location and name of our control files is defined by the `control_files` initialization parameter. The actual filename and path within the operating system must match what is defined by the parameter. From within the data dictionary, we can also query the **v$controlfile** view to see control file information, as shown in the following screenshot:

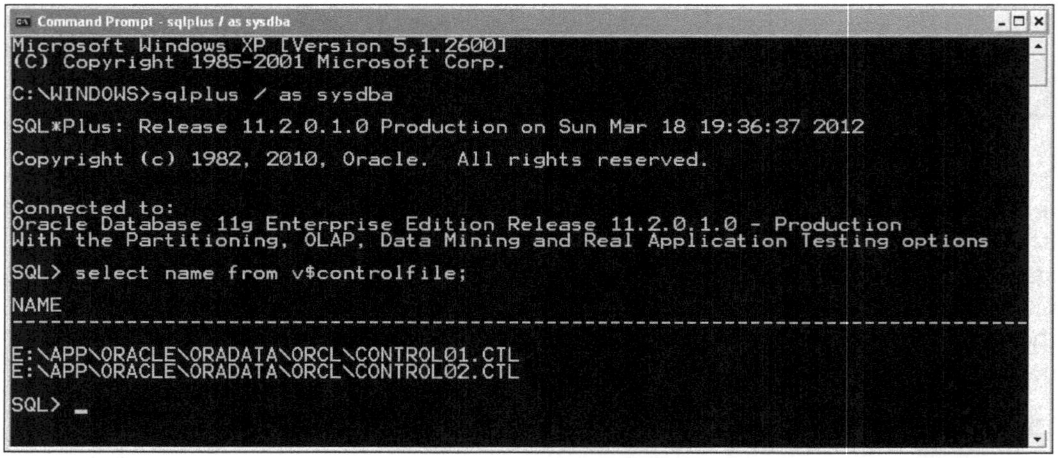
Command Prompt - sqlplus / as sysdba
Microsoft Windows XP [Version 5.1.2600]
(C) Copyright 1985-2001 Microsoft Corp.
C:\WINDOWS>sqlplus / as sysdba
SQL*Plus: Release 11.2.0.1.0 Production on Sun Mar 18 19:36:37 2012
Copyright (c) 1982, 2010, Oracle. All rights reserved.
Connected to:
Oracle Database 11g Enterprise Edition Release 11.2.0.1.0 - Production
With the Partitioning, OLAP, Data Mining and Real Application Testing options
SQL> select name from v$controlfile;
NAME
E:\APP\ORACLE\ORADATA\ORCL\CONTROL01.CTL
E:\APP\ORACLE\ORADATA\ORCL\CONTROL02.CTL
SQL> _

Exploring the redo logfiles

We've already discussed Oracle's redo log structure considerably in our discussion of both the redo log buffer and the LGWR process. By way of review, we learned that when changes occur in the database, they are recorded from a backup for the purpose of database recovery. They are first written to the redo log buffer and then written out by the LGWR process to the redo logfiles. Thus, the online redo logfiles contain the changes that occur in the database in sequential form. In the event that a database recovery is required, the redo logs can be read and the changes therein can be applied to the backup to "roll forward" a database into a desired state. Let's take a look at how LGWR writes to the redo logfiles:

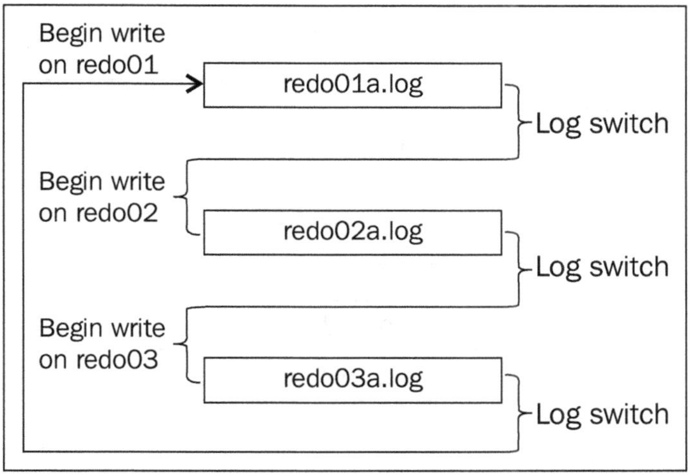
Begin write on redo01
redo01a.log
Log switch
Begin write on redo02
redo02a.log
Log switch
Begin write on redo03
redo03a.log
Log switch

For the sake of argument, let's say that LGWR begins writing to **redo01a.log**, the first redo logfile in the database. LGWR writes buffers from the log buffer to **redo01a.log** in batches. It continues to write until **redo01a.log** is full. At that point, a log switch occurs and LGWR begins writing to **redo02a.log**, the second redo log. Once it's full, another log switch occurs and LGWR begins writing to **redo03a.log**. Once that log is full, a third log switch occurs. At this point, LGWR begins writing to **redo01a.log** again, overwriting its contents, and the process continues. As we pointed out earlier in the chapter, overwriting a redo log defeats the purpose of redo data since the point is to preserve the data necessary for recovery. For that reason, ARCHIVELOG mode is used to ensure that a database is fully recoverable. More on that shortly.

The preceding diagram is the simplest representation of the way redo data is written. Each redo log in the previous example is the member of a group. Thus, **redo01a.log** is a redo log member of redo log group 1. The other logfiles belong to groups 2 and 3 respectively. Each redo log group can have multiple members. Why would this be necessary? As with the control file, the redo logfiles are crucial to database operations as they deal with database recovery. If a single member is lost or corrupted, the chain of database changes is broken and a database cannot be recovered fully. Owing to this fact, it is highly recommended that we duplex redo logs in a similar fashion to multiplexing control files. In duplexing redo logs, we create multiple redo log members in each group. Each member within a group is an identical copy of the other. So even if one member is lost or corrupted, the chain of redo remains unbroken. Taking this new information into account, we might better represent the redo architecture in the following diagram:

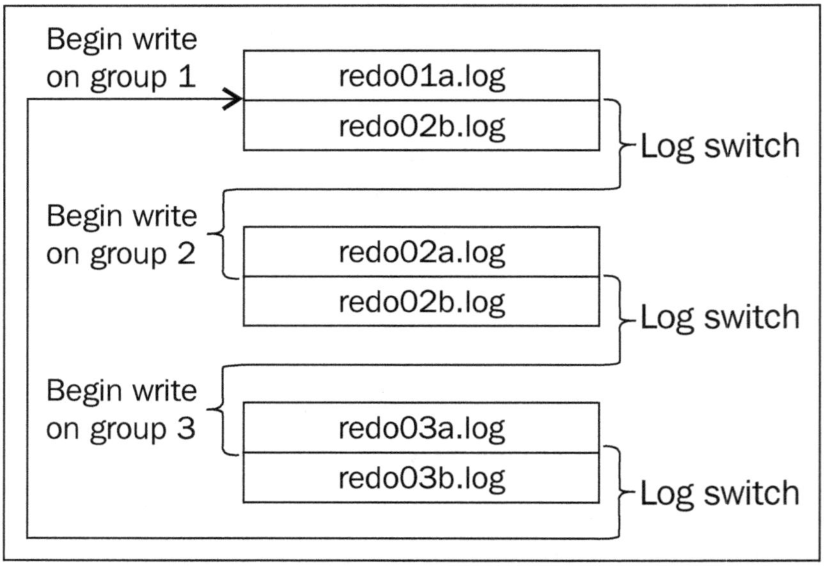
Begin write
on group 1
redo01a.log
redo02b.log
Log switch
Begin write
on group 2
redo02a.log
redo02b.log
Log switch
Begin write
on group 3
redo03a.log
redo03b.log
Log switch

Here, each member of a group is written to simultaneously. The group currently receiving writes from LGWR is called the **current log group**. When a log switch occurs, LGWR begins writing log buffers to each member of the next group simultaneously and that group becomes the current log group. By default, DBCA creates three, non-duplexed log groups with one member each. At a minimum, the database must contain at least two log groups with one log member each, since LGWR must be able to switch to a different group during a log switch and cannot switch to a non-existent group.

We can view the redo logfiles from the operating system itself. Our default database created by DBCA will place the redo logs in the same directory as our control files and other database files. An example of this is shown in the following screenshot in a Linux installation of Oracle. The Linux command displays files that begin with the name **redo**. The redo logs can be viewed in a Windows installation of Oracle using Windows Explorer:

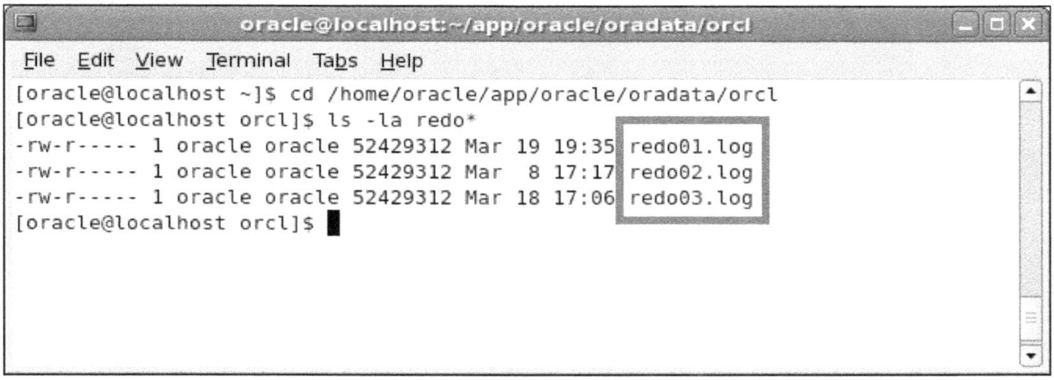
oracle@localhost:~/app/oracle/oradata/orcl
File Edit View Terminal Tabs Help
[oracle@localhost ~]$ cd /home/oracle/app/oracle/oradata/orcl
[oracle@localhost orcl]$ ls -la redo*
-rw-r----- 1 oracle oracle 52429312 Mar 19 19:35 redo01.log
-rw-r----- 1 oracle oracle 52429312 Mar 8 17:17 redo02.log
-rw-r----- 1 oracle oracle 52429312 Mar 18 17:06 redo03.log
[oracle@localhost orcl]$

Understanding the archived redo logs

We've discussed the manner in which the Oracle redo architecture operates. We also mentioned that database changes stored in the redo logs are overwritten during log switches if ARCHIVELOG mode is not enabled. We'll cover how to enable and disable ARCHIVELOG mode in a later chapter, but as part of our coverage of the Oracle architecture, we now address the output of ARCHIVELOG mode—archived redo logs.

ARCHIVELOG mode instructs the database that we intend to keep a static copy of the contents of each redo log. In this mode, when a log switch occurs, the contents of the current redo log are written out to an archived redo log by the ARCn process. These logs are also referred to as offline redo logs or simply archive logs. Let's extend our redo architecture diagram to include ARCHIVELOG mode and archived redo logs:

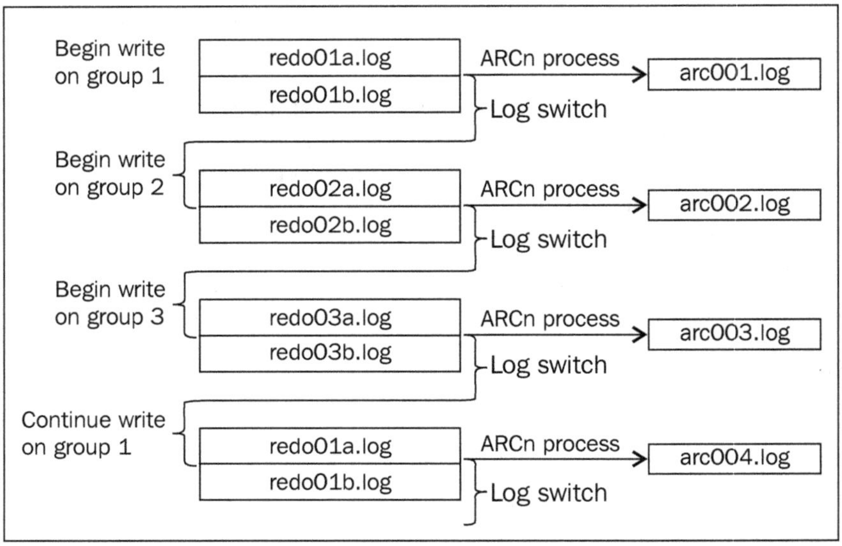
Begin write on group 1
redo01a.log
redo01b.log
ARCn process
arc001.log
Log switch
Begin write on group 2
redo02a.log
redo02b.log
ARCn process
arc002.log
Log switch
Begin write on group 3
redo03a.log
redo03b.log
ARCn process
arc003.log
Log switch
Continue write on group 1
redo01a.log
redo01b.log
ARCn process
arc004.log
Log switch

Each time a log switch occurs, the contents of the current redo log are written to an archived redo log. In the preceding example, let's say that redo log group 1 is the current group. When a log switch occurs from group 1 to group 2, the identical contents of **redo01a.log** and **redo01b.log** are written to an archived redo log **arc001.log**. Since the two redo log members contain the same data, only one archived redo log needs to be written. The changes in **arc001.log** called **change vectors** are the same as those found in **redo01a.log** and **redo01b.log**. This continues with groups 2 and 3. When group 3 completes a log switch back to group 1, the members of group 1 are overwritten. However, since we're running ARCHIVELOG mode in this example, we're not concerned with it. The contents of the members of group 1 have already been written to **arc001.log** and can be safely overwritten. When the members of group 1 have been filled a second time, a log switch occurs and a new archived redo log called **arc004.log** is written. By so doing, all the changes in the database are retained. The oldest changes are found in the oldest archived redo logs, continuing through the remainder of the newer archived redo logs, and then the newest changes are found in the redo logs themselves. When running in ARCHIVELOG mode, a database can be recovered up to the last write that occurred from the redo log buffer to the redo logfiles.

The naming and directory destination of archived redo logs are determined by the parameter values `log_archive_format` and `log_archive_dest_1`, respectively. As we mentioned earlier, the ARCn process can be configured as multiple processes that write to multiple destinations. These other destinations can be other filesystem directories, tape drives, and so on. We use the `log_archive_dest_1` parameter when our database is configured to have one destination, the `log_archive_dest_2` parameter to configure a second destination, and so on. We can use the **archive log list** command from a SQL*Plus prompt to determine our archiving status, as shown in the following screenshot; these commands work in Windows and Unix-based systems:

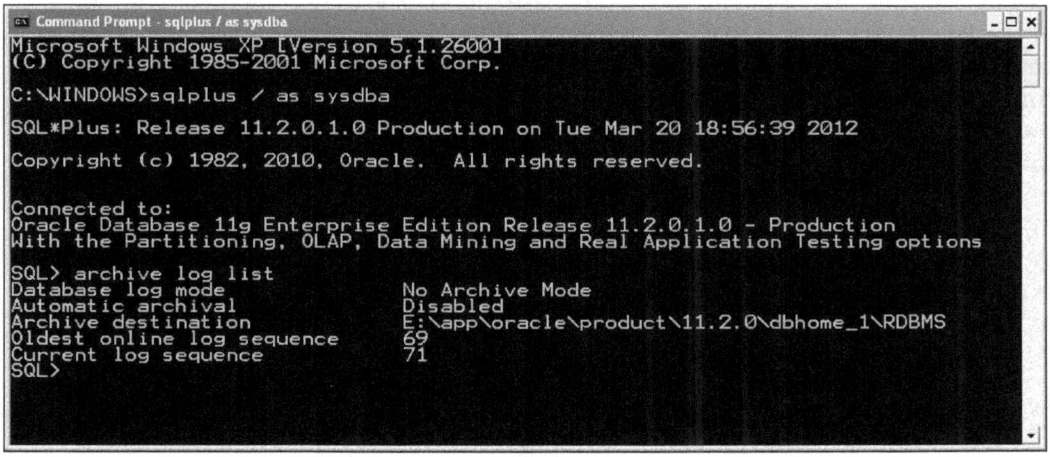
Command Prompt - sqlplus / as sysdba
Microsoft Windows XP [Version 5.1.2600]
(C) Copyright 1985-2001 Microsoft Corp.
C:\WINDOWS>sqlplus / as sysdba
SQL*Plus: Release 11.2.0.1.0 Production on Tue Mar 20 18:56:39 2012
Copyright (c) 1982, 2010, Oracle. All rights reserved.
Connected to:
Oracle Database 11g Enterprise Edition Release 11.2.0.1.0 - Production
With the Partitioning, OLAP, Data Mining and Real Application Testing options
SQL> archive log list
Database log mode No Archive Mode
Automatic archival Disabled
Archive destination E:\app\oracle\product\11.2.0\dbhome_1\RDBMS
Oldest online log sequence 69
Current log sequence 71
SQL>

From the information presented here, we can see from the values for **Database log mode** and **Automatic archival** that our database is not in ARCHIVELOG mode. We can also see the directory to which archived redo logs would be written by **Archive destination**, were ARCHIVELOG mode to be enabled. Lastly, we see the value for the current redo log sequence number from **Current log sequence**. Each time a log switch occurs, this value increases.

Examining Oracle's core infrastructure datafiles

The heart of any database is the data that it contains. The importance of concepts such as high availability, high performance, and high recoverability all stem from the idea that the database exists for the purpose of preserving and delivering data. The structure that contains this data is of the greatest importance. In Oracle, that structure is known as a datafile. All data that is readable to user sessions is stored in datafiles. The data contained in memory caches is transient—it is dynamic and can be lost by a simple loss of power to the database server. The data contained in datafiles is persistent—it survives beyond a server shutdown in non-volatile memory such as that found on the platters of a hard drive. Further, while the size of memory caches is limited by the total amount of memory in the system, the total data contained in the datafiles is essentially unlimited. Every datafile has a name associated with it called a tablespace. A **tablespace** is essentially the logical manifestation of a physical datafile. So, rather than referring to table data that is stored in `E:\APP\ORACLE\ORADATA\ORCL\USERS01.DBF datafile`, we can simply refer to it as the `USERS` tablespace. A tablespace can be composed of multiple datafiles, but a datafile can belong to only one tablespace. It's important to understand that a tablespace is only a logical name, as the physical files that make up a tablespace are stored on disk and can generally be viewed using operating system tools.

While the majority of customer data is held within datafiles, Oracle also keeps its own metadata within datafiles. So, there are certain datafiles that exist in any Oracle database, which we might refer to as its infrastructure. In the same manner as background processes and memory caches, each has a particular function.

Understanding the SYSTEM tablespace

If you recall from the last chapter, we stepped through the manual creation of a database. During this process, we ran the `catalog.sql` and `catproc.sql` scripts. We said that this was to create the data dictionary, the set of database objects that Oracle uses to store its metadata and Oracle-provided PL/SQL code. We've also learned that, in Oracle, table data is stored in datafiles. It follows, then, that the data dictionary must reside in datafiles as well. In fact, the data dictionary exists in the datafiles of the SYSTEM tablespace. Because it holds all of Oracle's metadata about itself, the SYSTEM tablespace is the most primary tablespace of all. Every datafile is given a number when it is created. The first datafile that makes up the SYSTEM tablespace is always given the number 1 since it is created first. The standard naming convention for the SYSTEM datafile is `system01.dbf`, with any additional datafiles being suffixed with `02`, `03`, and so on. The SYSTEM datafile is one of only two that are required to create a database, the second being the datafile for the SYSAUX tablespace.

Understanding the SYSAUX tablespace

Prior to Oracle Version 10*g*, getting performance-tuning metrics from the database could be a complicated task. Doing so required an extensive knowledge of the data dictionary, which is vast in its own right. As a result, there were many different performance-tuning methodologies, each with its own vocal proponents. With Version 10*g*, Oracle attempted, with a high degree of success, to consolidate (or perhaps replace) many of these methods with a single set of performance-oriented metadata tables called the **Automatic Workload Repository**, or **AWR**. As we mentioned earlier in the chapter, the MMON process collects performance information for the AWR in the form of snapshots containing database statistics—various point-in-time performance measurements. Sets of statistics can be compared to form metrics or measurements of statistical change, over time. The AWR is, in essence, a second data dictionary, one that focuses exclusively on database performance metrics. This data must be stored persistently in the database in order to be useful. The designers of Oracle 10*g* chose not to store this information in the SYSTEM tablespace where it might create contention with the data dictionary tables. Instead, they separated this data into its own tablespace—the SYSAUX tablespace. The SYSAUX tablespace contains the data that makes up the AWR. The amount and scope of the performance data stored in the datafile of the SYSAUX tablespace is immense. So, the AWR has its own mechanisms for aging this data out of the SYSAUX tablespace, keeping it to a reasonable size. The standard convention for naming the SYSAUX tablespace datafile is `sysaux01.dbf`.

Exploring the temporary tablespace

In our earlier discussion of the PGA, we mentioned the manner in which Oracle handles sorting. We learned that when a sort requires more memory than can be allocated in the PGA, the data is written out to the temporary tablespace. The **temporary tablespace** serves as a storage area for any temporary objects. When operations occur in the PGA, it is possible that the memory allocations given to users could expand beyond the boundaries that have been established. When this occurs, this PGA memory can be written out to temporary segments into the temporary tablespace, preventing the exhaustion of the PGA's memory for a user operation, such as a large sort. When the operation for a given session is complete, these segments are rejoined and returned to the user session. While we normally associate the temporary tablespace with the temporary segments that form during an overflow of a sort in the PGA, it is also used for many types of operations, including table joins and index creation. It can also store a special type of table known as a **temporary table**. The temporary tablespace allows us to make a distinction between permanent objects, such as tables, and temporary objects, such as the temporary segments from a sort.

In early versions of Oracle, this distinction was more or less in name only. In more recent versions, the structure of the temporary tablespace and the segments it holds has undergone a structural change that allows them to operate more efficiently. We even make a distinction between the files that make up a permanent tablespace and the files that make up a temporary tablespace. Instead of datafiles, we refer to them as tempfiles—the files that make up a temporary tablespace.

Understanding the Undo tablespace

Majority database operations exist in the form of a transaction—a unit of work done within the database. Transactions are formed when a DML statement is paired with a transaction control statement. A DML statement that initiates a transaction can be an `INSERT`, `UPDATE`, or `DELETE` statement, and transaction control is executed using a `COMMIT` or `ROLLBACK` statement. The primary concept behind a transaction is the understanding that the outcome of a DML statement is not truly realized within database tables until a transaction control statement has been executed. For instance, say that we change 100 rows in a table using an `UPDATE` statement. That change is not completed within the table until a `COMMIT` statement is executed. Although the change appears to the user that executes the `UPDATE` statement, no other user can see the change until `COMMIT` occurs. In a sense, the changes are not "real" until the `UPDATE` occurs. Why would an RDBMS operate in this way? Transaction control allows the RDBMS to operate under the principles of consistency that guarantee the reliability of transactions. Under this model, a transaction is not truly complete unless all statements complete. Transactions complete as a unit. This also allows for the concept of a `ROLLBACK` statement. If an incorrect statement occurs, the user is allowed to "roll back" that statement to its previous state.

In order for the principles of transaction control to work, a location for storing the before-image of the data—data as it was before a change was made—must exist. In the example of our 100 row `UPDATE` statement, the data that was in the columns before the statement was executed must be stored somewhere so it can be referenced in the event of a rollback. In Oracle, this data is primarily stored in the **Undo** tablespace. The Undo tablespace stores before-image transactional data in the form of undo segments. In previous versions of Oracle, before-image data was stored in the form of rollback segments. When a user session was created, a rollback segment was assigned to the user to store this transactional data. However, the rollback segment architecture was finite in its ability to assign disk resources for transactions, leading to many failed transactions. In later versions, Oracle introduced the concept of **automatic undo management**. Automatic undo management allows users to allocate undo segments for transactional storage from a pool of disks—the Undo tablespace. This creates a more flexible environment in which a user can be allocated more disk space for before-image data in the event of long-running DML operations that change a large amount of data.

Understanding non-specialized datafiles

While our previous examples of datafiles form the basic infrastructure of the database, the remainder of the physical file structures in Oracle are made up of the standard datafiles that contain application data. In most production databases, these datafiles take up a vast majority of the actual space used within the database. Datafiles such as these are non-specialized to any particular operations, other than the storage of database objects. Again, a tablespace is the logical name given to any set of datafiles.

> **The real-world DBA**
>
> Typically, database administrators create tablespaces with the goal of segregating different types of data. If an application uses certain tables that contain corporate financial data and other tables that represent personnel data, these two sets of tables are generally stored in two separate tablespaces—a FINANCE tablespace and a PERSONNEL tablespace, perhaps. Such a standard leads to a logical separation for clarity but can also improve database performance.

Taking our datafile architecture into account, we find that the maximum theoretical limits on the size of our database are almost difficult to imagine. The maximum size of a datafile in Oracle is 4,194,304 times the database block size. Given that the maximum size of a database block is 32 K, this gives us a max datafile size of 4,194,304 x 32,768 bytes equaling 137,438,953,472 bytes or 128 GB. Taking into account that the maximum number of datafiles present in our database can be up to 65,533, this allows us a maximum size of nearly 8 Petabytes for the database. However, Oracle also allows us to use a special kind of datafile called, a bigfile in tablespaces, **bigfile tablespaces**. Bigfiles can be an order of magnitude larger than typical datafiles (called smallfiles in this context), with a maximum size per bigfile of 128 TB. Thus, the maximum theoretical size limit for an Oracle database using bigfiles is 128 TB x 65,533 files, equaling 8 Exabytes or 9,007,199,254,740,992 bytes.

To complete our look at the database architecture, we refer once more to our architecture diagram and the section focusing on database files:

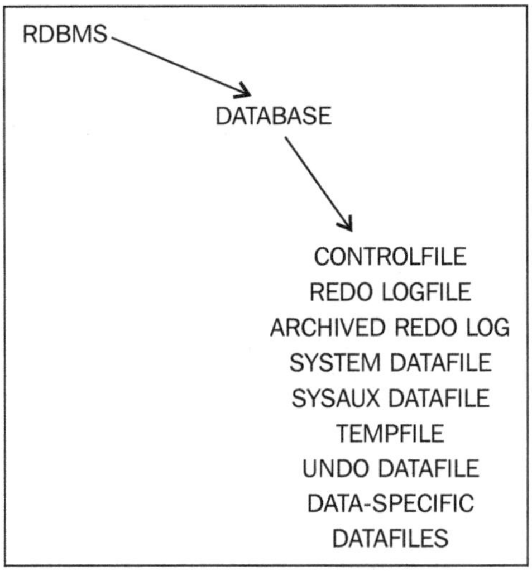
RDBMS
DATABASE
CONTROLFILE
REDO LOGFILE
ARCHIVED REDO LOG
SYSTEM DATAFILE
SYSAUX DATAFILE
TEMPFILE
UNDO DATAFILE
DATA-SPECIFIC
DATAFILES

Exploring Oracle Real Application Clusters

Now that we've fully explored the Oracle database architecture, a question might be raised. "Why make a distinction between the instance and the database at all? Don't they both operate on the same system?" By way of answer, yes; a vast majority of Oracle systems run on a single server. The background processes use a single set of CPUs and the caches run within a single set of memory chips. The database files exist on either storage that is within the machine or connected to it. Both the instance and database run on a single system. However, the Oracle RDBMS can be run in a different architecture—one in which the instance and database are physically independent.

Let's imagine an example for a moment. Let's say that we are DBAs for a small but growing company and we're responsible for the backend database that runs a customer billing system. We've chosen a small-sized server platform with two dual-core CPUs and 8 GB of RAM. This single machine connects to a small **SAN** (**Storage Area Network**) for the purpose of disk and power redundancy. After two years of running our system, we begin to notice performance problems at peak business hours. Upon further inspection, it becomes clear that the problem is the machine itself. When the database is the most active, the server resources are peaking at 100 percent utilization.

We address this by purchasing and configuring a new database server—one with more CPU and RAM. This works well for a few more years, but eventually the database usage of our growing company has once again overtaxed our server resources. We must then purchase another server, and so on. Our core problem in this case is scalability—our database architecture does not scale to meet the needs of our company. In addition to this, as our billing database becomes more and more important, it's clear that it exists on a single point of failure—the server itself. If the server loses power or malfunctions, there is no way for customers to access the database. Since our business requires 24 x 7 uptime, there is also an availability problem. What we really need is a scalable, high-availability solution. Oracle provides just such a solution (at an additional cost) in the form of **Oracle Real Application Clusters**, or **RAC**.

Oracle RAC first began as a product known as **Oracle Parallel Server**, or **OPS**. OPS was Oracle's first attempt at providing a clustered database solution. OPS was different from the single instance database architecture we've discussed. In OPS, multiple servers were connected to a single shared source of disk. These servers each operated with their own instance—their own background processes and memory caches. However, all of these machines shared the same, single source of database files. Thus, OPS systems ran multiple instances, but one database. With OPS, Oracle had created a system with both high scalability and high availability. It was scalable, since, if we possessed a two-machine system that was taxed in terms of server resources, we could simply add another server to the cluster. It was highly available as well, since in the event of the loss of a server, the connections to access database data could simply route through another instance. With the release of Oracle 9*i*, some significant, performance-oriented architecture changes were made, and Oracle Parallel Server was renamed as Oracle Real Application Clusters, or RAC.

In Oracle RAC, servers are connected to a single source of disk. This is usually a Storage Area Network (SAN) or **Network Attached Storage** (**NAS**). The data on the SAN or NAS can be "seen" by every server, referred to as a node, in the cluster. Each node has its own instance and can process user requests independently from the other nodes. However, the nodes in the cluster can also share information between instances. Each node is also connected to every other node by way of a high speed network switch or interconnect. In the event that one node has a particular block of data in the SGA that is needed by one of the other nodes, it doesn't have to write that block back to disk first. Instead, it can be shared directly across the interconnect to the node that needs it. We might diagram an RAC system as shown in the following screenshot:

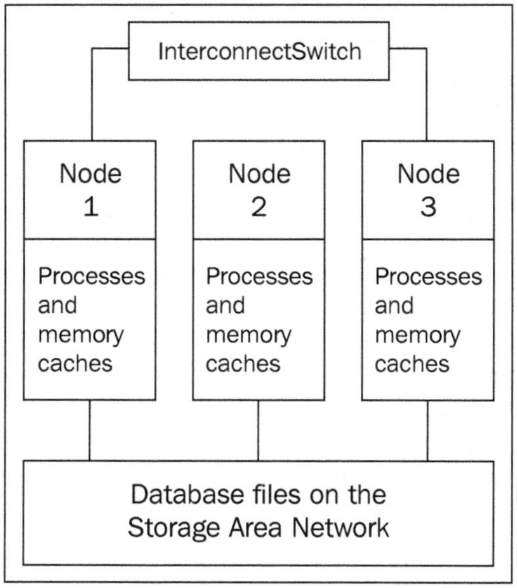
InterconnectSwitch
Node 1
Node 2
Node 3
Processes and memory caches
Processes and memory caches
Processes and memory caches
Database files on the Storage Area Network

Thus, with RAC, there is an important distinction between the instance and the database in Oracle. However, after this chapter, we will focus solely on the single instance architecture and use the term RDBMS and database interchangeably to refer to both the instance and the database as a whole.

Certification objectives covered

- Explain the Memory Structures
- Describe the Process Structures
- Overview of Storage Structures

Summary

In this chapter, we've introduced a lot of terms and concepts to explain the internal architecture of the Oracle RDBMS. Throughout the course of this book, we will continue to revisit these concepts and expand on them as we go, in an iterative fashion. We've examined the components of the Oracle instance, the background processes, and the memory caches. We've explored each of these components in greater detail, such as looking at each of the aspects of the caches. We've connected this to the other side of the Oracle RDBMS—the database. We've examined each of the core datafiles that make up the database. In the process, we've seen how both the instance and database work together to form the Oracle architecture. We've also examined Oracle RAC, an alternative to the single-instance architecture that offers scalability and high availability. In our next chapter, we'll learn more about the database side of the RDBMS; we'll learn to manage tablespaces and the data within them.

Test your knowledge

Q 1. Which of these terms describes the set of files that store the data contained in the RDBMS?

a. SGA
b. Database
c. Memory caches
d. Instance

Q 2. Which of these terms describes the set of background processes and memory structures that enable the Oracle kernel to operate?

a. SGA
b. Database
c. Memory caches
d. Instance

Q 3. Which of the following background processes is tasked with monitoring and regulating all other Oracle-related processes?

a. SMON
b. VKTM
c. PMON
d. LGWR

Q 4. Which of the following background processes is tasked with reading and writing the data that services user operations?

a. ARCn
b. MMON
c. Dnnn
d. DBWn

Q 5. Which command is used to force a full checkpoint?

a. `archive log list`
b. `alter system checkpoint;`
c. `alter system set checkpoint = TRUE;`
d. `alter system switch logfile;`

Q 6. Which background process is active only when ARCHIVELOG mode is enabled?

a. ARCn
b. LGWR
c. LGWn
d. PMON

Q 7. In which of these circumstances will the DBWn process write dirty buffers to disk?

a. When a COMMIT statement occurs
b. When the database is started
c. Every 10 seconds
d. When a checkpoint is reached

Q 8. Which of the following memory caches cannot be changed dynamically?

a. Shared pool
b. Database buffer cache
c. Log buffer
d. Large pool

Q 9. Which of these is NOT an area within the Shared pool?

a. Library cache
b. Data dictionary cache
c. Java area
d. PL/SQL area

Q 10. Which of these terms describes the algorithm used by Oracle to age data out of the database buffer cache?

a. Most recently used
b. Least recently used
c. Most recently changed
d. Least recently changed

Q 11. Which of the following is NOT a condition that causes LGWR to move changes from the log buffer into the redo logfiles?

a. When the log buffer fills to one-third of its capacity
b. When a COMMIT is issued
c. Every 3 seconds
d. When the shared pool allocates data to a resource

Q 12. What is the name given to the database file dealing with the state of the database that contains time-sensitive information?

a. Redo logfile
b. Control file
c. Initialization parameter file
d. SYSTEM tablespace

Q 13. Given a database that is in the NOARCHIVELOG mode and has three redo log groups, what is the state of the data in the first redo log group after three log switches?

a. Change vectors are being overwritten with no chance of recovery of the data
b. Change vectors are being overwritten but the data can be recovered
c. The data in the first redo log group has already been written to an archived redo log
d. All the redo data is unchanged regardless of what log mode is used

Q 14. What is the name of the tablespace that contains the data dictionary metadata created by the `catalog.sql` and `catproc.sql` scripts?

a. SYS
b. SYSTEM
c. SYSAUX
d. SYSTEMP

5
Managing Oracle Storage Structures

Our approach in this book is to learn Oracle from the ground up. Thus far, we've installed the Oracle database software, created a database, and taken a broad look at its architecture. Now that this is complete, we can begin to look more closely at each of the aspects we've covered. In this chapter, we'll examine the database side of RDBMS more closely by exploring the way in which Oracle stores data. We'll start deep within the datafiles, examine how data is stored, and then widen our look to actually work with tablespaces at the command level.

In this chapter we shall learn how to manage the following operations:

- Examining each of Oracle's physical storage structures
- Managing tablespaces
- Understanding Oracle-Managed Files

Examining Oracle's physical space paradigm

In the previous chapter, we explored the database side of the Oracle architecture. We said that a database is made up of datafiles. We have not as yet discussed what makes up the datafile itself. In this section, we break down the way that Oracle stores data within a datafile at the micro level.

Understanding the database block

During our discussion of the database buffer cache and database writer process, we mentioned that Oracle reads data from a disk and writes it into memory for faster manipulation. Now that we've defined a number of terms involved, we can more accurately say that *the DBWn process reads blocks of data from datafiles and writes them into the database buffer cache in the SGA in the form of database buffers*. We've defined the destination in memory for the data during this operation—the **database buffer cache**. We now want to take a closer look at the source of the data—the database block. The **database block** is the smallest atomic unit of storage in an Oracle database. This is to say, from an Oracle database's perspective, that DBWn will never read less than one block from a datafile in any given database read operation. The purpose of the database block is to hold row data from our tables. We "see" rows of data from a `SELECT` statement, but the rows are actually stored within database blocks. Suppose that our Oracle block is 8192 bytes in size and we execute a query against our database that returns a single row whose total size is 100 bytes. Will DBWn read 100 bytes worth of data? No. It will read the entire contents of the block that contains the row, no less than 8192 bytes in our example, and operate on the row within the block when it is moved into the database buffer cache. Isn't it inefficient to read more than you need? If every database query returned only one row, then perhaps this would be inefficient in the long run. However, most queries return multiple rows of data and our example doesn't take into account that we may need to scan *all* of the rows in the table to find the one we request.

Sizing the database block

We use this example to point out the importance of choosing the correct size for our database's blocks, as defined by the `db_block_size` parameter. If we recall from the DBCA session that we used to create our database, we were given the choice during one step to choose our **database block size**. We mentioned that database block sizes range from 2K to 32K. To be more accurate, there are five possible sizes for a database block, namely, 2K, 4K, 8K, 16K, and 32K. We chose the default size, 8K, for our database, but we could have chosen any of the other four instead. How does one determine the proper database block size for a given database? There is not necessarily one perfect block size in every case, but there are generally better choices than others. *The database block size should be based on the type of data that is held within the database and how it is used*. Let's look at the next diagram to help us understand the sizing of the database block:

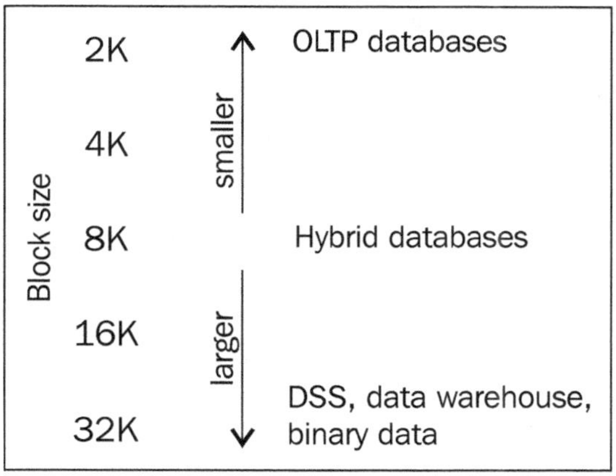
2K
4K
8K
16K
32K
Block size
smaller
larger
OLTP databases
Hybrid databases
DSS, data warehouse,
binary data

We can think of this diagram as a kind of "spectrum" of block sizes. At the top, we have the smallest block size, 2K and at the bottom, the largest, 32K. Databases with either of these extreme block sizes tend to be unusual, but they are valid sizes. If we imagine that any block is storing database rows, we need to determine how rows are fetched in a given database. Remember that our goal is to retrieve the required number of rows with the fewest blocks read into the database buffer cache. For the databases that operate on a limited number of rows at a time, a smaller block size is preferable, as a small number of rows is more likely to be returned by a small block size without excess overhead. We can understand it this way. If an operation that requires a total of only 500 bytes of row data stored in a 16K block, 15,884 bytes of data are needlessly read into the buffer cache. A smaller block size would be more appropriate. An example of such a database would be an **Online Transaction Processing (OLTP)** database. An OLTP database relies on the use of a limited number of discrete transactions to do its work. When we discuss OLTP databases, we usually think of high-speed ordering systems, such as an online bookstore.

At the other extreme are **Decision Support Systems (DSS)** and **Data Warehouses**. These types of systems tend to use large amounts of data at one time for purposes such as data mining and analytics. Because any given operation on these systems retrieves a large number of rows at a time, it is beneficial to use a larger block size that encapsulates the greatest number of rows in the fewest number of blocks.
We also include databases that contain a type of data that is growing in popularity: binary data, at the end of this spectrum. Oracle databases with binary data store unstructured data that is much different than typical row data. This type of data can come in the form of pictures, video files, or document files in proprietary formats, such as Microsoft Word and Adobe PDF. Because a single binary file can use more than even the largest database block size, it can be advantageous to use larger block sizes in such a database.

In the middle of the spectrum are the systems sometimes known as **hybrid databases**. These types of databases store a mixture of data that may be accessed differently by various users at different times of the day. For instance, it is common to see a database that serves users during business hours and then refreshes data at night in the form of data loads. During the day, such a database operates with smaller transaction-oriented operations that require a quick response from the user. At night, datasets are loaded into the database that operate on large numbers of rows at once. To "split the middle," a medium block size such as 8K (the default) is sometimes used. The choice of a block size can be extremely important to the long-term performance of an active database. Regardless of the block size chosen, the value for `db_block_size` cannot be changed after the database is created. Doing so would require a rebuild of the database, so we must choose our block size wisely.

Examining the anatomy of a database block

As the storage unit with the finest granularity in the Oracle database, the block is a very interesting component. The actual internals of the block are documented, so we can diagram the way that data would be stored within them. Examine the following diagram. Keep in mind that we're referring to a unit of space that is between 2048 bytes and 32,768 bytes.

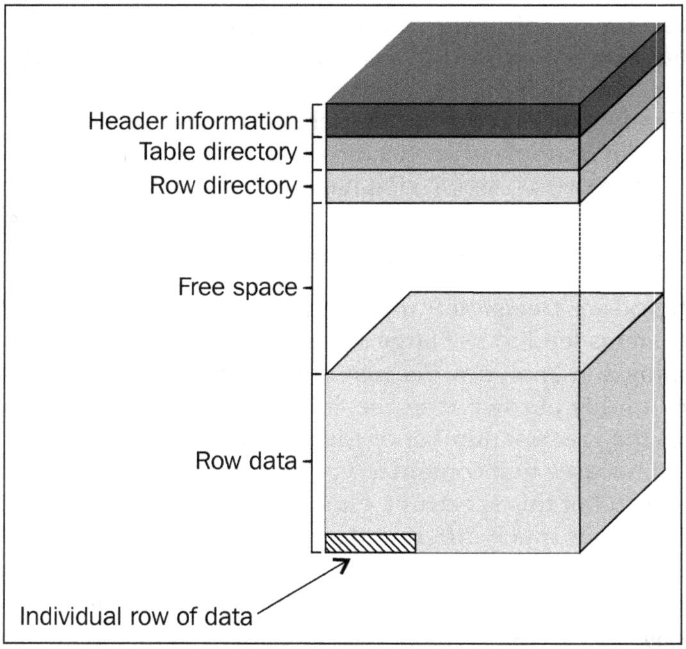
Header information
Table directory
Row directory
Free space
Row data
Individual row of data

The top of an Oracle block contains three sections of overhead data: **Header information**, **Table directory**, and **Row directory**. The **Header information** section includes data about the block itself, such as the **data block address** (called the **DBA** for short) and the type of data the block contains. The **Table directory** section contains information about the table that has rows within this block. The **Row directory** section similarly consists of information about the rows that are inside the block. The majority of the block consists of **Row data** and **Free space**. The **Row data** consists of what we'd expect—the rows of data that we actually see in tables. The **Free space** section shows the unallocated space that is available for new rows. Note the crosshatched section at the very bottom of the block marked **Individual row of data**. While we've noted that this contains row data, the row stored in a block also has its own overhead information. Examine the internals of a row, as shown in the next diagram:

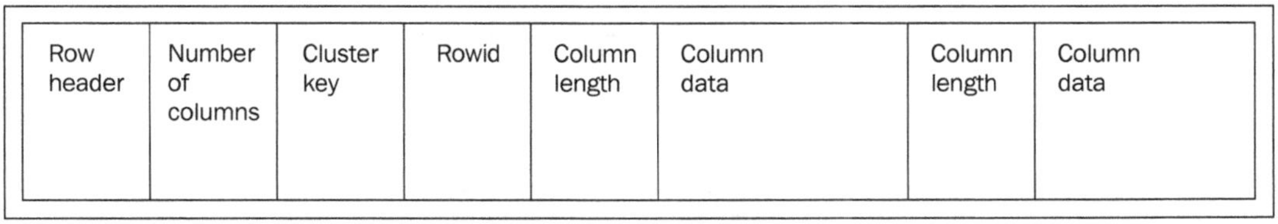
Row header
Number of columns
Cluster key
Rowid
Column length
Column data
Column length
Column data

Any row stored within a block contains the data itself, labeled here as **Column data**, but it also contains a number of overhead sections as well. The most important of these is the **Rowid**, shown in the fourth section. **Rowid** stores the information needed to precisely locate a row within the database. It contains information such as the object number of the row's parent object (such as a table), the row's data block address, the datafile number that contains the row's block, as well as the position of the row within the block.

Understanding the database extent

The next larger level of storage in the Oracle database is the extent. An **extent** is a physical grouping of database blocks for the purpose of efficient storage. When table data is stored in the database, the table rows are stored in blocks and these blocks are grouped into extents. Examine the example shown in the following diagram:

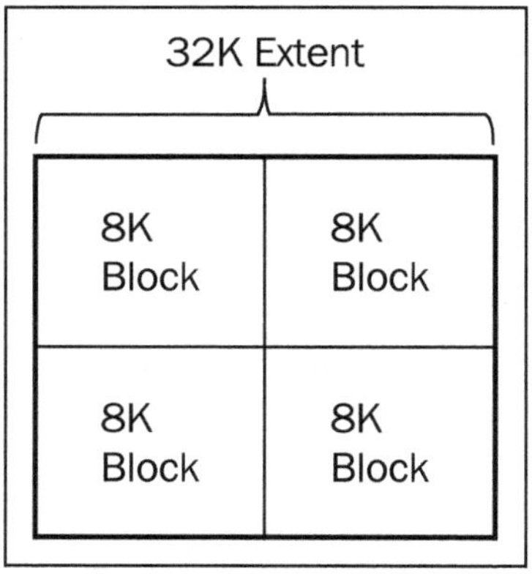
32K Extent
8K Block
8K Block
8K Block
8K Block

When a table is created, an **initial extent** made up of a given number of blocks is allocated to serve as storage for row data. When the initial extent is filled, a **next extent** is allocated and another next extent when that one is filled. We use the specific terms "initial extent" and "next extent" because it is possible to configure these values manually. For instance, we could create a table with an initial extent value of 320 M and a next extent value of 32 M. The first extent allocated would be 320 M in size, while all subsequent extents would be 32 M. This has the effect of being able to control the number of extents in a table. We might expect that our table is roughly 320 M in size, so the majority of its data would reside in a single extent. If there is an overflow, space would be allocated for that purpose in the amount specified by the next extent size. With the advent of **locally managed tablespaces**, extent sizes are dynamically controlled by Oracle, freeing the DBA from this task.

The real-world DBA

In previous versions of Oracle (otherwise known as "the old days"), the management of extents could be a tremendous burden for Oracle DBAs. Many theories existed about the performance impact of having too many extents, in effect resulting in table fragmentation. As the speed of disk subsystems improved, this became less of a concern. When locally managed tablespaces were introduced, extent management became more or less a non-issue altogether.

Understanding the database segment

We've discussed the manner in which blocks are combined into extents for efficient storage allocation within the database. We now turn to the next physical storage layer, the segment. A **segment** is a collection of extents that is the physical analogue of a table. We outlined the way in which extents are allocated for table rows: a first extent for initial storage and next extents for all subsequent storage. Thus, a table can be composed of many extents. We call this collection a segment. We say that a segment is the physical analogue of a table because the term "segment" denotes physical storage, while "table" denotes logical storage. For example, when we create a table, that table is a logical construct; it has no physical storage of its own. Strictly speaking, we cannot "find" a table on disk. The way a table is presented, in the form of rows and columns, is designed to interface with the user in a way that is easy to understand. It is a logical construct. The physical component of a table is the segment, there is, the actual physical storage of the table on disk. Thus, for every table that is created, it has a corresponding segment. We can see an example of this in the following screenshot using two queries from the data dictionary. As we have yet to create our example tables, you may not have this table in your database. For now, we examine this table just for the sake of an example.

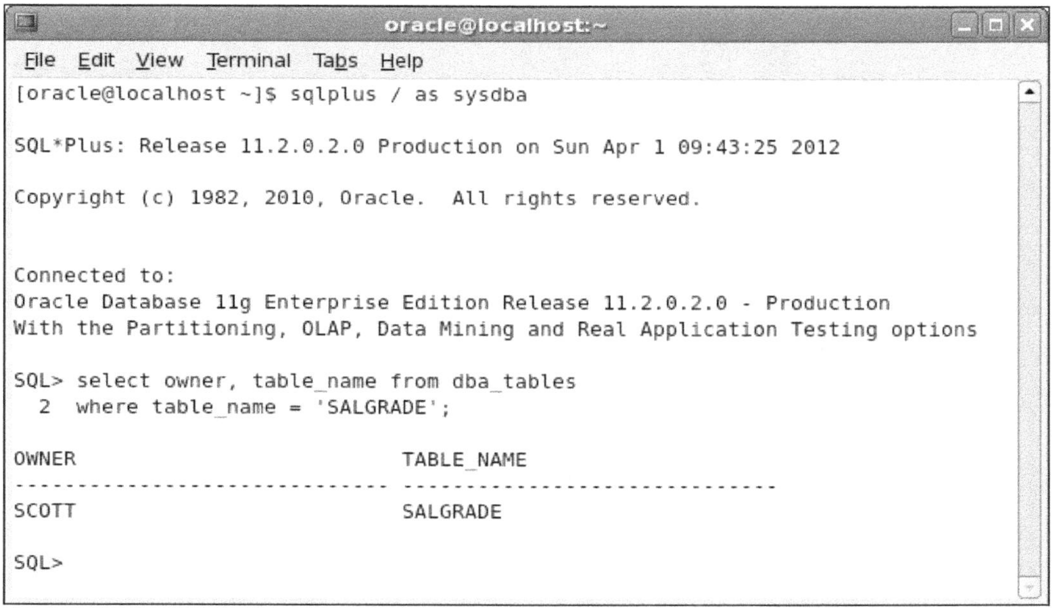
oracle@localhost:~
File Edit View Terminal Tabs Help
[oracle@localhost ~]$ sqlplus / as sysdba
SQL*Plus: Release 11.2.0.2.0 Production on Sun Apr 1 09:43:25 2012
Copyright (c) 1982, 2010, Oracle. All rights reserved.
Connected to:
Oracle Database 11g Enterprise Edition Release 11.2.0.2.0 - Production
With the Partitioning, OLAP, Data Mining and Real Application Testing options
SQL> select owner, table_name from dba_tables
2 where table_name = 'SALGRADE';
OWNER TABLE_NAME
SCOTT SALGRADE
SQL>

Here, we log in to the database and execute a simple query against the **dba_tables** data dictionary view. It shows us that we have a table named **SALGRADE** and that it is owned by the **SCOTT** user. Next, we query against a different data dictionary view.

```
oracle@localhost:~
File  Edit  View  Terminal  Tabs  Help

SQL*Plus: Release 11.2.0.2.0 Production on Sun Apr 1 09:43:25 2012

Copyright (c) 1982, 2010, Oracle.  All rights reserved.


Connected to:
Oracle Database 11g Enterprise Edition Release 11.2.0.2.0 - Production
With the Partitioning, OLAP, Data Mining and Real Application Testing options

SQL> select owner, table_name from dba_tables
  2  where table_name = 'SALGRADE';

OWNER                          TABLE_NAME
------------------------------ ------------------------------
SCOTT                          SALGRADE


SQL> select owner, segment_name from dba_segments
  2  where segment_name = 'SALGRADE';

OWNER                          SEGMENT_NAME
------------------------------ --------------------
SCOTT                          SALGRADE

SQL>
```

Here, we've executed a similar query against the **dba_segments** view. It shows us a corresponding segment named **SALGRADE** for the table of the same name.

> **Beyond the exam**
>
> It is interesting to note that when a table is created, it will not appear in the `dba_segments` view until a row has actually been inserted into it. It does appear in the `dba_tables` view, as that view represents the fact that the logical object has been created and is stored in the data dictionary. However, the table has no physical storage counterpart until a row is created. Once at least one row has been inserted, the table gains its "physicality" and a segment is allocated. This feature is known as **Deferred Segment Creation** and can be disabled using the `deferred_segment_creation` parameter.

While we've used table segments in our examples this far, there are many types of segments used within the Oracle database. In the previous chapter, we've mentioned other examples, such as **temporary segments** and **undo segments**. The following is a list of the types of segments. We will refer to some of these in greater detail, while others are beyond the scope of this book.

- Table segments
- Index segments
- Undo segments
- Temporary segments
- Table partition segments
- Index partition segments
- LOB segments
- LOB index segments
- LOB partition segments
- Cluster segments
- Nested table segments

Understanding the database datafile

Our final layer of storage in the Oracle database is one that we've already discussed, that is, the datafile. A **datafile** contains a group of segments representing the storage of various tables within the database. Just as a segment is the physical representation of a table, a datafile is the physical representation of a tablespace. As we've mentioned, a tablespace can contain multiple datafiles, but a datafile can only belong to one tablespace.

If we put all of our storage layers together, we might represent them visually as shown in the following diagram. We might sum it up this way. A datafile contains segments representing tables, segments contain extents, and extents are made up of blocks.

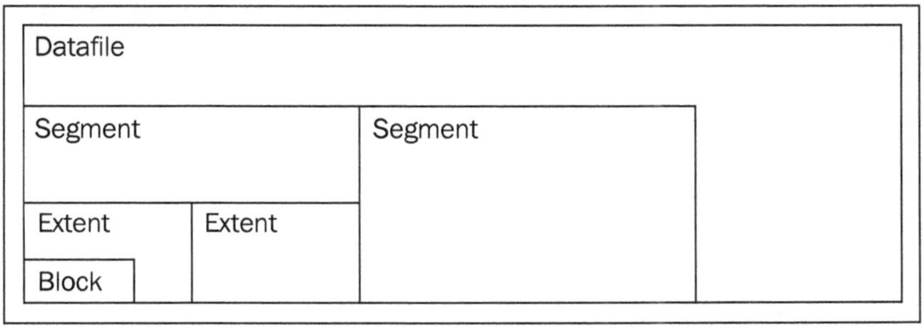
Datafile
Segment
Segment
Extent
Extent
Block

Managing tablespaces

Now that we've looked at how space is stored within the database at a micro level, it's time to get some hands-on experience working with space management. We'll examine creating and modifying tablespaces and their storage characteristics.

Starting SQL Developer

When we need to add space to a database, we do so by creating tablespaces and their associated datafiles with SQL commands. We'll execute these commands using our SQL Developer tool, so we need to take a moment to set it up. To do this on Windows, we navigate to **Start** | **All Programs** | **Oracle - Oradb11g** | **Application Development** | **SQL Developer**.

If we execute this on Windows, we'll be presented with the following window asking us the path to the Java executable:

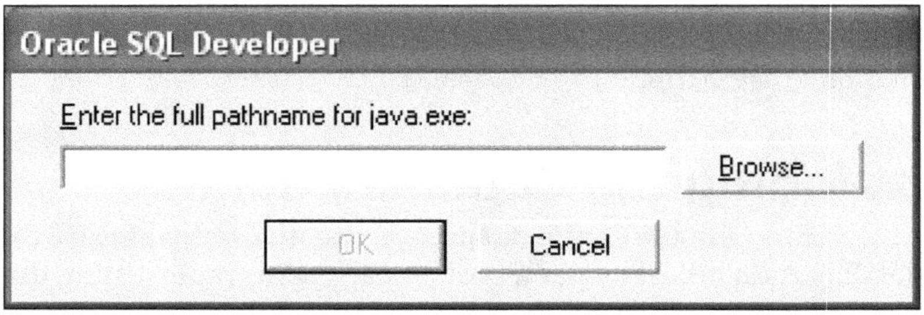
Oracle SQL Developer
Enter the full pathname for java.exe:
Browse...
OK
Cancel

Here we need to use the **Browse...** option to select the Java executable. The executable is within our installation of Oracle, so it will be found in the `ORACLE_HOME` directory in the `jdk\bin` subdirectory. In this example, the path is `E:\app\oracle\product\11.2.0\dbhome_1\jdk\bin\java.exe`.

If you used the same path we indicated during our Oracle software installation, yours should be the same. If you have difficulty finding it, you can do a search from Windows Explorer. Any `java.exe` file found within the `ORACLE_HOME` directory will suffice. Note that we only have to do this the first time we start SQL Developer.

For Linux, we simply type `sqldeveloper` in the command line. We're presented with the following screen. If you are asked to migrate settings from a previous release, simply click on **No**. You may also need to close the **Tip of the day** screen.

For the moment, we don't have much besides a blank screen. This is because we haven't yet set up any connections to our database. To do this, we need to click on the button for a new connection (indicated by **New Connection**), as shown in the following screenshot:

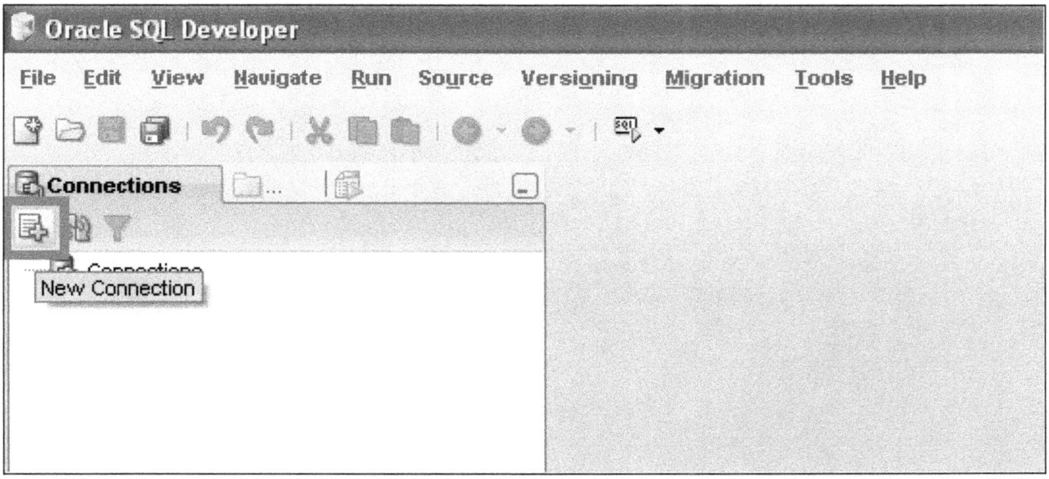
Oracle SQL Developer
File
Edit
View
Navigate
Run
Source
Versioning
Migration
Tools
Help
Connections
New Connection

This presents us with the **New / Select Database Connection** screen. This is the screen we use to fill in all the proper information to establish a connection to our database. We fill in the necessary data as shown in the following screenshot with two possible exceptions. First, the value for the **Hostname** box will be different on other computers. Enter the hostname of the machine on which your database resides. If you don't know the hostname of your machine, it can be found on running the `hostname` command from the command line in both Windows and Linux. Second, ensure that the value you enter for SID matches the one you chose during our database creation with DBCA. In our example, we chose `orcl`. If you chose a different one, enter it in the box labeled **SID**. Also, ensure that the password you enter matches the one you entered during the creation of the database.

In our example, we used `oracle` as the password.

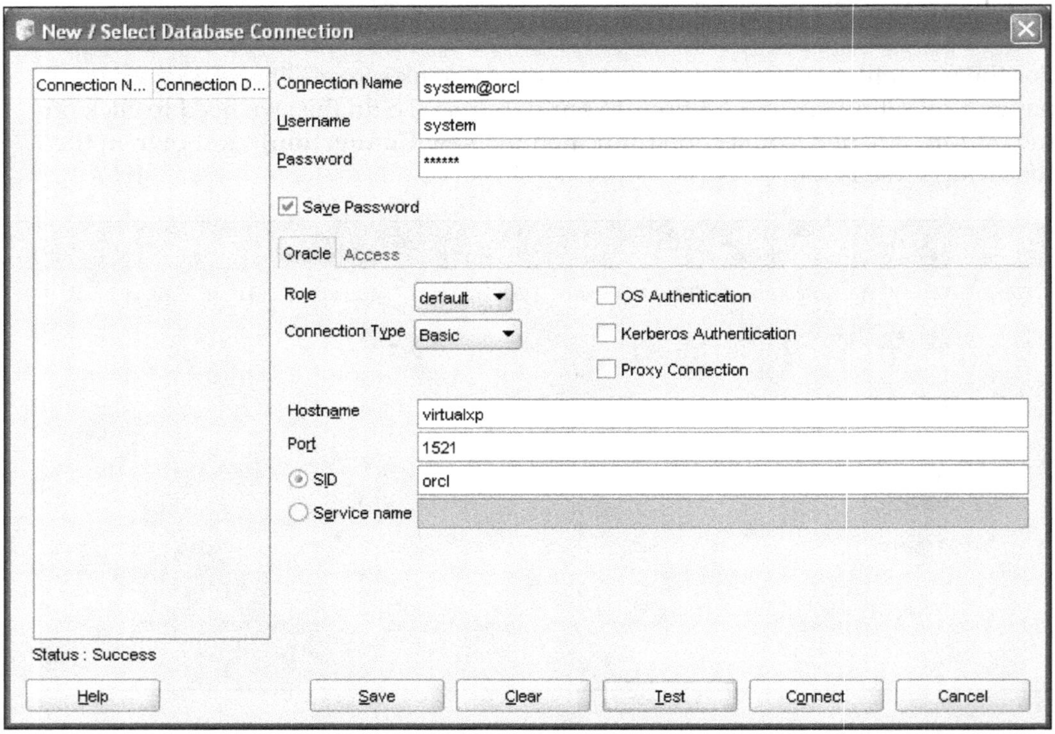
New / Select Database Connection
Connection N...
Connection D...
Connection Name
system@orcl
Username
system
Password
******
Save Password
Oracle
Access
Role
default
Connection Type
Basic
OS Authentication
Kerberos Authentication
Proxy Connection
Hostname
virtualxp
Port
1521
SID
orcl
Service name
Status : Success
Help
Save
Clear
Test
Connect
Cancel

Let's review what we've entered here. We've given our connection a memorable name, **system@orcl**, to signify that we're connecting the system user to a database named **orcl**. We enter **system** and its password as the account that connects. We click on the **Save Password** checkbox, so we won't be prompted for it during subsequent logins. We enter the hostname of the machine on which our database was created. The port indicated is the default port we set up in a previous chapter using NETCA. Our SID is the name of our database. Once all of this information has been correctly entered, we click on the **Test** button to attempt our connection. We should see **Status:Success** in the lower-left corner. We then click on **Save** and then on **Connect**. Remember that in order to connect successfully, our database must be up and running. If you've followed the steps correctly this far, your database should have started up. If it has not, ensure that the Oracle services (on Windows only) are started. We click on the plus sign (**+**) next to our connection name, **system@orcl**, to expand our view. Once we successfully connect, our SQL Developer window looks a bit different, as shown in the following screenshot:

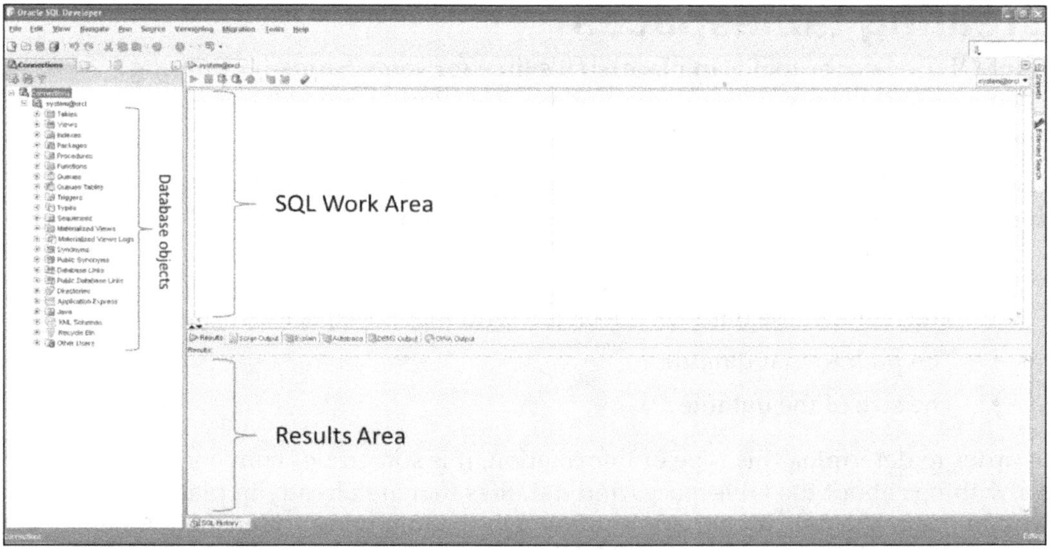
SQL Work Area
Results Area
Database objects

The top-left side of the window holds the database connections we've created. So far, we've only created one, **system@orcl**, so that is the only one shown. When we click on the plus sign next to our connection to expand it, we are shown a list of database object types that can be owned by our database user, **system**. Expanding any of these by clicking on the corresponding plus sign will display the objects of that type that are owned by the user designated in the connection, in this case, **system**. Feel free to click and expand any that you wish. The dominant right-hand side is made up of two areas: the **SQL Work Area** and the **Results Area**. Simply put, we enter SQL statements in the **SQL Work Area**, click on the **Execute Statement** button and the results are shown in the **Results Area**. We will step through this process in the next example.

While this might seem like a lot of work, the majority of it only needs to be done the first time we start SQL Developer. We've located the Java executable and have set up our connection already, so we only need to start up SQL Developer and double-click on the connection name any time we wish to log in to the database again. Feel free to explore some of the buttons and option menus in SQL Developer.

Creating tablespaces

Our SQL Developer tool is in place, so it's time for some hands-on learning. Keep in mind that if you wish, you can use SQL*Plus or any other SQL tool that supports Oracle to do these commands.

To create a tablespace, we'll use the `CREATE TABLESPACE` command. But we need to decide a few things first. For our command, we must determine the following:

- The name of the tablespace
- The name of the datafile associated with the tablespace
- The path to that datafile
- The size of the datafile

In order to determine this type of information, it is sometimes convenient to discover a few things about the tablespaces and datafiles that are already in place. To do this, we can query the data dictionary, as shown in the following screenshot. We enter the query into our **SQL Work Area** and click on the green arrow in the upper-left corner circled in the screenshot. By hovering over this button, we see that this is called the Execute Statement button. Alternatively, we can highlight the statement by selecting it and hitting the *F9* key.

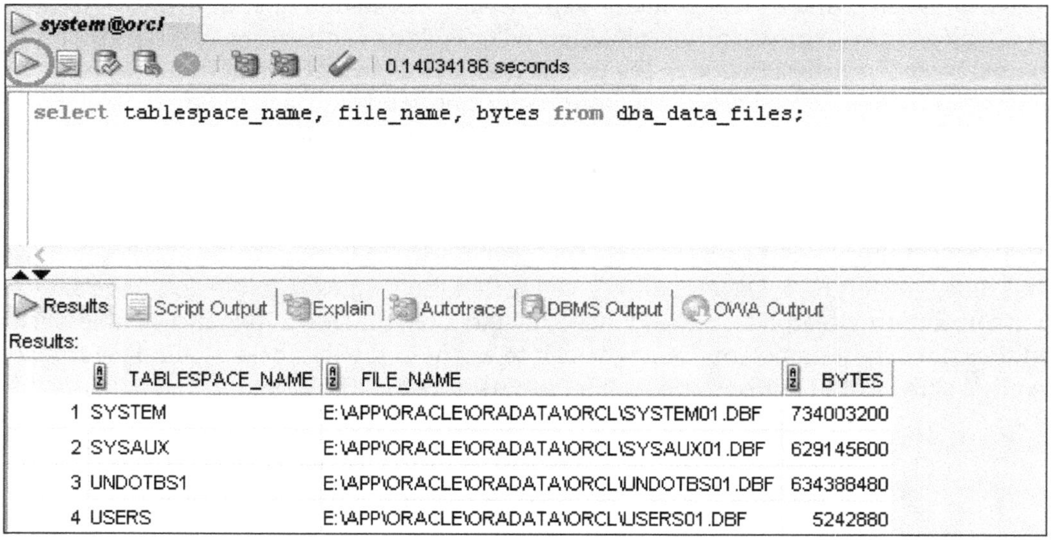
system@orcl
0.14034186 seconds
select tablespace_name, file_name, bytes from dba_data_files;
Results
Script Output
Explain
Autotrace
DBMS Output
OWA Output
Results:
TABLESPACE_NAME
FILE_NAME
BYTES
1 SYSTEM
E:\APP\ORACLE\ORADATA\ORCL\SYSTEM01.DBF
734003200
2 SYSAUX
E:\APP\ORACLE\ORADATA\ORCL\SYSAUX01.DBF
629145600
3 UNDOTBS1
E:\APP\ORACLE\ORADATA\ORCL\UNDOTBS01.DBF
634388480
4 USERS
E:\APP\ORACLE\ORADATA\ORCL\USERS01.DBF
5242880

Here we've consulted the **dba_data_files** view that contains information about tablespaces and datafiles in the database. We can see from here that there are four tablespaces in this database and the names of their associated datafiles. We also see the sizes of each displayed in the **BYTES** column. Note that although names of the datafiles themselves are different, the directory path to each of them is the same. It is logical, although not mandatory, that we use the same path for our datafile. Thus, we need to choose a name for a tablespace that is not in the list (as two tablespaces cannot have the same name within a database) and we'll use the same location for the directory as the other datafiles. To answer our previous questions, we'll use the following data:

- The name of the tablespace: `NEW_TS`
- The name of the datafile associated with the tablespace: `NEW_TS01.DBF`
- The path to that datafile: `E:\APP\ORACLE\ORADATA\ORCL`
- The size of the datafile: 100 MB

Putting this all together, we arrive at the following statement. We enter this in the SQL Work Area and click on the green arrow to execute the statement (**Execute Statement**). Remember that in SQL, case is ignored unless the characters in question are within quotations:

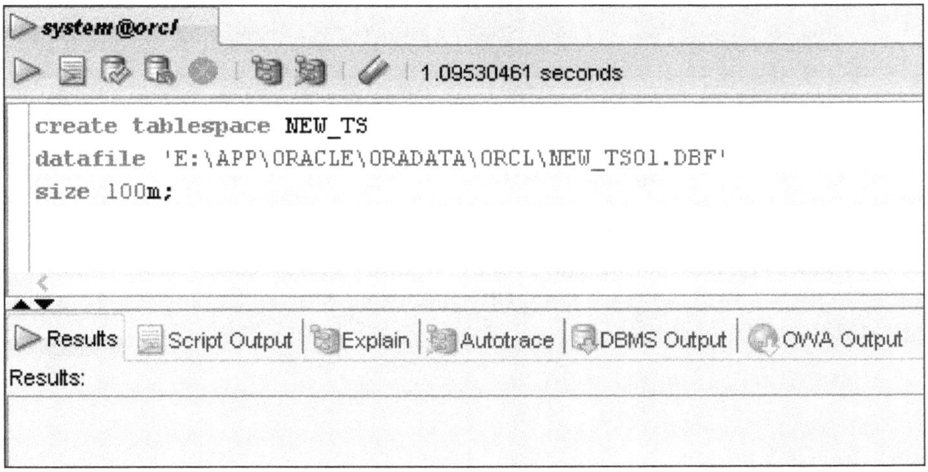
system@orcl
1.09530461 seconds
create tablespace NEW_TS
datafile 'E:\APP\ORACLE\ORADATA\ORCL\NEW_TS01.DBF'
size 100m;
Results
Script Output
Explain
Autotrace
DBMS Output
OWA Output
Results:

As we're not querying for any data, nothing is returned in the **Results** area. Instead, if we entered the information correctly, we see a message in the lower-left corner saying **Statement Processed**. Our **NEW_TS** tablespace has been created. If we want to verify this, we simply execute the same query against **dba_data_files** again, as shown in the following screenshot:

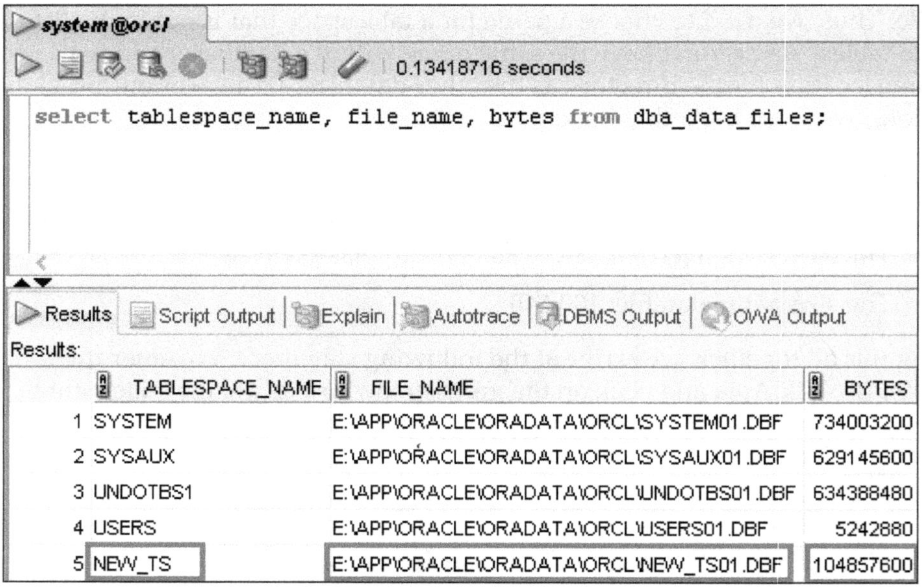
system@orcl
0.13418716 seconds
select tablespace_name, file_name, bytes from dba_data_files;
Results
Script Output
Explain
Autotrace
DBMS Output
OWA Output
Results:
TABLESPACE_NAME
FILE_NAME
BYTES
1 SYSTEM E:\APP\ORACLE\ORADATA\ORCL\SYSTEM01.DBF 734003200
2 SYSAUX E:\APP\ORACLE\ORADATA\ORCL\SYSAUX01.DBF 629145600
3 UNDOTBS1 E:\APP\ORACLE\ORADATA\ORCL\UNDOTBS01.DBF 634388480
4 USERS E:\APP\ORACLE\ORADATA\ORCL\USERS01.DBF 5242880
5 NEW_TS E:\APP\ORACLE\ORADATA\ORCL\NEW_TS01.DBF 104857600

As we can see, a new tablespace has been created with the specified tablespace name, datafile, and a datafile size of 104857600 bytes, or 100 M.

The previous examples are from a database on Windows. However, as `CREATE TABLESPACE` is a SQL command, the process is the same on other operating systems. Let's show a quick example from a slightly newer version of SQL Developer running against a database on Linux:

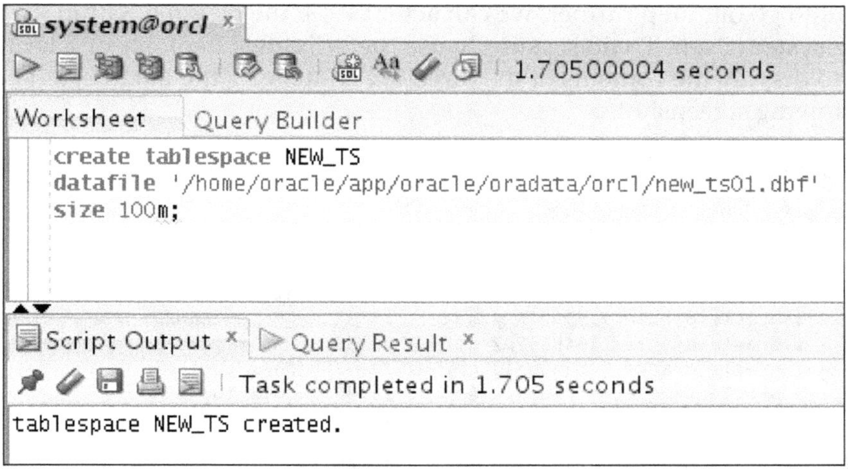
system@orcl
1.70500004 seconds
Worksheet
Query Builder
create tablespace NEW_TS
datafile '/home/oracle/app/oracle/oradata/orcl/new_ts01.dbf'
size 100m;
Script Output
Query Result
Task completed in 1.705 seconds
tablespace NEW_TS created.

Note the difference in the path to the datafile in Linux. As we mentioned in an earlier chapter, Linux-based directories use a different format than Windows. We can use the same query as before to verify our new tablespace.

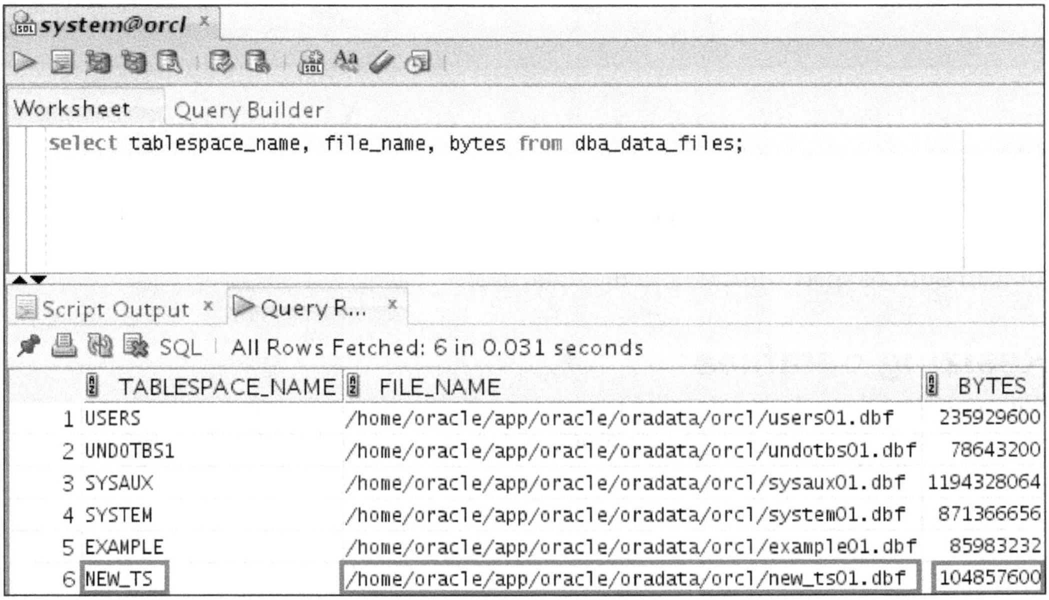
system@orcl
Worksheet
Query Builder
select tablespace_name, file_name, bytes from dba_data_files;
Script Output
Query R...
SQL
All Rows Fetched: 6 in 0.031 seconds
TABLESPACE_NAME
FILE_NAME
BYTES
1 USERS /home/oracle/app/oracle/oradata/orcl/users01.dbf 235929600
2 UNDOTBS1 /home/oracle/app/oracle/oradata/orcl/undotbs01.dbf 78643200
3 SYSAUX /home/oracle/app/oracle/oradata/orcl/sysaux01.dbf 1194328064
4 SYSTEM /home/oracle/app/oracle/oradata/orcl/system01.dbf 871366656
5 EXAMPLE /home/oracle/app/oracle/oradata/orcl/example01.dbf 85983232
6 NEW_TS /home/oracle/app/oracle/oradata/orcl/new_ts01.dbf 104857600

If we want to go one step further, we can actually see the new file within the operating system itself. To do so, simply use the Windows Explorer or a terminal in Linux to display the contents of the directory containing the datafile, as shown in the following screenshot:

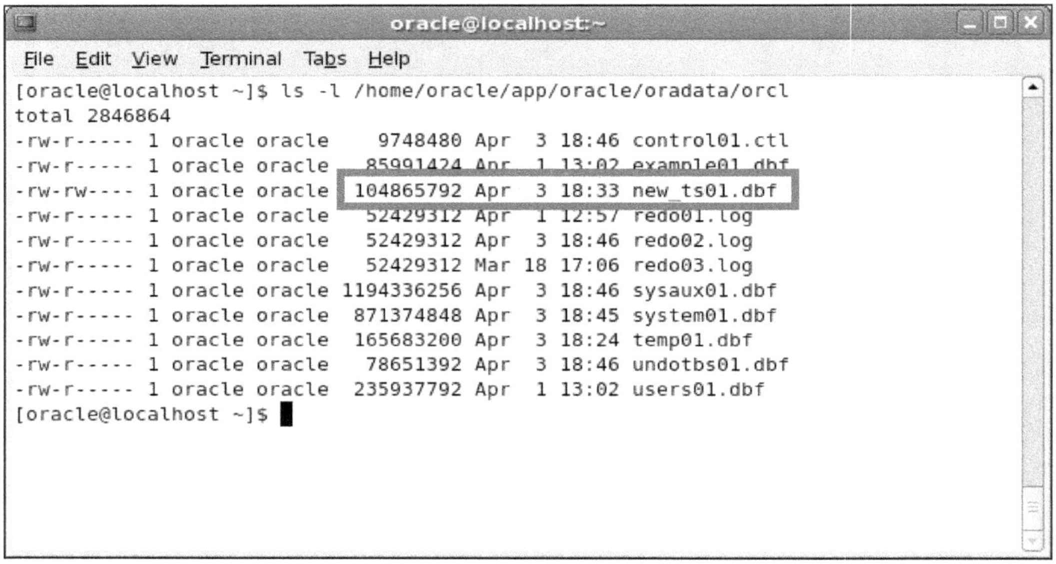
oracle@localhost:~
File Edit View Terminal Tabs Help
[oracle@localhost ~]$ ls -l /home/oracle/app/oracle/oradata/orcl
total 2846864
-rw-r----- 1 oracle oracle 9748480 Apr 3 18:46 control01.ctl
-rw-r----- 1 oracle oracle 85991424 Apr 1 13:02 example01.dbf
-rw-rw---- 1 oracle oracle 104865792 Apr 3 18:33 new_ts01.dbf
-rw-r----- 1 oracle oracle 52429312 Apr 1 12:57 redo01.log
-rw-r----- 1 oracle oracle 52429312 Apr 3 18:46 redo02.log
-rw-r----- 1 oracle oracle 52429312 Mar 18 17:06 redo03.log
-rw-r----- 1 oracle oracle 1194336256 Apr 3 18:46 sysaux01.dbf
-rw-r----- 1 oracle oracle 871374848 Apr 3 18:45 system01.dbf
-rw-r----- 1 oracle oracle 165683200 Apr 3 18:24 temp01.dbf
-rw-r----- 1 oracle oracle 78651392 Apr 3 18:46 undotbs01.dbf
-rw-r----- 1 oracle oracle 235937792 Apr 1 13:02 users01.dbf
[oracle@localhost ~]$

Modifying tablespaces

Once a tablespace is created and a datafile has been allocated to it, we can change its size in a number of ways. We do operations such as the following to manage the total amount of space allocated to the database.

Resizing datafiles

We can resize the existing datafile to either a larger size, or, in some cases, a smaller one. To resize a given datafile, we use the `ALTER DATABASE` command, specifying the datafile name we intend to change and its new size, as shown in the following screenshot:

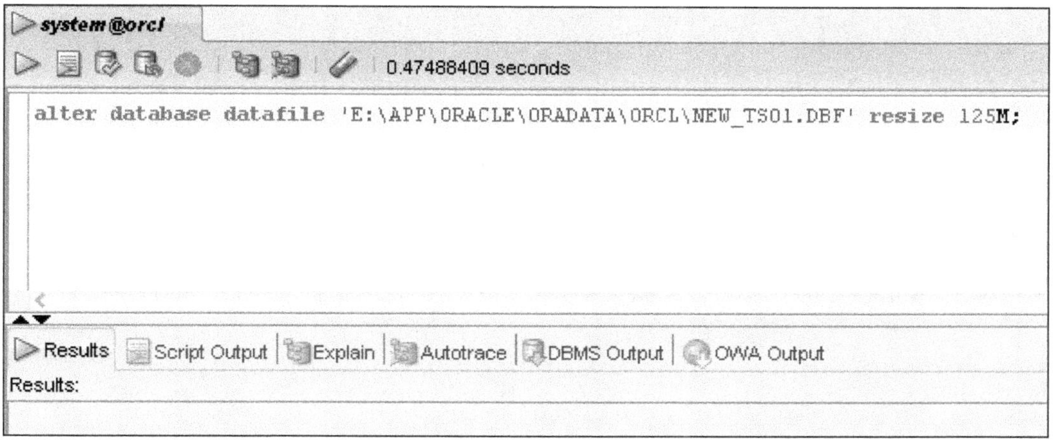
system@orcl
0.47488409 seconds
alter database datafile 'E:\APP\ORACLE\ORADATA\ORCL\NEW_TS01.DBF' resize 125M;
Results
Script Output
Explain
Autotrace
DBMS Output
OWA Output
Results:

In the previous screenshot, we've taken the datafile we created for our `NEW_TS` tablespace and increased its size from 100 M to 125 M. We specify the datafile we want to resize by indicating its full path and filename within single quotes. All of these are essential when using the datafile name to resize it. We can increase the size of a datafile by any amount we wish, provided that we have the necessary disk space and the size of the file does not exceed its maximum file size for a given block size. Remember that the maximum size of a datafile is dependent on the database block size. We're using an 8K database block, so the maximum datafile size is 4,194,304 bytes multiplied by the database block size. In our case, the maximum is 4,194,304 bytes x 8192 bytes equaling 32 GB.

It is sometimes cumbersome (and prone to error) to use the full path and filename for a resize operation. Every datafile has a unique ID number that can be used to identify it. We can use this ID instead of the full name and path, but we need to learn how to determine it first. As we're learning, we can utilize a query against the data dictionary as shown in the following screenshot:

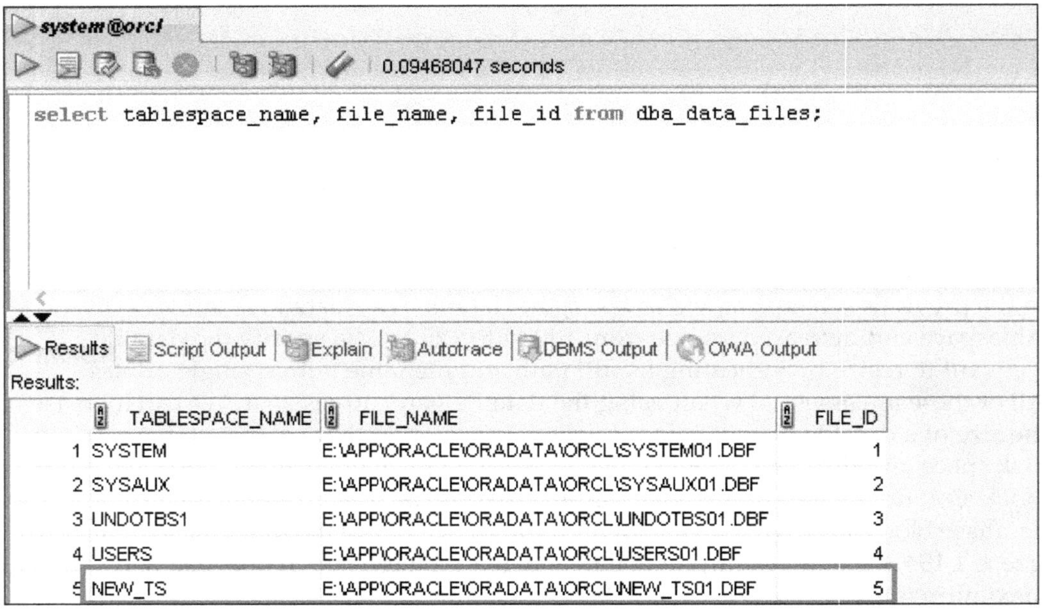
system@orcl
0.09468047 seconds
select tablespace_name, file_name, file_id from dba_data_files;
Results
Script Output
Explain
Autotrace
DBMS Output
OWA Output
Results:
TABLESPACE_NAME
FILE_NAME
FILE_ID
1 SYSTEM E:\APP\ORACLE\ORADATA\ORCL\SYSTEM01.DBF 1
2 SYSAUX E:\APP\ORACLE\ORADATA\ORCL\SYSAUX01.DBF 2
3 UNDOTBS1 E:\APP\ORACLE\ORADATA\ORCL\UNDOTBS01.DBF 3
4 USERS E:\APP\ORACLE\ORADATA\ORCL\USERS01.DBF 4
5 NEW_TS E:\APP\ORACLE\ORADATA\ORCL\NEW_TS01.DBF 5

We see that the `file_id` for our new datafile, shown in the third column, is **5**. We can then use this `file_id` value to refer to our datafile in other statements. Next, we'll attempt to shrink the size of the datafile below its original size of 100 M, as shown in the following screenshot:

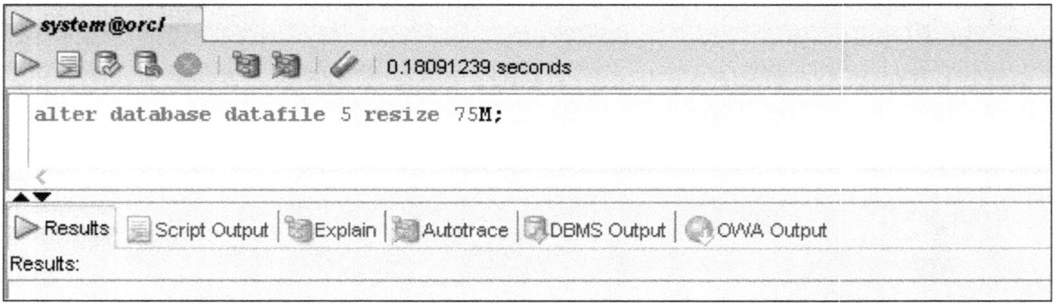
system@orcl
0.18091239 seconds
alter database datafile 5 resize 75M;
Results
Script Output
Explain
Autotrace
DBMS Output
OWA Output
Results:

Either method can be used to refer to the datafile. As we were able to shrink our datafile below its original size, how small can we make it? The limits to which we can shrink a datafile are determined by the amount of data within the datafile itself. For example, it should be obvious that we cannot shrink a 10 GB datafile that contains 5 GB of data down to 3 GB. What we also must remember, however, is that *we cannot shrink a datafile below the size of the largest amount of data that it ever contained*. Let's use a simple example to demonstrate this. Let's say that we have a tablespace datafile that is 10 GB in size. We'll also say that this datafile contains segments that total 5 GB in size. We might demonstrate this as shown in the following diagram:

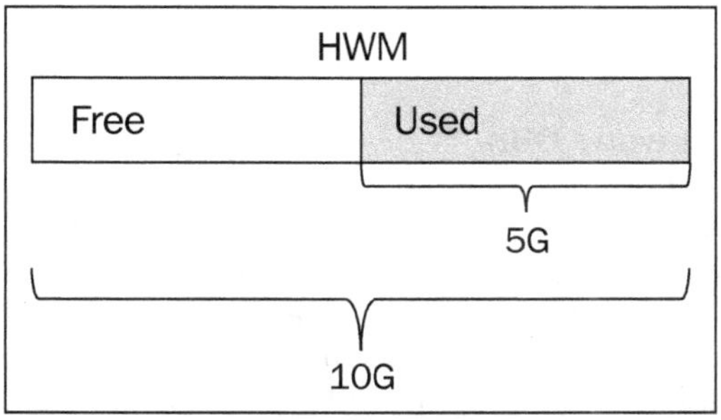
HWM
Free
Used
5G
10G

The line between the free and used space within the datafile is called the **High Water Mark** (**HWM**). The HWM establishes the upper limit of the used space within the datafile. As segments use more space within the datafile, the HWM level increases. However, we must remember that the HWM does not *decrease* when segments are removed and that a datafile cannot be shrunk below the HWM. Let's say in our example we drop all of the tables in this datafile and, thereby, their corresponding segments. Our example would then look like the following diagram:

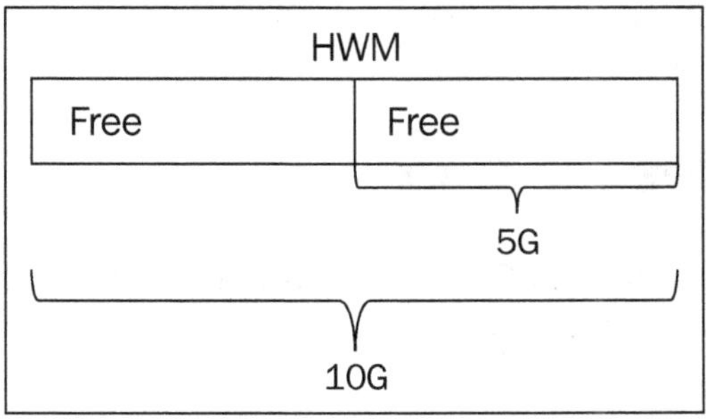
HWM
Free
Free
5G
10G

Even though our datafile is now completely empty, we still cannot resize it below 5 GB, as the HWM remains at the 5 GB point. If the amount of space in our filesystem demands that we shrink it below 5 GB, we really have no choice except to drop the tablespace and its corresponding datafile, and then recreate it with the proper size. This can be fairly involved if the datafile contains some segments that cannot be dropped. This underscores the importance of correctly sizing datafiles when they are initially created.

If we attempt to resize a datafile below the HWM level, we will receive an error indicating that the datafile contains data beyond the point of the requested `RESIZE` value.

The real-world DBA

Here's a true story that illustrates the importance of the HWM. A DBA once came to me and asked if the datafile for the `SYSTEM` tablespace could be shrunk. "Yes," I replied, "but not below the HWM." When I asked why he wanted to know, he responded with his current situation. He had allowed a large number of application tables to be created in the `SYSTEM` tablespace, rather than a separate data tablespace. In addition, the datafile for the `SYSTEM` tablespace had been set to automatically grow whenever it became full—a feature called `AUTOEXTEND` that we will discuss shortly. These application tables had been allowed to grow unchecked within the `SYSTEM` tablespace, causing the datafile to grow to such a size that it filled the entire hard drive the database was on. The DBA was willing to move the application tables out of the `SYSTEM` tablespace into a tablespace on another drive, but nothing could be done about the oversized datafile for the `SYSTEM` tablespace, as it cannot be dropped and recreated. Never keep application tables in the `SYSTEM` tablespace. That tablespace should be dedicated to the data dictionary.

Adding datafiles

In addition to resizing tablespaces by changing the sizes of the datafiles themselves, we can also allocate more space by simply adding another datafile. To do this, we use the `ALTER TABLESPACE` command, as shown in the following screenshot:

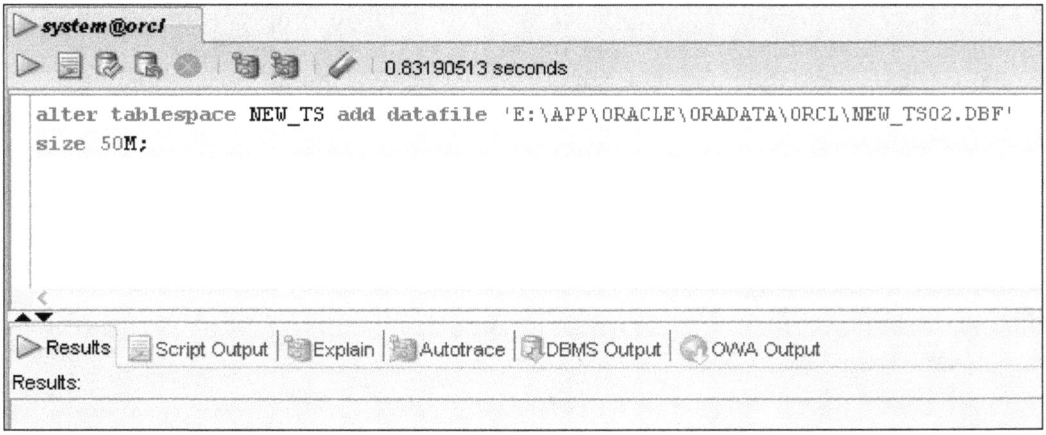
system@orcl
0.83190513 seconds
alter tablespace NEW_TS add datafile 'E:\APP\ORACLE\ORADATA\ORCL\NEW_TS02.DBF'
size 50M;
Results
Script Output
Explain
Autotrace
DBMS Output
OWA Output
Results:

Our `ALTER TABLESPACE ... ADD DATAFILE` command adds a new datafile to the `NEW_TS` tablespace with a size of 50 M. As we previously resized the `NEW_TS01.DBF` datafile down to 75 M, our `NEW_TS` tablespace now has a total of 125 M allocated to it. If we desire, we can locate separate datafiles on different mount points or separate disks, such as one tablespace datafile on `E:` and one on `F:`. When a datafile or datafiles have been allocated to a tablespace, there is no way to remove datafiles from the tablespace individually. The tablespace and its datafiles must be dropped together.

Automatically extending datafiles

Managing datafile sizes can be a time-consuming exercise. In a small database such as the one we're using for our examples, it's not very complicated. But in large multi-terabyte or larger databases, managing datafile sizes involves monitoring the amount of free space within the tablespaces and then resizing or adding datafiles. In a large, busy environment, this can lead to endless calls in the middle of the night to add space so that nightly jobs can complete. To mitigate this, we can set datafiles to be **automatically extensible**. When such a datafile becomes full, it automatically allocates space to itself. Thus, a running job that inserts enough data to fill the datafile's remaining space will not create any error because of insufficient space. The datafile continues to add space as needed.

We have a certain degree of control over this feature. If we simply want to set a datafile to be automatically extensible, regardless of limits, we use the `AUTOEXTEND ON` clause as a part of the `ALTER DATABASE DATAFILE` command, as shown in the following screenshot:

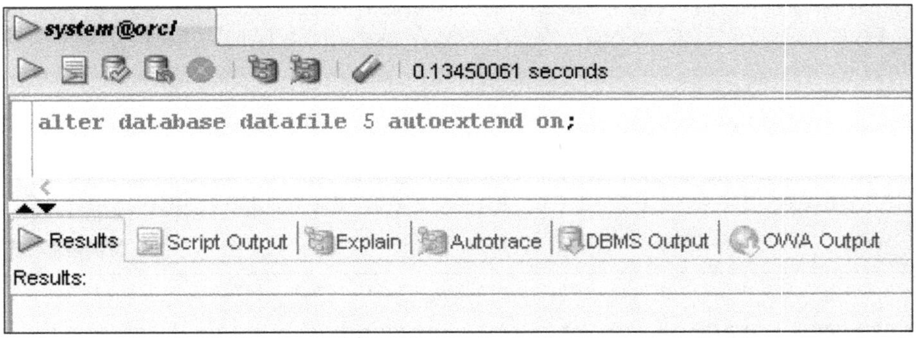
system@orcl
0.13450061 seconds
alter database datafile 5 autoextend on;
Results
Script Output
Explain
Autotrace
DBMS Output
OWA Output
Results:

If we want to control how the datafile extends and to what limit, we can use additional clauses to specify the amount of additional space added (`NEXT`) and the maximum size to which the datafile can extend (`MAXSIZE`), as shown in the following screenshot:

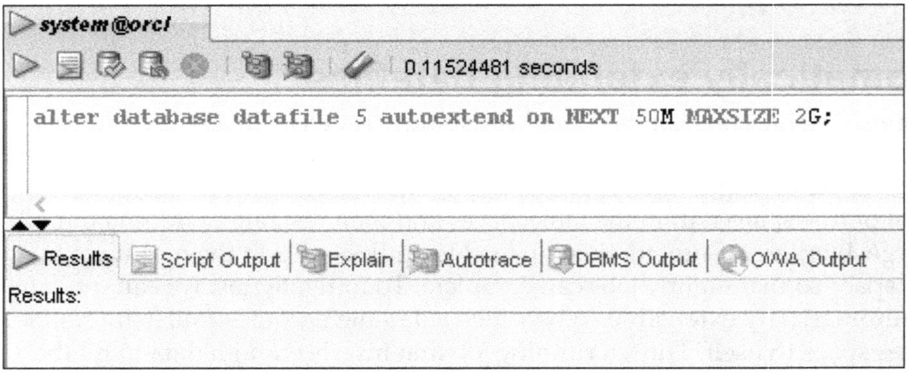
system@orcl
0.11524481 seconds
alter database datafile 5 autoextend on NEXT 50M MAXSIZE 2G;
Results
Script Output
Explain
Autotrace
DBMS Output
OWA Output
Results:

While the `AUTOEXTEND` feature is convenient (and can lead to a better night's sleep for an on-call DBA) it should be used with caution. Remember that there is always a practical limit to the amount of space available for an automatically extending datafile, either to the maximum datafile size or the amount of free space in the filesystem. `AUTOEXTEND` makes space management simpler, but doesn't remove the need for it altogether.

Managing tablespace availability

In addition to being used to manage space, tablespaces can be put in various states of availability. This is usually done by the DBA in certain cases involving various forms of maintenance. The first type of availability involves completely taking a tablespace offline that prevents all but a few operations from taking place on the tablespace and its datafiles. We can take a tablespace offline using the command shown in the next screenshot. Remember to highlight and execute the statements individually.

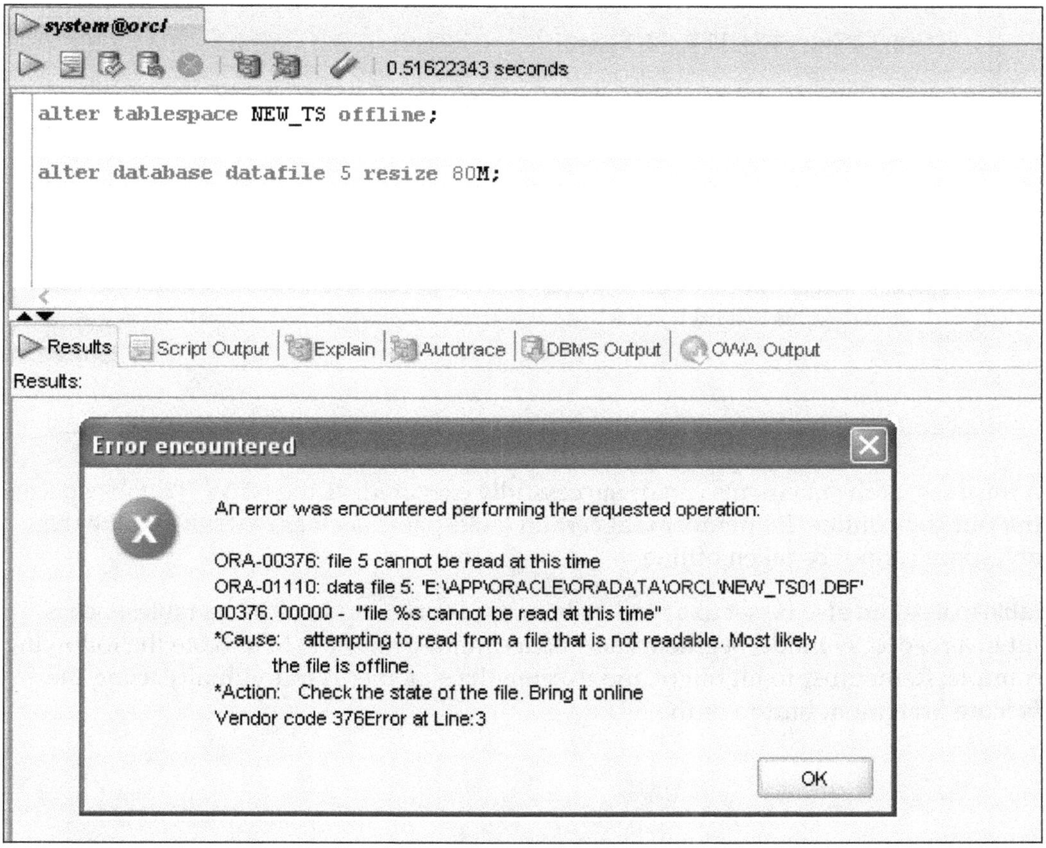
system@orcl
0.51622343 seconds
alter tablespace NEW_TS offline;
alter database datafile 5 resize 80M;
Results
Script Output
Explain
Autotrace
DBMS Output
OWA Output
Results:
Error encountered
An error was encountered performing the requested operation:
ORA-00376: file 5 cannot be read at this time
ORA-01110: data file 5: 'E:\APP\ORACLE\ORADATA\ORCL\NEW_TS01.DBF'
00376. 00000 - "file %s cannot be read at this time"
*Cause: attempting to read from a file that is not readable. Most likely the file is offline.
*Action: Check the state of the file. Bring it online
Vendor code 376Error at Line:3
OK

The first statement takes the **NEW_TS** tablespace offline successfully. The second statement attempts to resize a datafile (the datafile number 5 we used previously) but is unsuccessful. The operation does not succeed because the datafile we're attempting to resize has an associated tablespace that is offline. To place the tablespace online, we use a command similar to the one shown in the following screenshot:

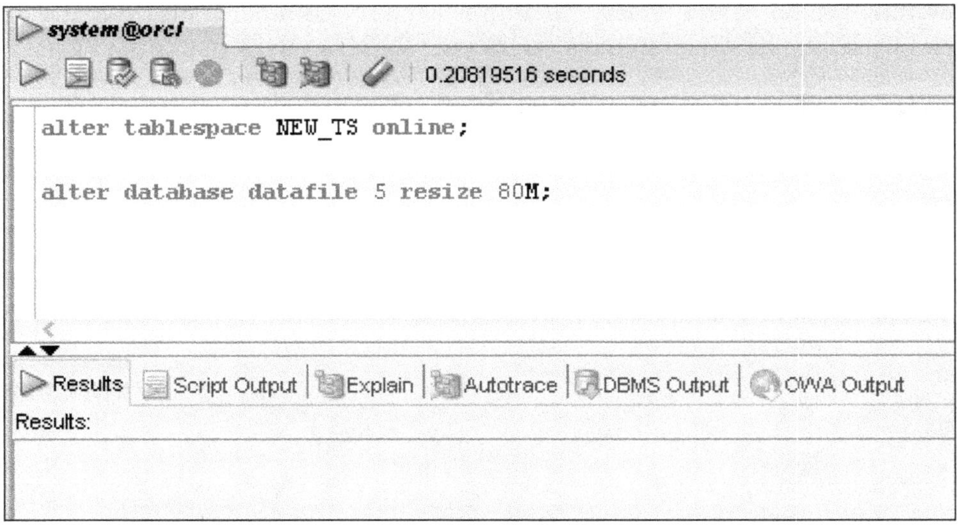
system@orcl
0.20819516 seconds
alter tablespace NEW_TS online;
alter database datafile 5 resize 80M;
Results
Script Output
Explain
Autotrace
DBMS Output
OWA Output
Results:

In this case, both statements can be successfully executed, as the **NEW_TS** tablespace is first put back online. Remember that certain tablespaces such as `SYSTEM` and the `UNDO` tablespace cannot be taken offline.

Tablespaces can also be set to a read-only or read-write mode. When a tablespace is put in a read-only mode, segments and data cannot be written to it. Note the following example. Remember to highlight and execute the statements individually using the **Execute Statement** button or the *F9* key.

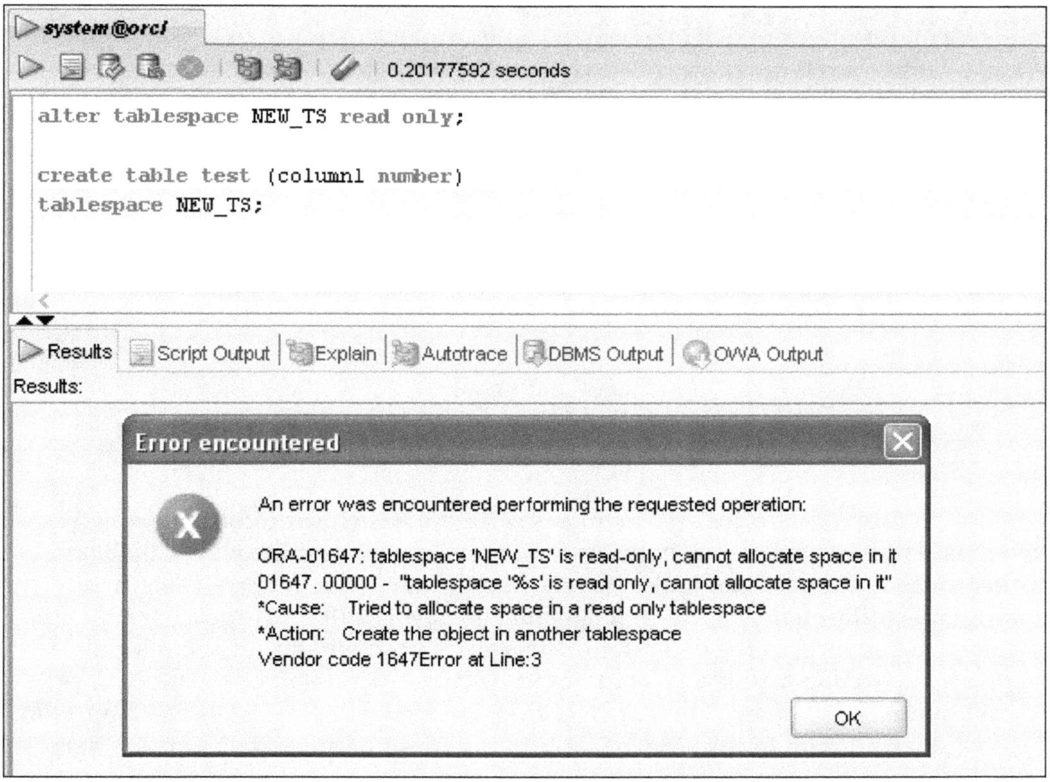
system@orcl
0.20177592 seconds
alter tablespace NEW_TS read only;
create table test (column1 number)
tablespace NEW_TS;
Results
Script Output
Explain
Autotrace
DBMS Output
OWA Output
Results:
Error encountered
An error was encountered performing the requested operation:
ORA-01647: tablespace 'NEW_TS' is read-only, cannot allocate space in it
01647. 00000 - "tablespace '%s' is read only, cannot allocate space in it"
*Cause: Tried to allocate space in a read only tablespace
*Action: Create the object in another tablespace
Vendor code 1647Error at Line:3
OK

As we can see from the error message numbered **ORA-01647**, space cannot be allocated within the `NEW_TS` tablespace as it is in read-only mode. We can return the tablespace to read-write mode using a command similar to the one shown in the following screenshot:

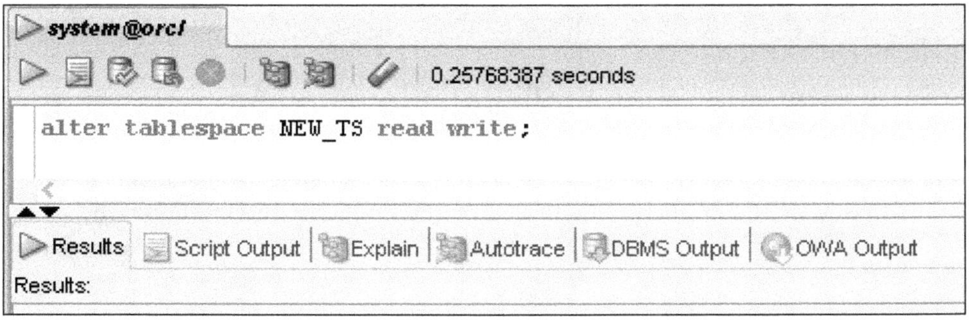
system@orcl
0.25768387 seconds
alter tablespace NEW_TS read write;
Results
Script Output
Explain
Autotrace
DBMS Output
OWA Output
Results:

Dropping a tablespace

When a tablespace is no longer needed, it can be dropped, removing it from the database. While the command is simple, certain factors must be considered before dropping a tablespace. First, let's look at the command itself:

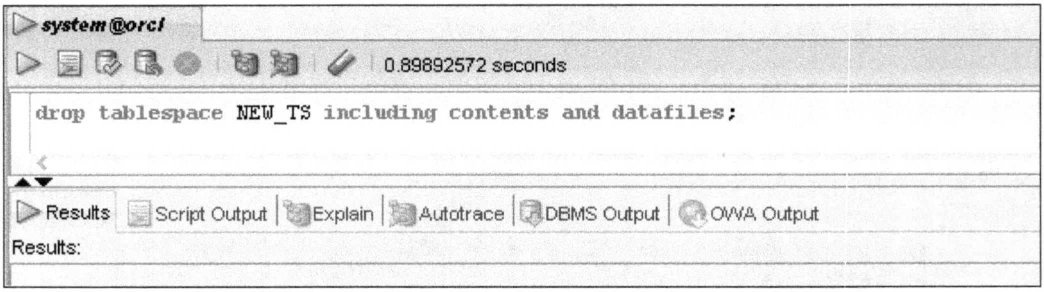
system@orcl
0.89892572 seconds
drop tablespace NEW_TS including contents and datafiles;
Results
Script Output
Explain
Autotrace
DBMS Output
OWA Output
Results:

We use the **drop tablespace** statement along with the **including contents and datafiles** clause to ensure that both the logical tablespace and the physical datafiles are removed at the same time. We can execute the `drop tablespace` statement without the additional clause but, while the tablespace will be dropped, its datafiles will continue to exist in the filesystem. This can be problematic for two reasons. First, when we drop a tablespace but not its datafiles, the datafiles are useless, yet no disk space is reclaimed. This can lead to space management issues at a later point. Second, if we attempt to recreate the tablespace using the same name for the datafile, we'll receive an error indicating that the filename is already in use. It is generally best to include both components of the statement when dropping a tablespace.

As we mentioned, we need to consider some other factors when dropping a tablespace. First, it is important that the objects within the tablespace are self-contained. What we mean by this is that the tablespace cannot contain objects, for instance, tables that are a part of a referential integrity relationship with other objects in another tablespace. For example, say our tablespace contains a table called TABLE_A that has a primary key that references a foreign key in another table, TABLE_B. If TABLE_B is stored in a different tablespace, it would be a parent/child key violation to remove TABLE_A and its primary key values by dropping the tablespace. Thus, this is not allowed and we would receive an error if we attempted to do so.

A second factor to consider is simply the safety issue of dropping an entire tablespace of objects with one command. It is important that we are aware of the impact of this. We have to ensure that we're not dropping unintended objects. Before dropping a tablespace, we may want to query the data dictionary to ensure that we're aware of all the objects that will be dropped with this command. An example query that we might use is as follows:

```
select segment_name from dba_segments
where tablespace_name = 'NEW_TS';
```

As we have dropped our example tablespace, let's create another one for future examples before we leave this subject. We will use this `COMPANYLINK` tablespace to store the database objects for our fictional `Companylink` database at a future point, as shown in the following screenshot:

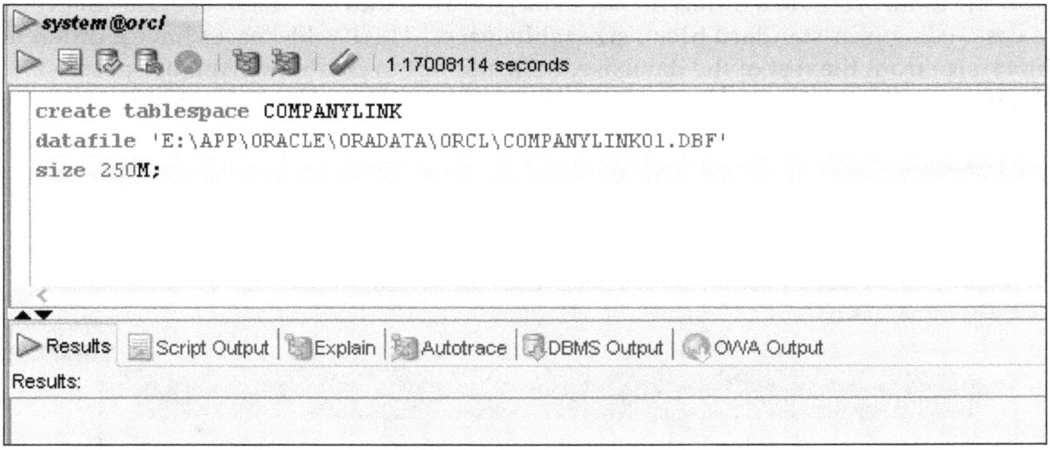
system@orcl
1.17008114 seconds
create tablespace COMPANYLINK
datafile 'E:\APP\ORACLE\ORADATA\ORCL\COMPANYLINK01.DBF'
size 250M;
Results
Script Output
Explain
Autotrace
DBMS Output
OWA Output
Results:

Using advanced tablespace management techniques

While the previous section covered the necessary basics for managing tablespaces, there are a few advanced topics that are important as well. While these techniques are not always needed in every database, they extend the basic functionality of Oracle space management in new and useful ways.

Using non-standard block size tablespaces

If we recall our earlier discussion of database block sizes, we presented a spectrum of block sizes and their applications. We said that certain types of databases can benefit from small block sizes, while others perform the best with larger sizes. While it is useful to be able to select from several different database block sizes when we create the database, the choice we make leaves us with certain limitations. Let's say, for instance, that we have a database that stores relatively typical data that best fits into the hybrid database category. We can be generally satisfied with the choice of an 8K block size to store this data. But let's say that we receive a requirement to add new tables, some of which store binary data, such as JPEG images. Because data such as this is considerably larger than typical character data, we may benefit from using a larger block size, at least with respect to these tables. But our database block size is already set at 8K and can't be changed without rebuilding the database. Can anything be done to incorporate a different block size, say 16K, into our database? The answer is yes—using **non-standard block size tablespaces**. These tablespaces have a different block size from the rest of the database. Let's attempt to create such a tablespace. We type a `CREATE TABLESPACE` command that uses the keyword `blocksize`:

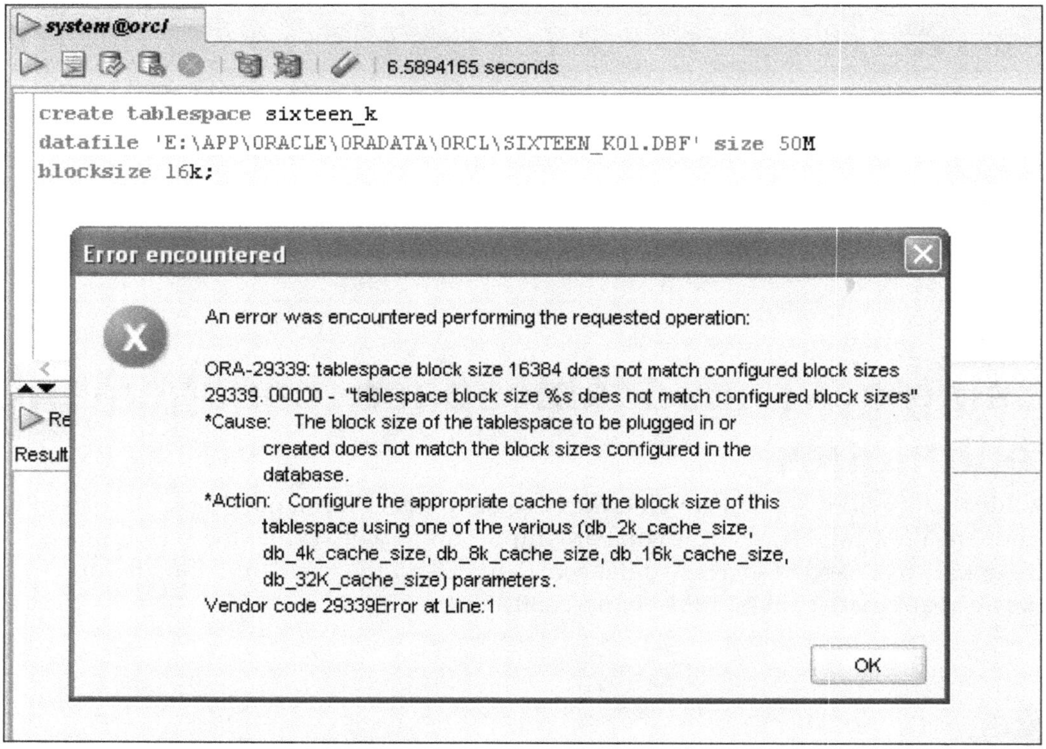
system@orcl
6.5894165 seconds
create tablespace sixteen_k
datafile 'E:\APP\ORACLE\ORADATA\ORCL\SIXTEEN_K01.DBF' size 50M
blocksize 16k;
Error encountered
An error was encountered performing the requested operation:
ORA-29339: tablespace block size 16384 does not match configured block sizes
29339. 00000 - "tablespace block size %s does not match configured block sizes"
*Cause: The block size of the tablespace to be plugged in or created does not match the block sizes configured in the database.
*Action: Configure the appropriate cache for the block size of this tablespace using one of the various (db_2k_cache_size, db_4k_cache_size, db_8k_cache_size, db_16k_cache_size, db_32K_cache_size) parameters.
Vendor code 29339Error at Line:1
OK
Result

Clearly, we enter the command and receive an error, but the error may not be what we might expect. In short, it says that *the tablespace block size does not match configured block sizes*. It also indicates that we could configure an appropriate cache. Why would we need to do this?

Recall our discussion of the Oracle memory caches, particularly the database buffer cache. We said that the buffer cache holds buffers. Database block buffers are essentially locations in memory that hold database blocks. Each buffer is sized to hold exactly one database block—no more, no less. In our case, our block size is 8K, so each of our buffers is also 8K. What this error is telling us is that Oracle cannot create a 16K block size tablespace because no buffers exist that can store 16K blocks. We can, however—as the advice in the error message indicates—create a secondary database buffer cache that *can* store 16K blocks. In fact, we can create tablespaces within a database with an 8K block size that are composed of 2K, 4K, 16K, and 32K blocks, provided that we create caches that can store blocks of those sizes. To do this, we'll need to modify some memory parameters to make room for the secondary cache. Let's open a SQL*Plus window and check the current size of our buffer cache as follows:

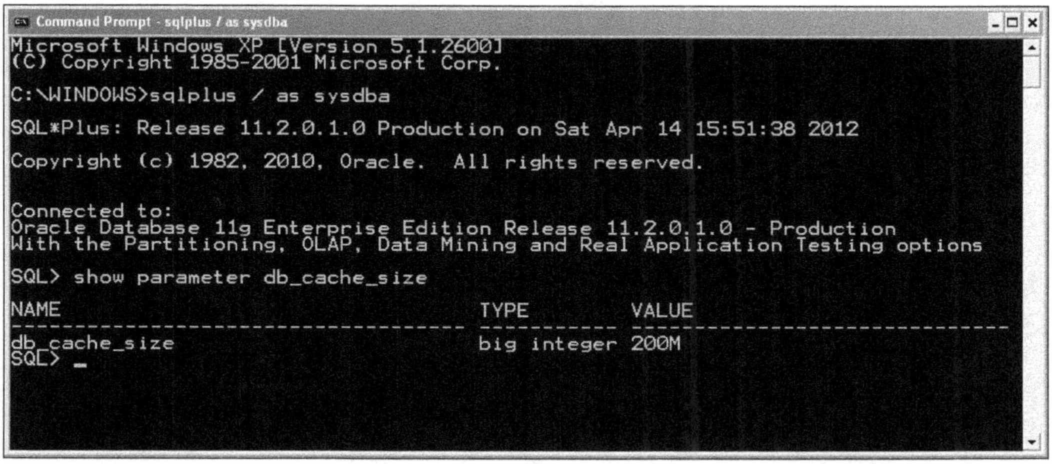
Command Prompt - sqlplus / as sysdba
Microsoft Windows XP [Version 5.1.2600]
(C) Copyright 1985-2001 Microsoft Corp.
C:\WINDOWS>sqlplus / as sysdba
SQL*Plus: Release 11.2.0.1.0 Production on Sat Apr 14 15:51:38 2012
Copyright (c) 1982, 2010, Oracle. All rights reserved.
Connected to:
Oracle Database 11g Enterprise Edition Release 11.2.0.1.0 - Production
With the Partitioning, OLAP, Data Mining and Real Application Testing options
SQL> show parameter db_cache_size
NAME TYPE VALUE
db_cache_size big integer 200M
SQL> _

We see that our database buffer cache is 200 M, as indicated by our **db_cache_size** parameter. We need to allocate additional memory for our 16K block size cache. Let's say we need 45 M for this cache, so we'll reduce the `db_cache_size` parameter by 50 M, just to make sure. We dynamically change this parameter to a value of 150 M as follows:

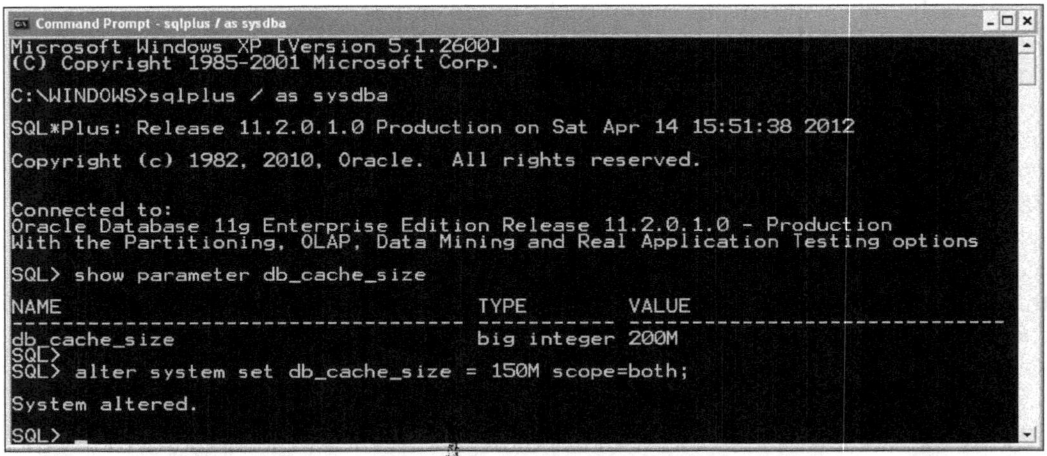

```
Command Prompt - sqlplus / as sysdba
Microsoft Windows XP [Version 5.1.2600]
(C) Copyright 1985-2001 Microsoft Corp.

C:\WINDOWS>sqlplus / as sysdba

SQL*Plus: Release 11.2.0.1.0 Production on Sat Apr 14 15:51:38 2012

Copyright (c) 1982, 2010, Oracle.  All rights reserved.


Connected to:
Oracle Database 11g Enterprise Edition Release 11.2.0.1.0 - Production
With the Partitioning, OLAP, Data Mining and Real Application Testing options

SQL> show parameter db_cache_size

NAME                                 TYPE        VALUE
------------------------------------ ----------- ------------------------------
db_cache_size                        big integer 200M
SQL>
SQL> alter system set db_cache_size = 150M scope=both;

System altered.

SQL> _
```

Next, we create the 16K block size cache, using the `db_16k_cache_size` parameter. This parameter allocates a cache for 16K blocks that is separate from the database buffer cache as follows:

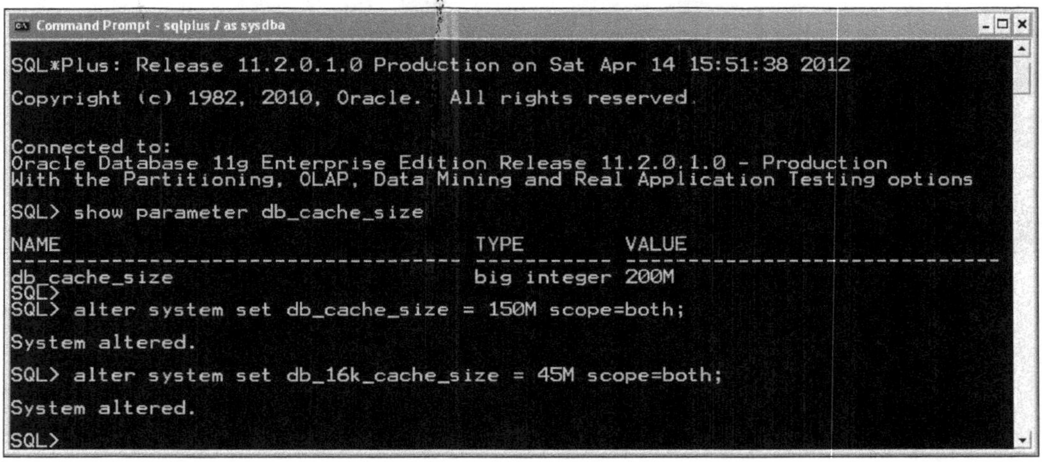

```
Command Prompt - sqlplus / as sysdba

SQL*Plus: Release 11.2.0.1.0 Production on Sat Apr 14 15:51:38 2012

Copyright (c) 1982, 2010, Oracle.  All rights reserved.


Connected to:
Oracle Database 11g Enterprise Edition Release 11.2.0.1.0 - Production
With the Partitioning, OLAP, Data Mining and Real Application Testing options

SQL> show parameter db_cache_size

NAME                                 TYPE        VALUE
------------------------------------ ----------- ------------------------------
db_cache_size                        big integer 200M
SQL>
SQL> alter system set db_cache_size = 150M scope=both;

System altered.

SQL> alter system set db_16k_cache_size = 45M scope=both;

System altered.

SQL>
```

We've now configured our database with a cache that can accept 16K blocks. Let's try our `CREATE TABLESPACE` command in SQL Developer again, as shown in the following screenshot:

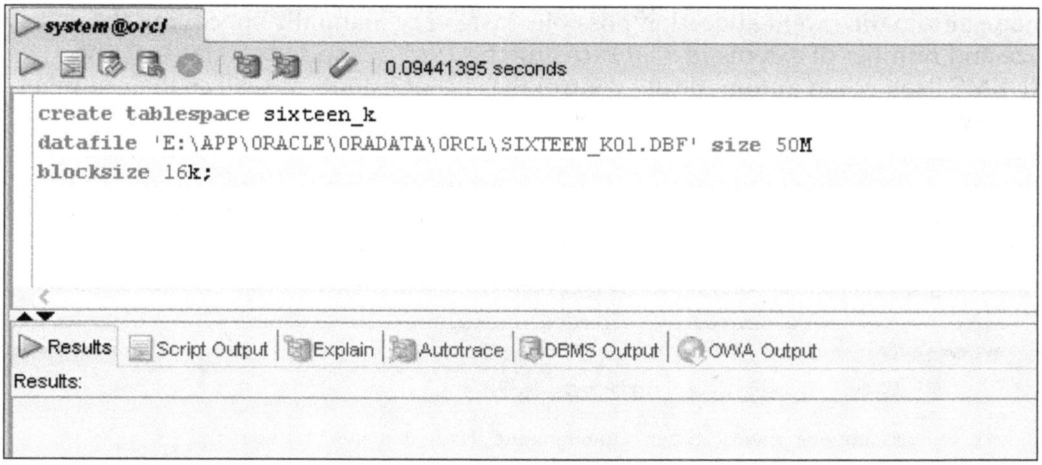
system@orcl
0.09441395 seconds
create tablespace sixteen_k
datafile 'E:\APP\ORACLE\ORADATA\ORCL\SIXTEEN_K01.DBF' size 50M
blocksize 16k;
Results
Script Output
Explain
Autotrace
DBMS Output
OWA Output
Results:

A tablespace has been created that can hold data segments with a block size of 16K.

Understanding locally managed tablespaces

If we recall from earlier in the chapter, we discussed a storage component of the Oracle database known as the extent, which is a collection of blocks. During the discussion, we mentioned that the subject of extent management is almost a non-issue with later versions of Oracle. This is due to the advent of a feature called **locally managed tablespaces**. In order to understand what makes these types of tablespaces unique, we must first review a little about the way those tablespaces *used* to be managed.

In versions of Oracle prior to Version 8*i*, all tablespaces were managed using a process known as dictionary managed tablespaces. With **dictionary managed tablespaces**, information about extents was stored in the base tables of the data dictionary. Over time, the data dictionary of a larger database could be required to hold massive amounts of data. In addition, DBAs were still required to manually size and maintain the extents of tables, demanding a significant amount of time.

With Version 8*i*, a new process was introduced, called locally managed tablespaces. With these new types of tablespaces, Oracle made two improvements at once. First, extent allocation information was stored as a bitmap within each datafile. In essence, each datafile "knew" about its own extents. Second, locally managed tablespaces made automatic extent allocation possible. Instead of manually specifying the size and number of extents in a table (using the `INITIAL` and `NEXT` clauses), the RDBMS itself could automatically control the size of extents as well as their number. Locally managed tablespaces were introduced in Version 8*i* and were used in a limited fashion in the first release of Version 9*i*, but were so successful that they were soon used almost universally throughout the database. Although we can still create dictionary managed tablespaces manually, in Version 11*g*, by default, every tablespace is automatically a locally managed tablespace. We can see this from the following query on the `dba_tablespaces` data dictionary view:

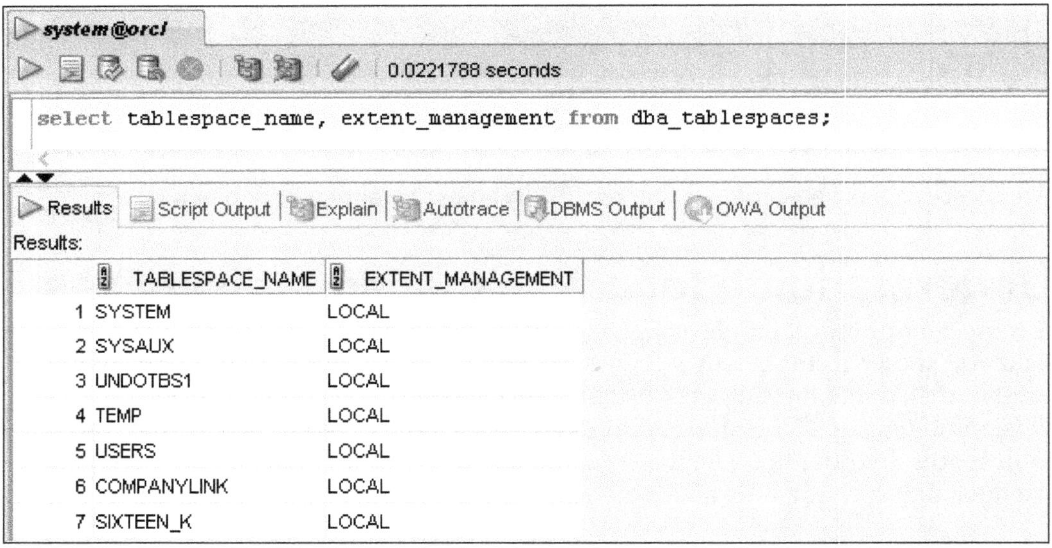
system@orcl
0.0221788 seconds
select tablespace_name, extent_management from dba_tablespaces;
Results
Script Output
Explain
Autotrace
DBMS Output
OWA Output
Results:
TABLESPACE_NAME
EXTENT_MANAGEMENT
1 SYSTEM LOCAL
2 SYSAUX LOCAL
3 UNDOTBS1 LOCAL
4 TEMP LOCAL
5 USERS LOCAL
6 COMPANYLINK LOCAL
7 SIXTEEN_K LOCAL

Locally managed tablespaces can be created with two options: `autoallocate` and `uniform size`. The `autoallocate` clause causes the tablespace to allocate extents automatically in the same manner that we've discussed and is the default. The `uniform size` clause gives us a little more control. While extent information is still stored in the bitmap of the datafile, we can directly control the size of the extent instead of giving control to the RDBMS. An example of creating a locally managed tablespace with uniform size is shown in the following screenshot. This statement creates a tablespace called `LOCAL` that is locally managed with a uniform extent size of 50K.

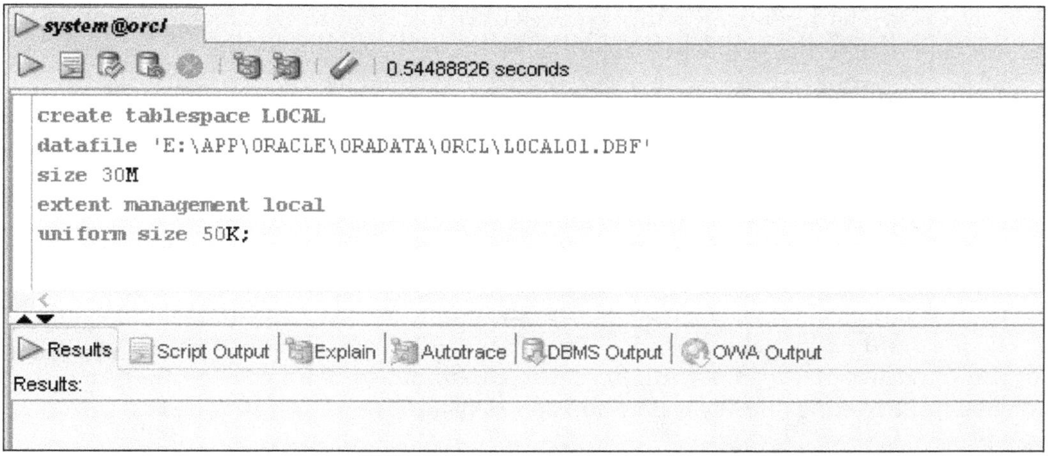
system@orcl
0.54488826 seconds
create tablespace LOCAL
datafile 'E:\APP\ORACLE\ORADATA\ORCL\LOCAL01.DBF'
size 30M
extent management local
uniform size 50K;
Results
Script Output
Explain
Autotrace
DBMS Output
OWA Output
Results:

Locally managed tablespaces also enable a feature called **Automatic Segment Space Management** (**ASSM**). ASSM is used to automatically manage the free space within blocks. Prior to ASSM, free space was managed using a construct known as a **freelist**. When a block possessed sufficient space to be available for more row data, that block was listed on a freelist. ASSM uses a much more efficient methodology, involving bitmaps to store information about free blocks. As a result, ASSM is the default space management mode for every tablespace except `SYSTEM`, `UNDO`, and temporary tablespaces.

Using Oracle Managed Files

One of the strengths of the Oracle RDBMS is its tremendous level of configurability. While some other RDBMS products take a fairly "black box" approach to their software that doesn't allow the DBA a great deal of control, Oracle allows the DBA to configure nearly every practical aspect of administration. However, even though Oracle allows a DBA to control many aspects of the database, we also have the option of releasing that control in order to ease the burden of certain administrative functions. We close this chapter by looking at **Oracle Managed Files** (**OMF**), one of the automation features of the Oracle RDBMS. With OMF, we can allow Oracle to control both the naming and sizing of datafiles that are created within the database. This can greatly simplify the process of creating tablespaces. Because, in our case, we want to maintain this control, we will simply step through the process here, rather than actually implementing OMF in our database.

Setting up OMF is a relatively simple process. We just need to set a few initialization parameters that define where our database files need to reside. The first is `db_create_file_dest`. This parameter defines the directory location we choose as a destination for our datafiles. The second is `db_create_online_log_dest_1`, which specifies the location of our redo logfiles. If we want to set up multiplexed redo logs, we can also specify additional redo log destinations with the `db_create_online_log_dest_2` parameter. We can define up to five destinations this way with the `db_create_online_log_dest_3` parameter, and so on. We can also use the `db_recovery_file_dest` parameter to designate a location for the archived redo logs and backup files. Thus, in its simplest form, OMF only requires setting two parameters, `db_create_file_dest` and `db_create_online_log_dest_1` in order to function. As an example for the Windows platform, we might set these parameters as follows in order to achieve multiplexing and file separation across disks:

```
db_create_file_dest = E:\APP\ORACLE\ORADATA\ORCL
db_create_online_log_dest_1 = E:\APP\ORACLE\ORADATA\ORCL\REDOLOG1
db_create_online_log_dest_2 = F:\APP\ORACLE\ORADATA\ORCL\REDOLOG2
db_recovery_file_dest = G:\APP\ORACLE\ORADATA\ORCL\RECOVERY
```

Now that we've defined the locations for these files, we no longer need to specify their locations and sizes when we create a tablespace. Take for example the following statement:

```
create tablespace TEST
datafile 'E:\APP\ORACLE\ORADATA\ORCL\TEST01.DBF'
size 100M;
```

With OMF it becomes:

```
create tablespace TEST;
```

Keep in mind that, when we implement OMF, it automatically controls both the naming and sizing of datafiles. It controls sizing by creating a datafile with `AUTOEXTEND ON` and extends the datafile as needed. It controls naming by creating a system-generated name based, in part, on the tablespace name. As a result, datafiles created by OMF often have non-descriptive names, such as `o1_mf_testtbs_4olzs_549_.dbf`.

> **The real-world DBA**
>
> Experienced DBAs sometimes have a certain reluctance to cede control of database functions to features like OMF. While automated features like OMF aren't necessarily appropriate for every database, such features shouldn't be dismissed without consideration. They can greatly reduce the amount of time spent doing basic, repetitive administration tasks. Regardless of your approach, the important thing is that Oracle allows you to "have it both ways."

Certification objectives covered

- Overview of tablespace and datafiles
- Creating and managing tablespaces
- Space-management in tablespaces

Summary

In this chapter, we've taken an in-depth look at space management in Oracle. We've examined blocks, extents, segments, and datafiles and seen how each is involved in managing data within the database. We've created and managed tablespaces and their respective datafiles. We've also examined some more advanced space management features of the Oracle RDBMS. We've seen how non-standard block size tablespaces can be used to more efficiently manage space. We explored locally managed tablespaces and automatic segment space management and saw the ways in which they can ease the burden of space administration. Finally, we've examined Oracle Managed Files and learned how OMF can simplify the creation of tablespaces.

In our next chapter, we will begin our examination of the various aspects of database administration—the types of activities that a DBA does on a day-to-day basis. We begin by examining startup and shutdown procedures, as well as exploring the data dictionary.

Test your knowledge

Q 1. Which of these block sizes cannot be used as the database block size for an Oracle database?

a. 1K
b. 2K
c. 16K
d. 32K

Q 2. Given a database with an 8 K block size, how many blocks must be read in order to return the results of a query that requests 100,000 rows that are 100 bytes in size?

a. 2
b. 14
c. 253
d. 1024

Q 3. Which of the following block sizes would be the best choice for a database used exclusively for data warehousing?

a. 1K
b. 2K
c. 12K
d. 16K

Q 4. Which of these units of data storage is a physical grouping of database blocks?

a. Table
b. Segment
c. Extent
d. Tablespace

Q 5. Which of these units of storage is the physical analogue of a table?

a. Block
b. Extent
c. Segment
d. Database

Q 6. Which of these statements will successfully create a tablespace?

a. `create tablespace test datafile "E:\test_area\test01.dbf" size 100M;`

b. `create tablespace test datafile 'E:\test_area\test01.dbf' size 100M;`

c. `create tablespace test datafile 'E:\test_area\test01.dbf';`

d. `create tablespace datafile 'E:\test_area\test01.dbf' size 100M;`

Q 7. Which of the following statements can be used to successfully retrieve the values for tablespace name, datafile name, and datafile size from the data dictionary?

a. `select tablespace_name, datafile_name, size from dba_data_files;`

b. `select tablespace_name, file_name, size from dba_data_files;`

c. `select tablespace_name, file_name, bytes from dba_data_files;`

d. `select tablespace_name, file_name, bytes from dba_tablespaces;`

Q 8. Which of the following commands can be used to change the size of a datafile?

a. `alter database datafile 'E:\test_area\test01.dbf' resize 125M;`

b. `alter database datafile 'E:\test_area\test01.dbf' size 125M;`

c. `alter tablespace datafile 'E:\test_area\test01.dbf' resize 125M;`

d. `alter datafile 'E:\test_area\test01.dbf' resize 125M;`

Q 9. Given a tablespace that contains a single datafile that is 1024 M in size and contains 782 M in segments, what is the smallest size to which the datafile can be reduced if all of the segments are removed?

a. 0 M

b. 782 M

c. 1025 M

d. Tablespace datafiles can never be reduced in size

Q 10. Which of the following commands can be used to add a datafile to an existing tablespace?

a. `alter tablespace test add datafile "E:\test_area\test02.dbf" size 50M;`

b. `alter datafile test01.dbf add datafile 'E:\test_area\test02.dbf' size 50M;`

c. `alter database add datafile 'E:\test_area\test02.dbf' size 50M to tablespace test;`

d. `alter tablespace test add datafile 'E:\test_area\test02.dbf' size 50M;`

Q 11. Which of the following commands can be used to make a datafile automatically extensible?

a. `alter datafile 8 autoextend;`

b. `alter datafile 8 autoextend on;`

c. `alter datafile 8 auto extend on;`

d. `alter datafile 8 automatically extend;`

Q 12. Which of the following commands will successfully remove a tablespace and its associated datafiles?

a. `drop tablespace test;`

b. `drop tablespace test all;`

c. `drop tablespace test including datafiles;`

d. `drop tablespace test including contents and datafiles;`

6
Managing the Oracle Instance

So far, much of what we've covered has been preparatory in nature. We've installed the Oracle software and created our first database. We've covered Oracle's use of storage, both physically with tablespaces and datafiles, and logically in the form of database objects. In this section of the book, we begin to examine the fundamentals of database administration, such as security, concurrency, networking, and performance. In this chapter, we cover the fundamentals of Oracle instance management. We'll look at startup and shutdown procedures. We'll examine database parameters and the data dictionary in greater depth. Finally, we'll explore gathering diagnostic information, patching, and using Oracle Support services.

In this chapter we will:

- Describe database startup and shutdown procedures
- Manage Oracle database parameters
- Explore the data dictionary
- Gather database diagnostic information
- Use Oracle Support services
- Understand the Oracle patching process

Understanding database startup and shutdown

One of the most fundamental operations in database administration is the ability to shut down and start up the database. However, this operation is considerably more involved than two simple commands. It is important to understand what happens "under the hood" during the process of starting and stopping an Oracle instance.

Understanding the startup process

To comprehend the startup process for the database, it is important to first understand the state of the database *before* it is started. Currently, our database has been started and is open—we've used it to run several queries in the previous chapters. This is because, at some point, either during the creation of the database using DBCA, or by Windows services, a `startup` command was issued to the database. However, before that command is issued, the database is in an inert state that is referred to as **cold**. In this state, we should understand several points about the instance and database. First, no memory has been allocated to the Oracle instance from the operating system. Second, no Oracle background processes are running on the database server itself. From what we learned in *Chapter 4, Examining the Oracle Architecture*, we recall that the Oracle instance consists of the memory caches and background processes that support Oracle. Thus, in a cold state, we can say that the instance has not started, and is down. Third, the datafiles that make up the database are not being used. Data is not being read from or written to them. This includes the datafiles that we have discussed; the control files, redo logfiles, archive logfiles, and tablespace datafiles. Before the startup process, we say that the database is not open; it is in a closed state.

When the `startup` command is issued, several important steps occur. The first stage is where the initialization parameter file is read. The parameter file—which we discussed briefly in *Chapter 3, Creating the Oracle Database*, and will explore further in this chapter—contains all of the configurable database parameters available to us. These parameters will determine the characteristics of our instance: the size of various memory caches, the number of background processes that will be spawned, the location of the control files, and much more. During this first stage, the instance is started. The memory caches, the sizes of which are determined by the database parameters in the parameter file, are allocated within the system memory on the server. In fact, if you are observing the server's memory usage during the instance startup, you will usually see a large jump in the amount of memory used. This is Oracle allocating the SGA and PGA to system memory.

Once this section of memory is allocated to Oracle, it is reserved for the SGA and PGA and cannot be used by other programs. Next, the background processes including PMON, SMON, DBWn, and others are spawned based on the configuration specified in the database parameters. Thus, if the `db_writer_processes` parameter is set to `4` in the initialization parameter file, four DBWn processes will be spawned. Once these operations have completed successfully, the database is in what is referred to as the NOMOUNT state.

The next stage of startup takes the database to the MOUNT state. During this stage, the control file is located and its existence is verified. If the control file is missing or corrupt, an error will be displayed at this point. As we recall from *Chapter 4, Examining the Oracle Architecture*, the control file is the "brain" of the database, in that it contains all the locations of the various datafiles, as well as such information as the current redo log sequence number and the System Change Number (SCN). This information is necessary in order to take the database to the next stage.

During the final stage of database startup, the information in the control file is used to locate and open the various database datafiles. If, for some reason, one of these datafiles is missing or damaged, the database will remain in the MOUNT state. Once every datafile has been located and opened, Oracle allows user sessions to connect to the database. The database is now in the OPEN state.

When the database is taken through the process of a shutdown, the process is essentially reversed. The database is first closed, meaning sessions are disconnected and datafiles are closed. In most cases of shutdown, active sessions are rolled back and any changed blocks in the SGA are flushed to disk. Then the database is dismounted and the control file is closed. Lastly, the instance is stopped. The background processes are terminated cleanly and any memory caches are released back to the operating system.

Controlling the startup and shutdown process

Now that we understand what occurs, we turn our attention to how a DBA can control the process of startup and shutdown. First, we need to understand how to establish a privileged connection.

Establishing a connection with SYSDBA privileges

For security reasons, not everyone has sufficient privileges to start and stop a database. Doing so requires a special level of access. First, we need to make a local connection to the database from the host server. Next, we need to make that connection using a special role that gives us the necessary privileges. There are two database roles that provide a DBA with the necessary privileges to control startup and shutdown—**SYSDBA** and **SYSOPER**.

> **The real-world DBA**
>
> Ordinarily, a user must actually be connected to the server that hosts the database in order to connect with this level of access. In short, remote administrative access is normally disallowed. This helps to prevent attackers on remote machines from connecting to the database. Remote administrative access, however, can be configured if needed.

The `SYSDBA` role grants the user the widest range of permissions possible on the Oracle database. With it, the user can create databases, manage startup and shutdown, and perform database backups and recoveries. The `SYSOPER` role is similar, although it does not allow the user to create databases or to create other `SYSDBA` and `SYSOPER` users. Normally, DBAs use the `SYSDBA` role for these operations. `SYSOPER` can be used in environments where it is necessary to separate job roles within DBA teams. Senior DBAs can be given the ability to become `SYSDBA` while junior DBAs might operate as `SYSOPER`. When we connect to the database as `SYSDBA` or `SYSOPER`, we must note that these are only roles—they are not users themselves. These roles must be explicitly granted to users. However, by default, there is one user that already possesses the `SYSDBA` role—the `SYS` user.

While we will learn how to create database users in the next chapter, we should understand that an Oracle database has two important users by default—`SYS` and `SYSTEM`. The `SYS` user is the highest administrative user that can connect to the database. It is comparable to the `root` user on Linux and Unix or the `Administrator` user on Windows. It has unlimited permissions within the database. A user that connects as `SYS` can see or modify any table in any schema and perform any administrative activity. In addition, `SYS` is the user that actually owns the data dictionary. All of the base tables and PL/SQL packages that form the data dictionary reside in the `SYS` schema. As such, `SYS` even has the power to directly modify the data dictionary tables—which should never be attempted. Most importantly for our purposes in this section, `SYS` has been granted the `SYSDBA` role. The `SYSTEM` user is the second highest user in the database in terms of access. Like `SYS`, the `SYSTEM` user has the ability to see or modify any table in any schema and perform any administrative activity.

However, since `SYSTEM` doesn't actually own the base data dictionary objects, it has been given indirect access to them through permissions. Additionally, by default, `SYSTEM` does not possess the `SYSDBA` role, preventing this user from starting and stopping the database.

From this information, we can deduce that, in order to start and stop the database, we'll need to connect as the `SYS` user. As we've seen, when we connect to the database, we provide a username and a password, as we've done when establishing a connection in SQL Developer. However, when starting and stopping the database, we're going to use the SQL*Plus tool instead. We can start SQL*Plus by invoking the `sqlplus` program from the command line, either in Windows or Unix/Linux. In general, we will be showing examples from an Oracle installation on Linux in this section, but the commands will be the same. From a command line, let's attempt to connect to the database as the `SYS` user with the password `oracle`, as we indicated when we created the database:

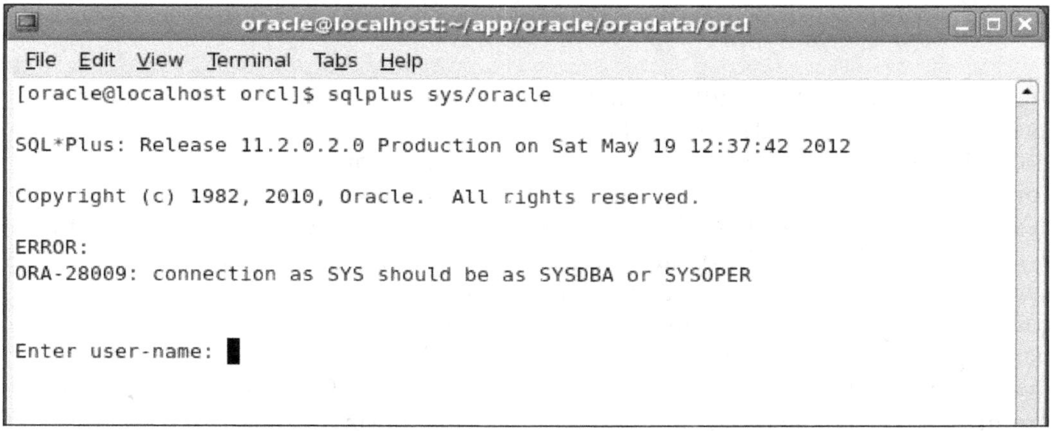
oracle@localhost:~/app/oracle/oradata/orcl
File Edit View Terminal Tabs Help
[oracle@localhost orcl]$ sqlplus sys/oracle
SQL*Plus: Release 11.2.0.2.0 Production on Sat May 19 12:37:42 2012
Copyright (c) 1982, 2010, Oracle. All rights reserved.
ERROR:
ORA-28009: connection as SYS should be as SYSDBA or SYSOPER
Enter user-name:

As we can see in the preceding screenshot, we receive an error message and are instructed to make any connections using `SYS` as `SYSDBA` or `SYSOPER`. We'll try this again, this time specifying the clause `as sysdba`:

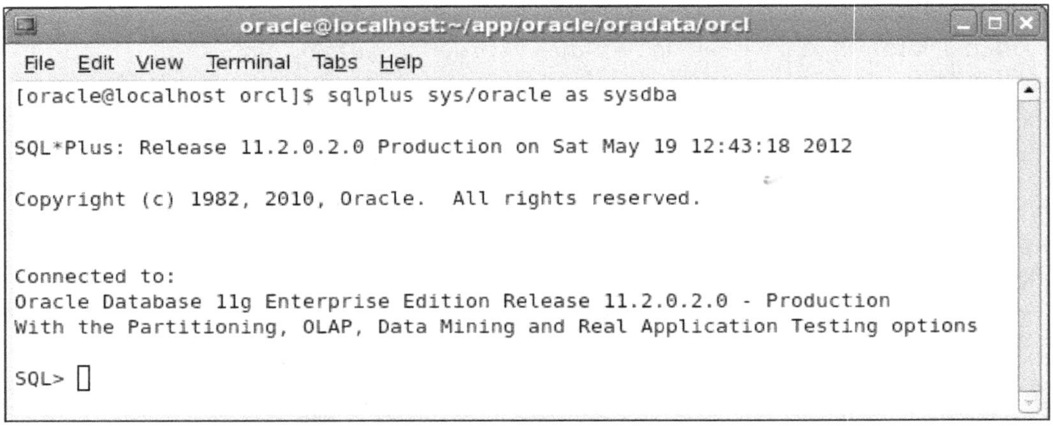
oracle@localhost:~/app/oracle/oradata/orcl
File Edit View Terminal Tabs Help
[oracle@localhost orcl]$ sqlplus sys/oracle as sysdba
SQL*Plus: Release 11.2.0.2.0 Production on Sat May 19 12:43:18 2012
Copyright (c) 1982, 2010, Oracle. All rights reserved.
Connected to:
Oracle Database 11g Enterprise Edition Release 11.2.0.2.0 - Production
With the Partitioning, OLAP, Data Mining and Real Application Testing options
SQL>

Our connection is successfully made. However, it might be interesting to note that, even though we connected using the password, `oracle`, it was not even necessary to do so. In fact, we could have used any password and would have been successfully connected. How could that be possible? It's possible because Oracle uses **operating system authentication**. This allows Oracle to authenticate our user using operating system credentials, not the database credentials that other users require. However, several conditions must apply in order for this to happen. First, the user we're connecting with, by default, must connect using the `SYSDBA` role. Second, since we're passing authentication rights back to the operating system, the operating system user being used must be a member of a certain OS group. For instance, in our Linux example, we've already logged on to the server that hosts the database using the `oracle` user. This is an operating system account, not a database account, and we used it to install the database software. One of the requirements during installation is that we specify an OS group for the installation user. On Linux and Unix, this group is normally called `dba`. Thus, we log in to the server using `oracle`, which is a member of the `dba` group.

When this is true, operating system authentication can occur and no password is necessary to connect to the database if we're using the `SYSDBA` role. On Windows, the process is similar. We log in to Windows using our OS user and install Oracle. During installation, the installer creates a Windows group called `ORA_DBA` and places the user in that group. When we connect with that user, operating system authentication can occur. Because of this, we can use a certain type of syntax to connect to the database that will make use of OS authentication. We've seen this before, but this will be the first time we've used it while being aware that we're invoking OS authentication. Understand that we can only use this if we're making a local connection to the database on the server where the database resides. The syntax is `sqlplus / as sysdba`, as shown in the following screenshot:

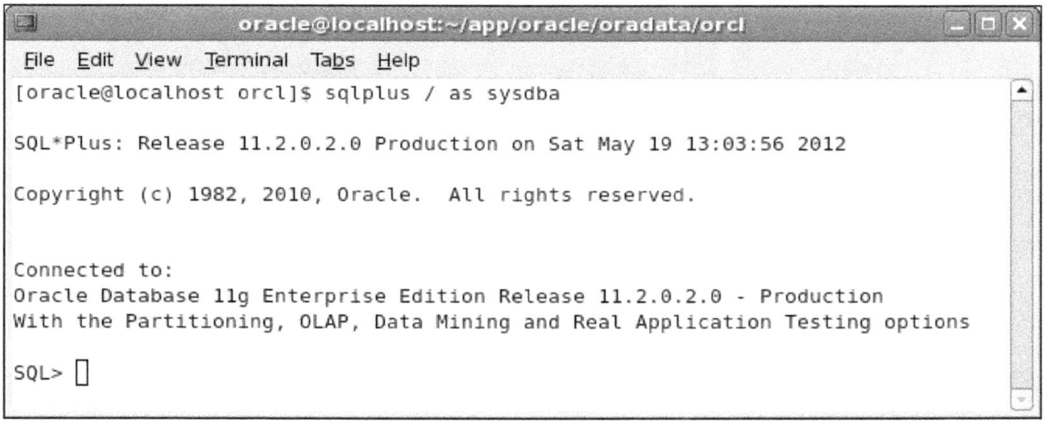
oracle@localhost:~/app/oracle/oradata/orcl
File Edit View Terminal Tabs Help
[oracle@localhost orcl]$ sqlplus / as sysdba
SQL*Plus: Release 11.2.0.2.0 Production on Sat May 19 13:03:56 2012
Copyright (c) 1982, 2010, Oracle. All rights reserved.
Connected to:
Oracle Database 11g Enterprise Edition Release 11.2.0.2.0 - Production
With the Partitioning, OLAP, Data Mining and Real Application Testing options
SQL>

Thus, we've essentially used an "empty" username and password, separated by a / to invoke OS authentication. This establishes the privileged connection we require in order to start and stop the database.

Controlling the database startup process

Now that we're connected, we can step through the process of starting the database. Ordinarily, we simply type the `startup` command and Oracle steps through the three stages—NOMOUNT, MOUNT, and OPEN. However, we can also choose to execute a startup directly to any of these stages and then stop. For instance, in the following example, we use the `startup nomount` command to take the database to the NOMOUNT state. Our database is already started, so we must first enter the `shutdown immediate` command, which we will cover shortly:

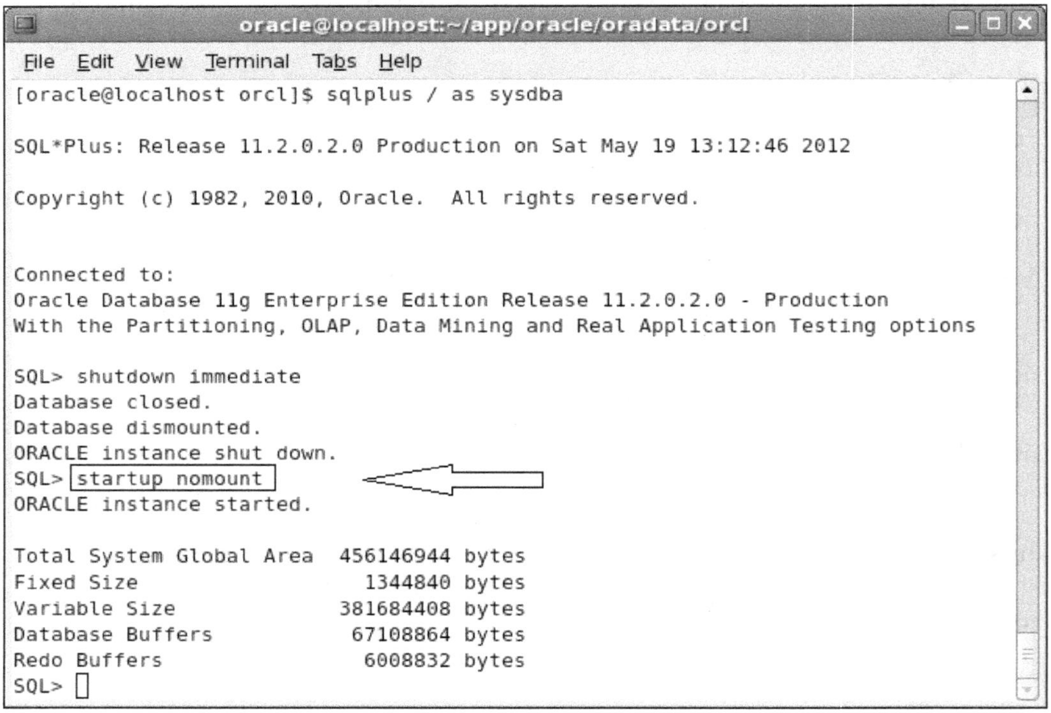
oracle@localhost:~/app/oracle/oradata/orcl
File Edit View Terminal Tabs Help
[oracle@localhost orcl]$ sqlplus / as sysdba
SQL*Plus: Release 11.2.0.2.0 Production on Sat May 19 13:12:46 2012
Copyright (c) 1982, 2010, Oracle. All rights reserved.
Connected to:
Oracle Database 11g Enterprise Edition Release 11.2.0.2.0 - Production
With the Partitioning, OLAP, Data Mining and Real Application Testing options
SQL> shutdown immediate
Database closed.
Database dismounted.
ORACLE instance shut down.
SQL> startup nomount
ORACLE instance started.
Total System Global Area 456146944 bytes
Fixed Size 1344840 bytes
Variable Size 381684408 bytes
Database Buffers 67108864 bytes
Redo Buffers 6008832 bytes
SQL>

Notice that we receive the message **ORACLE instance started**. This is consistent with what we've already learned about the startup process. During the NOMOUNT state, the instance is started and the background processes and memory caches are allocated. From the information at the bottom of the screenshot, we can see the specifics of how the SGA is allocated. However, in this state, we're only in NOMOUNT, so we need a way to continue to the MOUNT state. We use the `alter database mount` command, as shown in the next screenshot. Note that this is a SQL command, so in SQL*Plus the inclusion of the semicolon at the end of the statement is mandatory:

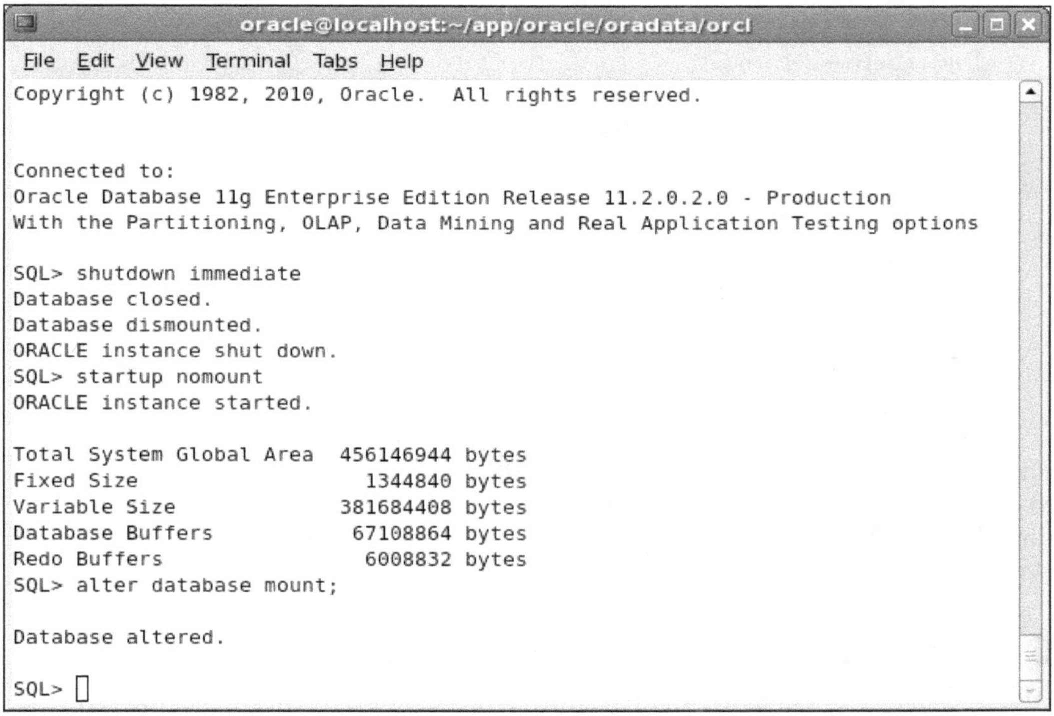
oracle@localhost:~/app/oracle/oradata/orcl
File Edit View Terminal Tabs Help
Copyright (c) 1982, 2010, Oracle. All rights reserved.
Connected to:
Oracle Database 11g Enterprise Edition Release 11.2.0.2.0 - Production
With the Partitioning, OLAP, Data Mining and Real Application Testing options
SQL> shutdown immediate
Database closed.
Database dismounted.
ORACLE instance shut down.
SQL> startup nomount
ORACLE instance started.
Total System Global Area 456146944 bytes
Fixed Size   1344840 bytes
Variable Size   381684408 bytes
Database Buffers   67108864 bytes
Redo Buffers   6008832 bytes
SQL> alter database mount;
Database altered.
SQL>

We're now in the MOUNT state. In order to completely open the database, we use a similar command. Let us see how this is done:

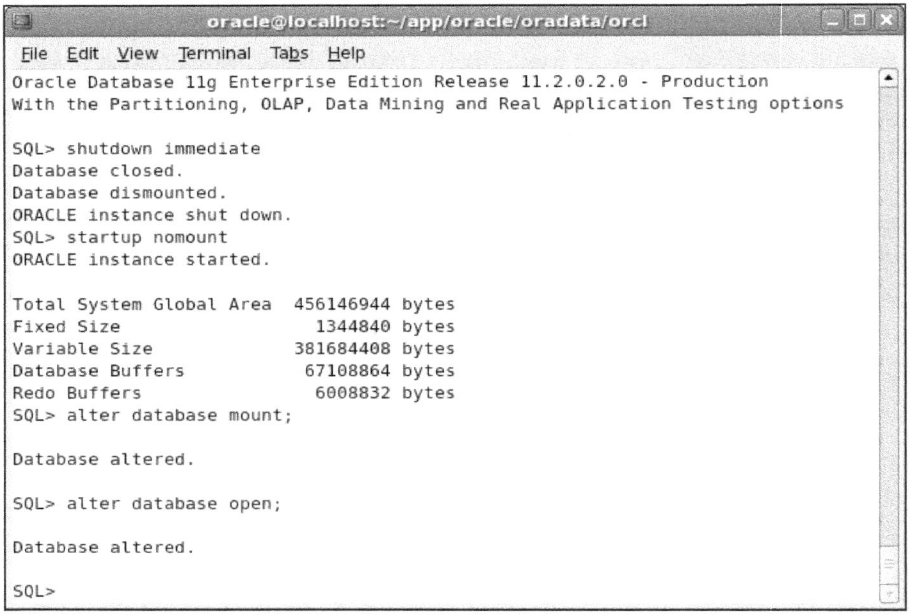
oracle@localhost:~/app/oracle/oradata/orcl
File Edit View Terminal Tabs Help

```
Oracle Database 11g Enterprise Edition Release 11.2.0.2.0 - Production
With the Partitioning, OLAP, Data Mining and Real Application Testing options

SQL> shutdown immediate
Database closed.
Database dismounted.
ORACLE instance shut down.
SQL> startup nomount
ORACLE instance started.

Total System Global Area  456146944 bytes
Fixed Size                  1344840 bytes
Variable Size             381684408 bytes
Database Buffers           67108864 bytes
Redo Buffers                6008832 bytes
SQL> alter database mount;

Database altered.

SQL> alter database open;

Database altered.

SQL>
```

The database is now in a fully OPEN state. Although we used our `startup` command to go to the NOMOUNT stage, we can also use the `startup mount` command to go directly to the MOUNT state, or the `startup` command by itself to go through all three stages and open the database with one command.

Controlling the database shutdown process

Although we've not discussed it, we've already used the `shutdown immediate` command to stop the database. As we've mentioned, during database shutdown, the database is closed and dismounted. Then, the instance is released. We can use the following commands to close and dismount the database:

```
alter database close;
alter database dismount;
```

However, ordinarily, DBAs don't need to control the shutdown process in the same way that they do the startup process. Instead, the process of controlling a shutdown is more dependent on the conditions under which the shutdown occurs. There are several types of `shutdown` commands available to us, although only one of them is the preferred method.

The default method for shutdown is the `shutdown normal` or `shutdown` command. During a shutdown initiated using this command, no new connections to the database are allowed. Current connections are allowed to remain connected. In fact, all users must explicitly log off their current sessions in order for the shutdown to commence. During an emergency situation or even scheduled maintenance, this can be problematic to say the least. Ordinarily, a DBA cannot wait for every user to voluntarily log off. Additionally, any software agents or monitoring tools that connect to the database must be explicitly stopped as well. Thus, although this default method for shutdown is the safest from a user perspective, it is not typically used. The following example shows a `shutdown` command that is hung:

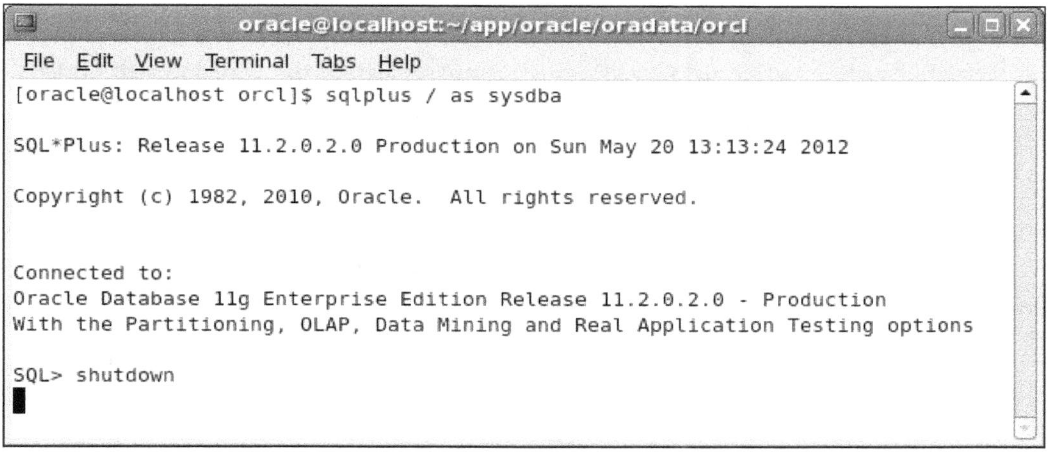
oracle@localhost:~/app/oracle/oradata/orcl
File Edit View Terminal Tabs Help
[oracle@localhost orcl]$ sqlplus / as sysdba
SQL*Plus: Release 11.2.0.2.0 Production on Sun May 20 13:13:24 2012
Copyright (c) 1982, 2010, Oracle. All rights reserved.
Connected to:
Oracle Database 11g Enterprise Edition Release 11.2.0.2.0 - Production
With the Partitioning, OLAP, Data Mining and Real Application Testing options
SQL> shutdown

During a `shutdown transactional` command, no new users are allowed to connect, and any existing sessions that are idle are terminated. However, any sessions that are actively involved in a running transaction will be allowed to complete. While this is more conducive to the shutdown process from the DBA's perspective, it can still affect the ability to properly complete scheduled maintenance activities. Any long-running transaction can prevent the DBA from stopping the database for maintenance. In fact, a simple `INSERT` statement that has not committed will not allow the shutdown to commence. For this reason, `shutdown transactional` is not commonly used, although it is available should the situation require it.

The most commonly used `shutdown` command is the one we've already seen—`shutdown immediate`. During this command, no new sessions are allowed and any idle sessions are disconnected. Additionally, any active sessions are immediately rolled back and the database begins the close and dismount process. Using the `shutdown immediate` command ensures that the process of stopping the database will execute in a timely fashion.

The last type of `shutdown` command is one that we want to use as little as possible. When a DBA executes a `shutdown abort` command, the instance itself is immediately terminated. All sessions are terminated without rolling back. No checkpointing occurs and no dirty buffers are flushed to disk. A `shutdown abort` command is considered a hard crash and will require the SMON process to execute instance recovery during the next startup. Nevertheless, it would be wrong to call it a dangerous command, since instance recovery will restore the database to its previous state. Still, it should be used as a last resort only after `shutdown immediate` has failed.

Controlling startup and shutdown on Windows platforms

To close this section, we should make a few points regarding the way startups and shutdowns are handled on Oracle installations on Windows. We looked at Oracle services on Windows in *Chapter 3, Creating the Oracle Database*. First and foremost, we must remember that in order to start an Oracle database on Windows, the service for that database must be started. The database service itself will be named `OracleService<SID>`, where `SID` is the name of the database. In our case, the service will be `OracleServiceORCL`, since `ORCL` is the name of our database. This service is essentially the pipeline by which Oracle talks to shared memory in the operating system. By default, this service is set to automatically start the database whenever the service starts. The `oradim` command can be used to change this behavior if so desired. We should also note that shutting down the database does not shut down the service. Provided the service is up and running properly, we can take the database up and down repeatedly without affecting the service. However, if we stop the `OracleServiceORCL` service, the database will be shut down as well. If attempt to login to a database on Windows on which the service is not running, we will receive the following error:

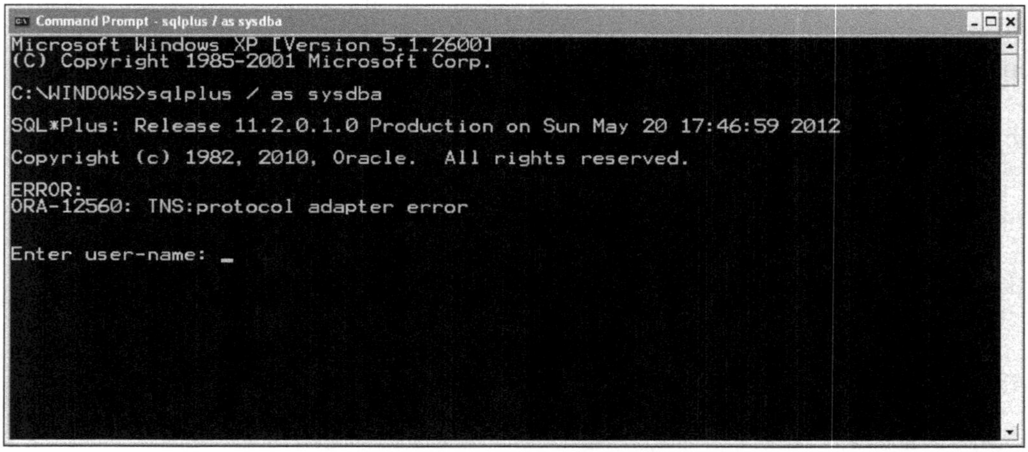
Command Prompt - sqlplus / as sysdba
Microsoft Windows XP [Version 5.1.2600]
(C) Copyright 1985-2001 Microsoft Corp.
C:\WINDOWS>sqlplus / as sysdba
SQL*Plus: Release 11.2.0.1.0 Production on Sun May 20 17:46:59 2012
Copyright (c) 1982, 2010, Oracle. All rights reserved.
ERROR:
ORA-12560: TNS:protocol adapter error
Enter user-name:

Setting database initialization parameters

In *Chapter 3, Creating the Oracle Database,* we introduced the concept of database initialization parameters. We said that these parameters can be used to control nearly every aspect of database operations. In this section, we examine the concept of the parameter file and learn how to change initialization parameters.

Understanding the PFILE and SPFILE

During the process of creating our database in *Chapter 3, Creating the Oracle Database,* we were presented with the following screen:

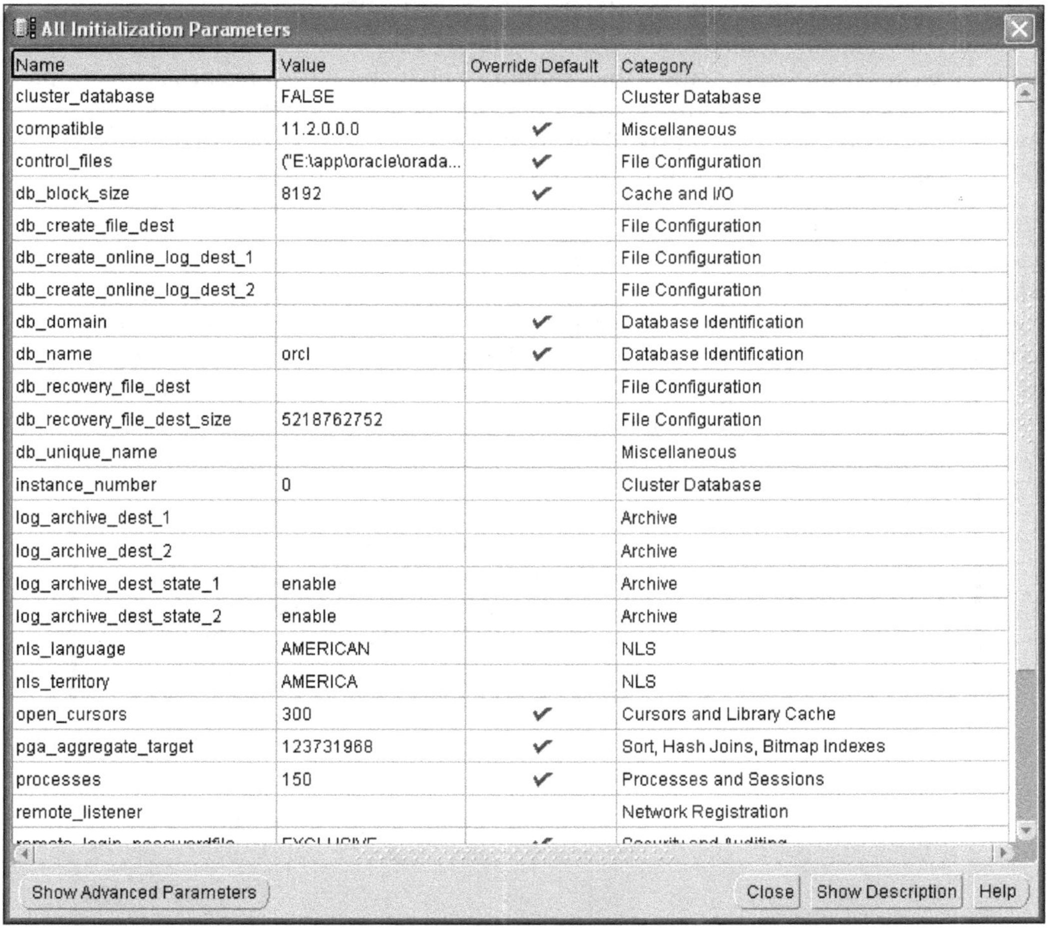
All Initialization Parameters
Name | Value | Override Default | Category
cluster_database | FALSE | | Cluster Database
compatible | 11.2.0.0.0 | ✔ | Miscellaneous
control_files | ("E:\app\oracle\orada... | ✔ | File Configuration
db_block_size | 8192 | ✔ | Cache and I/O
db_create_file_dest | | | File Configuration
db_create_online_log_dest_1 | | | File Configuration
db_create_online_log_dest_2 | | | File Configuration
db_domain | | ✔ | Database Identification
db_name | orcl | ✔ | Database Identification
db_recovery_file_dest | | | File Configuration
db_recovery_file_dest_size | 5218762752 | | File Configuration
db_unique_name | | | Miscellaneous
instance_number | 0 | | Cluster Database
log_archive_dest_1 | | | Archive
log_archive_dest_2 | | | Archive
log_archive_dest_state_1 | enable | | Archive
log_archive_dest_state_2 | enable | | Archive
nls_language | AMERICAN | | NLS
nls_territory | AMERICA | | NLS
open_cursors | 300 | ✔ | Cursors and Library Cache
pga_aggregate_target | 123731968 | ✔ | Sort, Hash Joins, Bitmap Indexes
processes | 150 | ✔ | Processes and Sessions
remote_listener | | | Network Registration
Show Advanced Parameters
Close
Show Description
Help

As the title of this window, **All Initialization Parameters**, would suggest, we use this screen to define the initialization parameters that control the inner-workings of the database. Although it happened without our knowledge at the time, these parameters, including any changes we made, were written out to a file called a **parameter file**. This is the file that holds all of the individual parameters that control our database. There are two types of parameter files available to us, and one is greatly preferred with current versions of Oracle.

The **initialization parameter file**, or **PFILE**, is a text file that records database parameters. As we mentioned earlier in the chapter, during startup of the database prior to the NOMOUNT state, the parameter file is read. In the case of the initialization parameter file, those plain text parameters are read only during startup. Changing one of the values has no effect until the database is started again and the parameters are re-read. Thus, starting a database instance using a PFILE means that the parameters themselves are completely static—they cannot be changed with a restart. An example of a PFILE is shown later in this section. Prior to Oracle Version 9*i*, this was the only way to make parameter corrections in the database. Every change required the database to be shut down and restarted.

With the advent of Oracle 9*i*, this paradigm was changed for the better. The **server parameter file**, or **SPFILE**, was introduced in order to allow DBAs to alter parameters while the database is still operating, negating the need for a restart. The SPFILE is not a simple text file—it is a binary file stored on the database server that is structured so that only the Oracle kernel can read and change it. It is read into memory during startup and is maintained there until the database is shut down. Since its contents exist in memory, many of the parameters can be changed.

> **The real-world DBA**
>
> In truth, the SPFILE can be read by most text editors. If you open it with one, you'll actually be able to make out some of the parameters, although they'll be somewhat disorganized and padded with non-printable characters. However, you should never change the parameters of an SPFILE with a text editor. It will result in a corrupted SPFILE that cannot be read by Oracle.

Working with the PFILE and SPFILE

The default location of both the PFILE and SPFILE on a Windows installation is `$ORACLE_HOME/database`, which means the `database` directory within the Oracle Home directory that we specified during database creation. On Linux, the default directory is `$ORACLE_HOME/dbs`. Our previous Windows example in *Chapter 2, Installing the Oracle Database Software*, used the following directory, although yours may be different:

```
E:\app\username\product\11.2.0\dbhome_1
```

Within that directory is the `database` directory. This directory contains several files, but at this point we are concerned only with the **SPFILEORCL.ORA** file, which is shown in the next screenshot. This is the server parameter file for our `ORCL` database. On a Linux installation, a similarly named file would be found in `$ORACLE_HOME/dbs`:

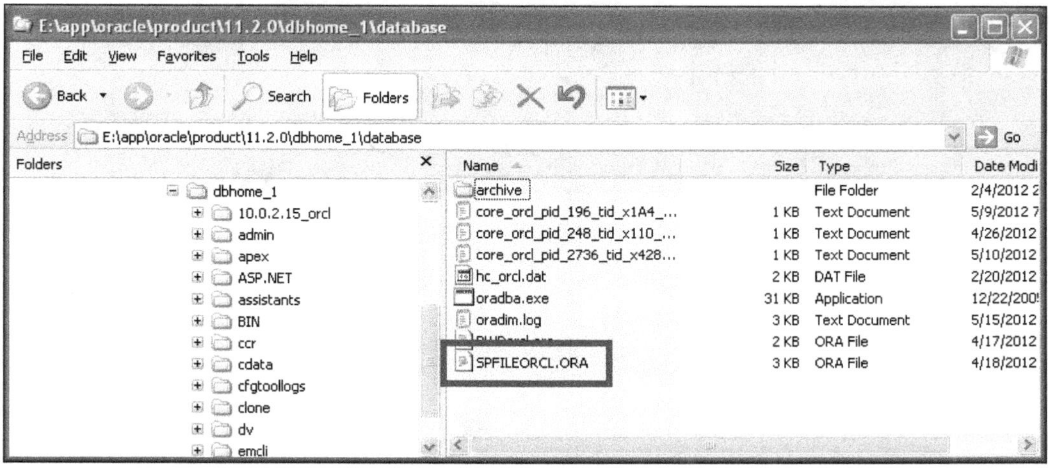
E:\app\oracle\product\11.2.0\dbhome_1\database
File Edit View Favorites Tools Help
Back Search Folders
Address E:\app\oracle\product\11.2.0\dbhome_1\database
Go
Folders
dbhome_1
10.0.2.15_orcl
admin
apex
ASP.NET
assistants
BIN
ccr
cdata
cfgtoollogs
clone
dv
emcli
Name Size Type Date Modi
archive File Folder 2/4/2012
core_orcl_pid_196_tid_x1A4_... 1 KB Text Document 5/9/2012
core_orcl_pid_248_tid_x110_... 1 KB Text Document 4/26/2012
core_orcl_pid_2736_tid_x428... 1 KB Text Document 5/10/2012
hc_orcl.dat 2 KB DAT File 2/20/2012
oradba.exe 31 KB Application 12/22/200
oradim.log 3 KB Text Document 5/15/2012
2 KB ORA File 4/17/2012
SPFILEORCL.ORA 3 KB ORA File 4/18/2012

At this point, we don't have a PFILE, since the DBCA tool only creates an SPFILE. Although the use of an SPFILE is greatly preferred because of its ability to change parameters dynamically, it is sometimes useful to be able to view our parameters in text form. It is not recommended that we open the SPFILE manually, but we can create a PFILE from our existing SPFILE from SQL*Plus using the `create pfile` command as shown in the following screenshot:

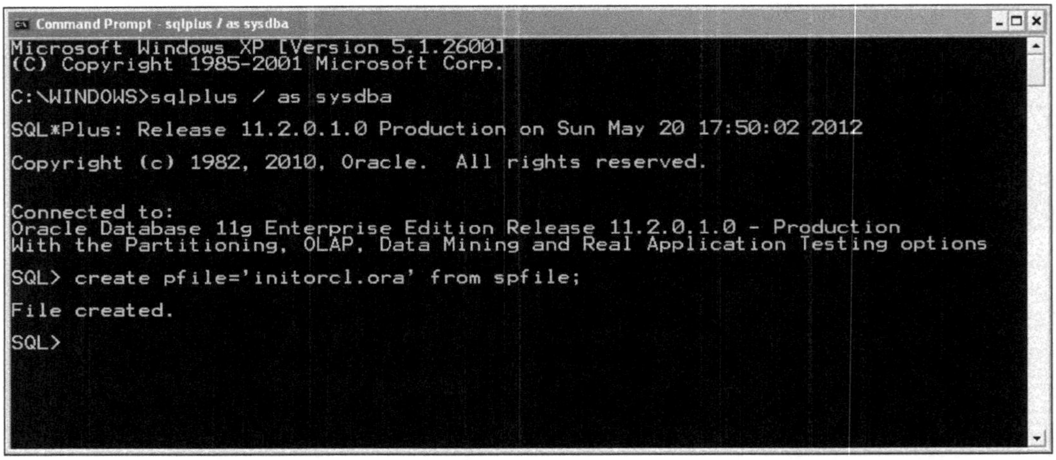
Command Prompt - sqlplus / as sysdba
Microsoft Windows XP [Version 5.1.2600]
(C) Copyright 1985-2001 Microsoft Corp.
C:\WINDOWS>sqlplus / as sysdba
SQL*Plus: Release 11.2.0.1.0 Production on Sun May 20 17:50:02 2012
Copyright (c) 1982, 2010, Oracle. All rights reserved.
Connected to:
Oracle Database 11g Enterprise Edition Release 11.2.0.1.0 - Production
With the Partitioning, OLAP, Data Mining and Real Application Testing options
SQL> create pfile='initorcl.ora' from spfile;
File created.
SQL>

If we return to our `$ORACLE_HOME/database` directory, we see that the `initorcl.ora` file is now present:

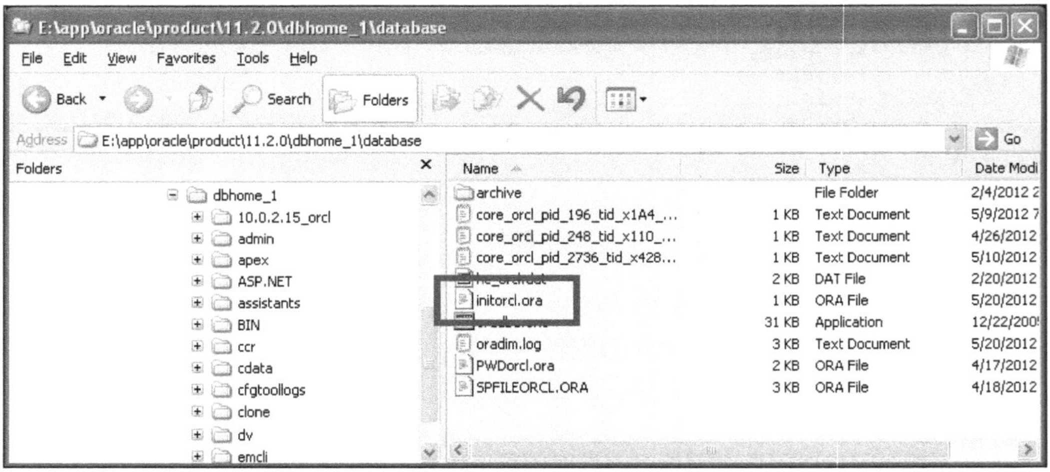
E:\app\oracle\product\11.2.0\dbhome_1\database
File Edit View Favorites Tools Help
Back
Search
Folders
Address E:\app\oracle\product\11.2.0\dbhome_1\database
Go
Folders
dbhome_1
10.0.2.15_orcl
admin
apex
ASP.NET
assistants
BIN
ccr
cdata
cfgtoollogs
clone
dv
emcli
Name
Size
Type
Date Modi
archive
File Folder
2/4/2012
core_orcl_pid_196_tid_x1A4_...
1 KB
Text Document
5/9/2012
core_orcl_pid_248_tid_x110_...
1 KB
Text Document
4/26/2012
core_orcl_pid_2736_tid_x428...
1 KB
Text Document
5/10/2012
2 KB
DAT File
2/20/2012
initorcl.ora
1 KB
ORA File
5/20/2012
31 KB
Application
oradim.log
3 KB
Text Document
5/20/2012
PWDorcl.ora
2 KB
ORA File
4/17/2012
SPFILEORCL.ORA
3 KB
ORA File
4/18/2012

If we open it, we can see the parameters it contains. Both the PFILE and SPFILE only contain parameters with non-default values. If a parameter is not mentioned, the default value is used. We can also do the reverse and create an SPFILE from a PFILE. Doing so allows us to manually edit the PFILE and read those changes into an SPFILE. By default, Oracle looks for an SPFILE in the default directory first. If the SPFILE is not present, it looks for a PFILE for the given database SID. Thus, the choice of which type of file to use is dependent on which file we place in this directory. Both of the types will never be read together:

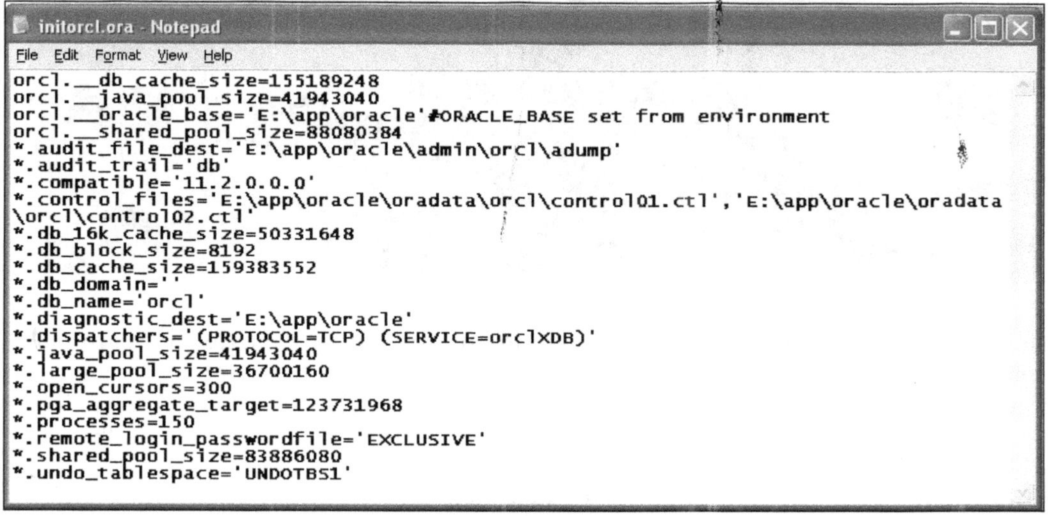
initorcl.ora - Notepad

File Edit Format View Help

```
orcl.__db_cache_size=155189248
orcl.__java_pool_size=41943040
orcl.__oracle_base='E:\app\oracle'#ORACLE_BASE set from environment
orcl.__shared_pool_size=88080384
*.audit_file_dest='E:\app\oracle\admin\orcl\adump'
*.audit_trail='db'
*.compatible='11.2.0.0.0'
*.control_files='E:\app\oracle\oradata\orcl\control01.ctl','E:\app\oracle\oradata
\orcl\control02.ctl'
*.db_16k_cache_size=50331648
*.db_block_size=8192
*.db_cache_size=159383552
*.db_domain=''
*.db_name='orcl'
*.diagnostic_dest='E:\app\oracle'
*.dispatchers='(PROTOCOL=TCP) (SERVICE=orclXDB)'
*.java_pool_size=41943040
*.large_pool_size=36700160
*.open_cursors=300
*.pga_aggregate_target=123731968
*.processes=150
*.remote_login_passwordfile='EXCLUSIVE'
*.shared_pool_size=83886080
*.undo_tablespace='UNDOTBS1'
```

> **The real-world DBA**
>
> If we have determined that the SPFILE is the preferred method, why will we ever need a PFILE? It is useful to store a PFILE copy of an SPFILE in case the SPFILE is ever corrupted or lost.

In the preceding example, we can see several parameters that we have already discussed, such as `db_cache_size` and `pga_aggregate_target`. Others we have not discussed, but their purpose should be evident, such as `db_name`. Many other parameters, however, appear to be quite a mystery. Additionally, the ones shown here are only the parameters that have non-default values; in total, there are hundreds of database parameters in Oracle. However, it is important to understand that, while a working knowledge of the purposes of some parameters is important, it is not necessary for a DBA, even an experienced one, to completely understand every parameter. If we have started the database with an SPFILE, we can also display our parameters by querying the `v$spparameter` view.

We mentioned that using an SPFILE allows us to change many database parameters dynamically. To do so, we log in to command-line SQL*Plus and use the command shown in the following screenshot:

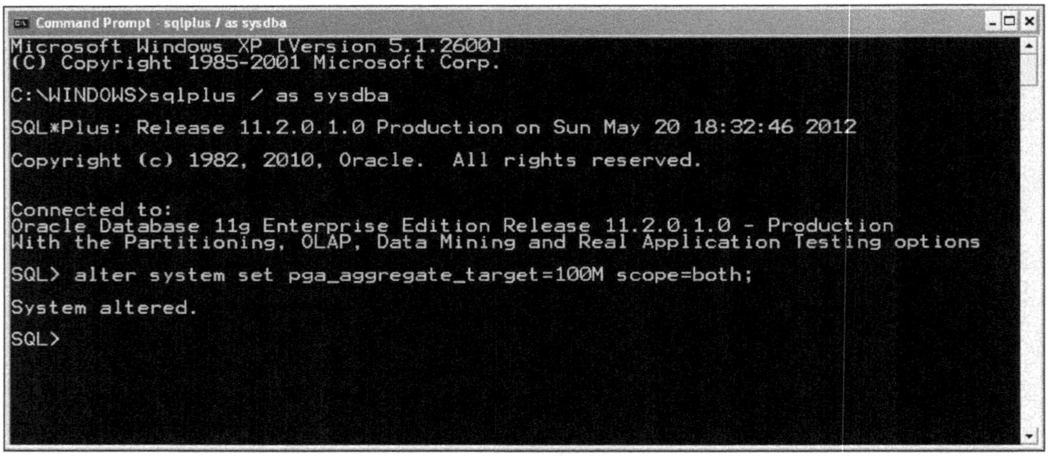
Command Prompt - sqlplus / as sysdba
Microsoft Windows XP [Version 5.1.2600]
(C) Copyright 1985-2001 Microsoft Corp.
C:\WINDOWS>sqlplus / as sysdba
SQL*Plus: Release 11.2.0.1.0 Production on Sun May 20 18:32:46 2012
Copyright (c) 1982, 2010, Oracle. All rights reserved.
Connected to:
Oracle Database 11g Enterprise Edition Release 11.2.0.1.0 - Production
With the Partitioning, OLAP, Data Mining and Real Application Testing options
SQL> alter system set pga_aggregate_target=100M scope=both;
System altered.
SQL>

Here, we enter the `alter system set` command followed by the desired parameter name, `pga_aggregate_target`, and the parameter's new value, `100M`. Following that, we use the `scope` clause. The `scope` clause specifies how the parameter will be changed, either in memory, directly in the SPFILE or, in our case, both. When a parameter is changed in memory with `scope=memory`, the assigned value will remain active in memory, but only until the database has been restarted, since it was not changed in the SPFILE. When a parameter is changed with `scope=spfile`, it will not be changed immediately and will only be active after the instance is restarted and the PFILE is re-read.

Clearly, using an SPFILE to allow dynamic parameter changes is beneficial. However, not every parameter can be dynamically changed, even when using an SPFILE. Certain parameter changes require a database restart to be instantiated:

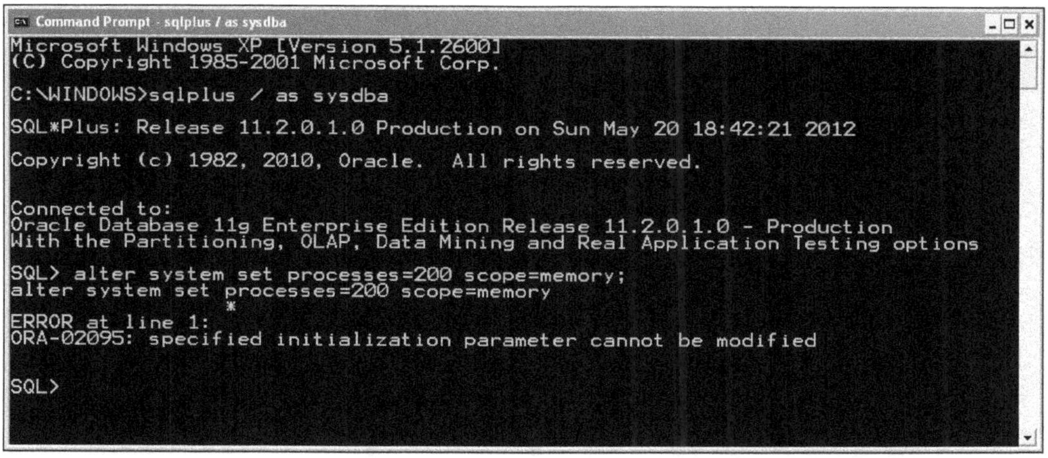
Command Prompt - sqlplus / as sysdba
Microsoft Windows XP [Version 5.1.2600]
(C) Copyright 1985-2001 Microsoft Corp.
C:\WINDOWS>sqlplus / as sysdba
SQL*Plus: Release 11.2.0.1.0 Production on Sun May 20 18:42:21 2012
Copyright (c) 1982, 2010, Oracle. All rights reserved.
Connected to:
Oracle Database 11g Enterprise Edition Release 11.2.0.1.0 - Production
With the Partitioning, OLAP, Data Mining and Real Application Testing options
SQL> alter system set processes=200 scope=memory;
alter system set processes=200 scope=memory
*
ERROR at line 1:
ORA-02095: specified initialization parameter cannot be modified
SQL>

As can be seen in the previous screenshot, the `processes` parameter is not dynamically modifiable, so we receive an error when we attempt to change it. This parameter defines the maximum number of processes that can run against the database, including background processes and the server processes that are given to user sessions. The solution to changing this parameter is to modify it using `scope=spfile` and restart the instance, as is done in the following screenshot:

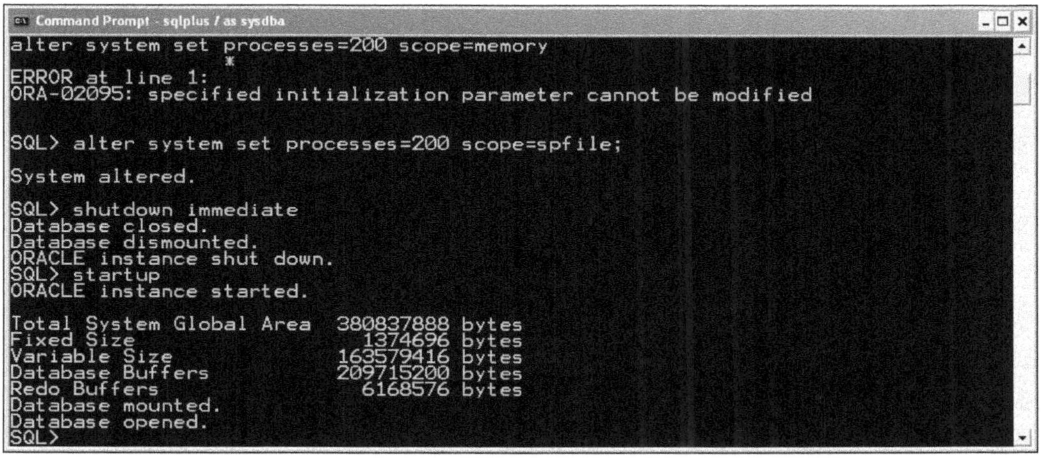
Command Prompt - sqlplus / as sysdba
alter system set processes=200 scope=memory
*
ERROR at line 1:
ORA-02095: specified initialization parameter cannot be modified
SQL> alter system set processes=200 scope=spfile;
System altered.
SQL> shutdown immediate
Database closed.
Database dismounted.
ORACLE instance shut down.
SQL> startup
ORACLE instance started.
Total System Global Area 380837888 bytes
Fixed Size 1374696 bytes
Variable Size 163579416 bytes
Database Buffers 209715200 bytes
Redo Buffers 6168576 bytes
Database mounted.
Database opened.
SQL>

In order to ensure that our change to the `processes` parameter was made, we use the `show parameter` command, followed by the name of the parameter. Note that `show parameter` will show all the parameters that contain the string `processes`, so other parameters are shown as well:

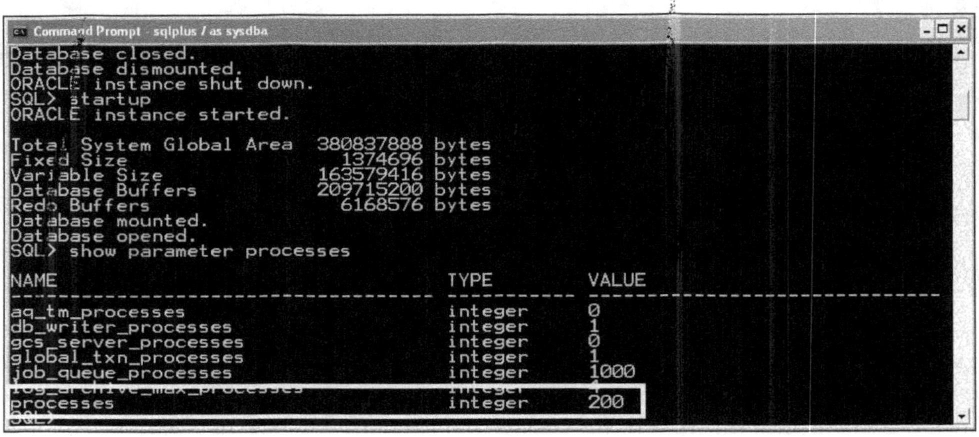
Command Prompt - sqlplus / as sysdba
Database closed.
Database dismounted.
ORACLE instance shut down.
SQL> startup
ORACLE instance started.
Total System Global Area 380837888 bytes
Fixed Size 1374696 bytes
Variable Size 163579416 bytes
Database Buffers 209715200 bytes
Redo Buffers 6168576 bytes
Database mounted.
Database opened.
SQL> show parameter processes
NAME TYPE VALUE
aq_tm_processes integer 0
db_writer_processes integer 1
gcs_server_processes integer 0
global_txn_processes integer 1
job_queue_processes integer 1000
processes integer 200

As we can see in the preceding screenshot, the value for the processes parameter was successfully changed to `200` following database restart.

> **The real-world DBA**
>
> Understanding a large number of the available database parameters can be a career-long pursuit. This is further complicated by the fact that, with new versions, many new parameters are introduced and some existing parameters are deprecated. Much of this learning comes by experience. You can also consult Oracle's documentation, specifically their online book titled simply **Reference**, to get information.

Understanding the data dictionary

We've mentioned the concept of the data dictionary several times thus far. The data dictionary is the metadata repository that holds all of the information about the database and its internal operations. It consists of base tables and views to those tables and is stored in the `SYSTEM` tablespace. As DBAs, the data dictionary is perhaps the most important tool at our disposal, other than our own problem-solving abilities. It is possible to complete many of our DBA tasks using GUI tools and completely ignore the data dictionary. Doing so, however, is inadvisable. While tools have limitations based on their programming, the data dictionary is a complex, but nearly unlimited, source of information about the database.

Exploring the Oracle base tables

In order to understand the data dictionary, it is important to understand that our interaction with it comes primarily in the form of data dictionary views. In SQL, we can create views on tables to simplify our queries. The same is true of data dictionary views, although we do not need to create them—they already exist. These views simplify interaction with the base tables of the data dictionary. Although the base tables of the data dictionary actually store the information about the database, they are not in any way user-friendly. Their table and column names are intentionally cryptic and difficult to read. This is because the base tables are never meant to be queried directly; the views are intended for that purpose. While the base tables are not, strictly speaking, read-only, they should never be operated on directly using `INSERT`, `UPDATE`, or `DELETE` statements, and their storage characteristics should never be tampered with. For the purpose of understanding Oracle's base tables, let's query one directly. We'll need to connect using our **system@orcl** connection:

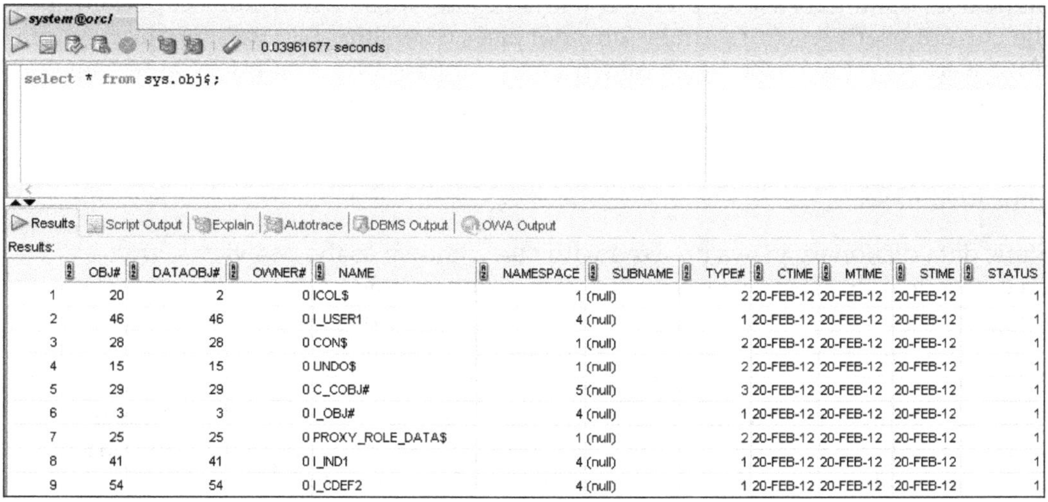
system@orcl
0.03961677 seconds
select * from sys.obj$;
Results
Script Output
Explain
Autotrace
DBMS Output
OWA Output
Results:

	OBJ#	DATAOBJ#	OWNER#	NAME	NAMESPACE	SUBNAME	TYPE#	CTIME	MTIME	STIME	STATUS
1	20	2	0	ICOL$	1	(null)	2	20-FEB-12	20-FEB-12	20-FEB-12	1
2	46	46	0	I_USER1	4	(null)	1	20-FEB-12	20-FEB-12	20-FEB-12	1
3	28	28	0	CON$	1	(null)	2	20-FEB-12	20-FEB-12	20-FEB-12	1
4	15	15	0	UNDO$	1	(null)	2	20-FEB-12	20-FEB-12	20-FEB-12	1
5	29	29	0	C_COBJ#	5	(null)	3	20-FEB-12	20-FEB-12	20-FEB-12	1
6	3	3	0	I_OBJ#	4	(null)	1	20-FEB-12	20-FEB-12	20-FEB-12	1
7	25	25	0	PROXY_ROLE_DATA$	1	(null)	2	20-FEB-12	20-FEB-12	20-FEB-12	1
8	41	41	0	I_IND1	4	(null)	1	20-FEB-12	20-FEB-12	20-FEB-12	1
9	54	54	0	I_CDEF2	4	(null)	1	20-FEB-12	20-FEB-12	20-FEB-12	1

Here, we query from the **obj$** table, which is owned by the `SYS` user and contains information about database objects. The columns and their contents are fairly mystifying. We can't even use a limiting condition, say, by object owner, because the **OWNER#** column only contains numeric values. We would actually have to join to another base table in order to get that information. In short, while it's important to understand the concept of the base table, we want to use the predefined views to query the data dictionary. There are two types of data dictionary views, static and dynamic

Exploring the static data dictionary views

Static data dictionary views are the set of views so named due to their infrequently changing nature. Static data dictionary views are not truly static; rather, they are comparatively slow changing compared to the dynamic data dictionary views. There are three basic types of static data dictionary views, and these are differentiated by their prefixes, `USER_`, `ALL_`, and `DBA_`.

Static data dictionary views prefixed with `USER_` are those whose subject pertains to the ownership of the user itself. For example, if we were logging in to the database with our `companylink` user and query the `USER_TABLES` view, we would see all of the tables owned by our current user `companylink`. If we query from `USER_INDEXES`, we see a list of indexes owned by the `companylink` user. The `USER` views, as they are sometimes called, are useful for data dictionary information as it pertains to the current user.

Static data dictionary views prefixed with `ALL_` are those whose subject pertains to the current user's level of permissions, not just ownership. To continue our example, if we were to log in to the database with user `companylink` and query `ALL_TABLES`, we would see not only those tables that the `companylink` user owns, but any that it has permission to see as well. Thus, ordinarily, a query from `ALL_TABLES` includes everything found in `USER_TABLES` plus any other tables that the current user is permitted to see.

Static data dictionary views prefixed with `DBA_`, known as the `DBA` views, are accessible to only those users who possess a database role known as the `DBA` role, not to be confused with the `SYSDBA` role. Use of the `DBA` role should be restricted to only those personnel who perform database administration—it is a highly inclusive set of permissions. For instance, the user `SYSTEM` possesses the `DBA` role. Thus as user `SYSTEM`, we can query any of the `DBA_` views. These views contain every occurrence of a given subject. For example, querying from `DBA_TABLES` presents an unrestricted list of every table within the database. Querying from `DBA_SEQUENCES` provides a list of every sequence in the database, and so on. The `DBA_` views provide the highest level of access to the static portion of the data dictionary.

Exploring the dynamic data dictionary views

Contrasting with the static data dictionary views are the **dynamic data dictionary views**, which are prefixed with `V$`. These views, sometimes referred to as the **V$ views**, are considered more dynamic because of the information they store. To give an example, we may say that `DBA_TABLES` is considered static because, although the list of database tables can change, it isn't likely that it changes moment to moment. But consider the sessions that connect to the database as a different example. Users, agents, and application servers can connect to and disconnect from a database at an extremely rapid pace. Their activity is more dynamic. Thus, while there is no `DBA_SESSIONS` static view, there is a `V$SESSION` view—a dynamic data dictionary view. This is certainly a broad generalization, and there are times that static and dynamic views contain information that overlaps. For instance, there is a static view called `DBA_DATA_FILES` and a dynamic view called `V$DATAFILE`. While they don't contain exactly the same information, some of it overlaps. However, very generally speaking, the `V$` views store information that changes more dynamically than the static `USER_`, `ALL_`, and `DBA_` views. Most of the `V$` views also have a global version of the view known as a `GV$` view, such as `gv$session`. These global views are only used with Oracle Real Application Clusters, since they are specific to each instance in the cluster.

> **The real-world DBA**
>
> It can be difficult to remember the specific names of both static and dynamic data dictionary views. Say, for instance, that we want to query the data dictionary for tablespace information. As it happens, there exists both a static and a dynamic view for tablespace information. Let's say that we are trying to remember these view names to write a query. Is it the singular `V$TABLESPACE` view or the plural `V$TABLESPACES` view? Is it `DBA_TABLESPACE` or `DBA_TABLESPACES`? The singular and plural forms of these views can be confusing. One very general rule of thumb to remember is that dynamic views tend to be singular, while static views tend to be plural. Thus, our view names are `V$TABLESPACE` and `DBA_TABLESPACES`.

Querying the data dictionary views

When we need to query these data dictionary views, we do so in the same manner that we would query any other table or view—by row and column. One of the challenges of becoming proficient using data dictionary views is figuring out exactly which columns we need to select in order to find the information we require. Although this is a learning process that occurs over time, we can use the `DESCRIBE` command to help us. Let's say that, as a member of the DBA team for `Companylink`, we need to make some determinations regarding the use of disk space in our database. We need datafile and tablespace information regarding sizing in megabytes. To find this, we query the **dba_data_files** data dictionary view, as shown below in the following screenshot; We log in to the database with SQL Developer using the **system@orcl** connection:

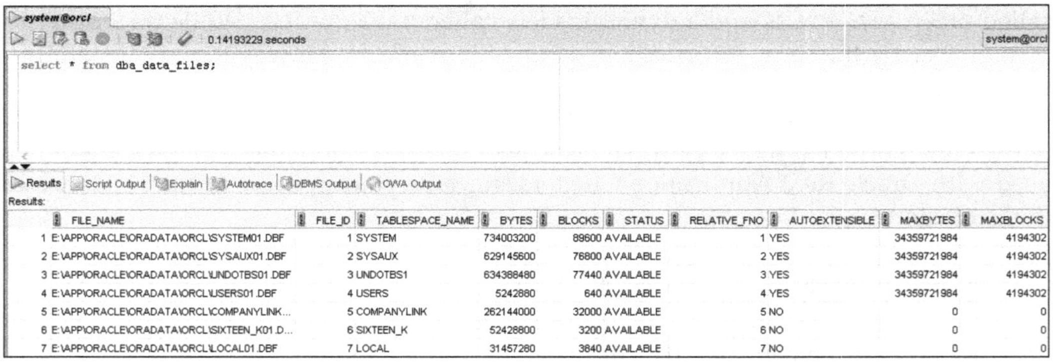
system@orcl
0.14193229 seconds
system@orcl
select * from dba_data_files;
Results
Script Output
Explain
Autotrace
DBMS Output
OWA Output
Results:
FILE_NAME FILE_ID TABLESPACE_NAME BYTES BLOCKS STATUS RELATIVE_FNO AUTOEXTENSIBLE MAXBYTES MAXBLOCKS
1 E:\APP\ORACLE\ORADATA\ORCL\SYSTEM01.DBF 1 SYSTEM 734003200 89600 AVAILABLE 1 YES 34359721984 4194302
2 E:\APP\ORACLE\ORADATA\ORCL\SYSAUX01.DBF 2 SYSAUX 629145600 76800 AVAILABLE 2 YES 34359721984 4194302
3 E:\APP\ORACLE\ORADATA\ORCL\UNDOTBS01.DBF 3 UNDOTBS1 634388480 77440 AVAILABLE 3 YES 34359721984 4194302
4 E:\APP\ORACLE\ORADATA\ORCL\USERS01.DBF 4 USERS 5242880 640 AVAILABLE 4 YES 34359721984 4194302
5 E:\APP\ORACLE\ORADATA\ORCL\COMPANYLINK... 5 COMPANYLINK 262144000 32000 AVAILABLE 5 NO 0 0
6 E:\APP\ORACLE\ORADATA\ORCL\SIXTEEN_K01.D... 6 SIXTEEN_K 52428800 3200 AVAILABLE 6 NO 0 0
7 E:\APP\ORACLE\ORADATA\ORCL\LOCAL01.DBF 7 LOCAL 31457280 3840 AVAILABLE 7 NO 0 0

We see the required information here under the **FILE_NAME**, **TABLESPACE_NAME**, and **BYTES** columns. But what we've selected is certainly more information than we need, so let's change the query to limit the data to what we actually need. Additionally, since we need the sizing information in megabytes, we'll do some math on the **BYTES** column, which represents the number of bytes in each datafile:

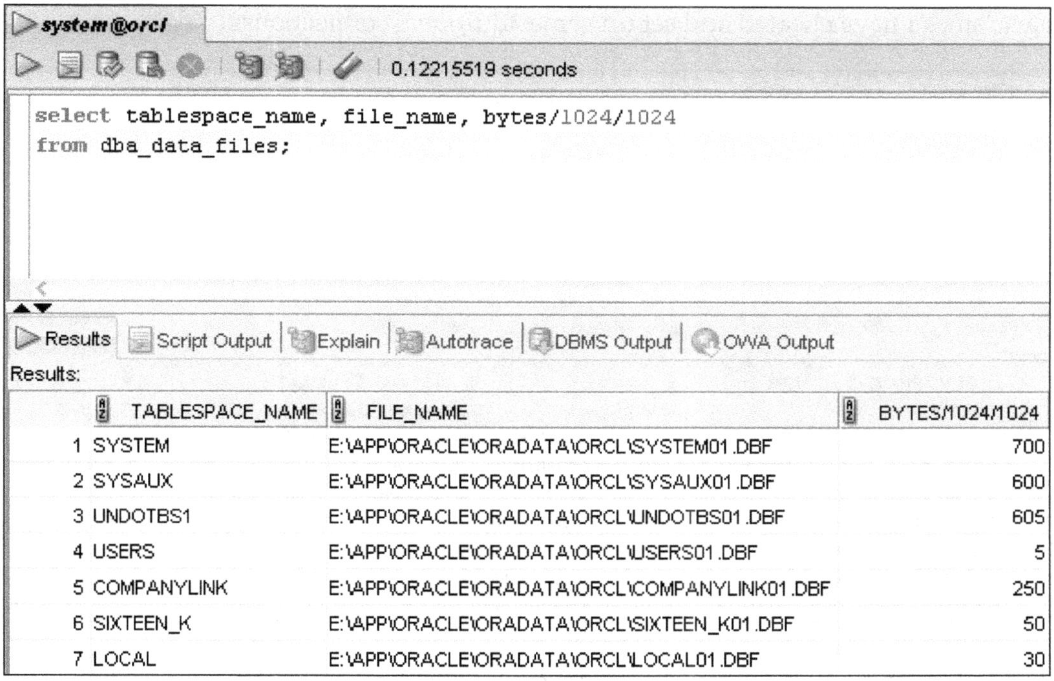
system@orcl
0.12215519 seconds
select tablespace_name, file_name, bytes/1024/1024
from dba_data_files;
Results
Script Output
Explain
Autotrace
DBMS Output
OWA Output
Results:
TABLESPACE_NAME
FILE_NAME
BYTES/1024/1024
1 SYSTEM E:\APP\ORACLE\ORADATA\ORCL\SYSTEM01.DBF 700
2 SYSAUX E:\APP\ORACLE\ORADATA\ORCL\SYSAUX01.DBF 600
3 UNDOTBS1 E:\APP\ORACLE\ORADATA\ORCL\UNDOTBS01.DBF 605
4 USERS E:\APP\ORACLE\ORADATA\ORCL\USERS01.DBF 5
5 COMPANYLINK E:\APP\ORACLE\ORADATA\ORCL\COMPANYLINK01.DBF 250
6 SIXTEEN_K E:\APP\ORACLE\ORADATA\ORCL\SIXTEEN_K01.DBF 50
7 LOCAL E:\APP\ORACLE\ORADATA\ORCL\LOCAL01.DBF 30

As you can see in the preceding screenshot, this is a much more concise query that gives us the information we need. For instance, we see that the tablespace **USERS** is 5 MB in size, since we've divided the **BYTES** column by **1024** twice (number of bytes/1024/1024 = megabytes). Next, let's say we need information about user sessions that are connected to our `Companylink` database. To find this information, we query the `V$SESSION` dynamic data dictionary view. The results you see may vary, since I have cheated and set up some additional connections:

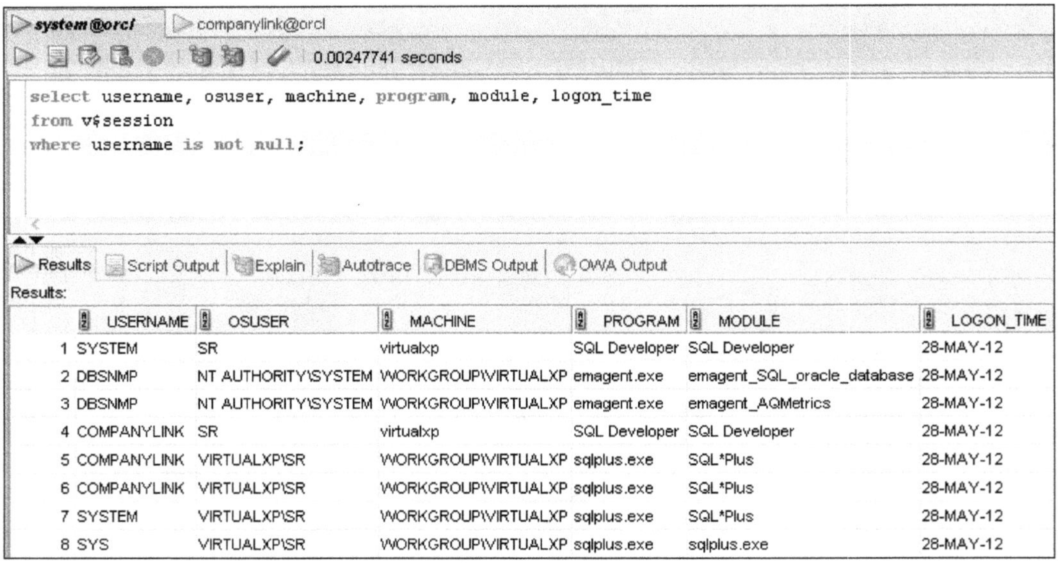
system@orcl
companylink@orcl
0.00247741 seconds
select username, osuser, machine, program, module, logon_time
from v$session
where username is not null;
Results
Script Output
Explain
Autotrace
DBMS Output
OWA Output
Results:
USERNAME OSUSER MACHINE PROGRAM MODULE LOGON_TIME
1 SYSTEM SR virtualxp SQL Developer SQL Developer 28-MAY-12
2 DBSNMP NT AUTHORITY\SYSTEM WORKGROUP\VIRTUALXP emagent.exe emagent_SQL_oracle_database 28-MAY-12
3 DBSNMP NT AUTHORITY\SYSTEM WORKGROUP\VIRTUALXP emagent.exe emagent_AQMetrics 28-MAY-12
4 COMPANYLINK SR virtualxp SQL Developer SQL Developer 28-MAY-12
5 COMPANYLINK VIRTUALXP\SR WORKGROUP\VIRTUALXP sqlplus.exe SQL*Plus 28-MAY-12
6 COMPANYLINK VIRTUALXP\SR WORKGROUP\VIRTUALXP sqlplus.exe SQL*Plus 28-MAY-12
7 SYSTEM VIRTUALXP\SR WORKGROUP\VIRTUALXP sqlplus.exe SQL*Plus 28-MAY-12
8 SYS VIRTUALXP\SR WORKGROUP\VIRTUALXP sqlplus.exe sqlplus.exe 28-MAY-12

Here, we see several different users connected to the database using different tools. The **USERNAME** column tells us the name of the database user that is connected. The **OSUSER** column gives us the name of the user that is connected at the operating system layer. **MACHINE** tells us the name of the machine that is being used to connect to the database. **PROGRAM** and **MODULE** give us the tool being used to connect to the database. In this case, we use SQL*Plus and SQL Developer to establish database connections, along with the sessions that the Enterprise Manager agent uses.

We mentioned previously that, although we can see the instance background processes in Linux at the operating system level using the `ps` command, we can't look at them on a Windows system in the same way. However, we can use a data dictionary view, **v$process**, to see this information, regardless of which operating system we're using, as shown in the following screenshot:

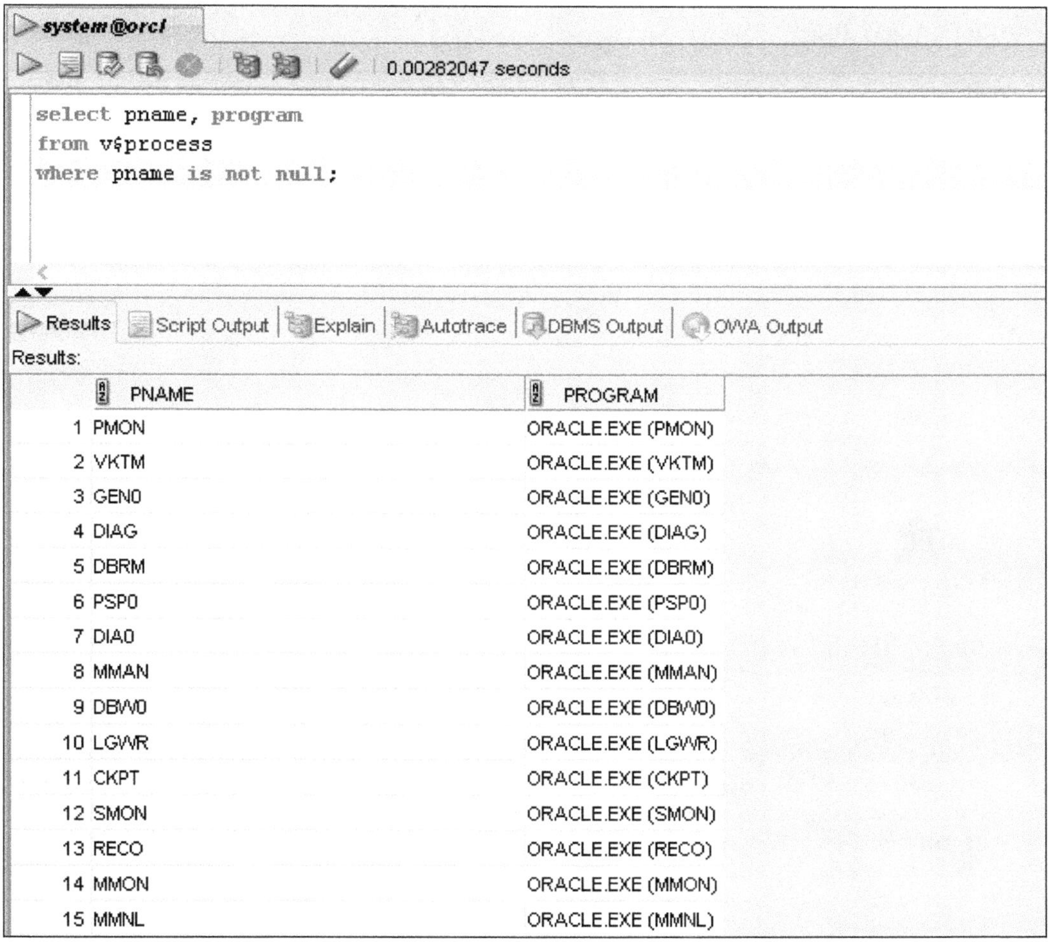
system@orcl
0.00282047 seconds
select pname, program
from v$process
where pname is not null;
Results
Script Output
Explain
Autotrace
DBMS Output
OWA Output
Results:
PNAME
PROGRAM
1 PMON
ORACLE.EXE (PMON)
2 VKTM
ORACLE.EXE (VKTM)
3 GEN0
ORACLE.EXE (GEN0)
4 DIAG
ORACLE.EXE (DIAG)
5 DBRM
ORACLE.EXE (DBRM)
6 PSP0
ORACLE.EXE (PSP0)
7 DIA0
ORACLE.EXE (DIA0)
8 MMAN
ORACLE.EXE (MMAN)
9 DBW0
ORACLE.EXE (DBW0)
10 LGWR
ORACLE.EXE (LGWR)
11 CKPT
ORACLE.EXE (CKPT)
12 SMON
ORACLE.EXE (SMON)
13 RECO
ORACLE.EXE (RECO)
14 MMON
ORACLE.EXE (MMON)
15 MMNL
ORACLE.EXE (MMNL)

We should recognize a number of these processes, such as **PMON**, **SMON**, **DBW0**, **LGWR**, and **MMON**, from our discussion of the background processes that make up the Oracle instance.

At times, we need information from two different data dictionary views that are related but do not exist as the same view. In situations like this, we simply use a SQL join between the two views on a common column. Say, for instance, we need to examine each background process, what that process is doing, and the location of the trace file of the process. We could use a join between the `V$SESSION` and `V$PROCESS` views, joining the `PADDR` and `ADDR` columns, which contain complementary information:

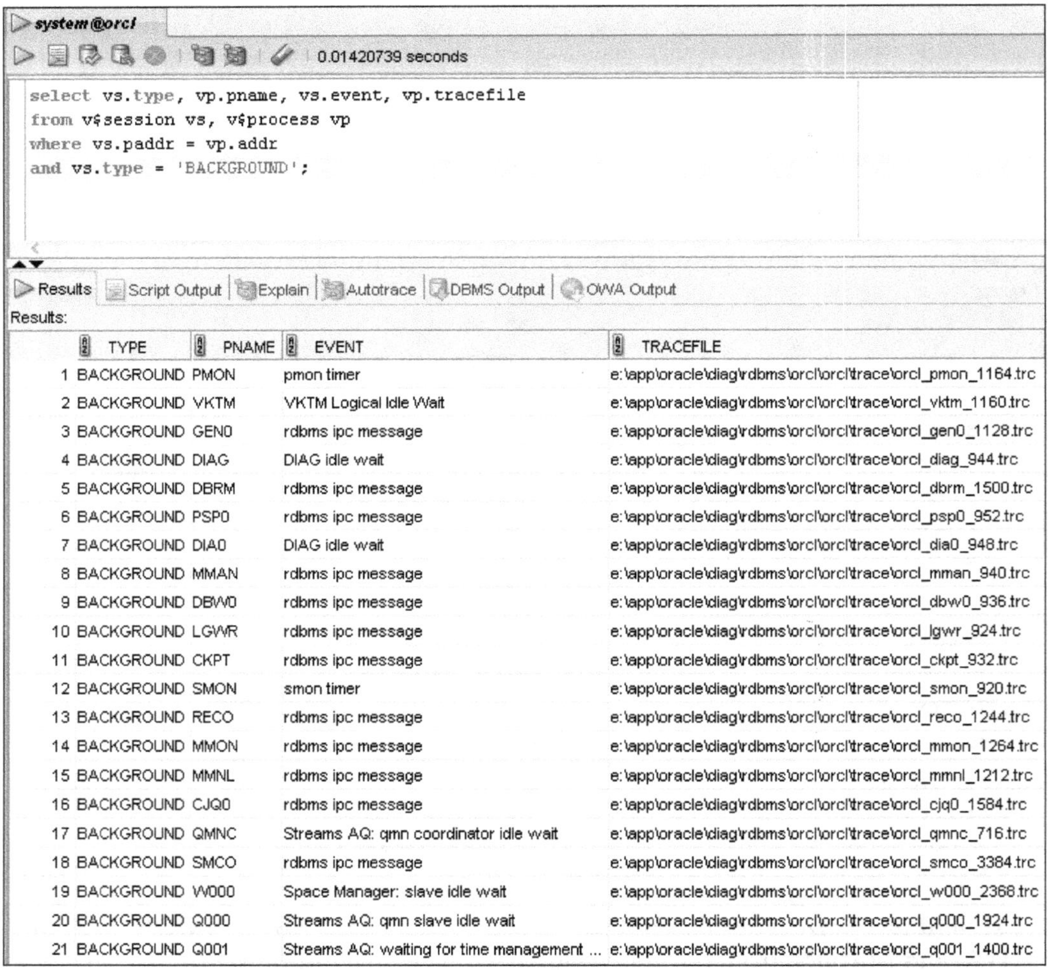
system@orcl
0.01420739 seconds
Results
Script Output
Explain
Autotrace
DBMS Output
OWA Output
Results:

```
select vs.type, vp.pname, vs.event, vp.tracefile
from v$session vs, v$process vp
where vs.paddr = vp.addr
and vs.type = 'BACKGROUND';
```

	TYPE	PNAME	EVENT	TRACEFILE
1	BACKGROUND	PMON	pmon timer	e:\app\oracle\diag\rdbms\orcl\orcl\trace\orcl_pmon_1164.trc
2	BACKGROUND	VKTM	VKTM Logical Idle Wait	e:\app\oracle\diag\rdbms\orcl\orcl\trace\orcl_vktm_1160.trc
3	BACKGROUND	GEN0	rdbms ipc message	e:\app\oracle\diag\rdbms\orcl\orcl\trace\orcl_gen0_1128.trc
4	BACKGROUND	DIAG	DIAG idle wait	e:\app\oracle\diag\rdbms\orcl\orcl\trace\orcl_diag_944.trc
5	BACKGROUND	DBRM	rdbms ipc message	e:\app\oracle\diag\rdbms\orcl\orcl\trace\orcl_dbrm_1500.trc
6	BACKGROUND	PSP0	rdbms ipc message	e:\app\oracle\diag\rdbms\orcl\orcl\trace\orcl_psp0_952.trc
7	BACKGROUND	DIA0	DIAG idle wait	e:\app\oracle\diag\rdbms\orcl\orcl\trace\orcl_dia0_948.trc
8	BACKGROUND	MMAN	rdbms ipc message	e:\app\oracle\diag\rdbms\orcl\orcl\trace\orcl_mman_940.trc
9	BACKGROUND	DBW0	rdbms ipc message	e:\app\oracle\diag\rdbms\orcl\orcl\trace\orcl_dbw0_936.trc
10	BACKGROUND	LGWR	rdbms ipc message	e:\app\oracle\diag\rdbms\orcl\orcl\trace\orcl_lgwr_924.trc
11	BACKGROUND	CKPT	rdbms ipc message	e:\app\oracle\diag\rdbms\orcl\orcl\trace\orcl_ckpt_932.trc
12	BACKGROUND	SMON	smon timer	e:\app\oracle\diag\rdbms\orcl\orcl\trace\orcl_smon_920.trc
13	BACKGROUND	RECO	rdbms ipc message	e:\app\oracle\diag\rdbms\orcl\orcl\trace\orcl_reco_1244.trc
14	BACKGROUND	MMON	rdbms ipc message	e:\app\oracle\diag\rdbms\orcl\orcl\trace\orcl_mmon_1264.trc
15	BACKGROUND	MMNL	rdbms ipc message	e:\app\oracle\diag\rdbms\orcl\orcl\trace\orcl_mmnl_1212.trc
16	BACKGROUND	CJQ0	rdbms ipc message	e:\app\oracle\diag\rdbms\orcl\orcl\trace\orcl_cjq0_1584.trc
17	BACKGROUND	QMNC	Streams AQ: qmn coordinator idle wait	e:\app\oracle\diag\rdbms\orcl\orcl\trace\orcl_qmnc_716.trc
18	BACKGROUND	SMCO	rdbms ipc message	e:\app\oracle\diag\rdbms\orcl\orcl\trace\orcl_smco_3384.trc
19	BACKGROUND	W000	Space Manager: slave idle wait	e:\app\oracle\diag\rdbms\orcl\orcl\trace\orcl_w000_2368.trc
20	BACKGROUND	Q000	Streams AQ: qmn slave idle wait	e:\app\oracle\diag\rdbms\orcl\orcl\trace\orcl_q000_1924.trc
21	BACKGROUND	Q001	Streams AQ: waiting for time management ...	e:\app\oracle\diag\rdbms\orcl\orcl\trace\orcl_q001_1400.trc

In the preceding screenshot, we can see the active event in the **EVENT** column for each background process and its respective trace file, which we'll discuss shortly in another section.

Listing common data dictionary views

Clearly, there is a remarkable amount of information contained in the data dictionary. Learning how to leverage it is extremely important in becoming a better DBA. We will use data dictionary queries throughout this book, but here are small lists of some of the more common ones and their usages:

Object-related views

View name	Description
DBA_TABLES	Information on database tables
DBA_OBJECTS	Information on all types of database objects
DBA_INDEXES	Index-related information
DBA_VIEWS	Information on database views
DBA_PART_TABLES	Information regarding partitioned tables
DBA_TAB_COLUMNS	Information on specific columns in tables
DBA_IND_COLUMNS	Information on specific indexed columns
DBA_CONSTRAINTS	Database constraint information
DBA_SYNONYMS	Synonym-related information

Administration-related views

View name	Description
V$CONTROLFILE	Controlfile information
V$LOG	Information on redo log groups
V$LOGFILE	Information on individual redo logfiles
V$PARAMETER	List of database parameters and their values
V$ARCHIVED_LOG	Information on logs that have been archived
V$INSTANCE	General instance information
V$DATABASE	General information on the database

Security-related views

View name	Description
DBA_USERS	Information regarding users in the database
DBA_TAB_PRIVS	Table privilege information as it relates to specific users
DBA_SYS_PRIVS	System privilege information as it relates to specific users

Storage-related views

DBA_TABLESPACES	General tablespace information
DBA_FREE_SPACE	Information on free space within tablespaces
DBA_DATA_FILES	Information related to data files
V$TABLESPACE	Information on tablespaces
V$DATAFILE	Information related to data files
DBA_TEMP_FILES	Temporary file information
V$TEMPFILE	Temporary file information

Understanding database diagnostic information

One of the most important abilities needed for a DBA is the ability to diagnose database problems. The data dictionary is often used for this task. However, Oracle has several other tools that we can use to diagnose problems, including logfiles, trace files, and the Automatic Diagnostic Repository.

Understanding the alert log

The most primary diagnostic tool used by DBAs is the **database alert log**. The alert log is a plain text log (with an exception for Version 11*g* that we will discuss shortly) that contains both messages and errors regarding the functioning of the database. As such, many DBAs consider the alert log to be the "first stop" when attempting to diagnose a database problem.

Up until Oracle Version 11*g*, the alert log was stored in a standard directory. This directory is usually referred to as the `BDUMP` directory, for background dump. This directory held the alert log as well as files known as trace files, particularly those for the instance background processes. Prior to Version 11*g*, there were essentially two locations for logfiles and trace files, the `BDUMP` directory and a directory known as `UDUMP`, for user dump. While `BDUMP` held the alert log and trace files for instance background processes, the `UDUMP` directory stored trace files from user sessions. With the advent of the Automatic Diagnostic Repository in Oracle 11*g*, this distinction has been blurred. However, we can still use the parameters used in previous versions to help us locate these files. From SQL*Plus, we display the value for the **background_dump_dest** parameter:

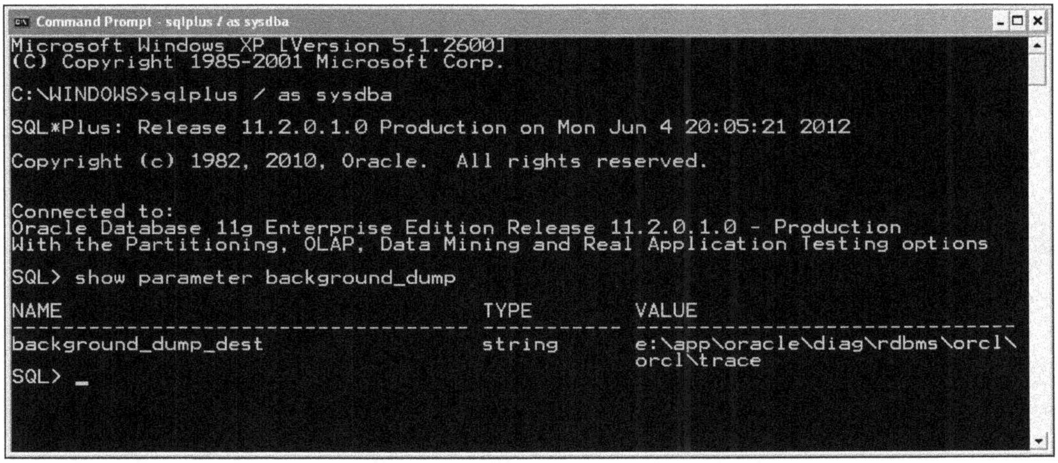
Command Prompt - sqlplus / as sysdba
Microsoft Windows XP [Version 5.1.2600]
(C) Copyright 1985-2001 Microsoft Corp.
C:\WINDOWS>sqlplus / as sysdba
SQL*Plus: Release 11.2.0.1.0 Production on Mon Jun 4 20:05:21 2012
Copyright (c) 1982, 2010, Oracle. All rights reserved.
Connected to:
Oracle Database 11g Enterprise Edition Release 11.2.0.1.0 - Production
With the Partitioning, OLAP, Data Mining and Real Application Testing options
SQL> show parameter background_dump
NAME
TYPE
VALUE
background_dump_dest
string
e:\app\oracle\diag\rdbms\orcl\orcl\trace
SQL> _

The parameter indicates that the alert log is stored in the `e:\app\oracle\diag\rdbms\orcl\orcl\trace` directory. We navigate to this directory and open the `alert_orcl.log` file. The following screenshot shows the contents of the file:

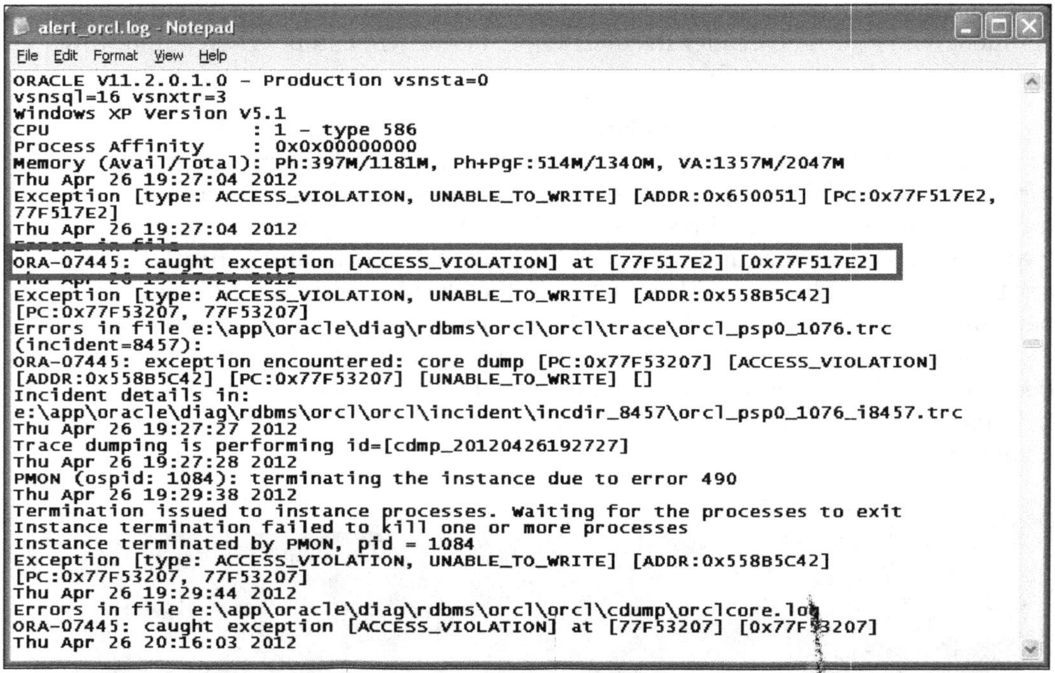

```
alert_orcl.log - Notepad
File  Edit  Format  View  Help
ORACLE V11.2.0.1.0 - Production vsnsta=0
vsnsql=16 vsnxtr=3
Windows XP Version V5.1
CPU                 : 1 - type 586
Process Affinity    : 0x0x00000000
Memory (Avail/Total): Ph:397M/1181M, Ph+PgF:514M/1340M, VA:1357M/2047M
Thu Apr 26 19:27:04 2012
Exception [type: ACCESS_VIOLATION, UNABLE_TO_WRITE] [ADDR:0x650051] [PC:0x77F517E2,
77F517E2]
Thu Apr 26 19:27:04 2012
[illegible]
ORA-07445: caught exception [ACCESS_VIOLATION] at [77F517E2] [0x77F517E2]
[illegible]
Exception [type: ACCESS_VIOLATION, UNABLE_TO_WRITE] [ADDR:0x558B5C42]
[PC:0x77F53207, 77F53207]
Errors in file e:\app\oracle\diag\rdbms\orcl\orcl\trace\orcl_psp0_1076.trc
(incident=8457):
ORA-07445: exception encountered: core dump [PC:0x77F53207] [ACCESS_VIOLATION]
[ADDR:0x558B5C42] [PC:0x77F53207] [UNABLE_TO_WRITE] []
Incident details in:
e:\app\oracle\diag\rdbms\orcl\orcl\incident\incdir_8457\orcl_psp0_1076_i8457.trc
Thu Apr 26 19:27:27 2012
Trace dumping is performing id=[cdmp_20120426192727]
Thu Apr 26 19:27:28 2012
PMON (ospid: 1084): terminating the instance due to error 490
Thu Apr 26 19:29:38 2012
Termination issued to instance processes. Waiting for the processes to exit
Instance termination failed to kill one or more processes
Instance terminated by PMON, pid = 1084
Exception [type: ACCESS_VIOLATION, UNABLE_TO_WRITE] [ADDR:0x558B5C42]
[PC:0x77F53207, 77F53207]
Thu Apr 26 19:29:44 2012
Errors in file e:\app\oracle\diag\rdbms\orcl\orcl\cdump\orclcore.log
ORA-07445: caught exception [ACCESS_VIOLATION] at [77F53207] [0x77F53207]
Thu Apr 26 20:16:03 2012
```

In the previous screenshot we can see a lot of information, although most of it seems undecipherable at this point. In the preceding example, we see the following error highlighted:

```
ORA-07445: caught exception [ACCESS_VIOLATION]
```

This indicates that an Oracle error has occurred. While this particular error might require the intervention of Oracle Support services, some are more descriptive. Although it is more readable than the trace files we will examine shortly, the alert log can still be difficult to fully understand. It contains many types of information, such as, but not limited to, the following:

- Startup and shutdown information
- System parameter with non-default values
- Information regarding the switch of one redo log group to another
- Database creation information

- Instance recovery information
- Missing controlfile, redo logfile, or datafile information
- Certain operating system errors
- Tablespace and datafile creation events
- Deadlock information
- Any other database-level errors or warning regarding the state of the database

The alert log does not contain the errors generated from most table-oriented operations such as constraint violations and datatype errors. Several examples from alert logs are shown in the next screenshot. Here, we see the point in the log where our database was created, followed by the full statement:

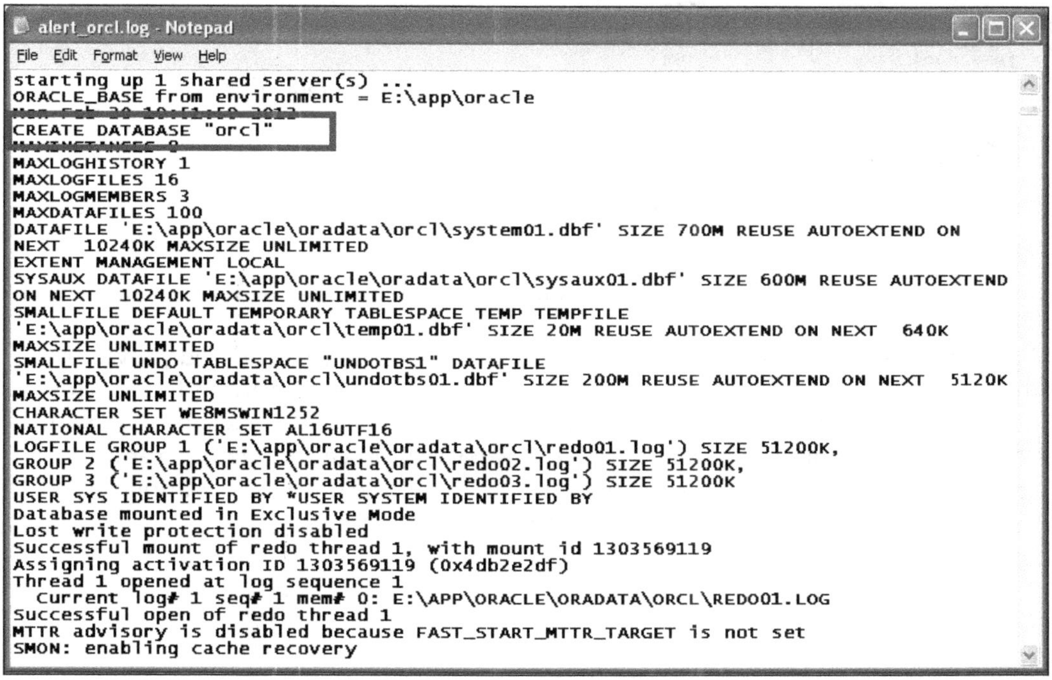

```
alert_orcl.log - Notepad
File Edit Format View Help
starting up 1 shared server(s) ...
ORACLE_BASE from environment = E:\app\oracle
Mon Feb 28 10:51:59 2011
CREATE DATABASE "orcl"
MAXINSTANCES 8
MAXLOGHISTORY 1
MAXLOGFILES 16
MAXLOGMEMBERS 3
MAXDATAFILES 100
DATAFILE 'E:\app\oracle\oradata\orcl\system01.dbf' SIZE 700M REUSE AUTOEXTEND ON
NEXT  10240K MAXSIZE UNLIMITED
EXTENT MANAGEMENT LOCAL
SYSAUX DATAFILE 'E:\app\oracle\oradata\orcl\sysaux01.dbf' SIZE 600M REUSE AUTOEXTEND
ON NEXT  10240K MAXSIZE UNLIMITED
SMALLFILE DEFAULT TEMPORARY TABLESPACE TEMP TEMPFILE
'E:\app\oracle\oradata\orcl\temp01.dbf' SIZE 20M REUSE AUTOEXTEND ON NEXT  640K
MAXSIZE UNLIMITED
SMALLFILE UNDO TABLESPACE "UNDOTBS1" DATAFILE
'E:\app\oracle\oradata\orcl\undotbs01.dbf' SIZE 200M REUSE AUTOEXTEND ON NEXT  5120K
MAXSIZE UNLIMITED
CHARACTER SET WE8MSWIN1252
NATIONAL CHARACTER SET AL16UTF16
LOGFILE GROUP 1 ('E:\app\oracle\oradata\orcl\redo01.log') SIZE 51200K,
GROUP 2 ('E:\app\oracle\oradata\orcl\redo02.log') SIZE 51200K,
GROUP 3 ('E:\app\oracle\oradata\orcl\redo03.log') SIZE 51200K
USER SYS IDENTIFIED BY *USER SYSTEM IDENTIFIED BY
Database mounted in Exclusive Mode
Lost write protection disabled
Successful mount of redo thread 1, with mount id 1303569119
Assigning activation ID 1303569119 (0x4db2e2df)
Thread 1 opened at log sequence 1
  Current log# 1 seq# 1 mem# 0: E:\APP\ORACLE\ORADATA\ORCL\REDO01.LOG
Successful open of redo thread 1
MTTR advisory is disabled because FAST_START_MTTR_TARGET is not set
SMON: enabling cache recovery
```

Next, the alert log records a database startup command, followed by non-default parameters:

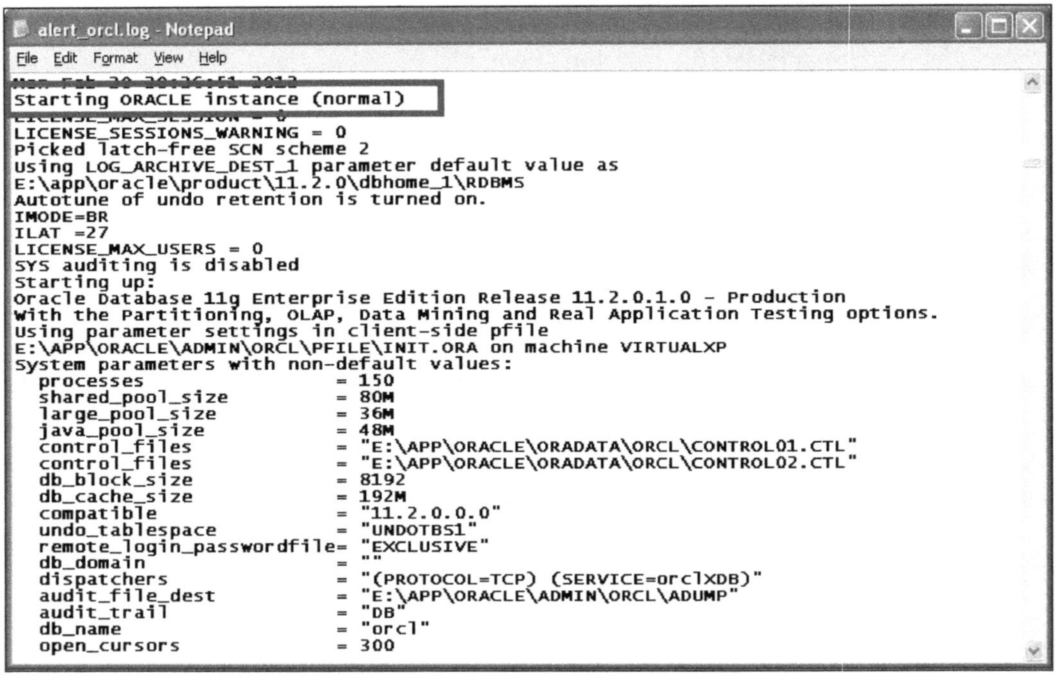

```
alert_orcl.log - Notepad
File Edit Format View Help
Starting ORACLE instance (normal)
LICENSE_SESSIONS_WARNING = 0
Picked latch-free SCN scheme 2
Using LOG_ARCHIVE_DEST_1 parameter default value as
E:\app\oracle\product\11.2.0\dbhome_1\RDBMS
Autotune of undo retention is turned on.
IMODE=BR
ILAT =27
LICENSE_MAX_USERS = 0
SYS auditing is disabled
Starting up:
Oracle Database 11g Enterprise Edition Release 11.2.0.1.0 - Production
With the Partitioning, OLAP, Data Mining and Real Application Testing options.
Using parameter settings in client-side pfile
E:\APP\ORACLE\ADMIN\ORCL\PFILE\INIT.ORA on machine VIRTUALXP
System parameters with non-default values:
  processes                = 150
  shared_pool_size         = 80M
  large_pool_size          = 36M
  java_pool_size           = 48M
  control_files            = "E:\APP\ORACLE\ORADATA\ORCL\CONTROL01.CTL"
  control_files            = "E:\APP\ORACLE\ORADATA\ORCL\CONTROL02.CTL"
  db_block_size            = 8192
  db_cache_size            = 192M
  compatible               = "11.2.0.0.0"
  undo_tablespace          = "UNDOTBS1"
  remote_login_passwordfile= "EXCLUSIVE"
  db_domain                = ""
  dispatchers              = "(PROTOCOL=TCP) (SERVICE=orclXDB)"
  audit_file_dest          = "E:\APP\ORACLE\ADMIN\ORCL\ADUMP"
  audit_trail              = "DB"
  db_name                  = "orcl"
  open_cursors             = 300
```

Finally, we see an example of an instance recovery. As we've discussed previously, an instance recovery occurs whenever the database has been improperly shut down, such as during a hard power-off of the host server or a `shutdown abort` command. When such an event occurs, it is the job of the SMON process to stabilize and synchronize the various components of the database. We see this operation in the alert log as indicated by the **Beginning crash recovery** phrase:

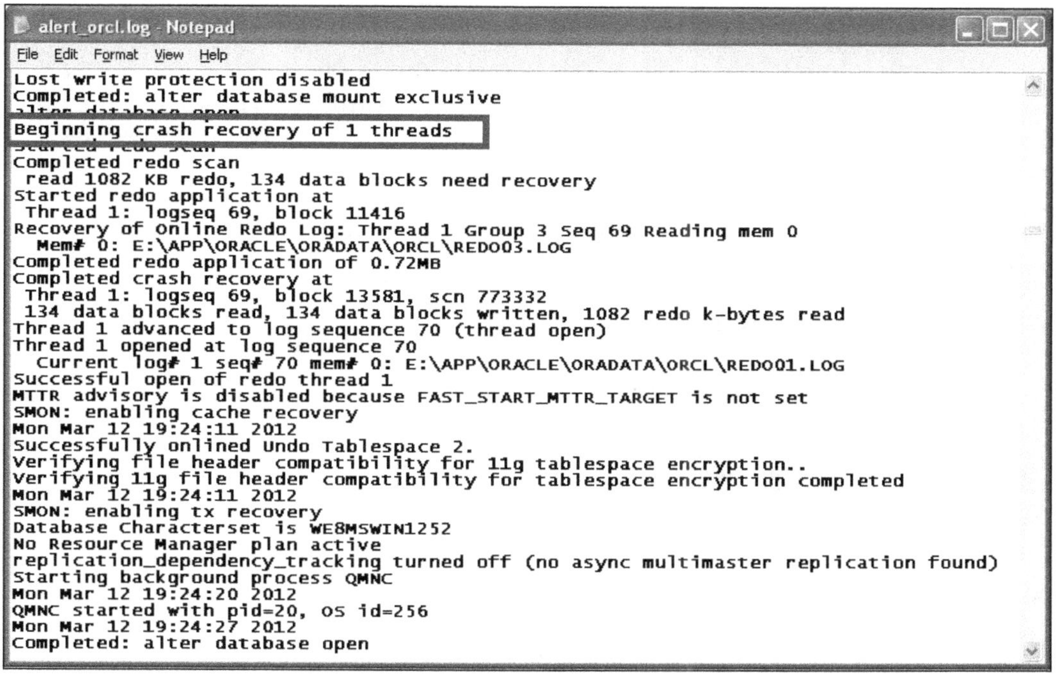

```
alert_orcl.log - Notepad
File Edit Format View Help
Lost write protection disabled
Completed: alter database mount exclusive
alter database open
Beginning crash recovery of 1 threads
Started redo scan
Completed redo scan
 read 1082 KB redo, 134 data blocks need recovery
Started redo application at
 Thread 1: logseq 69, block 11416
Recovery of Online Redo Log: Thread 1 Group 3 Seq 69 Reading mem 0
  Mem# 0: E:\APP\ORACLE\ORADATA\ORCL\REDO03.LOG
Completed redo application of 0.72MB
Completed crash recovery at
 Thread 1: logseq 69, block 13581, scn 773332
 134 data blocks read, 134 data blocks written, 1082 redo k-bytes read
Thread 1 advanced to log sequence 70 (thread open)
Thread 1 opened at log sequence 70
  Current log# 1 seq# 70 mem# 0: E:\APP\ORACLE\ORADATA\ORCL\REDO01.LOG
Successful open of redo thread 1
MTTR advisory is disabled because FAST_START_MTTR_TARGET is not set
SMON: enabling cache recovery
Mon Mar 12 19:24:11 2012
Successfully onlined Undo Tablespace 2.
Verifying file header compatibility for 11g tablespace encryption..
Verifying 11g file header compatibility for tablespace encryption completed
Mon Mar 12 19:24:11 2012
SMON: enabling tx recovery
Database Characterset is WE8MSWIN1252
No Resource Manager plan active
replication_dependency_tracking turned off (no async multimaster replication found)
Starting background process QMNC
Mon Mar 12 19:24:20 2012
QMNC started with pid=20, OS id=256
Mon Mar 12 19:24:27 2012
Completed: alter database open
```

Essentially, we use the alert log to examine a history of what has occurred in our database. If a problem with an unknown cause is present in our database, the alert log can be a good place to start.

Understanding the trace files

As we mentioned in the previous section, along with the alert log, we also have trace files at our disposal. A **trace file** is a text file of almost purely diagnostic information that is generated when an exception occurs within Oracle. Background processes as well as user processes can generate trace files. For instance, if during the course of database processing, the PMON process encounters an exception or warning, the event will be written out to a trace file with `pmon` in the name. The following screenshot is an example showing a trace file involving PMON:

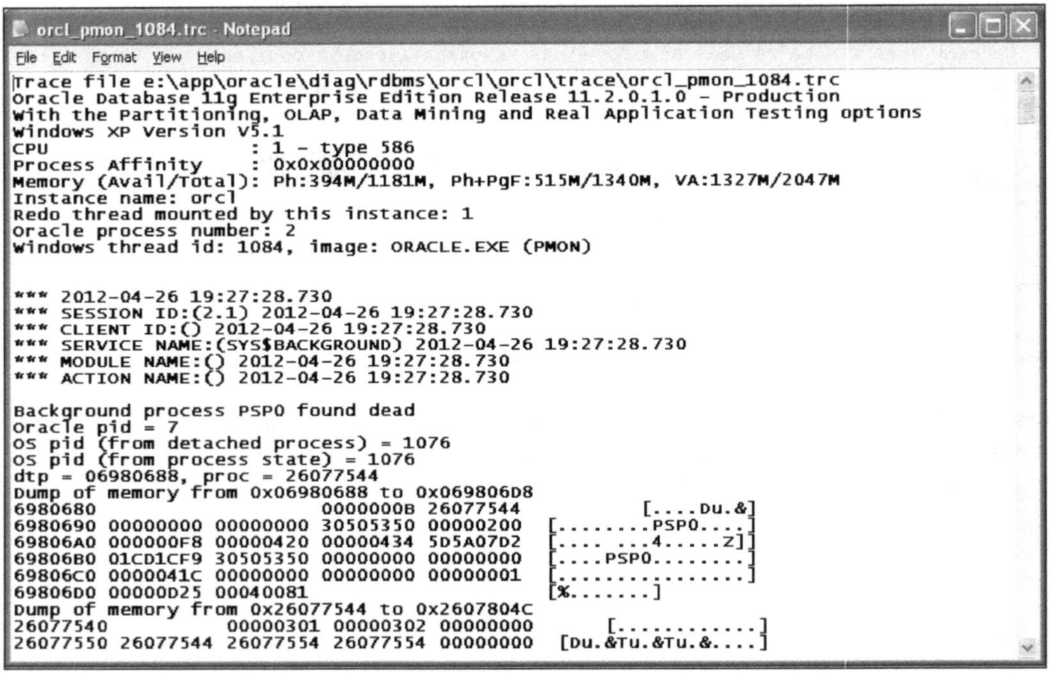

```
orcl_pmon_1084.trc - Notepad
File Edit Format View Help
Trace file e:\app\oracle\diag\rdbms\orcl\orcl\trace\orcl_pmon_1084.trc
Oracle Database 11g Enterprise Edition Release 11.2.0.1.0 - Production
With the Partitioning, OLAP, Data Mining and Real Application Testing options
Windows XP Version V5.1
CPU                 : 1 - type 586
Process Affinity    : 0x0x00000000
Memory (Avail/Total): Ph:394M/1181M, Ph+PgF:515M/1340M, VA:1327M/2047M
Instance name: orcl
Redo thread mounted by this instance: 1
Oracle process number: 2
Windows thread id: 1084, image: ORACLE.EXE (PMON)


*** 2012-04-26 19:27:28.730
*** SESSION ID:(2.1) 2012-04-26 19:27:28.730
*** CLIENT ID:() 2012-04-26 19:27:28.730
*** SERVICE NAME:(SYS$BACKGROUND) 2012-04-26 19:27:28.730
*** MODULE NAME:() 2012-04-26 19:27:28.730
*** ACTION NAME:() 2012-04-26 19:27:28.730

Background process PSP0 found dead
Oracle pid = 7
OS pid (from detached process) = 1076
OS pid (from process state) = 1076
dtp = 06980688, proc = 26077544
Dump of memory from 0x06980688 to 0x069806D8
6980680                   0000000B 26077544          [....Du.&]
6980690 00000000 00000000 30505350 00000200  [........PSP0....]
69806A0 000000F8 00000420 00000434 5D5A07D2  [.... ...4.....Z]]
69806B0 01CD1CF9 30505350 00000000 00000000  [....PSP0........]
69806C0 0000041C 00000000 00000000 00000001  [................]
69806D0 00000D25 00040081                    [%.......]
Dump of memory from 0x26077544 to 0x2607804C
26077540          00000301 00000302 00000000      [............]
26077550 26077544 26077554 26077554 00000000   [Du.&Tu.&Tu.&....]
```

When a user session encounters an internal exception, the results will be written out to a user trace file. These files are distinct from background trace files in that they do not contain the name of an Oracle background process in their filename. Rather, they generally are named by their operating system process ID number. For instance, a user trace file might be named `orcl_ora_3668.trc`—`orcl` for the database name and `3668` for the process ID. An example of a user trace file is shown in the following screenshot:

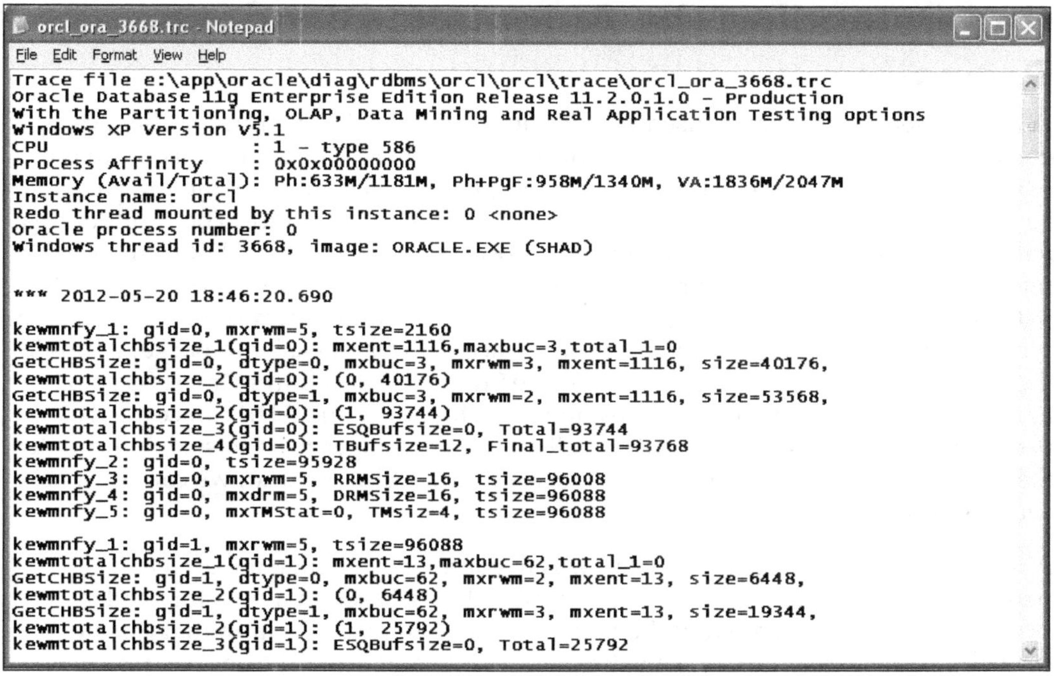

orcl_ora_3668.trc - Notepad

File Edit Format View Help

```
Trace file e:\app\oracle\diag\rdbms\orcl\orcl\trace\orcl_ora_3668.trc
Oracle Database 11g Enterprise Edition Release 11.2.0.1.0 - Production
With the Partitioning, OLAP, Data Mining and Real Application Testing options
Windows XP Version V5.1
CPU                 : 1 - type 586
Process Affinity    : 0x0x00000000
Memory (Avail/Total): Ph:633M/1181M, Ph+PgF:958M/1340M, VA:1836M/2047M
Instance name: orcl
Redo thread mounted by this instance: 0 <none>
Oracle process number: 0
Windows thread id: 3668, image: ORACLE.EXE (SHAD)


*** 2012-05-20 18:46:20.690

kewmnfy_1: gid=0, mxrwm=5, tsize=2160
kewmtotalchbsize_1(gid=0): mxent=1116,maxbuc=3,total_1=0
GetCHBSize: gid=0, dtype=0, mxbuc=3, mxrwm=3, mxent=1116, size=40176,
kewmtotalchbsize_2(gid=0): (0, 40176)
GetCHBSize: gid=0, dtype=1, mxbuc=3, mxrwm=2, mxent=1116, size=53568,
kewmtotalchbsize_2(gid=0): (1, 93744)
kewmtotalchbsize_3(gid=0): ESQBufsize=0, Total=93744
kewmtotalchbsize_4(gid=0): TBufsize=12, Final_total=93768
kewmnfy_2: gid=0, tsize=95928
kewmnfy_3: gid=0, mxrwm=5, RRMSize=16, tsize=96008
kewmnfy_4: gid=0, mxdrm=5, DRMSize=16, tsize=96088
kewmnfy_5: gid=0, mxTMStat=0, TMSiz=4, tsize=96088

kewmnfy_1: gid=1, mxrwm=5, tsize=96088
kewmtotalchbsize_1(gid=1): mxent=13,maxbuc=62,total_1=0
GetCHBSize: gid=1, dtype=0, mxbuc=62, mxrwm=2, mxent=13, size=6448,
kewmtotalchbsize_2(gid=1): (0, 6448)
GetCHBSize: gid=1, dtype=1, mxbuc=62, mxrwm=3, mxent=13, size=19344,
kewmtotalchbsize_2(gid=1): (1, 25792)
kewmtotalchbsize_3(gid=1): ESQBufsize=0, Total=25792
```

The vast majority of trace file information is not decipherable, nor is it meant to be. These types of diagnostic files have limited use to DBAs. They are, however, very useful to Oracle Support services should a database problem require their assistance. Typically, Oracle Support will request the alert log and relevant trace files as a part of their problem resolution process. Occasionally during a serious database problem, a core dump of the various memory caches may occur. If so, Oracle Support will generally request those as well.

Understanding the Automatic Diagnostic Repository

For many years, DBAs have used the alert log and trace files to assist in diagnosing database problems, either themselves or with the help of Oracle Support. With the advent of database Version 11*g*, Oracle attempted to redesign the structure and location of various types of logfiles into a more coherent structure. The result of this redesign was the Automatic Diagnostic Repository, or ADR. The ADR is intended to represent a self-managed approach to database diagnostics. While the actual content within such files as the alert log has not changed, the ADR centralizes these files in a central repository to make them more easily accessible and easier to package should these files need to be digitally sent to Oracle Support. This allows Oracle Support to resolve customer's database issues more quickly, since the ADR can correctly package all the relevant files. Additionally, DBAs no longer need to search through the operating system to locate various logs and trace files. Instead, we can use a new command-line interface.

A major part of introducing the ADR was to completely change the directory structure in which the logs are held. Instead of being based in a directory called `admin`, the ADR is based out of the `$ORACLE_BASE` directory. Within that directory is a subdirectory called `diag`. This directory essentially holds the entire substructure of the ADR. The directories we see under `diag` are dependent on what products we have installed. Our simple database installation shows subdirectories for `rdbms` and `tnslsnr`—the database and the database listener, respectively. If we had installed other Oracle products, such as the Grid Infrastructure that allows the use of Real Application Clusters, we would see other homes. Let's navigate to our main ADR directory for the database on a Linux installation of Oracle.

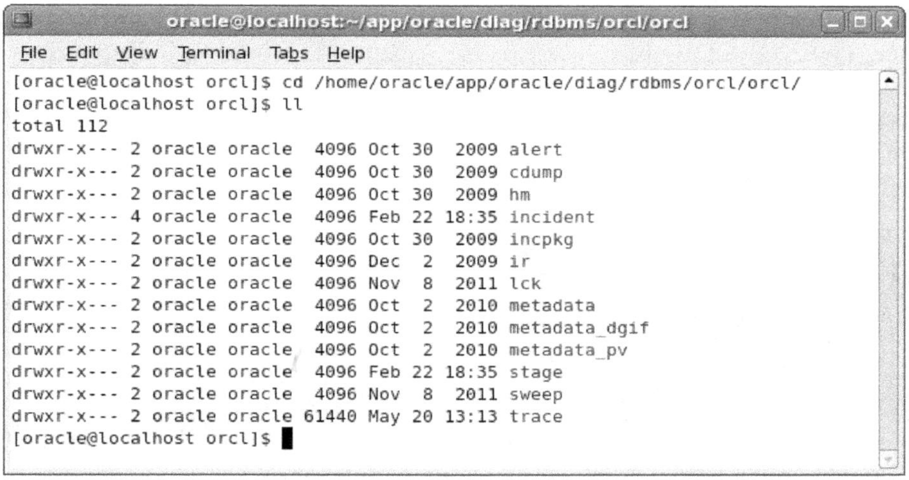
oracle@localhost:~/app/oracle/diag/rdbms/orcl/orcl
File Edit View Terminal Tabs Help
[oracle@localhost orcl]$ cd /home/oracle/app/oracle/diag/rdbms/orcl/orcl/
[oracle@localhost orcl]$ ll
total 112
drwxr-x--- 2 oracle oracle 4096 Oct 30 2009 alert
drwxr-x--- 2 oracle oracle 4096 Oct 30 2009 cdump
drwxr-x--- 2 oracle oracle 4096 Oct 30 2009 hm
drwxr-x--- 4 oracle oracle 4096 Feb 22 18:35 incident
drwxr-x--- 2 oracle oracle 4096 Oct 30 2009 incpkg
drwxr-x--- 2 oracle oracle 4096 Dec 2 2009 ir
drwxr-x--- 2 oracle oracle 4096 Nov 8 2011 lck
drwxr-x--- 2 oracle oracle 4096 Oct 2 2010 metadata
drwxr-x--- 2 oracle oracle 4096 Oct 2 2010 metadata_dgif
drwxr-x--- 2 oracle oracle 4096 Oct 2 2010 metadata_pv
drwxr-x--- 2 oracle oracle 4096 Feb 22 18:35 stage
drwxr-x--- 2 oracle oracle 4096 Nov 8 2011 sweep
drwxr-x--- 2 oracle oracle 61440 May 20 13:13 trace
[oracle@localhost orcl]$

> For our default Oracle installation on Windows, the directory will be `E:\app\oracle\diag\rdbms\orcl\orcl`.

As we can see in the preceding screenshot, there are a number of directories here that store ADR information. We will highlight a few of them:

- **alert**: Stores alert log information in an XML format. Read by the ADRCI
- **cdump**: Stores memory core dump information
- **incident**: Maintains information for incidents that occur in the database
- **incpkg**: Packaged incidents are located here
- **trace**: Location of many plaintext logs and trace files

The true power of the ADR is unlocked when we employ its new command-line interface. The **ADRCI**, mercifully short for **Automatic Diagnostic Repository Command Interface**, provides a single command-line interface with which to view any number of logs or trace files. Using the ADRCI, we can more easily access log and trace file information. To invoke the ADRCI, we simply type **adrci** from the command line, as shown in the following screenshot:

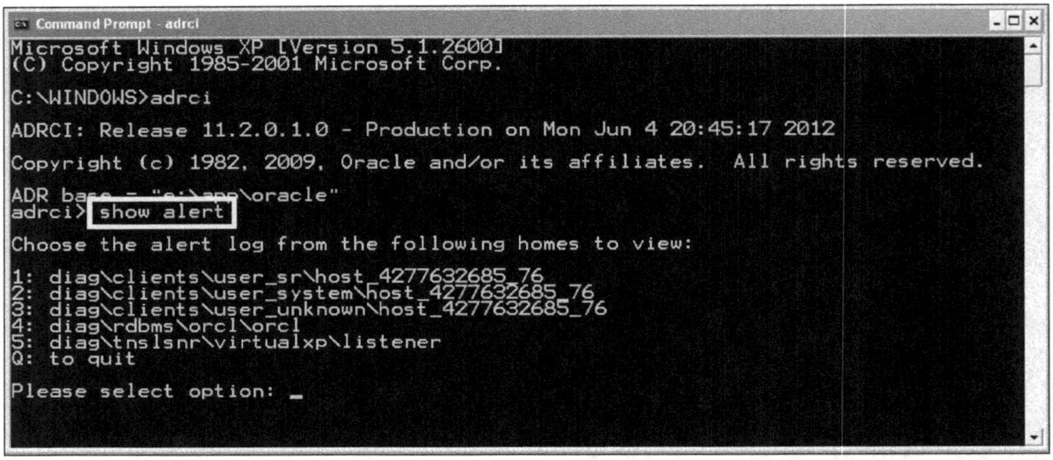
Command Prompt - adrci
Microsoft Windows XP [Version 5.1.2600]
(C) Copyright 1985-2001 Microsoft Corp.
C:\WINDOWS>adrci
ADRCI: Release 11.2.0.1.0 - Production on Mon Jun 4 20:45:17 2012
Copyright (c) 1982, 2009, Oracle and/or its affiliates. All rights reserved.
\oracle"
adrci> show alert
Choose the alert log from the following homes to view:
1: diag\clients\user_sr\host_4277632685_76
2: diag\clients\user_system\host_4277632685_76
3: diag\clients\user_unknown\host_4277632685_76
4: diag\rdbms\orcl\orcl
5: diag\tnslsnr\virtualxp\listener
Q: to quit
Please select option:

When we type **show alert** from the ADRCI command line, we're presented with a number of related alert logs. We simply select the log we wish to view, in this case **4** for the database alert log, and the log is displayed:

alert_856_3676_orcl_1.ado - Notepad
File Edit Format View Help
2012-02-20 19:51:55.274000 -06:00
Starting ORACLE instance (normal)
2012-02-20 19:51:56.365000 -06:00
LICENSE_MAX_SESSION = 0
LICENSE_SESSIONS_WARNING = 0
Shared memory segment for instance monitoring created
Picked latch-free SCN scheme 2
Using LOG_ARCHIVE_DEST_1 parameter default value as
E:\app\oracle\product\11.2.0\dbhome_1\RDBMS
Autotune of undo retention is turned on.
IMODE=BR
ILAT =27
LICENSE_MAX_USERS = 0
SYS auditing is disabled
2012-02-20 19:51:57.807000 -06:00
Starting up:
Oracle Database 11g Enterprise Edition Release 11.2.0.1.0 - ProductionWith the
Partitioning, OLAP, Data Mining and Real Application Testing options.
Using parameter settings in client-side pfile
E:\APP\ORACLE\ADMIN\ORCL\PFILE\INIT.ORA on machine VIRTUALXP
System parameters with non-default values:
processes = 150
shared_pool_size = 80M
large_pool_size = 36M
java_pool_size = 48M
control_files = "E:\APP\ORACLE\ORADATA\ORCL\CONTROL01.CTL"
control_files = "E:\APP\ORACLE\ORADATA\ORCL\CONTROL02.CTL"
db_block_size = 8192
db_cache_size = 192M
compatible = "11.2.0.0.0"
undo_tablespace = "UNDOTBS1"
remote_login_passwordfile= "EXCLUSIVE"
db_domain = ""
dispatchers = "(PROTOCOL=TCP) (SERVICE=orclXDB)"
audit_file_dest = "E:\APP\ORACLE\ADMIN\ORCL\ADUMP"

Even though the file is shown in text, the ADRCI is actually reading an XML file stored within the ADR.

The ADRCI can be used to package incidents—occurrences that are deemed by the database to be serious error situations that could require the help of Oracle Support. To display any incidents, we use the `set home` and `show incident` commands, as shown in the following screenshot, and a list of incidents is displayed:

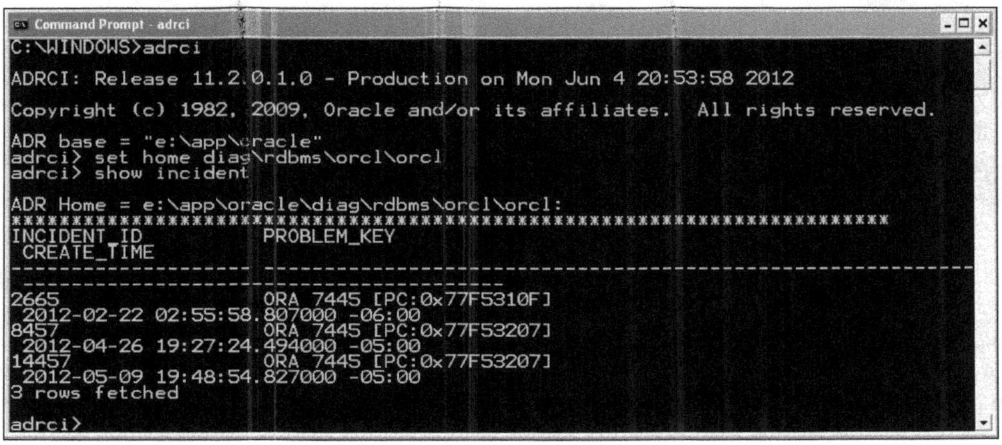
Command Prompt - adrci
C:\WINDOWS>adrci
ADRCI: Release 11.2.0.1.0 - Production on Mon Jun 4 20:53:58 2012
Copyright (c) 1982, 2009, Oracle and/or its affiliates. All rights reserved.
ADR base = "e:\app\oracle"
adrci> set home diag\rdbms\orcl\orcl
adrci> show incident
ADR Home = e:\app\oracle\diag\rdbms\orcl\orcl:
INCIDENT_ID PROBLEM_KEY
CREATE_TIME
2665 ORA 7445 [PC:0x77F5310F]
2012-02-22 02:55:58.807000 -06:00
8457 ORA 7445 [PC:0x77F53207]
2012-04-26 19:27:24.494000 -05:00
14457 ORA 7445 [PC:0x77F53207]
2012-05-09 19:48:54.827000 -05:00
3 rows fetched
adrci>

Once we know the incident ID, we can use the **Incident Packaging Service**, or **IPS**, to collect a set of relevant log and trace files for Oracle Support. We first create a package, and then add an incident to it. In this case, our incident ID is **2665**:

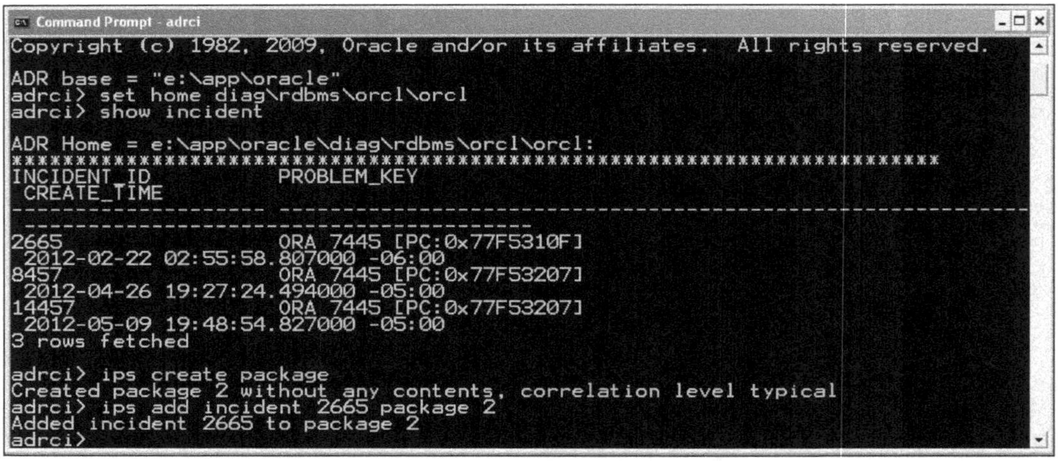
Command Prompt - adrci
Copyright (c) 1982, 2009, Oracle and/or its affiliates. All rights reserved.
ADR base = "e:\app\oracle"
adrci> set home diag\rdbms\orcl\orcl
adrci> show incident
ADR Home = e:\app\oracle\diag\rdbms\orcl\orcl:
INCIDENT_ID PROBLEM_KEY
CREATE_TIME
2665 ORA 7445 [PC:0x77F5310F]
2012-02-22 02:55:58.807000 -06:00
8457 ORA 7445 [PC:0x77F53207]
2012-04-26 19:27:24.494000 -05:00
14457 ORA 7445 [PC:0x77F53207]
2012-05-09 19:48:54.827000 -05:00
3 rows fetched
adrci> ips create package
Created package 2 without any contents, correlation level typical
adrci> ips add incident 2665 package 2
Added incident 2665 to package 2
adrci>

Once the package is created, we can use it to generate a physical file that contains the necessary trace files with the **ips generate** package command:

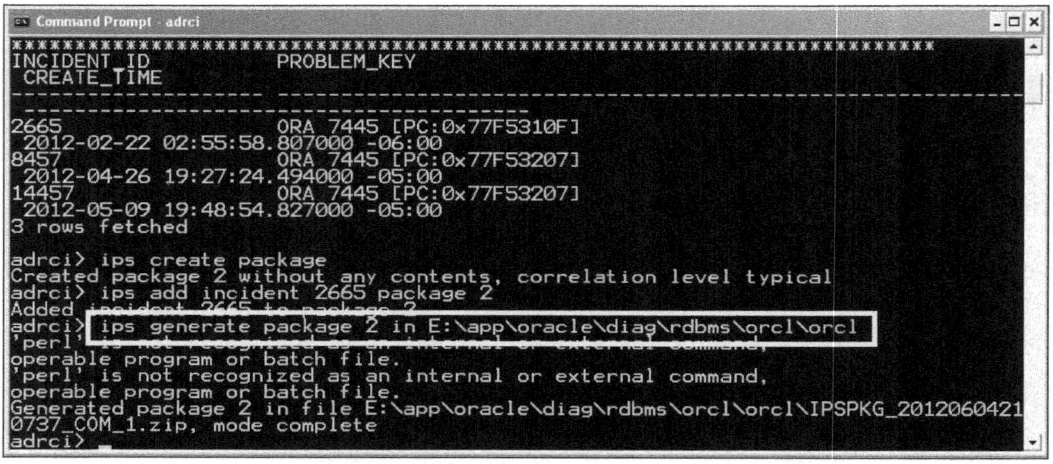
Command Prompt - adrci
INCIDENT_ID PROBLEM_KEY
CREATE_TIME
2665 ORA 7445 [PC:0x77F5310F]
2012-02-22 02:55:58.807000 -06:00
8457 ORA 7445 [PC:0x77F53207]
2012-04-26 19:27:24.494000 -05:00
14457 ORA 7445 [PC:0x77F53207]
2012-05-09 19:48:54.827000 -05:00
3 rows fetched
adrci> ips create package
Created package 2 without any contents, correlation level typical
adrci> ips add incident 2665 package 2
Added
adrci> ips generate package 2 in E:\app\oracle\diag\rdbms\orcl\orcl
'perl'
operable program or batch file.
'perl' is not recognized as an internal or external command,
operable program or batch file.
Generated package 2 in file E:\app\oracle\diag\rdbms\orcl\orcl\IPSPKG_20120604210737_COM_1.zip, mode complete
adrci>

This indicates that a ZIP file of the relevant log and trace information was generated in the requested directory. This file can then be sent to Oracle Support for more efficient diagnosis of the problem. This file can contain a number of other informational files besides trace files, including SQL test cases. Additionally, we can incrementally update the package with new information as our incident progresses.

Understanding the Oracle Support model

No matter how we might try to solve every problem on our own, DBAs sometimes still have to ask for help. Certain Oracle errors, such as the dreaded `ORA-0600` error, can be extremely difficult to solve without the intervention of Oracle Support services. Fortunately, Oracle provides an extremely useful website, **My Oracle Support** (formerly called **Metalink**), which can be found at `https://support.oracle.com`.

Using My Oracle Support

Note that support services are only available to paying customers of Oracle software. Those downloading Oracle for their own non-commercial use do not have access to the site. At the preceding URL, we are directed to log in with an authenticated username and password to the site, which we acquire as a result of the purchase process. Once we log in, we see the following startup screen that loads the necessary components to run the content-rich site:

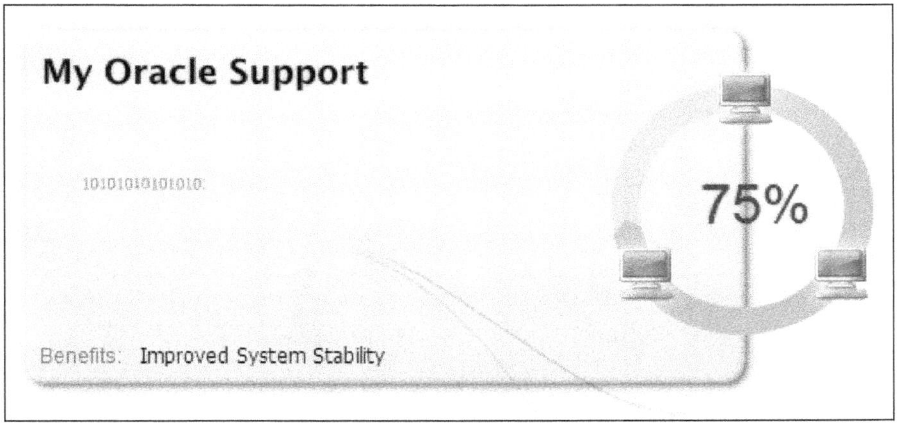
My Oracle Support
10101010101010
75%
Benefits: Improved System Stability

My Oracle Support can be an extremely useful site for help and problem resolution. The following is just a small example of the types of information we can gain from the site:

- A customizable dashboard tailored to our individual systems and configurations
- Latest news regarding Oracle releases
- Summary of bug reports

- List of technical service requests made
- Knowledge base of technical alerts and links to solutions
- Patches and updates
- List of certified Oracle systems, including operating systems

The following screenshot shows a partial look at the customizable dashboard that serves as the starting point for many of these features:

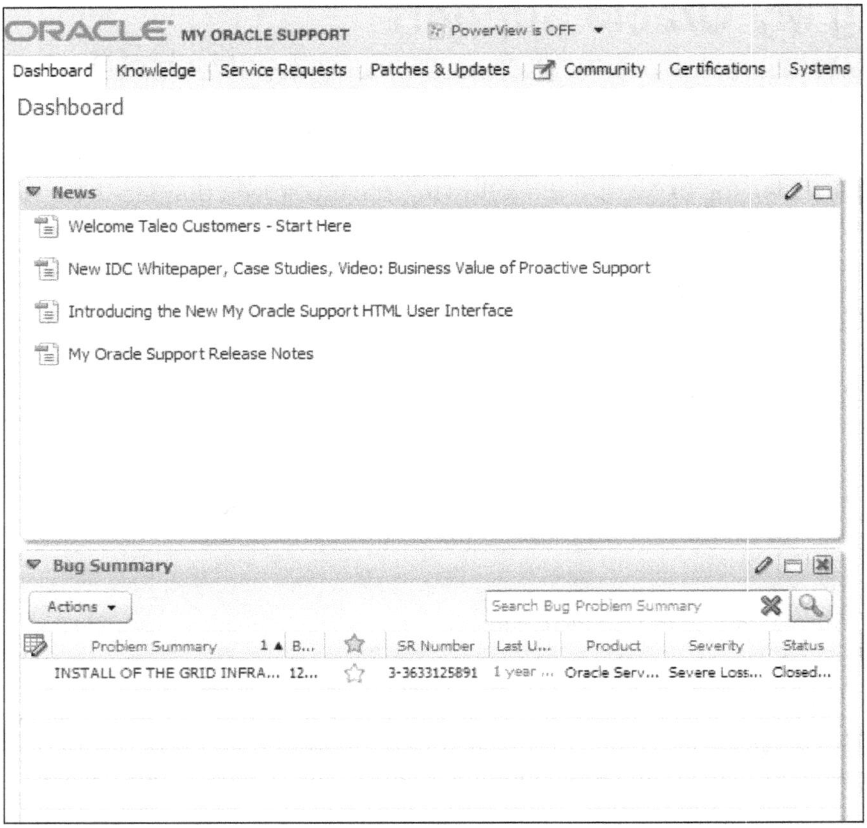
ORACLE MY ORACLE SUPPORT
PowerView is OFF
Dashboard
Knowledge
Service Requests
Patches & Updates
Community
Certifications
Systems
Dashboard
News
Welcome Taleo Customers - Start Here
New IDC Whitepaper, Case Studies, Video: Business Value of Proactive Support
Introducing the New My Oracle Support HTML User Interface
My Oracle Support Release Notes
Bug Summary
Actions
Search Bug Problem Summary
Problem Summary
SR Number
Last U...
Product
Severity
Status
INSTALL OF THE GRID INFRA... 12...
3-3633125891
1 year ...
Oracle Serv...
Severe Loss...
Closed...

In order to use the **My Oracle Support** website to request service, the user must possess a **Customer Support Identifier**, or **CSI**, that is linked to his or her licensing. This CSI covers only the Oracle products purchased by the customer. When a customer has a problem that requires the intervention of Oracle Support, he or she opens a **Service Request**, or **SR**. This SR is handled by members of the Oracle Support team, who work with the customer to resolve the problem. When an SR is opened, a severity level can be attached to it, indicating the level of support needed.

> **The real-world DBA**
>
> When opening an SR, it is prudent to assess your own availability or the availability of DBA team members to resolve the problem. Although all technical problems are important, be aware that opening an SR with the highest severity level, **SEV 1**, requires that a customer representative be available on a 24 x 7 basis to resolve the problem.

Patching Oracle

Like many other software companies, Oracle provides software updates and patches on a regular basis. These patches are used to fix software bugs, close security holes, and improve the general functionality of the product.

Updates and patches come in three basic forms. Patch sets are cumulative collections of product fixes. Upgrading a patch set will cause the version number to increment, such as patching a Version 11.2.0.1 installation to 11.2.0.2. Interim patches are released to fix a particular problem, and may be included in future patch bundles. **Critical Patch Updates** are a set of the latest fixes for a given release level and are often associated with security-related fixes. **Patch Set Updates**, or **PSU**, are related to Critical Patch Updates, but allow the DBA to select only those fixes that are recommended or proactive.

As an example of installing a Critical Patch Update patch, let's look at the next example. A Critical Patch Update patch has been downloaded from the **My Oracle Support** site. This patch contains a number bug and security fixes for Version 11.2.0.1. To apply the patch, we use the **OPatch** tool, invoked using the command `opatch`. We download and unzip the file, then navigate to the `patch` directory. In order to run the patch, we must shut down the database and listener with the proper commands. On Windows, we must also stop all Oracle-related services. We then run the `opatch apply` command, referencing the full path to the `opatch` executable. On Windows, this executable is called `opatch.bat`. The patch then runs and is applied:

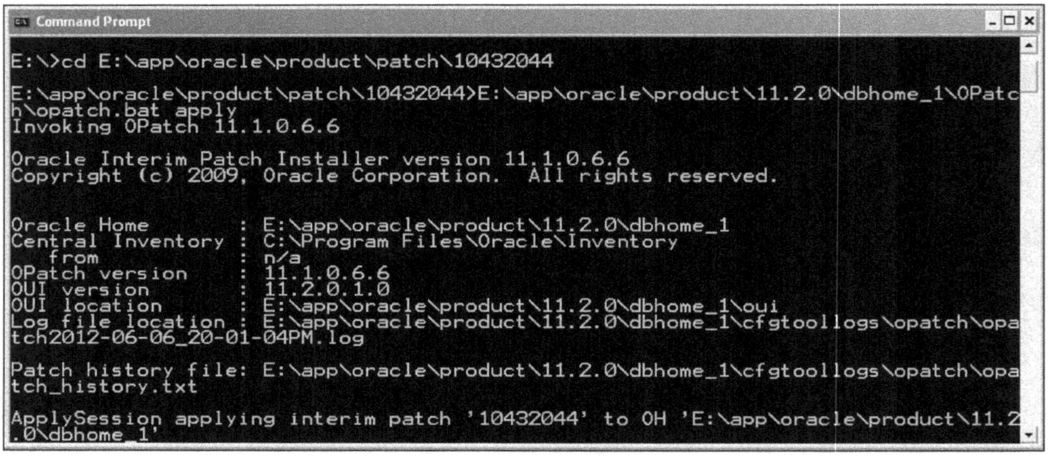
Command Prompt
E:\>cd E:\app\oracle\product\patch\10432044
E:\app\oracle\product\patch\10432044>E:\app\oracle\product\11.2.0\dbhome_1\OPatch\opatch.bat apply
Invoking OPatch 11.1.0.6.6
Oracle Interim Patch Installer version 11.1.0.6.6
Copyright (c) 2009, Oracle Corporation. All rights reserved.
Oracle Home : E:\app\oracle\product\11.2.0\dbhome_1
Central Inventory : C:\Program Files\Oracle\Inventory
from : n/a
OPatch version : 11.1.0.6.6
OUI version : 11.2.0.1.0
OUI location : E:\app\oracle\product\11.2.0\dbhome_1\oui
Log file location : E:\app\oracle\product\11.2.0\dbhome_1\cfgtoollogs\opatch\opatch2012-06-06_20-01-04PM.log
Patch history file: E:\app\oracle\product\11.2.0\dbhome_1\cfgtoollogs\opatch\opatch_history.txt
ApplySession applying interim patch '10432044' to OH 'E:\app\oracle\product\11.2.0\dbhome_1'

Certification objectives covered

The following certification objectives have been covered throughout this chapter:

- Setting database initialization parameters
- Describing the stages of database startup and shutdown
- Using alert log and trace files
- Using data dictionary and dynamic performance views

Summary

In this chapter, we've begun to dig deeper into the day-to-day activities of an Oracle DBA. We've examined the processes of database startup and shutdown, and learned to control those processes. We've managed Oracle database parameters using the PFILE and SPFILE. We've explored the data dictionary and learned to query it in order to retrieve valuable database information. We've learned about the process of gathering database diagnostics, and used the alert log and trace files to do so. We've also looked at the new ADR and ADRCI diagnostic command tools. Finally, we've examined the Oracle Support model, including the **My Oracle Support** website and the patching process. In our next chapter, we explore the concept of database security, including the ability to grant and revoke various types of database permissions.

Test your knowledge

Q 1. Which of the following is NOT available following the startup of the instance?

a. Background processes
b. Database
c. Memory caches
d. The SGA

Q 2. During which database state is the control file located and its existence verified?

a. NOMOUNT
b. MOUNT
c. OPEN
d. DISMOUNT

Q 3. Which of these does NOT occur during a `shutdown immediate` command?

a. Active sessions are rolled back
b. Changed blocks in the SGA are flushed to disk
c. Database parameters are re-read
d. Database is dismounted

Q 4. Which database role gives the user the widest possible range of permissions when connecting to the database?

a. `SYSOPER`
b. `SYSDBA`
c. `SYSTEM`
d. `SYSOSDBA`

Q 5. Which is the highest administrative user possible in an Oracle database?

a. `SYS`
b. `SYSTEM`
c. `DBA`
d. `OSDBA`

Q 6. When a user executes the `sqlplus / as sysdba` command, how is the user authenticated?

a. Using a local LDAP server
b. Using database credentials
c. Using operating system credentials
d. Using a remote RADIUS server

Q 7. Which command could be used to instantiate the instance and stop before the control file is read?

a. `startup nomount`
b. `startup mount`
c. `startup open`
d. `startup conditional`

Q 8. When the `shutdown` command is executed, which type of shutdown is executed?

a. `shutdown normal`
b. `shutdown transactional`
c. `shutdown immediate`
d. `shutdown abort`

Q 9. Which type of shutdown will still allow users to connect?

a. `shutdown normal`
b. `shutdown transactional`
c. `shutdown immediate`
d. None of the above

Q 10. Which types of shutdown will promptly disconnect user sessions? (Choose two)

a. `shutdown normal`
b. `shutdown transactional`
c. `shutdown immediate`
d. `shutdown abort`

Q 11. Which type of shutdown will require an instance recovery during the next startup?

a. `shutdown normal`
b. `shutdown transactional`
c. `shutdown immediate`
d. `shutdown abort`

Q 12. Which type of parameter file will allow certain parameters to be changed while the database is open?

a. PFILE
b. SPFILE
c. `init.ora`
d. None. Changing database parameters while the database is open is not possible.

Q 13. Which command could be used to change the value of the `pga_aggregate_target` parameter in the existing instance as well as the SPFILE?

a. `alter system set pga_aggregate_target = 150M scope=spfile;`
b. `alter system set pga_aggregate_target = 150M scope=memory;`
c. `alter system set pga_aggregate_target = 150M scope=both;`
d. `alter system set pga_aggregate_target = 150M scope=all;`

Q 14. Which of the following is NOT an example of a static data dictionary view?

a. `all_tables`
b. `user_synonyms`
c. `v$session_wait`
d. `dba_data_files`

Q 15. What parameter can be used to determine the location of the alert log?

a. `background_dump_dest`
b. `diagnostic_dump_dest`
c. `core_dump_dest`
d. `alert_dump_dest`

Q 16. For what purpose are trace files most useful?

a. Determining the values of database parameters
b. Determining the location of the ADR
c. Observing the startup and shutdown process of the database
d. Providing Oracle Support aid in problem resolution

Q 17. Which of the following is NOT a task designed for the ADR?

a. Opening a Service Request with Oracle Support
b. Packaging incremental diagnostic information for Oracle Support
c. Displaying serious internal database incidents
d. Viewing the alert log

7
Managing Security

Of the many trending issues in information technology today, perhaps none is more important than security. With an increasing rise in everything from malicious attacks to the theft of corporate intellectual property, there has never been a more pressing need for DBAs who are knowledgeable and vigilant to preserve the security of the data for which they are responsible. Consider this: Of all the possible targets to an attacker, what could be more attractive than a database filled with customer information, credit card numbers, billing addresses, or **Personally Identifiable Information** (**PII**)? In this chapter, we will learn the basics of securing an Oracle database. We'll look at the concept of security and what it means from a database perspective, how to enable privileged access to information, and how to audit what happens in our database even when we're not looking.

In this chapter, we shall:

- Understand the fundamentals of database security
- Manage user accounts
- Administer system and object privileges
- Explore roles
- Explain the purpose of profiles
- Understand database auditing

Understanding the fundamentals of database security

The purpose of a database is to store data. That data can come in many forms, but if someone takes the time and money to hire DBAs to organize and store it, that data is important in some way. As a DBA, it is easy to focus on the practicalities of administration, such as performance tuning, backup and recovery, or database and object creation. In the day-to-day life of a DBA, which often consists of "fighting fires", it is easy to lose sight of security. The security of the data is not a subject about which someone will complain to a DBA—until that data has been compromised. Security is a responsibility that a DBA must often bear alone. Compound this with the fact that so few people really *understand* what's involved in securing a database. This leaves us with an extremely important facet of administering a database that is often neither understood nor valued by those outside of the database administration team. Nevertheless, that responsibility falls on us as DBAs. We can never let negligence open the doors of our database to malicious intent.

Exploring the principles behind security

When we think of a person or group of individuals attempting to gain illegal access to a computer system, we often think of the overused and somewhat inaccurate term "hacker". Such an attacker gains access to the system from some remote site, far beyond the jurisdiction of the laws that protect a given nation. While these types of attacks are important and tend to make the evening news more often, it may be surprising to learn that they are *not* the most common form of attack. The majority of system-compromising attacks actually come from *within* an organization. These types of attacks often come in the form of disgruntled or compromised employees that steal or destroy data for their own purposes. Considering this fact, the practice of focusing security on the *boundaries* of a system is grossly insufficient. A DBA cannot simply defer the responsibility of security to network administrators and trust that their firewalls will prevent an attack. A DBA must also consider internal threats.

One of the most fundamental privileges in the realm of security is the principle of **least privilege**. It states that *a user should only be granted the privileges that are absolutely necessary for that user to accomplish their given tasks*. Unfortunately, this is one area in which a DBA can encounter resistance when formulating a security plan. It is common for users to request, or even feel that they require, more privileges than their job demands. One of the most egregious violations of the principle of least privilege can come from a DBA's own supervisors.

Take for example, a person in IT management that feels that, because they are responsible for the technological aspects of the company, they should have all the rights of an administrator. Nothing could be further from the truth. If this manager doesn't have the training and skills of an administrator, their user account could pose a threat to the security of the company's data. Even if they did possess the skills, their job role does not require such an elevated access level. In the principle of least privilege, less is best.

Note that we've used the word "feel" a number of times while discussing this subject. The security of the database is not a matter of personal feelings or whether someone thinks they "deserve" higher levels of access. Administrative access should be looked at as a responsibility. To combat such perceptions, it is invaluable for a DBA to create and implement a database **security policy** for their organization. This policy should be detailed and comprehensive, and should be endorsed by the organization's management. Such policies are often neglected, since they can be difficult to formulate. It requires the DBA to gain a thorough understanding of the various users and applications that use the database. Often, it necessitates interviewing users and reviewing the SQL code that is executed against the database. However, such a policy can prevent many of the internal threats that are possible, and even aid in limiting the amount of exposure posed by an external attack.

Another principle that is important in securing the database is the concept of separating users from data. In an earlier chapter, we discussed Oracle's schema-based approach. We said that some RDBMS systems make a distinction between database users and object owners. In these systems, a **database user** is defined as an account that allows access to the database. Converse to this is an **object owner**, which, in a system that makes such a distinction, is an account that exists only to create and own database objects. In Oracle, no such distinction exists. User accounts can own objects and objects can be owned by users. This, however, doesn't mean that we can't put such a division in place. As DBAs, we can designate that certain users have the ability to log in to the database and that these users have certain privileges to do certain operations and manipulate certain objects. We can also create other users that do not have the ability to log in, but instead own the tables, indexes, and other objects that make up the database. These object owners can be locked to prevent login access, even if someone knows the password. Thus, a division is put between users and database objects. To do this, however, we'll need to learn about the ways in which users are created and access is granted.

Creating and managing user accounts

One of the primary security principles is authentication. **Authentication** is the process of confirming the identity of a user. Users access the database by way of user accounts. In order to successfully log in to a database, a user must pass through some form of authentication, often by way of a user account name and password. To review what we've learned in previous chapters, there are two major default administrative accounts in Oracle called `SYS` and `SYSTEM`. The `SYS` account is the highest administrative account available. It owns the data dictionary and has the power to do any type of administrative activity. The `SYSTEM` account is comparable in terms of authority, but does not own the data dictionary. `SYSTEM` is often used by DBAs to administer the database, although `SYS` is used in certain cases, such as starting and stopping the database. We can, however, create other database user accounts with varying degrees of access.

Many of the following examples refer to database objects. These database objects can be created using the downloadable code from the Packt support website. In order to complete these examples, you will need to download and run that code. Instructions for executing the code are included in the zip file. For more detailed instructions, refer to the *Online Chapter 1, Managing Oracle Tables* available for download from the Packt support website.

Creating users

A user is created using the `CREATE USER` command. There are many clauses we can add to this statement to change various aspects of the user, but for now we'll use the most basic form of the command. Creating users requires a certain level of permissions, so we'll log in to SQL Developer using our `system@orcl` connection.

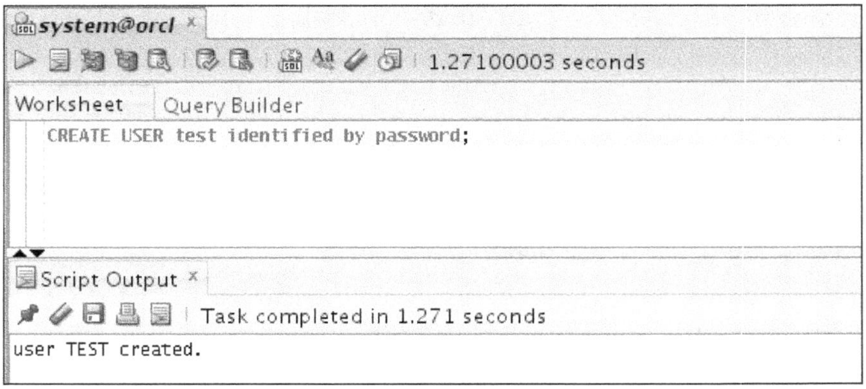
system@orcl
1.27100003 seconds
Worksheet
Query Builder
CREATE USER test identified by password;
Script Output
Task completed in 1.271 seconds
user TEST created.

Here we've created a user named `test`. The `identified by` clause indicates that the user is authenticated using database authentication with the password `password`. Other possible values for `identified` include `IDENTIFIED EXTERNALLY` and `IDENTIFIED GLOBALLY`. `EXTERNALLY` is used when an external authentication service is used, such as a Kerberos or Radius server. `GLOBALLY` indicates that the user is authenticated using a **Lightweight Directory Access Protocol** (**LDAP**) server or Oracle Internet Directory. For our purposes, we'll only focus on **local authentication**—database authentication using a password.

When we create a user, such as our `test` user, using the previous statement, we are implicitly accepting the default values for a number of other possible clauses that can more specifically control the characteristics of our user. Let's look at an example that shows ways we can more thoroughly define our user. Say we need to create a user login for one of our Companylink employee participants. Even though the Companylink users are listed in the `employee` table, their access is limited to connections that occur through the application. We want to give an employee, Laura Thrace, connectivity directly to the database itself.

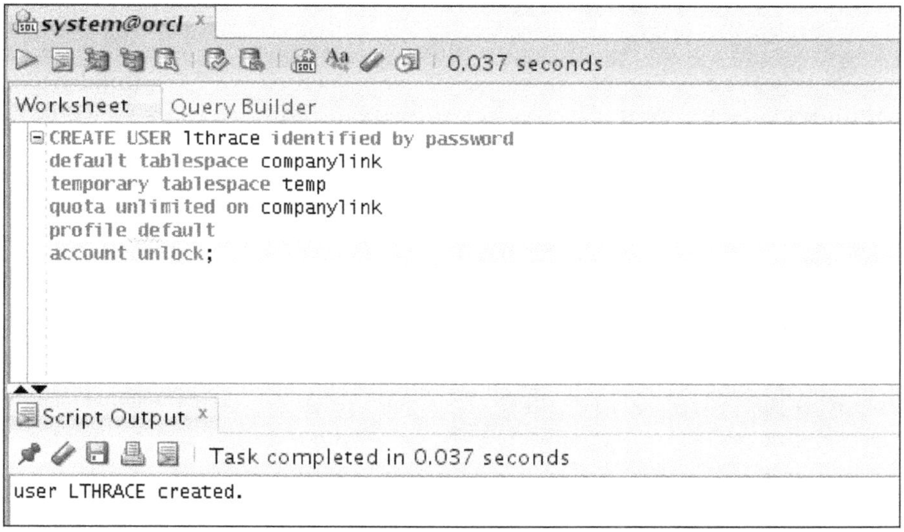
system@orcl
0.037 seconds
Worksheet
Query Builder
CREATE USER lthrace identified by password
default tablespace companylink
temporary tablespace temp
quota unlimited on companylink
profile default
account unlock;
Script Output
Task completed in 0.037 seconds
user LTHRACE created.

We've added a number of options to this statement, so let's define each of them.

- `default tablespace`: This is the default location in which this user's objects will be created. Thus, if the **lthrace** user logs in and creates an object, such as a table, without specifying its tablespace location, will be created in her default tablespace, shown here as **companylink**.

- `temporary tablespace`: This is the default location where any operations, such as sorting, that require temporary space will be performed. Because it is possible to have multiple temporary tablespaces in a database, this clause specifies where that temporary space is for the given user.
- `quota`: This defines the amount of space that can be used by the specified user in any given tablespace. Since we have used the keyword **unlimited** here, this means that the **lthrace** user has unlimited use of the **companylink** tablespace.
- `profile`: We will examine `profiles` shortly, but for now, this option is used to set a number of limits on a user that pertain to everything from password characteristics to a user's ability to consume a certain amount of CPU. For this user, we've indicated that the **default** profile should be used.
- `account unlock`: This indicates that the account will be unlocked and accessible to the user upon creation. This is the default behavior, although `account lock` can also be specified, which immediately locks the account once it is created and prevents anyone from using it to log in to the database. However, any objects owned by that user will still be available to all users. Only the account itself is locked.
- `password expire`: We didn't use this clause in our example, but this is an optional clause that indicates that the password we've defined will immediately expire upon creation of the user. This forces users to change their password the first time they log in.

To bring all of these options together, let's examine the syntax tree for `CREATE USER`.

```
CREATE USER <username> IDENTIFIED | BY <password> | EXTERNALLY AS
<certificate> | GLOBALLY AS <directory>
DEFAULT TABLESPACE <tablespace_name>
TEMPORARY TABLESPACE <temp_tablespace_name>
QUOTA <size> ON <tablespace_name>
PROFILE <profile_name>
PASSWORD EXPIRE
ACCOUNT LOCK | UNLOCK;
```

Now that we've created our new user, let's use it to connect to our database using SQL*Plus.

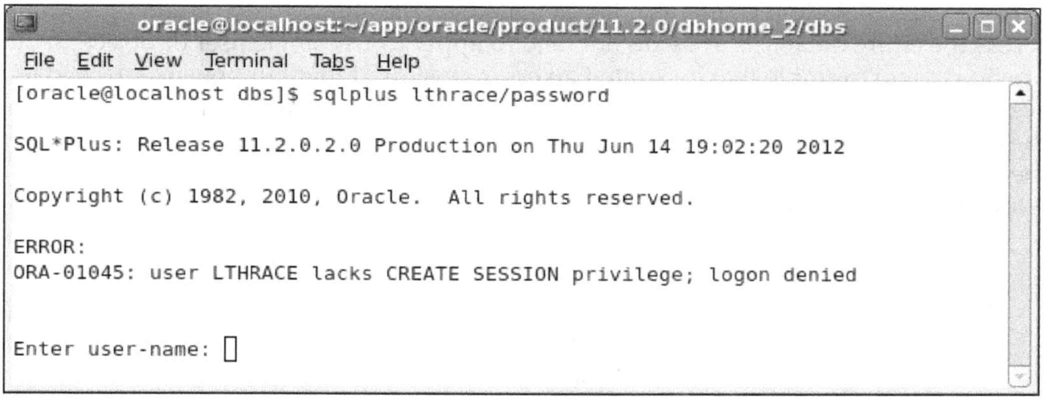
oracle@localhost:~/app/oracle/product/11.2.0/dbhome_2/dbs
File Edit View Terminal Tabs Help
[oracle@localhost dbs]$ sqlplus lthrace/password
SQL*Plus: Release 11.2.0.2.0 Production on Thu Jun 14 19:02:20 2012
Copyright (c) 1982, 2010, Oracle. All rights reserved.
ERROR:
ORA-01045: user LTHRACE lacks CREATE SESSION privilege; logon denied
Enter user-name:

Not quite the experience we were expecting. Note that the error message indicates that we lack a privilege called `CREATE SESSION`. Clearly, we're going to need to understand more about privileges before we can continue.

Understanding privileges

Any system that allows individual users to be created must also have some form of user access control. This prevents users from accessing or affecting components that should not be available to them. Access control is critical to establishing system security and contributes to the overall health and safety of a computer system. We see examples of access control in everything from operating systems to web mail accounts. In Oracle, we administer access control using a number of methods, the most primary of which is through the use of **privileges**.

Granting system privileges

The first type of privilege we will examine is a **system privilege**. System privileges define a class of wide-reaching privileges that affect the ability to do certain operations across the entire database. They do not tend to apply to any single user or object. In our previous login example that generated an error, we found that our new user lacked a system privilege called `CREATE SESSION`. When we "give" a privilege to a user, we use the `GRANT` command. Thus, the recipient of a privilege is called a **grantee**. Although there are hundreds of system privileges, at this point we do not need to be concerned with all of them. Let's examine a few of them here.

- `CREATE SESSION`: This allows the user to connect to the database.
- `ALTER DATABASE`: This allows the grantee to run commands (those beginning with `ALTER DATABASE`) that change the physical structure of the database.
- `ALTER SYSTEM`: This allows commands to be run that can change database parameters.
- `CREATE/ALTER/DROP TABLESPACE`: These three separate privileges allow the grantee to manage tablespace-related operations.
- `CREATE/ALTER/DROP ROLE`: They allow the grantee to manage roles that encapsulate multiple privileges (discussed later in the chapter).
- `CREATE/ALTER/DROP PROFILE`: They allow the grantee to manage user profiles.
- `CREATE TABLE`: This allows the grantee to create any number of tables within their schema. Note that there is no `ALTER` or `DROP TABLE` privilege. Any grantee that has received the `CREATE TABLE` privilege has the implicit rights to change and/or drop that table.
- `CREATE ANY TABLE`: This is not to be confused with the previous system privilege; this privilege allows the grantee to create a table in schemas besides its own. Thus, the `lthrace` user with this privilege would be able to create tables in the `companylink` schema.
- `DROP ANY TABLE`: Although there is no `DROP TABLE` privilege, this privilege allows the grantee to drop tables in other users' schemas. Clearly, grantees of this privilege should be chosen carefully.
- `SELECT ANY TABLE`: This allows the grantee to query the data from any table in the database, regardless of the schema in which it resides. This is a far-reaching system privilege that should be granted with caution.

We now understand why our `lthrace` user couldn't log in to the database; it lacked the `CREATE SESSION` system privilege. However, we as DBAs can grant this privilege; first, using our `system@companylink` connection, we grant `lthrace` this system privilege.

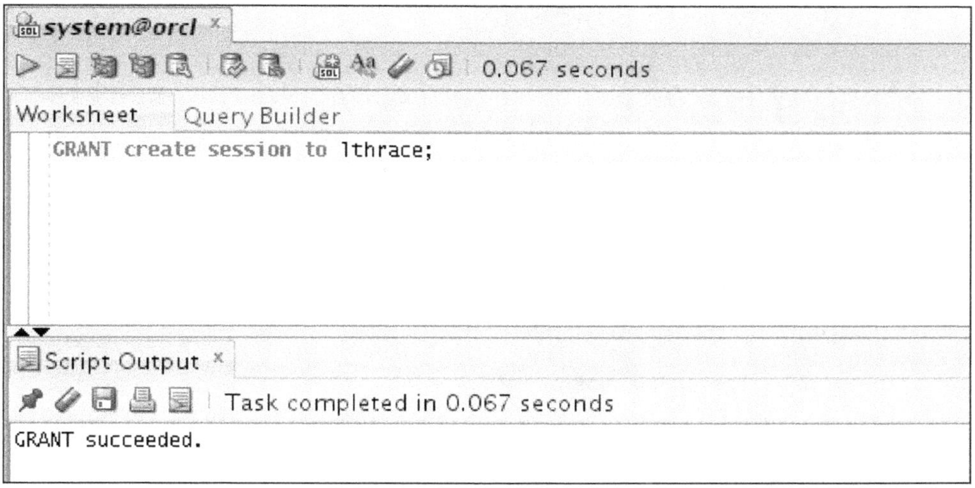
system@orcl
0.067 seconds
Worksheet
Query Builder
GRANT create session to lthrace;
Script Output
Task completed in 0.067 seconds
GRANT succeeded.

Next, we attempt to use SQL*Plus to connect `lthrace` to the database. We're using SQL*Plus in this example to avoid switching between SQL Developer connection tabs, although the reader is free to do so.

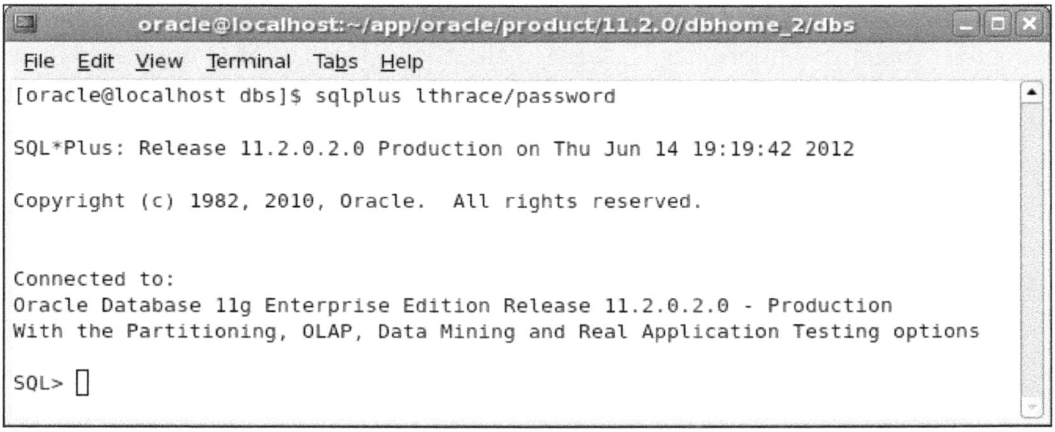
oracle@localhost:~/app/oracle/product/11.2.0/dbhome_2/dbs
File Edit View Terminal Tabs Help
[oracle@localhost dbs]$ sqlplus lthrace/password
SQL*Plus: Release 11.2.0.2.0 Production on Thu Jun 14 19:19:42 2012
Copyright (c) 1982, 2010, Oracle. All rights reserved.
Connected to:
Oracle Database 11g Enterprise Edition Release 11.2.0.2.0 - Production
With the Partitioning, OLAP, Data Mining and Real Application Testing options
SQL>

Now that `lthrace` is connected, let's create a simple table within its schema.

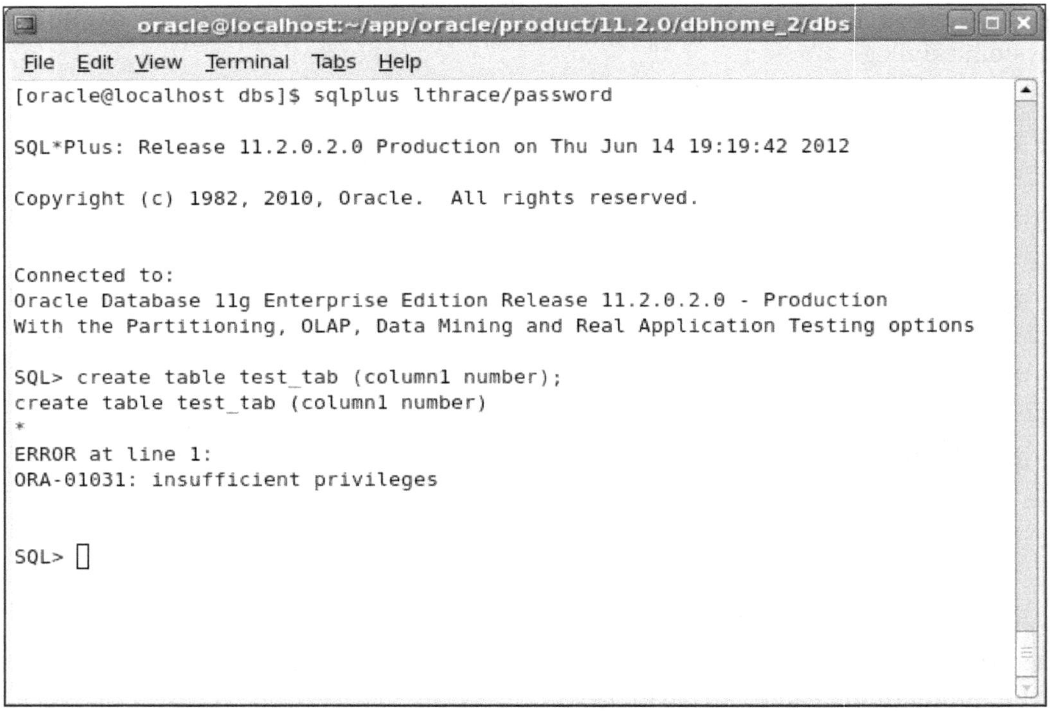
oracle@localhost:~/app/oracle/product/11.2.0/dbhome_2/dbs
File Edit View Terminal Tabs Help
[oracle@localhost dbs]$ sqlplus lthrace/password
SQL*Plus: Release 11.2.0.2.0 Production on Thu Jun 14 19:19:42 2012
Copyright (c) 1982, 2010, Oracle. All rights reserved.
Connected to:
Oracle Database 11g Enterprise Edition Release 11.2.0.2.0 - Production
With the Partitioning, OLAP, Data Mining and Real Application Testing options
SQL> create table test_tab (column1 number);
create table test_tab (column1 number)
*
ERROR at line 1:
ORA-01031: insufficient privileges
SQL>

As we can see, the `lthrace` user fails to create a table. Why? Again, because this user lacks the proper system privilege, `CREATE TABLE`, in order to create a database table. Once again, we can *grant* the proper privilege as the `SYSTEM` user.

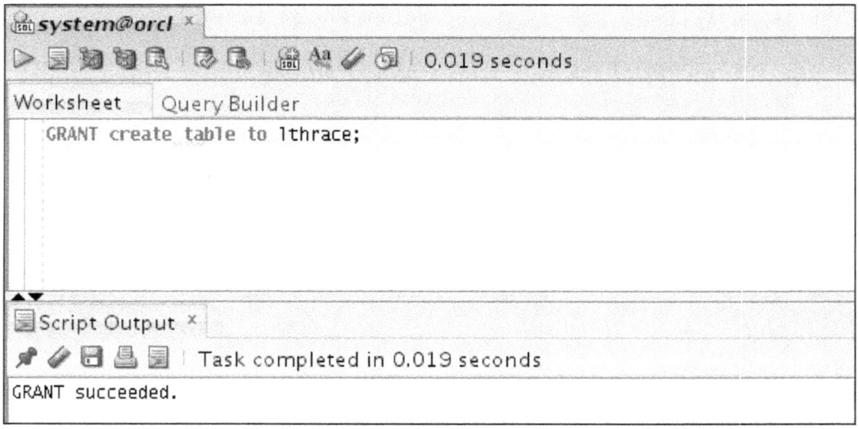
system@orcl
0.019 seconds
Worksheet
Query Builder
GRANT create table to lthrace;
Script Output
Task completed in 0.019 seconds
GRANT succeeded.

Now `lthrace` attempts to create the table again, this time succeeding. Note that it is not necessary to log out and log in again for this grant to take effect.

```
oracle@localhost:~/app/oracle/product/11.2.0/dbhome_2/dbs
File Edit View Terminal Tabs Help
[oracle@localhost dbs]$ sqlplus lthrace/password

SQL*Plus: Release 11.2.0.2.0 Production on Thu Jun 14 19:19:42 2012

Copyright (c) 1982, 2010, Oracle.  All rights reserved.


Connected to:
Oracle Database 11g Enterprise Edition Release 11.2.0.2.0 - Production
With the Partitioning, OLAP, Data Mining and Real Application Testing options

SQL> create table test_tab (column1 number);
create table test_tab (column1 number)
*
ERROR at line 1:
ORA-01031: insufficient privileges


SQL> create table test_tab (column1 number);

Table created.

SQL> 
```

When a system privilege is granted, it can be given in two ways. It can be granted solely to the grantee or using the `WITH ADMIN OPTION` clause. `WITH ADMIN OPTION` allows the grantee to grant that privilege to anyone they wish. So, if we grant `lthrace` to the `CREATE SESSION` privilege using the `WITH ADMIN OPTION` clause, `lthrace` can now grant that `CREATE SESSION` privilege to anyone. We see an example of this in the following screenshot. Note that it is perfectly acceptable to "re-grant" a privilege in doing so.

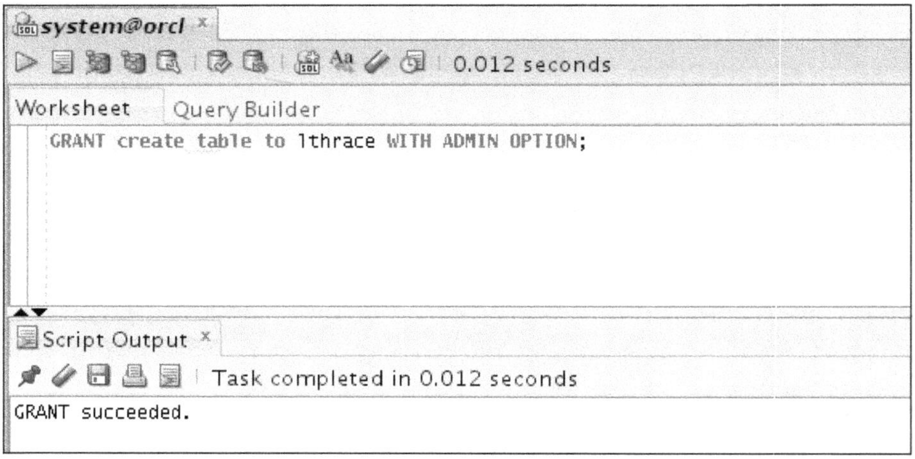
system@orcl
0.012 seconds
Worksheet
Query Builder
GRANT create table to lthrace WITH ADMIN OPTION;
Script Output
Task completed in 0.012 seconds
GRANT succeeded.

The real-world DBA

The improper allocation of system privileges is an act that can quickly weaken a database's security posture. System privileges can have wide-reaching effects. This is particularly true when system privileges are granted with the `WITH ADMIN OPTION` clause. As an example, never grant a user the `CREATE ANY TABLE` permission when all they really need is the ability to create tables within their own schema. The principle of least privilege always applies.

Granting object privileges

The second type of privilege we can grant has more direction. This type of permission called the **object privilege** allows a user to do a specific type of action on a specific object. Object privileges generally come in the form of a permission that allows a DML statement, such as `SELECT`, `INSERT`, `UPDATE`, or `DELETE`, to be executed against a certain table. For instance, if we wanted to allow our `lthrace` user to view data in the employee table of the `companylink` schema, we would grant a permission as shown in the following screenshot:

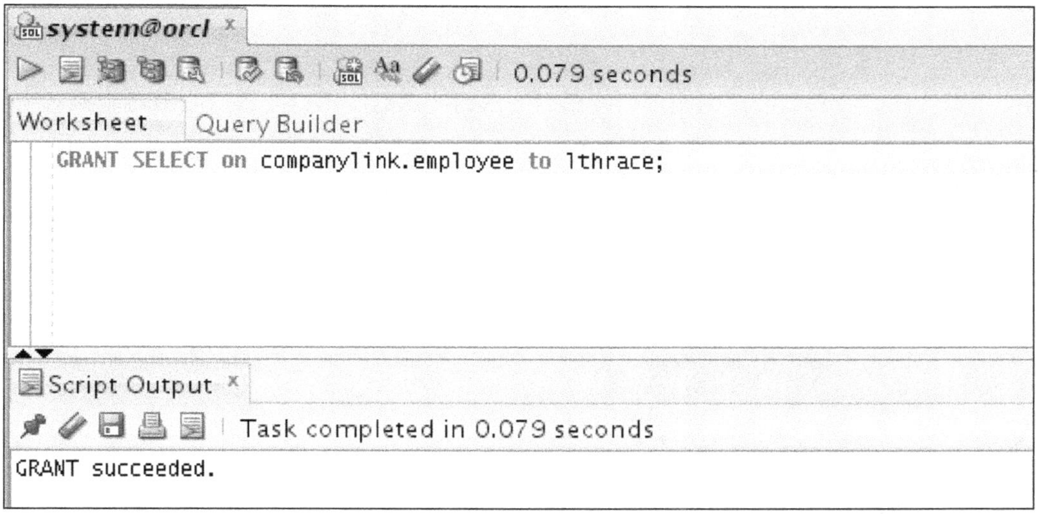
system@orcl
0.079 seconds
Worksheet
Query Builder
GRANT SELECT on companylink.employee to lthrace;
Script Output
Task completed in 0.079 seconds
GRANT succeeded.

If we log in through SQL*Plus as the `lthrace` user and execute the following statement, we see the data displayed. Remember that when we log in as `lthrace`, we are operating in the `lthrace` schema. Thus, because the employee table exists in the `companylink` schema, we must specify the `companylink` schema when selecting from the table using a dot notation.

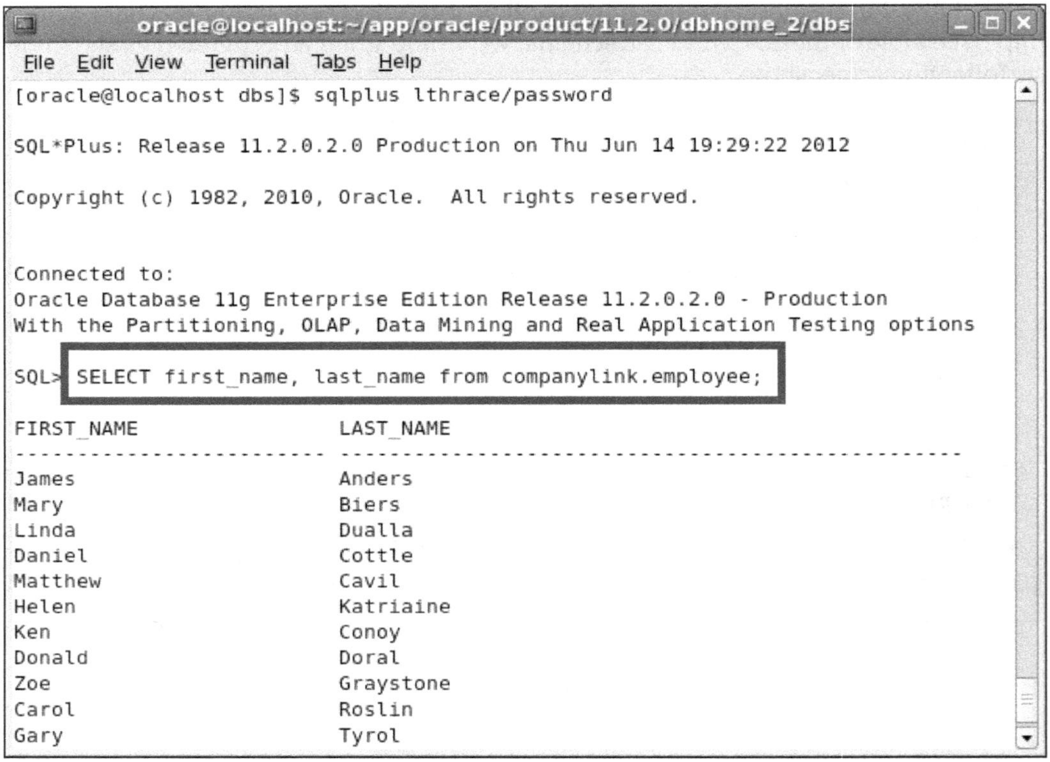
oracle@localhost:~/app/oracle/product/11.2.0/dbhome_2/dbs
File Edit View Terminal Tabs Help
[oracle@localhost dbs]$ sqlplus lthrace/password
SQL*Plus: Release 11.2.0.2.0 Production on Thu Jun 14 19:29:22 2012
Copyright (c) 1982, 2010, Oracle. All rights reserved.
Connected to:
Oracle Database 11g Enterprise Edition Release 11.2.0.2.0 - Production
With the Partitioning, OLAP, Data Mining and Real Application Testing options
SQL> SELECT first_name, last_name from companylink.employee;
FIRST_NAME LAST_NAME
James Anders
Mary Biers
Linda Dualla
Daniel Cottle
Matthew Cavil
Helen Katriaine
Ken Conoy
Donald Doral
Zoe Graystone
Carol Roslin
Gary Tyrol

We can perform the `SELECT` operation on this table because `lthrace` has been granted an explicit object privilege to do so. What would happen if we attempt to perform an operation on the table other than `SELECT`, such as a `DELETE` operation?

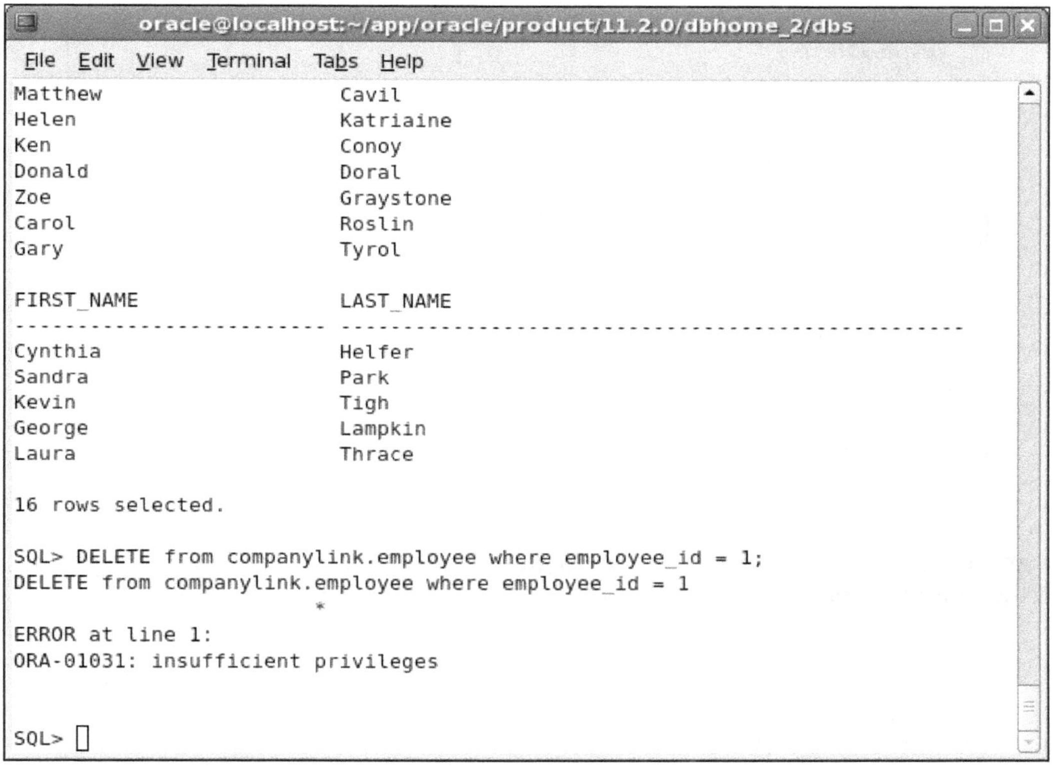
oracle@localhost:~/app/oracle/product/11.2.0/dbhome_2/dbs
File Edit View Terminal Tabs Help
Matthew Cavil
Helen Katriaine
Ken Conoy
Donald Doral
Zoe Graystone
Carol Roslin
Gary Tyrol
FIRST_NAME LAST_NAME
Cynthia Helfer
Sandra Park
Kevin Tigh
George Lampkin
Laura Thrace
16 rows selected.
SQL> DELETE from companylink.employee where employee_id = 1;
DELETE from companylink.employee where employee_id = 1
*
ERROR at line 1:
ORA-01031: insufficient privileges
SQL>

As we can see, we're denied the access needed to delete rows from the `companylink.employee` table because the `lthrace` user has not received explicit permission to do so. When we give object privileges, we can grant several together, separated by commas, as shown in the following screenshot:

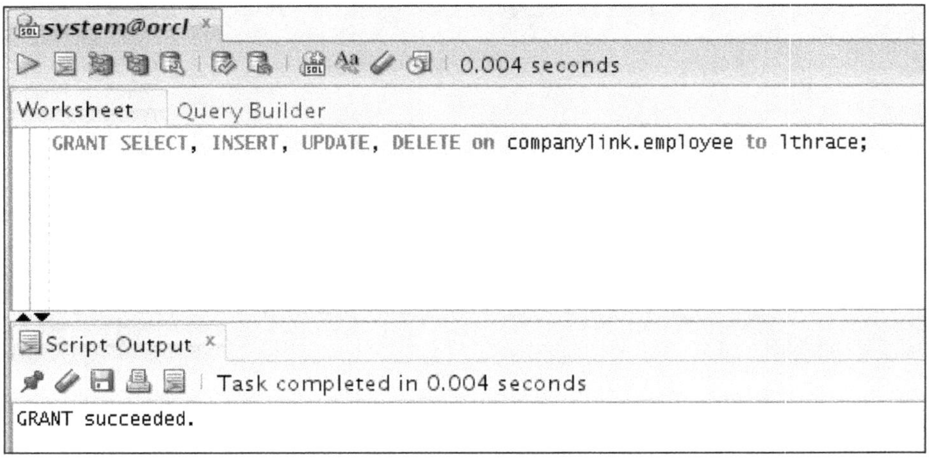
system@orcl
0.004 seconds
Worksheet
Query Builder
GRANT SELECT, INSERT, UPDATE, DELETE on companylink.employee to lthrace;
Script Output
Task completed in 0.004 seconds
GRANT succeeded.

In a similar manner to the `WITH ADMIN OPTION` clause used with system privileges, a grantee can also be given the ability to grant a given permission to any other user if the grant is done with the `WITH GRANT OPTION` clause. An example is shown here:

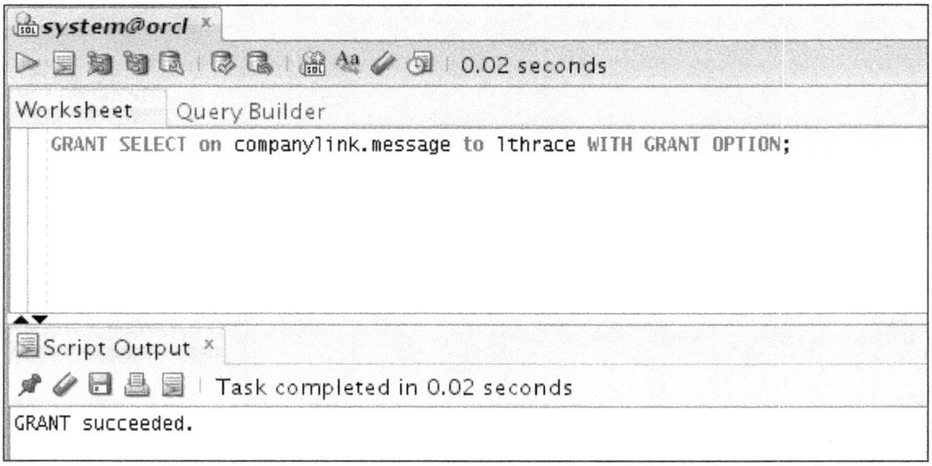
system@orcl
0.02 seconds
Worksheet
Query Builder
GRANT SELECT on companylink.message to lthrace WITH GRANT OPTION;
Script Output
Task completed in 0.02 seconds
GRANT succeeded.

The `lthrace` user now has the ability to perform a `SELECT` operation on the message table in the `companylink` schema, as well as the ability to grant that specific permission to other users. Alternatively, when we wish to grant all privileges to a user on a certain object, we can use the `ALL` keyword.

Removing privileges with REVOKE

Just as permissions need to be granted to users, we sometimes need to remove them as well. This need arises for several reasons. We may find that a user has been granted unnecessary privileges, or we may decide that the user requires a different set of privileges. When we need to remove privileges, we use the `REVOKE` command. For instance, we previously granted the `lthrace` user the `SELECT`, `INSERT`, `UPDATE`, and `DELETE` permissions on the `companylink.employee` table. We've decided that it isn't necessary for that user to delete rows from tables, and we want to remove that privilege while maintaining the others. We could do this with `REVOKE`, as shown in the following screenshot:

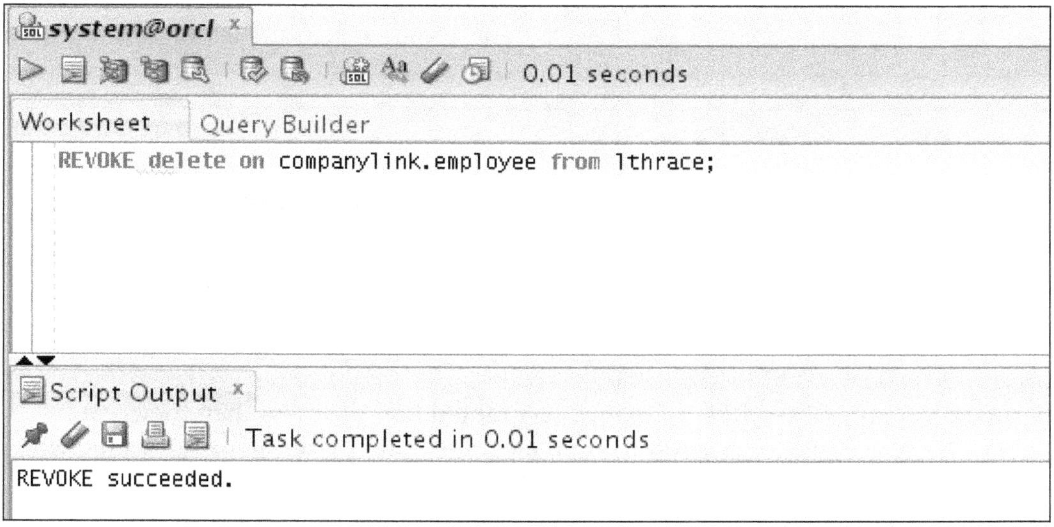
system@orcl
0.01 seconds
Worksheet
Query Builder
REVOKE delete on companylink.employee from lthrace;
Script Output
Task completed in 0.01 seconds
REVOKE succeeded.

Now, if the `lthrace` user attempts to delete from that table, access will be denied.

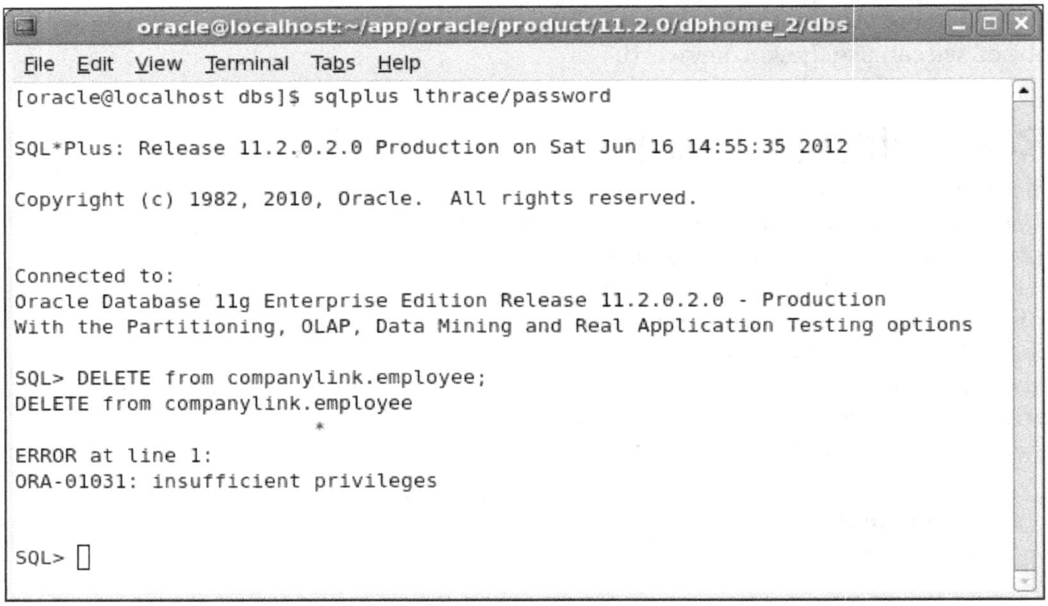
oracle@localhost:~/app/oracle/product/11.2.0/dbhome_2/dbs
File Edit View Terminal Tabs Help
[oracle@localhost dbs]$ sqlplus lthrace/password
SQL*Plus: Release 11.2.0.2.0 Production on Sat Jun 16 14:55:35 2012
Copyright (c) 1982, 2010, Oracle. All rights reserved.
Connected to:
Oracle Database 11g Enterprise Edition Release 11.2.0.2.0 - Production
With the Partitioning, OLAP, Data Mining and Real Application Testing options
SQL> DELETE from companylink.employee;
DELETE from companylink.employee
*
ERROR at line 1:
ORA-01031: insufficient privileges
SQL>

Understanding role-based security

When our task is limited to granting permissions to a select few users, what we've learned this far using `GRANT` and `REVOKE` would likely suffice. However, a real-world security approach may require us to manage the grants of thousands of users for hundreds of database objects. Were we to use individual grants for each of these users, mistakes would likely be made. Certain users would not have the necessary permissions and, worse still, users may be granted higher access than they require. We need a way to ease this burden and make managing permissions more efficient. To this end, we discuss the subject of role-based security.

Using system roles

In Oracle, a **role** is simply a container for a group of any other directly granted permissions, including both system privileges and object privileges. By creating a role and granting permissions to it, any user who receives that role receives all the permissions it contains. Before we examine the process of creating our own roles, let's look at the roles that Oracle provides us in the form of predefined roles. Dozens of predefined roles are provided by Oracle. Some of these roles must be used with a certain amount of care. Here, we look at a few of the most common ones.

- `CONNECT`: In previous releases of Oracle, the `CONNECT` role provided many more permissions than its name might imply. In addition to `CREATE SESSION`, which we might expect, `CONNECT` provided the permissions to create various database objects. In the most current version, it only provides `CREATE SESSION` and exists for backward compatibility. Generally, it is more secure to use `CREATE SESSION` and the grants necessary for individual system privileges than to use `CONNECT`.
- `RESOURCE`: Another role that is generally used for backward compatibility, `RESOURCE` provides this ability to database objects, such as tables and indexes, as well as PL/SQL objects. Again, `RESOURCE` often provides more privileges than necessary, and should be avoided.
- `DBA`: Probably the most well-known role, `DBA` should be granted only to database administrators. `DBA` contains nearly all system privileges and allows the grantee a wide range of administrative access. However, it differs from the `SYSDBA` role that we have discussed in that it does not allow the grantee to start and stop the database.
- `SELECT_CATALOG_ROLE`: This role allows the grantee to view the data dictionary, although it lacks the ability to view user data. In situations where a user needs to see data dictionary views, the `SELECT_CATALOG_ROLE` role can be used. However, the data within the data dictionary itself contains vital information and should not be viewable by every user.

In addition to these roles, Oracle also provides a unique type of role named `PUBLIC`. This role is owned by every user in the database. Whatever permissions are granted to `PUBLIC` are automatically granted to every user in the database. Thus, if we grant `CREATE SESSION` to `PUBLIC`, any user that is created within the database will be allowed to establish a database connection.

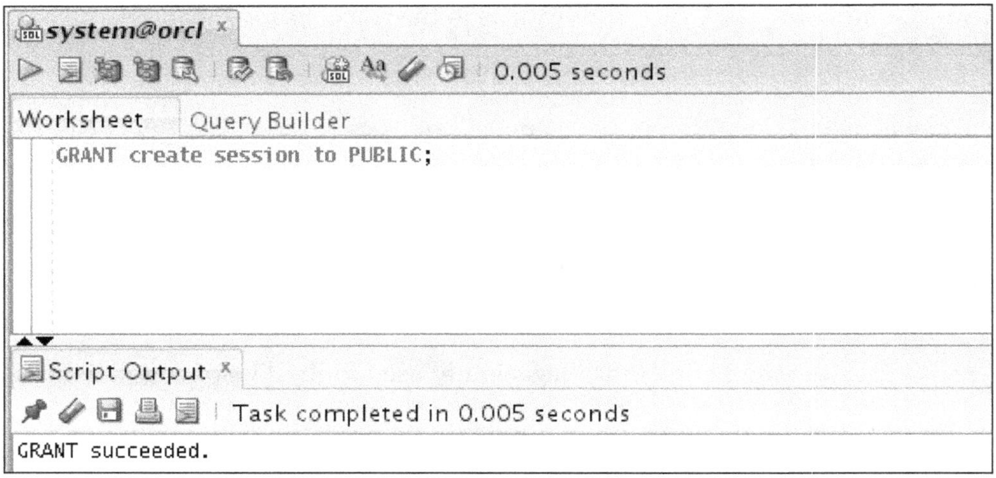
system@orcl
0.005 seconds
Worksheet
Query Builder
GRANT create session to PUBLIC;
Script Output
Task completed in 0.005 seconds
GRANT succeeded.

Managing user roles

In addition to the roles that Oracle provides, we can easily create our own roles and assign permissions to them. To do so, we use the `CREATE ROLE` command, as shown in the following screenshot:

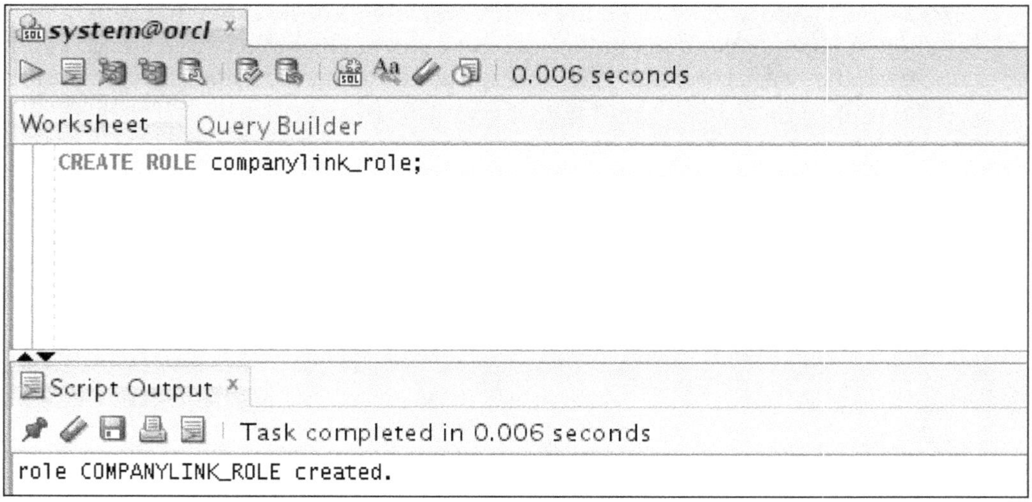
system@orcl
0.006 seconds
Worksheet
Query Builder
CREATE ROLE companylink_role;
Script Output
Task completed in 0.006 seconds
role COMPANYLINK_ROLE created.

What we have now is an empty role called `companylink_role`. It is now necessary to grant specific permissions to that role. In the following example, we grant a number of permissions to our new role. In SQL Developer, note that in order to execute these commands as a batch, we click the **Run Script** button just to the right-hand side of the **Execute** button. Optionally, we can simply highlight each statement individually and execute them as we normally do.

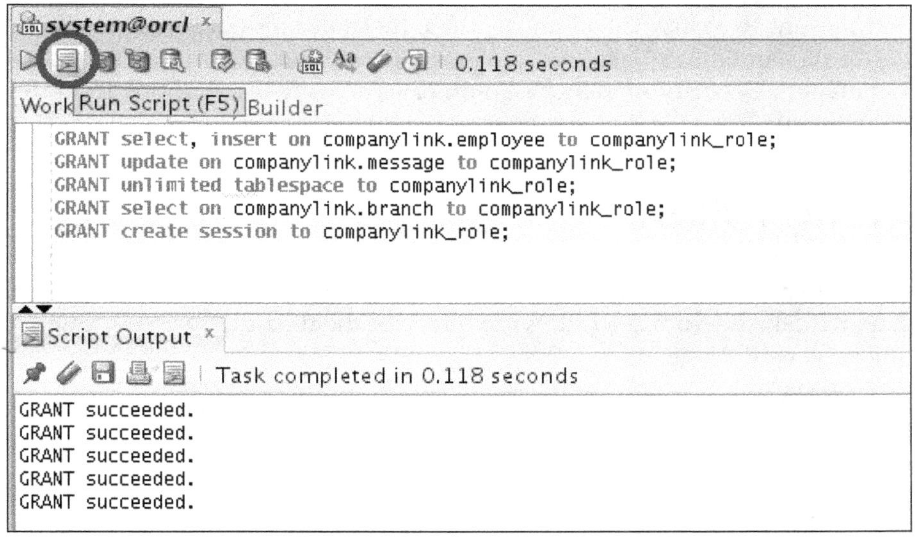
system@orcl
0.118 seconds
Work
Run Script (F5)
Builder
GRANT select, insert on companylink.employee to companylink_role;
GRANT update on companylink.message to companylink_role;
GRANT unlimited tablespace to companylink_role;
GRANT select on companylink.branch to companylink_role;
GRANT create session to companylink_role;
Script Output
Task completed in 0.118 seconds
GRANT succeeded.
GRANT succeeded.
GRANT succeeded.
GRANT succeeded.
GRANT succeeded.

Our role, `companylink_role`, now contains a number of both object and system permissions. In order to make use of this role and its new permissions, we now need to *grant* the role to a user. Once granted, the user will inherit all the permissions possessed by the role.

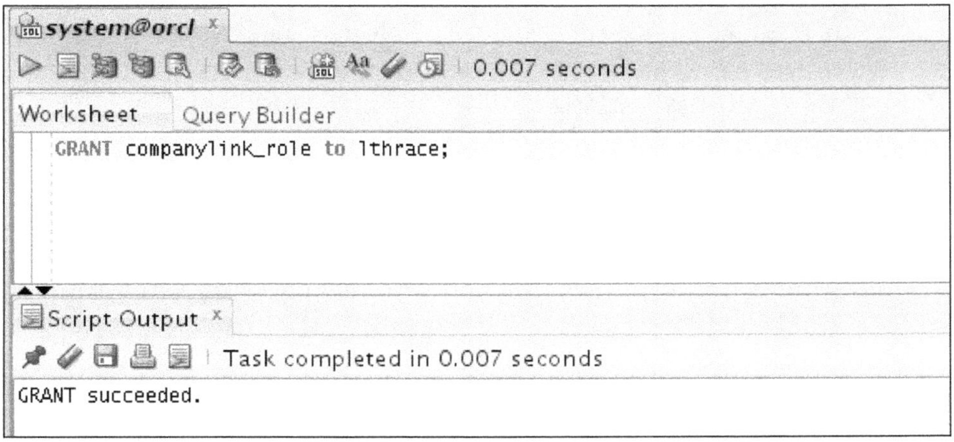
system@orcl
0.007 seconds
Worksheet
Query Builder
GRANT companylink_role to lthrace;
Script Output
Task completed in 0.007 seconds
GRANT succeeded.

Let's not miss the significance of this. Not only can `companylink_role` be granted to the `lthrace` user as an individual grant, but it can also be granted to any number of users at a time. Thus, a database role can represent the permissions required by a number of users. In the real world, a number of users may often require the same permissions. For instance, we may need to assign the necessary permissions to all of the project managers in our organization. These employees need the ability to write to a few tables and select data from most tables. Rather than individually granting these permissions, we can instead encapsulate these permissions in a role, for instance, a role named `proj_mgr_role`. That role can then be granted to each of our project managers. Security models based on roles are inherently more accurate and easier to manage.

Enabling roles

Although it is sometimes cumbersome to do so, roles granted to a user can be turned "on" or "off", in a manner of speaking. When we grant a role to a user, it is enabled by default, as we can see from the following query of the data dictionary shown in the following screenshot:

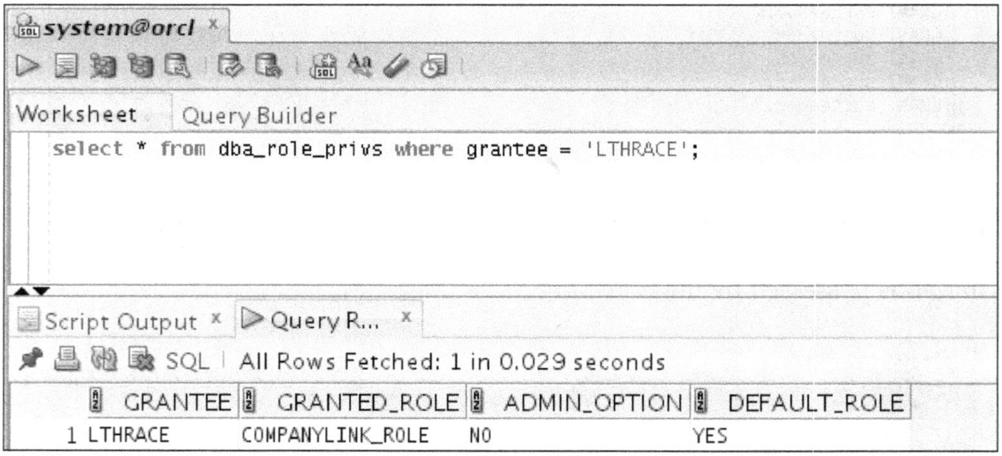
system@orcl
Worksheet
Query Builder
select * from dba_role_privs where grantee = 'LTHRACE';
Script Output
Query R...
SQL
All Rows Fetched: 1 in 0.029 seconds
GRANTEE
GRANTED_ROLE
ADMIN_OPTION
DEFAULT_ROLE
1 LTHRACE COMPANYLINK_ROLE NO YES

From this query, we can see that the `lthrace` user has been granted the `companylink_role` role, the `ADMIN OPTION` option has not been specified, and that it is a default role. A **default role** is one that is available to a user whenever they connect. We can disable a role anytime we wish to, using the command shown in the following screenshot:

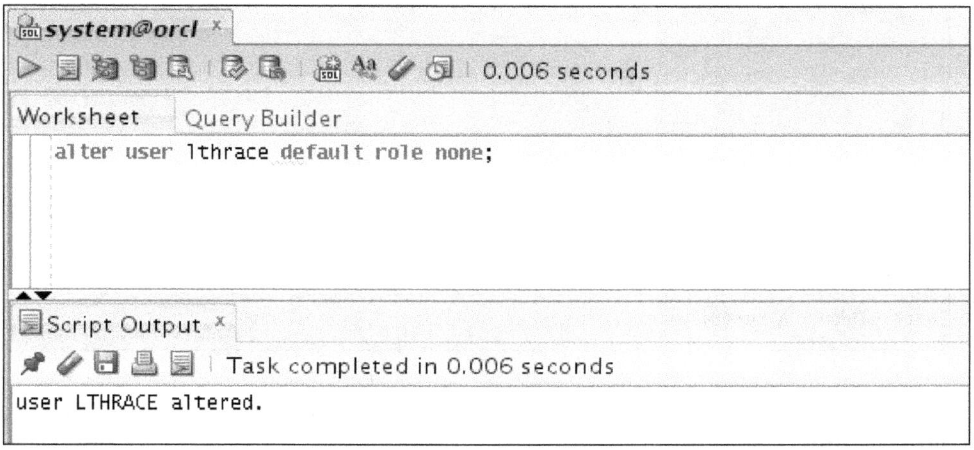
system@orcl
0.006 seconds
Worksheet
Query Builder
alter user lthrace default role none;
Script Output
Task completed in 0.006 seconds
user LTHRACE altered.

Now when we query the `dba_role_privs` view, we see a different result.

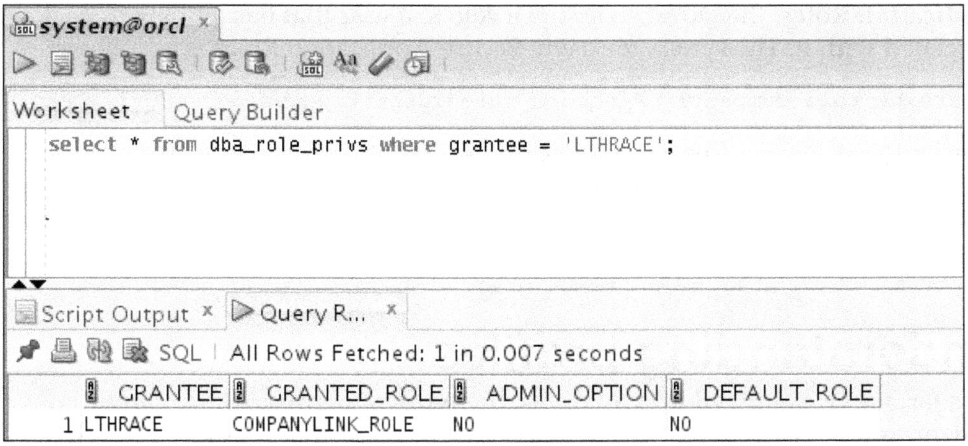
system@orcl
Worksheet
Query Builder
select * from dba_role_privs where grantee = 'LTHRACE';
Script Output
Query R...
SQL
All Rows Fetched: 1 in 0.007 seconds
GRANTEE
GRANTED_ROLE
ADMIN_OPTION
DEFAULT_ROLE
1 LTHRACE
COMPANYLINK_ROLE
NO
NO

As we can see, the companylink_role is no longer a default role for the lthrace user. In order to re-enable the role, we use the command shown in the following screenshot:

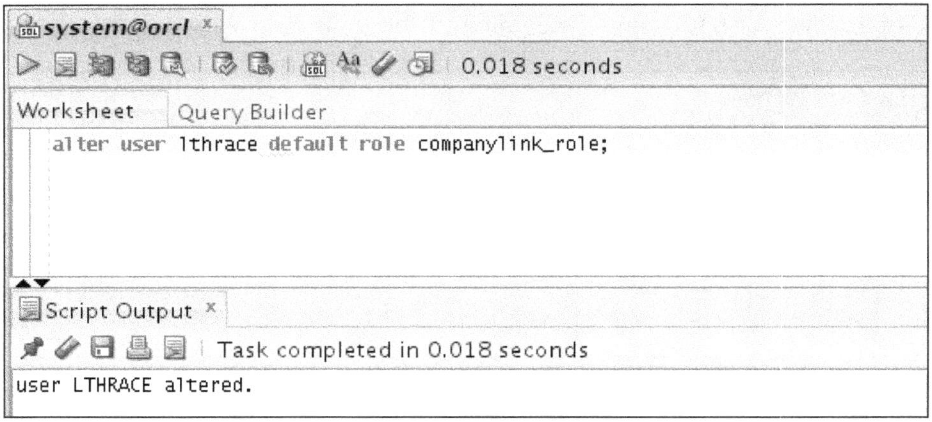
system@orcl
0.018 seconds
Worksheet
Query Builder
alter user lthrace default role companylink_role;
Script Output
Task completed in 0.018 seconds
user LTHRACE altered.

Default roles can also be enabled at the session level by a user with sufficient privileges. When this is done, the SET ROLE command is used.

We'll close this section by mentioning a different kind of role that, while conforming to the same structure of a standard role, allows for greater security. Using **Secure Application Roles**, the DBA can assign a role to a user that has a PL/SQL package associated with it. The syntax for using Secure Application Roles is as follows:

```
create role companylink_secure_role identified using security_pkg;
```

In order to use Secure Application Role, a user must have access to execute the package, in this case security_pkg, associated with it. The package itself can be written to perform any number of security checks that pertain to our organization's security policy.

Understanding profiles

Thus far, we've examined user accounts, the types of permission we can assign to them, and the ways in which we can encapsulate permissions into roles. In this section, we'll explore a topic that we saw previously in our section on creating users—database profiles. A **profile** is a combination of two, somewhat dissimilar, types of user controls. Profiles can be used to enforce user password characteristics as well as control a user's access to certain system resources.

Understanding password limits

Profiles make use of limits. A **limit** is a given characteristic of a profile. In order to change a profile, we change its limits. Thus, we can change the password characteristics of a profile by changing its limits. Every user is assigned a profile and will take on the password characteristics of the profile to which they've been assigned. A list of common, password-related profile limits is shown in the following list:

- `FAILED_LOGIN_ATTEMPTS`: This limit is used to specify the number of times a user can attempt to log in. When this limit is reached, the account is then locked and the user cannot connect. For example, if the limit for `FAILED_LOGIN_ATTEMPTS` is 5, a user can enter five incorrect passwords before the account is locked.
- `PASSWORD_LOCK_TIME`: This limit specifies the amount of time, in days, that a user account is locked after the `FAILED_LOGIN_ATTEMPTS` limit has been reached.
- `PASSWORD_LIFE_TIME`: As it suggests, this limit specifies the "lifetime" of a password, in days, before it must be changed. Thus, if we set `PASSWORD_LIFE_TIME` in a profile to `90`, a user with that profile must change their password every 90 days.
- `PASSWORD_GRACE_TIME`: This limit specifies the number of days that a user is prompted to change their password in after `PASSWORD_LIFE_TIME` has been reached. The grace period begins the first time the user connects to the database after the lifetime limit has been reached. During this time, their current password can still be used and their account has a status of `EXPIRED(GRACE)`.
- `PASSWORD_VERIFY_FUNCTION`: This limit is populated with the name of the verify function of our choice. A **verify function** is a piece of code that is run against every password when it is created. It is designed to check the password for various characteristics related to password complexity, such as overall length, number of special characters, and similarities to the previous password. By default, this value is `NULL`. However, we can create a verify function and assign its name here. A standard password verify function is created using the `utlpwdmg.sql` script; it is found in every Oracle installation.

- `PASSWORD_REUSE_MAX`: This limit specifies the number of times a password must be changed before it can be re-used. For instance, if this limit is set to `5`, a user must change their password five times before the current password can be used again.
- `PASSWORD_REUSE_TIME`: This limit specifies the number of days that must pass before an existing password can be re-used.

> **The real-world DBA**
> Never underestimate the importance of using password limits. These limits are a proactive way to prevent passwords from being too simple or overly re-used. Doing so can reduce the administrative burden of constantly checking to make sure users are maintaining strong passwords.

Using profiles to manage passwords

By default, every user possesses the profile named `DEFAULT`. Although this profile is somewhat lacking in proper security limits, it can be changed to reflect the type of restrictions needed. We can also, however, create our own profiles. Often, this is a good way to separate restrictions based on a user's job role. Some users may require certain limits that others do not. We create a profile using the `CREATE PROFILE` command, as shown in the following screenshot:

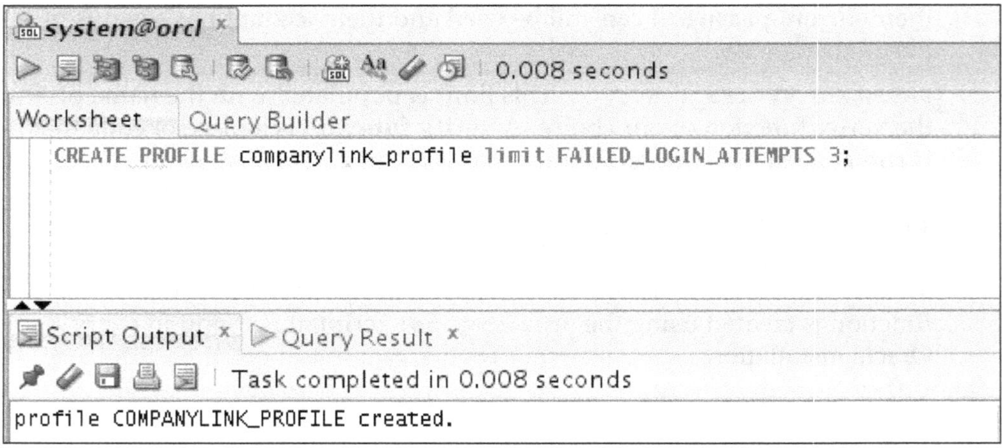
system@orcl
0.008 seconds
Worksheet
Query Builder
CREATE PROFILE companylink_profile limit FAILED_LOGIN_ATTEMPTS 3;
Script Output
Query Result
Task completed in 0.008 seconds
profile COMPANYLINK_PROFILE created.

Here, while creating the **companylink_profile** profile, we specify the **FAILED_LOGIN_ATTEMPTS** limit as **3**. When creating a profile, we must always specify at least one limit. At this point, all other limits in our new profile revert back to the `DEFAULT` profile, except for `FAILED_LOGIN_ATTEMPTS`. We can see this by examining the `DBA_PROFILES` data dictionary view.

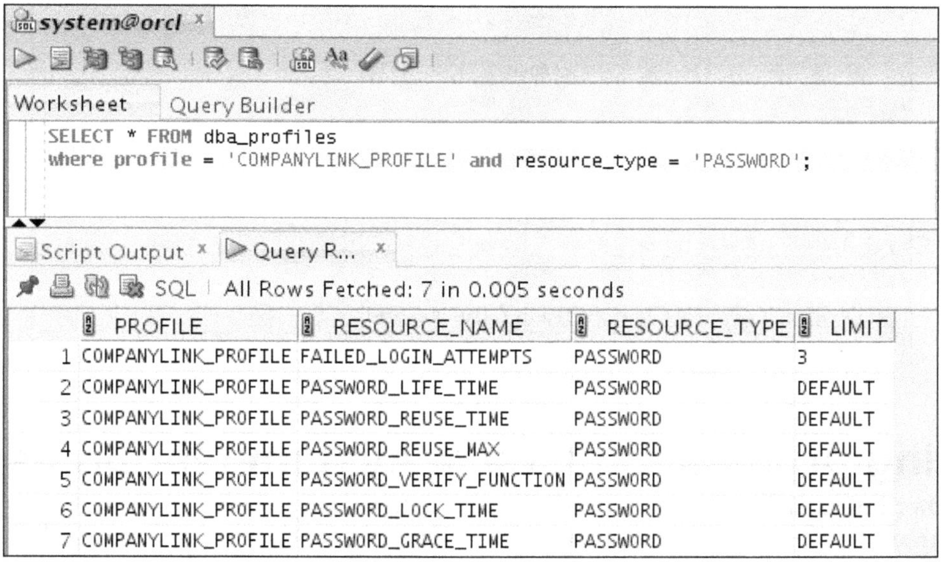
system@orcl
Worksheet
Query Builder
SELECT * FROM dba_profiles
where profile = 'COMPANYLINK_PROFILE' and resource_type = 'PASSWORD';
Script Output
Query R...
SQL
All Rows Fetched: 7 in 0.005 seconds

	PROFILE	RESOURCE_NAME	RESOURCE_TYPE	LIMIT
1	COMPANYLINK_PROFILE	FAILED_LOGIN_ATTEMPTS	PASSWORD	3
2	COMPANYLINK_PROFILE	PASSWORD_LIFE_TIME	PASSWORD	DEFAULT
3	COMPANYLINK_PROFILE	PASSWORD_REUSE_TIME	PASSWORD	DEFAULT
4	COMPANYLINK_PROFILE	PASSWORD_REUSE_MAX	PASSWORD	DEFAULT
5	COMPANYLINK_PROFILE	PASSWORD_VERIFY_FUNCTION	PASSWORD	DEFAULT
6	COMPANYLINK_PROFILE	PASSWORD_LOCK_TIME	PASSWORD	DEFAULT
7	COMPANYLINK_PROFILE	PASSWORD_GRACE_TIME	PASSWORD	DEFAULT

We can change this by using the `ALTER PROFILE` command to modify profile limits. This command can be used to change both single as well as multiple profile limits, as shown in the following screenshot:

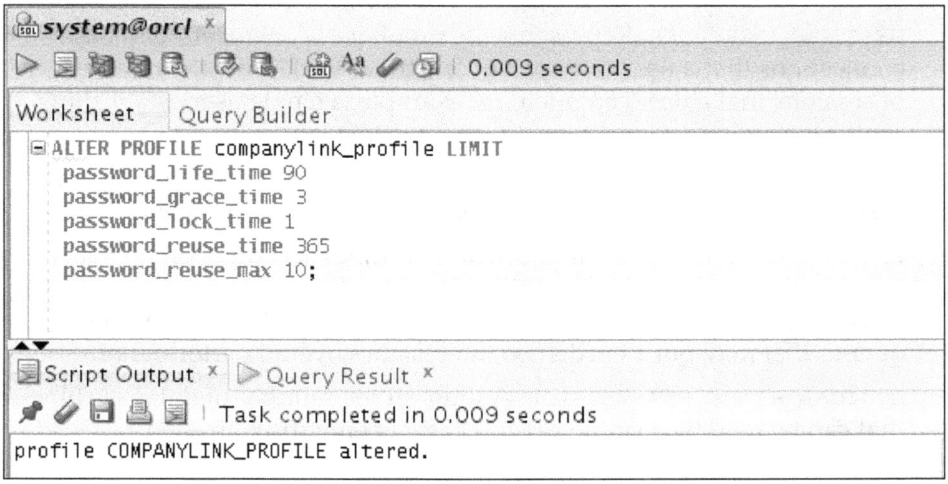
system@orcl
0.009 seconds
Worksheet
Query Builder
ALTER PROFILE companylink_profile LIMIT
password_life_time 90
password_grace_time 3
password_lock_time 1
password_reuse_time 365
password_reuse_max 10;
Script Output
Query Result
Task completed in 0.009 seconds
profile COMPANYLINK_PROFILE altered.

Once a profile is created and its limits are established, we can assign it to a user with the `ALTER USER` command. Here, we assign our new profile to the `lthrace` user. From this point on, `lthrace` will have these password restrictions in place.

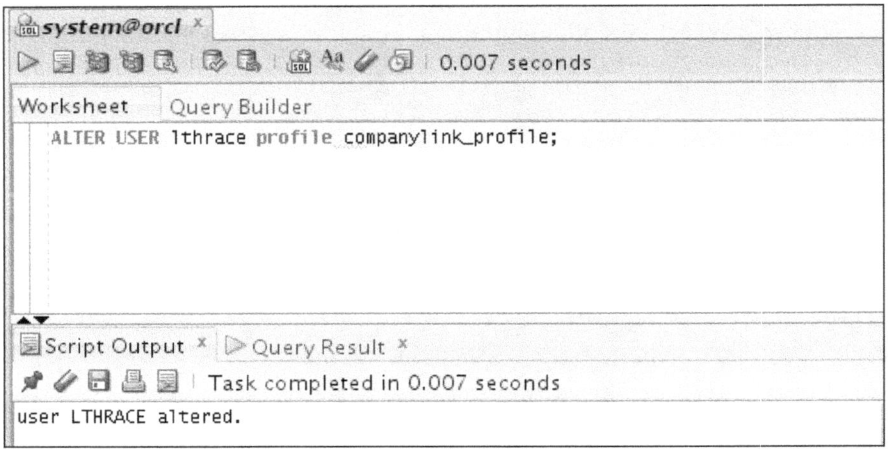
system@orcl
0.007 seconds
Worksheet
Query Builder
ALTER USER lthrace profile companylink_profile;
Script Output
Query Result
Task completed in 0.007 seconds
user LTHRACE altered.

Using profiles to manage system resources

Another interesting use of a profile is its ability to manage the usage of system resources. Using the profile limits with the `KERNEL` resource type, we can control a user's usage of various system resources, such as the CPU, memory, and disk. The use of these limits requires the `RESOURCE_LIMIT` initialization parameter to be set to `TRUE`. System resources can also be managed using Resource Manager, a more advanced and configurable administration tool. A list of `KERNEL` profile limits is shown in the following list:

- `SESSIONS_PER_USER`: Represents the number of concurrent database connections that a user can open at one time. This limits the number of sessions that a user can open, for example, a single user establishing multiple database connections to run multiple jobs.
- `CPU_PER_SESSION`: A limit on the number of centiseconds of CPU time that a single user's server process can use before being disconnected.
- `CPU_PER_CALL`: Limits the amount of CPU time (in centiseconds) that a user may consume in the execution of a single SQL statement before being disconnected. Useful in situations where users execute long-running, ad hoc queries that may put a burden on the system's overall performance.
- `LOGICAL_READS_PER_SESSION`: A limit on the number of database blocks that can be read by a single session before being disconnected.

- LOGICAL_READS_PER_CALL: Limits the number of database blocks that can be read in the execution of a single SQL statement before being disconnected.
- IDLE_TIME: Establishes a limit on the number of minutes a user session can be idle for before being disconnected.
- CONNECT_TIME: Limits the maximum number of minutes a user session can be connected before being forcibly disconnected.
- PRIVATE_SGA: Limits the number of kilobytes of SGA used by a session for data. Only applies to databases using the shared server architecture.
- COMPOSITE_LIMIT: An advanced limit that computes a weighted sum of CPU_PER_SESSION, CONNECT_TIME, LOGICAL_READS_PER_SESSION, and PRIVATE_SGA. When that limit is reached, the user is disconnected. This requires additional setup and configuration.

We assign these limits in the same manner as those relating to passwords, using the ALTER PROFILE command. Here, we assign a few system resource limits to our companylink_profile profile.

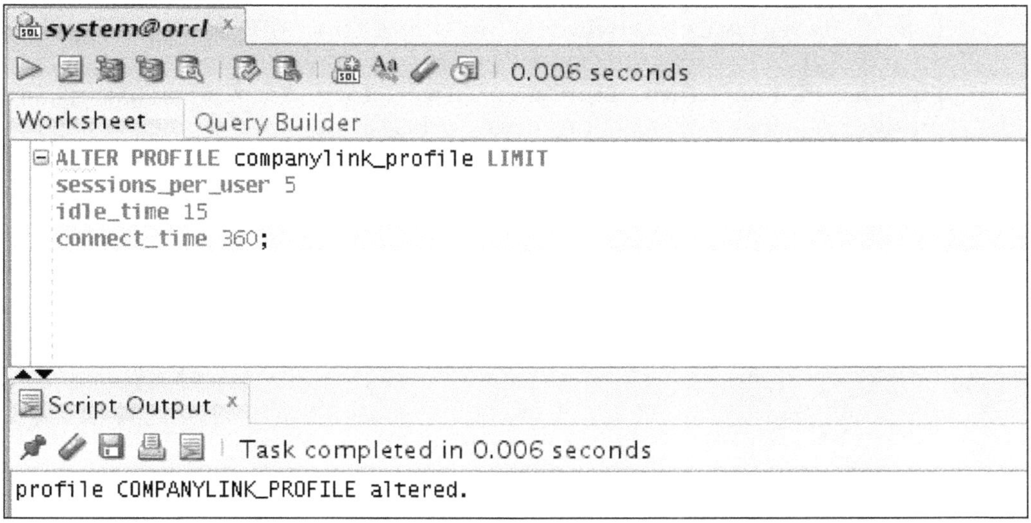
system@orcl
0.006 seconds
Worksheet
Query Builder
ALTER PROFILE companylink_profile LIMIT
sessions_per_user 5
idle_time 15
connect_time 360;
Script Output
Task completed in 0.006 seconds
profile COMPANYLINK_PROFILE altered.

Now, any users with the companylink_profile profile will also inherit these resource restrictions.

Understanding key security parameters

We've already seen the impact that database initialization parameters can have on the operation of the database. However, there are also several parameters that directly influence security, so we discuss them here.

- REMOTE_OS_AUTHENT: This parameter controls whether users can connect to the database remotely without providing a password. Possible values are TRUE and FALSE.
- O7_DICTIONARY_ACCESSIBILITY: If we recall our discussion of the ANY system privileges, such as SELECT ANY TABLE, we said that these privileges allow the grantee to do a given operation on any table, regardless of the schema. This parameter, when set it to FALSE (the default), ensures that these privileges do not include the data dictionary objects owned by SYS.
- REMOTE_LOGIN_PASSWORDFILE: This controls whether a user can log in remotely with the SYSDBA role. As we've discussed, the SYSDBA role allows a large number of privileges, including the ability to start and stop the database. When this parameter is set to NONE, this behavior is disallowed. Instead, it's necessary to go through the server's operating system to receive the role. When it is set to EXCLUSIVE, a user can connect remotely as SYSDBA, provided they have the appropriate password for a user with SYSDBA privilege, such as SYS. Also, this password is stored in the password file that exists for that database. The last possible parameter value is SHARED, which implies the same behavior as EXCLUSIVE, except that the same parameter file will be shared across all databases on that server.
- AUDIT_SYS_OPERATIONS: This is a very important parameter that, when set to TRUE, will cause all operations done by the SYS user as well as any user with the SYSDBA role to be audited. These records will be written to the operating system audit trail regardless of the value of the AUDIT_TRAIL parameter.
- SEC_CASE_SENSITIVE_LOGON: This enables or disables the ability to store and use case-sensitive passwords, a new feature in Version 11*g*.

- SEC_MAX_FAILED_LOGIN_ATTEMPTS: Specifies the number of attempts that can be made to authenticate a user to a server process. If the number of failed attempts reaches this value, the connection will be dropped.
- SEC_PROTOCOL_ERROR_FURTHER_ACTION: Specifies the action taken (either CONTINUE, DELAY, or DROP) when a server process receives bad network packets. Bad packets are often associated with an attack.
- SEC_PROTOCOL_ERROR_TRACE_ACTION: Specifies the action taken (either NONE, TRACE, LOG, or ALERT), related to tracing, when a server receives bad packets.
- SEC_RETURN_SERVER_RELEASE_BANNER: Controls the behavior of the software banner that returns software information (usually version) to clients that connect. When it is set to TRUE, the database returns complete database information. When set to FALSE, a generic version string is sent.

Understanding auditing

While the previous sections discussed proactive security measures, such as the granting of permissions and role-based security, there is also a time and a place for retroactive security measures. In the growing field of computer forensics, data collected during an attack becomes invaluable in determining the chain of events involved and learning the extent of the attack. In Oracle, the primary forensic tool available to us is auditing. **Auditing** is the act of recording a historical chain of events for various operations that take place in the database. Auditing plays an important part in satisfying one of the key principles of computer security. It states that *every action that occurs should be traceable to one and only one individual.*

Exploring the audit trail

The **audit trail** contains the list of audited events that take place in the database. The specific characteristics of the audit trail are controlled by the database administrator, and include the details of what information is audited, and where the information is written. Audit data can be written out in several different ways to different locations. This behavior is determined by the `AUDIT_TRAIL` database parameter. In order to determine if auditing is occurring and where that information is located, we can examine the parameter `AUDIT_TRAIL`, as shown in the following screenshot:

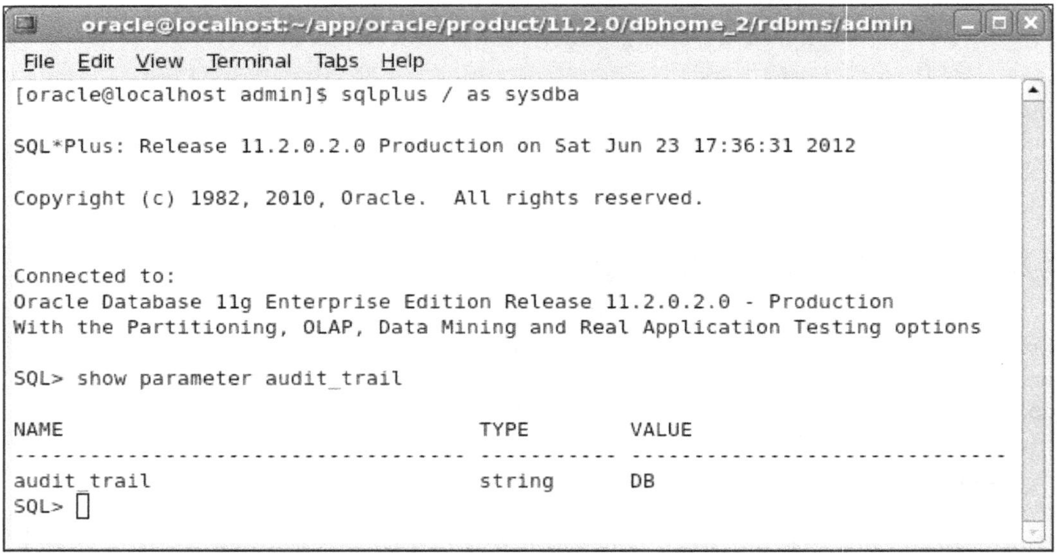
oracle@localhost:~/app/oracle/product/11.2.0/dbhome_2/rdbms/admin
File Edit View Terminal Tabs Help
[oracle@localhost admin]$ sqlplus / as sysdba
SQL*Plus: Release 11.2.0.2.0 Production on Sat Jun 23 17:36:31 2012
Copyright (c) 1982, 2010, Oracle. All rights reserved.
Connected to:
Oracle Database 11g Enterprise Edition Release 11.2.0.2.0 - Production
With the Partitioning, OLAP, Data Mining and Real Application Testing options
SQL> show parameter audit_trail
NAME TYPE VALUE
audit_trail string DB
SQL>

As we can see, by default the value for `AUDIT_TRAIL` is **DB**. `AUDIT_TRAIL` can have various values, as shown in the following list:

- `NONE` or `FALSE`: No auditing is done within the database. This is the case even if individual auditing commands are used.
- `OS`: Auditing information is written out at the operating system layer. In Windows, this information is written to the Application Log. In Unix-based systems, it is written as individual files to the directory specified by the `AUDIT_FILE_DEST` parameter.

- DB: Audit records are written to a base table SYS.AUD$ in the data dictionary. The DBA_AUDIT_TRAIL data dictionary view is the primary method for querying the information stored in SYS.AUD$.
- XML: Auditing information is stored in the same manner as in OS but is stored formatted with XML tags.
- DB/XML_EXTENDED: Same as DB or XML, but also contain the originating SQL statements with bind variables.

The AUDIT_TRAIL parameter is crucial for enabling auditing, but it is only the first step. In order to successfully put auditing in place, we must also specify exactly what events should be audited and in what manner.

Auditing database actions

Auditing is based on system and object privileges. In order to audit a system privilege, we use the AUDIT command, as shown in the following screenshot:

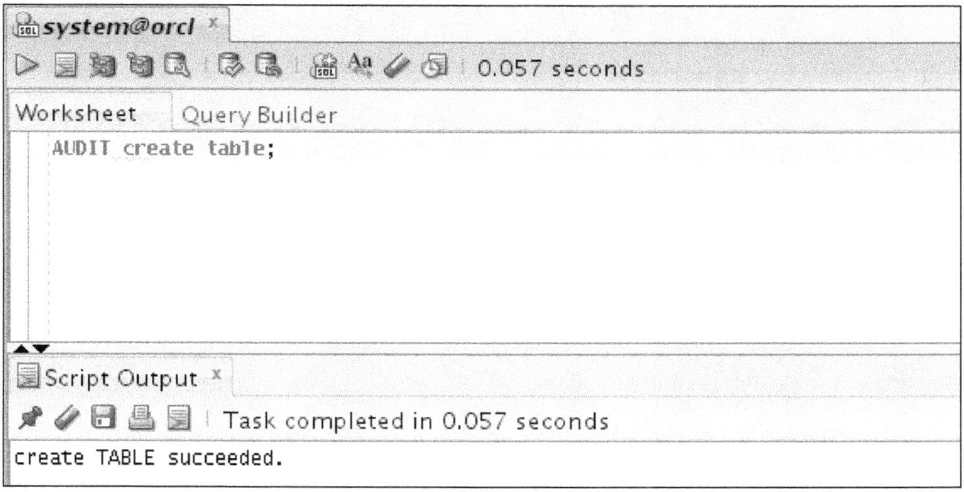
system@orcl
0.057 seconds
Worksheet
Query Builder
AUDIT create table;
Script Output
Task completed in 0.057 seconds
create TABLE succeeded.

Now that auditing of this system privilege is in place, any time a user makes use of the `CREATE TABLE` privilege, a row is entered in the `SYS.AUD$` base table that can be viewed through the `DBA_AUDIT_TRAIL` data dictionary view. As an example, we create a simple test table.

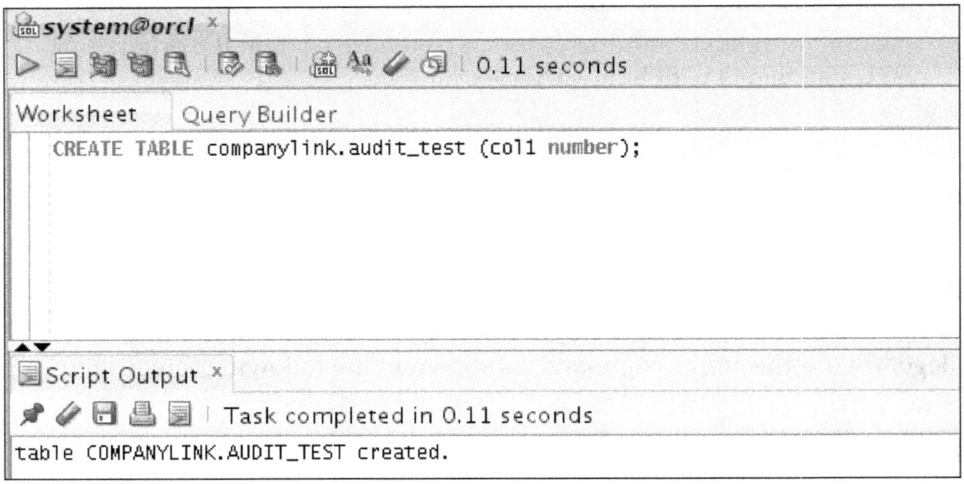
system@orcl
0.11 seconds
Worksheet
Query Builder
CREATE TABLE companylink.audit_test (col1 number);
Script Output
Task completed in 0.11 seconds
table COMPANYLINK.AUDIT_TEST created.

This action triggers Oracle to write an entry in `SYS.AUD$` that records several pieces of information about the event. Let's examine our query from `DBA_AUDIT_TRAIL` that allows us to see this information.

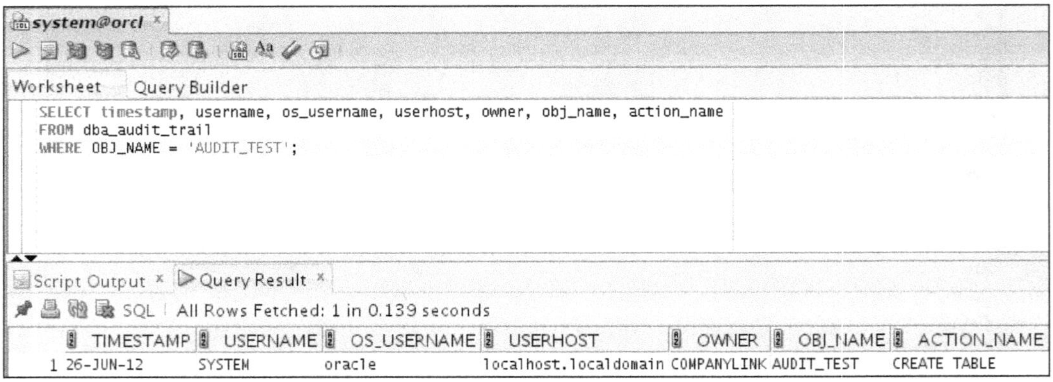
system@orcl
Worksheet
Query Builder
SELECT timestamp, username, os_username, userhost, owner, obj_name, action_name
FROM dba_audit_trail
WHERE OBJ_NAME = 'AUDIT_TEST';
Script Output
Query Result
SQL
All Rows Fetched: 1 in 0.139 seconds
TIMESTAMP USERNAME OS_USERNAME USERHOST OWNER OBJ_NAME ACTION_NAME
1 26-JUN-12 SYSTEM oracle localhost.localdomain COMPANYLINK AUDIT_TEST CREATE TABLE

Let's break down the information we've learned about this event. Although we're using a query to focus on certain information, a great deal of other information about the event is available in `DBA_AUDIT_TRAIL` as well.

- `TIMESTAMP`: The date and time at which the event occurred
- `USERNAME`: The database username that performed the action
- `OS_USERNAME`: The operating system username of the user that performed the action
- `USERHOST`: The hostname of the server that contains the database on which the event occurred
- `OWNER`: The owner of the target object
- `OBJ_NAME`: The name of the target object
- `ACTION_NAME`: The name of the event that occurred

So, here we see that our `CREATE TABLE` statement generated information indicating that the database user `SYSTEM` invoked the `CREATE TABLE` privilege on an object called `audit_test` owned by `companylink`.

As with system privileges, we can also audit the privilege usage on particular objects. Again, we use the `AUDIT` command for this purpose.

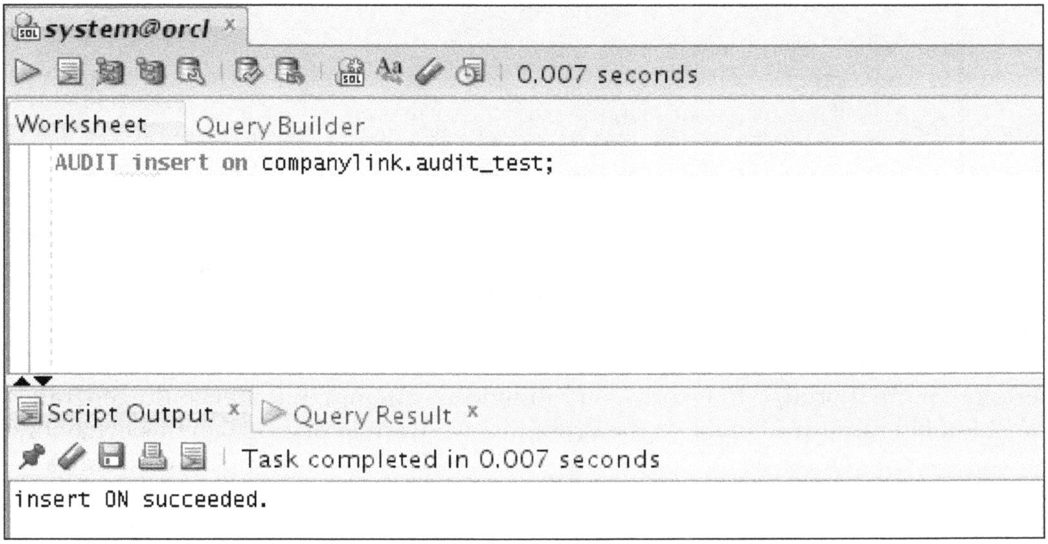
system@orcl
0.007 seconds
Worksheet
Query Builder
AUDIT insert on companylink.audit_test;
Script Output
Query Result
Task completed in 0.007 seconds
insert ON succeeded.

Now, when a user inserts values into the `companylink.audit_test` table, an audit entry will be made in `SYS.AUD$`.

The auditing of both system and object privileges can be done with options that specify *when* an audit entry is to be written. In essence, these are *conditions* on the writing of audit entries. For instance, we can specify that an entry be written either `WHENEVER SUCCESSFUL` or `WHENEVER NOT SUCCESSFUL`. By default, both operations are audited. So, in looking at the previous example, an audit record will be written whenever a successful insert occurs or even if an attempt is made to insert into the table that fails with an error. However, in order to reduce the volume of audit information stored in the database, we may come to the conclusion that it isn't important to audit successful inserts. What we want to record is events where someone is attempting to insert data into the table and fails to do so, perhaps because of a lack of object privileges on the table. Often, it's more important to track attempts by users who are unsuccessfully trying to do something they shouldn't. To do this, we can specify the clause required to restrict auditing to this condition.

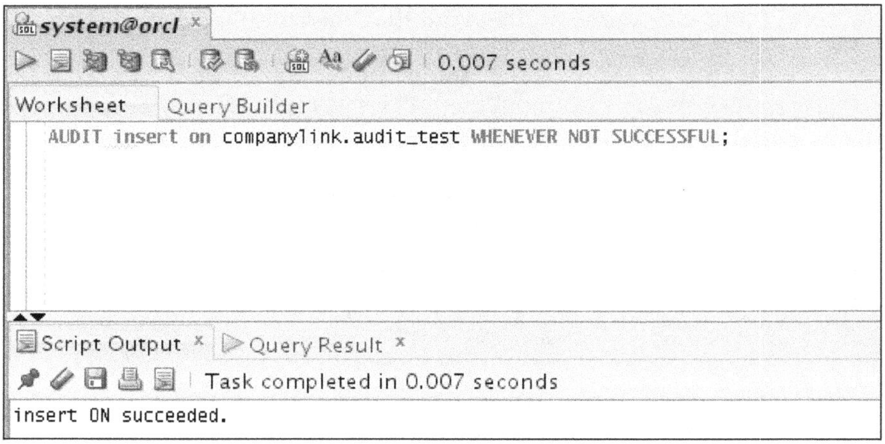
system@orcl
0.007 seconds
Worksheet
Query Builder
AUDIT insert on companylink.audit_test WHENEVER NOT SUCCESSFUL;
Script Output
Query Result
Task completed in 0.007 seconds
insert ON succeeded.

In addition to this type of condition, we can, in a way, change the level of aggregation in audit records. For instance, say a user logs in and repeatedly attempts to do an insert into `companylink.audit_test` without the `INSERT` privilege on that object. Do we want an audit record written out every time the attempt to insert records is made, or do we just want a single record written indicating the event occurred? It is certainly more thorough to record every individual attempt, but that could generate considerably more audit data. In the event that we want to distinguish this behavior, we can use the clauses `BY ACCESS` or `BY SESSION`. The `BY ACCESS` clause indicates that an audit record will be written to `SYS.AUD$` every time the audited event occurs. `BY SESSION` means that a single audit record will be written for a given session, no matter how many times the event occurs, and is the default behavior. Thus, we can combine these two types of conditions into a single `AUDIT` statement, as shown in the following screenshot:

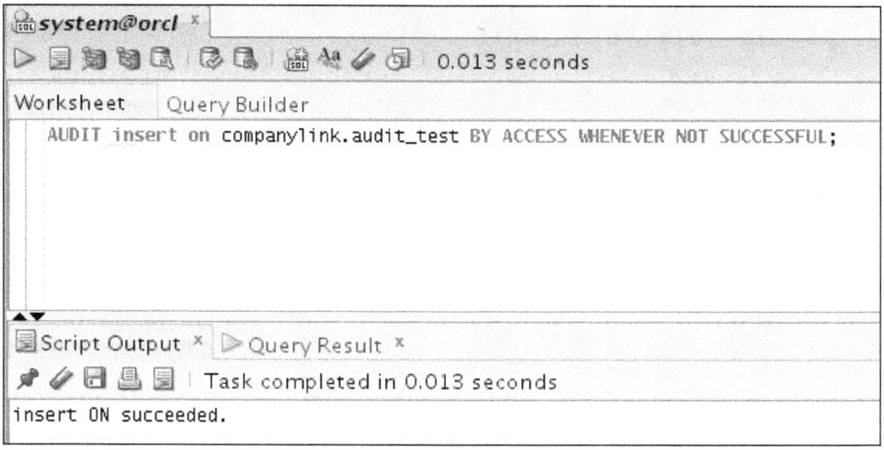
system@orcl
0.013 seconds
Worksheet
Query Builder
AUDIT insert on companylink.audit_test BY ACCESS WHENEVER NOT SUCCESSFUL;
Script Output
Query Result
Task completed in 0.013 seconds
insert ON succeeded.

In addition to these types of auditing, Oracle also offers another type of advanced auditing named **fine-grained auditing**. It allows an administrator to place auditing on database actions based on more specific conditions, such as auditing queries that are based on certain columns or particular row sets. Fine-grained auditing is accomplished through the creation of policies that define these conditions. For instance, we might create a fine-grained auditing policy that records an audit entry whenever a user queries against columns in a table that hold social security numbers.

Certification objectives covered

- Creating and managing database user accounts
- Granting and revoking privileges
- Creating and managing roles
- Creating and managing profiles

Summary

In this chapter, we've covered the fundamental concepts of Oracle database security. We've examined the responsibility for security that comes with being a DBA. We've explored ways to create database users and assign them privileges at both the system and object level. We've learned to use roles to encapsulate various system and object privileges. We've looked at profiles and the ways with which we can set limits on both password and resource usage characteristics. Finally, we've explored the subject of database auditing and how it can be used to monitor database activity. In our next chapter, we'll look at another important concept of the relational database, the subject of concurrency and undo management.

Test your knowledge

Q 1. Which term describes the process of confirming the identity of a user?

a. Verification
b. Repudiation
c. Authentication
d. Authorization

Q 2. When using local authentication, a user is authenticated using what?

a. An LDAP server
b. An external authentication service
c. KERBEROS
d. A password

Q 3. Which of the following lines in the `CREATE USER` statement will cause an error?

a. `CREATE USER janders identified by password`
b. `default tablespace example`
c. `quota 600M on example`
d. `profile limit set PASSWORD_REUSE_MAX = 10;`

Q 4. Which of the following is *incorrect* regarding the `CREATE ANY TABLE` privilege?

a. It allows a user to create a table in their own schema.
b. It allows a user to drop a table in any other schema.
c. It allows a user to create a table in any other schema.
d. It is a system privilege.

Q 5. Given that a new user is created and is granted the following privileges as shown, which of these statements is true?

```
create user janders identified by password;
grant create table to janders;
grant create index to janders;
```

a. The `janders` user will be able to log in and create tables in their own schema.
b. The `janders` user will be able to log in and drop tables in their own schema.

c. The janders user will be able to log in and create indexes in their own schema.

d. None of the above.

Q 6. Given the following set of statements, which of the following answers will be correct following their execution?

```
Grant insert, update, delete on companylink.employee to janders;
Revoke delete on companylink.employee from janders;
GRANT select on companylink.employee to janders;
REVOKE update on companylink.employee from janders;
```

a. The user janders will be able to update the companylink.employee table.

b. The user janders will be able to delete from the companylink.employee table.

c. The user janders will be able to insert into and select from the companylink.employee table.

d. All of the above are true.

Q 7. Which of these allows the least significant amount of administrative access?

a. The SELECT_CATALOG_ROLE role.

b. The SYS user.

c. The SYSTEM user.

d. The DBA role.

Q 8. When a privilege is granted to PUBLIC, which user owns this privilege?

a. Only SYS and SYSTEM.

b. Any user with the DBA role.

c. Any user with the SYSDBA role.

d. Any user in the database.

Q 9. Give that a new user is created and the following statements are issued, which of these answers are *incorrect*?

```
CREATE USER janders identified by password;
CREATE ROLE janders_role;
GRANT CREATE TABLE to janders_role;
GRANT SELECT on companylink.employee to janders_role;
GRANT SELECT ANY TABLE to janders_role;
GRANT janders_role to janders;
```

a. The user `janders` can select from tables in schemas other than his own.

b. The user `janders` can create tables in schemas other than his own.

c. The user `janders` can drop tables in his own schema.

d. The user `janders` can insert rows into the `companylink.employee` table.

Q 10. Which of the following profile limits could be used to enforce password complexity?

a. `PASSWORD_REUSE_TIME`

b. `PASSWORD_REUSE_MAX`

c. `PASSWORD_VERIFY_FUNCTION`

d. `PASSWORD_LIFE_TIME`

Q 11. Which of the following profile limits could be used to limit the number of times a password is changed before it can be re-used?

a. `PASSWORD_REUSE_TIME`

b. `PASSWORD_REUSE_MAX`

c. `PASSWORD_VERIFY_FUNCTION`

d. `PASSWORD_LIFE_TIME`

Q 12. Which of the following profile limits could be used to limit the amount of CPU cycles consumed in a single SQL statement?

a. `CPU_PER_USER`

b. `CPU_PER_SESSION`

c. `CPU_PER_CALL`

d. `IDLE_TIME`

Q 13. Given that the parameter value for `AUDIT_TRAIL` is `DB`, where will the audit information go after the following statement is executed and the database is restarted?

```
ALTER SYSTEM set AUDIT_TRAIL ='OS' scope=spfile;
```

a. The `SYS.AUD$` base table.
b. The `DBA_AUDIT_TRAIL` data dictionary table.
c. To an operating system directory in text format.
d. To an operating system directory in XML format.

Q 14. Given the following SQL statement, which of the following is the most accurate?

```
AUDIT insert on companylink.employee
BY SESSION WHENEVER NOT SUCCESSFUL;
```

a. An audit entry will be added whenever a user session selects from the `companylink.employee` table.
b. An audit entry will be added each time a user session successfully inserts into the `companylink.employee` table.
c. An audit entry will be added each time a user session unsuccessfully inserts into the `companylink.employee` table.
d. A single audit entry will be added whenever a user session unsuccessfully inserts into the `companylink.employee` table.

8
Managing Concurrency

One of the most difficult challenges that the real-world DBA faces is performance tuning. **Performance tuning** is the process of using database configuration mechanisms to achieve optimal application throughput. It is a career-long study that requires a keen understanding of the way that a database works, from memory caches to process configuration to the topic of this chapter—concurrency. **Concurrency** is the property that enables systems with many competing resources to function optimally. Maintaining concurrency in the Oracle RDBMS involves rules, mechanisms, and configuration settings.

In this chapter we shall:

- Understand the lifecycle of a transaction
- Explain the concept of the undo process
- Learn to manage undo data
- Explore database locking mechanisms
- Understand latches and mutexes

Understanding the lifecycle of a transaction

In order to understand concurrency, we need to understand the concept of a transaction. A **transaction**, in database terms, is a discrete unit of work within the database that accomplishes a certain task. Transactions allow groups of statements to be executed together, to allow for correct recovery in the event of failure. **Transaction control** is the act of manipulating the timing and execution of transactions. Let's begin this section with an example that demonstrates the importance of transaction control.

Examining the rules of a transaction

In database terms, transactions generally involve statements from the SQL sublanguage called **Data Manipulation Language** (**DML**). The `SELECT`, `INSERT`, `UPDATE`, and `DELETE` statements are generally categorized as DML, although some definitions exclude the `SELECT` statements. They also involve statements such as `COMMIT` and `ROLLBACK`, which are referred to as **Transaction Control Language** (**TCL**). In the following example, we will invoke two terminal windows on Linux, called `SESSION ONE` and `SESSION TWO`, and make two individual SQL*Plus connections to our database, using the `companylink` user. This establishes two different sessions.

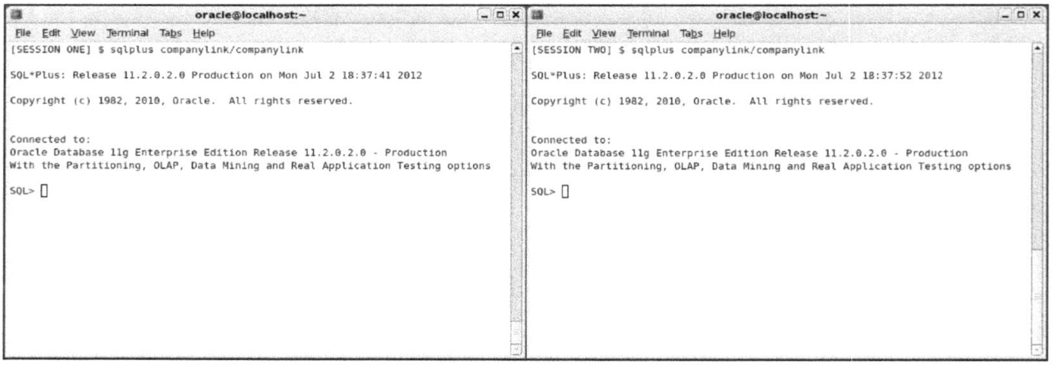
oracle@localhost:~
File Edit View Terminal Tabs Help
[SESSION ONE] $ sqlplus companylink/companylink
SQL*Plus: Release 11.2.0.2.0 Production on Mon Jul 2 18:37:41 2012
Copyright (c) 1982, 2010, Oracle. All rights reserved.
Connected to:
Oracle Database 11g Enterprise Edition Release 11.2.0.2.0 - Production
With the Partitioning, OLAP, Data Mining and Real Application Testing options
SQL>
oracle@localhost:~
File Edit View Terminal Tabs Help
[SESSION TWO] $ sqlplus companylink/companylink
SQL*Plus: Release 11.2.0.2.0 Production on Mon Jul 2 18:37:52 2012
Copyright (c) 1982, 2010, Oracle. All rights reserved.
Connected to:
Oracle Database 11g Enterprise Edition Release 11.2.0.2.0 - Production
With the Partitioning, OLAP, Data Mining and Real Application Testing options
SQL>

In `SESSION ONE`, we will create a `test_tab` table, and insert a row of data followed by a `COMMIT` operation:

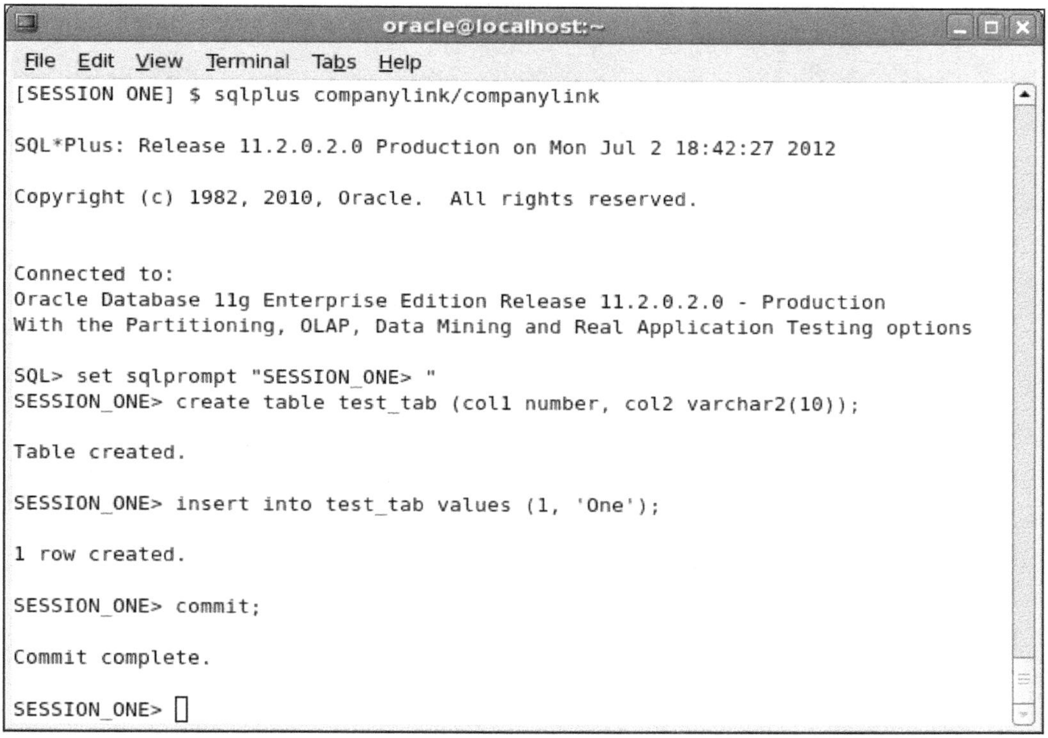
oracle@localhost:~
File Edit View Terminal Tabs Help

```
[SESSION ONE] $ sqlplus companylink/companylink

SQL*Plus: Release 11.2.0.2.0 Production on Mon Jul 2 18:42:27 2012

Copyright (c) 1982, 2010, Oracle.  All rights reserved.


Connected to:
Oracle Database 11g Enterprise Edition Release 11.2.0.2.0 - Production
With the Partitioning, OLAP, Data Mining and Real Application Testing options

SQL> set sqlprompt "SESSION_ONE> "
SESSION_ONE> create table test_tab (col1 number, col2 varchar2(10));

Table created.

SESSION_ONE> insert into test_tab values (1, 'One');

1 row created.

SESSION_ONE> commit;

Commit complete.

SESSION_ONE> 
```

When we query this table from `SESSION TWO`, we see the expected result:

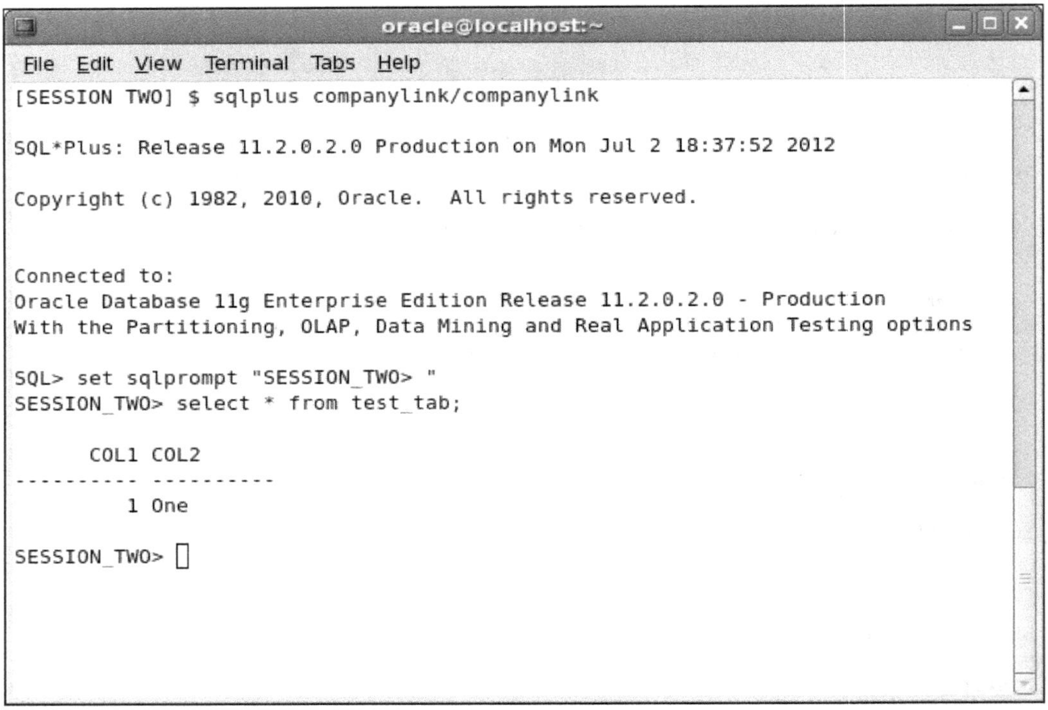

```
[SESSION TWO] $ sqlplus companylink/companylink

SQL*Plus: Release 11.2.0.2.0 Production on Mon Jul 2 18:37:52 2012

Copyright (c) 1982, 2010, Oracle.  All rights reserved.


Connected to:
Oracle Database 11g Enterprise Edition Release 11.2.0.2.0 - Production
With the Partitioning, OLAP, Data Mining and Real Application Testing options

SQL> set sqlprompt "SESSION_TWO> "
SESSION_TWO> select * from test_tab;

      COL1 COL2
---------- ----------
         1 One

SESSION_TWO>
```

Once again, we will insert values into our table from `SESSION ONE`, and query the result:

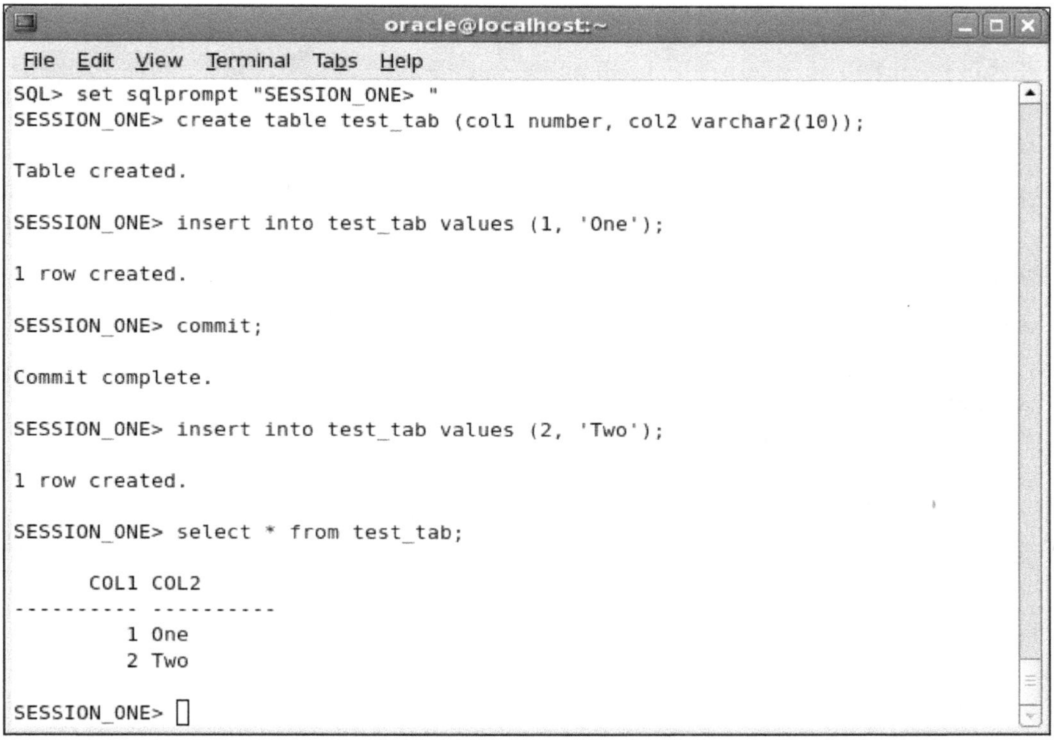
oracle@localhost:~
File Edit View Terminal Tabs Help
SQL> set sqlprompt "SESSION_ONE> "
SESSION_ONE> create table test_tab (col1 number, col2 varchar2(10));
Table created.
SESSION_ONE> insert into test_tab values (1, 'One');
1 row created.
SESSION_ONE> commit;
Commit complete.
SESSION_ONE> insert into test_tab values (2, 'Two');
1 row created.
SESSION_ONE> select * from test_tab;
COL1 COL2
---------- ----------
1 One
2 Two
SESSION_ONE>

As we've inserted a second row, we obviously see both rows returned from our query. However, what happens if we query the table from `SESSION TWO`? We might expect to see two rows, just as `SESSION ONE` does. But the results are different.

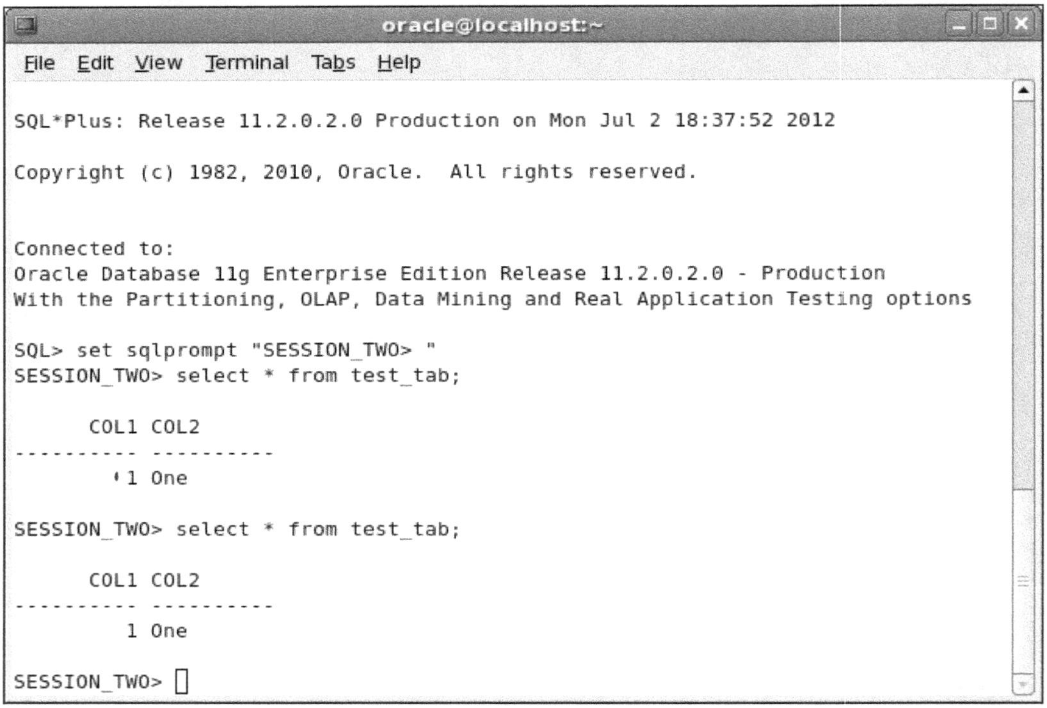
oracle@localhost:~
File Edit View Terminal Tabs Help
SQL*Plus: Release 11.2.0.2.0 Production on Mon Jul 2 18:37:52 2012
Copyright (c) 1982, 2010, Oracle. All rights reserved.
Connected to:
Oracle Database 11g Enterprise Edition Release 11.2.0.2.0 - Production
With the Partitioning, OLAP, Data Mining and Real Application Testing options
SQL> set sqlprompt "SESSION_TWO> "
SESSION_TWO> select * from test_tab;
COL1 COL2
---------- ----------
1 One
SESSION_TWO> select * from test_tab;
COL1 COL2
---------- ----------
1 One
SESSION_TWO>

Instead of seeing two rows, the user in `SESSION TWO` sees only one. How can this be? Clearly, a row was inserted from `SESSION ONE`, as `SESSION ONE` can see it. But why does `SESSION TWO` only see one? The answer lies in the rules of concurrency. After inserting the first row from `SESSION ONE`, the user issues a `COMMIT` statement. Following the `COMMIT` operation, both sessions see the same data. However, `SESSION ONE` does not issue a `COMMIT` after the second `INSERT`. Although `SESSION ONE` can see the data, `SESSION TWO` cannot. In a sense, it is not "real" to other sessions until the statement commits, allowing other sessions to see a consistent version of the data. Once a `COMMIT` is issued in `SESSION ONE`, `SESSION TWO` can see the data, as shown in the following screenshot:

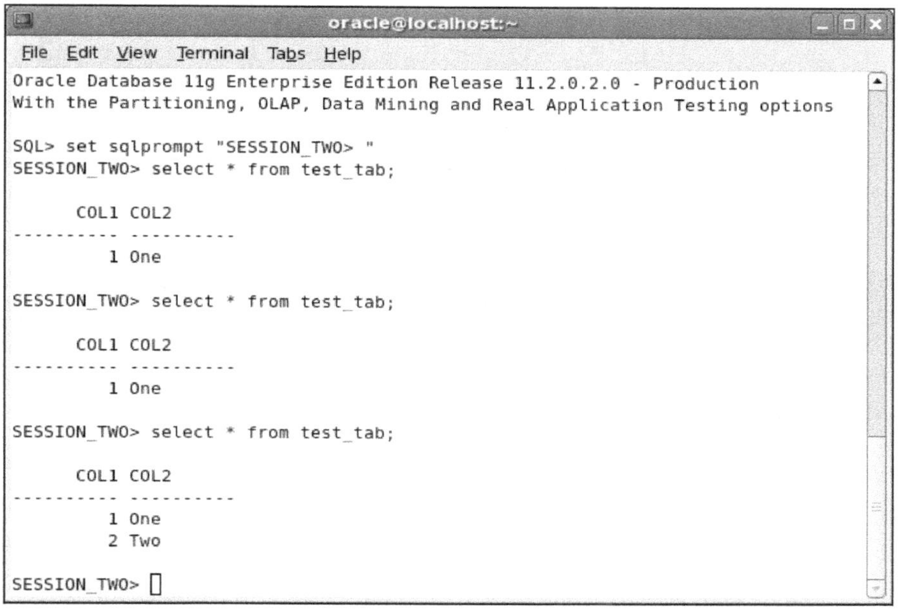
oracle@localhost:~
File Edit View Terminal Tabs Help
Oracle Database 11g Enterprise Edition Release 11.2.0.2.0 - Production
With the Partitioning, OLAP, Data Mining and Real Application Testing options
SQL> set sqlprompt "SESSION_TWO> "
SESSION_TWO> select * from test_tab;
COL1 COL2
---------- ----------
1 One
SESSION_TWO> select * from test_tab;
COL1 COL2
---------- ----------
1 One
SESSION_TWO> select * from test_tab;
COL1 COL2
---------- ----------
1 One
2 Two
SESSION_TWO>

This demonstrates the concept of **read consistency**. In order for an RDBMS to manage numerous sessions that work with the same data, it is sometimes necessary to maintain multiple versions of the same data to manage a consistent presentation of that data. We can look at this at the statement level, as shown here, but as DBAs, we can also think of this at the database block level. Since database blocks contain row data and the database block is the smallest unit of storage managed by Oracle, it is accurate to say that Oracle maintains multiple versions of the same database block at different points in time, a process called **multiversioning**. Let's examine the rules behind concurrency control.

In Oracle, concurrency control adheres to a set of rules known as **ACID**. Adherence to these rules, also known as ACID compliance, guarantees that transactions are processed reliably, regardless of how many user sessions are involved. ACID stands for Atomicity, Consistency, Isolation, and Durability. A description of these rules is as follows:

- **Atomicity** ensures the completeness of a transaction by enforcing the "all or nothing" rule. With an atomic transaction, all statements within the transaction must either succeed or all must fail.
- **Consistency** states that the data returned from a query will be consistent with the state of the data when the transaction began. If the data being selected is also being changed by other users, the data results will appear as they were when the transaction was executed.

- **Isolation** enforces the rule that the results of any query against data in the process of being changed must display the unchanged data until a transaction is complete. In short, the changes to the data must be hidden until a transaction is over. We saw this in our preceding example.
- **Durability** refers to the guarantee that, once committed, transactions cannot be "lost". Once a durable transaction is committed, its results are seen as "real", and cannot be reversed.

Taken together, the ACID rules enforce a level of consistency that allows many users to access data concurrently. Also note that, in the event of a database crash, such as a host server reboot or a `shutdown abort` command, any uncommitted transactions that were running at the time will automatically be rolled back during instance recovery. This ensures a read-consistent view of the data when the database is restarted, as ACID compliance requires.

The real-world DBA

Not all database systems are ACID-compliant. Much has been made recently of NoSQL databases. These systems offer significant performance increases, but usually at the cost of ACID compliance. Such systems require a tremendous amount of special application coding to ensure that data is displayed in a read-consistent manner and transactions complete normally.

Examining types of transactions

Now that we've clarified the rules behind a transaction, let's examine the steps that occur behind the scenes when a transaction is executed. First, let's look at what happens during a `SELECT` statement. We will then be able to relate that information to other DML statements.

During a `SELECT` statement, no changes are made to the data; thus, no "before" images of data are retained since one cannot roll back a query. When the `SELECT` statement is executed, the server process executing the query first checks to see whether the rows required are already in blocks within the buffer cache. If they are, the blocks needed to satisfy the query are read and the data is returned. If the blocks are not present in the buffer cache, the server process retrieves them from disk and writes them into the buffer, where they are made available to other server processes that may require the rows they contain. Once the blocks are copied into the buffer cache, the rows are read, and the values that satisfy the query are returned.

For a INSERT statement, the initial phase is similar to that of a SELECT statement. The user's server process either finds the required blocks in the buffer cache or reads them from the disk into the cache. However, since an INSERT statement actually represents a change in data, other steps must also occur. As we learned from our discussion of the log buffer cache and the redo logfiles, redo data must be recorded in order to provide for recoverability with a backup. Thus, first, the redo data representing the changes that will be made is written to the log buffer in the form of **change vectors**. This data ensures that a database is recoverable from backup in the event of a failure. Secondly, a "before" image of the data must be created for use in the event that a user rolls back the transaction using a ROLLBACK statement. This is known as **undo data**. Since an INSERT operation is adding new data, the only undo data that is kept is the ROWID value for the new row.

When a user executes an UPDATE statement, the user's server process either reads the required blocks from the buffer cache or from disk. Also, redo change vectors that represent the changes that are going to occur are written to the log buffer. Since an UPDATE statement changes the data, undo data is required to allow for a ROLLBACK operation. The table block changes are written to the buffer cache, and undo blocks are written out to the undo tablespace. Note that a type of SELECT statement exists that acts as an UPDATE statement. When we use SELECT...FOR UPDATE, the rows in question are handled as an UPDATE operation, even though the statement itself is SELECT.

In the event of a DELETE statement, the same steps occur. Blocks are read either from cache or disk, and redo change vectors are written to the log buffer. As DELETE removes an entire row, undo data must be generated for every value in the row. Consequently, a DELETE statement will generate significantly more undo blocks than an INSERT statement would.

> **The real-world DBA**
>
> This undo creation for every row is one of the reasons that DELETE statements can be costly in terms of performance—a great deal of system resources are used to generate the "before" image of the data. Special care must be taken to commit the changes in a reasonable time frame. In the event that every row in a table must be deleted, a TRUNCATE TABLE command should almost always be used, since it generates no undo.

Managing undo data

As so many of the statements executed against a database generate undo data, managing it is a crucial aspect of database administration. In the past, Oracle used resources called **rollback segments** to manage undo data. When a user connected to the database, they were assigned a rollback segment that would serve as storage for the undo data (called **rollback data**, back then) generated by that session. Unfortunately, these rollback segments were fairly finite in size, sometimes leading to the infamous `ORA-1555` error, "snapshot too old". This error was raised in situations where queries encountered an undo block that had been overwritten since the query was initiated. In version 9*i*, Oracle introduced new, more efficient ways to manage undo data, leading to fewer errors. This new approach has also allowed for new features that can use undo data even after it is expired following a `COMMIT` statement.

Understanding undo-related parameters

Let's examine the parameters that pertain to the management of undo space.

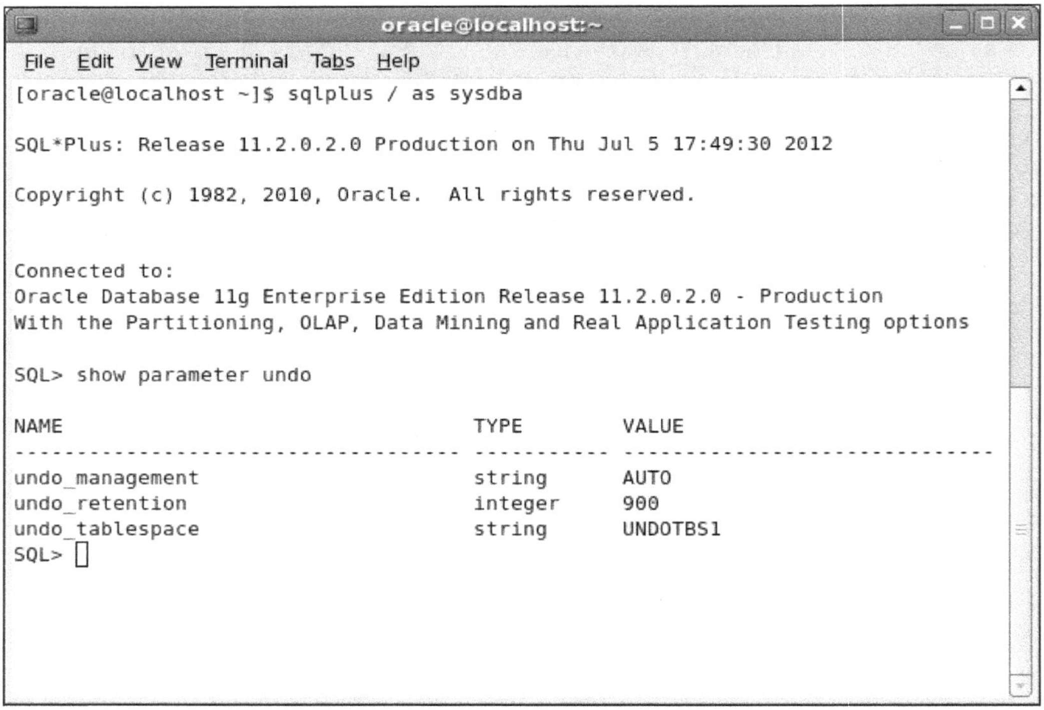
oracle@localhost:~
File Edit View Terminal Tabs Help
[oracle@localhost ~]$ sqlplus / as sysdba
SQL*Plus: Release 11.2.0.2.0 Production on Thu Jul 5 17:49:30 2012
Copyright (c) 1982, 2010, Oracle. All rights reserved.
Connected to:
Oracle Database 11g Enterprise Edition Release 11.2.0.2.0 - Production
With the Partitioning, OLAP, Data Mining and Real Application Testing options
SQL> show parameter undo
NAME TYPE VALUE
undo_management string AUTO
undo_retention integer 900
undo_tablespace string UNDOTBS1
SQL>

We'll examine these parameters one at a time, beginning with `undo_management`. As we mentioned, previous versions of Oracle made use of fixed-size rollback segments to provide space to user sessions. In versions of Oracle since 9*i*, we have the ability to make use of **Automatic Undo Management** (**AUM**). Rather than having users attached to a given rollback segment, AUM does what its name implies—it automatically manages the undo process. Rather than a DBA creating and managing a set of rollback segments, with AUM, we need only define an **undo tablespace**. AUM allocates, extends, and shrinks **undo segments** as needed to accommodate user activity. In essence, rather than managing each individual rollback segment, with AUM, we present an area of disk, the undo tablespace, and AUM manages it as needed. AUM is enabled using the `undo_management` parameter. Setting it to `AUTO` ensures that AUM is active. This is the default in 11*g*. If desired, the older method of undo management can be enabled by setting the parameter to `MANUAL`.

If we enable AUM (as it is by default), we define the undo tablespace that will be used using the third parameter listed in the preceding screenshot, `undo_tablespace`. In our case, this value is `UNDOTBS1`. This tells us that this tablespace will be used for automatically managed undo. When manual undo management is used, the `undo_tablespace` parameter should not be set. We can see the characteristics of this tablespace by querying the data dictionary, as shown in the following screenshot. Note the `RETENTION` column, which we'll discuss later.

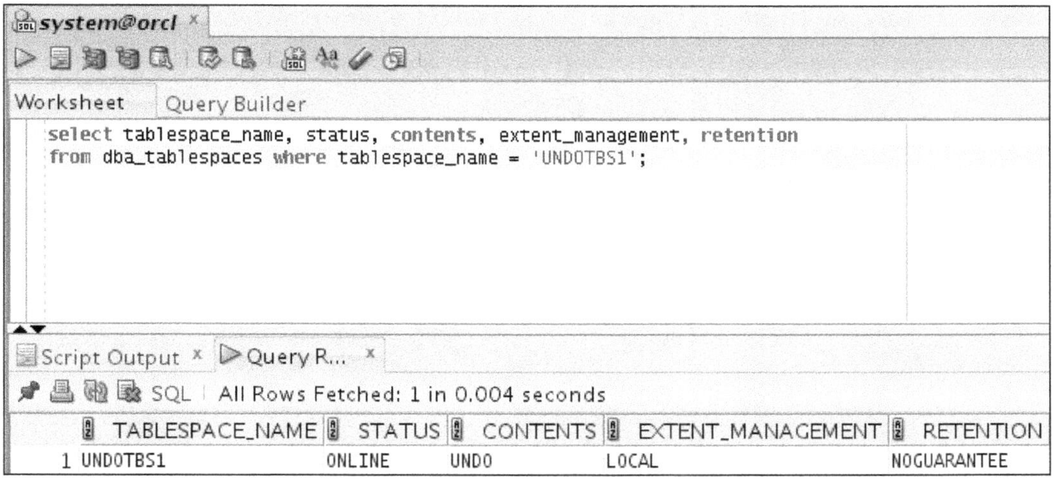
system@orcl
Worksheet
Query Builder
select tablespace_name, status, contents, extent_management, retention
from dba_tablespaces where tablespace_name = 'UNDOTBS1';
Script Output
Query R...
SQL
All Rows Fetched: 1 in 0.004 seconds
TABLESPACE_NAME STATUS CONTENTS EXTENT_MANAGEMENT RETENTION
1 UNDOTBS1 ONLINE UNDO LOCAL NOGUARANTEE

The second parameter in the list, `undo_retention`, is a little more complex. This parameter specifies the minimum amount of time, in seconds, for which undo data will be retained, beyond the point at which the transaction has been committed. In our example, `undo_retention` is set to `900` seconds, or 15 minutes. After the point of the commit, undo is said to be expired. AUM will attempt to retain expired undo data for the amount of time specified by `undo_retention` before overwriting it. Once the retention time has passed for a given piece of undo data, it is available to be overwritten. Why would this be of any benefit? Why should undo information be retained after the `COMMIT` statement has been executed?

The retention of undo data has several benefits. First, by allowing undo to exist past the point of commit, some errors involving long-running queries that query rapidly changing data can be avoided. However, most importantly, undo retention enables several of Oracle's **flashback** technologies. These features can be used to view data as it existed in the past. Let's demonstrate an example of a feature called **flashback query** using our recently created table `test_tab`. Here we query from the table in its current state:

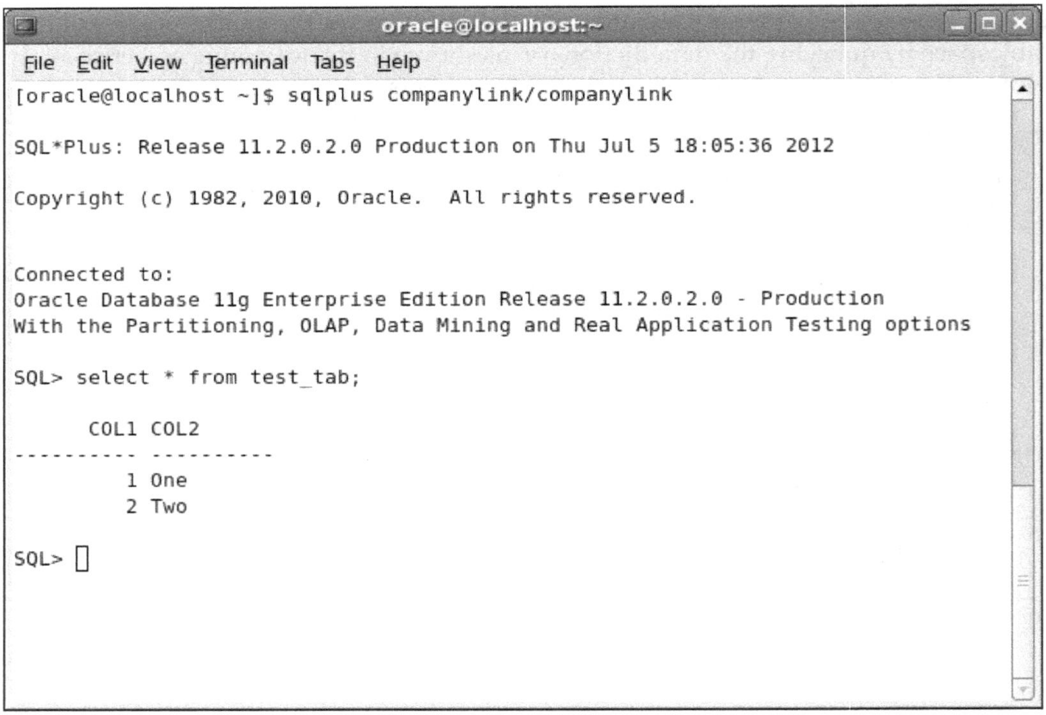
oracle@localhost:~
File Edit View Terminal Tabs Help
[oracle@localhost ~]$ sqlplus companylink/companylink
SQL*Plus: Release 11.2.0.2.0 Production on Thu Jul 5 18:05:36 2012
Copyright (c) 1982, 2010, Oracle. All rights reserved.
Connected to:
Oracle Database 11g Enterprise Edition Release 11.2.0.2.0 - Production
With the Partitioning, OLAP, Data Mining and Real Application Testing options
SQL> select * from test_tab;
COL1 COL2
---------- ----------
1 One
2 Two
SQL>

As we expect, we see the two rows of data that we inserted. Now, we'll delete a row and view the results.

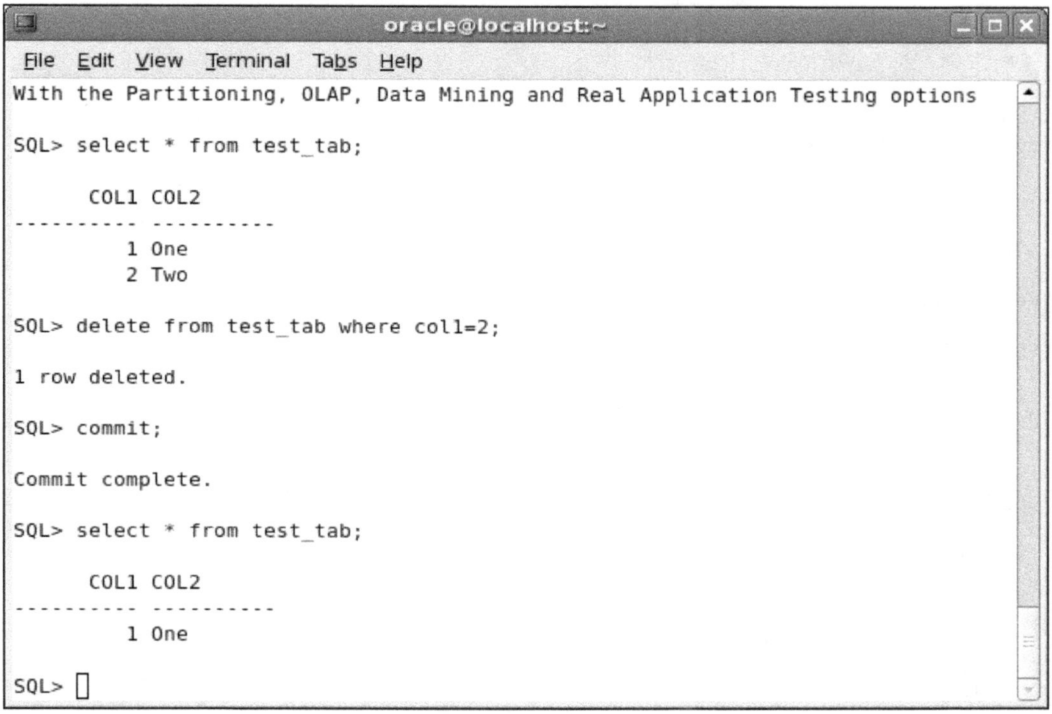
oracle@localhost:~
File Edit View Terminal Tabs Help
With the Partitioning, OLAP, Data Mining and Real Application Testing options
SQL> select * from test_tab;
COL1 COL2
---------- ----------
1 One
2 Two
SQL> delete from test_tab where col1=2;
1 row deleted.
SQL> commit;
Commit complete.
SQL> select * from test_tab;
COL1 COL2
---------- ----------
1 One
SQL>

We can use flashback query to view the table as it existed at a previous time. To do this, we use the `AS OF TIMESTAMP` clause in our `SELECT` statement.

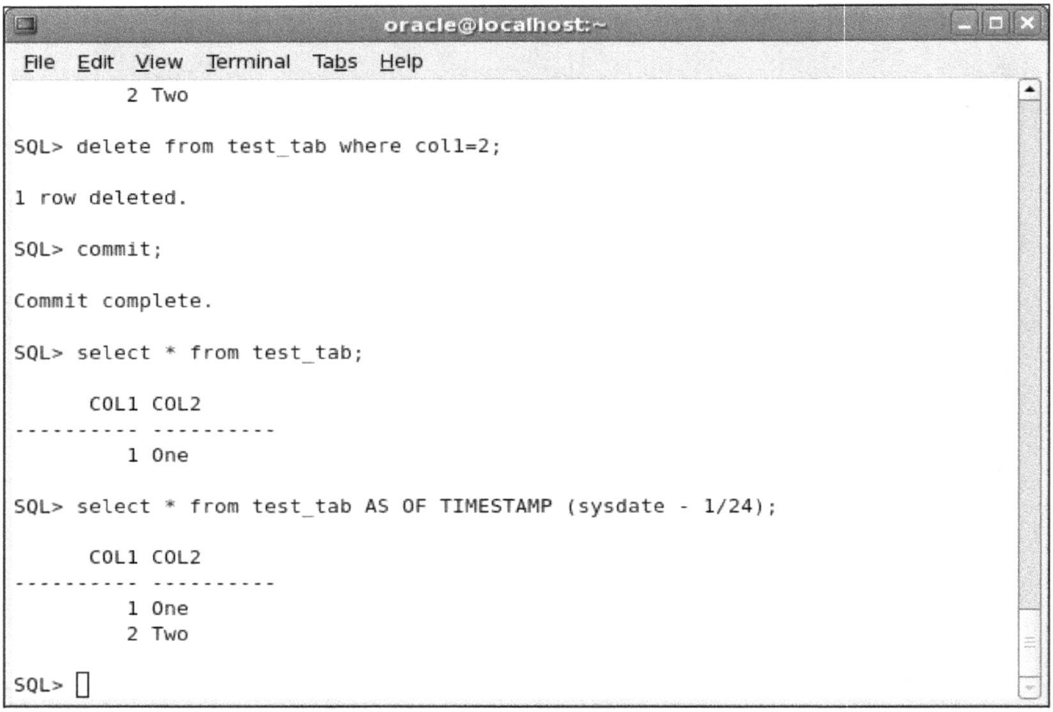
oracle@localhost:~
File Edit View Terminal Tabs Help
2 Two
SQL> delete from test_tab where col1=2;
1 row deleted.
SQL> commit;
Commit complete.
SQL> select * from test_tab;
COL1 COL2
---------- ----------
1 One
SQL> select * from test_tab AS OF TIMESTAMP (sysdate - 1/24);
COL1 COL2
---------- ----------
1 One
2 Two
SQL>

We use `sysdate - 1/24` for our timestamp, which represents the table as it was one hour prior. As if by magic, the row we deleted is now visible. But how is this possible? We committed the deleted row, which should mean that the row is gone. From where is this data coming? The answer isn't magic at all; it lies in the use of the `undo_retention` parameter. As `undo_retention` attempts to retain undo data for at least the number of seconds specified by the parameter value, the data we're seeing is actually coming from an undo segment in the undo tablespace. We're actually seeing a "before" image of the data, rather than the actual data in the table. Also notice that although our `undo_retention` parameter is set to 900 seconds, our flashback query views the data as it was 60 minutes in the past. Oracle will always attempt to save undo data for features such as flashback query. The `undo_retention` parameter represents the minimum amount of time Oracle will attempt to retain undo data. If the system is not actively seeking to write undo data, the data can be retained for a longer period of time.

Even though our example shows the flexibility of flashback query, Oracle cannot always guarantee that undo data will be available for flashback features. In a sufficiently active system, it is possible that undo data will be overwritten, even within the boundaries set by `undo_retention`. One way to guarantee that undo data will not be overwritten is to set the undo tablespace to `GUARANTEE` retention. In our previous example in which we viewed the undo tablespace, we made a note of the `RETENTION` column, which had the value `NOGUARANTEE`. This means that our undo tablespace, in its current form, cannot always guarantee that undo data will not be overwritten. If a system is sufficiently active, this undo data might be overwritten to service other transactions that require undoing. We can, however, ensure that our undoing will be retained for no fewer seconds than specified by `undo_retention`. This will be true even if doing so causes transactions to fail due to lack of space. To enable this, we can alter our undo tablespace with `GUARANTEE` retention, as shown in the following screenshot:

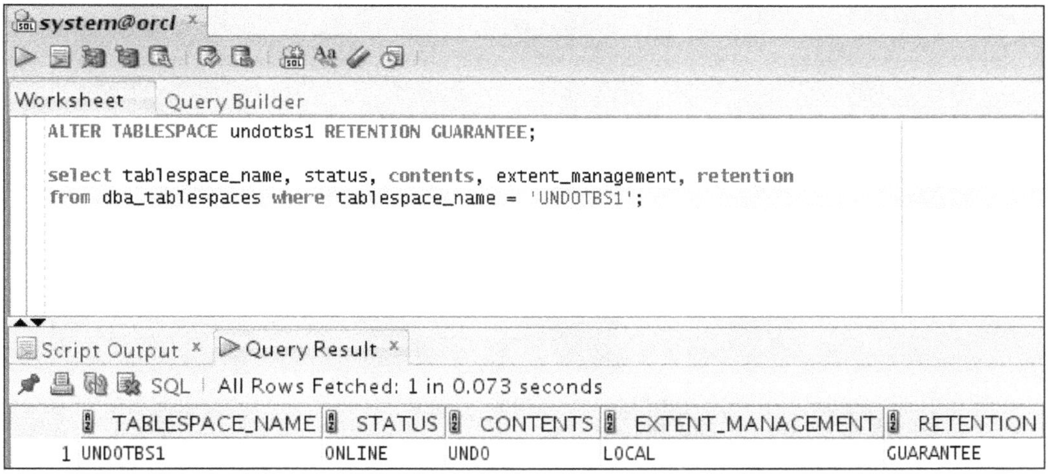
system@orcl
Worksheet
Query Builder
ALTER TABLESPACE undotbs1 RETENTION GUARANTEE;
select tablespace_name, status, contents, extent_management, retention
from dba_tablespaces where tablespace_name = 'UNDOTBS1';
Script Output
Query Result
SQL
All Rows Fetched: 1 in 0.073 seconds
TABLESPACE_NAME
STATUS
CONTENTS
EXTENT_MANAGEMENT
RETENTION
1 UNDOTBS1
ONLINE
UNDO
LOCAL
GUARANTEE

Our undo tablespace will now guarantee that undo data will be retained for no less than 900 seconds, as specified in our `undo_retention` parameter.

> **The real-world DBA**
>
> As tempting as it may be, it is not always advisable to turn on guaranteed retention for an active production system when the tablespace was previously set to `NOGUARANTEE`. When retention is guaranteed, the amount of undo retained can significantly increase. This could cause transactions to fail due to a lack of available undo space. Many times, this problem can be alleviated by increasing the size of the undo tablespace. Always activate guaranteed retention with caution and only after sufficient testing has been done.

As a final note on `undo_retention`, we will take a look at a particular characteristic that can cause the parameter to be ignored entirely. To begin with, let's look at the characteristics of the datafile for the undo tablespace, particularly whether its datafile is autoextensible.

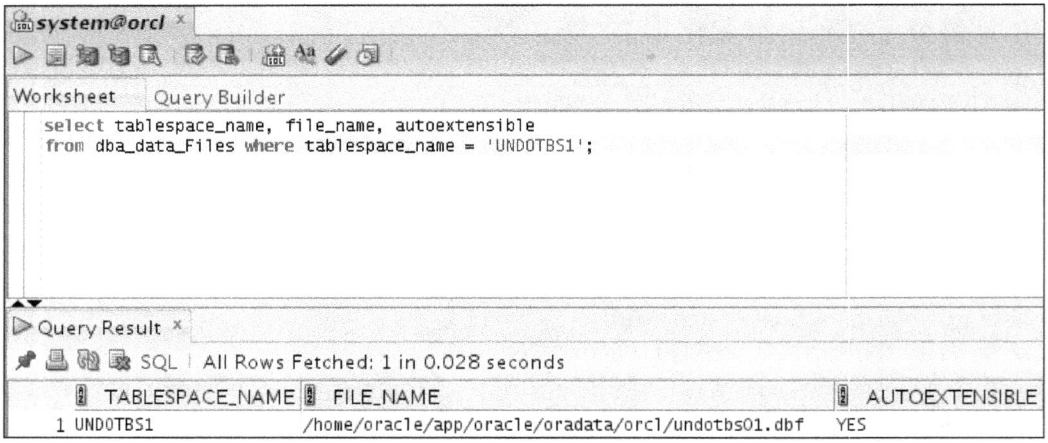
system@orcl
Worksheet
Query Builder
select tablespace_name, file_name, autoextensible
from dba_data_Files where tablespace_name = 'UNDOTBS1';
Query Result
SQL
All Rows Fetched: 1 in 0.028 seconds
TABLESPACE_NAME
FILE_NAME
AUTOEXTENSIBLE
1 UNDOTBS1
/home/oracle/app/oracle/oradata/orcl/undotbs01.dbf
YES

We see that the value `YES` in the `AUTOEXTENSIBLE` column indicates that the datafile for our undo tablespace will automatically extend when the datafile is full. In this configuration, Oracle will use the value we specify for `undo_retention` to retain undo data for the specified number of seconds. However, it is important to note that, if the datafile is not autoextensible, Oracle will ignore the value for `undo_retention`, instead choosing to calculate an optimal value for the parameter on its own. This can affect the usefulness of features such as flashback query, so it is important to recognize.

Managing undo tablespaces

As we've discussed, an undo tablespace is necessary in order to use Automatic Undo Management. Thus, if our `undo_management` parameter is set to `AUTO`, we must specify an undo tablespace in the `undo_tablespace` parameter. Since AUM was turned on when we created our database using DBCA, it was necessary for DBCA to create an undo tablespace during the actual creation of the database. If not, we would have never been able to start the database with the `undo_management` parameter set to `AUTO`. If we return to the database creation script we generated in *Chapter 3, Creating the Oracle Database,* we can see that an undo tablespace was created with the `CREATE DATABASE` command. The portion that involves the undo tablespace is highlighted in the following screenshot:

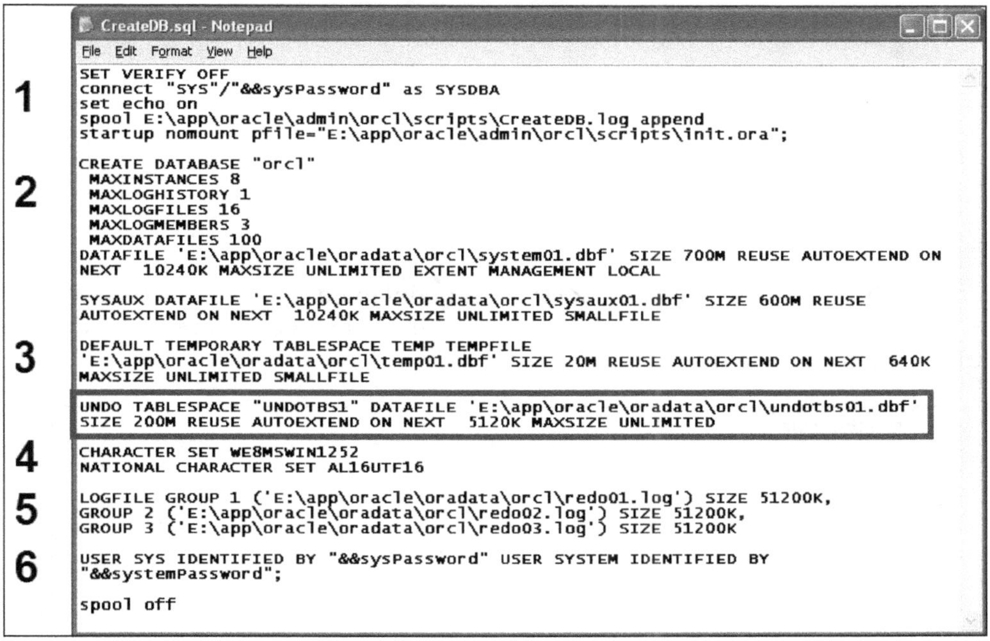
CreateDB.sql - Notepad
File Edit Format View Help
1
2
3
4
5
6

```
SET VERIFY OFF
connect "SYS"/"&&sysPassword" as SYSDBA
set echo on
spool E:\app\oracle\admin\orcl\scripts\CreateDB.log append
startup nomount pfile="E:\app\oracle\admin\orcl\scripts\init.ora";

CREATE DATABASE "orcl"
 MAXINSTANCES 8
 MAXLOGHISTORY 1
 MAXLOGFILES 16
 MAXLOGMEMBERS 3
 MAXDATAFILES 100
DATAFILE 'E:\app\oracle\oradata\orcl\system01.dbf' SIZE 700M REUSE AUTOEXTEND ON
NEXT  10240K MAXSIZE UNLIMITED EXTENT MANAGEMENT LOCAL

SYSAUX DATAFILE 'E:\app\oracle\oradata\orcl\sysaux01.dbf' SIZE 600M REUSE
AUTOEXTEND ON NEXT  10240K MAXSIZE UNLIMITED SMALLFILE

DEFAULT TEMPORARY TABLESPACE TEMP TEMPFILE
'E:\app\oracle\oradata\orcl\temp01.dbf' SIZE 20M REUSE AUTOEXTEND ON NEXT  640K
MAXSIZE UNLIMITED SMALLFILE

UNDO TABLESPACE "UNDOTBS1" DATAFILE 'E:\app\oracle\oradata\orcl\undotbs01.dbf'
SIZE 200M REUSE AUTOEXTEND ON NEXT  5120K MAXSIZE UNLIMITED

CHARACTER SET WE8MSWIN1252
NATIONAL CHARACTER SET AL16UTF16

LOGFILE GROUP 1 ('E:\app\oracle\oradata\orcl\redo01.log') SIZE 51200K,
GROUP 2 ('E:\app\oracle\oradata\orcl\redo02.log') SIZE 51200K,
GROUP 3 ('E:\app\oracle\oradata\orcl\redo03.log') SIZE 51200K

USER SYS IDENTIFIED BY "&&sysPassword" USER SYSTEM IDENTIFIED BY
"&&systemPassword";

spool off
```

If we desire, we can also create undo tablespaces for an existing database. Any given database can have multiple undo tablespaces. An undo tablespace can be managed in much the same way as any other tablespace. We can resize or add the datafiles of the tablespace or put the tablespace in offline or online mode. To create a new undo tablespace, we use the `CREATE UNDO TABLESPACE` command, rather than `CREATE TABLESPACE`.

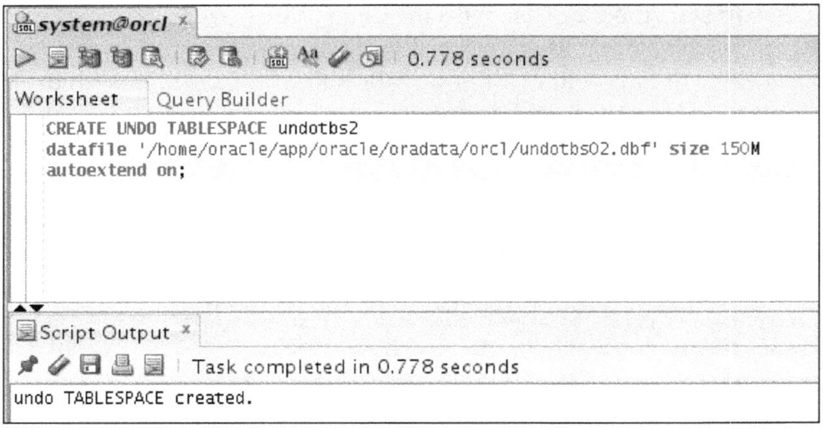
system@orcl
0.778 seconds
Worksheet
Query Builder
CREATE UNDO TABLESPACE undotbs2
datafile '/home/oracle/app/oracle/oradata/orcl/undotbs02.dbf' size 150M
autoextend on;
Script Output
Task completed in 0.778 seconds
undo TABLESPACE created.

An undo tablespace only contains the system-maintained undo segments that AUM uses to manage undo data. We cannot create other segments, such as table segments, within it; attempting to do so results in an error.

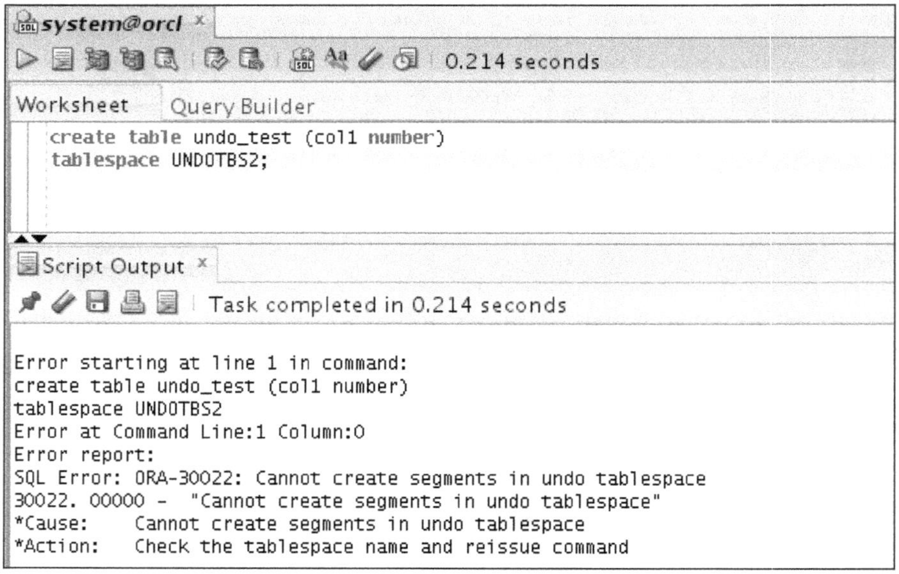
system@orcl
0.214 seconds
Worksheet
Query Builder
create table undo_test (col1 number)
tablespace UNDOTBS2;
Script Output
Task completed in 0.214 seconds
Error starting at line 1 in command:
create table undo_test (col1 number)
tablespace UNDOTBS2
Error at Command Line:1 Column:0
Error report:
SQL Error: ORA-30022: Cannot create segments in undo tablespace
30022. 00000 - "Cannot create segments in undo tablespace"
*Cause: Cannot create segments in undo tablespace
*Action: Check the tablespace name and reissue command

If we need to manage space within the undo tablespace, we can do so using the `ALTER DATABASE DATAFILE` command:

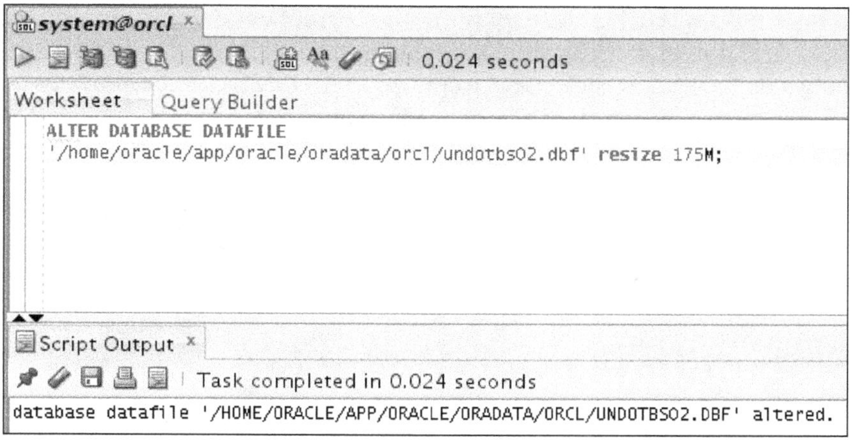
system@orcl
0.024 seconds
Worksheet
Query Builder
ALTER DATABASE DATAFILE
'/home/oracle/app/oracle/oradata/orcl/undotbs02.dbf' resize 175M;
Script Output
Task completed in 0.024 seconds
database datafile '/HOME/ORACLE/APP/ORACLE/ORADATA/ORCL/UNDOTBS02.DBF' altered.

At this point, we could make use of our new undo tablespace by setting the `undo_tablespace` parameter to a value `UNDOTBS2`. Generally, any given database has only one active undo tablespace at a time. An exception to this is the **Real Application Clusters** (**RAC**) architecture, which has one undo tablespace for each instance. However, if it is necessary, we can use the `undo_tablespace` parameter to switch between the undo tablespaces. We can do this while the database is open. If we wish to drop an undo tablespace, we use the `DROP TABLESPACE` command. Note that there is no `UNDO` clause in the command, unlike the `CREATE UNDO TABLESPACE` command. It is dropped in the same way that any other tablespace is dropped.

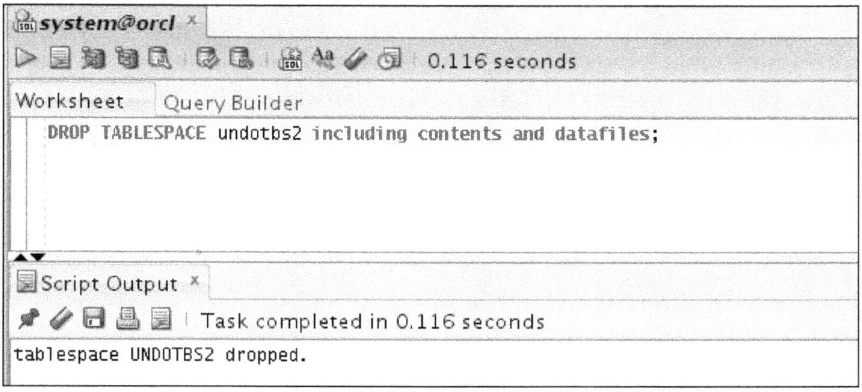
system@orcl
0.116 seconds
Worksheet
Query Builder
DROP TABLESPACE undotbs2 including contents and datafiles;
Script Output
Task completed in 0.116 seconds
tablespace UNDOTBS2 dropped.

We cannot drop an undo tablespace if it is specified in the `undo_tablespace` parameter or if it has active undo segments.

Managing serialization mechanisms

The concurrency mechanisms that we explored thus far involve mainly maintaining multiple versions of a block and displaying the correct version of a given block to a user. There are, however, other mechanisms that serialize access to table rows, database objects, or other system resources. As an RDBMS cannot allow two users to operate on the same piece of data at exactly the same time, it must have rules in place that prevent such an occurrence. As a simple example, imagine a four-way traffic stop. As more than one automobile cannot cross the same space at the intersection at exactly the same time, control mechanisms such as a traffic light must be employed to prevent collisions. In a similar manner, Oracle uses locks, latches, and mutexes to serialize access to objects and resources.

Understanding Oracle's locking scheme

Oracle's locking rules are designed to facilitate proper row and object concurrency between users. This locking is handled by the Oracle kernel and is therefore automatic. There are, however, coding issues that can come into play regarding locking that can greatly affect performance.

Oracle employs two broad categories of lock modes—exclusive and share. An **exclusive lock** places a lock on an entity—a row, for instance—and no other session is allowed write access or allowed to lock the entity until the lock is released. Any session that requests a read operation for the given row, however, is allowed that access. This is the type of lock that occurs during a `UPDATE` statement. The row or rows to be updated are locked until a `COMMIT` or `ROLLBACK` operation occurs. During the update, read access is allowed, but remember that this correlates with the rules of read consistency, which only allow other sessions to see the "before" image of the data. Tables can also be locked in exclusive mode. One of the most common examples of an exclusive lock on a table occurs when DDL statements are performed against it. The exclusive lock prevents alteration until a DDL statement, such as adding a column to a table, is complete.

The second type of lock is a **share lock**, which allows more than one lock per entity. Share locks are used on database objects, particularly tables, and prevent any other user from obtaining an exclusive lock on the same object. Thus, a share lock on a table by user A prevents an exclusive lock by user B from occurring. For instance, when a row is updated in a table, an exclusive lock is acquired on the row in question, and a share lock is obtained on the table itself. Thus, the table cannot be altered until the share lock is released. This promotes concurrency because it prevents object characteristics from being changed at the same time that the data is being altered. Whichever session acquires the proper lock first is the session that is allowed to execute the operation. To summarize, exclusive locks are generally used to modify an entity, although share locks generally prevent modification.

Row-level locks are generally referred to as **TX locks**. There is no restriction on the number of rows that can be locked using a TX lock, and this type of lock provides a low-level, highly concurrent method of transaction consistency. Table-level locks are referred to as **TM locks**, and can be either shared or exclusive.

Examining locking in action

We can witness locking occurring in the database by referencing the data dictionary. Basic locking information can be found in a view called `v$lock` although this view is usually joined with other views to see more detailed information. Let's look at some examples. We open two sessions in SQL Developer—one for the `companylink` user and one for `system`. In the following screenshots, we pay close attention to which session's tab is highlighted. First, we'll set up a test scenario by creating a table as the `companylink` user, and then we'll insert and commit a row. We can execute these individually or as a script with the appropriate button.

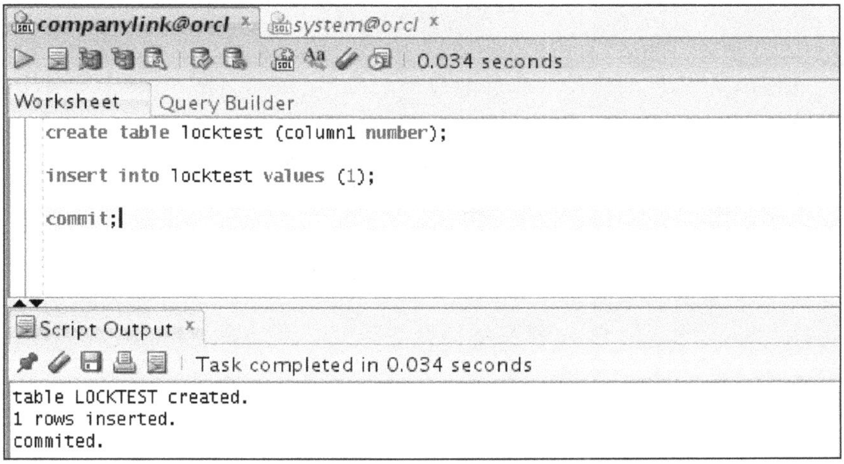
companylink@orcl
system@orcl
0.034 seconds
Worksheet
Query Builder
create table locktest (column1 number);
insert into locktest values (1);
commit;
Script Output
Task completed in 0.034 seconds
table LOCKTEST created.
1 rows inserted.
commited.

Next, we insert a row into the `locktest` table, but do not issue a commit.

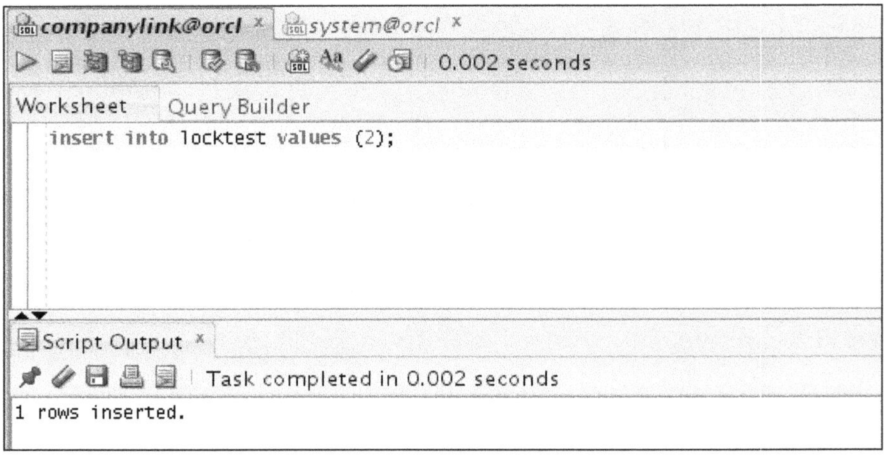
companylink@orcl
system@orcl
0.002 seconds
Worksheet
Query Builder
insert into locktest values (2);
Script Output
Task completed in 0.002 seconds
1 rows inserted.

In the tab for the `system` user, we execute a join against the `v$lock`, `v$locked_object`, and `dba_objects` data dictionary views. This will give us the username, object name, and lock type for this transaction:

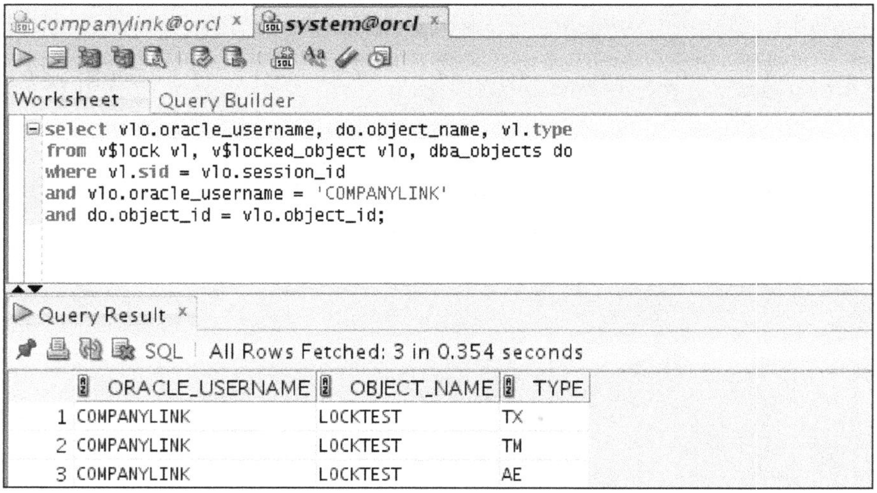
companylink@orcl
system@orcl
Worksheet
Query Builder
select vlo.oracle_username, do.object_name, vl.type
from v$lock vl, v$locked_object vlo, dba_objects do
where vl.sid = vlo.session_id
and vlo.oracle_username = 'COMPANYLINK'
and do.object_id = vlo.object_id;
Query Result
SQL
All Rows Fetched: 3 in 0.354 seconds
ORACLE_USERNAME
OBJECT_NAME
TYPE
1 COMPANYLINK LOCKTEST TX
2 COMPANYLINK LOCKTEST TM
3 COMPANYLINK LOCKTEST AE

Note that our query shows the typical locking scheme that occurs during a DML transaction. No commit has been issued, so two locks remain—a **TX**, or row-level lock, and a **TM**, or table-level lock. The third lock that is shown, `AE`, is a special lock in 11*g* that deals with the subject of "editioning", which is beyond the scope of this book. For our purposes, we will ignore this type of lock. These locks remain until a `COMMIT` statement is issued in the `companylink` session. If we open a third session before committing this one in SQL*Plus for the sake of simplicity, we see an interesting result that occurs from the use of a TM share lock.

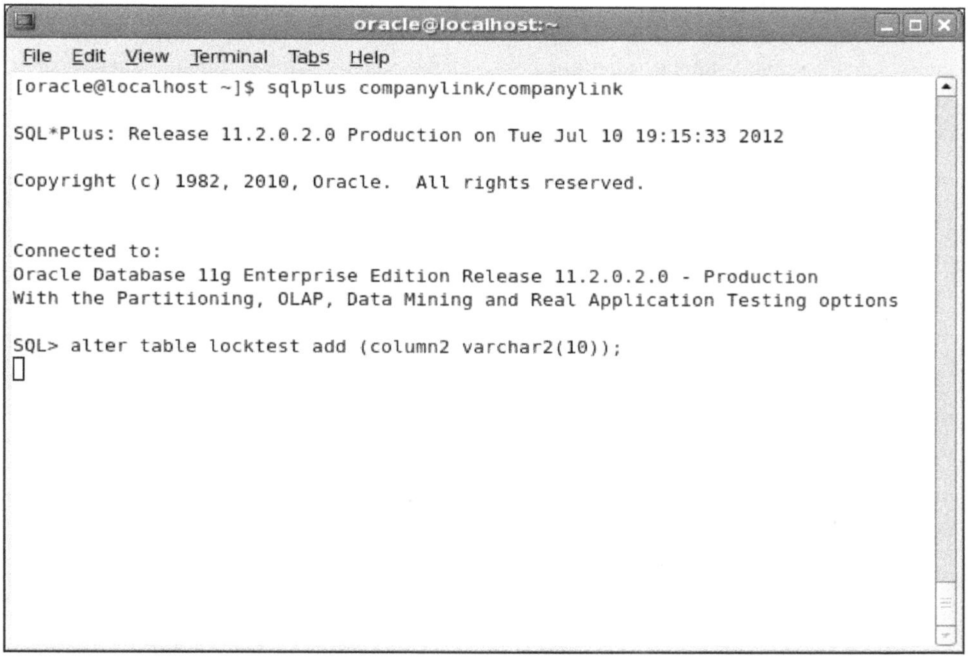
oracle@localhost:~
File Edit View Terminal Tabs Help
[oracle@localhost ~]$ sqlplus companylink/companylink
SQL*Plus: Release 11.2.0.2.0 Production on Tue Jul 10 19:15:33 2012
Copyright (c) 1982, 2010, Oracle. All rights reserved.
Connected to:
Oracle Database 11g Enterprise Edition Release 11.2.0.2.0 - Production
With the Partitioning, OLAP, Data Mining and Real Application Testing options
SQL> alter table locktest add (column2 varchar2(10));

Notice that we've executed an `ALTER TABLE` DDL statement against the `locktest` table, which currently has a shared TM lock in the other `companylink` session. The rules of Oracle's locking scheme say that a share lock prevents any exclusive locks from being made on the locked table. An `ALTER TABLE` statement is DDL and therefore requires an exclusive lock. Since this is not possible, the DDL statement enters a wait state, and cannot be completed while the original share lock is in place. Note that the DDL statement does not generate an error; it simply waits until a `COMMIT` operation occurs in the original `companylink` session in SQL Developer. Let's complete that `COMMIT` operation.

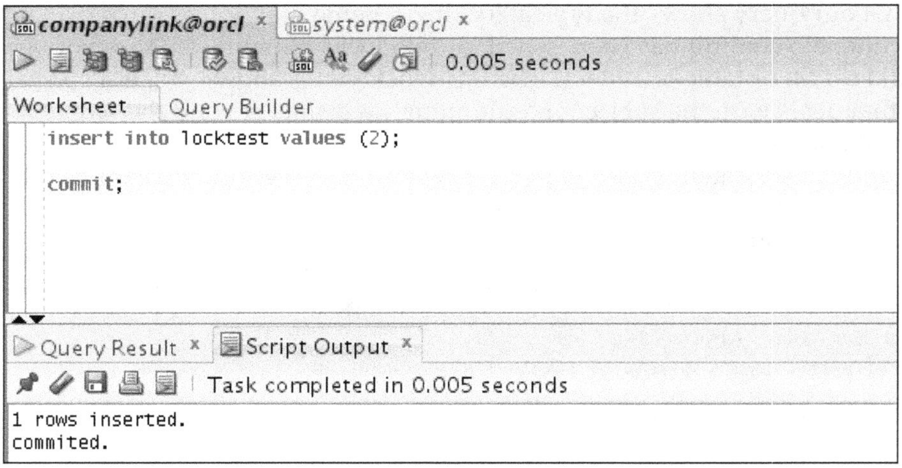
companylink@orcl
system@orcl
0.005 seconds
Worksheet
Query Builder
insert into locktest values (2);
commit;
Query Result
Script Output
Task completed in 0.005 seconds
1 rows inserted.
commited.

When we execute a `COMMIT` statement in this session, several events occur. First, we can see from our data dictionary query that locks are released:

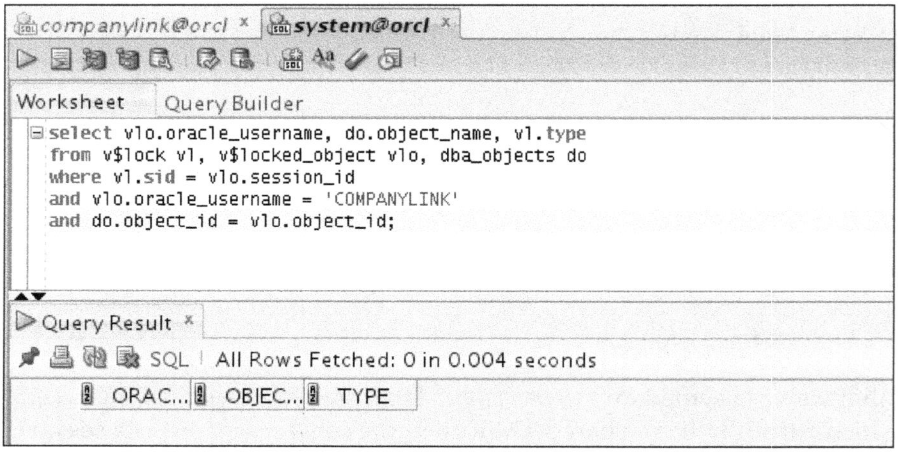
companylink@orcl
system@orcl
Worksheet
Query Builder
select vlo.oracle_username, do.object_name, vl.type
from v$lock vl, v$locked_object vlo, dba_objects do
where vl.sid = vlo.session_id
and vlo.oracle_username = 'COMPANYLINK'
and do.object_id = vlo.object_id;
Query Result
SQL
All Rows Fetched: 0 in 0.004 seconds
ORAC...
OBJEC...
TYPE

Second, just after the commit occurs, our `ALTER TABLE` statement is completed successfully, as the share TX lock is released after `COMMIT`:

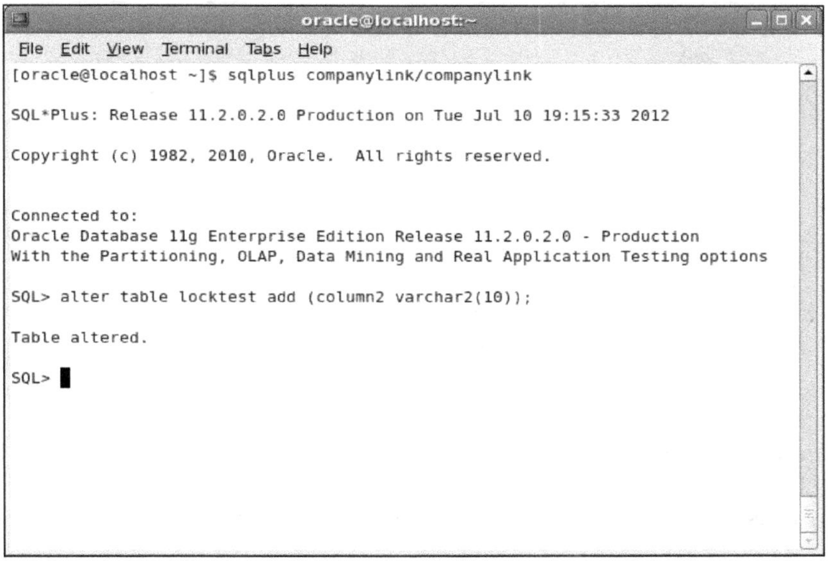
oracle@localhost:~
File Edit View Terminal Tabs Help
[oracle@localhost ~]$ sqlplus companylink/companylink
SQL*Plus: Release 11.2.0.2.0 Production on Tue Jul 10 19:15:33 2012
Copyright (c) 1982, 2010, Oracle. All rights reserved.
Connected to:
Oracle Database 11g Enterprise Edition Release 11.2.0.2.0 - Production
With the Partitioning, OLAP, Data Mining and Real Application Testing options
SQL> alter table locktest add (column2 varchar2(10));
Table altered.
SQL>

This type of locking can occur both ways. We can also initiate an exclusive TM table-level lock that blocks DML statements. We lock a table with an exclusive lock using the `LOCK TABLE` command, as shown in the following screenshot:

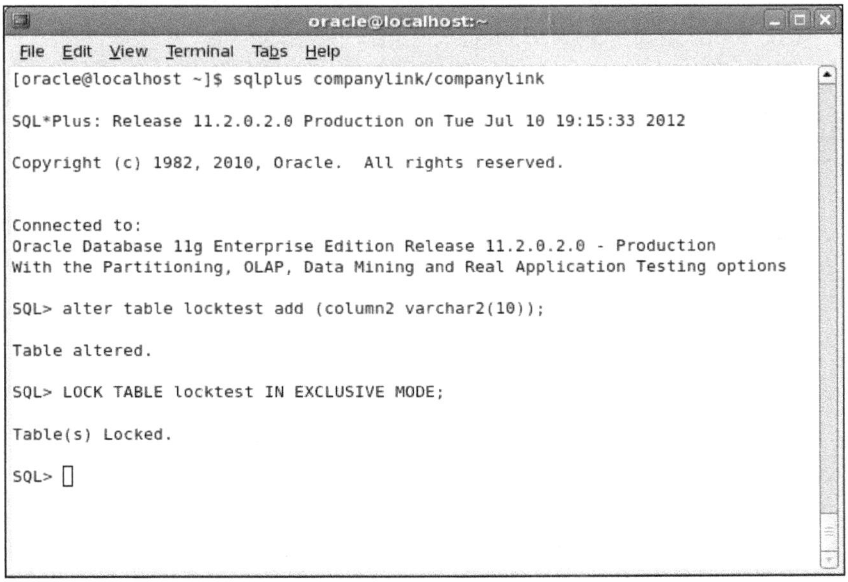
oracle@localhost:~
File Edit View Terminal Tabs Help
[oracle@localhost ~]$ sqlplus companylink/companylink
SQL*Plus: Release 11.2.0.2.0 Production on Tue Jul 10 19:15:33 2012
Copyright (c) 1982, 2010, Oracle. All rights reserved.
Connected to:
Oracle Database 11g Enterprise Edition Release 11.2.0.2.0 - Production
With the Partitioning, OLAP, Data Mining and Real Application Testing options
SQL> alter table locktest add (column2 varchar2(10));
Table altered.
SQL> LOCK TABLE locktest IN EXCLUSIVE MODE;
Table(s) Locked.
SQL>

Now, we will attempt to insert a row into the `locktest` table from our `companylink` session in SQL Developer:

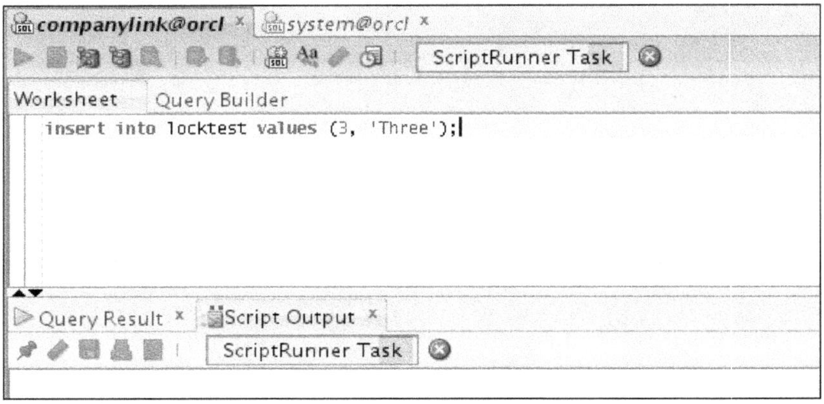
companylink@orcl
system@orcl
ScriptRunner Task
Worksheet
Query Builder
insert into locktest values (3, 'Three');
Query Result
Script Output
ScriptRunner Task

The statement does not return. It simply spins while the table is exclusively locked by the SQL*Plus session. In order to release this lock, we issue a `COMMIT` statement in the SQL*Plus session. The following screenshot shows both sessions:

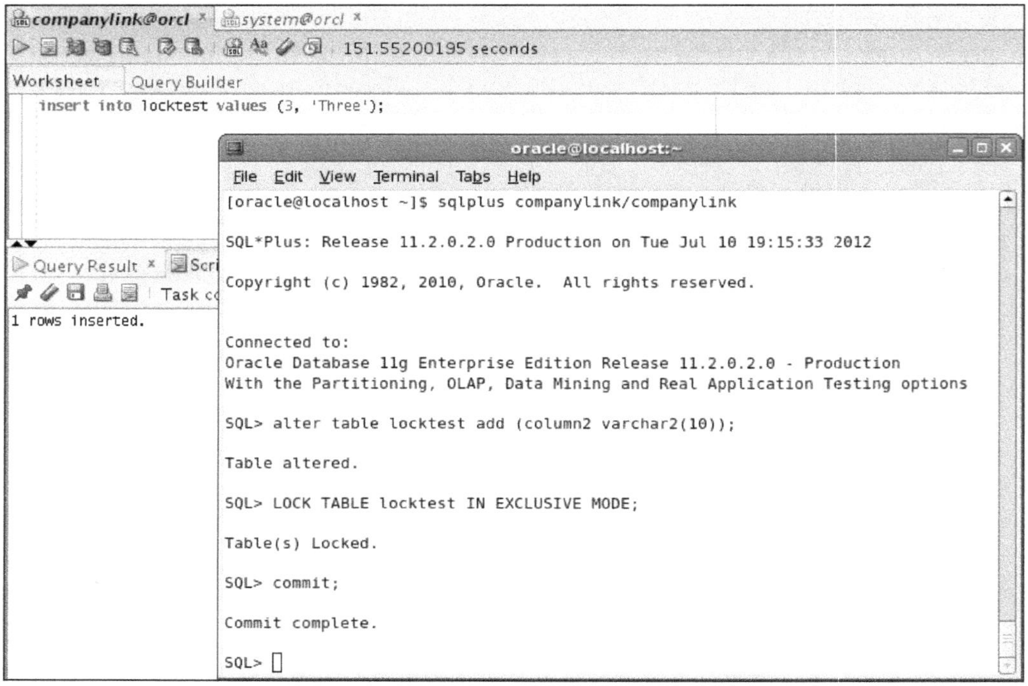
companylink@orcl
system@orcl
151.55200195 seconds
Worksheet
Query Builder
insert into locktest values (3, 'Three');
Query Result
1 rows inserted.
oracle@localhost:~
File Edit View Terminal Tabs Help
[oracle@localhost ~]$ sqlplus companylink/companylink
SQL*Plus: Release 11.2.0.2.0 Production on Tue Jul 10 19:15:33 2012
Copyright (c) 1982, 2010, Oracle. All rights reserved.
Connected to:
Oracle Database 11g Enterprise Edition Release 11.2.0.2.0 - Production
With the Partitioning, OLAP, Data Mining and Real Application Testing options
SQL> alter table locktest add (column2 varchar2(10));
Table altered.
SQL> LOCK TABLE locktest IN EXCLUSIVE MODE;
Table(s) Locked.
SQL> commit;
Commit complete.
SQL>

We can see that the COMMIT statement issued releases the exclusive TM lock, and allows the INSERT statement to be completed without error. From these examples, it should become clear that proper timing of the COMMIT statements is crucial to database performance. Improperly issued COMMIT statements can cause **lock contention**, a common database performance issue.

> **The real-world DBA**
>
> Although we've used the LOCK TABLE command here to illustrate an exclusive lock, the command itself should rarely be used. Oracle's locking scheme issues the proper type of locks at the appropriate time to maintain concurrency. Attempting to override that scheme can lead to performance problems.

Recognizing deadlocks

Our final type of lock is more similar to a condition than a lock, but it is often referred to as a special type of lock. A **deadlock** occurs when two or more sessions are competing for the same locks that are necessary to maintain transaction consistency. Deadlocks do not occur because of resource starvation or incorrect database parameters. Rather, they occur as a result of poorly written or timed SQL statements. The base SQL that underlies applications must always be written in a way that considers the possibility of deadlocks. Deadlocks are resolved by the Oracle kernel—one of the sessions causing the deadlock is forcibly rolled back and an Oracle ORA-00060 error is generated. There is little that a DBA can do to prevent deadlocks other than offering advice about an application's SQL statements. DBAs can, however, detect deadlocks by looking in the alert log and viewing the corresponding trace file. Let's examine a deadlock as it happens. To do so, we'll again use two different sessions, both logging in as the companylink user. One will be run in SQL Developer and the other in SQL*Plus, to help distinguish the two. We will begin by creating two tables, deadlock1 and deadlock2, and inserting rows to facilitate the test. From the SQL Developer session, we will execute command as follows:

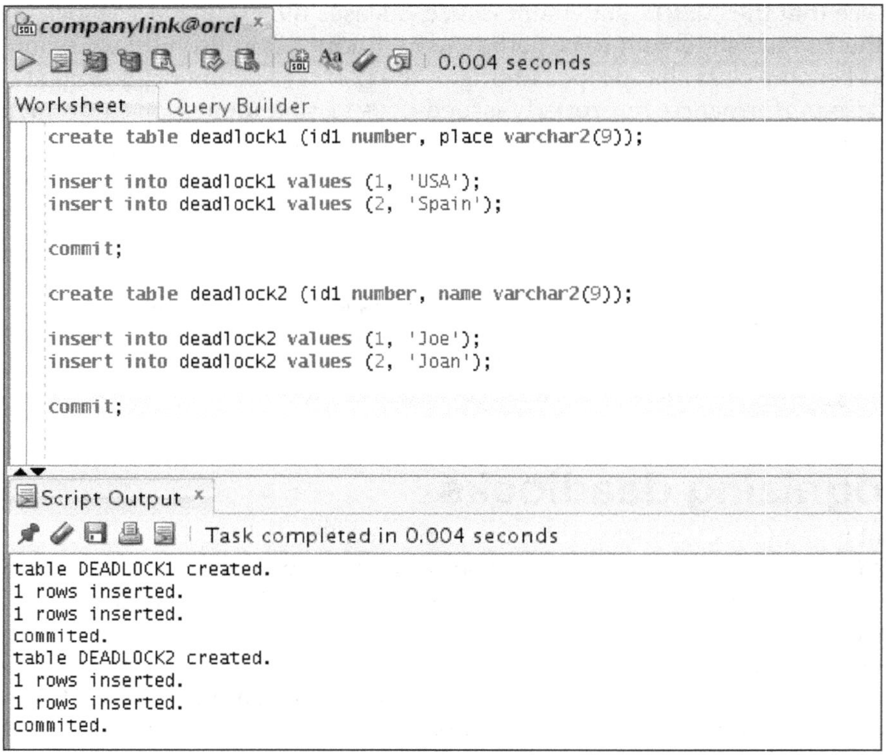
companylink@orcl
0.004 seconds
Worksheet
Query Builder
create table deadlock1 (id1 number, place varchar2(9));
insert into deadlock1 values (1, 'USA');
insert into deadlock1 values (2, 'Spain');
commit;
create table deadlock2 (id1 number, name varchar2(9));
insert into deadlock2 values (1, 'Joe');
insert into deadlock2 values (2, 'Joan');
commit;
Script Output
Task completed in 0.004 seconds
table DEADLOCK1 created.
1 rows inserted.
1 rows inserted.
commited.
table DEADLOCK2 created.
1 rows inserted.
1 rows inserted.
commited.

Next, again in our first session, we run a statement that updates the `place` column for `deadlock1` but does not commit.

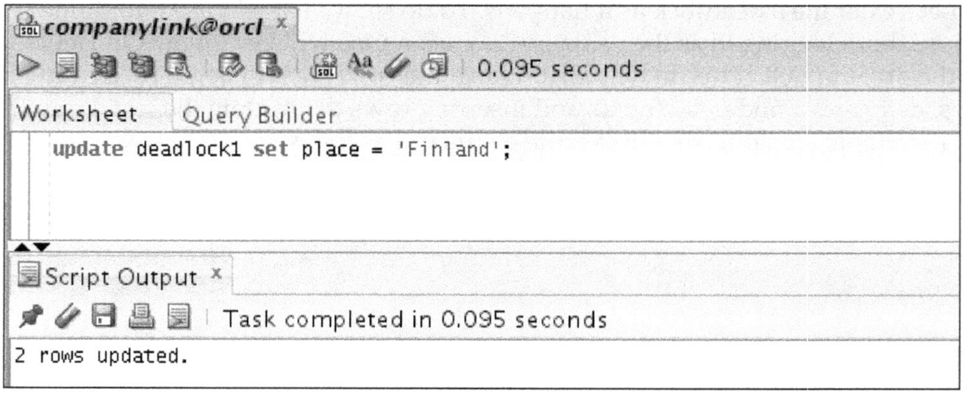
companylink@orcl
0.095 seconds
Worksheet
Query Builder
update deadlock1 set place = 'Finland';
Script Output
Task completed in 0.095 seconds
2 rows updated.

Then, we execute a similar statement that updates the `name` column in `deadlock2` from our second session, SQL*Plus:

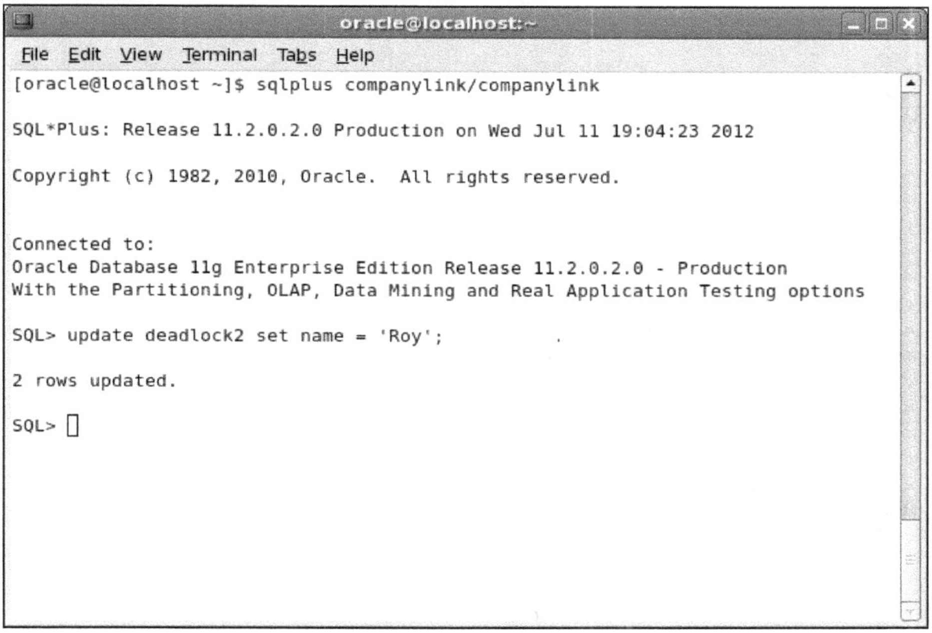
oracle@localhost:~
File Edit View Terminal Tabs Help
[oracle@localhost ~]$ sqlplus companylink/companylink
SQL*Plus: Release 11.2.0.2.0 Production on Wed Jul 11 19:04:23 2012
Copyright (c) 1982, 2010, Oracle. All rights reserved.
Connected to:
Oracle Database 11g Enterprise Edition Release 11.2.0.2.0 - Production
With the Partitioning, OLAP, Data Mining and Real Application Testing options
SQL> update deadlock2 set name = 'Roy';
2 rows updated.
SQL>

So far so good. Next, we will execute another statement in our first session that updates rows in the `deadlock2` table:

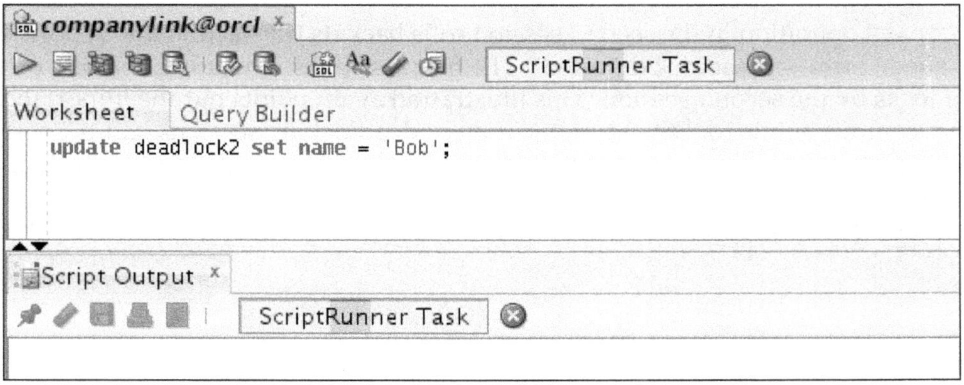
companylink@orcl
ScriptRunner Task
Worksheet
Query Builder
update deadlock2 set name = 'Bob';
Script Output
ScriptRunner Task

Note that the session hangs. This session is waiting for the locks acquired by the second session to be released. It is not a deadlocking situation yet, at least until the next statement is executed in the second session.

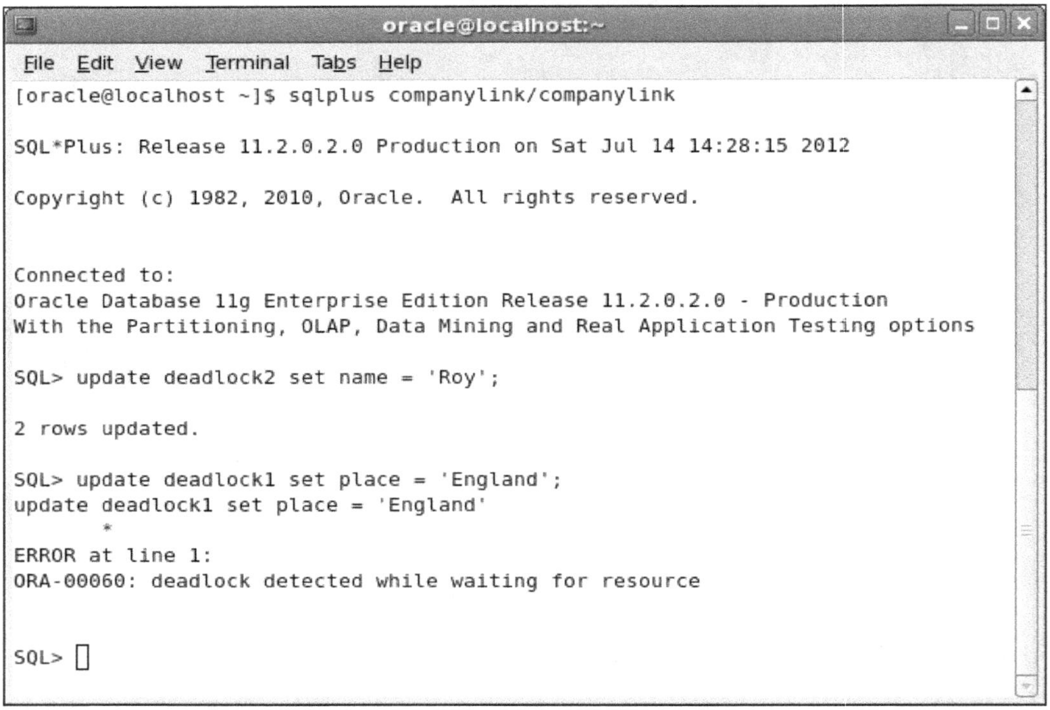
oracle@localhost:~
File Edit View Terminal Tabs Help
[oracle@localhost ~]$ sqlplus companylink/companylink
SQL*Plus: Release 11.2.0.2.0 Production on Sat Jul 14 14:28:15 2012
Copyright (c) 1982, 2010, Oracle. All rights reserved.
Connected to:
Oracle Database 11g Enterprise Edition Release 11.2.0.2.0 - Production
With the Partitioning, OLAP, Data Mining and Real Application Testing options
SQL> update deadlock2 set name = 'Roy';
2 rows updated.
SQL> update deadlock1 set place = 'England';
update deadlock1 set place = 'England'
*
ERROR at line 1:
ORA-00060: deadlock detected while waiting for resource
SQL>

The UPDATE operation in the second session rolls back its transaction and reports the ORA-00060 error—"deadlock detected". The first session is now hung, waiting on the set of locks by the second session. This illustration again points out the importance of proper commit points for SQL sessions. If these deadlocking sessions had properly committed their transactions, no deadlock would have occurred. As we mentioned previously, deadlocks are recorded in the alert log, as shown in the following screenshot. The referenced trace file would contain the specific statements involved.

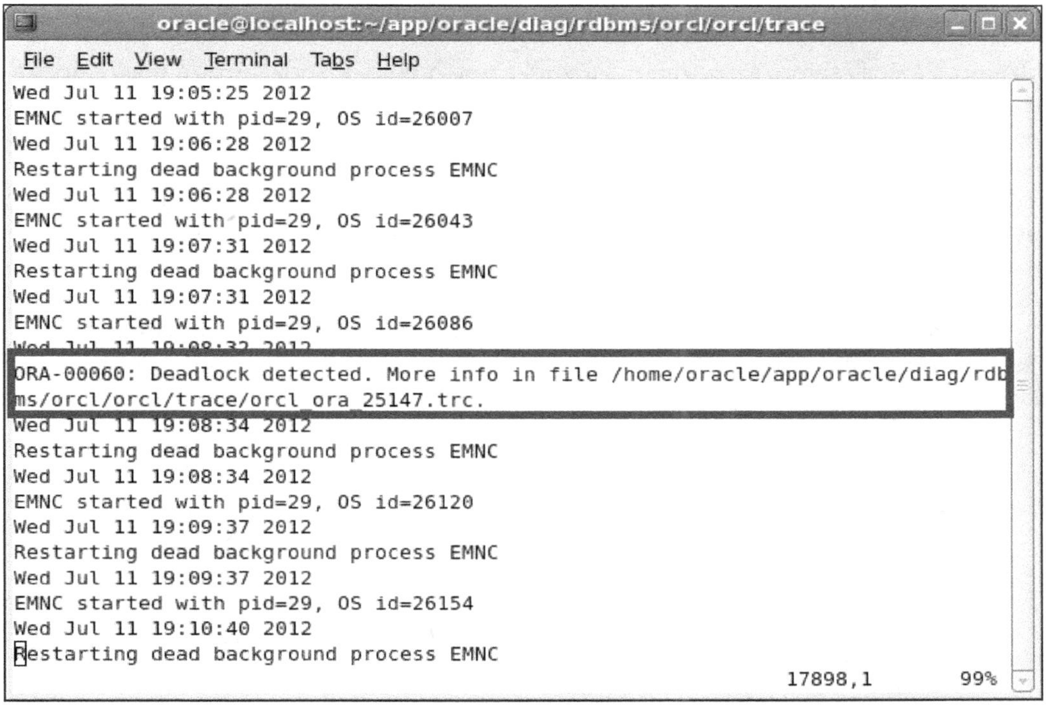
oracle@localhost:~/app/oracle/diag/rdbms/orcl/orcl/trace
File Edit View Terminal Tabs Help
Wed Jul 11 19:05:25 2012
EMNC started with pid=29, OS id=26007
Wed Jul 11 19:06:28 2012
Restarting dead background process EMNC
Wed Jul 11 19:06:28 2012
EMNC started with pid=29, OS id=26043
Wed Jul 11 19:07:31 2012
Restarting dead background process EMNC
Wed Jul 11 19:07:31 2012
EMNC started with pid=29, OS id=26086
ORA-00060: Deadlock detected. More info in file /home/oracle/app/oracle/diag/rdbms/orcl/orcl/trace/orcl_ora_25147.trc.
Wed Jul 11 19:08:34 2012
Restarting dead background process EMNC
Wed Jul 11 19:08:34 2012
EMNC started with pid=29, OS id=26120
Wed Jul 11 19:09:37 2012
Restarting dead background process EMNC
Wed Jul 11 19:09:37 2012
EMNC started with pid=29, OS id=26154
Wed Jul 11 19:10:40 2012
Restarting dead background process EMNC
17898,1 99%

The real-world DBA

The fact that deadlocks are recorded in the alert log is important for DBAs to remember. Although our demonstration displayed the deadlock error in one of the sessions, most of today's applications are not run using SQL Developer or SQL*Plus. Rather, they use coded applications in languages such as Java, which issue SQL statements against the database. If database errors, such as the `ORA-00060` error, are not being trapped or logged at the application layer, they may not specifically be identified. Instead, it would simply appear that one of the sessions has rolled back. A DBA can use the alert log and trace file to determine the error itself and the SQL statements involved in the deadlock.

Understanding latches and mutexes

Although locks are probably the most well-known type of serialization mechanism in Oracle, there are other types that are also important. A **latch** is a low-level mechanism that allows uncorrupted, concurrent access to data structures in memory, usually in the SGA. The basic principle for a latch is similar to that of a lock—shared access is allowed for read operations, while exclusive access can be used when a modification is necessary. Latches are generally faster than locks, and are therefore used where fast access to memory structures is needed. Latches are controlled by the Oracle kernel to provide quick, concurrent access to memory structures, and as such, they stand beyond a DBA's control for the most part. We can, however, view statistics about them in the data dictionary, as shown in the following screenshot:

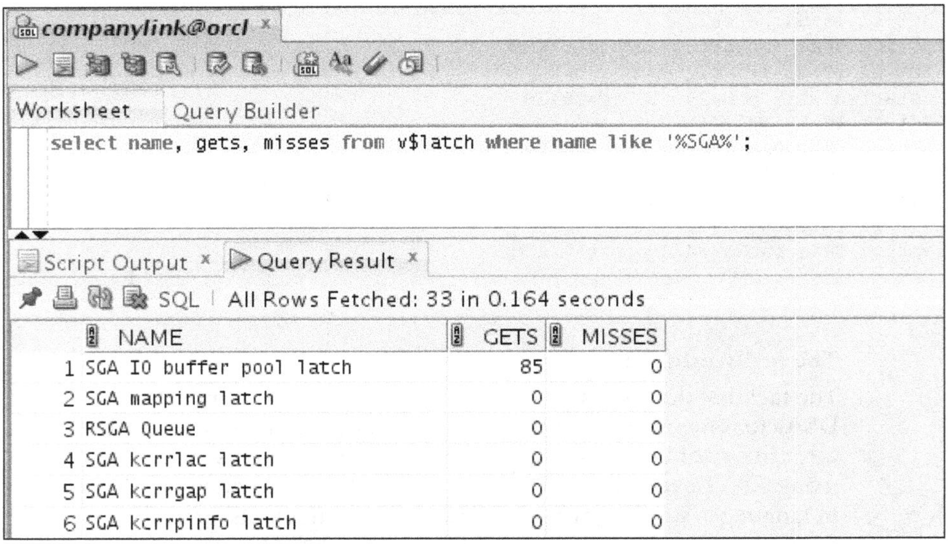
companylink@orcl
Worksheet
Query Builder
select name, gets, misses from v$latch where name like '%SGA%';
Script Output
Query Result
SQL
All Rows Fetched: 33 in 0.164 seconds
NAME
GETS
MISSES
1 SGA IO buffer pool latch 85 0
2 SGA mapping latch 0 0
3 RSGA Queue 0 0
4 SGA kcrrlac latch 0 0
5 SGA kcrrgap latch 0 0
6 SGA kcrrpinfo latch 0 0

A **mutex**, or mutual exclusion object, is another type of serialization mechanism that is similar in many ways to a latch. Like latches, mutexes serve to provide processes with a high level of concurrent access to shared memory resources. Mutexes have certain benefits, however, and have replaced some latches in recent versions of Oracle. Mutexes are smaller and faster than latches, owing to the fact that they generally consist of fewer instructions. A mutex takes less space in memory than a latch. Mutexes also have less potential for serialization contention since latches often protect multiple resources. Mutexes are generally created to protect a single resource, reducing the likelihood of contention. Latches and mutexes are independent of each other; a process can utilize both a latch and a mutex if needed.

Certification objectives covered

- Monitoring and resolving locking conflicts
- Overview of undo
- Transactions and undo data
- Managing undo

Summary

In this chapter, we've examined the principles and practices behind maintaining good levels of concurrency in the database. We've explored the lifecycle of a transaction and introduced the concept of undo data. We've learned how to manage this undo data in an undo tablespace and use database parameters to enable Automatic Undo Management. Finally, we've examined database serialization mechanisms, including locks, latches, and mutexes. In our next chapter, we explore an entirely new subject—the way networking operates in Oracle.

Test your knowledge

Q 1. User A executes only the following statements in a table with 100 rows:

```
INSERT of 50 rows
COMMIT
INSERT of 10 rows
DELETE of 20 rows
```

If User B logs in and executes a `SELECT` statement that returns every row in the table, how many rows will User B see?

a. 140
b. 150
c. 160
d. 180

Q 2. What is the term that states that Oracle maintains multiple versions of the same database block at different points in time to ensure read consistency?

a. Transaction control
b. Multiplexing
c. Multiversioning
d. Atomicity

Q 3. Which type of statement does not write change vectors to the log buffer?

a. `SELECT`
b. `INSERT`
c. `UPDATE`
d. `DELETE`

Q 4. Which Oracle error is raised in situations where a query encounters an undo block that had been overwritten since the query was initiated, also known as "snapshot too old"?

a. `ORA-00060`
b. `ORA-00600`
c. `ORA-1555`
d. `ORA-2306`

Q 5. Which of the following is not a valid database parameter related to the usage of undo data?

a. `undo_management`
b. `undo_segments`
c. `undo_retention`
d. `undo_tablespace`

Q 6. A user executes a `DROP TABLE` command within the `Companylink` database. While the `DROP TABLE` command is running, a second user executes an `UPDATE` statement against the same table, attempting to update all records within the table. Which of the following is a true statement regarding the `UPDATE` statement?

a. The `UPDATE` fails because the rows in question are locked in `SHARE` mode.
b. The `UPDATE` fails because the table is locked in `SHARE` mode.

c. The `UPDATE` fails because the table is locked in `EXCLUSIVE` mode.

d. The `UPDATE` succeeds.

Q 7. Which two of the following statements are true regarding the characteristics of undo tablespaces?

a. Undo segments can automatically grow and shrink to accommodate the needs of users when AUM is enabled.

b. Undo tablespaces are automatically created whenever `undo_management` is set to `AUTO`.

c. The `undo_tablespace` parameter can be used with both automatic and manual undo management.

d. A database can have multiple undo tablespaces.

Q 8. We administer a database that has three undo tablespaces with `undo_retention` set to `900`. The enabled undo tablespace is 100 percent full and no `COMMIT` statements have occurred for 16 minutes. A user executes an `UPDATE` statement at this point. What will happen to this user's `UPDATE` statement?

a. The `UPDATE` operation will succeed, and its required undo segment will be written to one of the non-enabled undo tablespaces.

b. The `UPDATE` operation will succeed, and its required undo segment will be written to the `SYSTEM` tablespace.

c. The `UPDATE` will succeed, and its required undo segment will be written to the `SYSAUX` tablespace.

d. The `UPDATE` will fail.

Q 9. Which of these statements is true regarding the `undo_retention` parameter when retention guarantee is disabled?

a. The parameter represents the time after which undo data is automatically deleted.

b. The parameter represents the time after which undo data is automatically overwritten.

c. The parameter represents the minimum time undo data is kept, provided that free space is available.

d. The parameter represents the time after which undo data is written to the `SYSTEM` tablespace.

Q 10. The `Companylink` database is configured to use Automatic Undo Management with an undo tablespace called `UNDOTBS` and `undo_retention` set to `1800`. Which of the following commands could be used to enable guaranteed retention?

a. `ALTER TABLESPACE UNDOTBS guarantee retention;`

b. `ALTER TABLESPACE UNDOTBS guarantee retention FOR 1800 SECONDS;`

c. `ALTER TABLESPACE UNDOTBS retention guarantee;`

d. `ALTER TABLESPACE retention guaranteed FOR UNDOTBS;`

Q 11. A user is executing a long running `UPDATE` statement in the `Companylink` database. Before the session can `COMMIT`, the host server is forcibly shut down while the database is still open. What is the state of the user's transaction when the server and database are restarted?

a. The uncommitted transaction is automatically committed during restart.

b. The uncommitted transaction is automatically rolled back during restart.

c. The uncommitted transaction can be manually recovered using the archive logs.

d. The uncommitted transaction can be manually recovered using full database recovery.

Q 12. Which two of the following operations use undo data?

a. A `FLASHBACK TABLE` operation.

b. A long-running uncommitted transaction.

c. A committed transaction.

d. A mutex.

Q 13. User A executes a `UPDATE` statement and receives the following error:

```
ORA-00060: deadlock detected while waiting for resource
```

Which of the following statements regarding this situation is false?

a. A message regarding the deadlock will be written to the alert log.

b. The `UPDATE` statement, executed by User A, that initiated the error is rolled back.

c. User A's session is automatically disconnected from the database.
d. Another session involved in the deadlock is most likely hung.

Q 14. In which situation would the value for the `undo_retention` parameter most likely be ignored?

a. When the undo tablespace is of a fixed size and retention guarantee is enabled.
b. When the undo tablespace is autoextensible and retention guarantee is enabled.
c. When the undo tablespace is of a fixed size and retention guarantee is not enabled.
d. When the undo tablespace is autoextensible and retention guarantee is not enabled.

Q 15. Which two of the following would most likely be used to protect serialized access to a memory structure?

a. A TX lock
b. A TM lock
c. A latch
d. A mutex

9
Configuring an Oracle Network

When one thinks of databases, networking is probably not the first subject that comes to mind. However, the addition of networking components to early versions of the Oracle database was one of the most important innovations in the evolution of database technology. It has become possible for clients and applications from all over the world to connect to an Oracle database. In this chapter, we'll examine these components and the tools we use to administer them.

In this chapter we shall:

- Understand the concepts behind Oracle networking
- Control and verify listeners with command-line utilities
- Examine name resolution as it relates to Oracle networking
- Explore the process of database listener registration

Understanding Oracle networking concepts

We rarely consider what actually goes on when we access data from our home computer. Take the example of signing up to use a site that allows us to order products online. We bring up the site in our web browser and navigate to the products we wish to purchase, which go into some kind of "shopping cart". If we are new to the site, we are usually prompted to enter information, such as our name, address, and date of birth, into a web form. When we fill out the form and click on **Submit**, a lot happens behind the scenes. To simplify it somewhat, when we click a button to submit our personal information, that data is passed to a web server over a network via the Internet. That web server passes the information to an application server, which does whatever logic it is designed for, and then passes the data to the database. The database processes the data request itself using resources from the host server and operating system. Then, the results are passed back by way of a reverse path, sending a notification that the transaction was completed successfully. All of this requires some form of network interaction between each of these distinct systems.

Exploring Oracle Net

The original networking components devised by Oracle were designed with a particular network access model in mind, called the client-server model. In the **client-server model**, a client machine makes a connection to a server machine. Once this connection is established, the client makes use of server resources to do work. Thus, from an Oracle perspective with this two-tier model, a client machine running some type of program—whether it's SQL*Plus or a custom-designed application—makes a direct connection into the server that hosts the database. The server grants resources to this connection so that work can be done. More directly, a user process connects to the server, and a server process is allocated to directly access the database. The server process can interact with the background processes of the instance, which in turn interact with the database. Today, this client-server model has evolved into various multitier models that accommodate the greater complexity of today's enterprise architectures and ensure efficient usage of server resources. In our previous example of a web form, the web server, application server, and database are each considered a tier in the overall architecture. There are three tiers in our example, so we might refer to it as a three-tier model. With the complexity of today's systems, there can be numerous tiers between a user and the data, including clusters of web, application, and database servers. Thus, an *n*-tier system defines the number of tiers involved. While the n-tier model is more common today, many systems continue to make use of the client-server model.

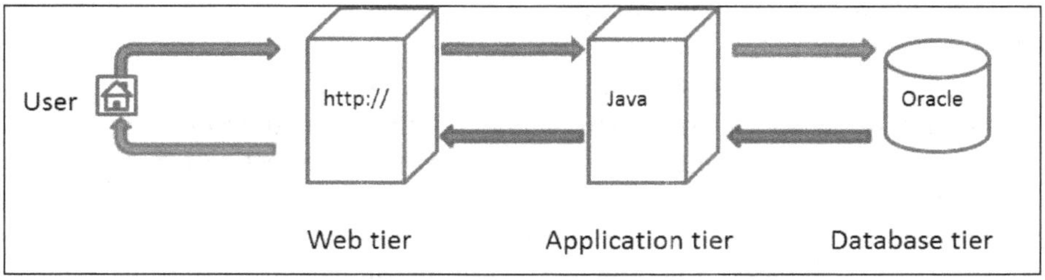
User
http://
Java
Oracle
Web tier
Application tier
Database tier

Although Oracle's networking components were designed with the client-server model in mind, they are just as valid and useful today. These components, known as **Oracle Net** today, are still used to route database network traffic using common protocols, such as TCP/IP, of the OSI network model. The most important feature that Oracle Net provides is its ability to allow client machines to connect to database servers across common networks, regardless of what operating system either machine uses. Oracle clients on Windows machines can seamlessly communicate with database servers hosted on Solaris, AIX, Linux, or other Windows machines.

Understanding the dedicated and shared server architectures

In the scenario we just mentioned, we said that when a connection is established, a user process connects to the server and a server process is allocated to directly access the database. This configuration is known as **dedicated server architecture** and is the most common type of configuration used in databases. Each user process that connects to the database and is validated using the listener is given a dedicated process with which to do work. These processes can even be seen at the operating system level using the `ps` command on Linux and Unix. However, Oracle can also be configured to use the shared server mode. In **shared server architecture** (formerly known as multithreaded server or MTS), instead of being given a dedicated process, the incoming session is connected to a **dispatcher** that serves to direct user processes to a shared server process. These shared server processes act much like dedicated server processes, except that they are fixed in number and can service multiple user processes, although not concurrently.

User processes connect to the dispatcher, which passes the user process to an available shared server. Thus, only a finite number of direct connections to the database need to be spawned (in the form of shared servers), and users share those connections as directed by the dispatcher. Because the dispatchers serve as intermediaries between user and server processes, both requests for data, and data returned are placed in queue. The request queue contains user requests, such as queries, from the user processes. The response queue contains the result sets from the request. When a dispatcher is busy servicing the queued information of one user session, the other sessions enter a **wait state**. Thus, it is often important to configure multiple dispatchers in large systems with many concurrent users. One important architectural point to remember about shared server mode is that, rather than storing the queued information in the PGA, both the request and response queues are actually stored in an area referred to as the **User Global Area** (**UGA**), which is stored in the large pool area of the SGA.

Understanding the listener

So far throughout this book, we've made a number of connections to our Oracle database using both SQL Developer and SQL*Plus, but we've yet to really discuss the details of what happens during these connections. Let's examine a simple connection that we've already used.

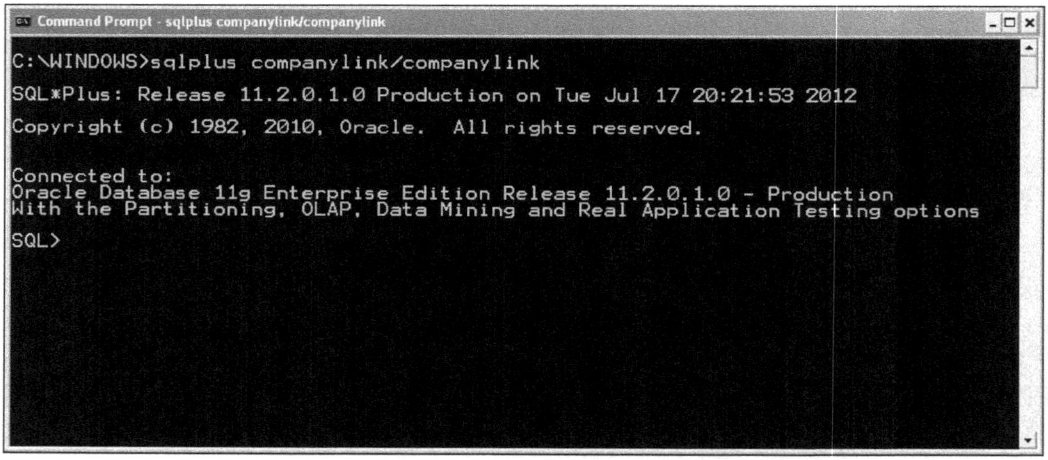
Command Prompt - sqlplus companylink/companylink
C:\WINDOWS>sqlplus companylink/companylink
SQL*Plus: Release 11.2.0.1.0 Production on Tue Jul 17 20:21:53 2012
Copyright (c) 1982, 2010, Oracle. All rights reserved.
Connected to:
Oracle Database 11g Enterprise Edition Release 11.2.0.1.0 - Production
With the Partitioning, OLAP, Data Mining and Real Application Testing options
SQL>

We make a connection to the database using SQL*Plus by providing a username and password, as we mentioned in our chapter on database security. This type of connection is known as a **local connection**—no remote database is specified. Thus, when no connection information other than a username and password are specified, an assumption is made that the connection is local, and it is determined only by the value for the `ORACLE_SID` environment variable. Rather than using a network protocol, such as TCP/IP, local connections use the **Inter-Process Communication** (**IPC**) protocol. Thus, our SQL*Plus can use IPC, since our client SQL*Plus session is on the same machine as our database. This is only true if we specify no database name in the connection string. Specifying the connection name of the local database would require TCP/IP.

However, the key to Oracle Net is its ability to make a remote connection that lets us communicate with databases that are not local to the machine on which we're working. In order to make a connection to a remote database, we must know four pieces of information about the remote destination.

- Hostname or IP address
- Network protocol (usually TCP/IP today)
- Network port number used
- Database name or SID

These four pieces of information define the remote database to which we want to connect. We saw an example using three of these when we created a SQL Developer connection using the `companylink` user.

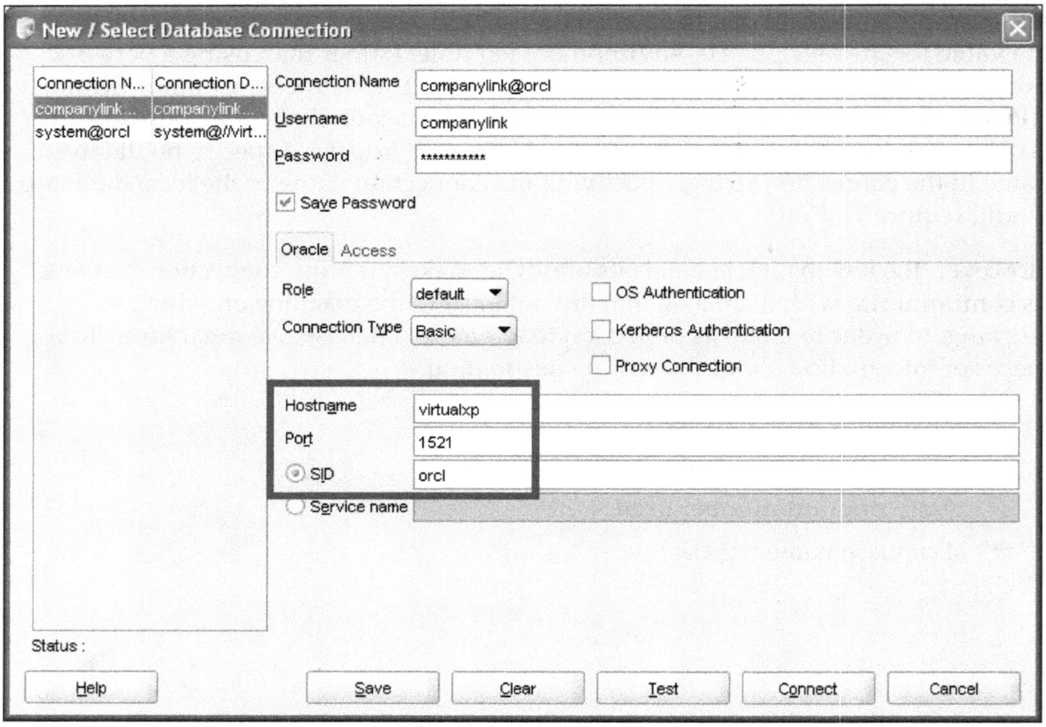
New / Select Database Connection
Connection N...
Connection D...
companylink...
companylink...
system@orcl
system@//virt...
Connection Name
companylink@orcl
Username
companylink
Password
Save Password
Oracle
Access
Role
default
Connection Type
Basic
OS Authentication
Kerberos Authentication
Proxy Connection
Hostname
virtualxp
Port
1521
SID
orcl
Service name
Status :
Help
Save
Clear
Test
Connect
Cancel

In this example, our hostname is **virtualxp**, our port is **1521**, and our SID or database name is **orcl**. SQL Developer assumes that the connection will be made via TCP/IP. Thus, these four pieces of information are used to establish the location of the remote database.

We can use SQL*Plus to examine a little more about the standard way to express the name of a database connection. A remote connection is usually expressed as a connection name that encapsulates all four required pieces of connection information into a single, easy-to-remember name. We'll explore how connection naming and name resolution works a little later in the chapter. When we wish to make a remote connection from SQL*Plus, we use a more standard method of address using the @ sign. We designate this sign, followed by the connection name, which includes hostname, port, protocol, and SID. An example is shown in the following screenshot. In this example, our connection name is **orcl**, which also happens to be the name of the database. As we can see, a service name can also be used.

The SID refers to the actual name of the database as defined by the `ORACLE_SID` environment variable. A **service name** is an alias to an instance that doesn't necessarily have to match the SID. For instance, service names are often used in RAC environments to refer to a database cluster as a whole, and not a particular instance.

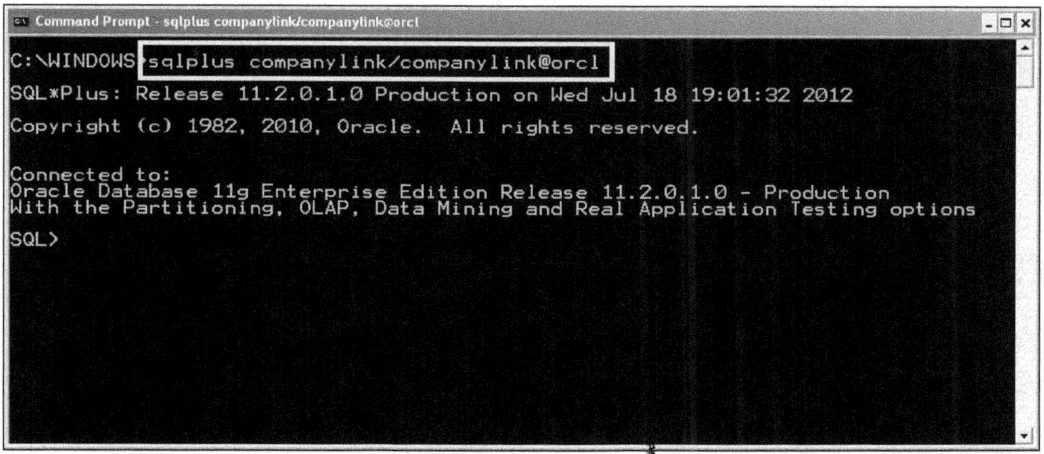
Command Prompt - sqlplus companylink/companylink@orcl
C:\WINDOWS>sqlplus companylink/companylink@orcl
SQL*Plus: Release 11.2.0.1.0 Production on Wed Jul 18 19:01:32 2012
Copyright (c) 1982, 2010, Oracle. All rights reserved.
Connected to:
Oracle Database 11g Enterprise Edition Release 11.2.0.1.0 - Production
With the Partitioning, OLAP, Data Mining and Real Application Testing options
SQL>

In order for remote connections to be received at the destination database, we must have a process running, called the **listener**, that listens for incoming connections to all Oracle instances on that machine. So, in our connection name, the **hostname** is the name of the host on which the listener (and consequently the database) is running. The **port** is the network port on which the listener receives incoming connections. The **SID** is the name of the database that the listener is listening for. The **protocol** is the network path by which the connection will be received. The listener listens for incoming connections, validates them, and then spawns a server process to service the needs of the incoming user process. Multiple listeners can be created on a given host, provided that they use a different port number. Additionally, multiple database instances on the same machine can be serviced by one listener. We configured a listener for our database in *Chapter 3, Creating the Oracle Database*, prior to creating the database, using DBCA. To do this, we used a GUI tool called NETCA, which stands for Network Configuration Assistant. Refer to that chapter for a refresher on the procedure to create a listener.

> **The real-world DBA**
>
> For new DBAs, the most unfamiliar of the four components of a database connection is often the **network port**. A port is used to separate the endpoints of a network connection and is usually associated with a particular service. For instance, the Hypertext Transfer Protocol (HTTP) is most commonly "run" on port 80. For the Oracle database listener, the port 1521 is most commonly used and is the default, although it can work on other ports as well. In fact, some DBAs consider deliberately assigning a different port number, since 1521 is widely known to be associated with Oracle databases, and can be seen as a common target for malicious attackers.

Controlling the listener

In order to control the services the listener provides, we use the `lsnrctl` (for listener control) command-line interface. To enter this interface, we simply type `lsnrctl` from the command line, either in Windows or Linux.

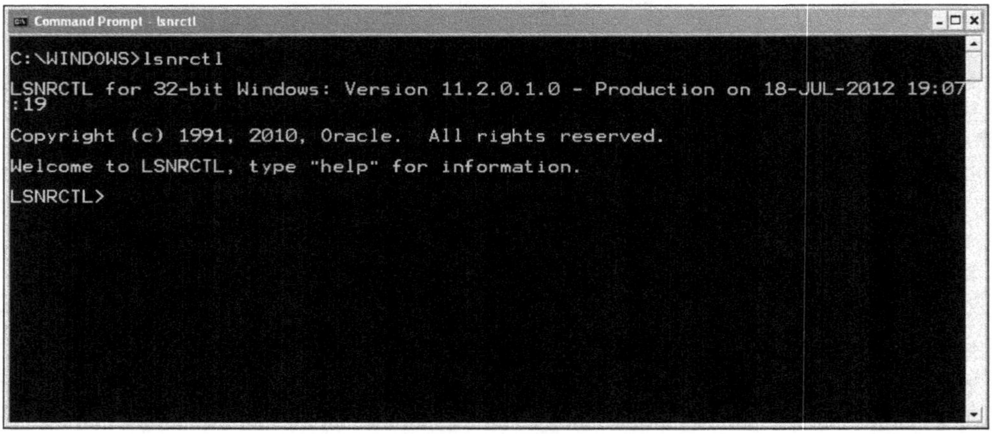
Command Prompt - lsnrctl
C:\WINDOWS>lsnrctl
LSNRCTL for 32-bit Windows: Version 11.2.0.1.0 - Production on 18-JUL-2012 19:07:19
Copyright (c) 1991, 2010, Oracle. All rights reserved.
Welcome to LSNRCTL, type "help" for information.
LSNRCTL>

For an overview of the types of commands we can use within `lsnrctl`, type `help` at the `LSNRCTL` prompt. To begin, let's get a report on the status of the listener itself; is it running?

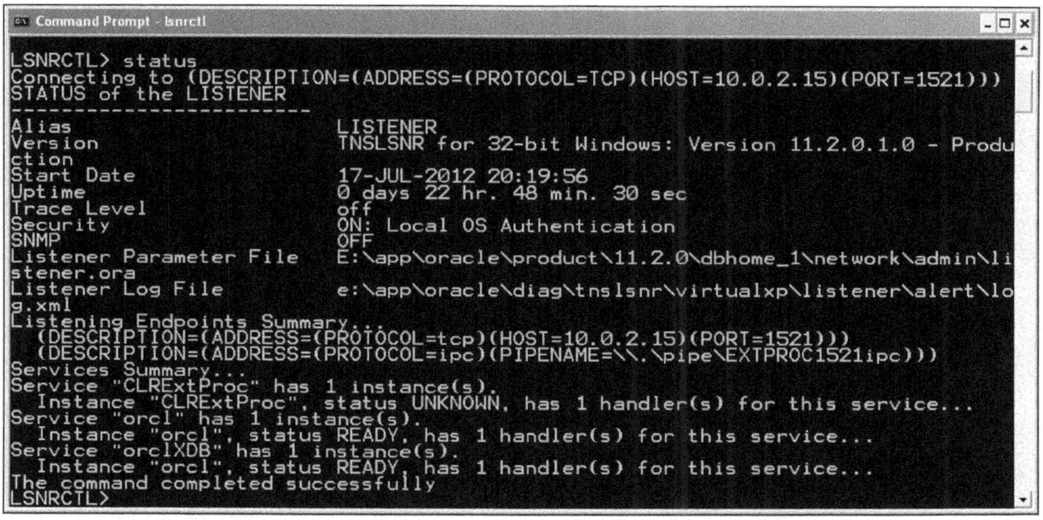
Command Prompt - lsnrctl
LSNRCTL> status
Connecting to (DESCRIPTION=(ADDRESS=(PROTOCOL=TCP)(HOST=10.0.2.15)(PORT=1521)))
STATUS of the LISTENER

Alias LISTENER
Version TNSLSNR for 32-bit Windows: Version 11.2.0.1.0 - Production
Start Date 17-JUL-2012 20:19:56
Uptime 0 days 22 hr. 48 min. 30 sec
Trace Level off
Security ON: Local OS Authentication
SNMP OFF
Listener Parameter File E:\app\oracle\product\11.2.0\dbhome_1\network\admin\listener.ora
Listener Log File e:\app\oracle\diag\tnslsnr\virtualxp\listener\alert\log.xml
Listening Endpoints Summary...
(DESCRIPTION=(ADDRESS=(PROTOCOL=tcp)(HOST=10.0.2.15)(PORT=1521)))
(DESCRIPTION=(ADDRESS=(PROTOCOL=ipc)(PIPENAME=\\.\pipe\EXTPROC1521ipc)))
Services Summary...
Service "CLRExtProc" has 1 instance(s).
Instance "CLRExtProc", status UNKNOWN, has 1 handler(s) for this service...
Service "orcl" has 1 instance(s).
Instance "orcl", status READY, has 1 handler(s) for this service...
Service "orclXDB" has 1 instance(s).
Instance "orcl", status READY, has 1 handler(s) for this service...
The command completed successfully
LSNRCTL>

We can see that the listener is, in fact, up and running. The status report gives us a lot of information on the listener. We can see several things here:

- Our listener is called **LISTENER**.
- It was started on **17-JUL-2012 20:19:56**.
- It has an uptime of **0 days 22 hr. 48 min. 30 sec**.
- In the **Services Summary...** section, we can see that an instance called **orcl** is using the listener. Thus, **LISTENER** is listening for remote connections to the **orcl** database.

Anytime we wish to check to see if our listener is up and accepting connections, we use the `status` keyword. This can also be done directly from the command line without entering the `lsnrctl` utility, as shown in the following screenshot:

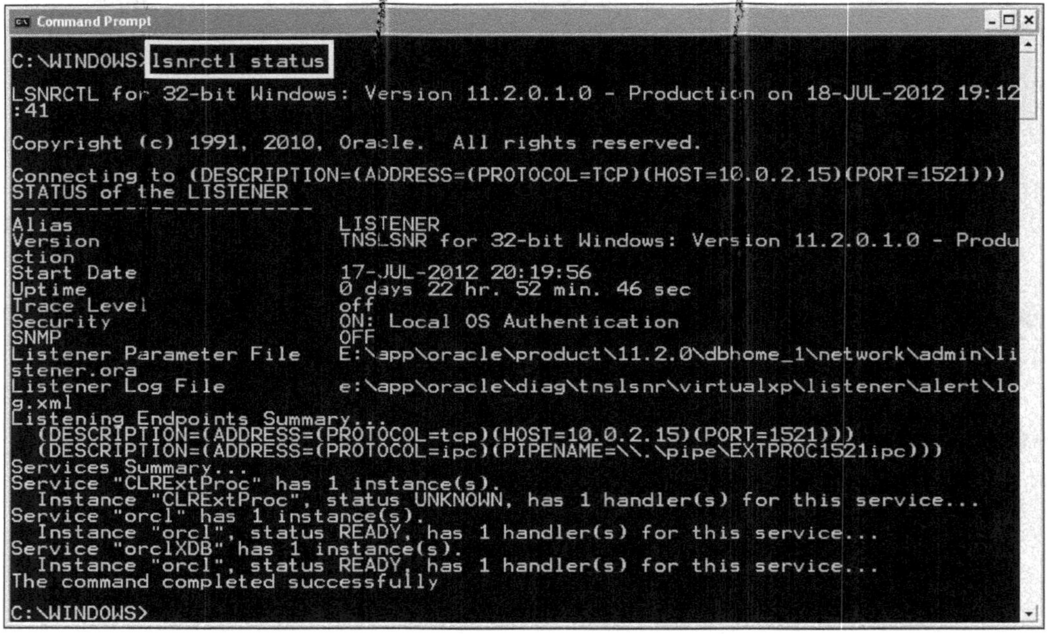
Command Prompt
C:\WINDOWS>lsnrctl status
LSNRCTL for 32-bit Windows: Version 11.2.0.1.0 - Production on 18-JUL-2012 19:12:41
Copyright (c) 1991, 2010, Oracle. All rights reserved.
Connecting to (DESCRIPTION=(ADDRESS=(PROTOCOL=TCP)(HOST=10.0.2.15)(PORT=1521)))
STATUS of the LISTENER

Alias LISTENER
Version TNSLSNR for 32-bit Windows: Version 11.2.0.1.0 - Production
Start Date 17-JUL-2012 20:19:56
Uptime 0 days 22 hr. 52 min. 46 sec
Trace Level off
Security ON: Local OS Authentication
SNMP OFF
Listener Parameter File E:\app\oracle\product\11.2.0\dbhome_1\network\admin\listener.ora
Listener Log File e:\app\oracle\diag\tnslsnr\virtualxp\listener\alert\log.xml
Listening Endpoints Summary...
(DESCRIPTION=(ADDRESS=(PROTOCOL=tcp)(HOST=10.0.2.15)(PORT=1521)))
(DESCRIPTION=(ADDRESS=(PROTOCOL=ipc)(PIPENAME=\\.\pipe\EXTPROC1521ipc)))
Services Summary...
Service "CLRExtProc" has 1 instance(s).
Instance "CLRExtProc", status UNKNOWN, has 1 handler(s) for this service...
Service "orcl" has 1 instance(s).
Instance "orcl", status READY, has 1 handler(s) for this service...
Service "orclXDB" has 1 instance(s).
Instance "orcl", status READY, has 1 handler(s) for this service...
The command completed successfully
C:\WINDOWS>

If we return to the interactive `lsnrctl` utility, we can also stop and start the listener from here. Since our status told us that the listener is currently up, let's use the `stop` command to take the listener down.

Command Prompt - lsnrctl
C:\WINDOWS>lsnrctl
LSNRCTL for 32-bit Windows: Version 11.2.0.1.0 - Production on 18-JUL-2012 19:15:01
Copyright (c) 1991, 2010, Oracle. All rights reserved.
Welcome to LSNRCTL, type "help" for information.
LSNRCTL> stop
Connecting to (DESCRIPTION=(ADDRESS=(PROTOCOL=TCP)(HOST=10.0.2.15)(PORT=1521)))
The command completed successfully
LSNRCTL>

At this point, the listener is down. No new incoming connections to the database are being received. However, note that any existing connections were not disconnected. Shutting down the listener just prevents new connections from from being established. When we wish to start the listener again, we simply type `start`.

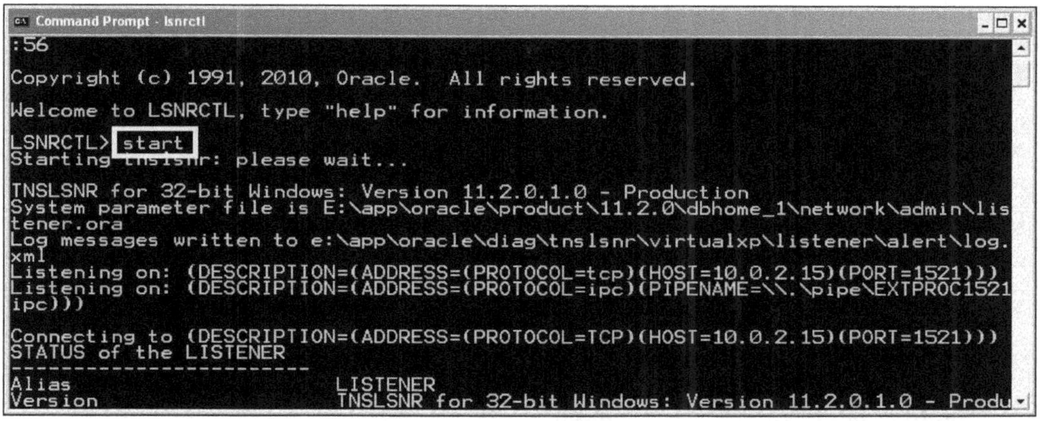
Command Prompt - lsnrctl
:56
Copyright (c) 1991, 2010, Oracle. All rights reserved.
Welcome to LSNRCTL, type "help" for information.
LSNRCTL> start
Starting tnslsnr: please wait...
TNSLSNR for 32-bit Windows: Version 11.2.0.1.0 - Production
System parameter file is E:\app\oracle\product\11.2.0\dbhome_1\network\admin\listener.ora
Log messages written to e:\app\oracle\diag\tnslsnr\virtualxp\listener\alert\log.xml
Listening on: (DESCRIPTION=(ADDRESS=(PROTOCOL=tcp)(HOST=10.0.2.15)(PORT=1521)))
Listening on: (DESCRIPTION=(ADDRESS=(PROTOCOL=ipc)(PIPENAME=\\.\pipe\EXTPROC1521ipc)))
Connecting to (DESCRIPTION=(ADDRESS=(PROTOCOL=TCP)(HOST=10.0.2.15)(PORT=1521)))
STATUS of the LISTENER
Alias LISTENER
Version TNSLSNR for 32-bit Windows: Version 11.2.0.1.0 - Produ

The listener returns to its previous state and can receive incoming connections. At times, we may need to change the characteristics of the listener through its configuration files. Since the configuration files are only read during the startup of the listener, it would be necessary to stop and start the listener in order to pick up any configuration changes. However, `lsnrctl` includes a command called `reload` that allows the configuration files to be reread without stopping the listener.

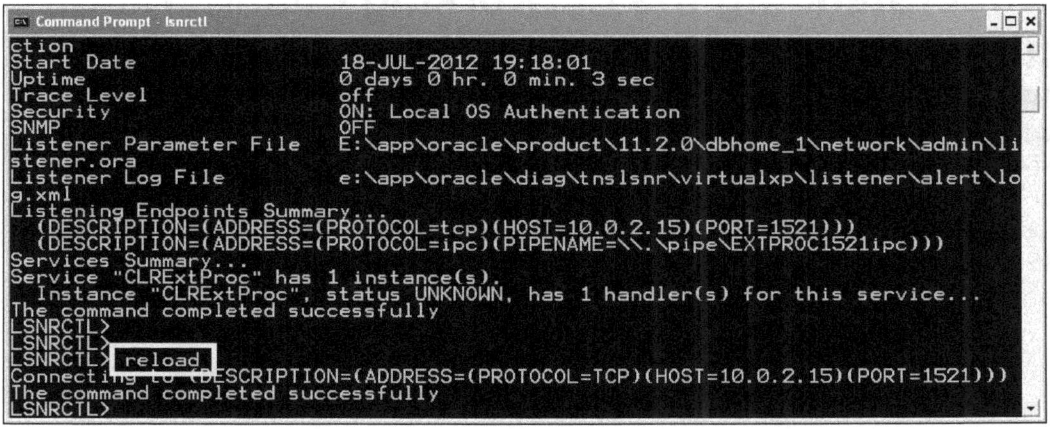
Command Prompt - lsnrctl
ction
Start Date 18-JUL-2012 19:18:01
Uptime 0 days 0 hr. 0 min. 3 sec
Trace Level off
Security ON: Local OS Authentication
SNMP OFF
Listener Parameter File E:\app\oracle\product\11.2.0\dbhome_1\network\admin\listener.ora
Listener Log File e:\app\oracle\diag\tnslsnr\virtualxp\listener\alert\log.xml
Listening Endpoints Summary...
(DESCRIPTION=(ADDRESS=(PROTOCOL=tcp)(HOST=10.0.2.15)(PORT=1521)))
(DESCRIPTION=(ADDRESS=(PROTOCOL=ipc)(PIPENAME=\\.\pipe\EXTPROC1521ipc)))
Services Summary...
Service "CLRExtProc" has 1 instance(s).
Instance "CLRExtProc", status UNKNOWN, has 1 handler(s) for this service...
The command completed successfully
LSNRCTL>
LSNRCTL>
LSNRCTL> reload
Connecting to (DESCRIPTION=(ADDRESS=(PROTOCOL=TCP)(HOST=10.0.2.15)(PORT=1521)))
The command completed successfully
LSNRCTL>

Any new configuration parameters are reread and the listener continues to operate normally. As with the status, any of these commands can be run directly from the command line by typing `lsnrctl <command>`. When we wish to leave the interactive `lsnrctl`, we type `exit`.

In addition to the commonly used commands, `lsnrctl` supports several others, as shown in the following list:

- `SERVICES`: This displays the details of services and the instances associated with them.
- `VERSION`: This displays the version information of the listener.
- `TRACE`: This is used to turn on listener-tracing information at various levels. The possible values are `OFF`, `USER`, `ADMIN`, and `SUPPORT`. Each level provides increasingly detailed trace information, with `SUPPORT` being the most detailed. It is typically only used to provide detailed trace information to Oracle Support.
- `SET TRC_FILE`: This is used to change the name of the listener trace file, which is `listener.trc` by default.
- `SET TRC_DIRECTORY`: This is used to change the default directory that stores the listener trace file, which is `ORACLE_HOME/network/trace` by default.
- `SET PASSWORD`: This is used to set a password for listener administration.
- `CHANGE_PASSWORD`: This is used to change the administrative password.

Understanding the networking configuration files

We mentioned that when we issue a `lsnrctl reload` command, the Oracle Net configuration files are re-read. At this point, we should explore these files and see the types of information that they contain. There are three primary network configuration files for Oracle Net. By default, they are found in the `$ORACLE_HOME/network/admin` directory. We show this location in the following screenshot on a Windows server. The three files in question are the `listener.ora`, `sqlnet.ora`, and `tnsnames.ora` files.

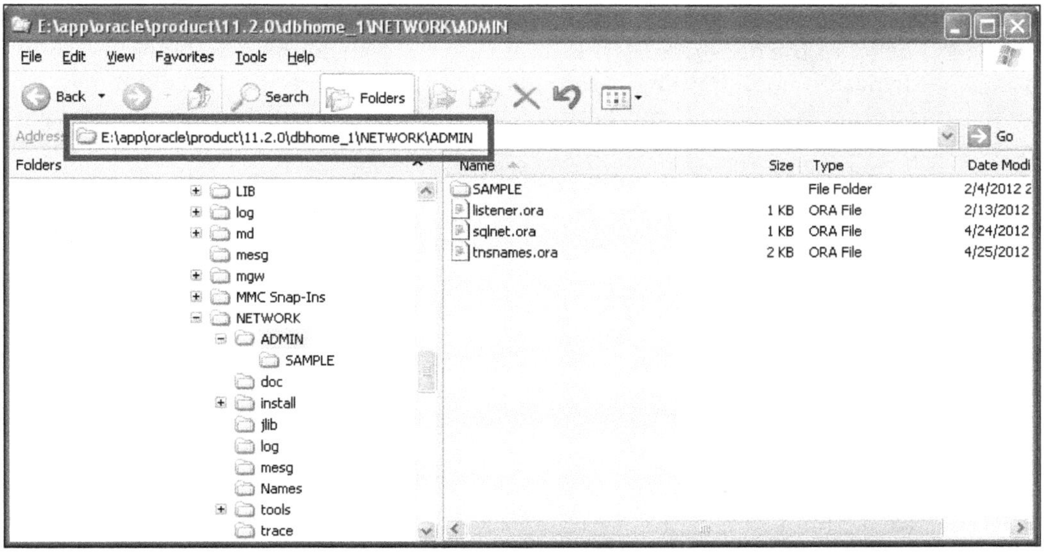

The `listener.ora` file contains all of the necessary information to run the listener. If we recall our previous section, we said that four pieces of information, that is, hostname, port, protocol, and database SID, were necessary to establish the destination location of a remote connection. Let's examine the `listener.ora` file to see if we find this information.

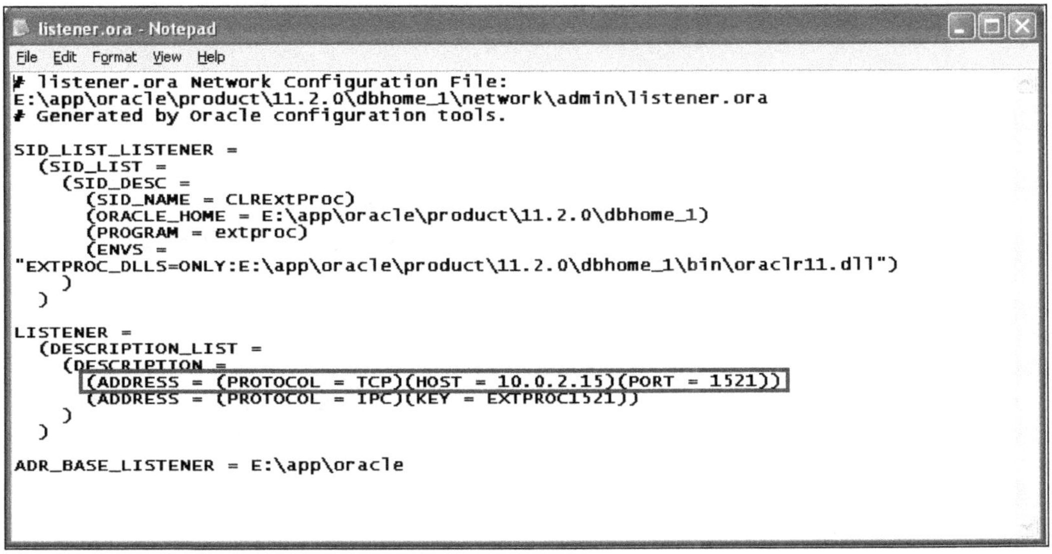

There are two basic sections to a `listener.ora` file. The first section, `SID_LIST_LISTENER`, lists out the database SIDs that the listener is listening for. Note that, while there is information here, nothing is said about our database—`orcl`. We'll touch on the reason for that later. The second section, `LISTENER`, contains the information we want. This section lists the different network addresses that the listener is running under. If we were listening on a number of different network protocols, we would see an `ADDRESS` line for each. However, we're concerned with the highlighted line. Note that we see three of the four pieces of information needed for a remote database connection—protocol (**TCP**), hostname or IP address (**10.0.2.15**), and port (**1521**). This tells us that our listener is running on the server at 10.0.2.15 on port 1521 using the TCP/IP protocol. Let's look at our second configuration file, the `tnsnames.ora` file.

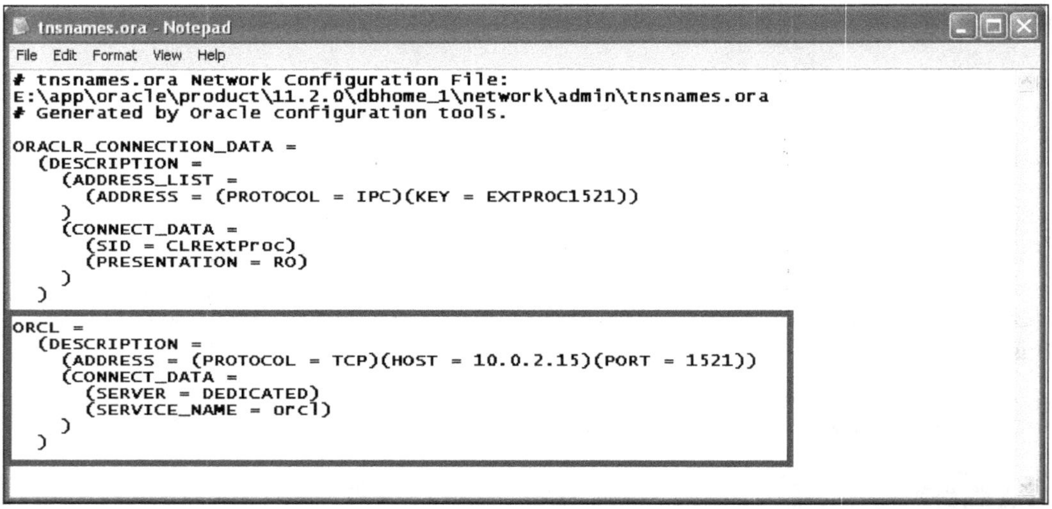

tnsnames.ora - Notepad
File Edit Format View Help
tnsnames.ora Network Configuration File:
E:\app\oracle\product\11.2.0\dbhome_1\network\admin\tnsnames.ora
Generated by Oracle configuration tools.
ORACLR_CONNECTION_DATA =
(DESCRIPTION =
(ADDRESS_LIST =
(ADDRESS = (PROTOCOL = IPC)(KEY = EXTPROC1521))
)
(CONNECT_DATA =
(SID = CLRExtProc)
(PRESENTATION = RO)
)
)
ORCL =
(DESCRIPTION =
(ADDRESS = (PROTOCOL = TCP)(HOST = 10.0.2.15)(PORT = 1521))
(CONNECT_DATA =
(SERVER = DEDICATED)
(SERVICE_NAME = orcl)
)
)

The `tnsnames.ora` file is a client-side file that contains the connection information for every remote database to which the client can connect. Once again, we see the protocol, hostname, port, and database SID, which is listed here as **SERVICE_NAME**. We might wonder why the information in the client-side `tnsnames.ora` file is the same as that in the `listener.ora` file. This is because, in our example, our host acts as both client and server. The `tnsnames.ora` file provides name resolution. In our example, we have a connection name, **ORCL**, that just happens to be the same as the name of our database. This is a common practice used to simplify the names of connections. However, the connection name does not have to match the database name, it can be anything we wish. The following is an example of a connection entry with some different information.

```
A_NEW_DATABASE =
  (DESCRIPTION =
    (ADDRESS = (PROTOCOL = TCP) (HOST = myserver) (PORT = 1521))
    (CONNECT_DATA =
      (SERVER = DEDICATED)
      (SERVICE_NAME = mynewdb)
    )
  )
```

> **The real-world DBA**
>
> One of the most common mistakes that new DBAs make when editing the `tnsnames.ora` and `listener.ora` files is to leave out or misplace the parentheses, which are needed for the listener to parse the files correctly. Often, it is good practice to copy an existing entry and edit it as needed, rather than writing one from scratch.

Our final configuration file is optional on both the client and server side. The `sqlnet.ora` file (named after an older version of Oracle Net called SQL Net) contains configuration parameters that apply to both listeners and incoming connections. It is shown in the following screenshot:

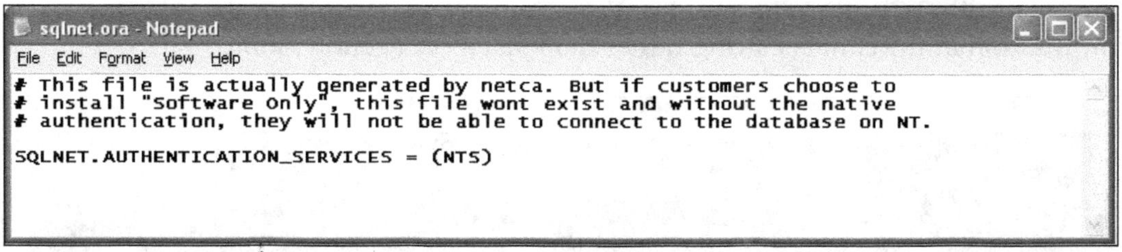
sqlnet.ora - Notepad
File Edit Format View Help
# This file is actually generated by netca. But if customers choose to
# install "Software Only", this file wont exist and without the native
# authentication, they will not be able to connect to the database on NT.
SQLNET.AUTHENTICATION_SERVICES = (NTS)

In our case, this file is very small, containing only one parameter called `SQLNET.AUTHENTICATION_SERVICES = (NTS)`. This parameter is used primarily on Windows and allows users to be authenticated using Windows NT security. There are a number of optional parameters possible in this file. They can be used to configure a number of different behaviors, including network encryption, connection timeouts, alternative authentication services, and even a basic software firewall.

Using Oracle name resolution

The concept of **name resolution** is one of the cornerstone principles in networking. People use name resolution every day without realizing it. Anytime we type in the URL for a website, we're using a name that refers to a particular Internet resource—a web server for instance. When we type `www.companylink.com/login/index.html` into a browser, that domain name actually resolves to the IP address of a web server. The path after the URL domain usually refers to a directory structure present on that web server. The HTML file itself is a document within those directories. So, rather than knowing the IP address, directory structure, and file structure of every site we visit, we only need to know a name that resolves that information. The same is true of a name resolution in Oracle. Rather than requiring users to know every aspect of a connection, we can provide a name resolution solution that simplifies this. Oracle provides several types of name resolutions that users can use to connect to databases.

Understanding Easy Connect

Easy Connect (once referred to as EZCONNECT) is a simplified method of name resolution that doesn't require any type of external resolution resource. We simply provide the hostname, port, and SID of the database we wish to connect to, all in one string. It does not require the protocol to be given since Easy Connect only supports one protocol—TCP/IP. When we use Easy Connect, we supply all the relevant information in the connect string rather than just a connection name.

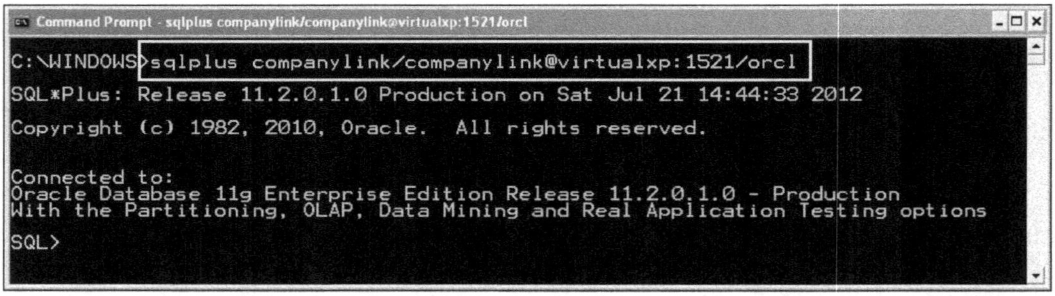
Command Prompt - sqlplus companylink/companylink@virtualxp:1521/orcl
C:\WINDOWS>sqlplus companylink/companylink@virtualxp:1521/orcl
SQL*Plus: Release 11.2.0.1.0 Production on Sat Jul 21 14:44:33 2012
Copyright (c) 1982, 2010, Oracle. All rights reserved.
Connected to:
Oracle Database 11g Enterprise Edition Release 11.2.0.1.0 - Production
With the Partitioning, OLAP, Data Mining and Real Application Testing options
SQL>

As seen in the preceding screenshot, we supply **virtualxp** as the hostname, **1521** as the port, and **orcl** as the SID. This directly connects us to the database. When using Easy Connect, we must always be aware of using the correct syntax and punctuation; any deviations will result in an error.

Understanding local naming

The second type of name resolution supported by Oracle is one we've already seen. Local naming uses the `tnsnames.ora` file to resolve a connection name to hostname, port, protocol, and SID. As we've mentioned, connection names do not need to be named the same as any part of the connection information, although they are usually given the same name as the database. In the following screenshot, we see two `tnsnames.ora` entries that are named differently but resolve to the same database:

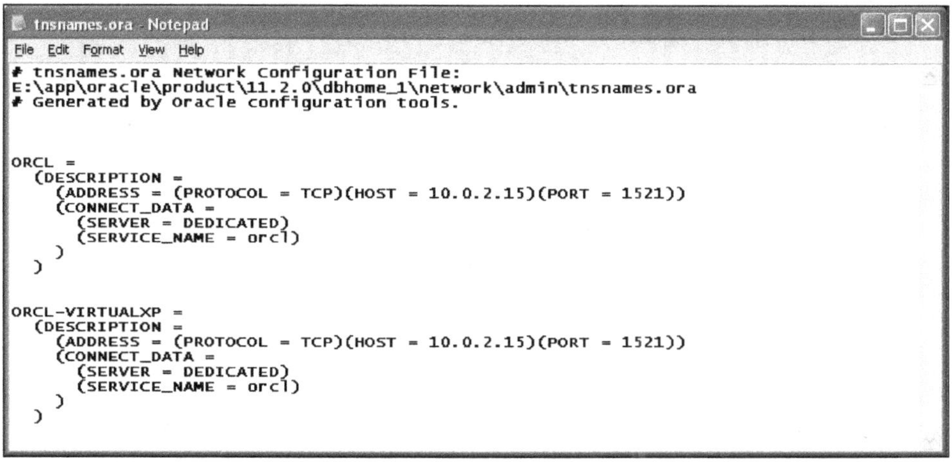

```
# tnsnames.ora Network Configuration File:
E:\app\oracle\product\11.2.0\dbhome_1\network\admin\tnsnames.ora
# Generated by Oracle Configuration tools.


ORCL =
  (DESCRIPTION =
    (ADDRESS = (PROTOCOL = TCP)(HOST = 10.0.2.15)(PORT = 1521))
    (CONNECT_DATA =
      (SERVER = DEDICATED)
      (SERVICE_NAME = orcl)
    )
  )

ORCL-VIRTUALXP =
  (DESCRIPTION =
    (ADDRESS = (PROTOCOL = TCP)(HOST = 10.0.2.15)(PORT = 1521))
    (CONNECT_DATA =
      (SERVER = DEDICATED)
      (SERVICE_NAME = orcl)
    )
  )
```

Whenever we wish to check the availability of a connection name, we can use the `tnsping` command from the command line. An example of the syntax is shown as follows:

```
tnsping orcl
```

Using directory naming and external naming

The last two types of name resolution methods are similar in some ways. Both use an external service to resolve connection information and authenticate users. **Directory naming** uses a **Lightweight Directory Access Protocol** (**LDAP**) server to accomplish this task. This requires the setup and configuration of an LDAP server on our network. This method can be advantageous in environments where vast numbers of users need direct connections to the database. Rather than maintaining and distributing an enormous `tnsnames.ora` file, an LDAP server retrieves connection information at a user's request. **External naming** is similar, although it requires the use of a third-party naming service, such as **Network Information Services** (**NIS+**). Neither directory naming nor external naming are covered on the exam; they are mentioned here for the sake of completeness.

> **The real-world DBA**
>
> At this point, we might wonder which of these name resolution methods is used by SQL Developer. As we recall, we directly provided the necessary information when we created a new connection. SQL Developer actually uses local naming, but does not use the `tnsnames.ora` file. Instead, it stores its connection information in a special XML file.

Understanding database registration

In our section on the `listener.ora` configuration file, we noted that the database SID was the only one of the four pieces of information needed to establish a connection that was missing. Prior to the latest versions of Oracle, it was necessary to explicitly declare, or register, the database name in the listener. In more recent versions, Oracle allows this process of registration to occur dynamically. In this section, we'll look at both types of database registration.

Using static registration

Static registration involves explicitly registering a database SID with a listener. When using static registration, we declare the SID in the **listener.ora** file in the **SID_LIST_LISTENER** section, as shown in the following screenshot:

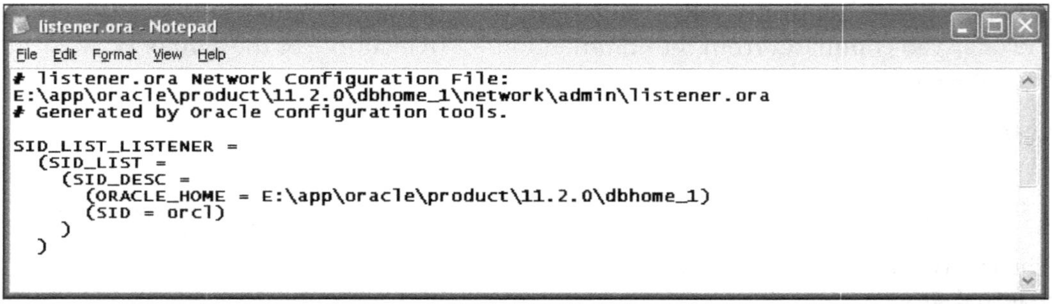
listener.ora - Notepad
File Edit Format View Help

```
# listener.ora Network Configuration File:
E:\app\oracle\product\11.2.0\dbhome_1\network\admin\listener.ora
# Generated by Oracle configuration tools.

SID_LIST_LISTENER =
  (SID_LIST =
    (SID_DESC =
      (ORACLE_HOME = E:\app\oracle\product\11.2.0\dbhome_1)
      (SID = orcl)
    )
  )
```

The SID `orcl` will be registered with the listener on startup. When using static registration, the listener is not aware of the state of the database—it could be started or it could be shut down. For this reason, dynamic registration is the preferred method. However, static registration can be used in situations where DBAs need to execute a remote startup of the database.

Using dynamic registration

This second method of registration uses a more simplified approach. **Dynamic registration** allows the listener to automatically register any running instances on the listener's host server. When a database is started and dynamic registration is being used, the database instance "talks" to the listener and is consequently registered.
In current versions of Oracle, dynamic registration does not require configuration; although if a port other than the default one (port 1521) is used, the DBA must set the `local_listener` parameter to either the listener name or the full protocol, hostname, and port. The benefit of dynamic registration is that only running database instances can be registered. If the database was started before the listener, it may be necessary to issue the following command to force the registration to occur:

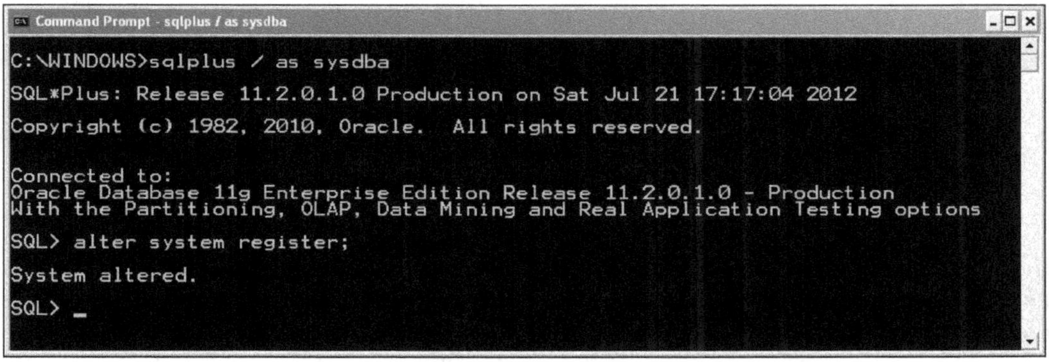
Command Prompt - sqlplus / as sysdba
C:\WINDOWS>sqlplus / as sysdba
SQL*Plus: Release 11.2.0.1.0 Production on Sat Jul 21 17:17:04 2012
Copyright (c) 1982, 2010, Oracle. All rights reserved.
Connected to:
Oracle Database 11g Enterprise Edition Release 11.2.0.1.0 - Production
With the Partitioning, OLAP, Data Mining and Real Application Testing options
SQL> alter system register;
System altered.
SQL> _

Using database links

One powerful type of database object that involves Oracle networking is the database link. A **database link** allows a user to directly connect from one database to another, giving them access to read and modify data and objects. There are several ways to create a database link, but the most straightforward way involves using local naming and the `tnsnames.ora` file to define the remote database. We can create a database link using the connection name specified for our database in the `tnsnames.ora` file. In the following example, we create a database link that actually loops back to our database, rather than reaching out to a remote database. The example is sound, because it uses the same method to specify the link information even though the database is actually local.

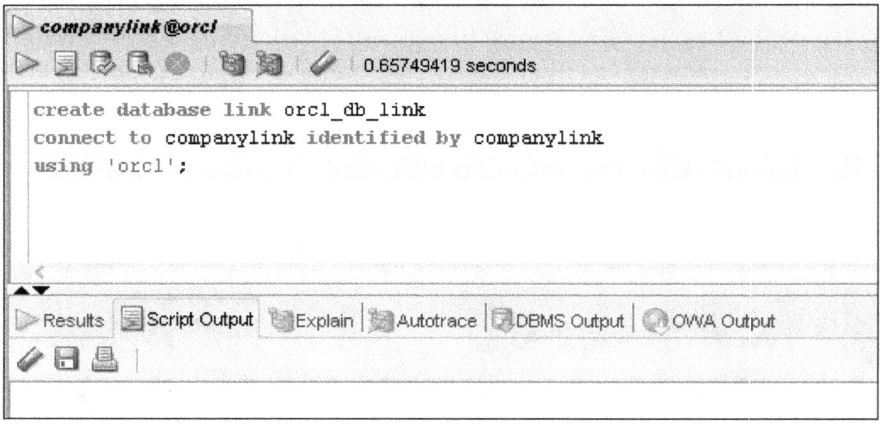
companylink@orcl
0.65749419 seconds
create database link orcl_db_link
connect to companylink identified by companylink
using 'orcl';
Results
Script Output
Explain
Autotrace
DBMS Output
OWA Output

In this example, we specify a database link named **orcl_db_link** that uses the username **companylink** with a password **companylink**. This means that when we invoke the database link, we will be logging into the target database as the `companylink` user. The last line specifies **orcl** as the connection name to be invoked. This is the same `orcl` listed in our `tnsnames.ora` file. Now, we can pull data over the database link using the `@orcl_db_link` link to specify our database link. In our case, the connection from our client session (in SQL*Plus) is actually reaching out to the listener and pulling the data back across the network via the database link, rather than making an internal connection using IPC.

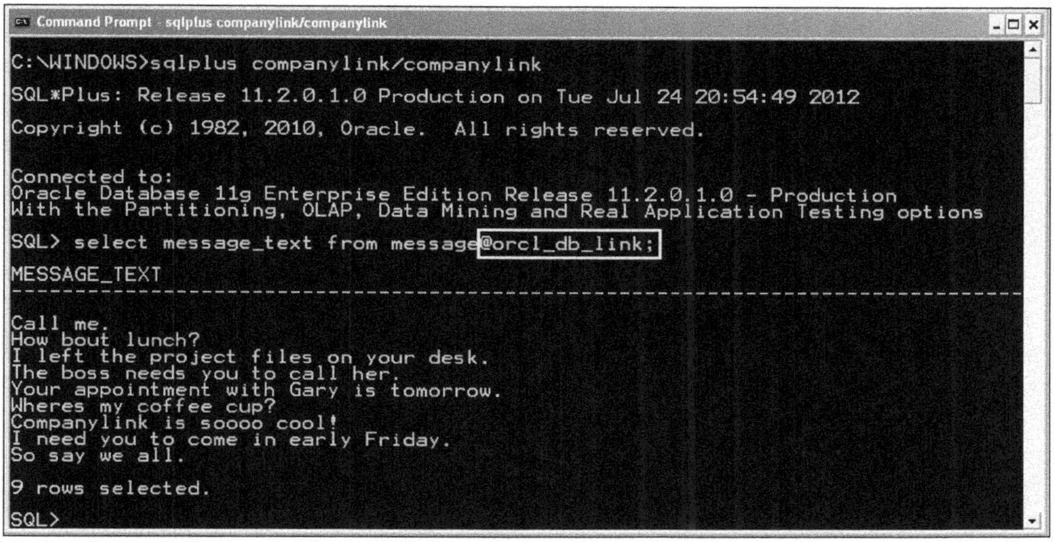
Command Prompt - sqlplus companylink/companylink
C:\WINDOWS>sqlplus companylink/companylink
SQL*Plus: Release 11.2.0.1.0 Production on Tue Jul 24 20:54:49 2012
Copyright (c) 1982, 2010, Oracle. All rights reserved.
Connected to:
Oracle Database 11g Enterprise Edition Release 11.2.0.1.0 - Production
With the Partitioning, OLAP, Data Mining and Real Application Testing options
SQL> select message_text from message@orcl_db_link;
MESSAGE_TEXT
Call me.
How bout lunch?
I left the project files on your desk.
The boss needs you to call her.
Your appointment with Gary is tomorrow.
Wheres my coffee cup?
Companylink is soooo cool!
I need you to come in early Friday.
So say we all.
9 rows selected.
SQL>

Certification objectives covered

- Configuring and managing the Oracle network
- Using the Oracle shared server architecture

Summary

In this chapter, we've examined the network architecture portion of the Oracle database. We've looked at the concepts behind Oracle Net, including the dedicated and shared server architectures and the listener. We've learned to manage the listener using the `lsnrctl` command-line utility. We've looked at the three major network configuration files for Oracle Net—`listener.ora`, `tnsnames.ora`, and `sqlnet.ora`. We've examined the concepts of database registration and name resolution. Finally, we've explored connecting to remote databases using database links. In our next chapter, we will learn about some of the newer features that Oracle provides to perform day-to-day administration.

Test your knowledge

Q 1. Which of the following describes an architecture that specifies the multiple layers between a user and data, and can include web servers and application servers?

a. Client-server
b. Multitier
c. Dedicated server
d. Shared server

Q 2. In the shared server architecture, which type of process is an incoming user process connected to first, after it has been validated by the listener?

a. Dedicated server process
b. Shared server process
c. Dispatcher process
d. A second user process

Q 3. Which of the following memory areas store session information when the shared server architecture is used?

a. Large pool
b. Shared server pool
c. Database buffer cache
d. Log buffer

Q 4. When a database administrator executes the `lsnrctl stop` command, what happens to any existing database connections?

a. Connections are immediately disconnected and their transactions are rolled back
b. Connections are immediately disconnected and their transactions are automatically committed
c. Connections are not disconnected, but any transactions in process are rolled back
d. Connections are unaffected.

Q 5. Which type of name resolution method uses the `tnsnames.ora` file to resolve connection names to their port, protocol, hostname, and SID information?

a. Easy connect
b. Local naming
c. Directory naming
d. External naming

Q 6. Which of the following statements is true regarding a listener?

a. A host can only run one listener at a time
b. Listeners in the newest versions of Oracle only support the TCP/IP protocol
c. Easy Connect does not make use of a listener to establish a connection
d. Multiple database instances can register to a single listener

Q 7. Which of the following is *not* one of the basic network configuration files used by Oracle Net?

a. `tnsnames.ora`
b. `sqlnet.ora`
c. `listener.ora`
d. `network.ora`

Q 8. Which database parameter must be set if the database is using dynamic registration and a port other than 1521 is being used?

a. `local_listener`
b. `remote_listener`
c. `listener_port`
d. `dynamic_listener_port`

Q 9. Examine the following statement to create a database link:

```
create database link my_dblink
connect to username identified by password
using 'orcl-myserver';
```

What does "`orcl-myserver`" refer to?

a. The name of the database link
b. The connection name in the `tnsnames.ora` file
c. The hostname of the remote server
d. The database name on the remote server in the `tnsnames.ora` file

10
Managing Database Performance

Up to this point, we've covered the basic topics of day-to-day database management. For the remainder of this book, we'll look at some of the more advanced topics in database administration, beginning with managing performance. At some point, every database administrator faces the problem where a user reports that "the database is slow." Where do we begin to tackle this problem? At the system level? The SQL statements themselves? Database parameters? Database performance tuning is perhaps the most intricate and complex of all the responsibilities of a DBA. Mastering it is a career-long pursuit that demands an in-depth understanding of the Oracle architecture. In the past (and perhaps still today), numerous theories and methodologies were discussed about the best way to approach performance tuning. Fortunately, in Version 10*g* and beyond, Oracle added an entire performance tuning framework that took much of the guesswork out of database performance tuning. In this chapter, we look at this tuning framework, as well as a number of other methods to maximize the performance of our database.

In this chapter we shall:

- Understand object-level tuning
- Explore the **Automatic Workload Repository** (**AWR**)
- Use the Advisory Framework
- Examine Automatic Memory Management

Understanding object-level tuning

Performance tuning boils down to the user experience. Bad performance derives from the very subjective notion that a given application is somehow different from the acceptable norms. The common complaint heard from the user is, "It was fast yesterday but it's slow today". It is the job of the DBA to take these subjective ideas and discover objective facts that point to the cause for this unacceptable performance. In the end, database performance tuning is an analysis of why SQL statements are executing at a suboptimal rate. Even if the root cause is CPU starvation, incorrect configuration parameters, or just a poorly written `DELETE` statement, the key is first finding out *what is slow* and then *what can be done* to rectify the situation. Thus, it is wise to look first at how SQL statements are executed against database objects and what conditions can affect how they are executed.

Understanding the Oracle optimizer

Let's take the following simple SQL statement as an example:

```
SELECT first_name, last_name
FROM employee
WHERE last_name = 'Thrace';
```

If we know the contents of the table beforehand, we might be able to predict the outcome of this statement. But how does the statement execute? A `SELECT` statement goes through three basic stages namely, parse, execute, and fetch, in order to return the data to the user. During the **parse** stage, a SQL statement is checked for syntactical correctness and object availability. The statement is then broken down into an execution plan, which we will examine shortly. During the **execute** stage, the statement is actually executed. If there are any execution-level errors in the statement, they will be reported during this stage. Finally, in the **fetch** stage, the data is returned to the user.

At this point, we should ask ourselves a question about the parse stage. How does Oracle decide the most optimal way to run the SQL statement? Does it choose a full table scan? A B-tree index? A bitmap index? What if the table is partitioned, does that make a difference? The entity that decides the answers to these and many more such questions is called the optimizer. The Oracle **optimizer** is the engine that determines the optimal execution plan for a SQL statement. Many database management systems use something analogous to the optimizer, but the algorithms for various optimizers can be very different. In fact, in older versions of Oracle, the only type of optimizer available was called the **rule-based optimizer**, which determines an execution plan based on a hierarchy of static rules.

Today, Oracle uses (for the most part) a type of optimizer called the **cost-based optimizer**. The cost-based optimizer uses a set of algorithms to generate a number of different paths, or **execution plans**, for the statement. It then uses a costing method to determine the best plan based on a number of different variables, including CPU and memory usage, table or index data distribution, and disk I/O, as well as other important factors. The result is, generally, an execution plan that can retrieve the requested data for the least amount of resource cost.

Gathering object statistics

The most crucial aspect that affects the optimizer's ability to choose an optimal execution path is the availability of the relevant information that the optimizer can use to make its determination. These pieces of information are collectively referred to as **optimizer statistics**. Optimizer statistics include, but are not limited to, the following types of information:

- The number of rows in a table
- The average length of a row
- The cardinality, or number of distinct rows, in a table
- The number of `NULL` values in a table
- The number of distinct keys in an index

Object statistics can be gathered either manually or, with newer versions of Oracle such as 11*g*, automatically. Statistics are stored within the data dictionary and should be updated in accordance with the rate of change within a table. For instance, if we manually gather statistics on a million-row table on Sunday and update 75 percent of these rows on Monday, it is unlikely that the statistics we gathered are going to be very useful, as the nature of the table has changed completely. This can dramatically affect the way the optimizer determines an optimal execution plan. Thus, how and when we gather statistics is extremely important.

Gathering statistics manually

There are two primary ways in which we can gather optimizer statistics on an object manually. We'll first examine the older method to introduce the concept, and then move on to the more recommended method.

To gather statistics for a given table, we can use the `ANALYZE TABLE` command from any SQL-based tool:

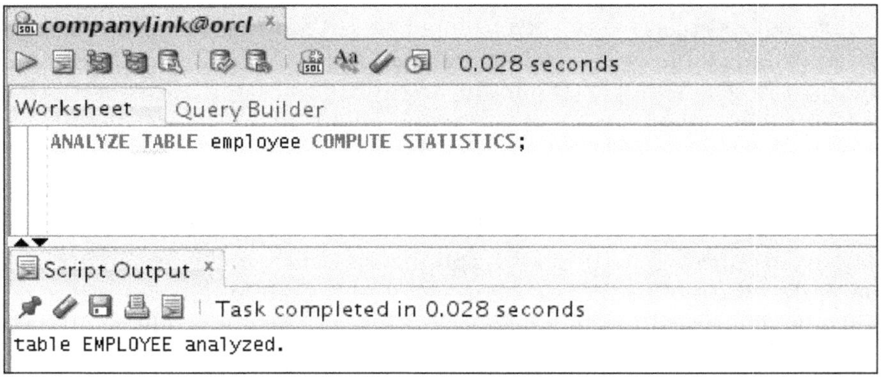
companylink@orcl
0.028 seconds
Worksheet
Query Builder
ANALYZE TABLE employee COMPUTE STATISTICS;
Script Output
Task completed in 0.028 seconds
table EMPLOYEE analyzed.

Using this command, Oracle examines every row in the `employee` table and computes all of the relevant statistics needed by the optimizer. Our table is small, so this analysis is relatively fast. However, in large tables, gathering statistics for an entire table can take a prohibitively long time. Thus, we can also use sampling methods to estimate the values for our object based on a given number of rows, or by a percentage of the rows in the table.

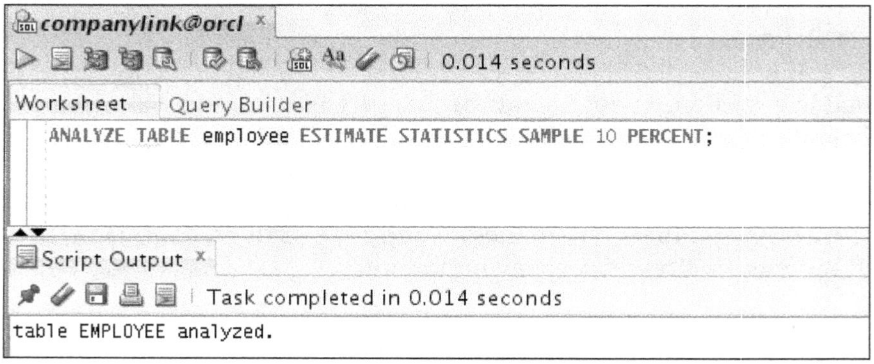
companylink@orcl
0.014 seconds
Worksheet
Query Builder
ANALYZE TABLE employee ESTIMATE STATISTICS SAMPLE 10 PERCENT;
Script Output
Task completed in 0.014 seconds
table EMPLOYEE analyzed.

In the preceding example, the statement gathers a sample of statistics on 10 percent of the table and extrapolates them as needed. While using `COMPUTE` will yield the most accurate statistics, using `ESTIMATE` is generally sufficient as well as faster for the optimizer to create optimal execution plans.

While ANALYZE is a serviceable way to gather statistics, Oracle recommends using a newer method for manual statistic collection that utilizes the Oracle supplied package, DBMS_STATS. The DBMS_STATS package is a PL/SQL package that includes a number of different procedures that can be used to gather statistics at the object level, schema level, and even the database level. It allows a greater degree of control over the granularity of the analysis, and can be used to lock or delete existing statistics. In the following example, we analyze the same table that we saw previously, but this time with DBMS_STATS:

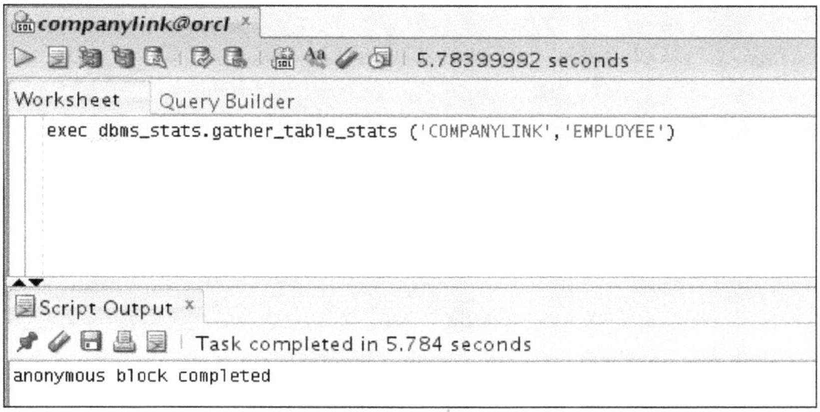
companylink@orcl
5.78399992 seconds
Worksheet
Query Builder
exec dbms_stats.gather_table_stats ('COMPANYLINK','EMPLOYEE')
Script Output
Task completed in 5.784 seconds
anonymous block completed

The first value we pass to the procedure, COMPANYLINK, is the schema name. The second value, EMPLOYEE, is the name of the table. The DBMS_STATS package allows us to gather statistics using sample estimation, degree of parallelism, and sub-objects. It is the preferred method of gathering statistics. Another subprogram called DBMS_STATS.GATHER_SCHEMA_STATS can be used to gather the statistics for all tables in an entire schema. If our schema has many tables, this can be a much simpler way to gather the statistics for every table in a schema, rather than running hundreds of ANALYZE TABLE statements. The DBMS_STATS.GATHER_DATABASE_STATS subprogram can be used to gather database-wide statistics.

In most cases, fresh statistics are beneficial to performance. However, in the event that the DBA wishes to preserve the existing statistics from being overwritten with newer ones, those statistics can be locked. Also note that in the event that the new statistics cause less than optimal performance, the previous statistics can be restored. Both of these actions are accomplished using the sub-programs of the DBMS_STATS package.

Gathering statistics automatically

Because of the importance of gathering fresh object statistics for the optimizer, Oracle has included a facility in the newer versions of the database that runs statistic collections automatically. In 11*g*, this facility is a part of the Autotask feature that automatically runs several types of maintenance jobs. We can see the content of the Autotask jobs from the data dictionary.

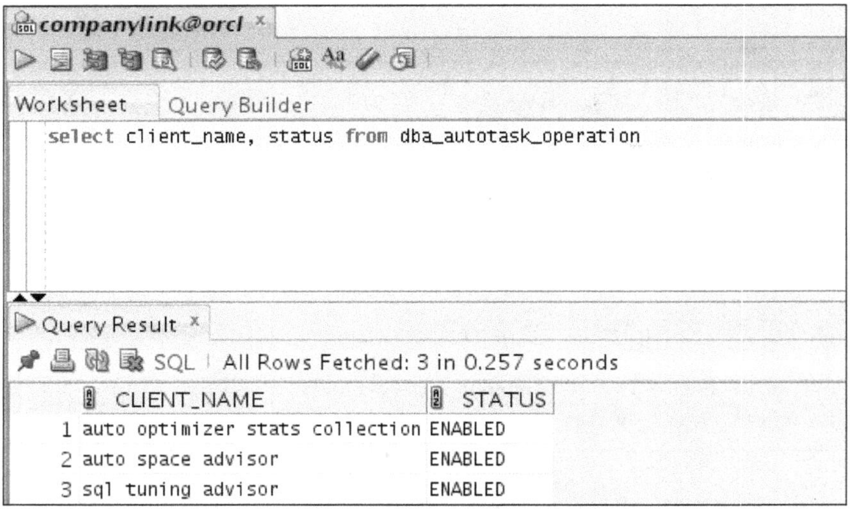
companylink@orcl
Worksheet
Query Builder
select client_name, status from dba_autotask_operation
Query Result
SQL
All Rows Fetched: 3 in 0.257 seconds
CLIENT_NAME
STATUS
1 auto optimizer stats collection ENABLED
2 auto space advisor ENABLED
3 sql tuning advisor ENABLED

As we can see in the previous screenshot, one of the jobs is called `auto optimizer stats collection`. This job automatically collects statistics for all the objects in the database using a special job that executes every night, by default. This statistics collection job is intelligent, it uses the existing database metrics to determine if an object has changed enough to warrant statistics collection. Thus, if a table needs to be analyzed, the job will do so. If not, it will skip the table. This gives us a highly efficient way to collect statistics automatically.

The job executes during a defined period of time known as a **window** which, by default, is set to 10:00 PM to 2:00 AM for each night during the week, and 6:00 AM to 2:00 AM on the weekends. If necessary, this time window can be changed to better suit the operation of our environment. If the job does not complete during the time defined by the window, it is terminated and run again during the next scheduled time period.

> **The real-world DBA**
>
> If Autotask takes care of statistics collection automatically, we should never need to collect them manually, right? Not necessarily. With very large tables, it is possible that Autotask cannot complete statistics collection within the predefined time window. When this occurs, we can either gather the statistics manually or extend the time window to include all the tables that are required.

Discovering invalid objects

The final area we should examine on the subject of object-level performance tuning is that of invalid or unusable objects. Certain types of database objects can become invalid in the course of daily use. They include:

- Views
- Packages
- Procedures
- Functions
- Triggers

In database terms, an **invalid object** is one that references an entity whose state has changed in some meaningful way. For instance, a view references the columns in a table. If one of those referenced columns is dropped, the view will become invalid as its underlying structure has been changed. The following steps will show the process of a valid object becoming invalid:

1. First, we will create an example table and an example view in order to stage our test case. Remember to use the **Run Script** button to run both SQL statements in sequence, or highlight them individually and use **Execute**.

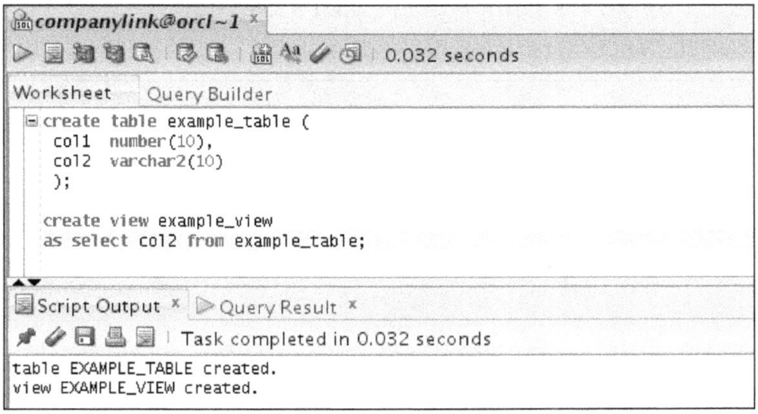
companylink@orcl~1
0.032 seconds
Worksheet
Query Builder
create table example_table (
col1 number(10),
col2 varchar2(10)
);
create view example_view
as select col2 from example_table;
Script Output
Query Result
Task completed in 0.032 seconds
table EXAMPLE_TABLE created.
view EXAMPLE_VIEW created.

2. Next, we'll query the `dba_objects` data dictionary view to determine the state of our view.

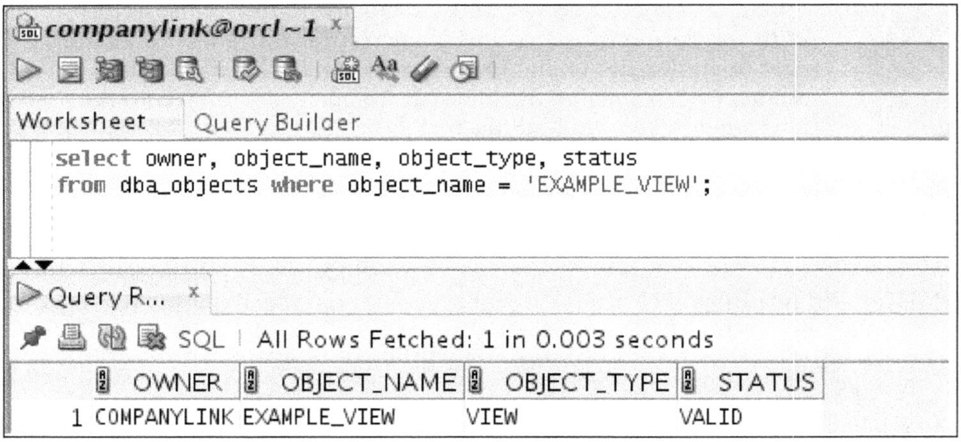
companylink@orcl~1
Worksheet
Query Builder
select owner, object_name, object_type, status
from dba_objects where object_name = 'EXAMPLE_VIEW';
Query R...
SQL
All Rows Fetched: 1 in 0.003 seconds
OWNER
OBJECT_NAME
OBJECT_TYPE
STATUS
1 COMPANYLINK EXAMPLE_VIEW VIEW VALID

As we can see in the previous screenshot, our view has a **VALID** status. Next, we'll change the view's underlying table by dropping a column.

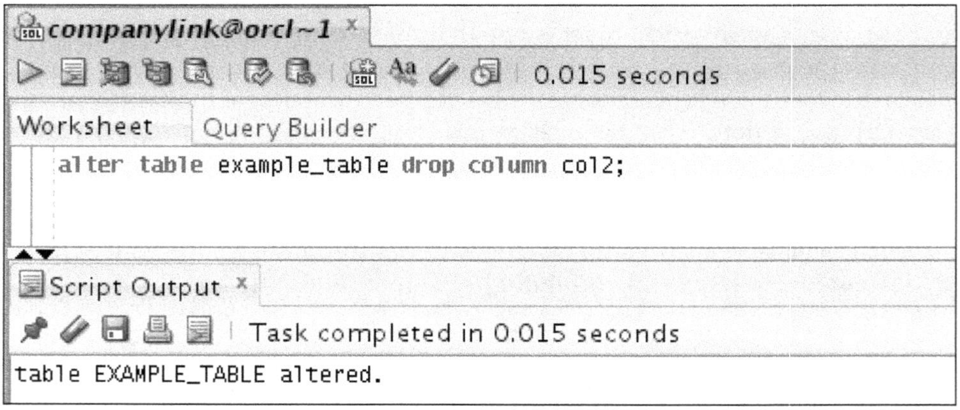
companylink@orcl~1
0.015 seconds
Worksheet
Query Builder
alter table example_table drop column col2;
Script Output
Task completed in 0.015 seconds
table EXAMPLE_TABLE altered.

3. Lastly, we'll check the status of the view again after dropping the column.

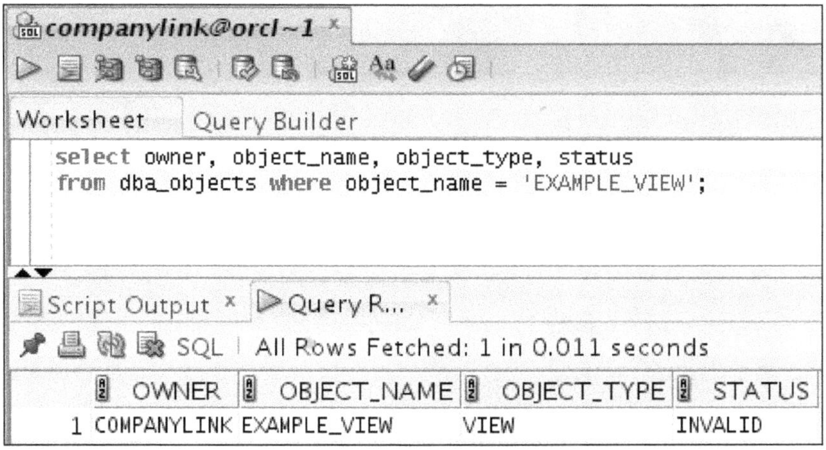
companylink@orcl~1
Worksheet
Query Builder
select owner, object_name, object_type, status
from dba_objects where object_name = 'EXAMPLE_VIEW';
Script Output
Query R...
SQL
All Rows Fetched: 1 in 0.011 seconds
OWNER
OBJECT_NAME
OBJECT_TYPE
STATUS
1 COMPANYLINK EXAMPLE_VIEW VIEW INVALID

4. As we can see, the status of the `EXAMPLE_VIEW` view is now `INVALID`. Why? The view references the `col2` column of the `EXAMPLE_TABLE` table. When we dropped `col2`, the view no longer had a valid column to reference. The same would have been true had we dropped `EXAMPLE_TABLE` itself. Similar to views, PL/SQL objects, such as procedures and packages, will become invalid when any referenced object or column is removed or changed in a way that affects the referencing of the PL/SQL object. Objects can also become invalid if they are created with syntactical errors. Once an object becomes invalid, it will remain so until the underlying condition that affects it is rectified and the object is recompiled. We can recompile an object using the `COMPILE` keyword.

5. As shown in the following screenshot, we correct the error in the referenced table and manually recompile the view

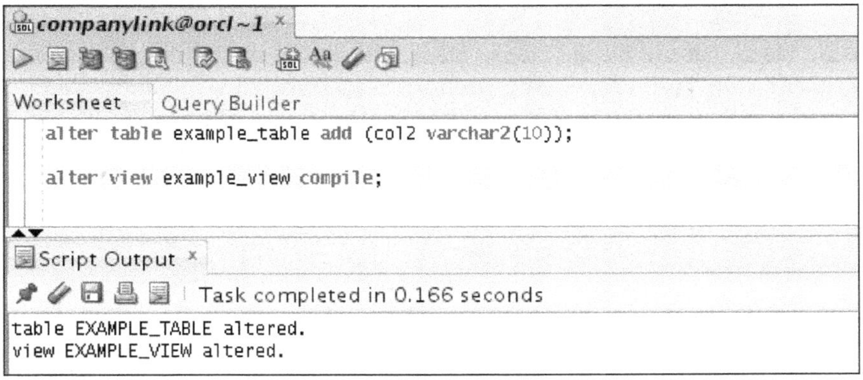
companylink@orcl~1
Worksheet
Query Builder
alter table example_table add (col2 varchar2(10));
alter view example_view compile;
Script Output
Task completed in 0.166 seconds
table EXAMPLE_TABLE altered.
view EXAMPLE_VIEW altered.

If we examine the status of the object now, it has returned to `VALID`:

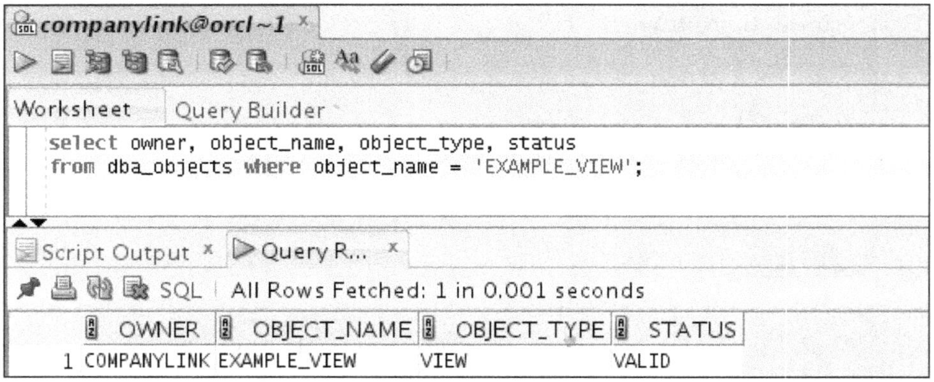
companylink@orcl~1
Worksheet
Query Builder
select owner, object_name, object_type, status
from dba_objects where object_name = 'EXAMPLE_VIEW';
Script Output
Query R...
SQL
All Rows Fetched: 1 in 0.001 seconds
OWNER
OBJECT_NAME
OBJECT_TYPE
STATUS
1 COMPANYLINK EXAMPLE_VIEW VIEW VALID

Oracle automatically attempts to recompile any invalid object when it is referenced so manual recompilation is not always necessary. Still, it is a good practice to check for invalid objects from time to time and correct them as needed. To do so, a good standard query is shown as follows:

```
select owner, object_name, object_type, status
from dba_objects
where status = 'INVALID';
```

> **The real-world DBA**
>
> It is not uncommon for certain Oracle default schemas to have invalid objects, depending on which features you use. Use your own judgment when attempting to recompile them. Also, Oracle provides a script called `utlrp.sql` in the `admin` directory under `$ORACLE_HOME/rdbms` that will recompile all the invalid objects in the database. This can be useful when you need to "bulk recompile" a large number of objects.

Finally, indexes can change the state to `UNUSABLE` when their underlying table is moved to a different tablespace. Any such **unusable index** will be ignored during the processing of a query, even if it could cause the query to perform better. This can have a tremendous impact on performance. To detect unusable indexes, we can use the following query:

```
select owner, index_name, table_owner, table_name, status
from dba_indexes
where status = 'UNUSABLE';
```

If an unusable index is detected, we can rebuild the index using the following statement:

```
alter index example_index REBUILD;
```

Managing the Automatic Workload Repository

At the beginning of the chapter, we mentioned that there have been many different methodologies regarding the best way to go about performance tuning in an Oracle database. In the past, the Oracle database lent itself to a vast spectrum of ideas, as it is one of the most configurable pieces of software in existence. A DBA could spend hours examining various data dictionary views and testing different database parameters to find the perfect balance for a system. However, in Version 10*g*, Oracle attempted to create a consolidated performance tuning methodology by creating the Automatic Workload Repository, or AWR. In this section, we'll learn how to use the AWR to formulate performance tuning strategies.

Understanding the AWR

In the earlier versions of Oracle, a tool called **Statspack** (as well as an even earlier tool called **bstat/estat**) was available in order to diagnose performance problems. Statspack was what we might call a static collection performance tool. Whenever a performance problem occurred, a DBA would take a Statspack snapshot, a point in time collection of various performance measurements from the data dictionary. After a period of diagnosis, the DBA would take a second snapshot. A report could then be run that would compare the diagnostic measurements from both snapshots and some causal determinations could be made. Additionally, Statspack could be set up as an automatic job that collected snapshots during a standard time interval, such as hourly.

While Statspack proved to be a useful tool, it was still limited by what performance information could be collected from the existing data dictionary. In Version 10*g*, Oracle took a huge leap forward by adding an entirely new performance framework to the database called the **Automatic Workload Repository**. The AWR, amounts to a second data dictionary, one that only collects performance-related data.

Using statistics, metrics, and baselines

The AWR uses some of the same terminology as Statspack. Like Statspack, the AWR collects **snapshots** that can be used to produce performance reports. However, the architecture of the AWR is completely different. The AWR collects its performance measurements directly from the memory used by the instance and not from the data dictionary views. Thus, the measurements done by the AWR are far more timely and accurate than Statspack or any other manual collection method. Because they are read from the memory, they have an almost negligible effect on performance. The **Manageability Monitor** (**MMON**) process directly accesses the instance memory structures and writes these measurements at set time intervals to the AWR tables, which are stored in the `SYSAUX` tablespace. This set of data is called a **statistic**, a point in time collection of a given performance measurement. An example of a statistic might be the amount of shared pool memory used by any given user session. The number and breadth of statistics collected by the MMON process for the AWR is staggering; nearly every detail related to performance is collected. Any two statistics can be compared to form a **metric**, a measurement of the rate of change between any two statistics. Metrics provide the ability for the AWR to record more than just point-in-time measurements. They can be used to examine trending and change in performance. For instance, a statistic can be used to determine whether a performance measurement is high or low. But a metric can demonstrate that the memory usage for a given session is rising or falling. Metrics can be gathered into collections called the baselines. A **baseline** is a set of metrics that can be stored for future reference. For an example of how useful this can be, let's say that `companylink` is about to add new functionalities to its website, and will make a number of changes to do so. New tables, new indexes, and new SQL code will be added, along with a number of application coding changes. Rather than taking the "wait and see" approach as to how these changes will affect the performance, we could take a baseline before the changes are made. Then, after the changes have been applied, we could run another baseline and compare the differences from a performance perspective. From this, we may determine if the CPU usage is dramatically affected, database parameters need to be modified, or any other number of effects that arise from the changes.

All of this functionality depends primarily on a single database initialization parameter, called `STATISTICS_LEVEL`, which has three possible settings. When `STATISTICS_LEVEL` is set to `BASIC`, almost no performance statistics will be collected, essentially rendering the AWR useless. If the value is set to `ALL`, a massive amount of extremely detailed statistics will be collected. In fact, setting `STATISTICS_LEVEL` to `ALL` can have a dramatically negative effect on overall performance, and is only recommended when sending certain information to Oracle Support.

By far the most recommended setting is `TYPICAL`, which is the default setting. `TYPICAL` allows the AWR to collect the standard amount of statistics to function normally, and provides the DBA with the necessary performance data. As shown in the following screenshot, we check the `STATISTICS_LEVEL` parameter to ensure that it is set to `TYPICAL`:

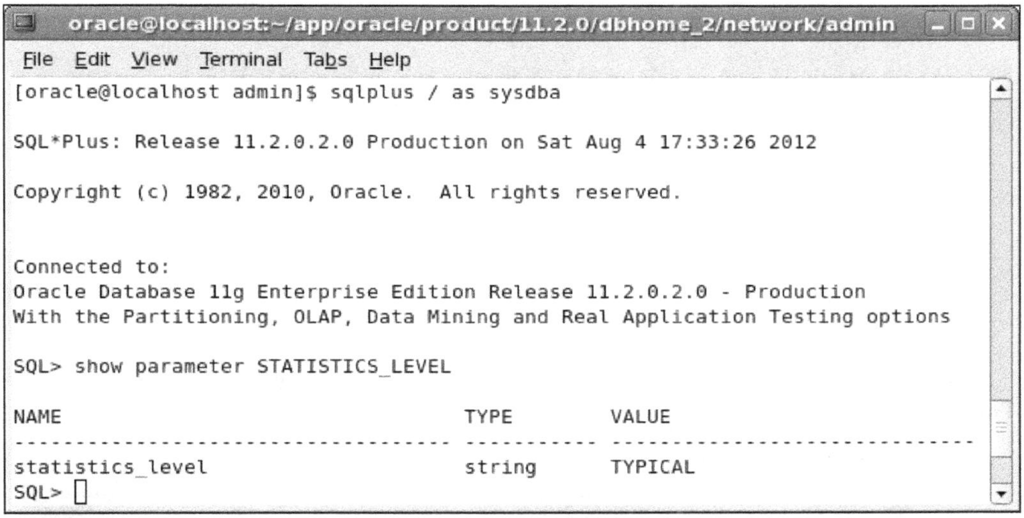
oracle@localhost:~/app/oracle/product/11.2.0/dbhome_2/network/admin
File Edit View Terminal Tabs Help
[oracle@localhost admin]$ sqlplus / as sysdba
SQL*Plus: Release 11.2.0.2.0 Production on Sat Aug 4 17:33:26 2012
Copyright (c) 1982, 2010, Oracle. All rights reserved.
Connected to:
Oracle Database 11g Enterprise Edition Release 11.2.0.2.0 - Production
With the Partitioning, OLAP, Data Mining and Real Application Testing options
SQL> show parameter STATISTICS_LEVEL
NAME TYPE VALUE
statistics_level string TYPICAL
SQL>

Generating an AWR report

The most useful application of the AWR to the everyday life of a DBA is found in reporting. While an extensive look at AWR reports is beyond the scope of the particular exam with which we're concerned, it is still the DBA's most vital tool in gaining an overall look at performance tuning. Generating an AWR report is simple; interpreting its findings is not. Understanding the scope of the information found in an AWR report can be a very in-depth pursuit. However, the AWR report can provide an excellent overview of the performance condition of our database, even without an extensive understanding of the vast amount of information in the report.

To generate an AWR report, it is generally easiest to navigate to the `./rdbms/admin` directory within our `ORACLE_HOME`, shown here for a database on the Linux platform.

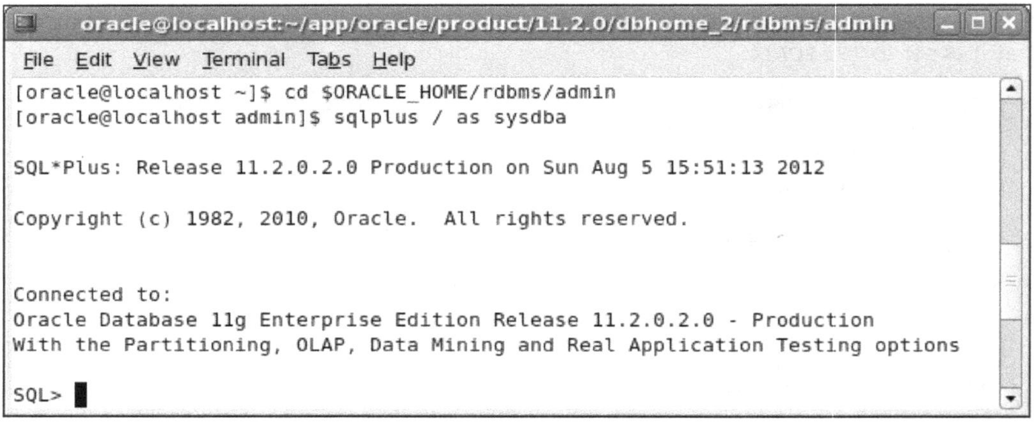
oracle@localhost:~/app/oracle/product/11.2.0/dbhome_2/rdbms/admin
File Edit View Terminal Tabs Help
[oracle@localhost ~]$ cd $ORACLE_HOME/rdbms/admin
[oracle@localhost admin]$ sqlplus / as sysdba
SQL*Plus: Release 11.2.0.2.0 Production on Sun Aug 5 15:51:13 2012
Copyright (c) 1982, 2010, Oracle. All rights reserved.
Connected to:
Oracle Database 11g Enterprise Edition Release 11.2.0.2.0 - Production
With the Partitioning, OLAP, Data Mining and Real Application Testing options
SQL>

On our default installation on Windows, the directory is shown in the following screenshot:

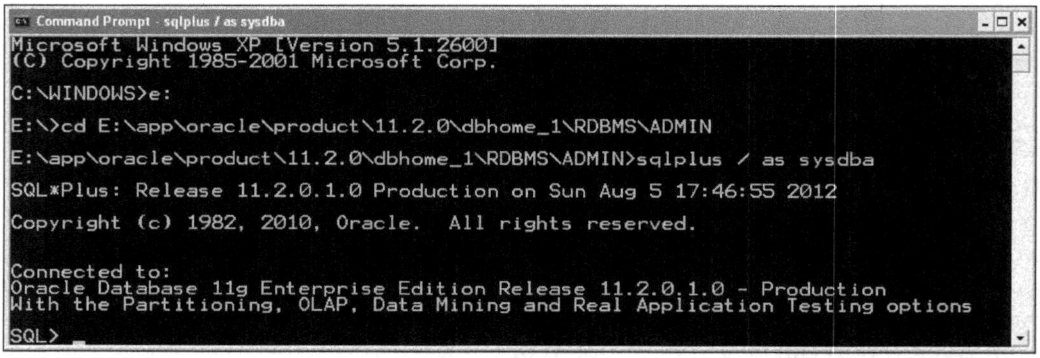
Command Prompt - sqlplus / as sysdba
Microsoft Windows XP [Version 5.1.2600]
(C) Copyright 1985-2001 Microsoft Corp.
C:\WINDOWS>e:
E:\>cd E:\app\oracle\product\11.2.0\dbhome_1\RDBMS\ADMIN
E:\app\oracle\product\11.2.0\dbhome_1\RDBMS\ADMIN>sqlplus / as sysdba
SQL*Plus: Release 11.2.0.1.0 Production on Sun Aug 5 17:46:55 2012
Copyright (c) 1982, 2010, Oracle. All rights reserved.
Connected to:
Oracle Database 11g Enterprise Edition Release 11.2.0.1.0 - Production
With the Partitioning, OLAP, Data Mining and Real Application Testing options
SQL> _

Once we're within SQL*Plus, the process is the same on either operating system. Run an Oracle-provided script, `awrrpt.sql`, that will access the data found in the AWR. This script will lead us through the process of choosing the AWR snapshots for comparisons and generating the final report. For our purposes, we'll choose the two most recent snapshots. Note that the snapshot numbers for your own testing will likely differ.

```
oracle@localhost:~/app/oracle/product/11.2.0/dbhome_2/rdbms/admin
File  Edit  View  Terminal  Tabs  Help
SQL> @awrrpt.sql

Current Instance
~~~~~~~~~~~~~~~~

   DB Id    DB Name      Inst Num Instance
----------- ------------ -------- ------------
 1229390655 ORCL                1 orcl


Specify the Report Type
~~~~~~~~~~~~~~~~~~~~~~~
Would you like an HTML report, or a plain text report?
Enter 'html' for an HTML report, or 'text' for plain text
Defaults to 'html'
Enter value for report_type: html
```

We're first prompted as to which type of report we want to generate. The `awrrpt.sql` script supports only HTML or text format. Enter `html` to choose an HTML-formatted report.

```
oracle@localhost:~/app/oracle/product/11.2.0/dbhome_2/rdbms/admin
File  Edit  View  Terminal  Tabs  Help
------------ -------- ------------ ------------ ------------
* 1229390655        1 ORCL         orcl         localhost.lo
                                                caldomain

Using 1229390655 for database Id
Using          1 for instance number


Specify the number of days of snapshots to choose from
~~~~~~~~~~~~~~~~~~~~~~~~~~~~~~~~~~~~~~~~~~~~~~~~~~~~~~
Entering the number of days (n) will result in the most recent
(n) days of snapshots being listed.  Pressing <return> without
specifying a number lists all completed snapshots.


Enter value for num_days: 1
```

We're prompted to enter the number of days of snapshots from which to choose. By default, the AWR will keep seven days of snapshot information. We'll shorten the list by choosing 1 day.

Next, we're asked to choose two snapshots to compare. Enter the `begin_snap` and `end_snap` of the two most recent snapshot numbers. After these two values are entered, we're prompted for the name of the report. We can simply hit the *Enter* key to accept the default value.

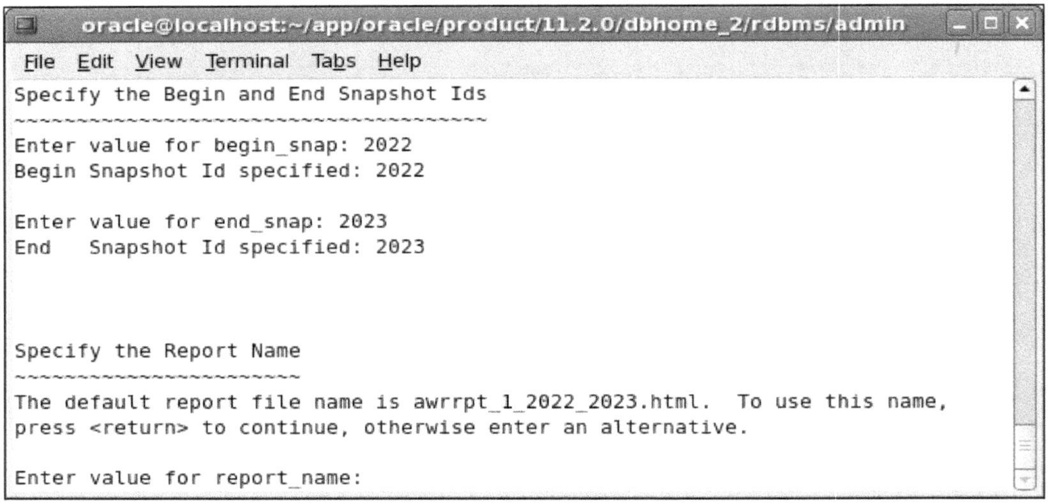

oracle@localhost:~/app/oracle/product/11.2.0/dbhome_2/rdbms/admin

File Edit View Terminal Tabs Help

```
Specify the Begin and End Snapshot Ids
~~~~~~~~~~~~~~~~~~~~~~~~~~~~~~~~~~~~~~
Enter value for begin_snap: 2022
Begin Snapshot Id specified: 2022

Enter value for end_snap: 2023
End   Snapshot Id specified: 2023



Specify the Report Name
~~~~~~~~~~~~~~~~~~~~~~~
The default report file name is awrrpt_1_2022_2023.html.  To use this name,
press <return> to continue, otherwise enter an alternative.

Enter value for report_name:
```

The report is then generated within the same directory from which we executed the script. To view it, we simply display it in a web browser. A brief portion of this very long report is shown in the following screenshot:

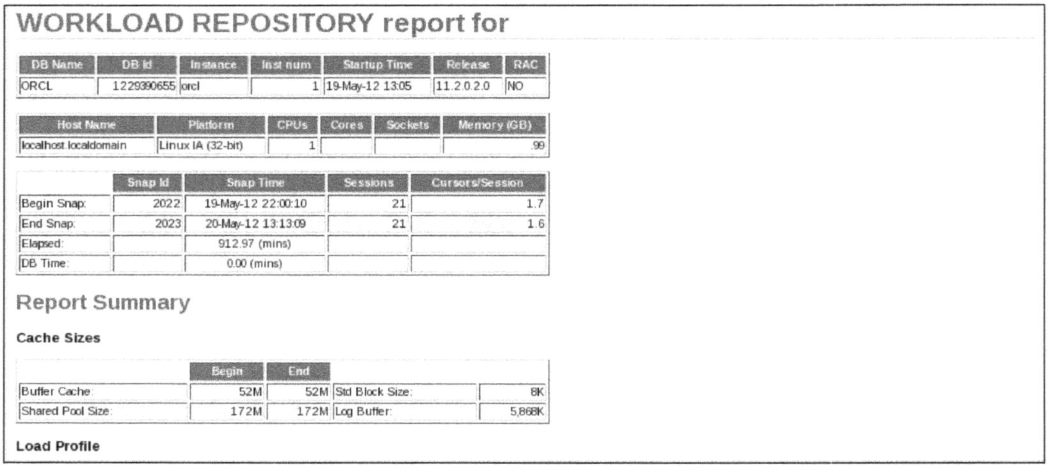

WORKLOAD REPOSITORY report for

DB Name	DB Id	Instance	Inst num	Startup Time	Release	RAC
ORCL	1229390655	orcl	1	19-May-12 13:05	11.2.0.2.0	NO

Host Name	Platform	CPUs	Cores	Sockets	Memory (GB)
localhost.localdomain	Linux IA (32-bit)	1			.99

	Snap Id	Snap Time	Sessions	Cursors/Session
Begin Snap:	2022	19-May-12 22:00:10	21	1.7
End Snap:	2023	20-May-12 13:13:09	21	1.6
Elapsed:		912.97 (mins)		
DB Time:		0.00 (mins)		

Report Summary

Cache Sizes

	Begin	End		
Buffer Cache:	52M	52M	Std Block Size:	8K
Shared Pool Size:	172M	172M	Log Buffer:	5,868K

Load Profile

> **The real-world DBA**
>
> Various parameters for the AWR, including the retention period for the AWR data, the frequency of snapshots, and the generation of reports can be controlled by the Oracle-supplied package `DBMS_WORKLOAD_REPOSITORY`. Alternatively, the Enterprise Manager tool can be used.

Understanding Oracle's Advisory Framework

While the AWR is revolutionary enough in its own right, the repository of performance information kept by the AWR provides DBAs with an entirely different set of tools, namely, the Advisory Framework. The Advisory Framework goes beyond the simple collection and presentation of statistics and metrics. It takes those metrics and uses them to give DBAs something all of us need at one time or another, that is, advice. The Advisory Framework can be a powerful tool in finding proactive and predictive solutions for several common performance problems.

Understanding the Automatic Database Diagnostic Monitor

Imagine that instead of spending hours interpreting the output of an AWR report, we could generate a report that lists, in order, the problems in our database, and even suggests possible actions to take to resolve them. That's exactly what the **Automatic Database Diagnostic Monitor**, or **ADDM**, provides. The ADDM is an intelligent set of algorithms that runs each time an AWR snapshot is taken and compares the results with the previous snapshot. It uses this comparison as the basis for a set of advisory tools that can help DBAs determine the root cause of various performance problems. The ADDM is the core of the Advisory Framework.

Generating an ADDM Report

The most straightforward use of ADDM is found by generating an ADDM report. This report can be used to quickly identify problems over a specified number of AWR snapshots. The process of running an ADDM report is very similar to that of the AWR report. Log in to SQL*Plus, run a script called `addmrpt.sql`, and choose your `begin_snap` and `end_snap` values. ADDM only supports text output, not HTML as AWR does, so that choice is removed.

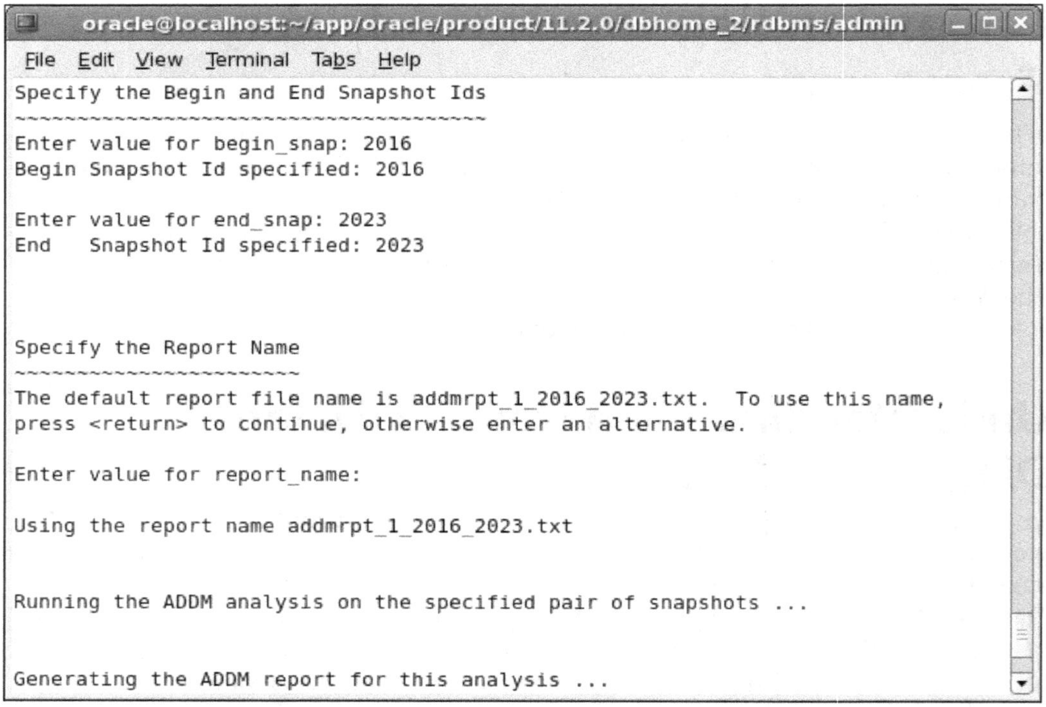
oracle@localhost:~/app/oracle/product/11.2.0/dbhome_2/rdbms/admin
File Edit View Terminal Tabs Help
Specify the Begin and End Snapshot Ids
Enter value for begin_snap: 2016
Begin Snapshot Id specified: 2016
Enter value for end_snap: 2023
End   Snapshot Id specified: 2023
Specify the Report Name
The default report file name is addmrpt_1_2016_2023.txt. To use this name,
press <return> to continue, otherwise enter an alternative.
Enter value for report_name:
Using the report name addmrpt_1_2016_2023.txt
Running the ADDM analysis on the specified pair of snapshots ...
Generating the ADDM report for this analysis ...

Hit *Enter* to accept the default name of the report and the report is generated:

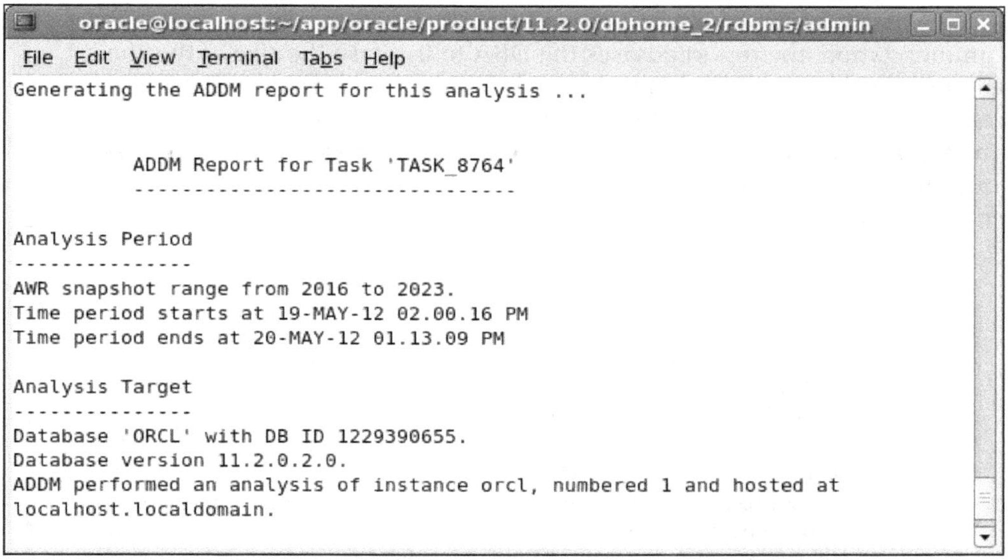
oracle@localhost:~/app/oracle/product/11.2.0/dbhome_2/rdbms/admin
File Edit View Terminal Tabs Help
Generating the ADDM report for this analysis ...
ADDM Report for Task 'TASK_8764'
Analysis Period
AWR snapshot range from 2016 to 2023.
Time period starts at 19-MAY-12 02.00.16 PM
Time period ends at 20-MAY-12 01.13.09 PM
Analysis Target
Database 'ORCL' with DB ID 1229390655.
Database version 11.2.0.2.0.
ADDM performed an analysis of instance orcl, numbered 1 and hosted at
localhost.localdomain.

Unlike the AWR report, the ADDM report is much more straightforward in nature. Rather than simply reporting on the raw statistics and metrics, ADDM uses its comparison algorithms to make concrete suggestions. These suggestions are reported as **findings**. The following screenshot is taken from an ADDM report:

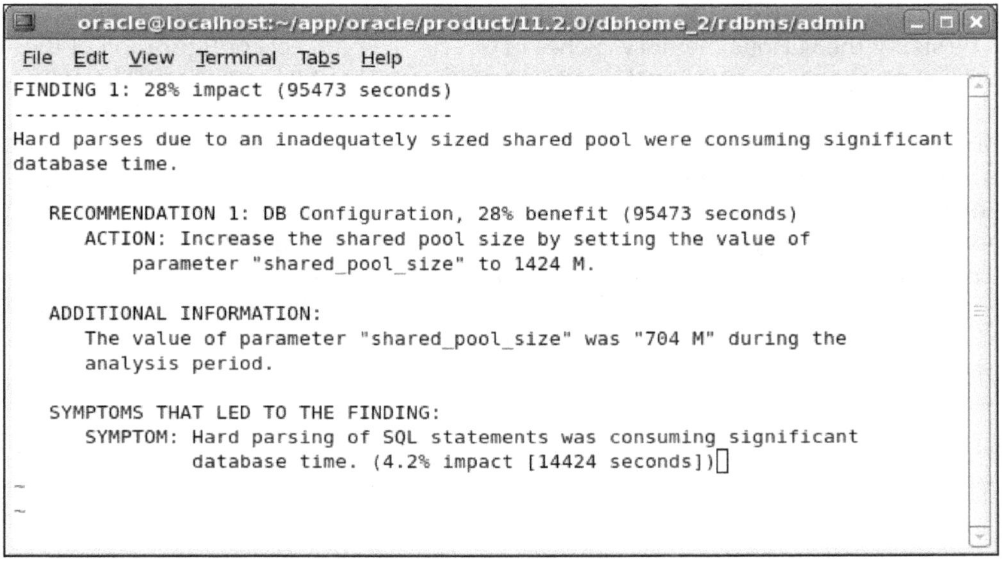
oracle@localhost:~/app/oracle/product/11.2.0/dbhome_2/rdbms/admin
File Edit View Terminal Tabs Help
FINDING 1: 28% impact (95473 seconds)
Hard parses due to an inadequately sized shared pool were consuming significant
database time.
RECOMMENDATION 1: DB Configuration, 28% benefit (95473 seconds)
ACTION: Increase the shared pool size by setting the value of
parameter "shared_pool_size" to 1424 M.
ADDITIONAL INFORMATION:
The value of parameter "shared_pool_size" was "704 M" during the
analysis period.
SYMPTOMS THAT LED TO THE FINDING:
SYMPTOM: Hard parsing of SQL statements was consuming significant
database time. (4.2% impact [14424 seconds])

`FINDING 1` is listed as having a quantifiable impact on database performance—28 percent to be exact. It lists the problem as `Hard parses due to an inadequately sized shared pool were consuming significant database time.` For a recommendation, the report advises the DBA to increase the size of the shared pool memory cache to 1424 M and reports that the current size is 704 M. This is an extremely simple and straightforward suggestion that can give you-according to the report-a 28 percent benefit in database performance, without any analysis of our own. ADDM can report on many types of findings, including insufficient memory configuration, inaccurate database parameters, and poorly structured SQL statements.

> **The real-world DBA**
>
> The simplicity of the ADDM report has led many DBAs to use it as a "first analysis" for performance problems. While it can certainly serve in that capacity, it should not be the only tool upon which a DBA relies. While an ADDM report can list various findings, it cannot always point to the exact root cause for a finding. When it comes to performance tuning, nothing can replace an experienced DBA who can interpret the AWR reports, examine the configuration of an operating system, or delve into the data dictionary to solve the problems.

Using Memory Advisors

As useful as the ADDM can be when reporting its findings, it supports many other types of advisors as well. One of the trickiest configuration tasks for a real-world DBA can be sizing the various memory caches in Oracle. The correct configuration of these caches is absolutely essential to the efficient performance of the database. The **memory advisors** provided by the ADDM can make this task much simpler. Note that while an in-depth knowledge of the ADDM's memory advisors is not needed for the exam, it is required to know and understand the basic functionality of each. In this section, we examine these advisors, including a look at how they are presented in the AWR report, as well as Enterprise Manager Database Control. Because the advisors must be run on a database with a significant amount of activity in order to display data, the screenshots in this section were taken from a database other than the sample one we have created. Still, they are good examples of how the memory advisors can help a DBA to configure memory.

Using the Buffer Pool Advisor

The Buffer Pool Advisor can be used as a predictive tool to determine the correct sizing of the database buffer cache. An example of the Buffer Pool Advisor demonstrated in an AWR report is shown as follows:

Buffer Pool Advisory

- Only rows with estimated physical reads >0 are displayed
- ordered by Block Size, Buffers For Estimate

P	Size for Est (M)	Size Factor	Buffers (thousands)	Est Phys Read Factor	Estimated Phys Reads (thousands)	Est Phys Read Time	Est %DBtime for Rds
D	176	0.09	21	2.04	79,046	1	1874830.00
D	352	0.18	42	1.65	63,672	1	1496705.00
D	528	0.28	62	1.40	54,080	1	1260785.00
D	704	0.37	83	1.37	52,836	1	1230190.00
D	880	0.46	104	1.34	51,873	1	1206482.00
D	1,056	0.55	125	1.32	51,027	1	1185679.00
D	1,232	0.65	145	1.30	50,282	1	1167358.00
D	1,408	0.74	166	1.28	49,405	1	1145785.00
D	1,584	0.83	187	1.19	45,951	1	1060849.00
D	1,760	0.92	208	1.02	39,455	1	901068.00
D	1,904	1.00	225	1.00	38,675	1	881890.00
D	1,936	1.02	228	1.00	38,525	1	878180.00
D	2,112	1.11	249	0.97	37,392	1	850315.00
D	2,288	1.20	270	0.94	36,383	1	825502.00
D	2,464	1.29	291	0.92	35,723	1	809265.00
D	2,640	1.39	312	0.91	35,098	1	793908.00
D	2,816	1.48	332	0.89	34,515	1	779566.00
D	2,992	1.57	353	0.88	34,008	1	767098.00
D	3,168	1.66	374	0.87	33,533	1	755409.00
D	3,344	1.76	395	0.85	33,011	1	742562.00
D	3,520	1.85	415	0.83	32,028	1	718394.00

The highlighted row in the previous screenshot is considered as our starting point. It shows a Size Factor of 1.00, which means this row represents the current size of our buffer cache, which is 1904 from the **Size For Est (M)** column. The rows following this starting point show the effect of increasing the buffer cache. For instance, if we look a few rows down where the Size for Est is 3168, the Est Phys Read Factor is 0.87. This means that if we increase the size of the buffer cache to 3168 M, we can roughly predict a reduction of physical reads by a factor of 0.13. Less physical reads is generally a good thing as it requires less disk I/O. Conversely, if we look at the rows above our baseline, we can predict an increase in the amount of physical reads if we were to decrease the size of the buffer cache.

Using the Shared Pool Advisory

The various memory advisors can also be accessed in a convenient GUI form using Enterprise Manager Database Control, which is included with any default install of Oracle 11*g*. When we access the Shared Pool Advisor via Database Control, we will see the following:

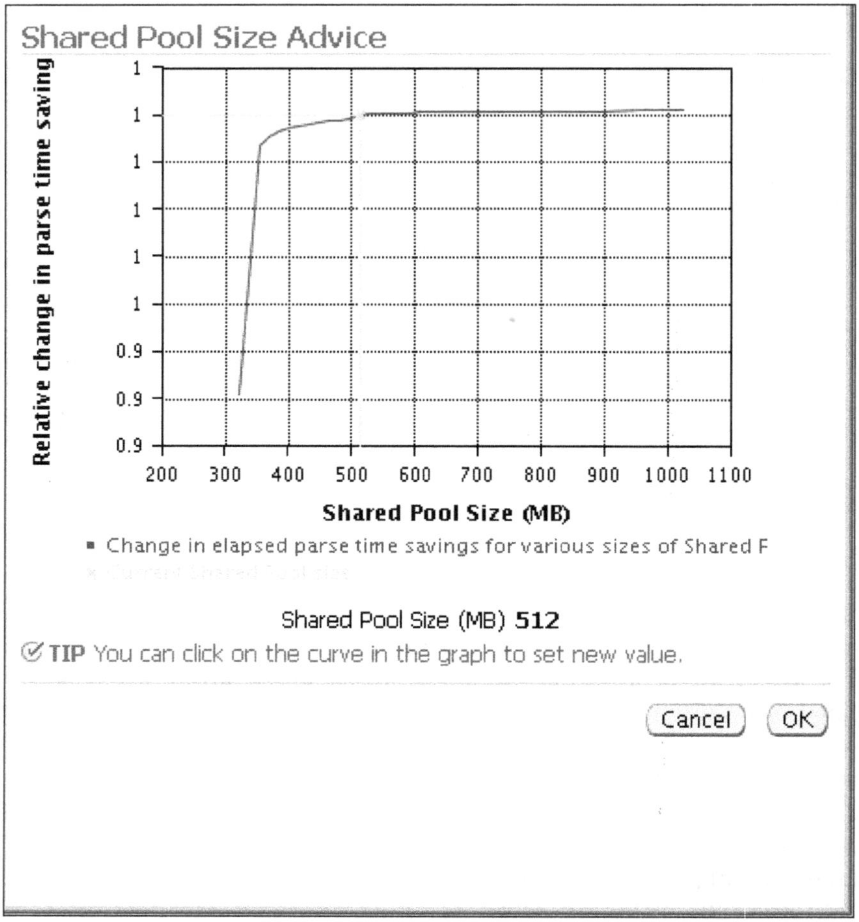
Shared Pool Size Advice
Relative change in parse time saving
1
1
1
1
1
1
0.9
0.9
0.9
200 300 400 500 600 700 800 900 1000 1100
Shared Pool Size (MB)
Change in elapsed parse time savings for various sizes of Shared F
Shared Pool Size (MB) 512
TIP You can click on the curve in the graph to set new value.
Cancel
OK

The previous advisor, for sizing the Shared Pool, shows our current shared pool size as 512 MB. The graph indicates that increasing the size of the `shared_pool_size` parameter will have negligible impact on our performance, as indicated by the left side of the graph, **Relative Change in parse time saving**. It does, however, indicate a fast drop-off in time savings if we decrease the size of the shared pool at about the 350 MB point.

Using the PGA Advisor

The final type of advisor we'll examine is one for the **Program Global Area** (**PGA**). As we've discussed, the PGA functions as a memory area for user-specific operations, such as sorting. The GUI advisor is shown as follows:

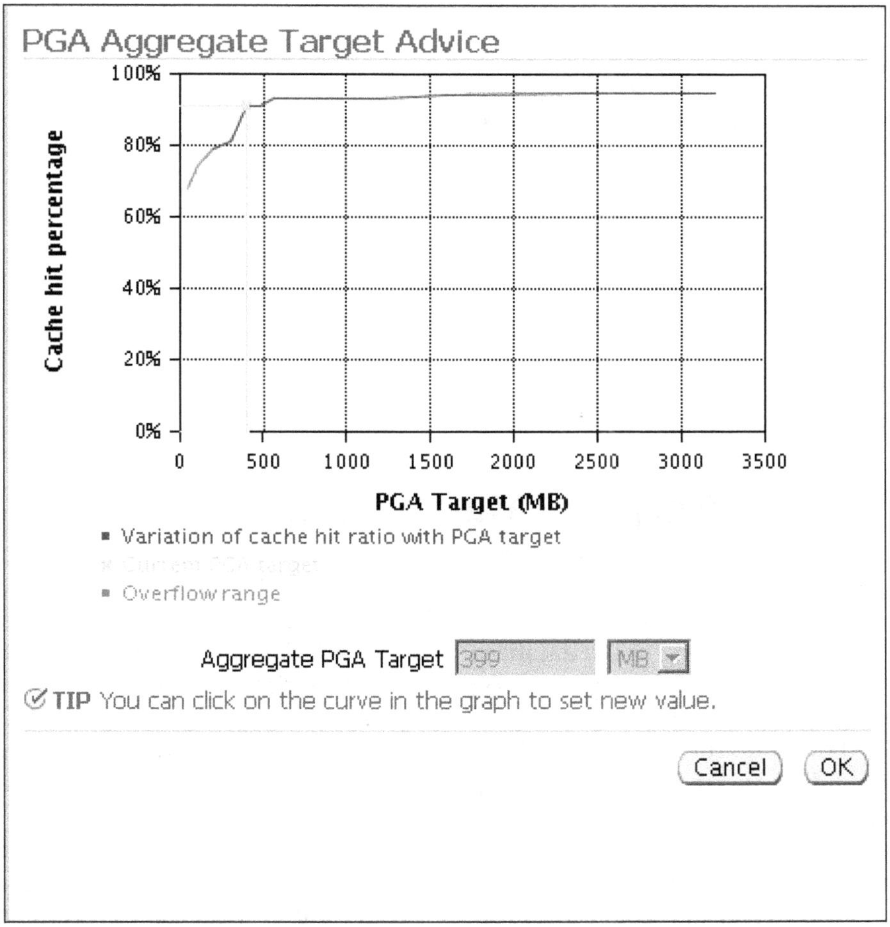
PGA Aggregate Target Advice
Cache hit percentage
100%
80%
60%
40%
20%
0%
0
500
1000
1500
2000
2500
3000
3500
PGA Target (MB)
Variation of cache hit ratio with PGA target
Overflow range
Aggregate PGA Target
399
MB
TIP You can click on the curve in the graph to set new value.
Cancel
OK

Based on what we can see in the previous graph, the PGA is almost optimally sized. Its size is 399 MB and it currently has a cache hit percentage (indicated on the left side of the graph) of somewhere above 90 percent. However, with an increase into the 600 MB range, the advisor predicts that we could see an increase in the hit percentage. Even small improvements in the PGA cache hit percentage can be noticeable; so it is worth considering in this situation to make the improvement by increasing the value of the `pga_aggregate_target` parameter.

Finally, Database Control also includes an overall dashboard view of memory usage that can be useful when determining how Oracle's caches are distributed as shown in the next screenshot. We will examine some of the terms mentioned on the following screen later in the chapter:

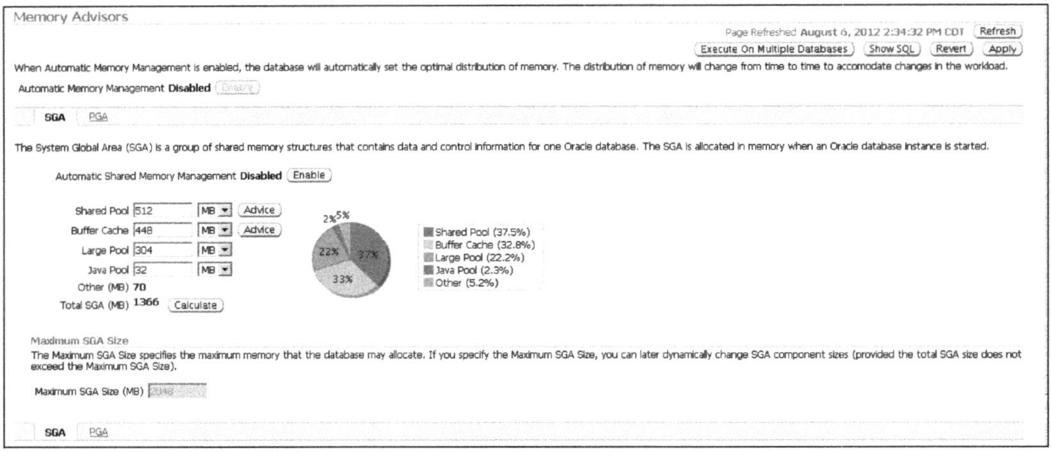
Memory Advisors
Page Refreshed August 6, 2012 2:34:32 PM CDT
Refresh
Execute On Multiple Databases
Show SQL
Revert
Apply
When Automatic Memory Management is enabled, the database will automatically set the optimal distribution of memory. The distribution of memory will change from time to time to accomodate changes in the workload.
Automatic Memory Management Disabled
SGA
PGA
The System Global Area (SGA) is a group of shared memory structures that contains data and control information for one Oracle database. The SGA is allocated in memory when an Oracle database instance is started.
Automatic Shared Memory Management Disabled
Enable
Shared Pool 512 MB
Advice
Buffer Cache 448 MB
Advice
Large Pool 304 MB
Java Pool 32 MB
Other (MB) 70
Total SGA (MB) 1366
Calculate
2%
5%
22%
37%
33%
Shared Pool (37.5%)
Buffer Cache (32.8%)
Large Pool (22.2%)
Java Pool (2.3%)
Other (5.2%)
Maximum SGA Size
The Maximum SGA Size specifies the maximum memory that the database may allocate. If you specify the Maximum SGA Size, you can later dynamically change SGA component sizes (provided the total SGA size does not exceed the Maximum SGA Size).
Maximum SGA Size (MB)
SGA
PGA

Understanding the Alert Framework

Our final piece of Oracle's Advisory Framework concerns some of the day-to-day performance-related activities of the real-world DBA. Much of a DBA's time is spent simply in monitoring various aspects of the database. How full are the tablespaces? What errors are occurring in the database? Are the redo logs switching too frequently? The list is endless. Many third-party programs are designed to help the DBAs check these and many other types of conditions. However, starting with Version 10*g*, Oracle has moved one step further by including the Alert Framework within the database. This set of tables and procedures is designed to monitor the internals of our database and even report to us when a problem arises. The Alert Framework attempts to provide a "self-managing" database. The two main components of this framework are thresholds and alerts. A **threshold** is a set of DBA-defined limits on a given measurable metric. Let's consider the tablespace capacity as a metric. When a tablespace becomes full, error conditions often arise as jobs cannot add data to the tables in that tablespace. To avoid this situation, we can set a threshold as to what an acceptable tablespace capacity limit would be. We can have warning and critical thresholds. We might set the **warning threshold** at 90 percent full for the tablespace, and the **critical threshold** at 95 percent. Then, when a given tablespace becomes more than 90 percent full, a warning alert is generated. When it passes 95 percent full, a critical alert is generated. These types of alerts are known as **server-generated alerts**. Server-generated alerts cannot be cleared automatically and generally require the intervention of the DBA.

The simplest way to interact with the alert framework is through **Oracle Enterprise Manager (OEM)**, either Grid Control or Database Control, which we have as a part of our default installation. Although the management of thresholds and alerts is normally associated with Enterprise Manager, OEM does not generate the alerts. The process responsible for issuing these alerts is the Manageability Monitor, or MMON process. To invoke Database Control for Windows, we will have to navigate the Oracle program group via **All Programs | Oracle-Ora11gDB_home1 | Database Control | orcl**.

In Linux, we point our browser to the location that is specified on the last window of our DBCA installation, usually `https://localhost:1158/em`. After logging in to Database Control with the `system` user (password `oracle` in our default installation), we're presented with a home page. This page contains a section near the middle that brings the alerts to our attention:

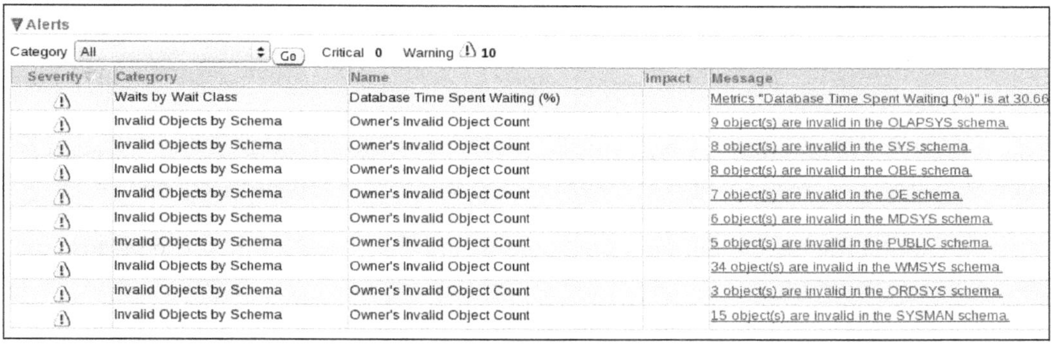
Alerts
Category All
Go
Critical 0
Warning 10
Severity
Category
Name
Impact
Message
Waits by Wait Class
Database Time Spent Waiting (%)
Metrics "Database Time Spent Waiting (%)" is at 30.66
Invalid Objects by Schema
Owner's Invalid Object Count
9 object(s) are invalid in the OLAPSYS schema.
8 object(s) are invalid in the SYS schema.
8 object(s) are invalid in the OBE schema.
7 object(s) are invalid in the OE schema.
6 object(s) are invalid in the MDSYS schema.
5 object(s) are invalid in the PUBLIC schema.
34 object(s) are invalid in the WMSYS schema.
3 object(s) are invalid in the ORDSYS schema.
15 object(s) are invalid in the SYSMAN schema.

We see here that our database has a number of warning alerts, but no critical ones. Note that this may differ on your own machine. Near the bottom of the page, in the **Related Links** section, is a link to **Metric and Policy Settings**. If we click on this link, the list of metrics for which thresholds can be edited is shown. Near the bottom of that page is the section for tablespace thresholds, shown in the following screenshot:

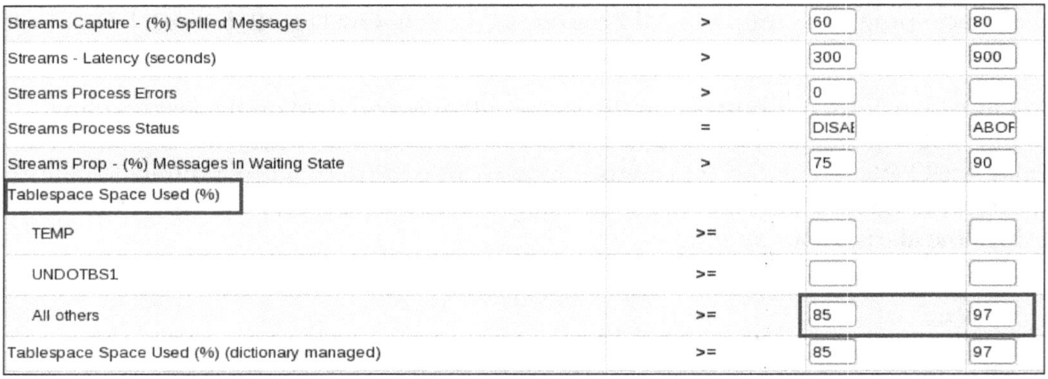
Streams Capture - (%) Spilled Messages > 60 80
Streams - Latency (seconds) > 300 900
Streams Process Errors > 0
Streams Process Status = DISAI ABOF
Streams Prop - (%) Messages in Waiting State > 75 90
Tablespace Space Used (%)
TEMP >=
UNDOTBS1 >=
All others >= 85 97
Tablespace Space Used (%) (dictionary managed) >= 85 97

We can see here that tablespace thresholds of 85 percent full for warning alerts and 97 percent full for critical alerts are currently in place. If we desire, we can change these thresholds to values that are more appropriate for our environment. We simply enter the new value in the relevant box and click on the **OK** button at the bottom of the page.

Server-generated alerts are listed in the `DBA_OUTSTANDING_ALERTS` data dictionary view. When alerts are generated, they can be cleared manually by the DBA by clicking on the link for the alert and then clicking on **Acknowledge**. The DBA may do this after a problem has been fixed. Note that not all of the alerts we see in Database Control are recorded in `DBA_OUTSTANDING_ALERTS`. Once cleared, the alerts are moved to the alert history, or the `DBA_ALERT_HISTORY` view, as shown in the following screenshot:

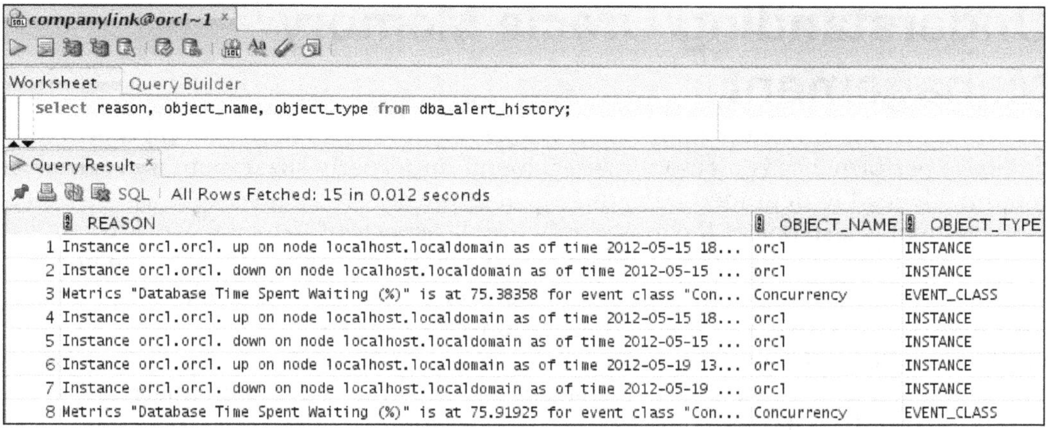
companylink@orcl~1
Worksheet
Query Builder
select reason, object_name, object_type from dba_alert_history;
Query Result
SQL | All Rows Fetched: 15 in 0.012 seconds
REASON
OBJECT_NAME
OBJECT_TYPE
1 Instance orcl.orcl. up on node localhost.localdomain as of time 2012-05-15 18... orcl INSTANCE
2 Instance orcl.orcl. down on node localhost.localdomain as of time 2012-05-15 ... orcl INSTANCE
3 Metrics "Database Time Spent Waiting (%)" is at 75.38358 for event class "Con... Concurrency EVENT_CLASS
4 Instance orcl.orcl. up on node localhost.localdomain as of time 2012-05-15 18... orcl INSTANCE
5 Instance orcl.orcl. down on node localhost.localdomain as of time 2012-05-15 ... orcl INSTANCE
6 Instance orcl.orcl. up on node localhost.localdomain as of time 2012-05-19 13... orcl INSTANCE
7 Instance orcl.orcl. down on node localhost.localdomain as of time 2012-05-19 ... orcl INSTANCE
8 Metrics "Database Time Spent Waiting (%)" is at 75.91925 for event class "Con... Concurrency EVENT_CLASS

The examples given in the previous screenshot show the value of using OEM to manage alerts and thresholds, but the Alert Framework can even go one step further and directly notify the DBA when alerts are generated. If we have access to an e-mail server, OEM can be configured to send out e-mails or even text messages when alerts arise. This allows OEM and the Alert Framework to proactively keep a DBA up-to-date with several types of problems in the system.

The real-world DBA

Oracle Enterprise Manager is not required to use the Alert Framework, but it does make leveraging its capabilities much easier. OEM is only a frontend to the framework itself. We can use the alert framework without it, but doing so requires running a lot of complex PL/SQL statements. Also, remember that when setting up e-mail or text notifications, many types of alerts can be generated. Not all of them require waking up a DBA in the middle of the night with a page or text message!

Understanding Oracle Memory Management

As we've mentioned a number of times earlier, one of the most crucial aspects of database performance is memory management. Improperly sized memory caches can quickly lead to degraded performance of applications and user queries. Memory management is also one of the most configurable aspects of the database. We can use the database initialization parameters to easily change the amount of memory used by Oracle, and how that memory is distributed. However, Oracle also gives us the opportunity to release some of that responsibility and allows the database kernel itself to handle memory management, increasing or decreasing the size of various caches as needed. When memory is managed in this way, there is no interruption of service and the database stays in an open state for the entire time, unnoticed by the user. In this section, we will examine the three different types of memory management available to the Oracle DBA.

Using Manual Memory Management

Historically, in the earlier versions of Oracle database, the only way to manage memory was to do it manually. Before the advent of the server parameter file in Oracle 9*i*, if a DBA needed to change a parameter that governed the size of a memory cache, such as `shared_pool_size`, the change would be made in the `init.ora` file and the database would be restarted to read the new parameter value. This would severely impact the uptime of high availability systems, as the database needed to be restarted every time a memory reallocation was required. The server parameter file (`SPFILE`) allowed DBAs to make changes to memory allocation while the database was still available. We can dynamically resize the following SGA memory cache parameters without restarting the database:

- `shared_pool_size`
- `db_cache_size`
- `large_pool`
- `streams_pool_size`
- `java_pool_size`

From this list, `shared_pool_size` and `db_cache_size` generally pertain to overall database performance. The other three can help performance in certain situations. This leaves only the `log_buffer` as a cache that cannot be resized while the database is open. Let's examine the process of managing memory manually. For example, say that based on the findings of an ADDM report, our `Companylink` database has an undersized shared pool. We cannot allocate any more memory to the SGA as a whole, so we're going to take some memory from the buffer cache and give it to the shared pool. We begin by logging in and executing a `show sga` command to determine our starting point:

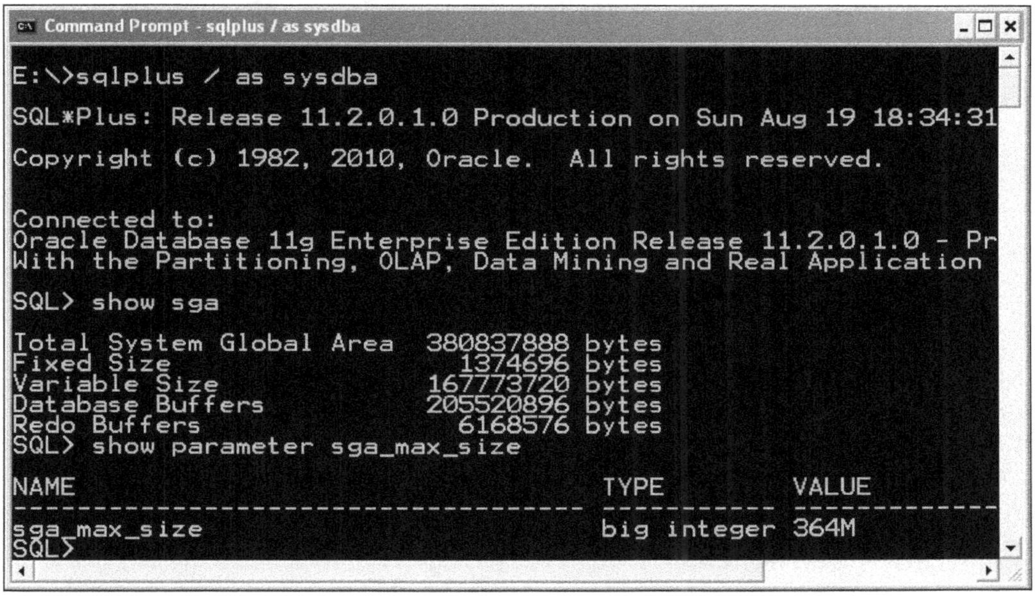
Command Prompt - sqlplus / as sysdba
E:\>sqlplus / as sysdba
SQL*Plus: Release 11.2.0.1.0 Production on Sun Aug 19 18:34:31
Copyright (c) 1982, 2010, Oracle. All rights reserved.
Connected to:
Oracle Database 11g Enterprise Edition Release 11.2.0.1.0 - Pr
With the Partitioning, OLAP, Data Mining and Real Application
SQL> show sga
Total System Global Area 380837888 bytes
Fixed Size 1374696 bytes
Variable Size 167773720 bytes
Database Buffers 205520896 bytes
Redo Buffers 6168576 bytes
SQL> show parameter sga_max_size
NAME TYPE VALUE
sga_max_size big integer 364M
SQL>

We can see that we have a total SGA of 380837888 bytes, which is about 364 MB. Not coincidentally, we also see that the value of `sga_max_size` is also 364 MB. This parameter governs the overall maximum size of the SGA. This parameter cannot be changed without restarting the database, so we'll need to work within that amount. Let's look at the individual settings for the buffer cache and shared pool.

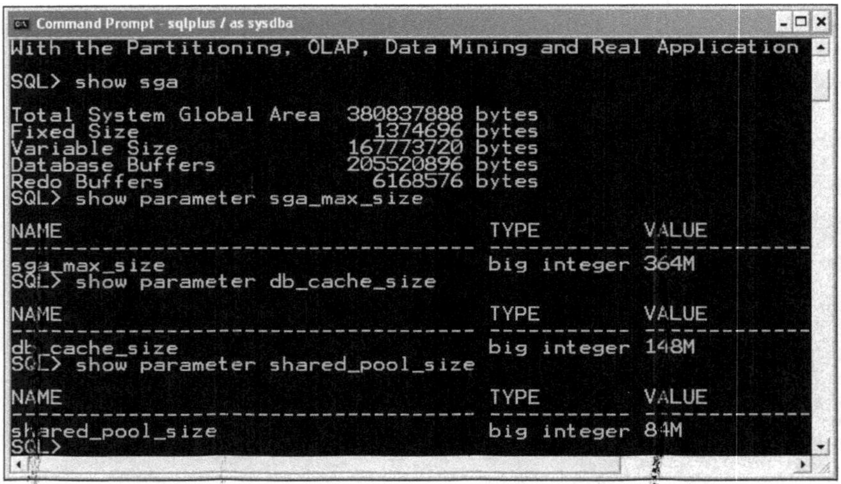
Command Prompt - sqlplus / as sysdba
With the Partitioning, OLAP, Data Mining and Real Application
SQL> show sga
Total System Global Area 380837888 bytes
Fixed Size 1374696 bytes
Variable Size 167773720 bytes
Database Buffers 205520896 bytes
Redo Buffers 6168576 bytes
SQL> show parameter sga_max_size
NAME TYPE VALUE
sga_max_size big integer 364M
SQL> show parameter db_cache_size
NAME TYPE VALUE
db_cache_size big integer 148M
SQL> show parameter shared_pool_size
NAME TYPE VALUE
shared_pool_size big integer 84M
SQL>

We see that our buffer cache is 148 MB and our shared pool is 84 MB, which makes a total of 232 MB. This is significantly less than `sga_max_size`. However, we need to remember that while these two caches make up the majority of the SGA, they're not the only caches that are allocated. We will reduce the buffer cache by 16 MB and add that 16 MB to the shared pool.

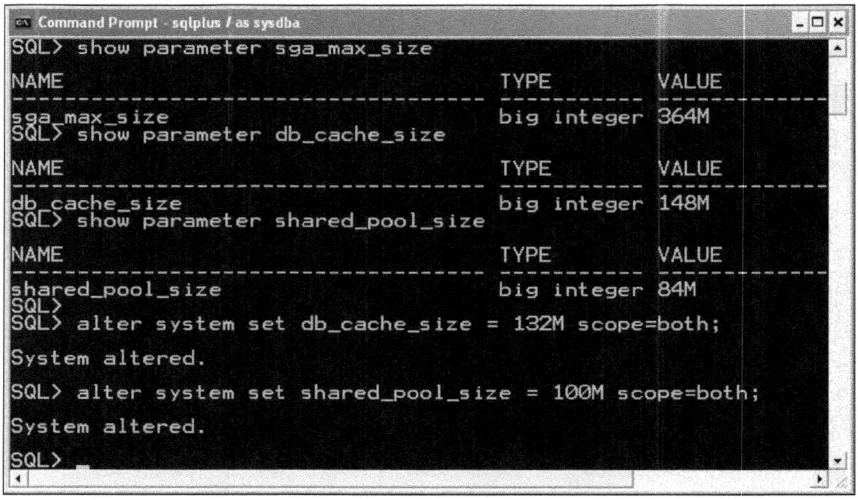
Command Prompt - sqlplus / as sysdba
SQL> show parameter sga_max_size
NAME TYPE VALUE
sga_max_size big integer 364M
SQL> show parameter db_cache_size
NAME TYPE VALUE
db_cache_size big integer 148M
SQL> show parameter shared_pool_size
NAME TYPE VALUE
shared_pool_size big integer 84M
SQL>
SQL> alter system set db_cache_size = 132M scope=both;
System altered.
SQL> alter system set shared_pool_size = 100M scope=both;
System altered.
SQL> _

Now if we review the new parameter sizes, we see that we have successfully used manual memory management. We should note that memory is allocated in units known as **granules**. Thus, when we specify the size for a memory cache, it is sometimes rounded to the closest granule size. In our case, we have used a size that matches the granule allocation unit for our database. A different size may yield slightly different results.

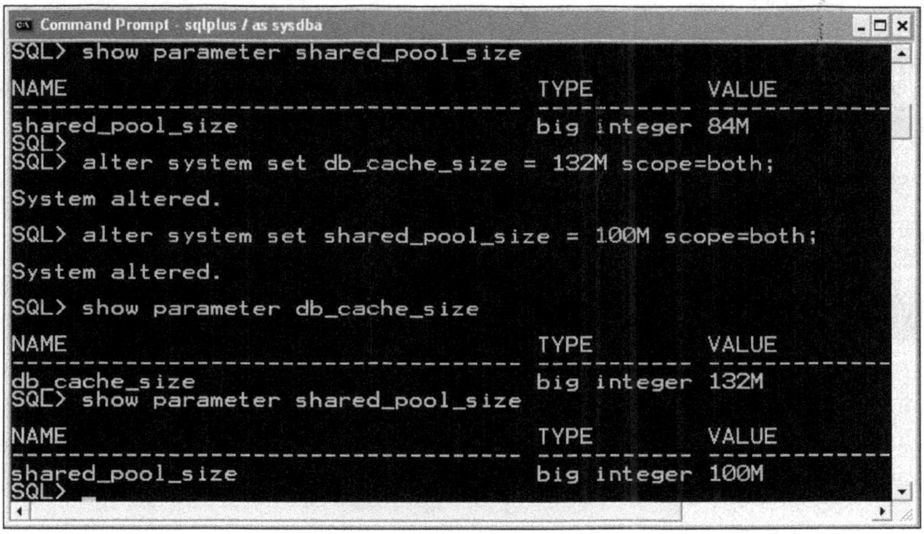
Command Prompt - sqlplus / as sysdba
SQL> show parameter shared_pool_size
NAME TYPE VALUE
shared_pool_size big integer 84M
SQL>
SQL> alter system set db_cache_size = 132M scope=both;
System altered.
SQL> alter system set shared_pool_size = 100M scope=both;
System altered.
SQL> show parameter db_cache_size
NAME TYPE VALUE
db_cache_size big integer 132M
SQL> show parameter shared_pool_size
NAME TYPE VALUE
shared_pool_size big integer 100M
SQL>

Using Automatic Shared Memory Management

While the introduction of the SPFILE allowed high uptime memory management, it was still a manual process. Oracle wanted to put an infrastructure in place that allowed DBAs to set an outer-boundary memory value and allow the kernel to adjust the individual caches within this boundary. The first iteration of this feature is known as **Automatic Shared Memory Management** (**ASMM**). ASMM allows the DBA to turn over memory management within the SGA to the Oracle kernel. ASMM will then grow and shrink the various caches within the SGA to sizes that it considers optimal, effectively freeing the DBA from manually sizing the individual caches. ASMM automatically resizes all of the caches that make up the SGA, with the exception of the log buffer.

The activation of ASMM is governed by one database parameter, that is, `sga_target`. Let's activate ASMM in our database by setting this parameter. We can see that it is currently set to `0`:

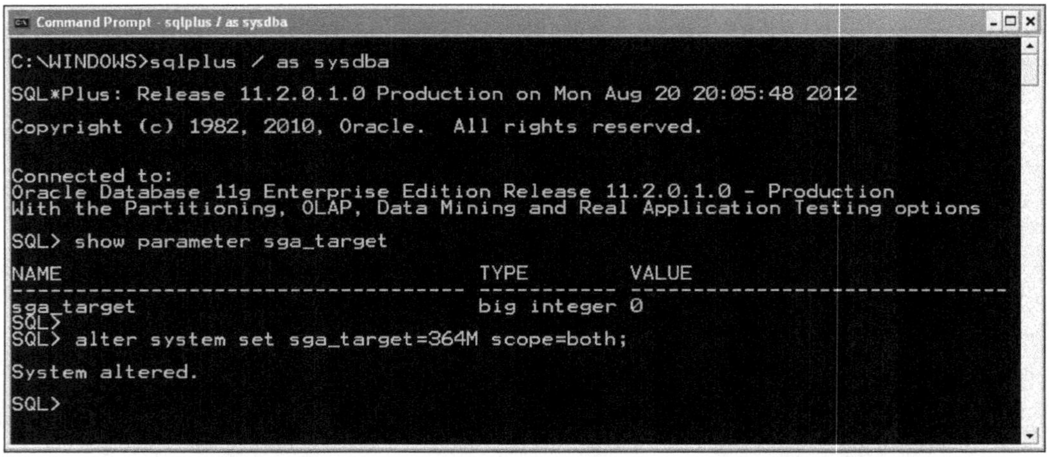
Command Prompt - sqlplus / as sysdba
C:\WINDOWS>sqlplus / as sysdba
SQL*Plus: Release 11.2.0.1.0 Production on Mon Aug 20 20:05:48 2012
Copyright (c) 1982, 2010, Oracle. All rights reserved.
Connected to:
Oracle Database 11g Enterprise Edition Release 11.2.0.1.0 - Production
With the Partitioning, OLAP, Data Mining and Real Application Testing options
SQL> show parameter sga_target
NAME TYPE VALUE
sga_target big integer 0
SQL>
SQL> alter system set sga_target=364M scope=both;
System altered.
SQL>

Here, we've set the value for `sga_target` to `364M`, the same as our `sga_max_size`. This value is now the outer boundary within which ASMM sizes the SGA caches. The value for `sga_target` cannot be greater than the value of `sga_max_size`.

If we've now allowed ASMM to manage memory, what happened to the parameters that governed the individual caches themselves? For example, earlier in the chapter, we resized both `shared_pool_size` and `db_cache_size` to explicit values. Are those values now set to zero? Actually, no—these, and any other values for the caches within the SGA that have been explicitly set, represent the lower boundary to which ASMM can size that cache. For instance, if the value for `shared_pool_size` is set to `100M`, ASMM can increase the size of the shared pool to any value greater than 100 MB, but never less than 100 MB. To give ASMM complete control, we can size the individual cache parameters to zero as shown in the following screenshot:

Command Prompt - sqlplus / as sysdba
System altered.
SQL>
SQL> alter system set shared_pool_size=0 scope=both;
System altered.
SQL> alter system set db_cache_size=0 scope=both;
System altered.
SQL> alter system set large_pool_size=0 scope=both;
System altered.
SQL> alter system set java_pool_size=0 scope=both;
System altered.
SQL> alter system set streams_pool_size=0 scope=both;
System altered.
SQL>

We've now given ASMM complete control to grow and shrink the memory caches of the SGA as it sees fit.

Using Automatic Memory Management

If we recall our previous discussions, the Program Global Area, or PGA, is a specialized memory cache used to store the data that is relevant to a single user's actions, such as sorting. When a sort occurs, the PGA is used to store the results of the sort before returning them to the user. The PGA is an automatic cache itself and is defined by the `pga_aggregate_target` parameter. In versions previous to Oracle 9*i*, numerous other parameters, such as `sort_area_size`, were used to apportion private memory areas to users. The PGA took that functionality and encapsulated it into a single cache. Thus, a single, global memory area is used to provide private memory to user sessions. The allocations within it are managed automatically.

With Oracle 11*g*, Oracle has taken automatic memory management to the next logical step. **Automatic Memory Management**, or **AMM**, allows the user to define a single memory area that contains both the SGA and the PGA. Thus, management of both memory areas is combined. We can think of AMM as taking ASMM and combining it with automatic management of the PGA. Just as ASMM is managed by setting the `sga_target` parameter, AMM is enabled using a parameter called `memory_target`. Also, as with ASMM, AMM does not automatically manage the size of the log buffer. Our database currently uses ASMM to manage the SGA; let's convert it to use AMM.

To begin, we need to define two parameters, `memory_max_target` and `memory_target`, that are analogous to `sga_max_size` and `sga_target` in ASMM. The `memory_max_target` parameter is not dynamic, so we must define it in the SPFILE and restart the database for the parameter to take effect. We'll set it larger than our previous settings for ASMM.

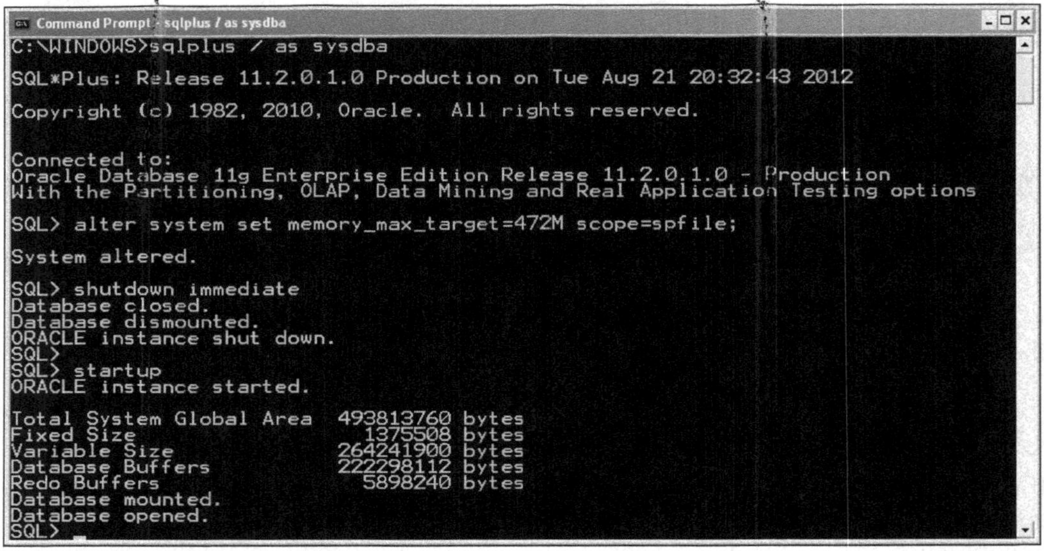
Command Prompt - sqlplus / as sysdba
C:\WINDOWS>sqlplus / as sysdba
SQL*Plus: Release 11.2.0.1.0 Production on Tue Aug 21 20:32:43 2012
Copyright (c) 1982, 2010, Oracle. All rights reserved.
Connected to:
Oracle Database 11g Enterprise Edition Release 11.2.0.1.0 - Production
With the Partitioning, OLAP, Data Mining and Real Application Testing options
SQL> alter system set memory_max_target=472M scope=spfile;
System altered.
SQL> shutdown immediate
Database closed.
Database dismounted.
ORACLE instance shut down.
SQL>
SQL> startup
ORACLE instance started.
Total System Global Area 493813760 bytes
Fixed Size 1375508 bytes
Variable Size 264241900 bytes
Database Buffers 222298112 bytes
Redo Buffers 5898240 bytes
Database mounted.
Database opened.
SQL>

In the following screenshot we've set `memory_max_target` to use 472 MB of system memory. We're no longer using ASMM; so let's set the boundary for `sga_target` to zero and then activate AMM using the `memory_target` parameter, both of which can be done dynamically. We'll set `memory_target` to the same value as `memory_max_target` in order to maximize our use of AMM.

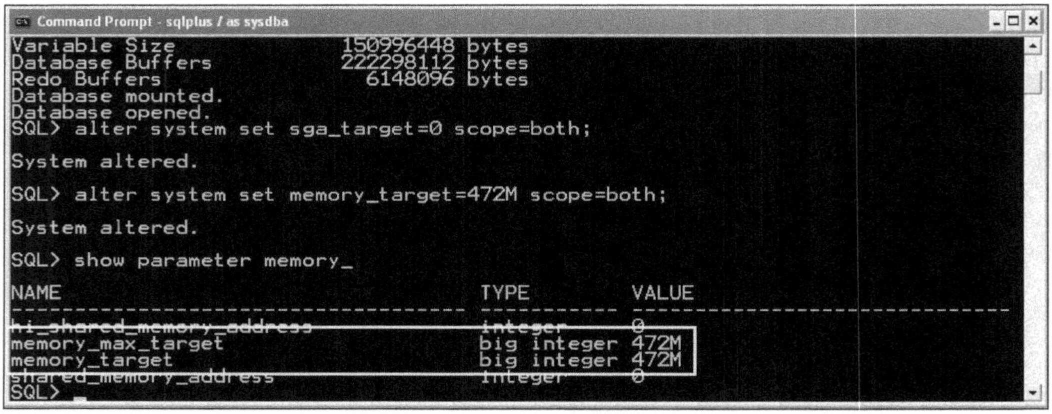
Command Prompt - sqlplus / as sysdba
Variable Size 150996448 bytes
Database Buffers 222298112 bytes
Redo Buffers 6148096 bytes
Database mounted.
Database opened.
SQL> alter system set sga_target=0 scope=both;
System altered.
SQL> alter system set memory_target=472M scope=both;
System altered.
SQL> show parameter memory_
NAME TYPE VALUE
hi_shared_memory_address integer 0
memory_max_target big integer 472M
memory_target big integer 472M
shared_memory_address integer 0
SQL>

Our individual caches, such as `shared_pool_size` and `db_cache_size`, are already set to `0`, so we're now managing both the SGA and PGA automatically using AMM. The current sizes of these caches can be viewed using the `v$memory_dynamic_components` data dictionary view.

> **The real-world DBA**
>
> While using ASMM or AMM can generally relieve the DBA from the task of calculating and resizing caches, it also can be beneficial in highly dynamic hybrid environments. For instance, let's say our `Companylink` database serves two types of functions. During business hours, it serves as an **Online Transaction Processing** (**OLTP**) database, but during the night hours, it hosts data loads and aggregate reporting. When it is serving as an OLTP database during the day, users are running smaller, discrete transactions, which generally require a larger shared pool to accommodate the number of different SQL statements being parsed. However, during the night, the data loads and reporting put a heavier strain on the database buffer cache as these operations use large amounts of data. Without ASMM or AMM, the DBA must usually "split the difference" for memory allocation, attempting to find compromise values for both caches. With automatically managed memory, the database will automatically resize to accommodate the change in the workload, and can lead to better performance with lesser memory.

Certification objectives covered

- Using and managing optimizer statistics
- Troubleshooting invalid and unusable objects
- Using and managing **Automatic Workload Repository** (**AWR**)
- Using Advisory Framework
- Using Memory Advisors
- Managing alerts and thresholds
- Using Automatic Memory Management

Summary

In this chapter, we've examined the concept of performance management in the Oracle database. We've examined object-level tuning using strategies to manage optimizer statistics and recompile invalid objects. We've explored the Automatic Workload Repository or AWR and used it to generate reports that can reveal statistics about database performance. We've looked at the 11*g* Advisory Framework and ADDM, which can give relevant performance advice to DBAs based on the statistics it has collected. We've examined how thresholds and alerts can be used to proactively notify us when problems arise. Finally, we've examined all the three methods of memory management, namely, manual, ASMM, and AMM. In our next chapter, we begin a section that addresses one of the most important facets of database administration, that is, backup and recovery. In the next several chapters, we'll look at the concepts of backup and recovery, learn to back up a database using Recovery Manager, and then perform database recoveries.

Test your knowledge

Q. 1. Which type of optimization is most commonly used today in the Oracle database?

a. Rule-based optimization
b. Cost-based optimization
c. Execution-based optimization
d. Run-based optimization

Q. 2. Which procedure of the `DBMS_STATS` package can be used to gather statistics for all the tables in one given schema?

a. `GATHER_TABLE_STATS`
b. `ANALYZE_TABLE_STATS`
c. `GATHER_SCHEMA_STATS`
d. `ANALYZE_DATABASE_STATS`

Q. 3. The `auto optimizer stats collection job` is enabled for our `Companylink` database. However, we notice that statistics are not being collected for all of the tables in our database. What could be the cause of the missed statistics?

a. The objects being missed are not within a single schema.
b. The objects being missed are in separate tablespaces.

c. The job is not completing within the Autotask scheduled window.
d. The Autotask feature has not been enabled using `DBMS_STATS`.

Q. 4. If the collection of new statistics causes a degradation of performance from the previous statistics, what action could be taken that would address the problem?

a. Statistics can dropped using `DBMS_STATS`.
b. Statistics can be re-run using `DBMS_STATS`.
c. Statistics can be restored using `DBMS_STATS`.
d. No action can be taken.

Q. 5. Which of the following statements could be used to compile an invalid view called `c_link_view` that overlays a table called `c_link_table`?

a. `alter object c_link_view compile immediate;`
b. `alter view c_link_view compile;`
c. `alter table c_link_table compile all views;`
d. `alter table c_link_table compile view c_link_view;`

Q. 6. Which value for the `STATISTICS_LEVEL` parameter will prevent the generation of AWR snapshots?

a. `BASIC`
b. `TYPICAL`
c. `ALL`
d. `FULL`

Q. 7. Which of the following is not true regarding the generation of an AWR report?

a. It can be generated in either text, HTML, or XML format.
b. It requires two snapshots to be specified.
c. The report's data is pulled from the `SYSAUX` tablespace.
d. By default, it can access snapshots that are up to 7 days old.

Q. 8. Which of the following is not true regarding the ADDM?

a. The ADDM is run automatically without the intervention of the DBA after each AWR snapshot is collected.
b. The ADDM requires a baseline to be established in order to run.
c. The ADDM can advise a DBA through an ADDM report.
d. ADDM results are stored in the Automatic Workload Repository.

Q. 9. Which memory advisor could assist a DBA in cases where too many physical reads are occurring?

a. The PGA memory advisor
b. The SGA memory advisor
c. The shared pool memory advisor
d. The buffer cache memory advisor

Q. 10. When an alert is cleared, where can it be viewed?

a. `DBA_OUTSTANDING_ALERTS`
b. `DBA_CLEARED_ALERTS`
c. `DBA_ALERT_HISTORY`
d. Cleared alerts cannot be viewed

Q. 11. Which database background process is responsible for issuing alerts when a threshold is crossed?

a. `PMON`
b. `SMON`
c. `LGWR`
d. `MMON`

Q. 12. Which of the following parameters must be set to zero in order to use manual memory management?

a. `SHARED_POOL_SIZE`
b. `SGA_TARGET`
c. `SGA_MAX_SIZE`
d. `LOG_BUFFER`

Q. 13. Our `Companylink` database has AMM enabled. What is the effect of setting the `SHARED_POOL_SIZE` parameter to `85M`?

a. The minimum amount of shared pool memory that can be used is 85 MB.

b. The maximum amount of shared pool memory that can be used is 85 MB.

c. The maximum amount of SGA that can be used is 85 MB.

d. Setting this parameter has no effect as AMM automatically manages all memory.

Q. 14. Which of the following parameters cannot be changed dynamically while the database is in an open state?

a. `SGA_TARGET`

b. `MEMORY_TARGET`

c. `MEMORY_MAX_TARGET`

d. `JAVA_POOL_SIZE`

Q. 15. Which of the following caches in the SGA is defined by a static parameter and cannot be changed dynamically while the database is in an open state?

a. The shared pool

b. The buffer cache

c. The larger pool

d. The log buffer

11

Understanding Backup and Recovery Concepts

Most of the daily life of a DBA is spent doing the types of tasks we've covered so far. Creating databases, allocating storage, building tables, and managing performance are all important daily considerations for a real-world DBA. Unfortunately, sometimes more serious problems arise. Hard drives fail, users drop important tables, and databases become corrupt. In these situations, all eyes fall on the DBA to save the day. In today's world, it is assumed that data is always recoverable. The inability to recover data is one of the few mistakes a DBA can make that can cost them their job. That's why, in this book, we spend three full chapters on the subject—to give it the attention it deserves. In this chapter, we'll outline the concepts and terminology in the area of backup and recovery. We'll look at the underlying architecture that makes Oracle recoverable. We'll examine the types of failures that occur in databases and what can be done about each, including a look at Oracle's Data Recovery Advisor. In the subsequent two chapters, we'll go hands-on with running backups and recoveries.

In this chapter, we shall:

- Understand Oracle's redo-based architecture
- Use the Flash Recovery Area
- Understand instance recovery
- Explain the types of failure that can occur within the database
- Explore the Data Recovery Advisor

Understanding the redo-based architecture

Recoverable databases don't happen by accident. They start with an RDBMS architecture that places a high degree of emphasis on recoverability. The goal of the Oracle RDBMS is to have a database that is completely recoverable—right up until the last committed transaction. A significant portion of the Oracle architecture exists specifically for the purpose of recoverability. We've mentioned a little already about Oracle's change-based redo architecture. Let's review this in more detail.

As changes accrue in the database, they are written to the redo log buffer. Then, periodically, the log buffer is written out to the redo logfiles. In *Chapter 4, Examining the Oracle Architecture*, we illustrated this. One of the three triggers for the log buffer to be flushed to the redo logs is when a COMMIT occurs. Thus every transaction has a "guaranteed write" to the redo logs. This is the cornerstone of why Oracle is recoverable until the last transaction. Generally speaking, even if the database's host server was to lose power in the middle of a transaction, and thus lose the contents of the log buffer in memory, the only transactions that would be lost are those that were uncommitted. This redo architecture exists solely to support complete database recovery up to the last transaction.

Because of the importance of redo logfiles (sometimes referred to as **online redo logs**), a DBA needs to be familiar with how to manage them. Redo logs are designated in **redo log groups** and each individual file within a group is called a **redo log member**. When a redo log group becomes full, it switches to the next group in the sequence. This sequence number continues to increase as log switches occur. The redo log group that is currently being written to is known as the **current log group**. The current log group will have the most recent log sequence number, known as the **current log sequence**.

Because of the critical nature of redo logs, Oracle recommends that redo logs be multiplexed. **Multiplexing redo logs** refers to the act of assigning more than one member to each redo log group. These members are simply copies of each other. In a multiplexed redo log configuration, if a redo log member is corrupted or compromised in some way, another member still exists with the redo information necessary for recovery. A multiplexed configuration can be taken even further to actually place different log members on different physical disk drives. In this way, if the drive containing one set of members fails, the other identical members still exist on an unaffected drive. Even if we do not physically separate logfile members on separate disks, it is still a very good practice, as it protects our database against file-level corruption. Our database is currently not multiplexed, so let's change that.

Adding redo log members

To begin with, we'll look at two very important data dictionary views—`v$log` and `v$logfile`.

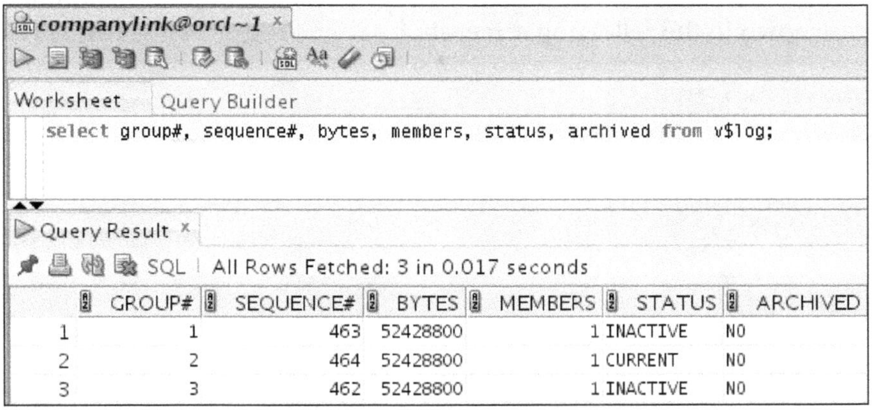
companylink@orcl~1
Worksheet
Query Builder
select group#, sequence#, bytes, members, status, archived from v$log;
Query Result
SQL
All Rows Fetched: 3 in 0.017 seconds
GROUP# SEQUENCE# BYTES MEMBERS STATUS ARCHIVED
1 1 463 52428800 1 INACTIVE NO
2 2 464 52428800 1 CURRENT NO
3 3 462 52428800 1 INACTIVE NO

Our first redo log-related view, `v$log`, gives us a look at redo logs from a group perspective. It indicates that we have three log groups, that each one is 52428800 bytes in size, and has one member each. The **STATUS** column shows that, here, group **2** is the current log group; that is to say, redo data is currently being written to the member in group **2**. The data you see regarding sequence numbers and status may be slightly different. Let's take a look at our next view:

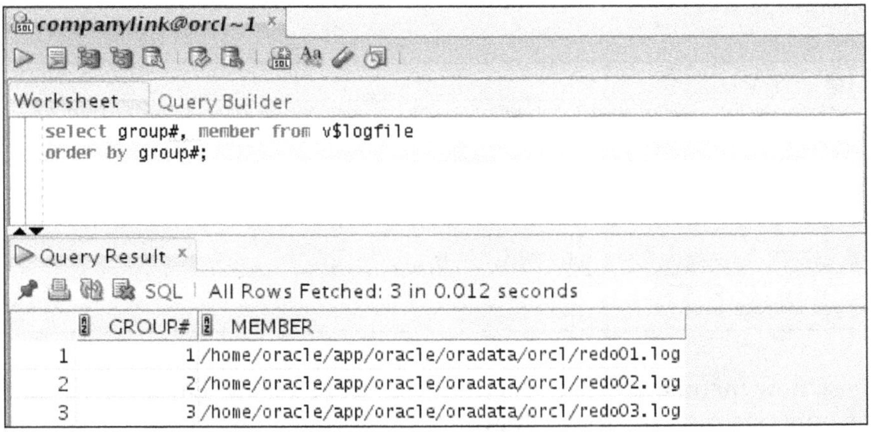
companylink@orcl~1
Worksheet
Query Builder
select group#, member from v$logfile
order by group#;
Query Result
SQL
All Rows Fetched: 3 in 0.012 seconds
GROUP# MEMBER
1 1 /home/oracle/app/oracle/oradata/orcl/redo01.log
2 2 /home/oracle/app/oracle/oradata/orcl/redo02.log
3 3 /home/oracle/app/oracle/oradata/orcl/redo03.log

The `v$logfile` view shows us redo log information from a logfile perspective. This view lists each member of a group and the directory where they are located in the filesystem. The `v$log` view indicated that we only have one member per group, and we can confirm that fact in `v$logfile` as well. In order to multiplex these groups, we'll need to add a logfile member to each group. We'll add the first one as shown in the following screenshot:

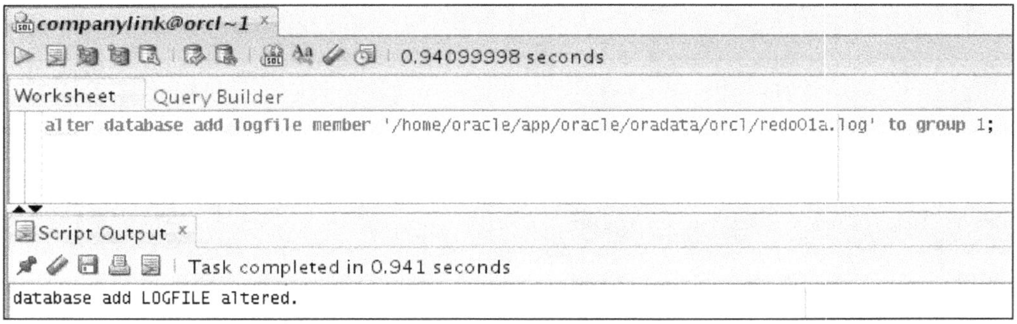
companylink@orcl~1
0.94099998 seconds
Worksheet
Query Builder
alter database add logfile member '/home/oracle/app/oracle/oradata/orcl/redo01a.log' to group 1;
Script Output
Task completed in 0.941 seconds
database add LOGFILE altered.

We use the `alter database add logfile member … to group` syntax to add a member to an existing group. We specify the full path and filename for our new log member and the group to which we're adding it. Obviously, we've given the new member a distinct name, `redo01a.log`, as members within the same directory cannot have the same filename. We'll complete our multiplexing by adding members to the other two groups as well.

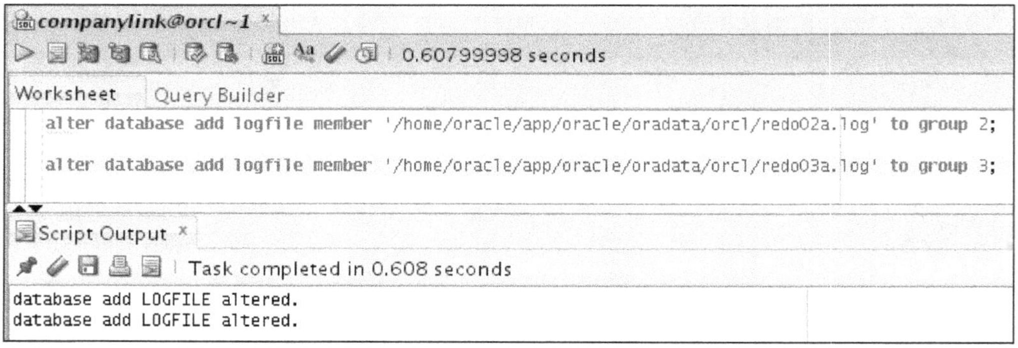
companylink@orcl~1
0.60799998 seconds
Worksheet
Query Builder
alter database add logfile member '/home/oracle/app/oracle/oradata/orcl/redo02a.log' to group 2;
alter database add logfile member '/home/oracle/app/oracle/oradata/orcl/redo03a.log' to group 3;
Script Output
Task completed in 0.608 seconds
database add LOGFILE altered.
database add LOGFILE altered.

To see these new members, we'll query the `v$logfile` view. Earlier, we noted that there was only one member for each group. Our results now are different.

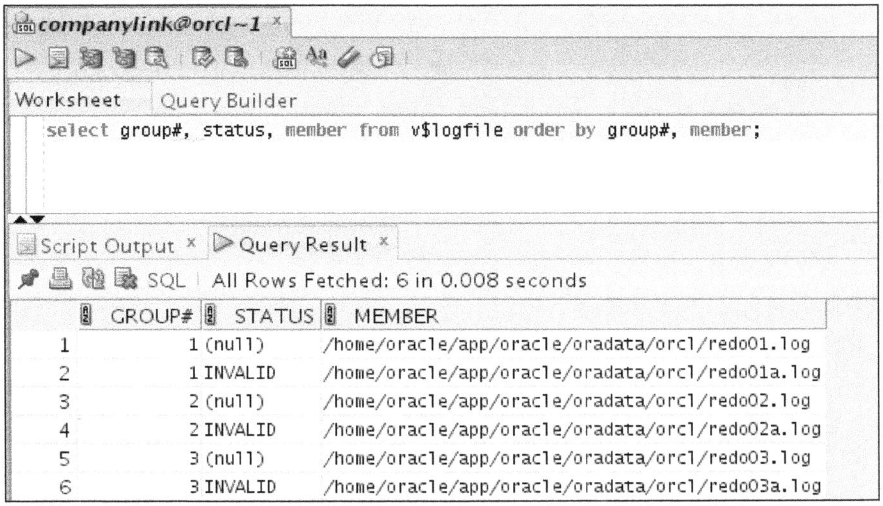
companylink@orcl~1
Worksheet
Query Builder
select group#, status, member from v$logfile order by group#, member;
Script Output
Query Result
SQL
All Rows Fetched: 6 in 0.008 seconds
GROUP#
STATUS
MEMBER
1 1 (null) /home/oracle/app/oracle/oradata/orcl/redo01.log
2 1 INVALID /home/oracle/app/oracle/oradata/orcl/redo01a.log
3 2 (null) /home/oracle/app/oracle/oradata/orcl/redo02.log
4 2 INVALID /home/oracle/app/oracle/oradata/orcl/redo02a.log
5 3 (null) /home/oracle/app/oracle/oradata/orcl/redo03.log
6 3 INVALID /home/oracle/app/oracle/oradata/orcl/redo03a.log

We can see our new members, so we've succeeded in multiplexing our redo log groups. However, we may be concerned to see their status as **INVALID**. If we recall our earlier definition of a redo log member, we said that members within the same group are exact copies of each other. We have added new members, but they've never been written to. We might say that these newly added members are essentially empty files that are formatted as redo logs. As such, they cannot be used for recovery. To remove the **INVALID** status, we'll need to manually force a log switch—the act of switching from one logfile group to another. This will effectively initialize the group to which we switch, as well as both of its members. We have three groups, so we'll need to make three log switches using the `alter system switch logfile` command.

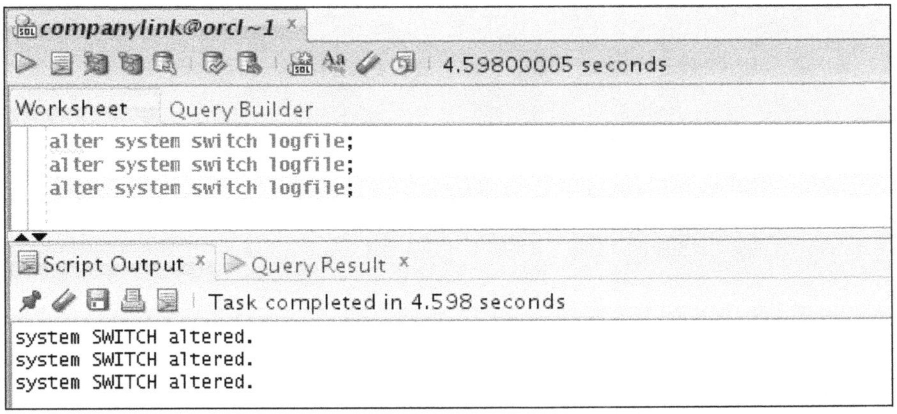
companylink@orcl~1
4.59800005 seconds
Worksheet
Query Builder
alter system switch logfile;
alter system switch logfile;
alter system switch logfile;
Script Output
Query Result
Task completed in 4.598 seconds
system SWITCH altered.
system SWITCH altered.
system SWITCH altered.

Now, if we view `v$logfile` again, we see results without the status of **INVALID**:

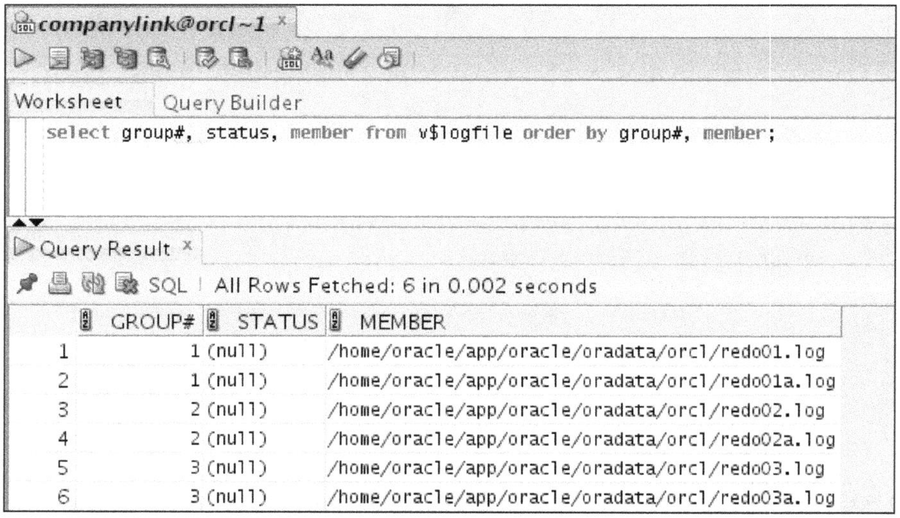
companylink@orcl~1
Worksheet
Query Builder
select group#, status, member from v$logfile order by group#, member;
Query Result
SQL
All Rows Fetched: 6 in 0.002 seconds
GROUP#
STATUS
MEMBER
1 1 (null) /home/oracle/app/oracle/oradata/orcl/redo01.log
2 1 (null) /home/oracle/app/oracle/oradata/orcl/redo01a.log
3 2 (null) /home/oracle/app/oracle/oradata/orcl/redo02.log
4 2 (null) /home/oracle/app/oracle/oradata/orcl/redo02a.log
5 3 (null) /home/oracle/app/oracle/oradata/orcl/redo03.log
6 3 (null) /home/oracle/app/oracle/oradata/orcl/redo03a.log

Adding a redo log group

As we learn about redo logs, we may ask the question, "How many redo log groups should a database have?" There is no exact answer to this question; it usually depends on several factors, including the size and activity of the database, the size of the redo logs themselves, and requirements for recoverability. However, it is reasonable that, in some circumstances, we may need more log groups than the three that were created by default with our DBCA installation. We can add a fourth redo log group as shown in the following screenshot:

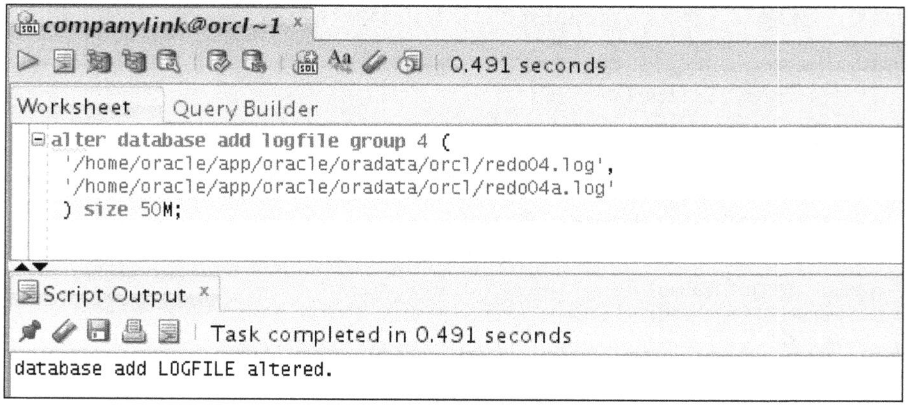
companylink@orcl~1
0.491 seconds
Worksheet
Query Builder
alter database add logfile group 4 (
'/home/oracle/app/oracle/oradata/orcl/redo04.log',
'/home/oracle/app/oracle/oradata/orcl/redo04a.log'
) size 50M;
Script Output
Task completed in 0.491 seconds
database add LOGFILE altered.

We've used the `alter database add logfile group` syntax to add our fourth redo log group. Note that, although not syntactically necessary, we've chosen to continue using our multiplexing scheme by specifying two members in our group. We've added the fourth group, but if we examine the `v$log` view, we'll see that we have a similar problem to the one we encountered when we added new members.

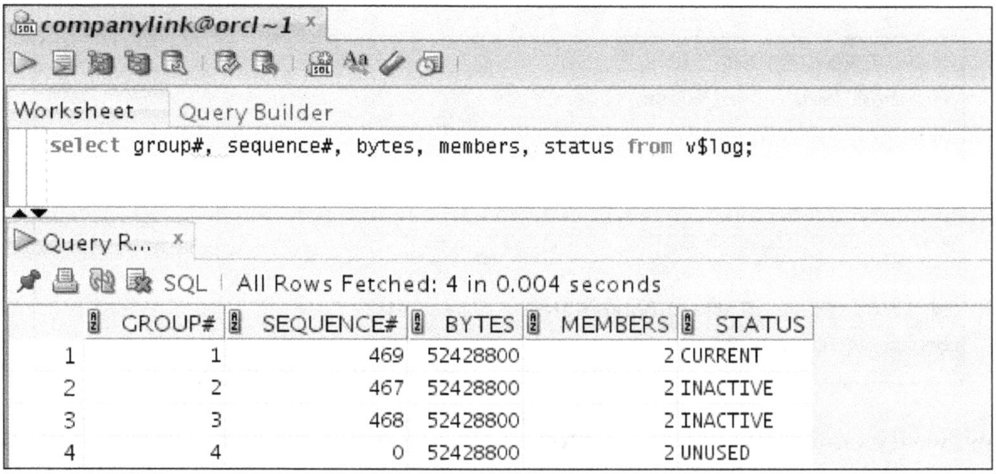
companylink@orcl~1
Worksheet
Query Builder
select group#, sequence#, bytes, members, status from v$log;
Query R...
SQL
All Rows Fetched: 4 in 0.004 seconds
GROUP# SEQUENCE# BYTES MEMBERS STATUS
1 1 469 52428800 2 CURRENT
2 2 467 52428800 2 INACTIVE
3 3 468 52428800 2 INACTIVE
4 4 0 52428800 2 UNUSED

We can see our new group **4**, and note that it is sized as 5243880 bytes, or 50 MB as the other groups are. The **MEMBERS** column shows that each group has two members. However, our **STATUS** shows group **4** as **UNUSED**. This is because our new group has not yet become the current log group, and is essentially empty. We need to actually switch to the new group to remove the **UNUSED** status. Our current group (in this example) is group number **1**. Therefore, we might assume that we must complete three manual log switches in order to switch to group number **4**. This is not always the case.

The group number does not always indicate the actual switching order of the groups. A much better indicator is the **SEQUENCE#** column. It indicates that group numbers **2** and **3** have sequence numbers of **467** and **468**, respectively. It is group number **1** that has the most recent sequence number. Therefore, switching to group number **4** will only require one manual log switch. Let's try this. First, we'll manually force a log switch once.

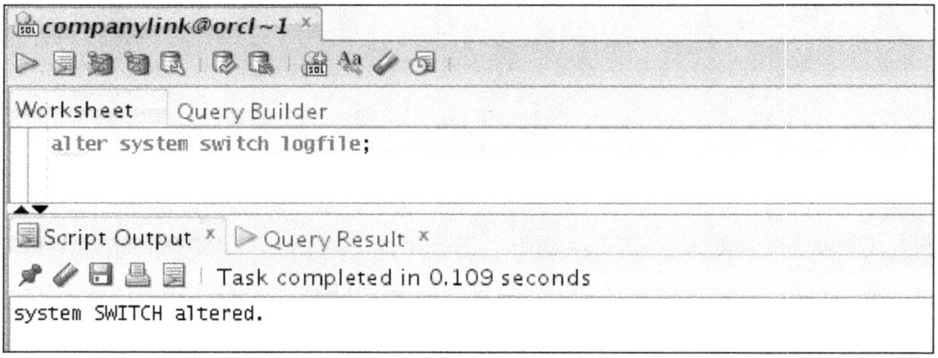
companylink@orcl~1
Worksheet
Query Builder
alter system switch logfile;
Script Output
Query Result
Task completed in 0.109 seconds
system SWITCH altered.

Now, we'll examine the `v$log` view to see if group number **4** is the current group, as we predict.

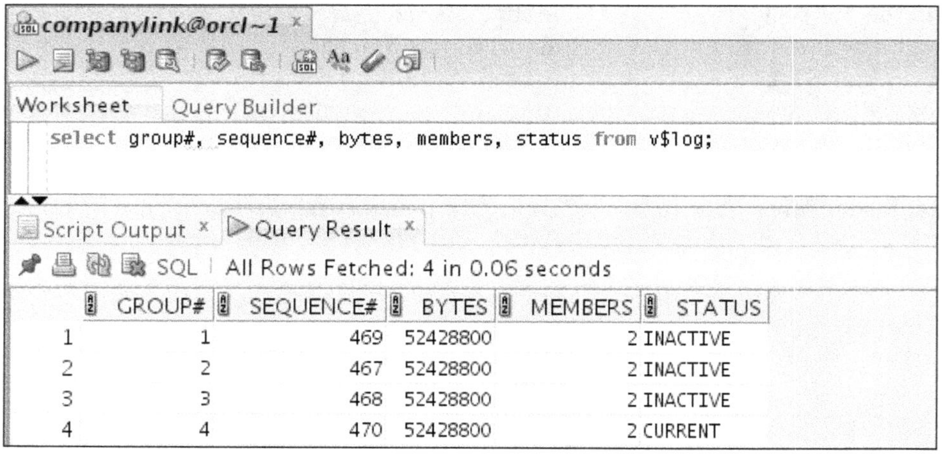
companylink@orcl~1
Worksheet
Query Builder
select group#, sequence#, bytes, members, status from v$log;
Script Output
Query Result
SQL
All Rows Fetched: 4 in 0.06 seconds
GROUP#
SEQUENCE#
BYTES
MEMBERS
STATUS
1 1 469 52428800 2 INACTIVE
2 2 467 52428800 2 INACTIVE
3 3 468 52428800 2 INACTIVE
4 4 470 52428800 2 CURRENT

As predicted, our current logfile group is number **4**, with a sequence number of **470**. Again, note that your own results will likely have different numbers, but the principle is the same.

Exploring ARCHIVELOG mode

Now that we've established *how* the redo architecture works, it's worth asking an important question. If the redo logs continually switch from group to group, they eventually overwrite each other. If the redo logs contain a sequential history of all database changes, what good are redo logs during recovery? If a redo log is overwritten, all of the changes recorded within it are lost. This is a crucial point to understand. In the configuration we've just described, we cannot apply the changes that have been written to the overwritten redo logs. In a practical situation, this would mean that, during a recovery, we could recover the data in the last backup, but none of the changes thereafter. In the beginning of this chapter, we mentioned that Oracle provided a recoverable architecture, even up to the point of the last transaction. Why don't we see that here?

The missing piece to this puzzle lies in the fact that an Oracle database can operate in two very different recoverability modes. The mode we've just described is known as **NOARCHIVELOG** mode. NOARCHIVELOG mode severely limits the recovery options available to a DBA. We cannot run "hot" backups while the database is available; we must shut down the database first. More importantly, we can only recover a database in NOARCHIVELOG mode up to the completion of the last backup. In NOARCHIVELOG mode, if we back up our database weekly on Sunday night and we have a failure, resulting in data loss on the following Friday, none of the database changes since the backup finished can be applied. Clearly, we need a better recoverability option than this.

The second, highly recommended mode in which the database can function is called ARCHIVELOG mode. In ARCHIVELOG mode, a secondary optional background process, the **ARCn** process, writes out the contents of each redo log group to a static file that is *not* overwritten. These static files are called **archived redo logs** or sometimes **offline redo logs**. ARCHIVELOG mode provides us with a number of advantages in the area of database backup and recovery. First and foremost, it provides us with the ability to run "hot backups"—backups of the database while the database is still open and available for use. ARCHIVELOG mode is crucial to a fully-recoverable backup plan, but there is a point we must consider—it requires a location on disk to store archived logs. If this location fills up to the point that no more archived logs can be written, the database will hang and no more changes will be allowed, effectively stopping our database. This shouldn't be unexpected. When we instruct the database to operate in ARCHIVELOG mode, we're saying that every change must be written out to a static file, the **archived log**. When the database can no longer guarantee that functionality, it hangs until the situation is resolved. That's why it is crucial that the destination directory for the archived logs be defined and maintained, clearing old logs when they are no longer needed.

The location of the archived logfiles is defined by the `log_archive_dest_1` parameter, as seen in the following screenshot:

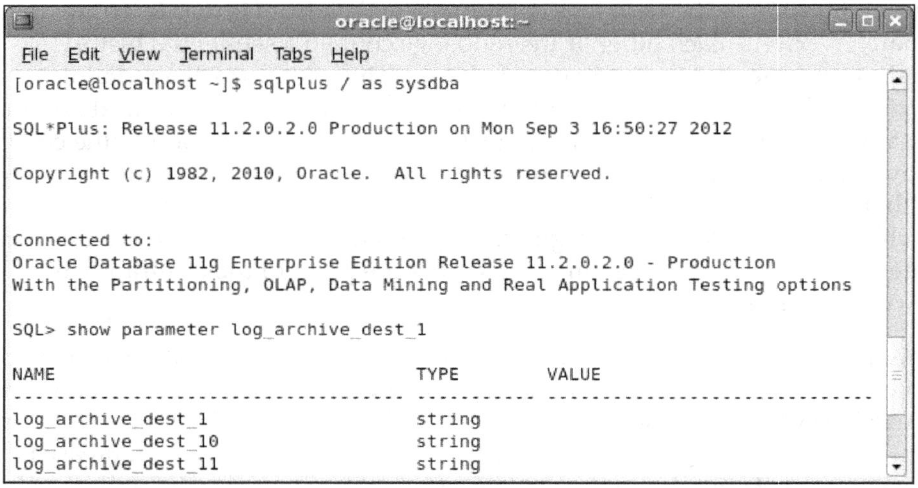
oracle@localhost:~
File Edit View Terminal Tabs Help
[oracle@localhost ~]$ sqlplus / as sysdba
SQL*Plus: Release 11.2.0.2.0 Production on Mon Sep 3 16:50:27 2012
Copyright (c) 1982, 2010, Oracle. All rights reserved.
Connected to:
Oracle Database 11g Enterprise Edition Release 11.2.0.2.0 - Production
With the Partitioning, OLAP, Data Mining and Real Application Testing options
SQL> show parameter log_archive_dest_1
NAME TYPE VALUE
log_archive_dest_1 string
log_archive_dest_10 string
log_archive_dest_11 string

As we can see, there are a number of other log destinations, up to 31 in fact, that can be defined. When running in ARCHIVELOG mode, it is sometimes required to keep multiple copies of the archived logs. This serves as an added protection against media failures, such as file corruption and the loss of a disk. As we can see, `log_archive_dest_1` is undefined at this point. In this situation, any archived logs would be written to the default location within the Oracle Home directory. However, since we're not in ARCHIVELOG mode at this point, we'll have the opportunity to change that.

The real-world DBA

DBAs sometimes face misconceptions about ARCHIVELOG mode, namely that it can negatively impact performance. This might have been a valid point ten years ago, but improvements in both the Oracle kernel and the speed of disk subsystems have improved the archiving process to a point where performance impacts are generally negligible. The benefits of ARCHIVELOG mode greatly outweigh these misconceptions—it is almost always the best choice. That being said, there might be certain scenarios where it is not possible to run in ARCHIVELOG mode, such as situations where disk space is limited or where a system generates so many changes that it is impossible to manage the archive space. On the whole, these situations are rare. ARCHIVELOG mode offers a tremendous number of advantages for recoverability.

Converting to an ARCHIVELOG mode

Converting to an ARCHIVELOG mode is a relatively simple process, but it does require a restart of the database. Here, we'll convert our database in NOARCHIVELOG mode to ARCHIVELOG mode. In the interest of simplicity, we'll leave the `log_archive_dest_1` parameter unset for now and use the default location. Later in the chapter, we'll move it to the Flash Recovery Area. Let's first determine our logging status using the `archive log list` command.

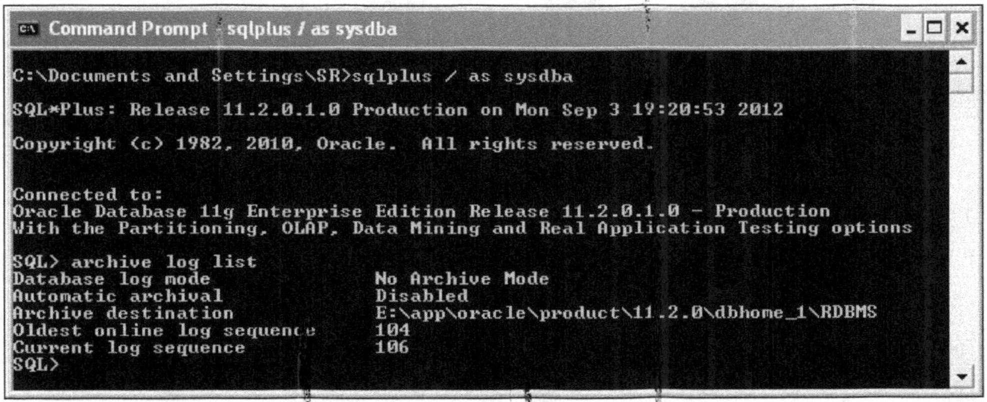
Command Prompt - sqlplus / as sysdba
C:\Documents and Settings\SR>sqlplus / as sysdba
SQL*Plus: Release 11.2.0.1.0 Production on Mon Sep 3 19:20:53 2012
Copyright (c) 1982, 2010, Oracle. All rights reserved.
Connected to:
Oracle Database 11g Enterprise Edition Release 11.2.0.1.0 - Production
With the Partitioning, OLAP, Data Mining and Real Application Testing options
SQL> archive log list
Database log mode No Archive Mode
Automatic archival Disabled
Archive destination E:\app\oracle\product\11.2.0\dbhome_1\RDBMS
Oldest online log sequence 104
Current log sequence 106
SQL>

As we can see, our current log mode is **No Archive Mode** and **Automatic archival** is set to **Disabled**. We need to change this. First, we'll shut down the database and then restart it in the MOUNT state.

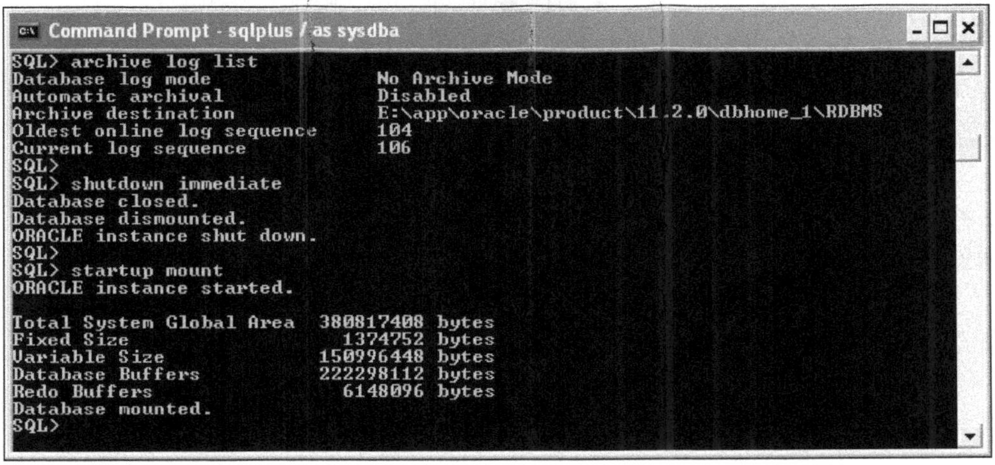
Command Prompt - sqlplus / as sysdba
SQL> archive log list
Database log mode No Archive Mode
Automatic archival Disabled
Archive destination E:\app\oracle\product\11.2.0\dbhome_1\RDBMS
Oldest online log sequence 104
Current log sequence 106
SQL>
SQL> shutdown immediate
Database closed.
Database dismounted.
ORACLE instance shut down.
SQL>
SQL> startup mount
ORACLE instance started.
Total System Global Area 380817408 bytes
Fixed Size 1374752 bytes
Variable Size 150996448 bytes
Database Buffers 222298112 bytes
Redo Buffers 6148096 bytes
Database mounted.
SQL>

Next we use the `alter database archivelog` command to enable archiving and then return the database to an open state.

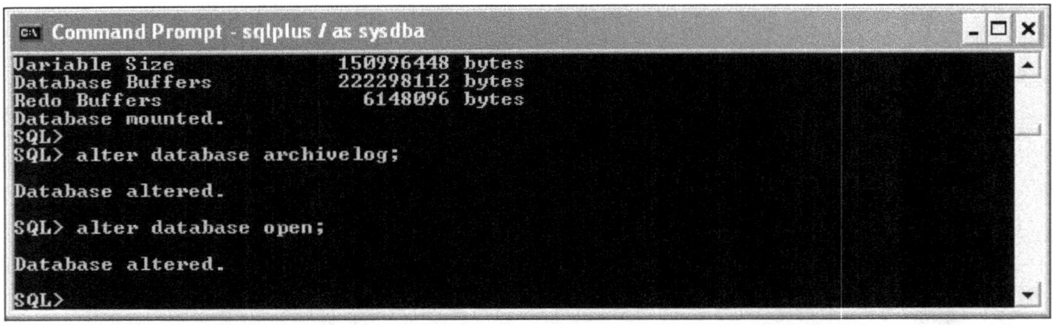
Command Prompt - sqlplus / as sysdba
Variable Size 150996448 bytes
Database Buffers 222298112 bytes
Redo Buffers 6148096 bytes
Database mounted.
SQL>
SQL> alter database archivelog;
Database altered.
SQL> alter database open;
Database altered.
SQL>

Now we'll execute our `archive log list` command again to verify that our log mode has changed. Since a log switch has not occurred, we'll also do a manual log switch. This will write out our archived logfile to the default location.

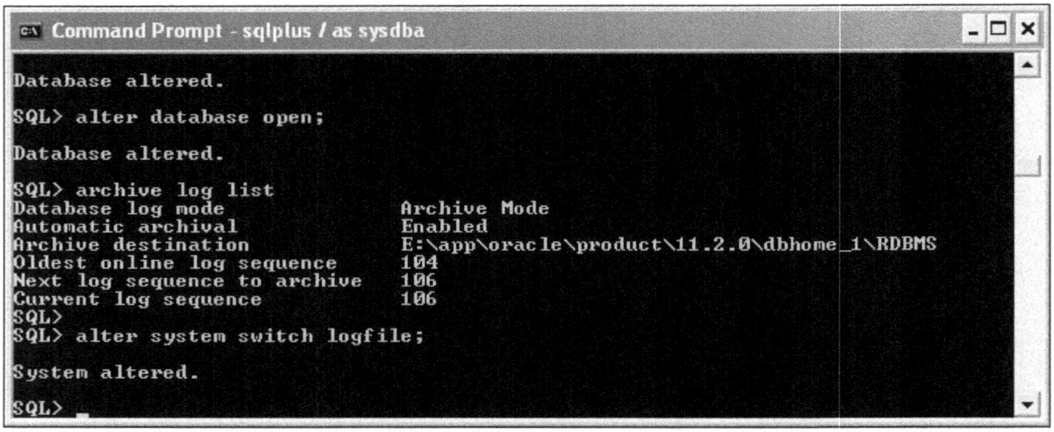
Command Prompt - sqlplus / as sysdba
Database altered.
SQL> alter database open;
Database altered.
SQL> archive log list
Database log mode Archive Mode
Automatic archival Enabled
Archive destination E:\app\oracle\product\11.2.0\dbhome_1\RDBMS
Oldest online log sequence 104
Next log sequence to archive 106
Current log sequence 106
SQL>
SQL> alter system switch logfile;
System altered.
SQL>

If we navigate to the default directory location (on Windows, in this case), we will be able to see the file for ourselves. The exact name of the file will differ from system to system.

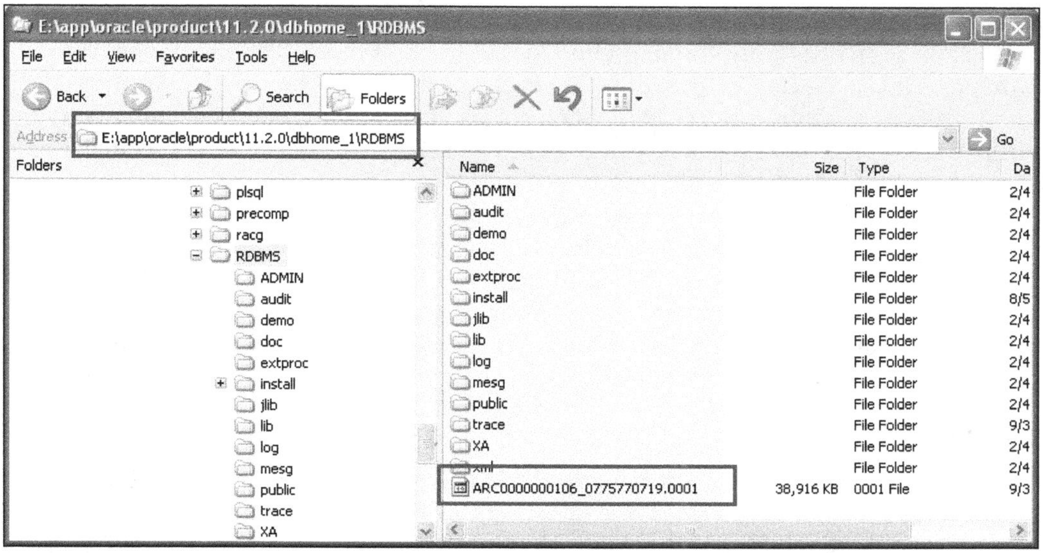
E:\app\oracle\product\11.2.0\dbhome_1\RDBMS
File Edit View Favorites Tools Help
Back
Search
Folders
Address
E:\app\oracle\product\11.2.0\dbhome_1\RDBMS
Go
Folders
plsql
precomp
racg
RDBMS
ADMIN
audit
demo
doc
extproc
install
jlib
lib
log
mesg
public
trace
XA
Name
Size
Type
ARC0000000106_0775770719.0001
38,916 KB
0001 File
File Folder

Understanding Flash Recovery Area

One of the most important disk areas for a recoverable database is the area used to store backups. If this area fails, the recoverability of the database is lost, even though temporarily, until another backup can be run. In earlier versions of Oracle, there was no specific backup area defined in the configuration of the database—any directory or disk area could be used. While we can still use any area we wish, Oracle has simplified backup management by allowing us to explicitly define a single destination for our backups—the Flash Recovery Area.

Configuring the Flash Recovery Area

The **Flash Recovery Area** (**FRA**) is a location we specify to hold all files related to recovery. Unless otherwise directed, the FRA holds the following:

- Backup files created using Oracle's backup tool, Recovery Manager
- Archived logfiles
- Database flashback logs

Thus, the FRA consolidates the files needed for recovery into one place, lessening the burden of maintaining them or even losing track of them. The FRA even manages files to the degree that obsolete backups and flashback logs are removed when needed, to clear space for the FRA. We use two initialization parameters to define the scope of the FRA. The `db_recovery_file_dest` parameter specifies the location of the FRA and simply points to a directory. The `db_recovery_file_dest_size` parameter defines the maximum size of the FRA. Once that limit is reached, Oracle will no longer write backups or archivelogs to that destination. As such, it's important to have an understanding of how much space is used for backups and archivelogs. Let's activate the FRA by defining these parameters now. But first, we need to create a directory for the FRA. We do so by using the following command from the Windows command line:

```
mkdir e:\app\oracle\flash_recovery_area
```

This example creates the directory from the Windows command line, but Linux users can use similar commands. Next, from SQL*Plus, we'll define two parameters needed to activate the FRA. It's important to set these parameters in the correct order —`db_recovery_file_dest_size` must be set first.

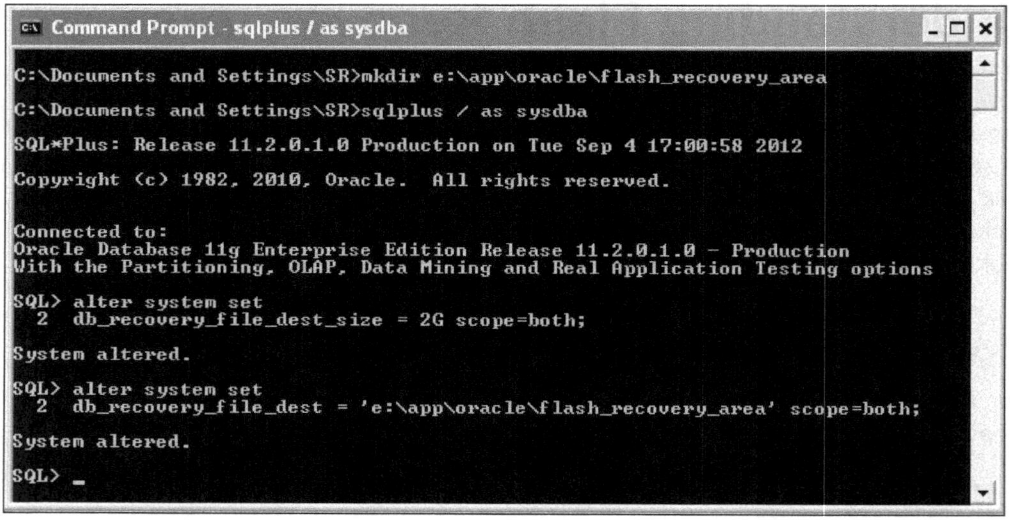
Command Prompt - sqlplus / as sysdba
C:\Documents and Settings\SR>mkdir e:\app\oracle\flash_recovery_area
C:\Documents and Settings\SR>sqlplus / as sysdba
SQL*Plus: Release 11.2.0.1.0 Production on Tue Sep 4 17:00:58 2012
Copyright (c) 1982, 2010, Oracle. All rights reserved.
Connected to:
Oracle Database 11g Enterprise Edition Release 11.2.0.1.0 - Production
With the Partitioning, OLAP, Data Mining and Real Application Testing options
SQL> alter system set
2 db_recovery_file_dest_size = 2G scope=both;
System altered.
SQL> alter system set
2 db_recovery_file_dest = 'e:\app\oracle\flash_recovery_area' scope=both;
System altered.
SQL> _

We've set our new FRA parameters to reflect our new `flash_recovery_area` directory with a maximum size of `2G`. Now, unless otherwise specified, Recovery Manager backup files (covered in the next chapter) will be written to the FRA, as well as database flashback logs. Flashback logs are used with some of Oracle's advanced flashback features. However, there is one type of file that is currently not being written to the FRA in our database. When we defined ARCHIVELOG mode, we specified a directory that is not within the FRA. Let's correct that now.

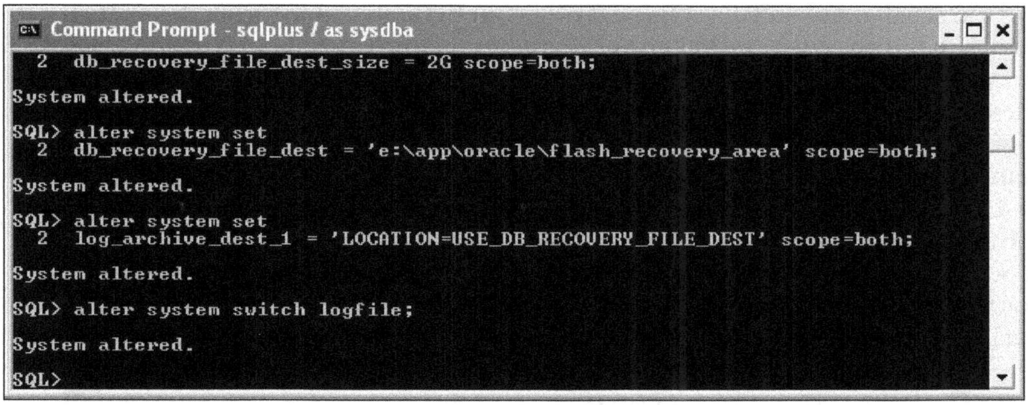
Command Prompt - sqlplus / as sysdba
2 db_recovery_file_dest_size = 2G scope=both;
System altered.
SQL> alter system set
2 db_recovery_file_dest = 'e:\app\oracle\flash_recovery_area' scope=both;
System altered.
SQL> alter system set
2 log_archive_dest_1 = 'LOCATION=USE_DB_RECOVERY_FILE_DEST' scope=both;
System altered.
SQL> alter system switch logfile;
System altered.
SQL>

By assigning the keyword, `USE_DB_RECOVERY_FILE_DEST`, to the `log_archive_dest_1` parameter, our archived log destination is inherited from the parameters governing the FRA. Now, any future archived logs will be written to the FRA. To demonstrate this, we've also done a manual log switch. Now we can go to the location of the FRA and see this for ourselves.

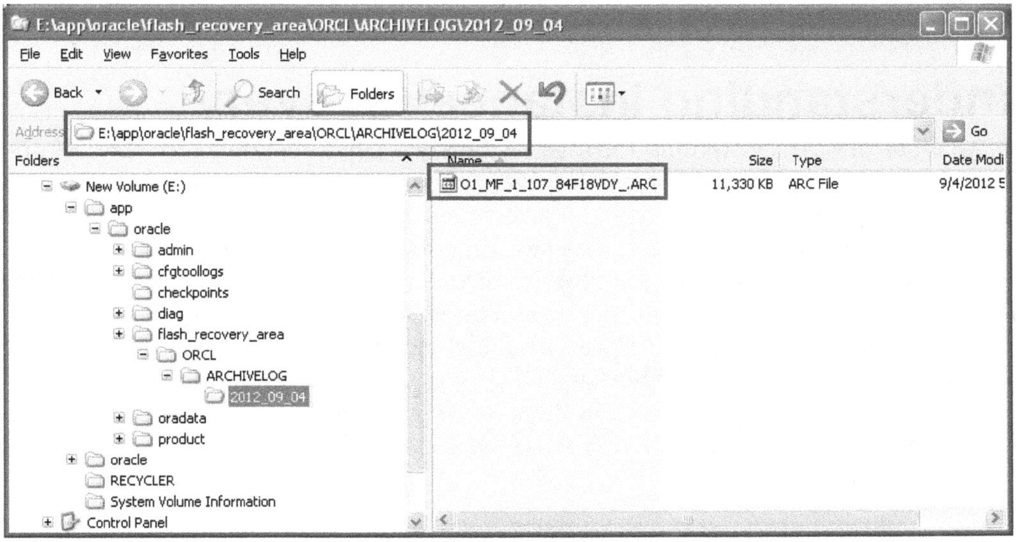
E:\app\oracle\flash_recovery_area\ORCL\ARCHIVELOG\2012_09_04
File Edit View Favorites Tools Help
Back Search Folders
Address E:\app\oracle\flash_recovery_area\ORCL\ARCHIVELOG\2012_09_04
Go
Folders
Name Size Type Date Modi
O1_MF_1_107_84F18VDY_.ARC 11,330 KB ARC File 9/4/2012
New Volume (E:)
app
oracle
admin
cfgtoollogs
checkpoints
diag
flash_recovery_area
ORCL
ARCHIVELOG
2012_09_04
oradata
product
oracle
RECYCLER
System Volume Information
Control Panel

We can see that not only has Oracle written out the archived log from the manual switch, but it has even created an entire directory structure to hold it. Below the FRA directory, we now have an **ORCL** directory to specify the database, an **ARCHIVELOG** directory to specify the type of file, and a directory named after the date the archived logfile was written. The FRA organizes different types of files this way, providing a standardized structure for the entire backup area. Note that if the FRA is activated and the value of `log_archive_dest_1` is null, Oracle will use the FRA directory as the default location for the archivelog destination. Now that we're in ARCHIVELOG mode, any backups we had done previously are no longer reliable as a recovery source. Thus after configuring ARCHIVELOG mode, a best practice is to run a backup as soon as possible.

> **The real-world DBA**
>
> Although using the Flash Recovery Area provides an excellent way to manage the files needed for recovery, it does tend to put "all the eggs in one basket." Because all of the files needed for recovery are kept there, it is crucial that this area is protected and, where possible, has a secondary backup of its own. This can include using disk storage with built-in redundancy and backups of the FRA to tape or secondary disk storage.

Understanding instance recovery

Not all types of recovery require the intervention of a DBA. **Instance recovery** occurs when some type of instance-terminating event occurs, such as a hard crash of the host server, a `shutdown abort`, or certain Oracle errors. When an instance terminates, the database is in an inconsistent state. The next time the database is started, the SMON process uses the contents of the redo logs to reconstruct the state of the database before the crash and rolls back uncommitted transactions. All database changes after the last recorded checkpoint are applied to datafiles. Instance recovery is completely automatic and doesn't require the intervention of a DBA. We can, however, monitor it when it occurs, from the alert log, as shown in the following screenshot. As a reminder, to view the alert log, we can invoke the `adrci` from the command line and choose the alert log for the database.

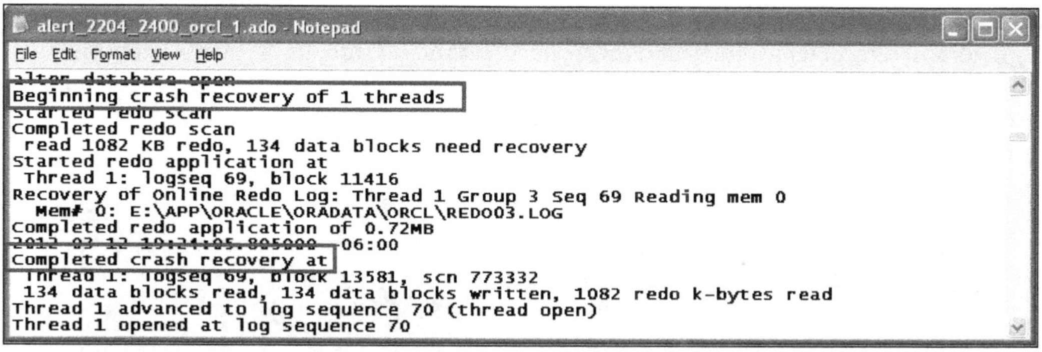
alert_2204_2400_orcl_1.ado - Notepad
File Edit Format View Help
alter database open
Beginning crash recovery of 1 threads
Started redo scan
Completed redo scan
read 1082 KB redo, 134 data blocks need recovery
Started redo application at
Thread 1: logseq 69, block 11416
Recovery of Online Redo Log: Thread 1 Group 3 Seq 69 Reading mem 0
Mem# 0: E:\APP\ORACLE\ORADATA\ORCL\REDO03.LOG
Completed redo application of 0.72MB
-06:00
Completed crash recovery at
13581, scn 773332
134 data blocks read, 134 data blocks written, 1082 redo k-bytes read
Thread 1 advanced to log sequence 70 (thread open)
Thread 1 opened at log sequence 70

We know that instance recovery has occurred when we see the phrase, **Beginning crash recovery of 1 threads**, in the alert log. Redo is applied and the message **Completed crash recovery** is shown.

Because instance recovery occurs without an action on the part of the DBA, it is important to understand how to control it. Instance recovery generally occurs in a relatively short period of time—in smaller databases, it is almost negligible. In larger databases, however, it can take long enough to impact database availability. In some organizations, service-level agreements may even stipulate the amount of time a database can remain down after a crash. This recovery time is referred to as **Mean Time To Recover** (**MTTR**). In these situations, the length of time used by SMON for instance recovery may impact business concerns. Thus Oracle allows us to do a certain amount of tuning with instance recovery. In past versions, this involved the configuration of several different parameters. In newer versions, we only need to configure one—`fast_start_mttr_target`. The `fast_start_mttr_target` parameter is used to specify the target amount of time in seconds that it takes to complete an instance recovery. While we may think that setting this value to a low amount is always best, this isn't necessarily the case. The frequency of database checkpoints affects instance recovery. Thus if `fast_start_mttr_target` is set to a low value, checkpoints must occur more frequently to ensure that MTTR is within our specified boundary; if it is set to a higher value, checkpoints aren't needed as frequently.

Checkpointing is generally a very efficient operation, but in larger databases with high concurrency, it can impact overall performance. Thus, in certain situations, we may need to sacrifice the speed of instance recovery in favor of higher performance. In other situations, the reverse may be true. By default, the `fast_start_mttr_target` parameter is set to zero. We can see this using SQL*Plus.

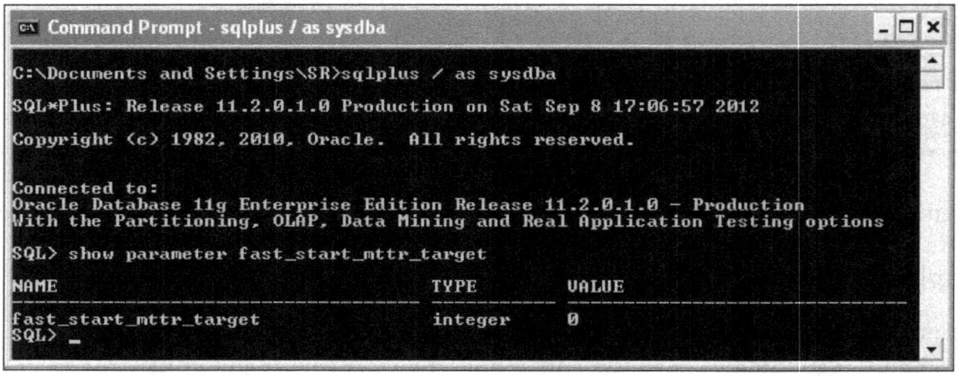
Command Prompt - sqlplus / as sysdba
C:\Documents and Settings\SR>sqlplus / as sysdba
SQL*Plus: Release 11.2.0.1.0 Production on Sat Sep 8 17:06:57 2012
Copyright (c) 1982, 2010, Oracle. All rights reserved.
Connected to:
Oracle Database 11g Enterprise Edition Release 11.2.0.1.0 - Production
With the Partitioning, OLAP, Data Mining and Real Application Testing options
SQL> show parameter fast_start_mttr_target
NAME TYPE VALUE
fast_start_mttr_target integer 0
SQL>

The default value of zero allows for the best performance in terms of checkpointing while sacrificing any particular need for quick instance recovery. Setting the parameter to a non-default value has three effects. Firstly, a target time allowed for instance recovery is established. This target time is only a target—if we set the value to `1`, we cannot guarantee that instance recovery will take only one second. Secondly, a non-zero value enables checkpoint auto-tuning, which surveys the resources on the database host system and uses any available CPU and I/O to checkpoint more frequently in an attempt to mitigate any performance impact. The maximum value we can set for `fast_start_mttr_target` is 3600 seconds. Thirdly, it enables the use of the `v$instance_recovery` data dictionary view, which can be used to estimate the optimal file size of redo logs based on the value we've set for MTTR. Let's set this parameter to a non-zero value:

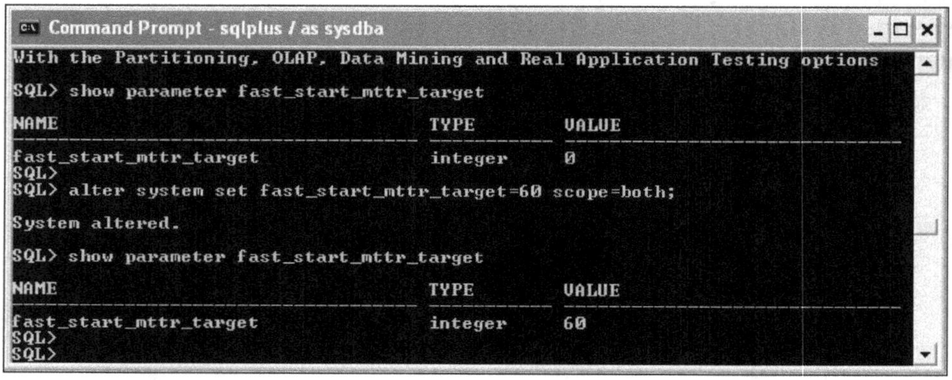
Command Prompt - sqlplus / as sysdba
With the Partitioning, OLAP, Data Mining and Real Application Testing options
SQL> show parameter fast_start_mttr_target
NAME TYPE VALUE
fast_start_mttr_target integer 0
SQL>
SQL> alter system set fast_start_mttr_target=60 scope=both;
System altered.
SQL> show parameter fast_start_mttr_target
NAME TYPE VALUE
fast_start_mttr_target integer 60
SQL>
SQL>

Now, when we examine `v$instance_recovery`, we can gain some specific information about our expected recovery times. This view is not populated with information when `fast_start_mttr_target` is set to zero.

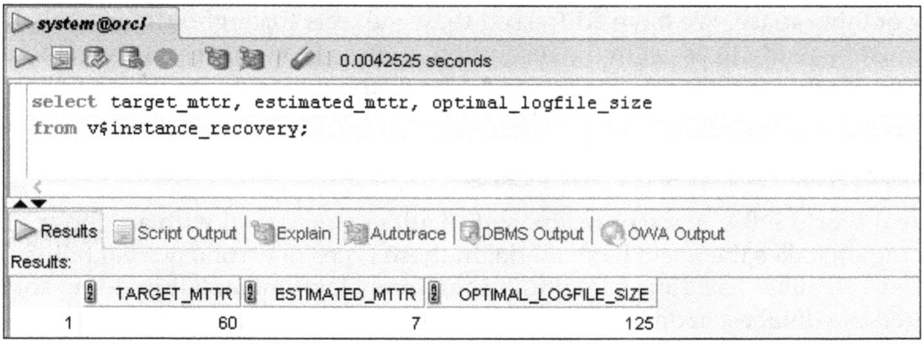
system@orcl
0.0042525 seconds
select target_mttr, estimated_mttr, optimal_logfile_size
from v$instance_recovery;
Results
Script Output
Explain
Autotrace
DBMS Output
OWA Output
Results:
TARGET_MTTR
ESTIMATED_MTTR
OPTIMAL_LOGFILE_SIZE
1
60
7
125

Understanding the categories of database failure

Although instance recovery does not require the intervention of a DBA, many other types of failure do. Not all of these failures are what we might consider true "recovery" scenarios, but the DBA may be called on to address such failures. We examine these categories here and end with those that do require database recovery.

Addressing statement failures

A **statement failure** occurs when a SQL statement, either DML or DDL, fails before its execution has completed. There are many situations that can cause a statement failure. One of the most basic is a DML statement that initiates a transaction, such as an `UPDATE`. If the `UPDATE` fails part of the way through execution, the transaction is automatically rolled back. Statements that cause constraint violations, such as the violation of a primary key to foreign key relationship, are types of statement failures. Datatype mismatch errors fall into this category as well. Another type of statement failure involves logical errors on the part of the application developer, such as locking contention, and failures to commit frequently. Logical errors may be difficult to detect, since they may run to normal completion during one time period, but may lead to problems when other conditions, such as a large number of connected users, occur.

Statement failures can occur when users attempt operations for which they have insufficient privileges, such as attempting to `SELECT` from a table without the proper permissions to view the table. Improper space management can cause statement failures, such as when a transaction attempting a large `INSERT` operation fails due to lack of table space. We have addressed these subjects throughout this book, but a DBA must be ready to assist in the resolution of these types of errors, even though a complete database recovery is not required for them.

Addressing user errors

For a real-world DBA, some of the most difficult errors to deal with are those involving mistakes the users have made. In these types of errors, no real failure has occurred—the user has done something completely legitimate, but in doing so, has damaged the database from a business perspective. Recovering from these types of mistakes presents a challenge, since there are few recovery methods for fixing "something done wrong that was done the right way". The most common type of user error is simply updating or deleting the wrong data in a table. The statement itself does not generate an error, but the consequences can be devastating. Even worse, the error might not even be recognized for a substantial period of time. Using Recovery Manager, a database can be recovered up to a point in the past, but all of the data that was changed after that recovery point will be lost. That leaves management with the difficult decision as to which data is more important. For a DBA, this is not an acceptable course of action.

The most important way to deal with user errors is through the principles of security that we discussed in *Chapter 7, Managing Security*. The principle of least privilege always applies. By minimizing the amount of accidental damage that can be done through restricted privileges, we reduce the risk that these types of errors occur. In short, if a developer accidentally drops a production table, the DBA should ask why a developer would have permission to do that operation at all. Asking those types of questions before an error occurs significantly reduces the risk of them occurring at all. DBAs are not exempt from these types of errors either. Considering the number of privileges that a DBA holds, they can really do the most damage. By accidentally dropping the wrong tablespace or datafile, a DBA can severely damage the database.

Oracle also includes a number of technologies to aid in these situations. Most of these are outside the scope of the DBA I exam, but we list them here for completeness. Recent versions of Oracle have provided flashback technologies to assist DBAs in recovering data lost through user error. We looked at one of these, flashback query, in *Chapter 8, Managing Concurrency*. The family of flashback technologies in Version 11*g* includes the following:

- **Flashback query**: This uses a previous image of table data to display it as it was in a past state
- **Flashback version query**: This displays different versions of row data over a fixed period of time
- **Flashback transaction query**: This retrieves metadata and historical data for a transaction over a specified time interval
- **Flashback drop**: This uses changes in the redo logs to reconstruct a dropped table
- **Flashback table**: This restores a table to a previous state
- **Flashback database**: This uses flashback logs to undo changes to a database, effectively rolling it back in time

All of these features require a certain amount of configuration and administration. However, they can provide a number of options when attempting to recover from user errors.

Addressing user process errors

User process errors are a broad class of failures that tend to involve some sort of system-related error condition. Some of these are dealt with automatically while some might require the intervention of a DBA or a system administrator. If a user abnormally terminates a session, for instance, by exiting a terminal session or rebooting their client machine, the **Process Monitor** (**PMON**) process handles this by polling the server processes allocated to users and rolling back any abnormally terminated sessions. Network failures can fall into the category of user process errors. If the network is down or only transmits intermittently, user processes may be unable to connect or maintain a session and may require the assistance of a system or network administrator. With certain internal Oracle errors, background processes may hang or be forcibly terminated, often generating the infamous ORA-600 error. The best course of action for these types of user process errors is often to open a ticket with Oracle Support.

Addressing media failure

While the DBA may only be tangentially involved in the types of failures we discussed so far, recovery from a media failure will almost certainly revolve around the actions taken by a DBA. A **media failure** occurs when the disks that store database data or the files on them are lost or corrupted in some way. This is the type of failure that most people associate with a true "database recovery". In the scenario where a disk is lost, the first step may not require the DBA at all. Generally, before any recovery actions by the DBA can take place, the disk failure itself must be resolved. This usually involves a system administrator replacing the disk itself.

Understanding RAID

What we term as disk failures can occur on a number of different levels. The majority of enterprise database systems today use some form of RAID technology. **Redundant Array of Inexpensive Disks** (**RAID**) is a storage technology that takes multiple disk drives and presents them as a single logical unit. Since RAID is not an Oracle-specific technology, it is not covered on the Oracle certification exam. However, it is crucial for a real-world DBA to understand as it significantly impacts the actions that must be taken by a DBA to recover data. With RAID, the disks that make up a RAID group are dependent on each other in some way. This dependency allows the disks to operate in union and can provide benefits in both disk performance and disk redundancy. This redundancy is key for our purposes, since properly configured RAID technologies can reduce the amount of manual effort needed by the DBA to recover database data. RAID technologies are defined at different levels and configurations. For simplicity's sake, we will discuss the most common forms of RAID that impact media failures from the database perspective. In addition to the ones we list here, there are a number of vendor-specific RAID levels that are associated with a number of products. Because of their specificity, we will not discuss them here. For these examples, we'll use a scenario on a Windows server where we have four physical hard drives. Out of these four drives, we will configure `C:` for the operating system and Oracle binaries, and `D:` for Oracle database data. This is a fairly simplified scenario, but it does demonstrate the functionality of each RAID level.

RAID 0

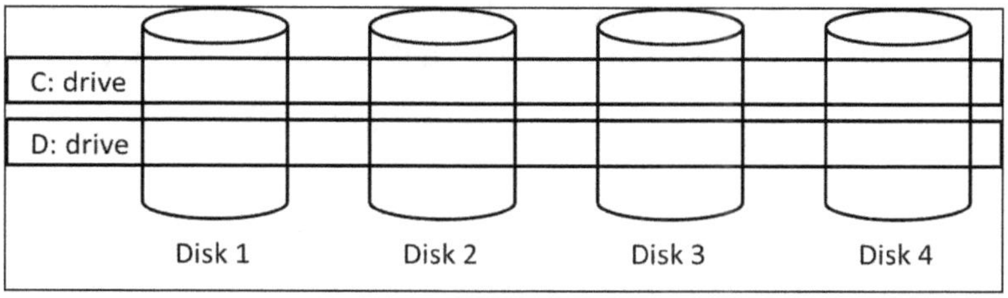
C: drive
D: drive
Disk 1
Disk 2
Disk 3
Disk 4

With **RAID 0**, or **striping**, a logical drive is physically spread across all of the disks in our RAID group. Here, we've striped both our `C:` and `D:` across all four of our physical disks. RAID 0 has a very positive effect on disk I/O performance, since it makes simultaneous use of the read/write heads on each disk to perform I/O. However, it does not provide any kind of redundancy, since the loss of any of the four disks would impact both `C:` and `D:`, and would require disk replacement and full recovery of both logical drives. In short, RAID 0 provides superior performance but no redundancy.

RAID 1

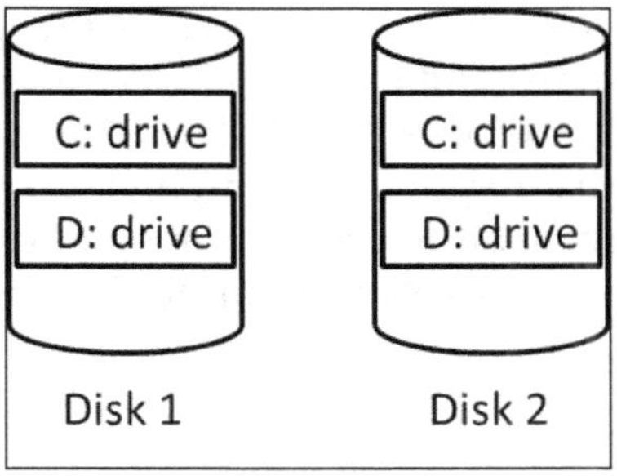
C: drive
D: drive
C: drive
D: drive
Disk 1
Disk 2

RAID 1, or **mirroring**, takes each logical drive, `C:` and `D:` and creates a mirror copy of them on each disk. Thus, both logical drives have complete, block-for-block copies on two disks. We have shown this example using only two disks since, strictly speaking, that is all that is required for RAID 1. Multiple mirrors can be constructed using multiple disks, if desired. RAID 1 has a high level of redundancy, so that if either physical disk fails, the other can support the full use of both logical drives with potentially no loss of service.

In a failure situation, the failed disk can be replaced and the mirror can be reconstructed on the new disk. RAID 1 has the drawback, however, of requiring double the amount of disk space to accomplish this redundancy. Thus if our `C:` and `D:` require 1 TB of space, 2 TB of physical disk must be allocated.

RAID 10

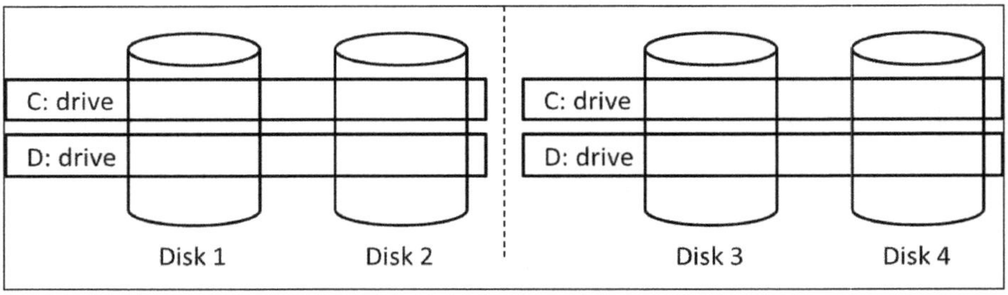
C: drive
D: drive
Disk 1
Disk 2
C: drive
D: drive
Disk 3
Disk 4

RAID 10 (known as "RAID one-zero" or "RAID ten"), or **striping with mirroring**, constructs the RAID group in such a way that leverages the benefits of both data striping and mirroring. In our example, each logical drive is striped across two physical drives, improving read/write performance over multiple disk drive heads. Additionally, each logical drive is mirrored on a separate pair of drives, providing redundancy in the event of a disk failure. Thus, we've achieved the redundancy of RAID 1, with the performance benefit of RAID 0. This configuration is highly desirable for database data that requires both high failure tolerance and high performance, such as high availability production systems. However, it comes with an added cost, since it requires a larger number of disks.

RAID 5

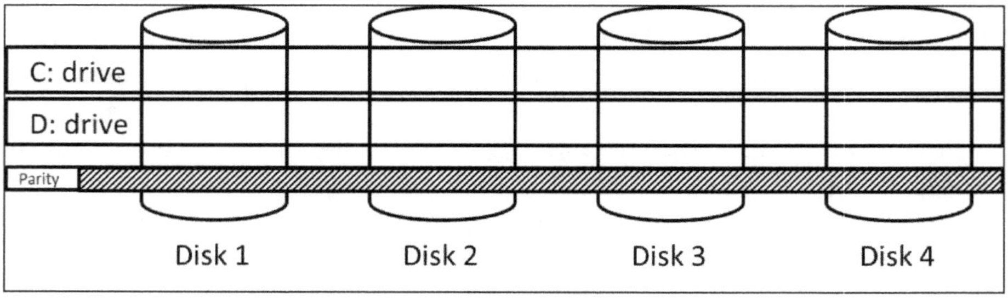
C: drive
D: drive
Parity
Disk 1
Disk 2
Disk 3
Disk 4

RAID 5, or **striping with parity**, attempts to provide a high level of redundancy at a reasonably low cost, using the concept of parity to achieve this. **Parity** provides a mechanism by which the information needed to reconstruct *any single disk* is striped across all disks. Thus, in the event that any of our four disks fails, the parity information on the other three can be used to reconstruct the information that was on the failed disk. This would be true even if our RAID group was composed of, not just four, but any number of disks, although three disks is the required minimum. It is important to note that RAID 5 is only designed to survive the loss of a *single disk*. Any more than that would require rebuilding and recovery. This configuration provides a DBA with a level of redundancy that would survive the failure of any disk in the group, without the added expense of mirroring. The amount of space required for parity is always equal to the size of one disk in the group. This amount of space is often referred to as the "parity disk," although this is not strictly accurate, since the parity is striped across all disks. As with the other types of RAID, there is a caveat to using RAID 5. While the read performance for RAID 5 is comparable to disks without RAID, write performance can suffer, since every write must also write parity information. Still, RAID 5 can be an excellent choice when balancing the need for redundancy with the realities of cost.

We take the time to cover RAID technologies because they are absolutely crucial to the manner in which a real-world DBA deals with media failures. Consider this example; our `Companylink` database uses the four-disk model we've discussed. One day, disk 4 fails when its disk armature malfunctions. In environments without RAID, there is no protection against the loss of this disk drive, which will inevitably lead to a full database recovery situation for a DBA. However, with RAID technologies, our database may not be impacted at all. Modern disk subsystems use hot-swappable technologies which allow failed disks to be removed and new ones to be inserted without even taking down the system. Thus, if our `Companylink` database is constructed on a disk subsystem using RAID 1, RAID 10, or RAID 5 with hot-swap technology, the disk is simply replaced with a new one on which the mirror or parity is then automatically reconstituted. While the user may experience some performance lag during this reconstitution, the database itself never becomes unavailable and high availability was maintained.

Understanding file-level media failure

While media failure most often represents failed disk drives, it can also refer to file-level corruption. File-level corruption is uncommon, but a DBA should know how to detect it. We can verify that a datafile has integrity using the `DBVERIFY` tool, which is invoked by executing `dbv` from the command line. `DBVERIFY` checks the physical integrity of a datafile or backup file at the block level. It can be run against datafiles regardless of whether the database is online or offline. `DBVERIFY` can be useful when you suspect that some sort of file-level corruption has occurred or merely to ensure that it hasn't occurred. The `dbv` command can take several possible parameters, but only two are generally required. We use the tool as follows. In our example, we'll use a small datafile to limit the amount of time required for the scan. On large datafiles, `dbv` can take a considerable amount of time.

```
C:\>dbv file=E:\APP\ORACLE\ORADATA\ORCL\USERS01.DBF blocksize=8192

DBVERIFY: Release 11.2.0.1.0 - Production on Wed Sep 12 19:58:21 2012

Copyright (c) 1982, 2009, Oracle and/or its affiliates.  All rights reserved.

DBVERIFY - Verification starting : FILE = E:\APP\ORACLE\ORADATA\ORCL\USERS01.DBF


DBVERIFY - Verification complete

Total Pages Examined         : 640
Total Pages Processed (Data) : 1
Total Pages Failing   (Data) : 0
Total Pages Processed (Index): 12
Total Pages Failing   (Index): 0
Total Pages Processed (Other): 193
Total Pages Processed (Seg)  : 0
Total Pages Failing   (Seg)  : 0
Total Pages Empty            : 434
Total Pages Marked Corrupt   : 0
Total Pages Influx           : 0
Total Pages Encrypted        : 0
Highest block SCN            : 1177664 (0.1177664)

C:\>
```

With the `dbv` command, we've specified the full path and name of our **USERS01.DBF** datafile along with a **blocksize** of **8192**, which matches our database block size. Incidentally, **8192** is the default for the **blocksize** parameter, so it is not necessary to specify it directly. What we're looking for in the output of the command is the number of **Pages Failing** for **Data**, **Index**, or **Seg** (segment) that is greater than zero. In our output, we see zero values for each of these, indicating that our datafile passed the integrity check.

Introducing the Data Recovery Advisor

Recovery from media failures can be a tricky process; it requires a thorough knowledge of the topics we cover in the next two chapters, as well as a good deal of practice. In order to simplify the process of recovery, Oracle introduced the **Data Recovery Advisor**, (**DRA**). The DRA is a facility to diagnose problems related to database recovery and advise the DBA on the necessary steps to solve them. It is specific to situations where a backup can be used to recover a database; thus it cannot assist a DBA with user failures or when no backup exists. Furthermore, it does not currently support advanced database features such as Real Application Clusters and standby databases with Data Guard. However, the DRA can be very useful in media failure situations such as the loss, corruption, or accidental renaming of datafiles.

The DRA can be invoked using RMAN or Enterprise Manager. As an example of the capabilities of the DRA, we'll see it at work through the Enterprise Manager Database Control interface. First, to log in and use the DRA, we need to start Database Control from a web browser, as we've done in previous chapters. Then, log in as the privileged `SYS` user with the `SYSDBA` role. If you have used the same password as indicated throughout the book, the password is `oracle`.

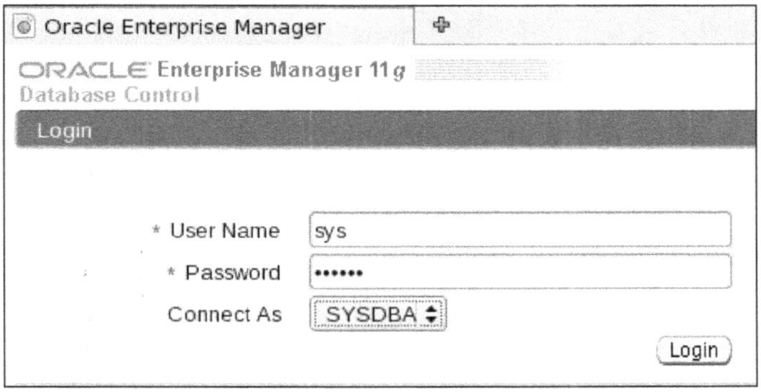
Oracle Enterprise Manager
ORACLE Enterprise Manager 11g
Database Control
Login
* User Name
sys
* Password
••••••
Connect As
SYSDBA
Login

Once within **Database Control**, we need to scroll to the bottom of the page to the **Related Links** section and click **Advisor Central**.

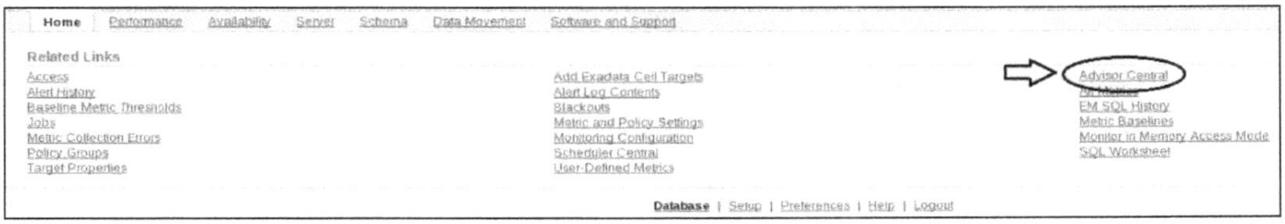
Home
Performance
Availability
Server
Schema
Data Movement
Software and Support
Related Links
Access
Alert History
Baseline Metric Thresholds
Jobs
Metric Collection Errors
Policy Groups
Target Properties
Add Exadata Cell Targets
Alert Log Contents
Blackouts
Metric and Policy Settings
Monitoring Configuration
Scheduler Central
User-Defined Metrics
Advisor Central
EM SQL History
Metric Baselines
Monitor in Memory Access Mode
SQL Worksheet
Database
Setup
Preferences
Help
Logout

In **Advisor Central**, we click **Data Recovery Advisor**.

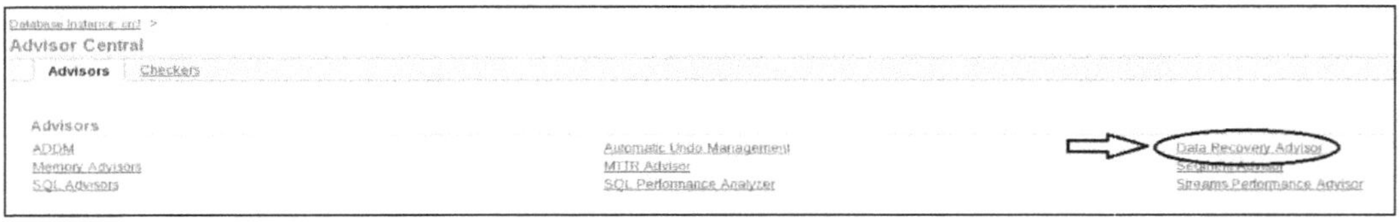
Advisor Central
Advisors
Checkers
Advisors
ADDM
Memory Advisors
SQL Advisors
Automatic Undo Management
MTTR Advisor
SQL Performance Analyzer
Data Recovery Advisor
Streams Performance Advisor

When we enter the DRA, we're presented with a screen that allows us to view and manage any database failures. If we click the **Go** button for failures with a status of **OPEN**, it shows us that no failures are present, as we would expect.

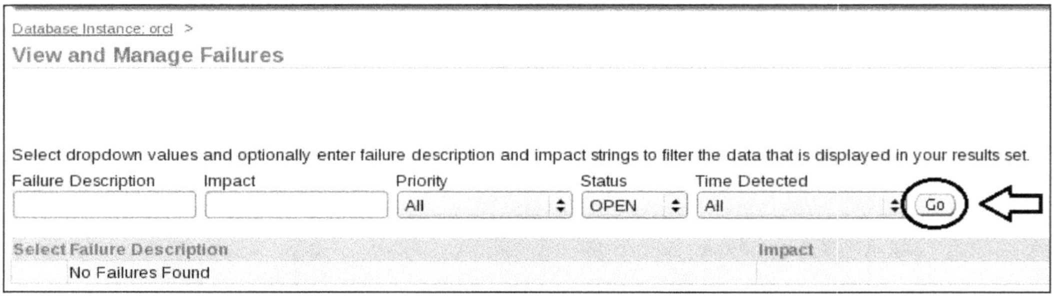
Database Instance: orcl >
View and Manage Failures
Select dropdown values and optionally enter failure description and impact strings to filter the data that is displayed in your results set.
Failure Description
Impact
Priority
Status
Time Detected
All
OPEN
All
Go
Select Failure Description
Impact
No Failures Found

Let's examine our interaction with the DRA in a recovery situation. In the following examples, a failure has already been simulated for us. In this failure, a datafile called `junk01.dbf` was inadvertently deleted. If we change the drop-down list for **Status** to **ALL**, we see the failure listed:

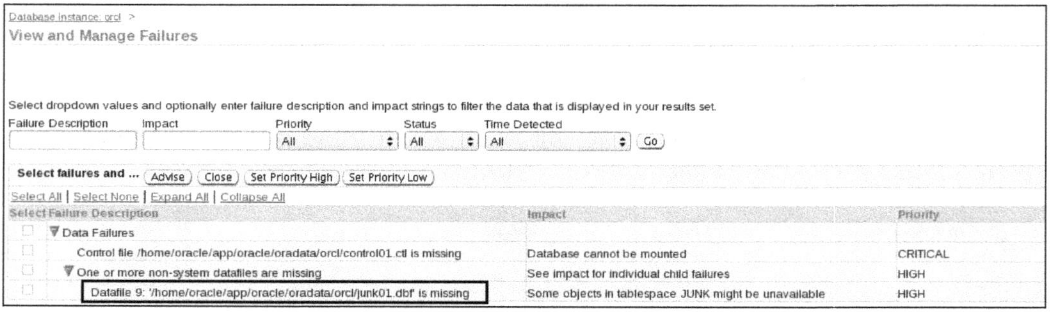
Database Instance: orcl >
View and Manage Failures
Select dropdown values and optionally enter failure description and impact strings to filter the data that is displayed in your results set.
Failure Description
Impact
Priority
Status
Time Detected
All
All
All
Go
Select failures and ...
Advise
Close
Set Priority High
Set Priority Low
Select All | Select None | Expand All | Collapse All
Select Failure Description
Impact
Priority
Data Failures
Control file /home/oracle/app/oracle/oradata/orcl/control01.ctl is missing
Database cannot be mounted
CRITICAL
One or more non-system datafiles are missing
See impact for individual child failures
HIGH
Datafile 9: '/home/oracle/app/oracle/oradata/orcl/junk01.dbf' is missing
Some objects in tablespace JUNK might be unavailable
HIGH

The process of recovery in a real-world, situation would be somewhat different than our earlier look at the DRA. If the datafile was missing, an error would occur and the database may be down. However, using Database Control, we could still log in to the database as `SYS` and begin the recovery. We would see a screen such as the one shown in the following screenshot:

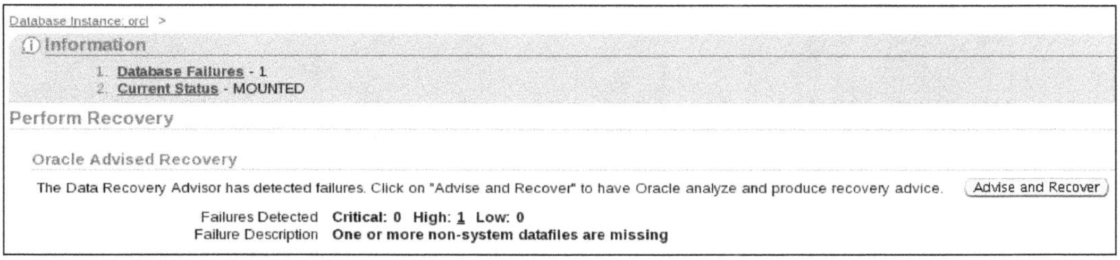
Database Instance: orcl >
Information
1. Database Failures - 1
2. Current Status - MOUNTED
Perform Recovery
Oracle Advised Recovery
The Data Recovery Advisor has detected failures. Click on "Advise and Recover" to have Oracle analyze and produce recovery advice.
Advise and Recover
Failures Detected Critical: 0 High: 1 Low: 0
Failure Description One or more non-system datafiles are missing

Here, the database is in the MOUNT , state and the DRA indicates that datafiles are missing. Our best choice in this situation is to click **Advise and Recover**, which presents us with this screen, which takes us back to the **View and Manage Failures** screen we've seen previously:

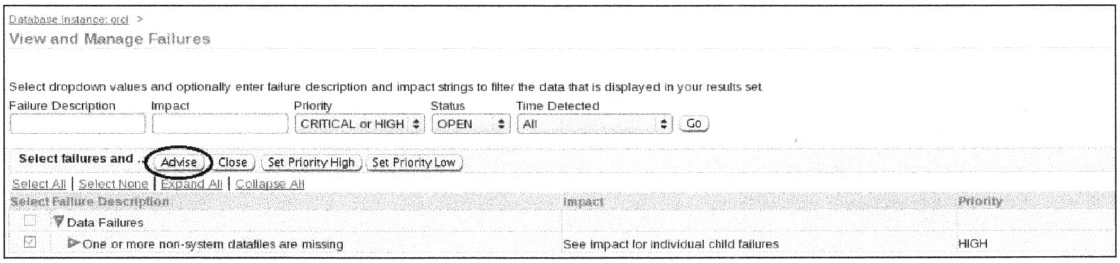
Database Instance: orcl >
View and Manage Failures
Select dropdown values and optionally enter failure description and impact strings to filter the data that is displayed in your results set.
Failure Description
Impact
Priority
Status
Time Detected
CRITICAL or HIGH
OPEN
All
Go
Select failures and ...
Advise
Close
Set Priority High
Set Priority Low
Select All | Select None | Expand All | Collapse All
Select Failure Description
Impact
Priority
Data Failures
One or more non-system datafiles are missing
See impact for individual child failures
HIGH

Clearly there is a critical problem, so we click the **Advise** button:

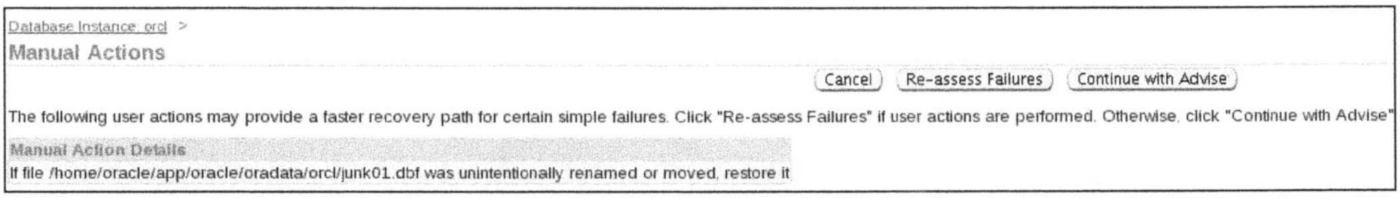
Database Instance: orcl >
Manual Actions
Cancel
Re-assess Failures
Continue with Advise
The following user actions may provide a faster recovery path for certain simple failures. Click "Re-assess Failures" if user actions are performed. Otherwise, click "Continue with Advise"
Manual Action Details
If file /home/oracle/app/oracle/oradata/orcl/junk01.dbf was unintentionally renamed or moved, restore it

This section details the problem itself—our datafile was renamed or removed and needs to be restored. We click **Continue with Advise** to gather more advice on what specific actions should be taken:

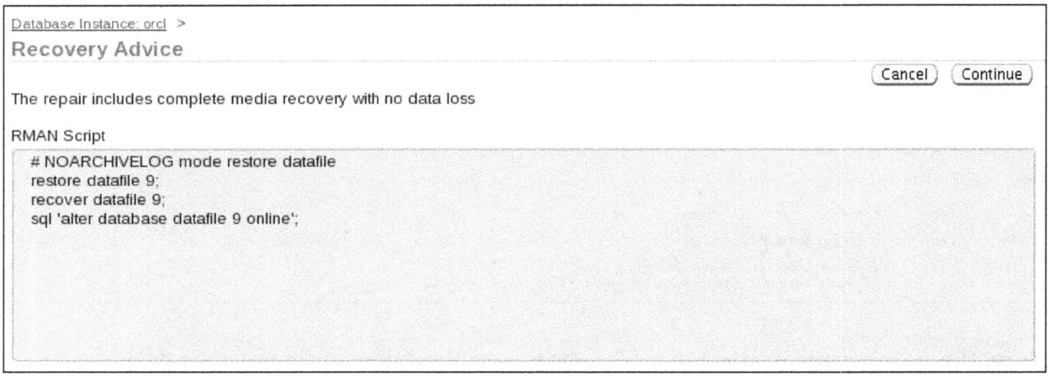
Database Instance: orcl >
Recovery Advice
Cancel
Continue
The repair includes complete media recovery with no data loss
RMAN Script
NOARCHIVELOG mode restore datafile
restore datafile 9;
recover datafile 9;
sql 'alter database datafile 9 online';

We finally arrive at the core advice of the , DRA. Here, the DRA actually generates a Recovery Manager script to recover the lost datafile. This script can be copied and pasted into Recovery Manager or simply used as a template for the steps we could use to proceed. We could also continue and allow the DRA to fix our database itself. Although using the DRA within Database Control has several steps, keep in mind what we've actually done here. We've used Database Control to connect to a database that wasn't even in an open state and received a generated script that details the steps needed for a complete recovery. In some recovery situations, the DRA can be extremely beneficial.

Certification objectives covered

- Identify the types of failures that can occur in an Oracle database
- Describe ways to tune instance recovery
- Identify the importance of checkpoints, redo logfiles, and archived logfiles
- Overview of Flash Recovery Area
- Configure ARCHIVELOG mode

Summary

In this chapter, we've taken our first steps to understanding backup and recovery concepts. We've looked at the core Oracle architecture that allows the database to be recovered. We've seen the ways that ARCHIVELOG mode can allow us to recover databases even up to the point of failure. We've examined the Flash Recovery Area and seen how it serves as a single source for recovery-related information. We've explored the concept of instance recovery and the ways in which we can tune it. We've examined the types of failure that can occur in databases and which ones require the intervention of a database administrator. Finally, we've explored the Data Recovery Advisor, which allows us to more easily identify the problems at the root of database failures, and can advise DBAs on how to proceed with recovery. In our next chapter, we'll examine the process of backing up databases with Oracle's Recovery Manager tool.

Test your knowledge

Q 1. Fill in the blanks in order. Multiplexing refers to the act of creating multiple redo log _______ for each redo log ________.

a. archives, group
b. groups, member
c. members, group
d. groups, group

Q 2. Which of the following data dictionary views allow us to look at redo logs from a group perspective?

a. `v$log`
b. `v$logfile`
c. `v$logfile_group`
d. `v$log_group`

Q 3. Which of the following commands allows the DBA to manually switch from the current redo log group to the next redo log group in the sequence?

a. `alter system switch archivelog;`
b. `alter system switch logfile sequence;`
c. `alter system switch to next log sequence;`
d. `alter system switch logfile;`

Q 4. Following are the steps needed to enable ARCHIVELOG mode. Place them in their proper sequence.

1. Open the database
2. Enable archiving using the `alter database archivelog` command
3. Shutdown the database
4. Start the database into the `MOUNT` state

   a. 4, 2, 3, 1
   b. 1, 4, 2, 3
   c. 3, 4, 2, 1
   d. 1, 2, 4, 3

Q 5. We want to configure our `Companylink` database for maximum recoverability—even up to the point of a failure. Which task is most important in accomplishing this requirement?

   a. Configuring ARCHIVELOG mode
   b. Configuring multiplexed redo logs
   c. Setting the `fast_start_mttr_target` parameter
   d. Configuring the Flash Recovery Area

Q 6. When configuring the Flash Recovery Area, which parameter must be set first?

   a. `fast_start_mttr_target`
   b. `flashback_recovery_area`
   c. `db_recovery_file_dest`
   d. `db_recovery_file_dest_size`

Q 7. Which of the following types of files is *not* stored in the FRA by default?

   a. Recovery Manager backup files
   b. Redo logfiles
   c. Flashback logs
   d. Archive logfiles

Q 8. Where can the DBA view information be found to confirm that an instance recovery has taken place?

a. The `v$recovery` data dictionary view
b. The Recovery Manager backup log
c. The alert log
d. The PMON trace file

Q 9. Which of the following statements is *not* true if we set `fast_start_mttr_target` to a non-zero value?

a. Use of the `v$instance_recovery` view is enabled
b. A target time for instance recovery is established
c. Checkpoint auto tuning is enabled
d. The fastest possible instance recovery is guaranteed

Q 10. Which of the following failure scenarios will most depend on the intervention of a DBA to do a database recovery?

a. The physical disk that stores the database datafiles fails
b. A `DELETE` statement fails midway through execution
c. An application developer deletes important rows from a production table
d. A network failure prevents users from accessing the database

Q 11. Which RAID configuration provides the highest level of combined performance and redundancy?

a. RAID 0
b. RAID 1
c. RAID 5
d. RAID 10

Q 12. In which type of failure scenario is the `DBVERIFY` tool most useful?

a. File-level media failure
b. User process failure
c. Statement failure
d. User errors

Q 13. In which type of failure scenario is the Data Recovery Advisor most useful?

a. A developer drops a production table
b. Datafiles are missing when the database is started
c. Network failure is preventing users from accessing the database.
d. A user job fails due to lack of tablespace

12
Performing Database Backups

Now that we've understood the nature and importance of database backups, it's time to delve into the details of actually running them. When running backups in Oracle, we have a number of choices to make. Will our backups run while the database is open or shut down? Will we back up using Oracle's tools, or will we do it manually? Will we back up the entire database or only a portion of it? How do these choices affect the steps that will be needed for recovery? In this chapter, we will answer these and many such questions. We will understand the details of how to run enterprise-level backups of an Oracle database, as well as how to maintain and automate them.

In this chapter, we shall:

- Create user-managed backups
- Explore the Recovery Manager tool
- Create RMAN offline backups
- Create RMAN online hot backups
- Create incremental backups
- Perform backup maintenance activities
- Automate backups

Creating user-managed backups

At one point in the history of the Oracle database, there was no integrated tool with which the DBAs could back up and recover databases. The DBAs used manual methods to back up databases in a way that they could be safely recovered. Truthfully, these methods, known as **user-managed backups**, are used much less often today, due in large part to their low tolerance for human error. However, using the right procedures, user-managed backups produce all the proper output needed to recover a database.

Creating user-managed cold backups

To begin, we need to create a directory location for our user-managed backups. We will use the Windows platform for these examples, so we'll create a directory in the base of one of our system drives, in this example, the `E:`.

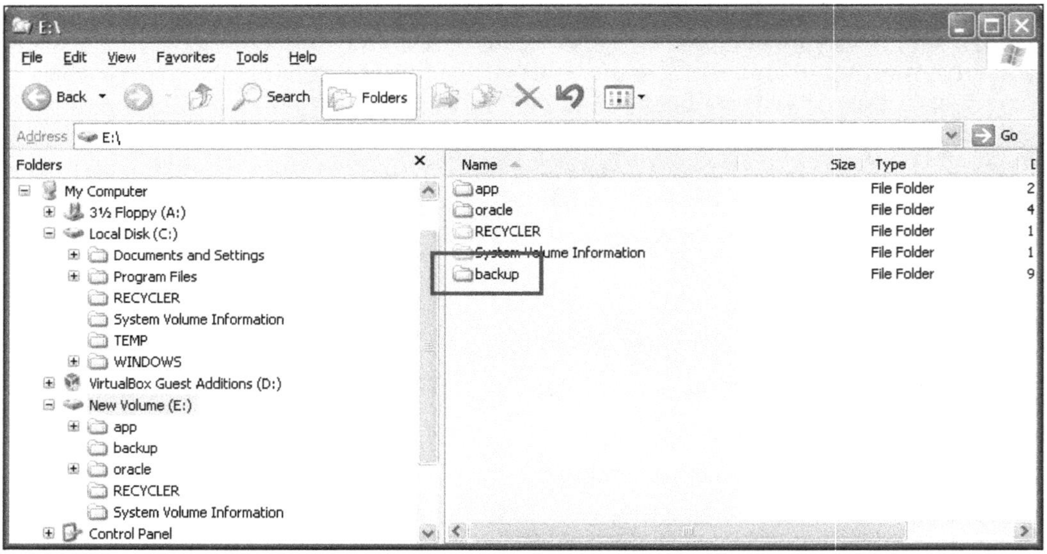
E:\
File Edit View Favorites Tools Help
Back
Search
Folders
Address E:\
Go
Folders
My Computer
3½ Floppy (A:)
Local Disk (C:)
Documents and Settings
Program Files
RECYCLER
System Volume Information
TEMP
WINDOWS
VirtualBox Guest Additions (D:)
New Volume (E:)
app
backup
oracle
RECYCLER
System Volume Information
Control Panel
Name
Size
Type
app
oracle
RECYCLER
backup
File Folder

We'll first examine the process behind performing a user-managed **offline backup**. The certification exam also refers to this as a **whole consistent backup**, indicating that all datafiles have been closed by the operating system. Thus, an offline backup is performed with the database in a closed state. So, we'll first need to shut the database down.

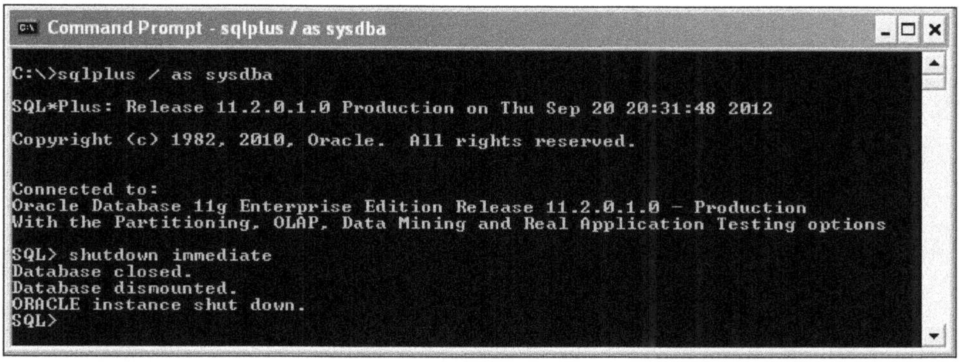
Command Prompt - sqlplus / as sysdba
C:\>sqlplus / as sysdba
SQL*Plus: Release 11.2.0.1.0 Production on Thu Sep 20 20:31:48 2012
Copyright (c) 1982, 2010, Oracle. All rights reserved.
Connected to:
Oracle Database 11g Enterprise Edition Release 11.2.0.1.0 - Production
With the Partitioning, OLAP, Data Mining and Real Application Testing options
SQL> shutdown immediate
Database closed.
Database dismounted.
ORACLE instance shut down.
SQL>

Once the database is shut down, the process to make a user-managed backup is to copy the following files to a backup location:

- The control files (located in the directory specified by `v$controlfile`)
- The redo logfiles (located in the directory specified by `v$logfile`)
- The datafiles (located in the directory specified by `v$datafile`)
- The temp files (located in the directory specified by `v$tempfile`)

This copying process can take place in any number of ways, depending on the operating system in use. In the case of our example database, all of these files are located in one directory, so it is easy to copy them. They are located as shown in the following screenshot:

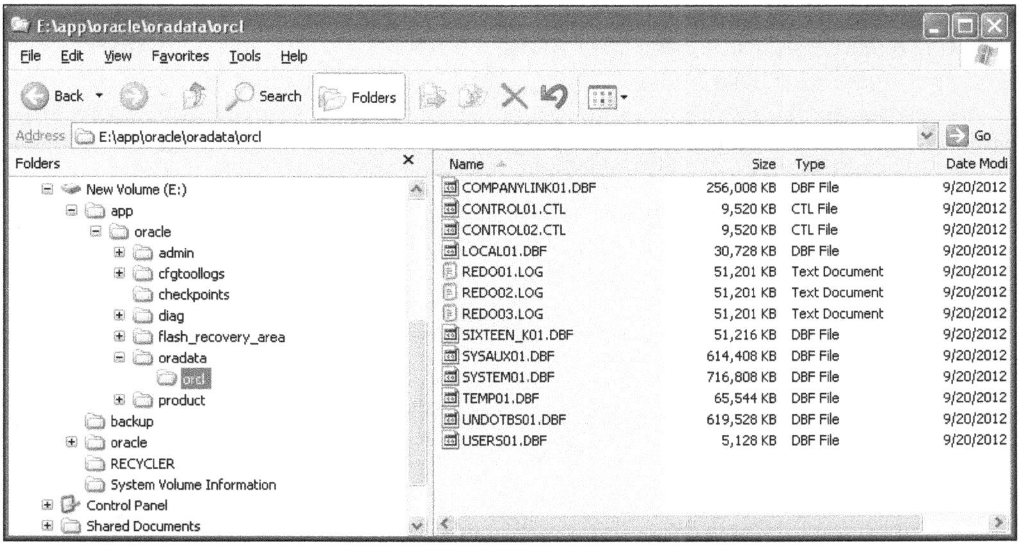
E:\app\oracle\oradata\orcl
File Edit View Favorites Tools Help
Back Search Folders
Address E:\app\oracle\oradata\orcl
Go
Folders
New Volume (E:)
app
oracle
admin
cfgtoollogs
checkpoints
diag
flash_recovery_area
oradata
orcl
product
backup
oracle
RECYCLER
System Volume Information
Control Panel
Shared Documents
Name Size Type Date Modi
COMPANYLINK01.DBF 256,008 KB DBF File 9/20/2012
CONTROL01.CTL 9,520 KB CTL File 9/20/2012
CONTROL02.CTL 9,520 KB CTL File 9/20/2012
LOCAL01.DBF 30,728 KB DBF File 9/20/2012
REDO01.LOG 51,201 KB Text Document 9/20/2012
REDO02.LOG 51,201 KB Text Document 9/20/2012
REDO03.LOG 51,201 KB Text Document 9/20/2012
SIXTEEN_K01.DBF 51,216 KB DBF File 9/20/2012
SYSAUX01.DBF 614,408 KB DBF File 9/20/2012
SYSTEM01.DBF 716,808 KB DBF File 9/20/2012
TEMP01.DBF 65,544 KB DBF File 9/20/2012
UNDOTBS01.DBF 619,528 KB DBF File 9/20/2012
USERS01.DBF 5,128 KB DBF File 9/20/2012

Copy them to the new backup directory we created.

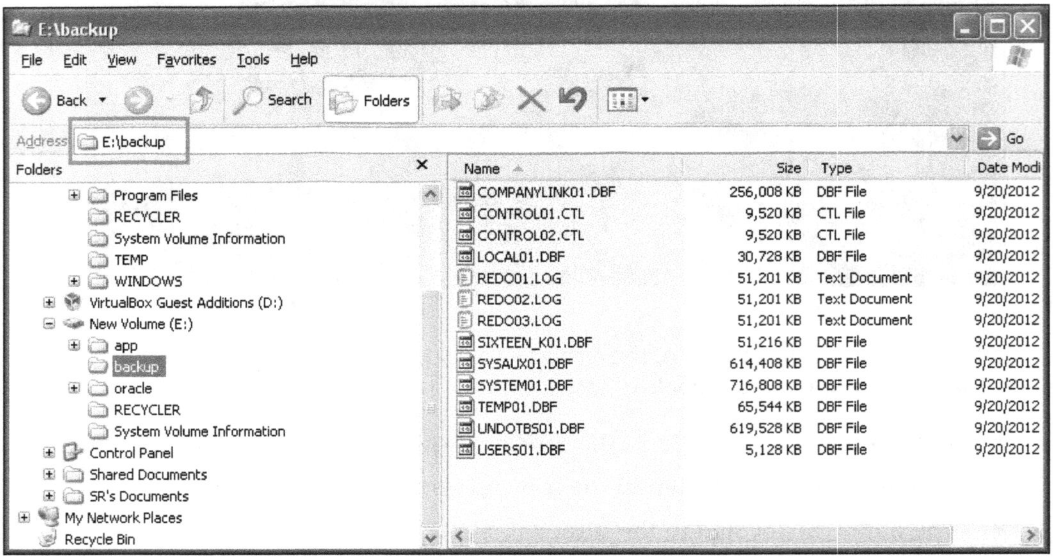
E:\backup
File Edit View Favorites Tools Help
Back
Search
Folders
Address E:\backup
Go
Folders
Program Files
RECYCLER
System Volume Information
TEMP
WINDOWS
VirtualBox Guest Additions (D:)
New Volume (E:)
app
backup
oracle
RECYCLER
System Volume Information
Control Panel
Shared Documents
SR's Documents
My Network Places
Recycle Bin
Name
Size
Type
Date Modi
COMPANYLINK01.DBF 256,008 KB DBF File 9/20/2012
CONTROL01.CTL 9,520 KB CTL File 9/20/2012
CONTROL02.CTL 9,520 KB CTL File 9/20/2012
LOCAL01.DBF 30,728 KB DBF File 9/20/2012
REDO01.LOG 51,201 KB Text Document 9/20/2012
REDO02.LOG 51,201 KB Text Document 9/20/2012
REDO03.LOG 51,201 KB Text Document 9/20/2012
SIXTEEN_K01.DBF 51,216 KB DBF File 9/20/2012
SYSAUX01.DBF 614,408 KB DBF File 9/20/2012
SYSTEM01.DBF 716,808 KB DBF File 9/20/2012
TEMP01.DBF 65,544 KB DBF File 9/20/2012
UNDOTBS01.DBF 619,528 KB DBF File 9/20/2012
USERS01.DBF 5,128 KB DBF File 9/20/2012

Once the copying process is completed, the database is restarted and made available for use. Obviously, this is an almost completely manual process. Later on in the chapter, we'll discuss ways that backups can be scheduled to run automatically.

Creating user-managed hot backups

In today's world, backing up the data while the database is up and available for use is greatly preferred. These types of backups are known as **online backups**, or more commonly, **hot backups**. The user-managed methods used to run hot backups are significantly different than those for offline backups. First and foremost, a database cannot be backed up online unless it is operating in ARCHIVELOG mode. Hot backups are accomplished using several SQL commands. But, as with offline user-managed backups, we must remember to back up all the necessary files. First, we must back up the control file using the command shown in the following screenshot:

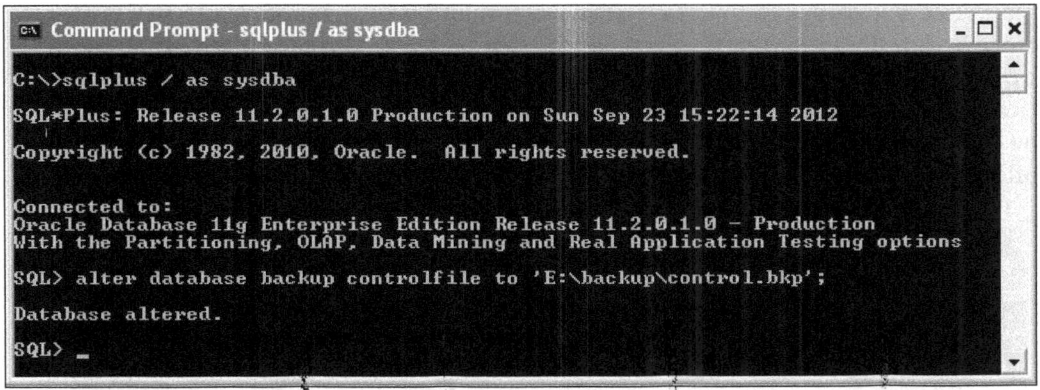
Command Prompt - sqlplus / as sysdba
C:\>sqlplus / as sysdba
SQL*Plus: Release 11.2.0.1.0 Production on Sun Sep 23 15:22:14 2012
Copyright (c) 1982, 2010, Oracle. All rights reserved.
Connected to:
Oracle Database 11g Enterprise Edition Release 11.2.0.1.0 - Production
With the Partitioning, OLAP, Data Mining and Real Application Testing options
SQL> alter database backup controlfile to 'E:\backup\control.bkp';
Database altered.
SQL> _

We can back up the datafiles associated with a given tablespace by placing the tablespace in the **backup mode**. Alternatively, we can place the entire database in the backup mode with one command. First, we'll look at doing this at the tablespace level.

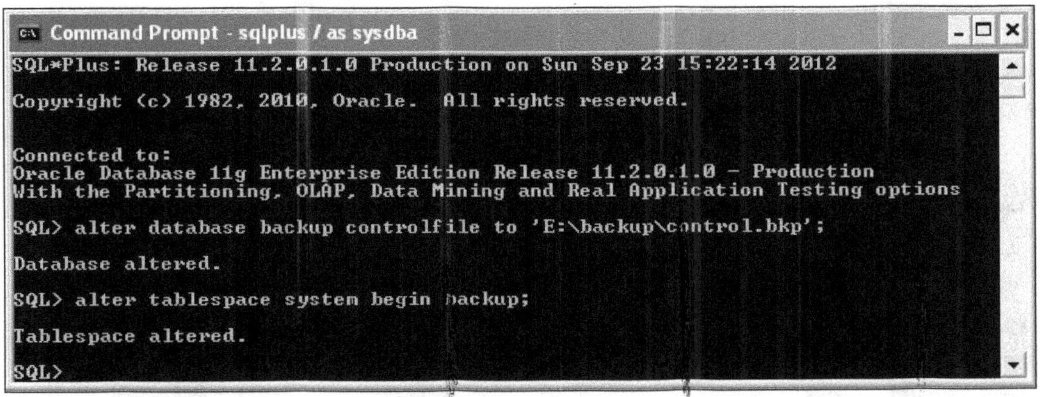
Command Prompt - sqlplus / as sysdba
SQL*Plus: Release 11.2.0.1.0 Production on Sun Sep 23 15:22:14 2012
Copyright (c) 1982, 2010, Oracle. All rights reserved.
Connected to:
Oracle Database 11g Enterprise Edition Release 11.2.0.1.0 - Production
With the Partitioning, OLAP, Data Mining and Real Application Testing options
SQL> alter database backup controlfile to 'E:\backup\control.bkp';
Database altered.
SQL> alter tablespace system begin backup;
Tablespace altered.
SQL>

The `alter tablespace...begin backup` command will suspend reads and writes to every datafile in that tablespace, in this case `system`, allowing them to be safely copied using any available operating system method. It is crucial that once we have completed copying the datafiles associated with the tablespace, we must execute the command to take the tablespace out of the backup mode, as shown in the following screenshot:

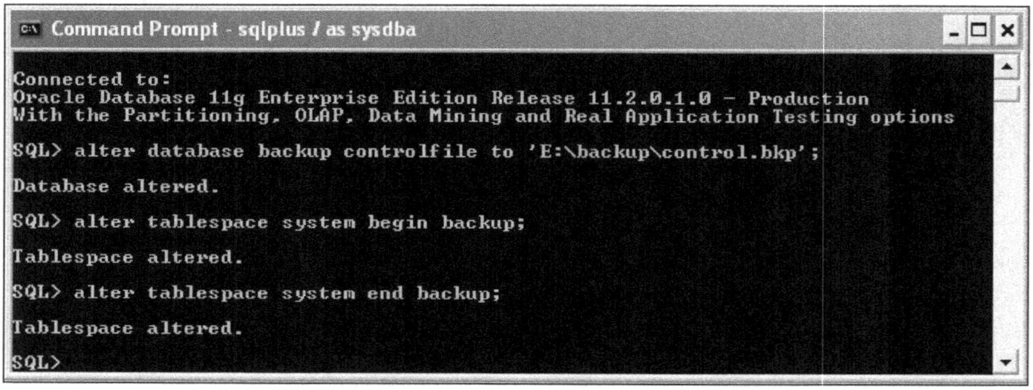
Command Prompt - sqlplus / as sysdba
Connected to:
Oracle Database 11g Enterprise Edition Release 11.2.0.1.0 - Production
With the Partitioning, OLAP, Data Mining and Real Application Testing options
SQL> alter database backup controlfile to 'E:\backup\control.bkp';
Database altered.
SQL> alter tablespace system begin backup;
Tablespace altered.
SQL> alter tablespace system end backup;
Tablespace altered.
SQL>

Alternatively, we can place all of the tablespaces and their corresponding datafiles, into backup mode using the `alter database...begin backup` command.

Command Prompt - sqlplus / as sysdba
Connected to:
Oracle Database 11g Enterprise Edition Release 11.2.0.1.0 - Production
With the Partitioning, OLAP, Data Mining and Real Application Testing options
SQL> alter tablespace system begin backup;
Tablespace altered.
SQL> alter tablespace system end backup;
Tablespace altered.
SQL> alter database begin backup;
Database altered.
SQL>

Once the entire database is in the backup mode, the datafiles can be copied to the backup location. At this point, we might ask "Why wouldn't we just use the `alter database...begin backup` command to perform a hot backup, since it is so much simpler than backing up individual tablespaces?" When a tablespace is put in the backup mode, no transactions can be written directly to that tablespace's datafiles; so they must be written somewhere else. In a user-managed backup, these changes are written to the redo logs. This means that a tremendous amount of redo can be generated during a user-managed hot backup. If all the tablespaces are placed in the backup mode using `alter database...begin backup`, that amount of redo grows exponentially. So, while it is certainly viable to put the entire database in the backup mode, it is not always advantageous.

Understanding Oracle Recovery Manager

Although, when done correctly, user-managed backups are a perfectly acceptable way to back up an Oracle database, it has probably become clear that these methods can easily introduce problems with human error. Using these methods, there is a possibility to omit needed files, back up the wrong files, or back them up in a wrong order, making recovery an extremely difficult proposition. In order to safely back up an enterprise-level database, Oracle felt that it was necessary to introduce an application that could be used as the standard tool. Today, that tool is called **Oracle Recovery Manager**.

Introducing RMAN

In Oracle Version 7, the **Enterprise Backup Utility** (**EBU**) was released as a part of the standard Oracle database software installation. It was Oracle's first attempt to provide an enterprise-grade solution for backing up and recovering databases. The original EBU was less than successful; so, in Version 8, Oracle retooled the EBU and released Oracle Recovery Manager, which is more commonly referred to as **RMAN**. Since its initial release, RMAN has continued to innovate and improve in functionality. Today, RMAN has a number of important features that make it the de facto standard for backing up and recovering Oracle databases. These features include:

- Providing true block-level backups, rather than file-level ones
- Including a simple and intuitive scripting language

- Capability of ignoring the whitespace in a datafile—that is, RMAN can ignore unused blocks during a backup, significantly reducing the amount of space used
- Ability to produce compressed backups that further reduce the space used
- Eliminating the need to place tablespaces in backup mode during a hot backup
- Providing a block-level error check during backup, which can detect block corruption in the database
- Allowing a validation mode to test backups and recoveries fully without writing them to the disk
- Supporting incremental backups
- Ability to be used to clone entire databases
- Providing advanced reporting features that can list the details of backups that have occurred, and even report on and delete backups that are no longer needed
- Allowing for the internal storage of backup scripts that can be used in automating backups
- Available free as a part of the Enterprise Edition installation

It should be clear from this list why RMAN has become the preferred choice of Oracle DBAs when performing backups and recoveries. In fact, there is essentially no reason to choose any other method, other than personal preference. RMAN is the easiest, safest way to back up an Oracle database.

Oracle also produces another backup product, called **Oracle Secure Backup**, which is integrated with RMAN. Oracle Secure Backup is a centrally managed product that is intended to integrate with many of its products, including Oracle Database, Weblogic, Exadata, and Enterprise Manager, with a particular focus on tape management. Oracle Secure Backup is sold as a separately priced option.

Understanding the RMAN architecture

To understand how to use RMAN effectively, we should explore the architectural components that allow RMAN to function. The four main components of RMAN are as follows:

- The RMAN executable
- The target database

- The repository
- The **Media Management Library**, or **MML** (optional)

These four components act in concert to facilitate backup and recovery in an Oracle database. We might diagram their interaction as follows:

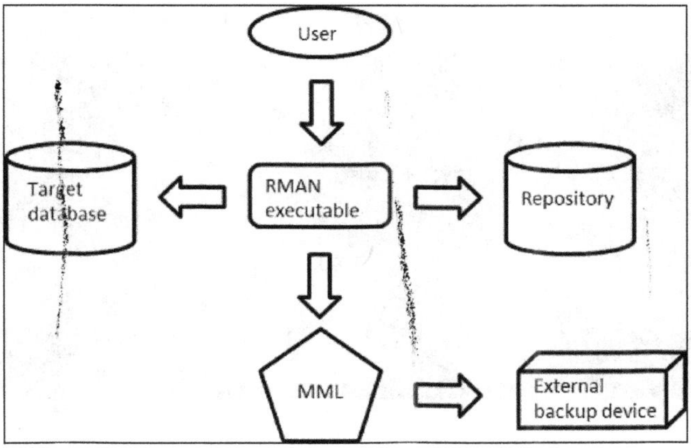
User
Target database
RMAN executable
Repository
MML
External backup device

The user, generally the DBA, interacts with the RMAN system using the RMAN executable, which I will introduce shortly. This executable is a command-line interface that allows the DBA to input various commands that control the actions of RMAN. The executable uses a proprietary scripting language, but the users familiar with SQL shouldn't have much trouble understanding it. Through the executable, we connect to the target database—the database that is being backed up or recovered. The executable can also be used to connect to the **RMAN repository**—a stored set of metadata that contains data about past and present backup operations. RMAN uses this repository to determine the history and current state of the target database. The repository can come in two forms. By default, the database control file is always used to store repository information. The repository can also be stored in database tables, named the **recovery catalog**. Optionally, the executable can also be used to connect to a **Media Management Library** (**MML**). The MML is a set of interfaces that can be used to directly communicate with an external backup device, such as a tape drive. Using the MML, RMAN can write backups directly to the tape.

The RMAN executable is invoked using the `rman` command, regardless of the operating system. The majority of the remaining examples will be shown from a Linux operating system. However, once we are within the command-line interface, the commands are the same. We'll first show an invocation of RMAN from a Windows command line.

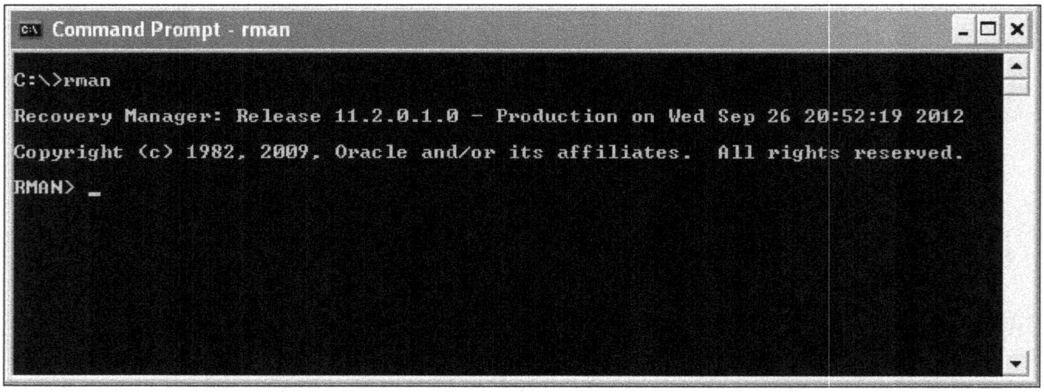
Command Prompt - rman
C:\>rman
Recovery Manager: Release 11.2.0.1.0 - Production on Wed Sep 26 20:52:19 2012
Copyright (c) 1982, 2009, Oracle and/or its affiliates. All rights reserved.
RMAN>

Next, an RMAN session is invoked from Linux.

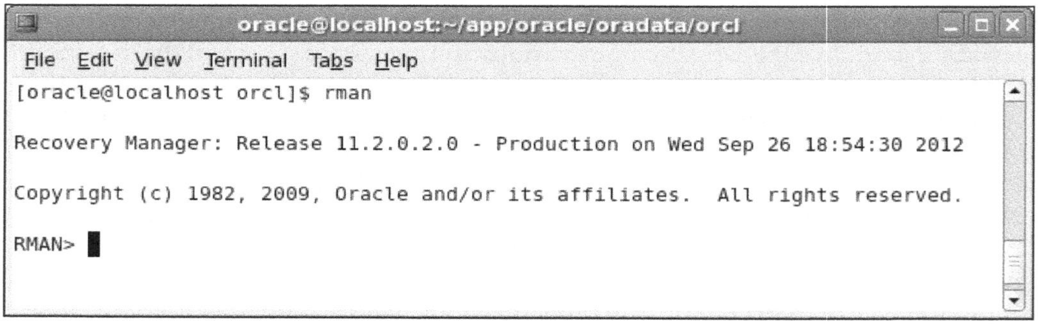
oracle@localhost:~/app/oracle/oradata/orcl
File Edit View Terminal Tabs Help
[oracle@localhost orcl]$ rman
Recovery Manager: Release 11.2.0.2.0 - Production on Wed Sep 26 18:54:30 2012
Copyright (c) 1982, 2009, Oracle and/or its affiliates. All rights reserved.
RMAN>

When RMAN backs up a database, it reads datafiles at the block level. Multiple datafiles can be read at once. The set of datafiles being read is defined as a **backup set**. As blocks are read from the backup set, they are then written to a backup file known as a **backup piece**. The output of a backup set is sequentially written to multiple backup pieces. Thus, any given backup piece can have blocks from any number of datafiles. The process of backing up using backup sets will also ignore any unused blocks or *whitespace* in the datafile. Thus, if a 1000M datafile only has 500M of used data in it, the resulting space required for this data is 500M rather that the 1000M in the source datafile. This paradigm is very dissimilar from the typical backup concept, where a backup file that is output is a one-for-one representation of a source datafile. This is because RMAN produces backups at the block level. RMAN can even recover a single corrupted datafile block from a backup. When compression is used, RMAN compresses database blocks as they are read before they are written to the backup pieces. This process is demonstrated as follows:

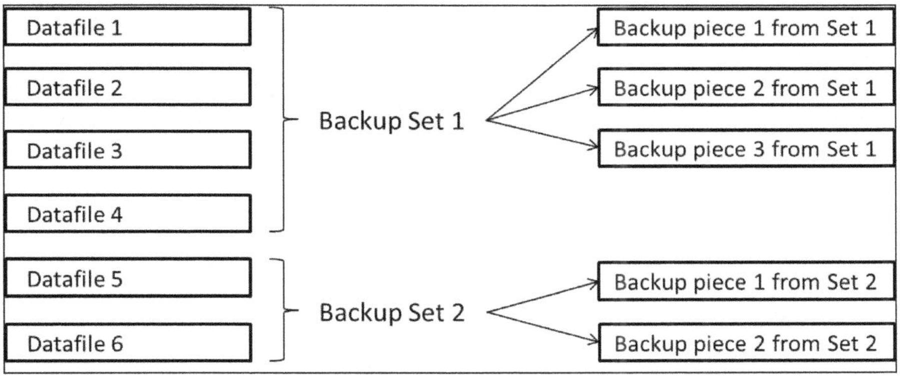
Datafile 1
Datafile 2
Datafile 3
Datafile 4
Datafile 5
Datafile 6
Backup Set 1
Backup Set 2
Backup piece 1 from Set 1
Backup piece 2 from Set 1
Backup piece 3 from Set 1
Backup piece 1 from Set 2
Backup piece 2 from Set 2

Although RMAN is typically used to perform block-for-block backups, it can also be used to create file-level backups. A file-level backup output file is known as an image copy. An **image copy** is a backup file that is identical to its input datafile. Image copies are sometimes used for certain database cloning operations, or if it is simply the preference of the DBA. Image copies can also lead to faster recovery as the datafile already exists in the complete form, rather than having its blocks reconstructed from a backup piece. However, image copies have a space disadvantage, in that they cannot ignore the whitespace in a datafile, resulting in no space savings for unused data.

Performing RMAN offline backups

Now that we've introduced some of the terminology, we can look at the process of performing an actual backup. In this section, we'll look at RMAN offline backups—backups that are run when the database is shut down. These are also sometimes referred to as **closed backups**. Although hot backups are more common when using RMAN, we'll find that the process is nearly identical, other than the state of the database. However, we should always remember the downside to offline backups. Although offline backups allow for complete recovery of a database, this is only the case if the database is in ARCHIVELOG mode. Generally, the only reason for a DBA to run offline backups is if the database is required to be in NOARCHIVELOG mode. This configuration does not allow for complete recovery up to the point of failure, as there are no archive logs to reconstruct the changes in the database since the backup occurred.

Performing a tablespace-level RMAN backup

Although it is less common than a full database backup, RMAN can be used to backup a single tablespace. In such a scenario, all of the datafiles that belong to a tablespace are treated as a single backup set and are written out to one or more backup pieces. First, we invoke the RMAN executable and connect to our target database.

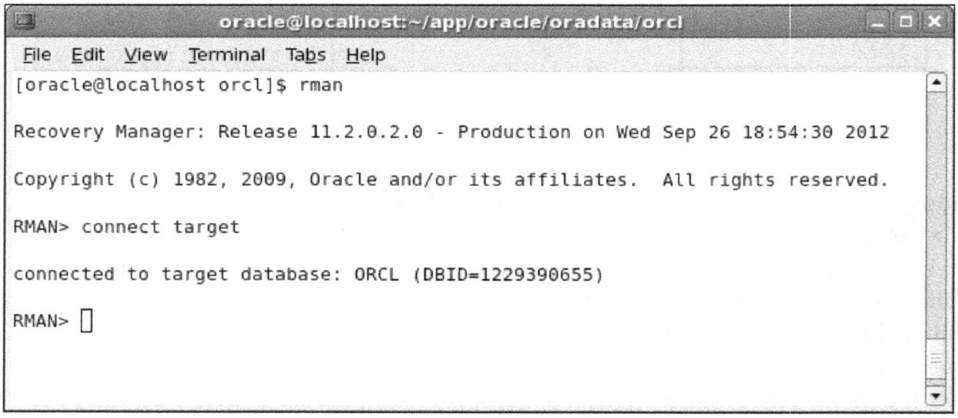
oracle@localhost:~/app/oracle/oradata/orcl
File Edit View Terminal Tabs Help
[oracle@localhost orcl]$ rman
Recovery Manager: Release 11.2.0.2.0 - Production on Wed Sep 26 18:54:30 2012
Copyright (c) 1982, 2009, Oracle and/or its affiliates. All rights reserved.
RMAN> connect target
connected to target database: ORCL (DBID=1229390655)
RMAN>

As we can see, RMAN returns the name of the target database, `ORCL`, as well as a value for `DBID`, which is required for certain database recoveries. Because this backup is to be an offline backup, we'll execute a `shutdown immediate` command, which we can do using RMAN. However, during an offline backup, the database cannot be completely shut down—it must be placed in a mounted state. This allows RMAN to read the blocks in the database. If the database was completely closed, these blocks could not be read. Thus, we also issue a `startup mount` command.

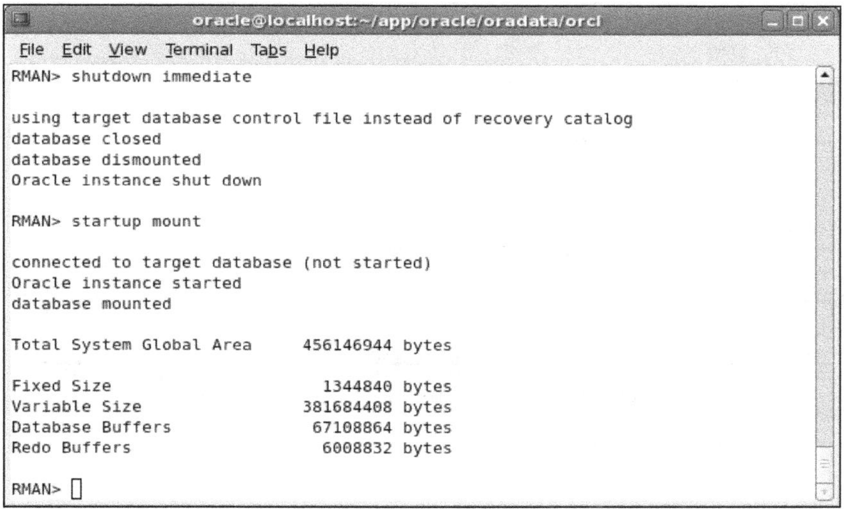
oracle@localhost:~/app/oracle/oradata/orcl
File Edit View Terminal Tabs Help
RMAN> shutdown immediate
using target database control file instead of recovery catalog
database closed
database dismounted
Oracle instance shut down
RMAN> startup mount
connected to target database (not started)
Oracle instance started
database mounted
Total System Global Area 456146944 bytes
Fixed Size 1344840 bytes
Variable Size 381684408 bytes
Database Buffers 67108864 bytes
Redo Buffers 6008832 bytes
RMAN>

As we can see in the preceding screenshot, the database is shut down and then mounted, but we can also see an interesting piece of information has returned after the `shutdown immediate` command. As can be seen in the previous screenshot, `using target database control file instead of recovery catalog` is part of the output. This informs us of a fact we've already discussed, namely, RMAN will use the control file as the RMAN repository by default. We did not specify a recovery catalog (as we're not using an external catalog), and the control file is used instead. Next, we will use the `backup tablespace` command along with the name of the tablespace to be backed up.

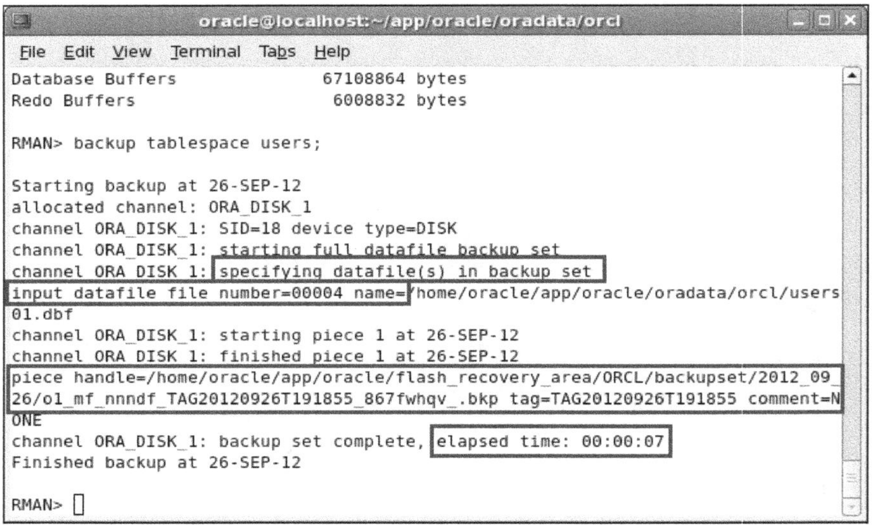
oracle@localhost:~/app/oracle/oradata/orcl
File Edit View Terminal Tabs Help
Database Buffers 67108864 bytes
Redo Buffers 6008832 bytes
RMAN> backup tablespace users;
Starting backup at 26-SEP-12
allocated channel: ORA_DISK_1
channel ORA_DISK_1: SID=18 device type=DISK
channel ORA_DISK_1: starting full datafile backup set
channel ORA_DISK_1: specifying datafile(s) in backup set
input datafile file number=00004 name=/home/oracle/app/oracle/oradata/orcl/users
01.dbf
channel ORA_DISK_1: starting piece 1 at 26-SEP-12
channel ORA_DISK_1: finished piece 1 at 26-SEP-12
piece handle=/home/oracle/app/oracle/flash_recovery_area/ORCL/backupset/2012_09_
26/o1_mf_nnndf_TAG20120926T191855_867fwhqv_.bkp tag=TAG20120926T191855 comment=N
ONE
channel ORA_DISK_1: backup set complete, elapsed time: 00:00:07
Finished backup at 26-SEP-12
RMAN>

The log following the execution of the `backup` command gives us a lot of information that reinforces what we've already discussed. First, we see `allocated channel`. Whenever a backup is run, a **backup channel** is allocated to handle the work being done. A channel will be allocated by default, or we can define one or more manually. Next, we see `specifying datafile(s) in backup set`. This indicates that a backup set has been established and the next line, `input datafile file number=00004 name=`, indicates the datafile number and name of the datafile in the backup set. If there were multiple files in the `USERS` tablespace, we would see multiple files listed. Following the log entries indicating that the backup pieces were started and finished, we see the name of the backup piece listed as `piece handle=`. Notice that the directory of the backup piece is in the **Flash Recovery Area** or **FRA** (`../flash_recovery_area/ORCL/..`). This indicates that the FRA we implemented in the last chapter is functioning normally. Finally, the output log tells us the time spent completing the backup set.

Performing a full backup

One of the strengths of RMAN's scripting language is its consistency. The syntax for backing up an entire database is very similar to that of a tablespace-level backup, and is very intuitive. When we backup an entire database and all of its respective datafiles, the backup is known as a **full backup**. To execute an RMAN full backup, we use the `backup database` command, as shown in the following screenshot:

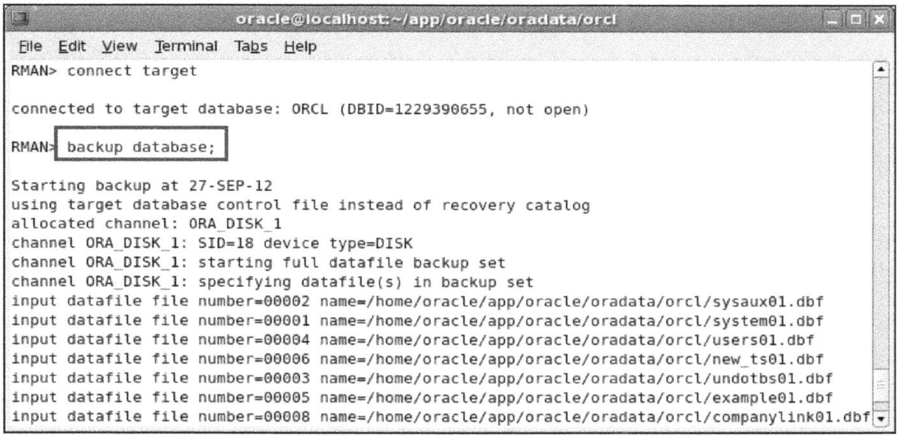
oracle@localhost:~/app/oracle/oradata/orcl
File Edit View Terminal Tabs Help
RMAN> connect target
connected to target database: ORCL (DBID=1229390655, not open)
RMAN> backup database;
Starting backup at 27-SEP-12
using target database control file instead of recovery catalog
allocated channel: ORA_DISK_1
channel ORA_DISK_1: SID=18 device type=DISK
channel ORA_DISK_1: starting full datafile backup set
channel ORA_DISK_1: specifying datafile(s) in backup set
input datafile file number=00002 name=/home/oracle/app/oracle/oradata/orcl/sysaux01.dbf
input datafile file number=00001 name=/home/oracle/app/oracle/oradata/orcl/system01.dbf
input datafile file number=00004 name=/home/oracle/app/oracle/oradata/orcl/users01.dbf
input datafile file number=00006 name=/home/oracle/app/oracle/oradata/orcl/new_ts01.dbf
input datafile file number=00003 name=/home/oracle/app/oracle/oradata/orcl/undotbs01.dbf
input datafile file number=00005 name=/home/oracle/app/oracle/oradata/orcl/example01.dbf
input datafile file number=00008 name=/home/oracle/app/oracle/oradata/orcl/companylink01.dbf

Although this backup takes considerably longer to run, note that the log output is very similar to what we've already seen. The datafiles are specified as a part of a backup set and written out to backup pieces. However, at the end of the backup log, we notice something different.

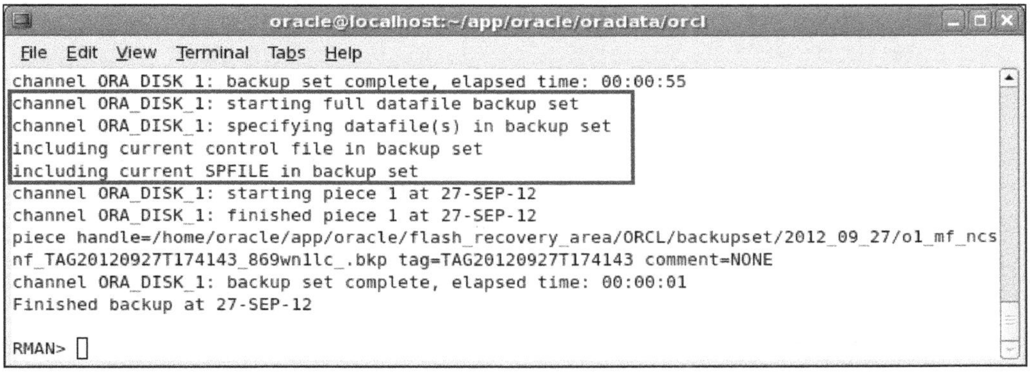
oracle@localhost:~/app/oracle/oradata/orcl
File Edit View Terminal Tabs Help
channel ORA_DISK_1: backup set complete, elapsed time: 00:00:55
channel ORA_DISK_1: starting full datafile backup set
channel ORA_DISK_1: specifying datafile(s) in backup set
including current control file in backup set
including current SPFILE in backup set
channel ORA_DISK_1: starting piece 1 at 27-SEP-12
channel ORA_DISK_1: finished piece 1 at 27-SEP-12
piece handle=/home/oracle/app/oracle/flash_recovery_area/ORCL/backupset/2012_09_27/o1_mf_ncs
nf_TAG20120927T174143_869wn1lc_.bkp tag=TAG20120927T174143 comment=NONE
channel ORA_DISK_1: backup set complete, elapsed time: 00:00:01
Finished backup at 27-SEP-12
RMAN>

After the datafiles are backed up, a second backup starts. According to the log, the current control file and SPFILE are both included in the backup set, which is allocated and run automatically. This automatic backup operation is extremely important when it's necessary to do a complete recovery from the loss of every database-related file. In such a scenario, it is vital to be able to restore the control file from backup, and very helpful to recover the SPFILE.

Performing compressed backups

Even with an RMAN backup that ignores the datafile's whitespace, backups of large databases require a great deal of space. In situations where the backup space is at a premium, backup compression can be extremely useful. It is also important to note that while we might expect that adding compression to our backups might substantially lengthen the amount of time needed for our backup, this generally isn't the case. The compression algorithms used with RMAN are extremely efficient and generally won't add a great deal to the amount of time needed for the backup, because the blocks are compressed on the fly. Running a compressed backup is as simple as adding a compression clause to the backup statement.

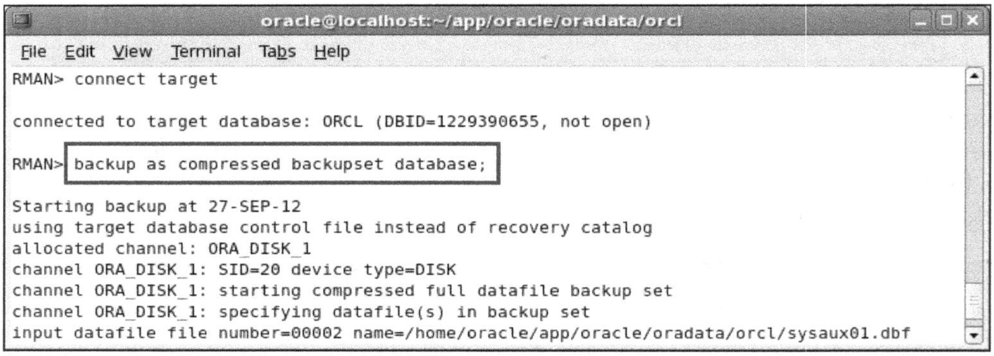
oracle@localhost:~/app/oracle/oradata/orcl
File Edit View Terminal Tabs Help
RMAN> connect target
connected to target database: ORCL (DBID=1229390655, not open)
RMAN> backup as compressed backupset database;
Starting backup at 27-SEP-12
using target database control file instead of recovery catalog
allocated channel: ORA_DISK_1
channel ORA_DISK_1: SID=20 device type=DISK
channel ORA_DISK_1: starting compressed full datafile backup set
channel ORA_DISK_1: specifying datafile(s) in backup set
input datafile file number=00002 name=/home/oracle/app/oracle/oradata/orcl/sysaux01.dbf

If we examine the output of the last two backups, the first uncompressed and the second compressed, we can see the size difference in the output files. The compressed piece is less than half the size of the uncompressed piece.

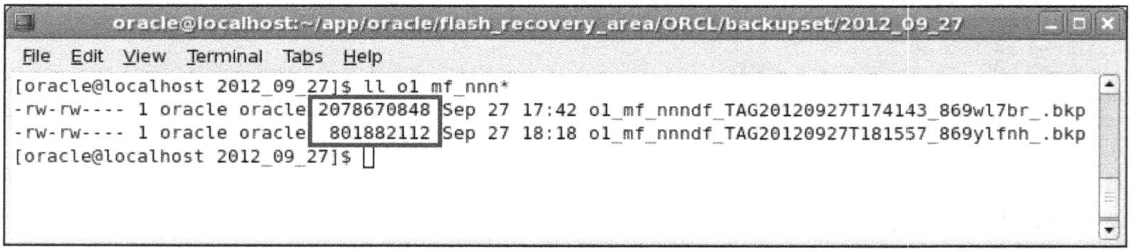
oracle@localhost:~/app/oracle/flash_recovery_area/ORCL/backupset/2012_09_27
File Edit View Terminal Tabs Help
[oracle@localhost 2012_09_27]$ ll o1_mf_nnn*
-rw-rw---- 1 oracle oracle 2078670848 Sep 27 17:42 o1_mf_nnndf_TAG20120927T174143_869wl7br_.bkp
-rw-rw---- 1 oracle oracle 801882112 Sep 27 18:18 o1_mf_nnndf_TAG20120927T181557_869ylfnh_.bkp
[oracle@localhost 2012_09_27]$

Backing up image copies

As we discussed earlier in the chapter, an image copy is a byte-for-byte copy of a datafile that is interchangeable with it. Image copies are sometimes created as a part of certain cloning strategies. To create an image copy of a tablespace, we run the backup command as shown in the following screenshot:

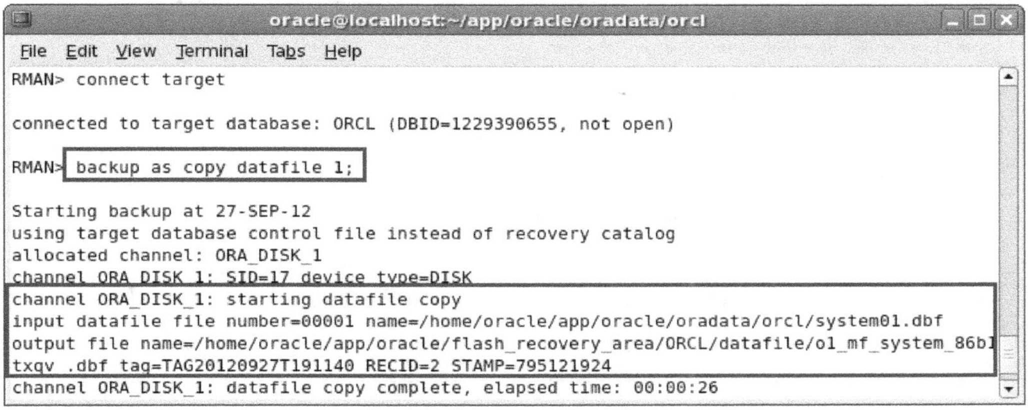
oracle@localhost:~/app/oracle/oradata/orcl
File Edit View Terminal Tabs Help
RMAN> connect target
connected to target database: ORCL (DBID=1229390655, not open)
RMAN> backup as copy datafile 1;
Starting backup at 27-SEP-12
using target database control file instead of recovery catalog
allocated channel: ORA_DISK_1
channel ORA_DISK_1: SID=17 device type=DISK
channel ORA_DISK_1: starting datafile copy
input datafile file number=00001 name=/home/oracle/app/oracle/oradata/orcl/system01.dbf
output file name=/home/oracle/app/oracle/flash_recovery_area/ORCL/datafile/o1_mf_system_86b]
txqv_.dbf tag=TAG20120927T191140 RECID=2 STAMP=795121924
channel ORA_DISK_1: datafile copy complete, elapsed time: 00:00:26

Using the `backup as copy` command, we create an image copy of `datafile 1` – the `SYSTEM` tablespace datafile. The log indicates to us that a copy is occurring, lists the input datafile, and states the name of the output datafile copy. Image copies can also be done at the database level using the `backup as copy database` command.

Performing RMAN hot backups

As we mentioned, the command-line syntax of RMAN is very similar, regardless of the type of backup being performed. Unlike user-managed backups, performing hot backups while the database is online is almost identical in process to offline backups. The main difference is the state of the database: hot backups run while the database is up and available.

Performing full hot backups

To begin with our hot backup, we should first bring it online. We can also do this from the RMAN command line. We must also remember that to run a hot backup, we must be in ARCHIVELOG mode. Our database is currently in a mount state, so we need to open it first.

```
Recovery Manager: Release 11.2.0.2.0 - Production on Sat Sep 29 13:37:59 2012

Copyright (c) 1982, 2009, Oracle and/or its affiliates.  All rights reserved.

RMAN> connect target

connected to target database: ORCL (DBID=1229390655, not open)

RMAN> alter database open;

using target database control file instead of recovery catalog
database opened

RMAN>
```

Now that the database is open, because we're already in ARCHIVELOG mode, we can simply execute a `backup database` command. However, let's expand our RMAN skill set by taking the opportunity to learn a little more about RMAN syntax.

We can interact with RMAN through the command line and execute many basic statements. However, we can also batch numerous commands together using a run script. A **run script** or **RMAN script** is a set of RMAN statements, which begin with `run`, that will execute the set in a batch. Often, it is desirable to back up both the database and the archive logs at the same time to maintain backup consistency. We'll use a run script to do this.

```
RMAN> run {
2> allocate channel c1 type disk;
3> backup as compressed backupset database;
4> backup as compressed backupset archivelog all delete all input;
5> }

allocated channel: c1
channel c1: SID=32 device type=DISK

Starting backup at 29-SEP-12
channel c1: starting compressed full datafile backup set
channel c1: specifying datafile(s) in backup set
input datafile file number=00002 name=/home/oracle/app/oracle/oradata/orcl/sysaux01.dbf
input datafile file number=00001 name=/home/oracle/app/oracle/oradata/orcl/system01.dbf
```

We will begin the script with the `run` command, and enclose it with brackets. The first line explicitly allocates a named backup channel, rather than allowing RMAN to define a default channel. With large backups, we can define numerous channels to improve performance. The second line of the script performs a compressed full database backup. The third backs up all archive logs and deletes them after they are backed up. This is helpful in maintaining the available space for our archived logs. The last portion of the log shows the actions that were taken by RMAN during the archivelog backup.

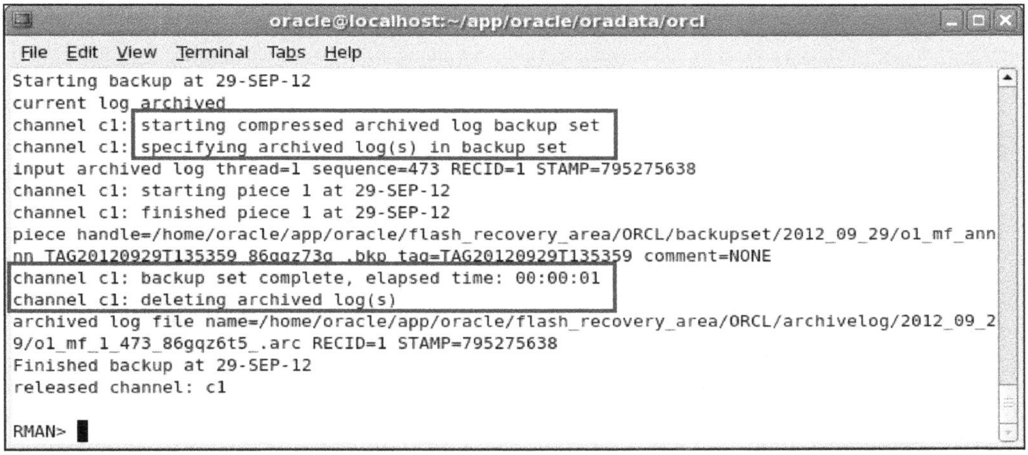
oracle@localhost:~/app/oracle/oradata/orcl
File Edit View Terminal Tabs Help
Starting backup at 29-SEP-12
current log archived
channel c1: starting compressed archived log backup set
channel c1: specifying archived log(s) in backup set
input archived log thread=1 sequence=473 RECID=1 STAMP=795275638
channel c1: starting piece 1 at 29-SEP-12
channel c1: finished piece 1 at 29-SEP-12
piece handle=/home/oracle/app/oracle/flash_recovery_area/ORCL/backupset/2012_09_29/o1_mf_ann
nn_TAG20120929T135359_86gqz73q_.bkp tag=TAG20120929T135359 comment=NONE
channel c1: backup set complete, elapsed time: 00:00:01
channel c1: deleting archived log(s)
archived log file name=/home/oracle/app/oracle/flash_recovery_area/ORCL/archivelog/2012_09_2
9/o1_mf_1_473_86gqz6t5_.arc RECID=1 STAMP=795275638
Finished backup at 29-SEP-12
released channel: c1
RMAN>

Creating incremental backups

One of the most desirable features for any backup application is the ability to do incremental backups. **Incremental backups** allow the DBA to take a base backup of the database and then take smaller, more frequent backups that only back up the changes since the last backup. As we've mentioned previously, RMAN supports this feature.

The default type of incremental backup used in RMAN is the **differential incremental backup**. This type of backup relies on various backup levels in order to achieve the most efficient incremental backups. For any type of incremental backup in RMAN, the first backup that must be taken is known as a level 0 (zero) backup. A level 0 backup backs up the database in the same way as a full backup; however, a level 0 can be used as the base for any additional incremental backups. Let's examine how a differential incremental works.

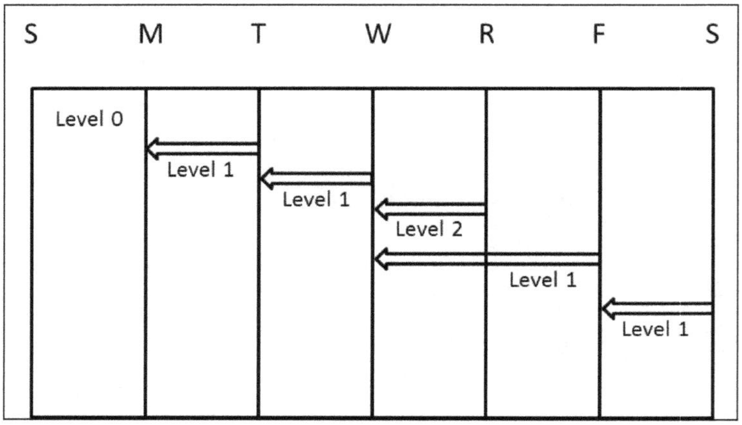
S
M
T
W
R
F
S
Level 0
Level 1
Level 1
Level 2
Level 1
Level 1

As we mentioned, RMAN incremental backups rely on various levels to organize which data is backed up. In the preceding diagram, a level 0 backup is taken on Sunday, forming the basis for other incrementals. By definition, differential incremental backups back up all the data blocks that have changed since the last level *n* or lower backup. Thus, when a level 1 incremental is taken on Monday, *n* is 1, and it backs up data that has changed since the last level 0 or 1 backup. On Tuesday, a new level 1 backup backs up data since the most recent level 0 or 1 backup. On Wednesday, a level 2 incremental is taken, which backs up changes since the last level 0, 1, or 2 backup. However, on Thursday, when a new level 1 is taken, it backs up data since the last level 0 or 1 backup, which requires it to back up changes since Tuesday. In this manner, a DBA has the flexibility to control the day on which certain backups can occur. We list three different levels in this example, but it is not uncommon in an incremental backup strategy to only use levels 0 and 1. One level 0 is taken during the week, such as Sunday, and daily level 1 backups are taken on other days. Finally, RMAN also allows for a different strategy, a cumulative incremental backup, to be taken in a similar fashion. However, a **cumulative incremental backup** backs up all changed blocks since the last *n-1* level backup. A cumulative backup requires the use of the `CUMULATIVE` keyword. Thus, a cumulative incremental level 1 will only back up the data changed since the last *n-1* backup, or level 0 backup. A level 2 cumulative would back up changes since the last *n-1* backup, meaning level 0 or 1.

Let's examine a differential incremental backup in practice. First, we create a level 0 backup that backs up all the blocks in the database.

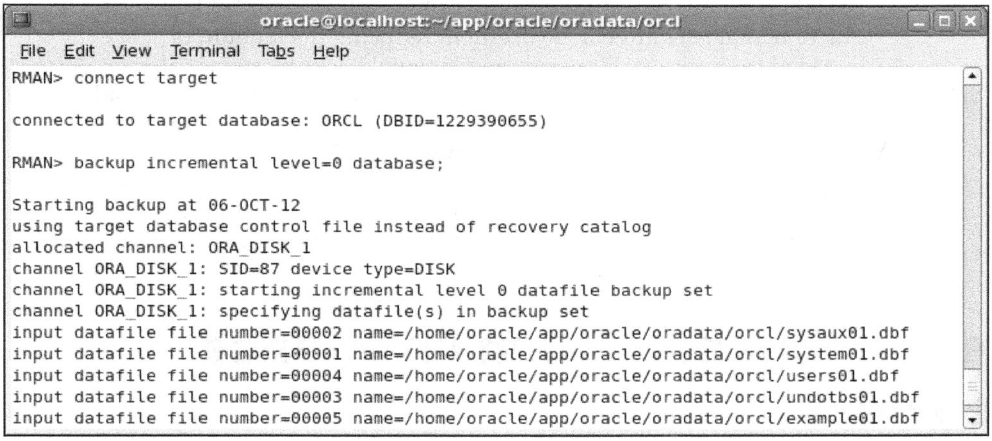

```
oracle@localhost:~/app/oracle/oradata/orcl
File Edit View Terminal Tabs Help
RMAN> connect target

connected to target database: ORCL (DBID=1229390655)

RMAN> backup incremental level=0 database;

Starting backup at 06-OCT-12
using target database control file instead of recovery catalog
allocated channel: ORA_DISK_1
channel ORA_DISK_1: SID=87 device type=DISK
channel ORA_DISK_1: starting incremental level 0 datafile backup set
channel ORA_DISK_1: specifying datafile(s) in backup set
input datafile file number=00002 name=/home/oracle/app/oracle/oradata/orcl/sysaux01.dbf
input datafile file number=00001 name=/home/oracle/app/oracle/oradata/orcl/system01.dbf
input datafile file number=00004 name=/home/oracle/app/oracle/oradata/orcl/users01.dbf
input datafile file number=00003 name=/home/oracle/app/oracle/oradata/orcl/undotbs01.dbf
input datafile file number=00005 name=/home/oracle/app/oracle/oradata/orcl/example01.dbf
```

Next, we'll assume that the changes have taken place in the database, say, over the course of a day. Our level 0 is in place; we can now take a differential incremental.

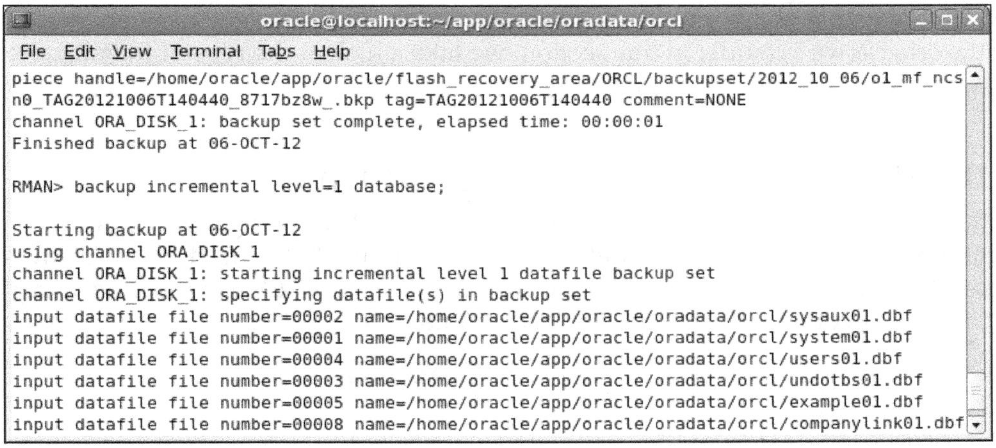

```
oracle@localhost:~/app/oracle/oradata/orcl
File Edit View Terminal Tabs Help
piece handle=/home/oracle/app/oracle/flash_recovery_area/ORCL/backupset/2012_10_06/o1_mf_ncs
n0_TAG20121006T140440_8717bz8w_.bkp tag=TAG20121006T140440 comment=NONE
channel ORA_DISK_1: backup set complete, elapsed time: 00:00:01
Finished backup at 06-OCT-12

RMAN> backup incremental level=1 database;

Starting backup at 06-OCT-12
using channel ORA_DISK_1
channel ORA_DISK_1: starting incremental level 1 datafile backup set
channel ORA_DISK_1: specifying datafile(s) in backup set
input datafile file number=00002 name=/home/oracle/app/oracle/oradata/orcl/sysaux01.dbf
input datafile file number=00001 name=/home/oracle/app/oracle/oradata/orcl/system01.dbf
input datafile file number=00004 name=/home/oracle/app/oracle/oradata/orcl/users01.dbf
input datafile file number=00003 name=/home/oracle/app/oracle/oradata/orcl/undotbs01.dbf
input datafile file number=00005 name=/home/oracle/app/oracle/oradata/orcl/example01.dbf
input datafile file number=00008 name=/home/oracle/app/oracle/oradata/orcl/companylink01.dbf
```

The resulting incremental backup takes significantly less time to run, as well as less space. To summarize these RMAN commands in a syntax tree, examine the following from the RMAN command prompt:

```
BACKUP [ FULL | INCREMENTAL LEVEL <x> ]
  [ DATABASE | DATAFILE <x> | TABLESPACE 'tablespace_name' ]
  AS [ COPY OF | COMPRESSED BACKUPSET ]
```

> **The real-world DBA**
>
> Incremental strategies are driven largely by the requirements for database recovery and the amount of time allowed for backups. Incremental backups can be useful in reducing the amount of space needed for backups. However, incremental backups are not always faster than their full counterparts. Because every block must be read before determining whether to back it up, an incremental can take almost as long as a full backup. To mitigate this, Oracle provides a feature called **block change tracking**, which can be used to keep a running list of blocks that change between the incrementals. This can result in a very significant reduction in time for incremental backups.

Performing backup maintenance activities

No matter what type of backup we use, it will require maintenance, particularly in terms of space. Thus, being able to maintain a sufficient amount of free space for new backups is crucial to any backup strategy. This is another area where RMAN shines. Instead of requiring manual calculations and dangerous file deletions, RMAN is capable of determining what backup files are needed for recovery, based on the criteria we provide. In this section, we take a look at the type of maintenance activities we can perform with RMAN.

Understanding RMAN Parameters

With RMAN, we can specify basic criteria, called **RMAN parameters**, for how we want our backups to operate by default. This can eliminate the need for a certain amount of scripting in some situations. We can view our RMAN parameters using the `show all` command from the RMAN command line.

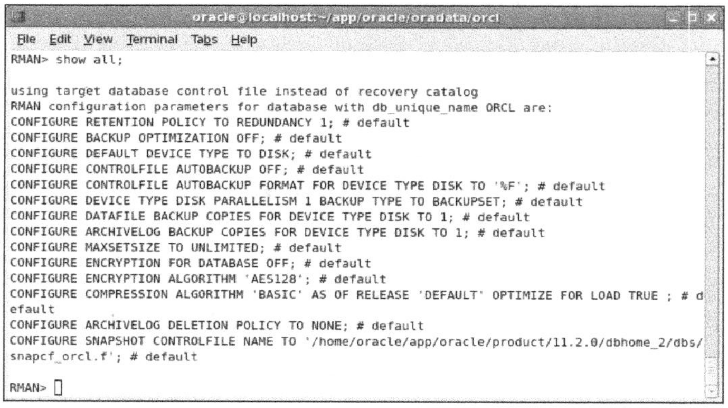
oracle@localhost:~/app/oracle/oradata/orcl
File Edit View Terminal Tabs Help
RMAN> show all;
using target database control file instead of recovery catalog
RMAN configuration parameters for database with db_unique_name ORCL are:
CONFIGURE RETENTION POLICY TO REDUNDANCY 1; # default
CONFIGURE BACKUP OPTIMIZATION OFF; # default
CONFIGURE DEFAULT DEVICE TYPE TO DISK; # default
CONFIGURE CONTROLFILE AUTOBACKUP OFF; # default
CONFIGURE CONTROLFILE AUTOBACKUP FORMAT FOR DEVICE TYPE DISK TO '%F'; # default
CONFIGURE DEVICE TYPE DISK PARALLELISM 1 BACKUP TYPE TO BACKUPSET; # default
CONFIGURE DATAFILE BACKUP COPIES FOR DEVICE TYPE DISK TO 1; # default
CONFIGURE ARCHIVELOG BACKUP COPIES FOR DEVICE TYPE DISK TO 1; # default
CONFIGURE MAXSETSIZE TO UNLIMITED; # default
CONFIGURE ENCRYPTION FOR DATABASE OFF; # default
CONFIGURE ENCRYPTION ALGORITHM 'AES128'; # default
CONFIGURE COMPRESSION ALGORITHM 'BASIC' AS OF RELEASE 'DEFAULT' OPTIMIZE FOR LOAD TRUE ; # d
efault
CONFIGURE ARCHIVELOG DELETION POLICY TO NONE; # default
CONFIGURE SNAPSHOT CONTROLFILE NAME TO '/home/oracle/app/oracle/product/11.2.0/dbhome_2/dbs/
snapcf_orcl.f'; # default
RMAN>

An exhaustive look at these parameters is outside the scope of this book, and, in fact, many of these parameters need not be changed at all, particularly if we are using the FRA. However, we should point out two of these—one, because it bears on our discussion of maintenance, and the other because it adds a measure of safety for our backups. In the preceding screenshot, we notice the following line:

```
CONFIGURE RETENTION POLICY TO REDUNDANCY 1;
```

This parameter indicates that our retention policy is set to 1, which means we always intend to retain one complete backup. This can be changed to another value for `REDUNDANCY`, or be changed to base our redundancy on a fixed time period instead of the number of backups. For instance, we could change our retention policy to 7 days instead of one complete backup. For our purposes, we'll keep the default value.

The second parameter is the one that we should change from the default value. The `CONTROLFILE AUTOBACKUP` parameter, when enabled, will automatically back up the control file and the SPFILE whenever a structural change occurs to the database, such as the addition of a datafile. This adds a measure of safety during recovery, so we should enable it. RMAN displays parameters in a manner that makes them easy to change. We will simply copy and paste the relevant line and make any changes we need. We can see this in the following screenshot:

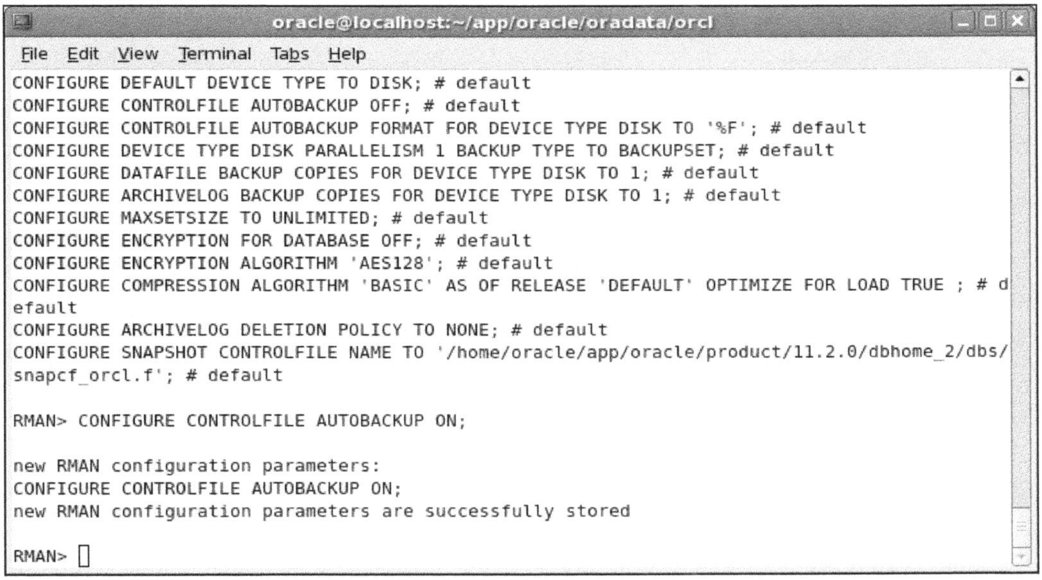
oracle@localhost:~/app/oracle/oradata/orcl
File Edit View Terminal Tabs Help
CONFIGURE DEFAULT DEVICE TYPE TO DISK; # default
CONFIGURE CONTROLFILE AUTOBACKUP OFF; # default
CONFIGURE CONTROLFILE AUTOBACKUP FORMAT FOR DEVICE TYPE DISK TO '%F'; # default
CONFIGURE DEVICE TYPE DISK PARALLELISM 1 BACKUP TYPE TO BACKUPSET; # default
CONFIGURE DATAFILE BACKUP COPIES FOR DEVICE TYPE DISK TO 1; # default
CONFIGURE ARCHIVELOG BACKUP COPIES FOR DEVICE TYPE DISK TO 1; # default
CONFIGURE MAXSETSIZE TO UNLIMITED; # default
CONFIGURE ENCRYPTION FOR DATABASE OFF; # default
CONFIGURE ENCRYPTION ALGORITHM 'AES128'; # default
CONFIGURE COMPRESSION ALGORITHM 'BASIC' AS OF RELEASE 'DEFAULT' OPTIMIZE FOR LOAD TRUE ; # d
efault
CONFIGURE ARCHIVELOG DELETION POLICY TO NONE; # default
CONFIGURE SNAPSHOT CONTROLFILE NAME TO '/home/oracle/app/oracle/product/11.2.0/dbhome_2/dbs/
snapcf_orcl.f'; # default
RMAN> CONFIGURE CONTROLFILE AUTOBACKUP ON;
new RMAN configuration parameters:
CONFIGURE CONTROLFILE AUTOBACKUP ON;
new RMAN configuration parameters are successfully stored
RMAN>

Using the LIST command in RMAN

As mentioned earlier, all of the metadata information about backups taken is stored in the RMAN repository. RMAN is capable of using the repository to generate a number of reports that give us information on what has, or even what has not, been backed up. The RMAN `LIST` command can be used as shown in the following screenshot:

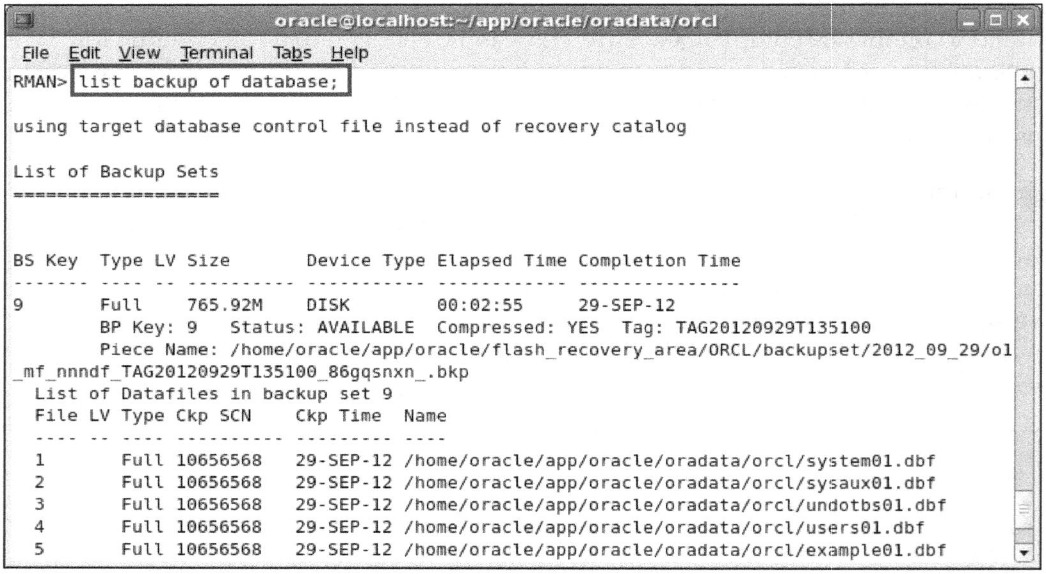
oracle@localhost:~/app/oracle/oradata/orcl
File Edit View Terminal Tabs Help
RMAN> list backup of database;
using target database control file instead of recovery catalog
List of Backup Sets
===================
BS Key Type LV Size Device Type Elapsed Time Completion Time
9 Full 765.92M DISK 00:02:55 29-SEP-12
BP Key: 9 Status: AVAILABLE Compressed: YES Tag: TAG20120929T135100
Piece Name: /home/oracle/app/oracle/flash_recovery_area/ORCL/backupset/2012_09_29/o1_mf_nnndf_TAG20120929T135100_86gqsnxn_.bkp
List of Datafiles in backup set 9
File LV Type Ckp SCN Ckp Time Name
1 Full 10656568 29-SEP-12 /home/oracle/app/oracle/oradata/orcl/system01.dbf
2 Full 10656568 29-SEP-12 /home/oracle/app/oracle/oradata/orcl/sysaux01.dbf
3 Full 10656568 29-SEP-12 /home/oracle/app/oracle/oradata/orcl/undotbs01.dbf
4 Full 10656568 29-SEP-12 /home/oracle/app/oracle/oradata/orcl/users01.dbf
5 Full 10656568 29-SEP-12 /home/oracle/app/oracle/oradata/orcl/example01.dbf

The `list backup of database` command presents us with a great deal of information about the backups we've taken, including sizing and timing information as well as a list of the files in the backup set. This information can be used to historically track how our backups are performing. An expanded summary of the types of `LIST` commands available to us is as follows:

```
LIST [ FAILURE | COPY | BACKUP [ OF DATABASE | SUMMARY | BY FILE ] ]
```

Using the REPORT command in RMAN

The second command used to leverage the RMAN metadata is `REPORT`. The `REPORT` command is slightly different than `LIST` in that, although it can return the metadata information, it can also actively use that information to do maintenance. The `REPORT` command is probably the most important of the maintenance commands in that it can actually tell us whether we're safe from a backup perspective. Let's examine the `REPORT` command.

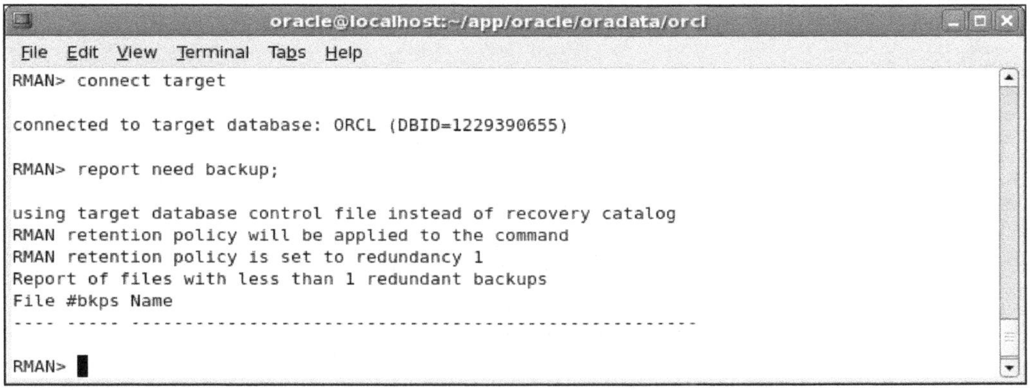
oracle@localhost:~/app/oracle/oradata/orcl
File Edit View Terminal Tabs Help
RMAN> connect target
connected to target database: ORCL (DBID=1229390655)
RMAN> report need backup;
using target database control file instead of recovery catalog
RMAN retention policy will be applied to the command
RMAN retention policy is set to redundancy 1
Report of files with less than 1 redundant backups
File #bkps Name
---- ----- ---
RMAN>

The `REPORT NEED BACKUP` command is crucial to the maintenance of our backup strategy. When we issue this command, RMAN examines its existing metadata to determine whether we have sufficient backups to satisfy our retention policy. Recall from our look at RMAN parameters that our retention policy is set to one complete backup. As long as the number of recorded backups meet that condition, our `REPORT` command will return no rows, indicating that we are sufficiently backed up. If it did return rows, they would indicate the datafiles that have not been backed up to satisfy our retention policy, and that our database may not be recoverable. In that situation, we should run a backup immediately. Thus, this command can act as a manual check to determine if our database is currently recoverable. This is especially useful in situations where a running backup has failed due to insufficient space or some other reason. It is absolutely crucial to understand that `REPORT NEED BACKUP` gets its information from the RMAN repository. If we have manually deleted the backup pieces using operating system commands, the repository will not be aware of this and will not report our recoverability status accurately. Thus, instead of using operating system commands, we should use our next `REPORT` command.

The second `REPORT` command is crucial in maintaining sufficient backup space – in our case, the flash recovery area. We use `REPORT OBSOLETE` to determine which backups are safe to remove. When used in conjunction with the `DELETE OBSOLETE` command, these operations can safely remove any backups or archive logs that are no longer needed, based on our retention policy. We execute this command as shown in the following screenshot:

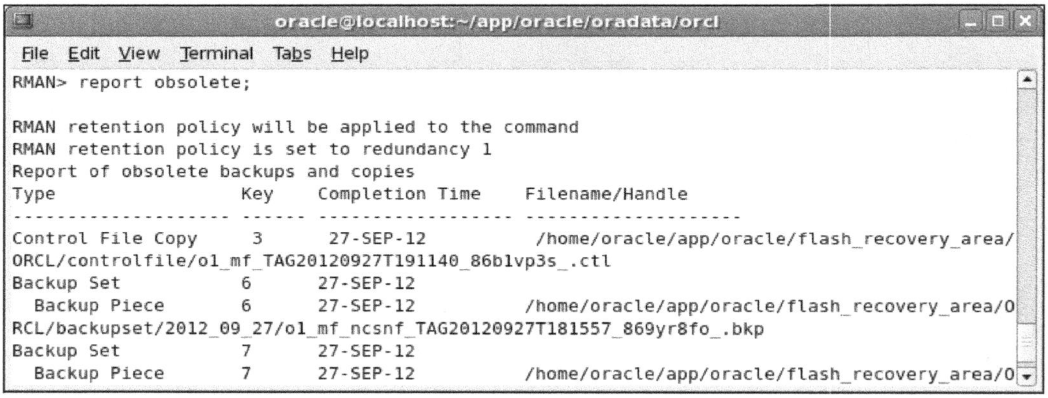

```
RMAN> report obsolete;

RMAN retention policy will be applied to the command
RMAN retention policy is set to redundancy 1
Report of obsolete backups and copies
Type                 Key    Completion Time    Filename/Handle
-------------------- ------ ------------------ --------------------
Control File Copy     3      27-SEP-12          /home/oracle/app/oracle/flash_recovery_area/
ORCL/controlfile/o1_mf_TAG20120927T191140_86blvp3s_.ctl
Backup Set           6      27-SEP-12
  Backup Piece       6      27-SEP-12          /home/oracle/app/oracle/flash_recovery_area/O
RCL/backupset/2012_09_27/o1_mf_ncsnf_TAG20120927T181557_869yr8fo_.bkp
Backup Set           7      27-SEP-12
  Backup Piece       7      27-SEP-12          /home/oracle/app/oracle/flash_recovery_area/O
```

When we issue the `REPORT OBSOLETE` command, we receive a list of various obsolete backups. RMAN has reviewed the repository and found that all of the blocks in these backups have newer backups in place and can be removed. Rather than deleting them manually, we can use the `DELETE OBSOLETE` command to ensure that no mistakes are made.

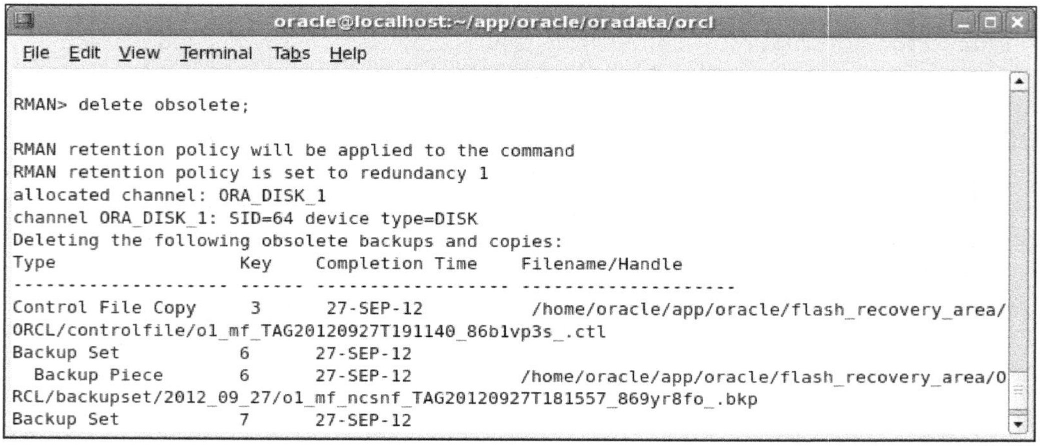

```
RMAN> delete obsolete;

RMAN retention policy will be applied to the command
RMAN retention policy is set to redundancy 1
allocated channel: ORA_DISK_1
channel ORA_DISK_1: SID=64 device type=DISK
Deleting the following obsolete backups and copies:
Type                 Key    Completion Time    Filename/Handle
-------------------- ------ ------------------ --------------------
Control File Copy     3      27-SEP-12          /home/oracle/app/oracle/flash_recovery_area/
ORCL/controlfile/o1_mf_TAG20120927T191140_86blvp3s_.ctl
Backup Set           6      27-SEP-12
  Backup Piece       6      27-SEP-12          /home/oracle/app/oracle/flash_recovery_area/O
RCL/backupset/2012_09_27/o1_mf_ncsnf_TAG20120927T181557_869yr8fo_.bkp
Backup Set           7      27-SEP-12
```

When this command is executed, a prompt will appear after a listing of the obsolete files.

```
Do you really want to delete the above objects (enter YES or NO)? YES
deleted control file copy
control file copy file name=/home/oracle/app/oracle/flash_recovery_area/ORCL/controlfile/o1_
mf_TAG20120927T191140_86blvp3s_.ctl RECID=3 STAMP=795121926
deleted backup piece
backup piece handle=/home/oracle/app/oracle/flash_recovery_area/ORCL/backupset/2012_10_06/o1
_mf_ncsn0_TAG20121006T140440_8717bz8w_.bkp RECID=13 STAMP=795967599
Deleted 2 objects

RMAN-06207: WARNING: 6 objects could not be deleted for DISK channel(s) due
RMAN-06208:          to mismatched status.  Use CROSSCHECK command to fix status
RMAN-06210: List of Mismatched objects
RMAN-06211: ==========================
RMAN-06212:   Object Type   Filename/Handle
RMAN-06213: --------------- ---------------------------------------------------
```

Respond with `YES` and the files are deleted. A warning message also appears, indicating that some files could not be removed due to "mismatched status". We will address this situation in the next section. A summary syntax tree for the `REPORT` command is shown as follows:

```
REPORT [ SCHEMA | OBSOLETE | UNRECOVERABLE | NEED BACKUP ]
```

> **The real-world DBA**
>
> The importance of the `REPORT` and `DELETE OBSOLETE` commands cannot be overstated. Without RMAN and these commands, a DBA must rely on operating system commands and manual date calculations to remove backup pieces. The results can be disastrous to our recoverability status. If *one* wrong file is removed, the database may not be recoverable. It is far safer to rely on RMAN to determine which pieces can be removed, especially because RMAN sees below the file level, all the way down to the database blocks themselves.

Checking files using CROSSCHECK

We made the observation in the previous section that the `RMAN REPORT` command looks into the repository for its information as to the status of existing RMAN backup pieces. We also observed a warning message indicating that some files had a "mismatched status". When the backup pieces are deleted without using the `REPORT` and `DELETE` commands, they can receive this status. Essentially, RMAN cannot reconcile the status of these files with what it sees in the repository. The `CROSSCHECK` command is used to perform this reconciliation between the repository and the actual files on the disk. It checks the files that should be present according to the repository against what is actually there. The command is used as shown in the following screenshot:

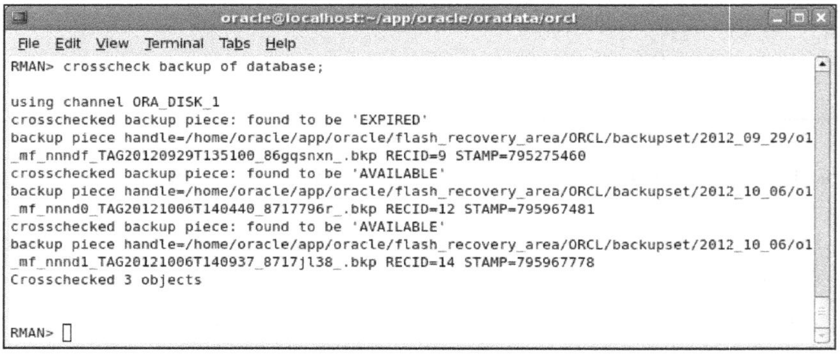

```
RMAN> crosscheck backup of database;

using channel ORA_DISK_1
crosschecked backup piece: found to be 'EXPIRED'
backup piece handle=/home/oracle/app/oracle/flash_recovery_area/ORCL/backupset/2012_09_29/o1
_mf_nnndf_TAG20120929T135100_86gqsnxn_.bkp RECID=9 STAMP=795275460
crosschecked backup piece: found to be 'AVAILABLE'
backup piece handle=/home/oracle/app/oracle/flash_recovery_area/ORCL/backupset/2012_10_06/o1
_mf_nnnd0_TAG20121006T140440_8717796r_.bkp RECID=12 STAMP=795967481
crosschecked backup piece: found to be 'AVAILABLE'
backup piece handle=/home/oracle/app/oracle/flash_recovery_area/ORCL/backupset/2012_10_06/o1
_mf_nnnd1_TAG20121006T140937_8717jl38_.bkp RECID=14 STAMP=795967778
Crosschecked 3 objects

RMAN>
```

When we issue the `crosscheck backup of database` command, some pieces are found to be available while others are expired. The pieces with the `AVAILABLE` status are present in both the repository and the backup location, while those with the `EXPIRED` status are not. Backups with the `EXPIRED` status can be removed from the repository using the `DELETE` command as shown in the following screenshot:

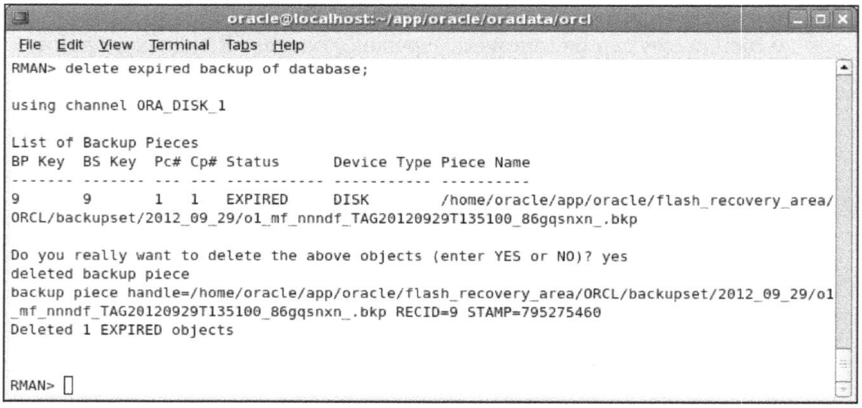

```
RMAN> delete expired backup of database;

using channel ORA_DISK_1

List of Backup Pieces
BP Key  BS Key  Pc# Cp# Status      Device Type Piece Name
------- ------- --- --- ----------- ----------- ----------
9       9       1   1   EXPIRED     DISK        /home/oracle/app/oracle/flash_recovery_area/
ORCL/backupset/2012_09_29/o1_mf_nnndf_TAG20120929T135100_86gqsnxn_.bkp

Do you really want to delete the above objects (enter YES or NO)? yes
deleted backup piece
backup piece handle=/home/oracle/app/oracle/flash_recovery_area/ORCL/backupset/2012_09_29/o1
_mf_nnndf_TAG20120929T135100_86gqsnxn_.bkp RECID=9 STAMP=795275460
Deleted 1 EXPIRED objects

RMAN>
```

When prompted with a confirmation, respond with `YES` to proceed with the deletion. The `CROSSCHECK` command we have used here is specific to database backup files. We can also use the following `CROSSCHECK` commands to reconcile other types of backups:

- `CROSSCHECK archivelog all;`
- `CROSSCHECK backup of archivelog all;`
- `CROSSCHECK backup of controlfile;`

Monitoring the Flash Recovery Area with Enterprise Manager

At times, the DBA should monitor the amount of space available for backup files. Although we can use filesystem tools to do this, when we're using the Flash Recovery Area, we are dealing with a defined limit on space. Thus, while the filesystem may show sufficient space, we may be close to the limit imposed by the FRA. In order to more accurately determine the available FRA space and its usage, we can use the Enterprise Manager tool—in our case, Database Control. Additionally, Database Control is an excellent tool to monitor a number of characteristics of the Flash Recovery Area beyond the disk usage. To navigate to the **Recovery Settings** page, log in to the Database Control from a web browser, click on the **Availability** tab, and then click on the **Recovery Settings** link. Let's examine the sections of this page:

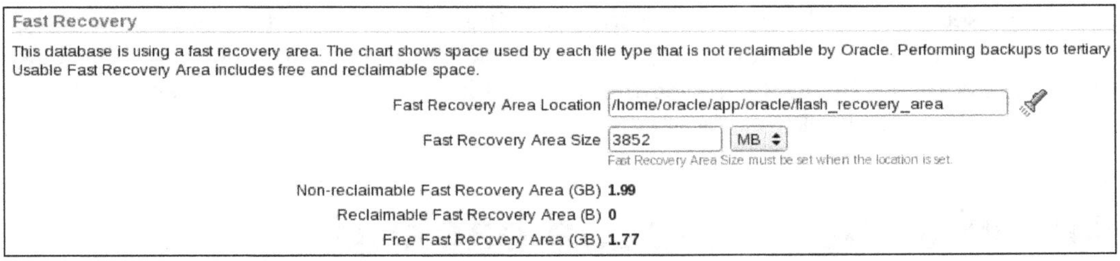
Fast Recovery
This database is using a fast recovery area. The chart shows space used by each file type that is not reclaimable by Oracle. Performing backups to tertiary
Usable Fast Recovery Area includes free and reclaimable space.
Fast Recovery Area Location
/home/oracle/app/oracle/flash_recovery_area
Fast Recovery Area Size
3852
MB
Fast Recovery Area Size must be set when the location is set.
Non-reclaimable Fast Recovery Area (GB) 1.99
Reclaimable Fast Recovery Area (B) 0
Free Fast Recovery Area (GB) 1.77

This portion of the page indicates the amount of space allocated to the FRA as well as its location on the disk. Notice that Enterprise Manager lists this section as "Fast Recovery Area". This is the new name for the Flash Recovery Area, although defaults still point to `flash_recovery_area` as the default directory.

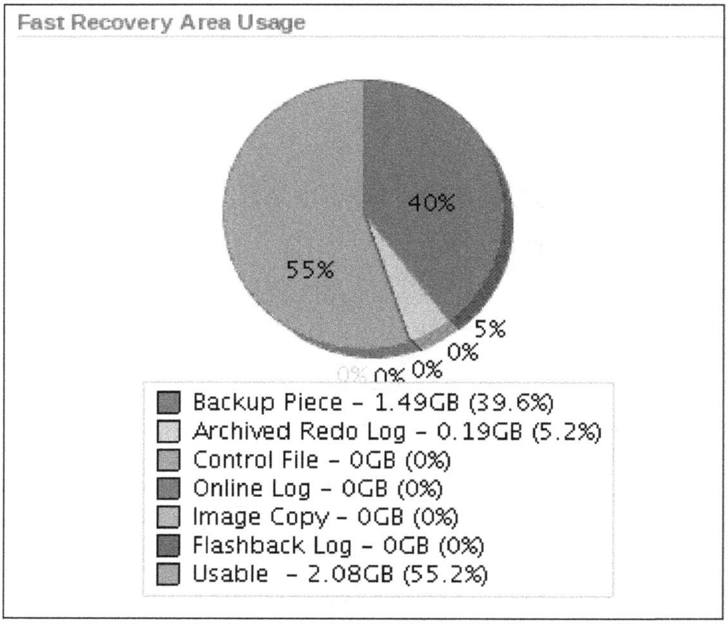
Fast Recovery Area Usage
40%
55%
5%
0%
0%
0%
0%
Backup Piece - 1.49GB (39.6%)
Archived Redo Log - 0.19GB (5.2%)
Control File - 0GB (0%)
Online Log - 0GB (0%)
Image Copy - 0GB (0%)
Flashback Log - 0GB (0%)
Usable - 2.08GB (55.2%)

The usage section details the manner in which the FRA is used. It can show the usage pattern for a number of different types of files, including backup pieces, archivelogs and image copies. This tool is particularly useful in environments that use a number of different types of backups.

Automating database backups

Everyone needs backups, but no one wants to wake up in the middle of the night to run them manually. That's why automation is so important. There are a number of ways to automate backups, from `cron` jobs in Linux and Unix to the Windows Task Scheduler. In this section, we'll examine two methods for backup automation.

Automating Backups with scripting

One of the most common ways to automate backups is through the use of OS scripting languages, such as shell scripting in Linux and Unix. A script is written and then placed in an OS scheduler mechanism such as `cron`. The process is simple, but the scripting can require a little experience. First, we need to create an RMAN script for the backup commands themselves, as shown in the following screenshot:

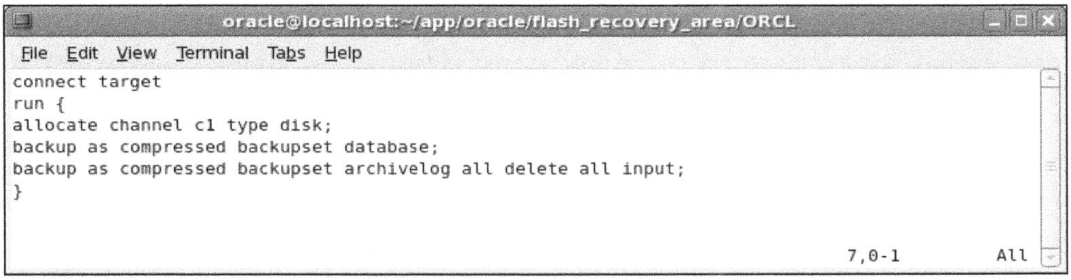
oracle@localhost:~/app/oracle/flash_recovery_area/ORCL
File Edit View Terminal Tabs Help
connect target
run {
allocate channel c1 type disk;
backup as compressed backupset database;
backup as compressed backupset archivelog all delete all input;
}
7,0-1
All

This is essentially the same script we used in an earlier backup example. Both the database and the archivelogs are backed up using compression, and the archivelogs are deleted as they are backed up. Next, we can put an entry in the Linux `crontab` command to schedule a job using the `cron` daemon, similar to the one shown in the following screenshot:

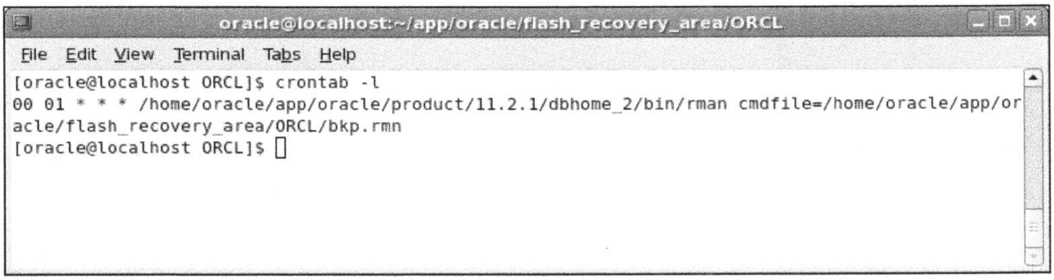
oracle@localhost:~/app/oracle/flash_recovery_area/ORCL
File Edit View Terminal Tabs Help
[oracle@localhost ORCL]$ crontab -l
00 01 * * * /home/oracle/app/oracle/product/11.2.1/dbhome_2/bin/rman cmdfile=/home/oracle/app/oracle/flash_recovery_area/ORCL/bkp.rmn
[oracle@localhost ORCL]$

This requires knowledge of the `cron` and `crontab` syntax; we can consult the proper documentation if this is unfamiliar. Essentially, we place the full path and name for the RMAN executable, and then the full path and name for our RMAN script, `bkp.rmn`. This entry will invoke RMAN at 1:00 A.M. and call the `bkp.rmn` script using the `cmdfile` clause.

Automating backups using Enterprise Manager

For a more GUI approach, we can use the Enterprise Manager tool to schedule our backups. From the Database Control home page, we once again click on the **Availability** tab, and then **Schedule Backup**. The following screen is presented:

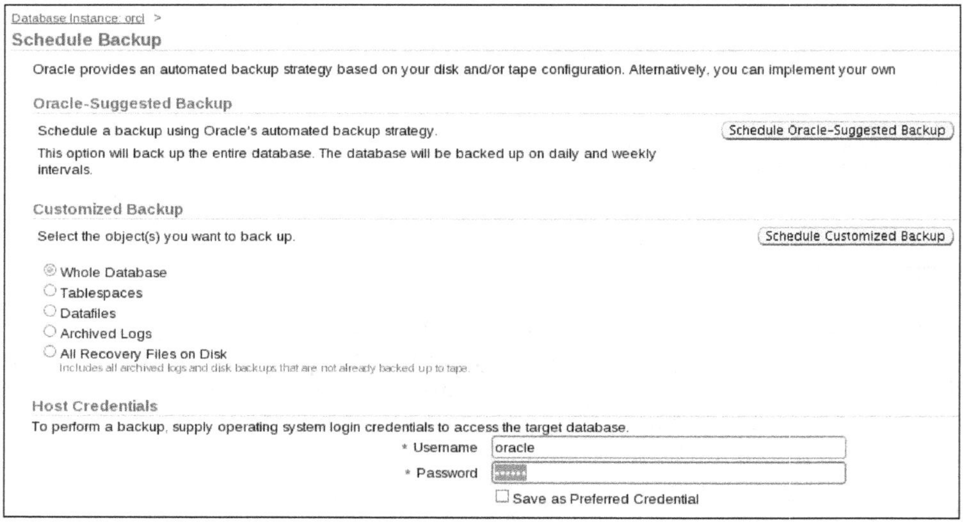
Database Instance: orcl >
Schedule Backup
Oracle provides an automated backup strategy based on your disk and/or tape configuration. Alternatively, you can implement your own
Oracle-Suggested Backup
Schedule a backup using Oracle's automated backup strategy.
Schedule Oracle-Suggested Backup
This option will back up the entire database. The database will be backed up on daily and weekly intervals.
Customized Backup
Select the object(s) you want to back up.
Schedule Customized Backup
Whole Database
Tablespaces
Datafiles
Archived Logs
All Recovery Files on Disk
Includes all archived logs and disk backups that are not already backed up to tape.
Host Credentials
To perform a backup, supply operating system login credentials to access the target database.
* Username
oracle
* Password
Save as Preferred Credential

From this screen we can choose an Oracle recommended backup or schedule a customized one of our own. Either choice requires entering the host credentials (not the database credentials) of the server on which the backup occurs. In this example, we'll enter our OS credentials and choose **Schedule Customized Backup**.

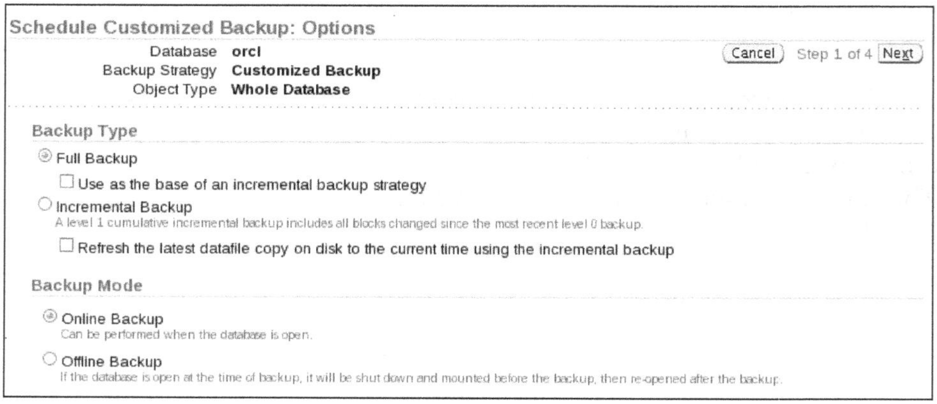
Schedule Customized Backup: Options
Database orcl
Backup Strategy Customized Backup
Object Type Whole Database
Cancel
Step 1 of 4
Next
Backup Type
Full Backup
Use as the base of an incremental backup strategy
Incremental Backup
A level 1 cumulative incremental backup includes all blocks changed since the most recent level 0 backup.
Refresh the latest datafile copy on disk to the current time using the incremental backup
Backup Mode
Online Backup
Can be performed when the database is open.
Offline Backup
If the database is open at the time of backup, it will be shut down and mounted before the backup, then re-opened after the backup.

Here, we'll select our backup options, choosing a full online backup. Then click on **Next**.

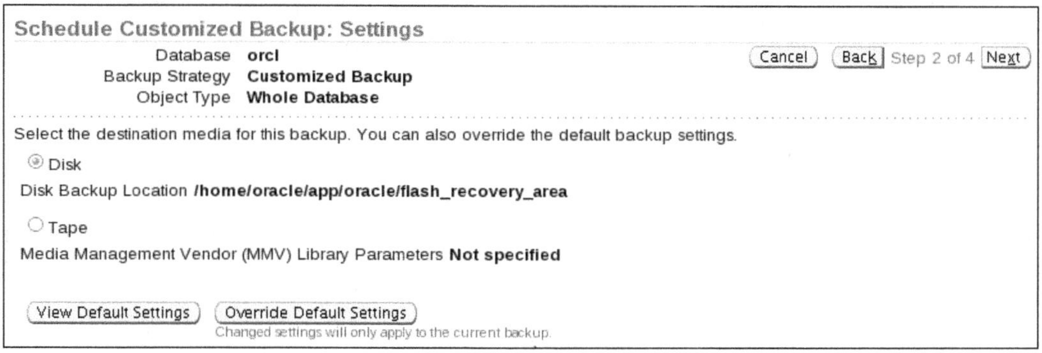
Schedule Customized Backup: Settings
Database orcl
Backup Strategy Customized Backup
Object Type Whole Database
Cancel
Back
Step 2 of 4
Next
Select the destination media for this backup. You can also override the default backup settings.
Disk
Disk Backup Location /home/oracle/app/oracle/flash_recovery_area
Tape
Media Management Vendor (MMV) Library Parameters Not specified
View Default Settings
Override Default Settings
Changed settings will only apply to the current backup.

We want our backup to be written to the disk (namely the FRA), so we choose **Disk** as the backup destination and click on **Next**.

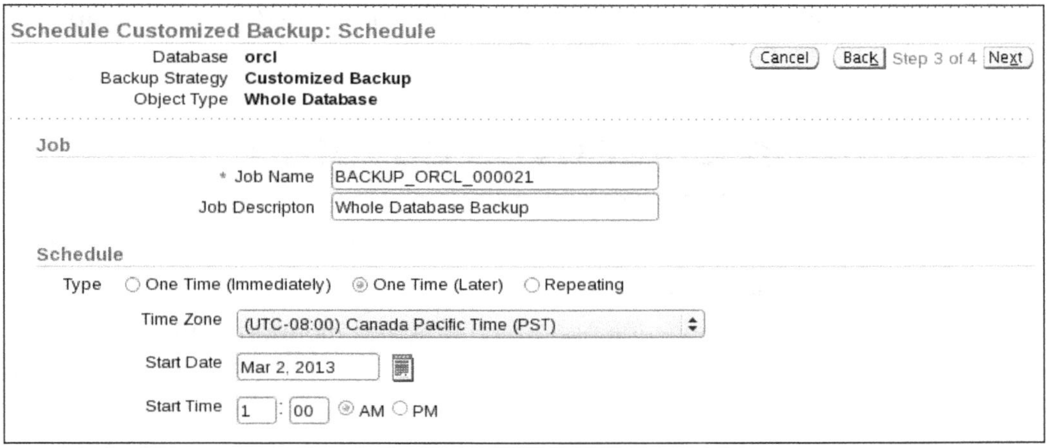
Schedule Customized Backup: Schedule
Database orcl
Backup Strategy Customized Backup
Object Type Whole Database
Cancel
Back
Step 3 of 4
Next
Job
* Job Name BACKUP_ORCL_000021
Job Descripton Whole Database Backup
Schedule
Type One Time (Immediately) One Time (Later) Repeating
Time Zone (UTC-08:00) Canada Pacific Time (PST)
Start Date Mar 2, 2013
Start Time 1 : 00 AM PM

The next screen allows us to select a time for our backup, presenting us with the date, time, and time zone options. Enter the information as required, and click on **Next**.

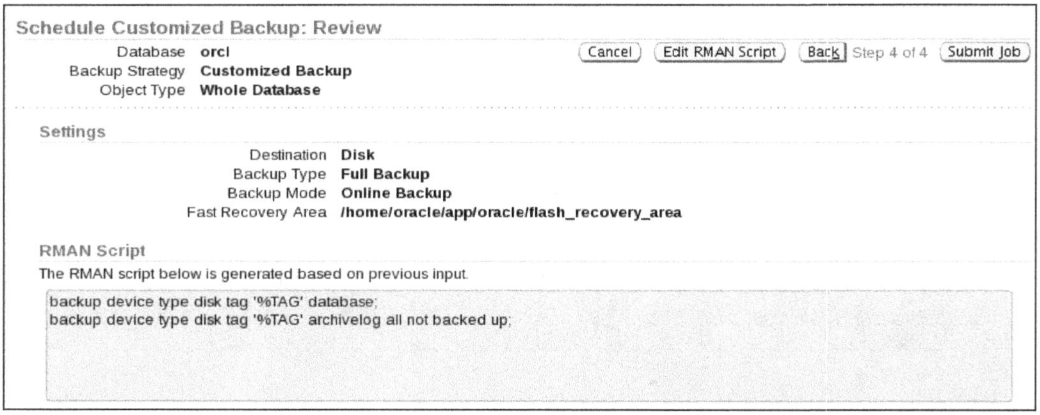
Schedule Customized Backup: Review
Database orcl
Backup Strategy Customized Backup
Object Type Whole Database
Cancel
Edit RMAN Script
Back
Step 4 of 4
Submit Job
Settings
Destination Disk
Backup Type Full Backup
Backup Mode Online Backup
Fast Recovery Area /home/oracle/app/oracle/flash_recovery_area
RMAN Script
The RMAN script below is generated based on previous input.
backup device type disk tag '%TAG' database;
backup device type disk tag '%TAG' archivelog all not backed up;

Finally, we will review our selections and click on **Submit Job** to schedule our backup. We can also choose to edit the RMAN script that is used for the backup if we wish to add any particular functionalities.

Certification objectives covered

- Creating consistent database backups
- Backing up your database without shutting it down
- Creating incremental backups
- Managing backups, viewing backup reports, and monitoring the Flash Recovery Area
- Automating database backups

Summary

In this chapter, we've taken a hands-on approach to backing up our database. We examined user-managed backups, both online and offline. We've introduced the RMAN tool and used it to perform many types of backups, including full, incremental, tablespace-level, and compressed. We've explored numerous RMAN commands that can be used to perform backup maintenance. Finally, we've examined ways to automate our backups. However, backups are really only useful for one thing - database recoveries. In our next chapter, we'll go hands-on again—this time with database recoveries.

Test your knowledge

Q. 1. When running user-managed backups, how are the datafiles moved to the backup area?

a. With RMAN copy commands
b. With RMAN backup commands
c. With operating system commands
d. The files are automatically moved, provided the FRA is used

Q. 2. Which of the following types of file(s) are not required to be backed up with a user-managed whole consistent backup?

a. The SPFILE
b. The redo logfiles
c. The database datafiles
d. The control files

Q. 3. You intend to execute a `ALTER TABLESPACE...BEGIN BACKUP` command. Which of the following conditions would most likely produce an error during the execution of this command?

a. A `ALTER DATABASE...BEGIN BACKUP` command was not executed previously
b. The Flash Recovery Area is not configured
c. The database is in NOARCHIVELOG mode
d. The database is currently in an open state

Q. 4. Which of the following is not a feature supported by RMAN?

a. Block-level backups
b. Incremental backups
c. Whitespace ignore
d. Table-level backups

Q. 5. Which two of the following can be used to store an RMAN repository?

a. The control file
b. The Media Management Library
c. The recovery catalog
d. The redo logs

Q. 6. Which of the following statements is true regarding closed database backups with RMAN?

a. The database must be in the `NOMOUNT` state
b. The database must be in the `MOUNT` state
c. The database must be in the `OPEN` state
d. The database can optionally be in the `OPEN` state, but this is not required

Q. 7. Which type(s) of backup can be used as the basis for an incremental backup strategy?

a. Full backup
b. Level 0 backup
c. Level 1 backup
d. Level 0 or level 1 backup

Q. 8. Which type of backup is created by the command that follows?

```
backup as copy database;
```

a. A block-level backup
b. An image copy backup
c. A differential incremental backup
d. A cumulative incremental backup

Q. 9. You perform differential incremental backups in your environment. On Sundays, you run a level 0 backup, and on each weeknight you run level 1 backups. Which of the following statements is true regarding the state of your backups?

a. The backups performed on weeknights contain the data blocks that have changed since Sunday
b. The backups performed on Sundays contain all the blocks that have changed since the previous weeknight
c. The backups performed on weeknights contain all the blocks in the database
d. The backups on Tuesday night contain all the blocks that have changed since Monday's backup

Q. 10. You perform cumulative incremental backups in your environment. On Sundays, you run a level 0 backup. On Wednesdays, you run a level 1 backup. On Fridays, you run a second level 1 backup. Which of the following is true regarding Friday's backup?

1. It contains all of the blocks in the database
2. It contains all of the changed blocks since Wednesday
3. It contains all of the changed blocks since Sunday
4. The backup will result in an error, as two level 1 backups cannot be run in succession without a level 0 backup in between

Q. 11. Which of the following statements would be used to determine whether your existing backups can be used to recover a database fully?

1. `REPORT NEED BACKUP;`
2. `REPORT OBSOLETE;`
3. `CONFIGURE CONTROLFILE AUTOBACKUP ON;`
4. `LIST BACKUP OF DATABASE;`

Q. 12. You are running backups configured with Flash Recovery Area. In viewing the output of a `CROSSCHECK` command, you find that five backup pieces are listed as `AVAILABLE`, although two others are shown to be `EXPIRED`. Which statement is true regarding this output?

1. Five files were recorded in the repository, but were not found in the FRA
2. Two files were recorded in the repository, but were not found in the FRA
3. Two files were overwritten in the FRA
4. The FRA has insufficient space to store the `EXPIRED` pieces

Q. 13. Which of the following is the best method to automate a database backup job?

1. Use the Enterprise Manager **Schedule Backup** page
2. Use a PL/SQL script
3. Use Oracle Data Pump
4. None of these can be used to automate a backup

13
Performing Database Recovery

Although we now know how to backup our Oracle database, this knowledge alone is not nearly enough. All the backups in the world will not save our data unless we know how to use them to recover a database. In this chapter, we'll examine the very important, and sometimes stressful, process of database recovery.

We'll be covering the following topics:

- Understanding the process of database recovery
- Performing cold backup recoveries
- Performing hot backup recoveries
- Examining the Data Recovery Advisor
- Using Data Recovery Advisor to perform recovery

Understanding the recovery process

Before delving too deeply into hands-on recovery techniques, it's important to first have a complete understanding of the process. **Database recovery** is the act of restoring data from a backup and then, optionally, rolling forward in time by applying the existing changes. However, the recovery process is one that doesn't always work "by the numbers". It requires a DBA who understands the Oracle architecture and can respond appropriately to the situations that are presented. There are very few "cookie-cutter" database recoveries; they require knowledge and flexibility on the part of the DBA. In this section, we'll explore the concepts that make this flexibility possible.

Understanding the importance of database recovery

Before venturing much further, we would be remiss if we did not take a moment to emphasize the importance of database recovery. Although the job of the DBA comes with a certain amount of stress, there is probably no event in the life of a DBA more stressful than the recovery of a crucial production database. In the life of a real-world DBA, when such as loss occurs, it gains instant visibility at a management level. In such a situation, the DBA may find that they have phone calls and visitors to their office cube from the highest levels of the company. The fate of the corporate data in that database rests in the hands of the DBA alone. Even good DBAs may find themselves looking for work if important data is lost. In today's world, it is *assumed* that corporate data is always safe and recoverable. This is a legitimate assumption; the safety and availability of data is the most important job of the DBA. It's a high-pressure situation and one that the DBA must be prepared to face. However, there are steps that a DBA can take *before* a recovery scenario occurs that can also prepare him or her to mitigate the risk. They are as follows:

- **Understand the concepts of recovery**: Recoveries can vary widely from one scenario to another. The process of restoring a complete database is somewhat different from simply restoring a single datafile. Recovering a database up to the point of failure is different from recovering it up to a point in the past. A DBA must understand these differences (plus many others) and know how to address them.
- **Practice database recovery**: No other responsibility of a DBA deserves more practice than database recovery. Thinking through a recovery is not the same as actually doing it. Practicing in a noncritical situation, such as a test environment, enables the DBA to work through all of the "gotchas" that can occur. We never want the first recovery we do to occur when our job depends on it. Practice provides the DBA with the skills and confidence to perform database recovery when everything is on the line. To that end, the DBA must have an environment where it is safe to actually break the database and attempt recoveries. Delete the SYSTEM tablespace datafile and see if we can recover it. Delete a redo log and see how much of the database we can save. Even a small environment, such as a testing database, can go a long way in preparing a DBA to recover a database successfully. But remember that this type of testing can result in a complete loss of the database; it must only be done in a nonessential system.

- **Design your backup strategy with recovery in mind**: It is not enough to simply take a backup. We must know from what scenarios can our backup save us. If our datafiles and backup files are all stored locally on the internal hard drives of a server, we are backed up, but we cannot recover from the loss of the server itself. The same is true of a storage area network (SAN) or other form of attached storage. Always identify the single points of failure that can prevent your recovery, and take them into consideration when designing your backup strategy. We should always be able to say that "we can save the database from this, but we cannot save the database from that".

> **The real-world DBA**
>
> Misunderstandings about what is involved in database backup and recovery are very common, even among computer professionals. It is common for system administrators to believe that a database has been "backed up", because all the datafiles were copied to some form of backup storage during a nightly backup of the system. This could not be further from the truth. In such a situation, the database would likely be lost. Oracle databases are not composed of static files; if datafiles are copied to another location while the database is open, those files are almost certainly inconsistent and cannot be used in a recovery. Techniques such as those used with user-managed backups and Recovery Manager (RMAN) are required in order to perform the level of backup needed for a recovery.

Understanding the different types of recovery

As we mentioned earlier, database recovery is the act of restoring the data from a backup and then, optionally, rolling forward in time by applying the existing changes. To understand a database recovery, it is usually helpful to consider it in terms of time. A backup occurs, then over time, database changes accrue and are stored in the redo logs and archivelogs. Thus, standard database recoveries do not "roll back" a database in time—they actually roll forward in time from a backup. We might illustrate it this way.

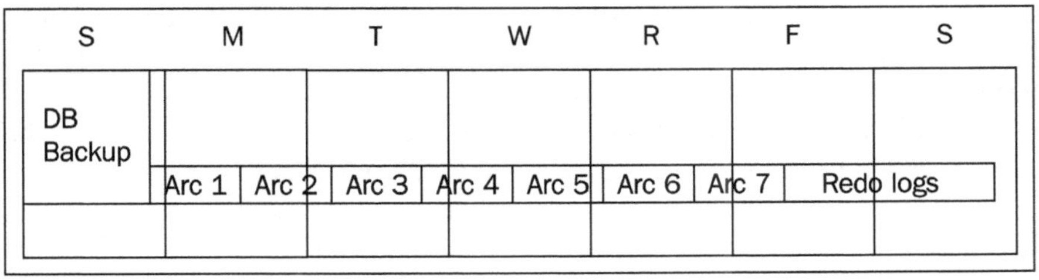
S
M
T
W
R
F
S
DB Backup
Arc 1
Arc 2
Arc 3
Arc 4
Arc 5
Arc 6
Arc 7
Redo logs

In this example, we show the weekly processing of a database in terms of database changes. On Sunday, a full backup is taken. From that point on, changes are written to the redo logs and then out to archivelogs, assuming we are running in ARCHIVELOG mode. So the entire chain of changes through time is contained in archivelogs, designated as **Arc 1**, **Arc 2**, and so on, with the most recent changes being stored in the redo logs. In order to fully recover every block of data, we would require the backup, that has stored all of the database blocks at that point in time, along with all of the changes that have occurred, which are stored in the archivelogs and redo logs.

There are two broad categories of recovery available to the Oracle DBA. A **complete recovery** occurs when the backup is restored, and all changes since the backup are re-applied to the database. The database is recovered all the way up to the point of the last committed transaction. This is due to, as we discovered in our last chapter, the recoverability architecture of the Oracle database. This type of recovery is generally, but not always, the preferred type of recovery, because it provides the least loss of data.

The second category of recovery is an incomplete recovery. An **incomplete recovery** occurs when the backup is restored and some, but not all, of the changes are applied. We might ask why we would ever want to do this. In certain situations, the conditions of the recovery may require this approach. For instance, say that a recovery is required, but due to a media failure, not all of the archivelogs are available. In this scenario, we can't perform a complete recovery, because the database changes, which are stored in the archivelogs, are not available to be used in the recovery. Thus, we may have to apply all of the changes that are possible, and then end the recovery at that point. Another possible scenario for incomplete recovery occurs when an important table has been dropped. In this situation, we're faced with a tough choice. We can recover the database up to the point in time just before the table was dropped. However, all of the changes made since that point will be lost. Such a choice is usually a business decision. The DBA may be called upon to perform an incomplete recovery to save the lost table.

The most important factor in our ability to recover a database is the log mode in which we're running. Our previous example diagram assumes we are running in ARCHIVELOG mode, which captures all of the changes in the redo logs before they are overwritten. If this is not the case and we're running our database in NOARCHIVELOG mode, our recovery options are severely limited. In fact, because the changes written to the redo logs are overwritten, we have no recourse during recovery other than to restore the backup and stop. Any changes after that are lost. Thus, if we back the database up on Sunday and experience a media failure during the course of Friday, all of the changes made from the end of the backup on Sunday to the state of the database on Friday will be unrecoverable.

Thus, recoveries up to a point of time in the past are also impossible, unless we're operating in ARCHIVELOG mode. Running in NOARCHIVELOG mode also prevents us from running hot backups and requires the database to be shut down. For these reasons, ARCHIVELOG mode is greatly preferred for our database. Complete and incomplete recoveries can be performed with both user-managed and RMAN backups, although RMAN simplifies the process.

Performing RMAN complete recoveries

The process for performing a complete recovery in RMAN involves two operations, namely restore and recover. **Restore** is the process of restoring the lost files from backup. **Recover** is the process of applying the changes from the archivelogs and redo logs. So, in order for a complete recovery to occur, both restore and recover must be performed in that order. In this section, we'll examine the process of complete recovery using RMAN. As a side note, although user-managed backups are covered on the DBA I exam, user-managed recoveries are not, even though they are possible. The actual syntax for user-managed recovery is very similar to that of RMAN, although it is performed in SQL*Plus instead of in the RMAN executable.

Performing datafile-level RMAN complete recovery

In the case of the loss of a non-SYSTEM datafile, we can use RMAN to recover the datafile without disturbing any other database files. As we will see, we can also do this while the rest of the database is up and available for use. We will actually simulate this loss by removing the file, so we need to ensure that our database is fully backed up. Thus, we'll first perform a full backup to ensure that our database is recoverable. Keep in mind that our examples will actually break the database. Every step should be followed to prevent permanent loss to the database. We'll run our backup using our RMAN commands.

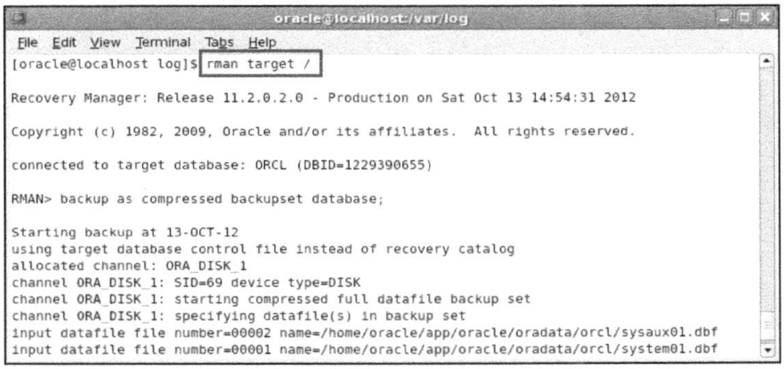
oracle@localhost:/var/log
File Edit View Terminal Tabs Help
[oracle@localhost log]$ rman target /
Recovery Manager: Release 11.2.0.2.0 - Production on Sat Oct 13 14:54:31 2012
Copyright (c) 1982, 2009, Oracle and/or its affiliates. All rights reserved.
connected to target database: ORCL (DBID=1229390655)
RMAN> backup as compressed backupset database;
Starting backup at 13-OCT-12
using target database control file instead of recovery catalog
allocated channel: ORA_DISK_1
channel ORA_DISK_1: SID=69 device type=DISK
channel ORA_DISK_1: starting compressed full datafile backup set
channel ORA_DISK_1: specifying datafile(s) in backup set
input datafile file number=00002 name=/home/oracle/app/oracle/oradata/orcl/sysaux01.dbf
input datafile file number=00001 name=/home/oracle/app/oracle/oradata/orcl/system01.dbf

To begin, note that we've used a slightly different syntax to invoke RMAN. Instead of simply invoking the executable file and then using `connect target`, we've started the executable file and connected to the database from the OS command line using a single command, `rman target /`. This has no bearing on the way backups and recoveries are done, and is simply shown as an alternate invocation that can be used when preferred. The backup completes normally, and we're now prepared to simulate a failure.

This will be a controlled failure of the loss of a datafile, so we need to identify the filename and path of the datafile that will "fail". We can execute the following query from SQL*Plus to make our choice:

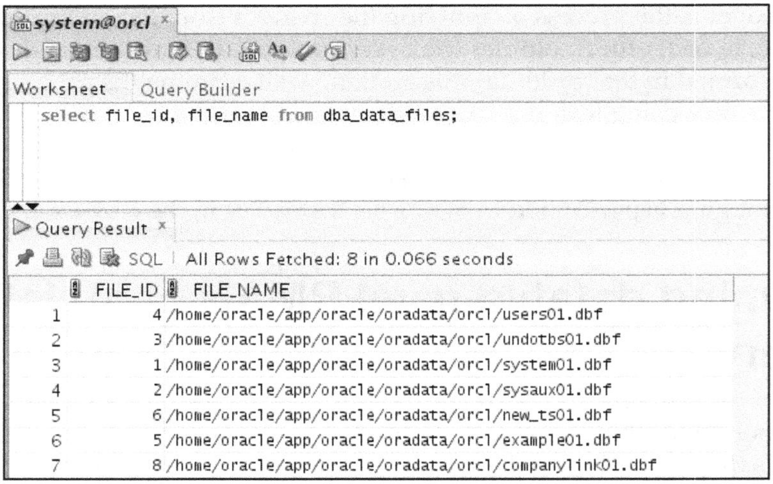
system@orcl
Worksheet
Query Builder
select file_id, file_name from dba_data_files;
Query Result
SQL
All Rows Fetched: 8 in 0.066 seconds
FILE_ID
FILE_NAME
1 4 /home/oracle/app/oracle/oradata/orcl/users01.dbf
2 3 /home/oracle/app/oracle/oradata/orcl/undotbs01.dbf
3 1 /home/oracle/app/oracle/oradata/orcl/system01.dbf
4 2 /home/oracle/app/oracle/oradata/orcl/sysaux01.dbf
5 6 /home/oracle/app/oracle/oradata/orcl/new_ts01.dbf
6 5 /home/oracle/app/oracle/oradata/orcl/example01.dbf
7 8 /home/oracle/app/oracle/oradata/orcl/companylink01.dbf

We've queried from the `dba_data_files` data dictionary view for a list of datafiles. Note that we've also queried the `file_id` column. We'll make use of that information during the recovery. Because of its relatively small size, we'll use the datafile with ID number 4 that is located at `/home/oracle/app/oracle/oradata/orcl/users01.dbf`.

Now that the file is identified, we'll shut down our database to remove the file. Although this isn't necessary for the simulation on Linux, a shutdown is necessary on Windows, because the operating system will lock the Oracle datafiles while the database is up.

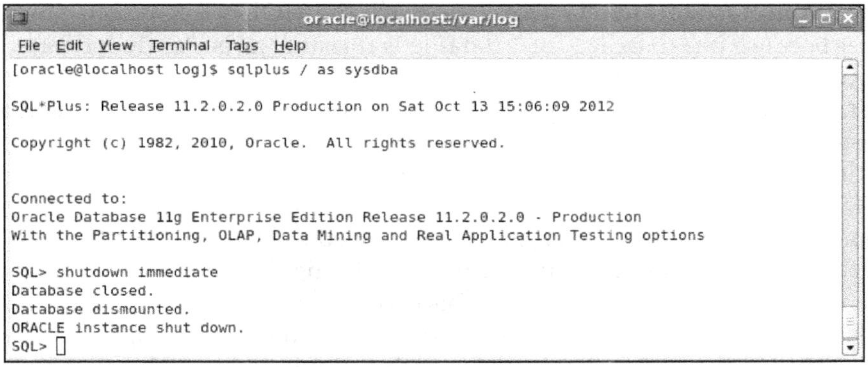
oracle@localhost:/var/log
File Edit View Terminal Tabs Help
[oracle@localhost log]$ sqlplus / as sysdba
SQL*Plus: Release 11.2.0.2.0 Production on Sat Oct 13 15:06:09 2012
Copyright (c) 1982, 2010, Oracle. All rights reserved.
Connected to:
Oracle Database 11g Enterprise Edition Release 11.2.0.2.0 - Production
With the Partitioning, OLAP, Data Mining and Real Application Testing options
SQL> shutdown immediate
Database closed.
Database dismounted.
ORACLE instance shut down.
SQL>

Next, we'll rename the `users01.dbf` file to `users01.dbf.old`. We could remove it, but we'll rename it just to be safe. Since the controlfile knows this datafile as `users01.dbf`, it will still consider it to be missing.

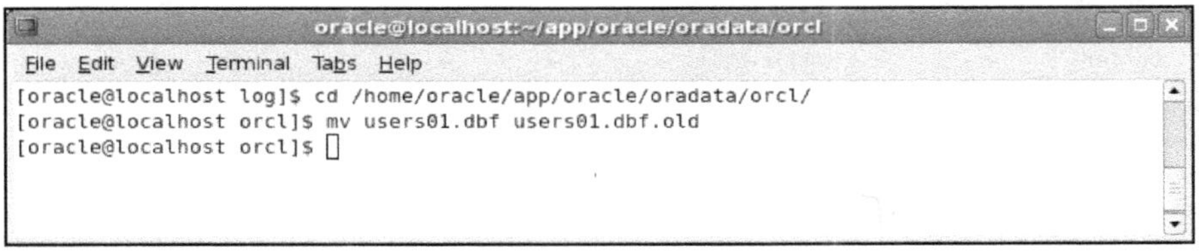
oracle@localhost:~/app/oracle/oradata/orcl
File Edit View Terminal Tabs Help
[oracle@localhost log]$ cd /home/oracle/app/oracle/oradata/orcl/
[oracle@localhost orcl]$ mv users01.dbf users01.dbf.old
[oracle@localhost orcl]$

Now, we'll attempt to start the database.

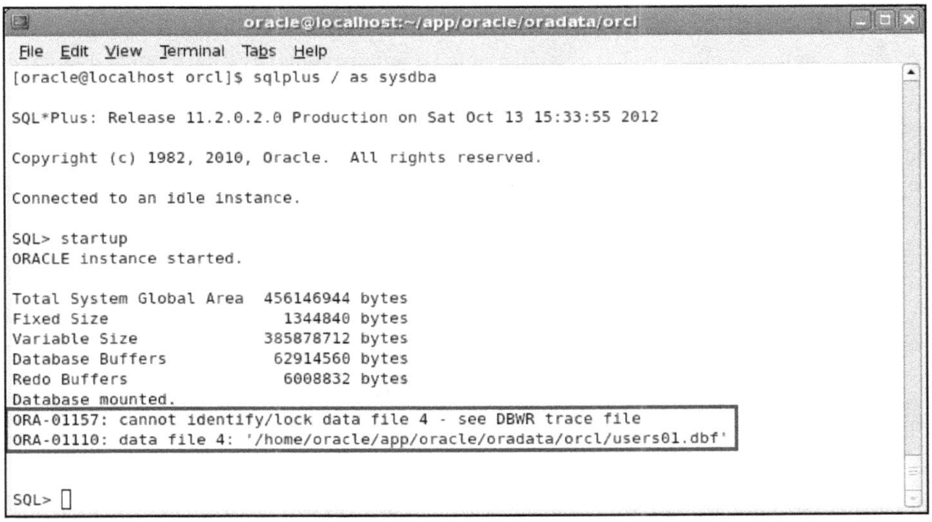
oracle@localhost:~/app/oracle/oradata/orcl
File Edit View Terminal Tabs Help
[oracle@localhost orcl]$ sqlplus / as sysdba
SQL*Plus: Release 11.2.0.2.0 Production on Sat Oct 13 15:33:55 2012
Copyright (c) 1982, 2010, Oracle. All rights reserved.
Connected to an idle instance.
SQL> startup
ORACLE instance started.
Total System Global Area 456146944 bytes
Fixed Size   1344840 bytes
Variable Size   385878712 bytes
Database Buffers   62914560 bytes
Redo Buffers   6008832 bytes
Database mounted.
ORA-01157: cannot identify/lock data file 4 - see DBWR trace file
ORA-01110: data file 4: '/home/oracle/app/oracle/oradata/orcl/users01.dbf'
SQL>

When we attempt to start the database, we reach the MOUNT state, but can go no further because our `users01.dbf` datafile is missing, as is clearly indicated by the error message. Take note of this message. This is the error that indicates that a media failure has occurred. We would see a similar message if any of the datafiles were missing or corrupted. Clearly, a database recovery is in order. However, it's worth noting that `users01.dbf` is a non-SYSTEM datafile—it does not belong to the SYSTEM tablespace. Thus, we can take the rest of the database to the OPEN state while attempting the recovery. First, we'll need to take this datafile offline because the database cannot be opened with a missing datafile. Then we can fully open the rest of the database. Note that this can have varying degrees of impact. If the missing datafile is crucial to the functioning of an application, it may not be advisable to bring the rest of the database online. But if the datafile contains data that is noncritical or isolated from other applications, this technique can be used to restore service quickly to our environment.

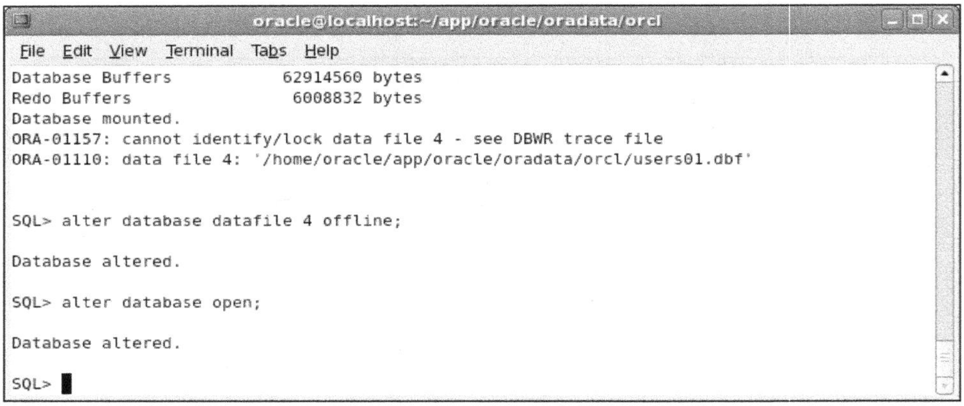
oracle@localhost:~/app/oracle/oradata/orcl
File Edit View Terminal Tabs Help
Database Buffers 62914560 bytes
Redo Buffers 6008832 bytes
Database mounted.
ORA-01157: cannot identify/lock data file 4 - see DBWR trace file
ORA-01110: data file 4: '/home/oracle/app/oracle/oradata/orcl/users01.dbf'
SQL> alter database datafile 4 offline;
Database altered.
SQL> alter database open;
Database altered.
SQL>

With our database opened, we're ready to begin the recovery process. We invoke RMAN and begin the first step—to restore the missing datafile.

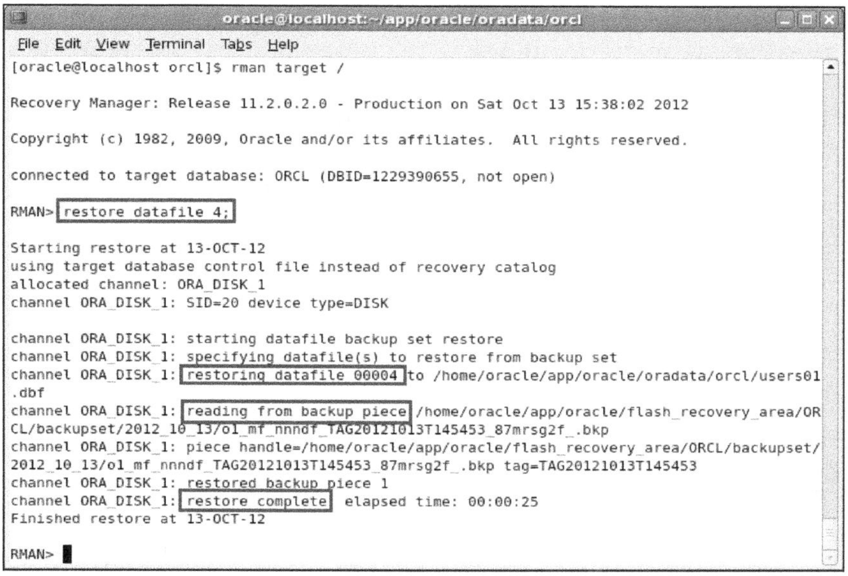

```
oracle@localhost:~/app/oracle/oradata/orcl
File Edit View Terminal Tabs Help
[oracle@localhost orcl]$ rman target /

Recovery Manager: Release 11.2.0.2.0 - Production on Sat Oct 13 15:38:02 2012

Copyright (c) 1982, 2009, Oracle and/or its affiliates.  All rights reserved.

connected to target database: ORCL (DBID=1229390655, not open)

RMAN> restore datafile 4;

Starting restore at 13-OCT-12
using target database control file instead of recovery catalog
allocated channel: ORA_DISK_1
channel ORA_DISK_1: SID=20 device type=DISK

channel ORA_DISK_1: starting datafile backup set restore
channel ORA_DISK_1: specifying datafile(s) to restore from backup set
channel ORA_DISK_1: restoring datafile 00004 to /home/oracle/app/oracle/oradata/orcl/users01
.dbf
channel ORA_DISK_1: reading from backup piece /home/oracle/app/oracle/flash_recovery_area/OR
CL/backupset/2012_10_13/o1_mf_nnndf_TAG20121013T145453_87mrsg2f_.bkp
channel ORA_DISK_1: piece handle=/home/oracle/app/oracle/flash_recovery_area/ORCL/backupset/
2012_10_13/o1_mf_nnndf_TAG20121013T145453_87mrsg2f_.bkp tag=TAG20121013T145453
channel ORA_DISK_1: restored backup piece 1
channel ORA_DISK_1: restore complete, elapsed time: 00:00:25
Finished restore at 13-OCT-12

RMAN>
```

Several things are occurring during this operation. First, we issue the `restore datafile 4` command, because we know from the error that datafile number 4, `users01.dbf`, is the missing file. The RMAN output indicates that it is performing the restore operation, and is doing so by reading from the backup piece. Thus, RMAN is restoring the missing datafile from the backup pieces created during our backup, as we would expect.

The next step is to recover the datafile; that is, apply any changes to the datafile since the backup occurred.

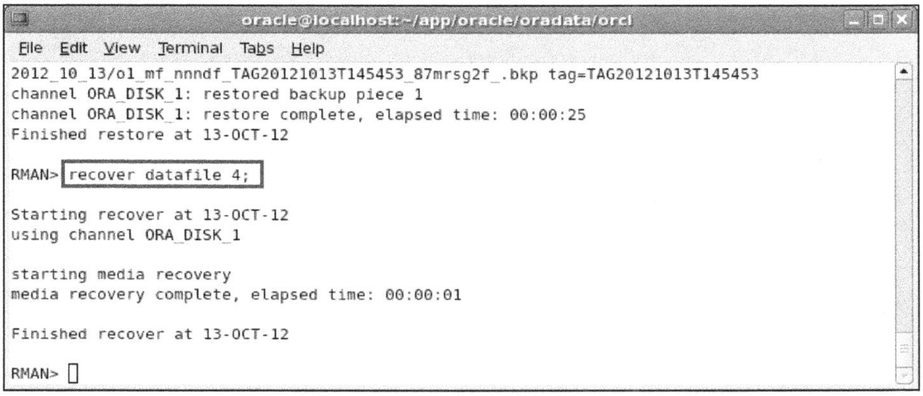

```
oracle@localhost:~/app/oracle/oradata/orcl
File Edit View Terminal Tabs Help
2012_10_13/o1_mf_nnndf_TAG20121013T145453_87mrsg2f_.bkp tag=TAG20121013T145453
channel ORA_DISK_1: restored backup piece 1
channel ORA_DISK_1: restore complete, elapsed time: 00:00:25
Finished restore at 13-OCT-12

RMAN> recover datafile 4;

Starting recover at 13-OCT-12
using channel ORA_DISK_1

starting media recovery
media recovery complete, elapsed time: 00:00:01

Finished recover at 13-OCT-12

RMAN>
```

Datafile number 4 has now been completely restored and recovered. The only step left is to bring the datafile back online.

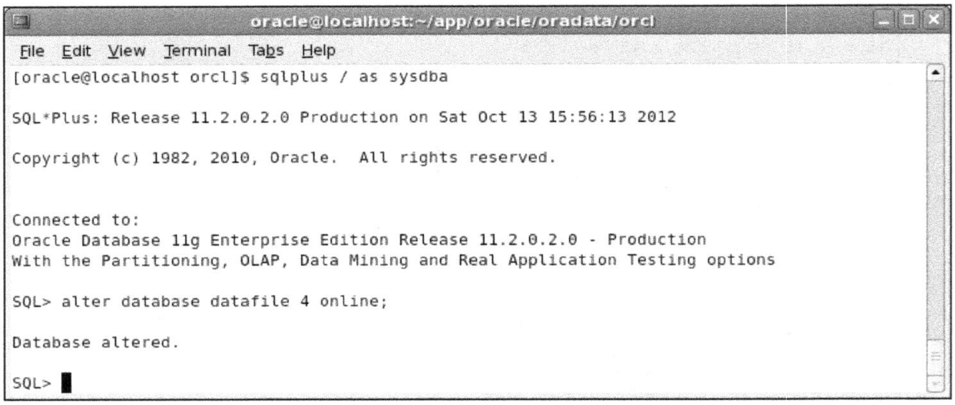
oracle@localhost:~/app/oracle/oradata/orcl
File Edit View Terminal Tabs Help
[oracle@localhost orcl]$ sqlplus / as sysdba
SQL*Plus: Release 11.2.0.2.0 Production on Sat Oct 13 15:56:13 2012
Copyright (c) 1982, 2010, Oracle. All rights reserved.
Connected to:
Oracle Database 11g Enterprise Edition Release 11.2.0.2.0 - Production
With the Partitioning, OLAP, Data Mining and Real Application Testing options
SQL> alter database datafile 4 online;
Database altered.
SQL>

As a final check, we can examine the data dictionary to ensure that all datafiles are restored and available.

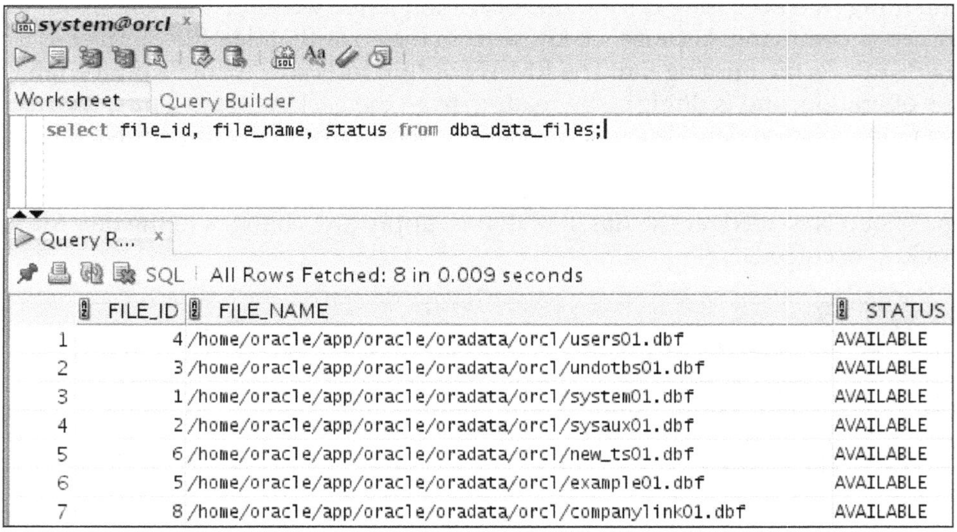
system@orcl
Worksheet
Query Builder
select file_id, file_name, status from dba_data_files;
Query R...
SQL
All Rows Fetched: 8 in 0.009 seconds
FILE_ID
FILE_NAME
STATUS
1 4 /home/oracle/app/oracle/oradata/orcl/users01.dbf AVAILABLE
2 3 /home/oracle/app/oracle/oradata/orcl/undotbs01.dbf AVAILABLE
3 1 /home/oracle/app/oracle/oradata/orcl/system01.dbf AVAILABLE
4 2 /home/oracle/app/oracle/oradata/orcl/sysaux01.dbf AVAILABLE
5 6 /home/oracle/app/oracle/oradata/orcl/new_ts01.dbf AVAILABLE
6 5 /home/oracle/app/oracle/oradata/orcl/example01.dbf AVAILABLE
7 8 /home/oracle/app/oracle/oradata/orcl/companylink01.dbf AVAILABLE

Performing complete recovery of the database

A database-level recovery is very similar to our previous datafile example, with one important difference. A database-level recovery implies that all of the database files are missing. Because this includes the datafile for the SYSTEM tablespace, we cannot bring the database online during recovery. In this case, the database will need to be in the MOUNT state. In this example, we won't actually rename or remove any files—in fact, we don't need to. Once we place the database into the MOUNT state, we can perform the restore and recover steps even though nothing is wrong with the database. The first step is to shut down the database and bring it into MOUNT, which we can do from RMAN.

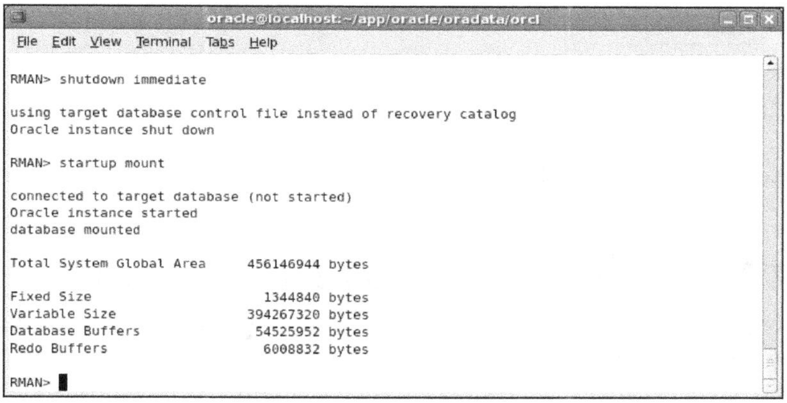
oracle@localhost:~/app/oracle/oradata/orcl
File Edit View Terminal Tabs Help
RMAN> shutdown immediate
using target database control file instead of recovery catalog
Oracle instance shut down
RMAN> startup mount
connected to target database (not started)
Oracle instance started
database mounted
Total System Global Area 456146944 bytes
Fixed Size 1344840 bytes
Variable Size 394267320 bytes
Database Buffers 54525952 bytes
Redo Buffers 6008832 bytes
RMAN>

We're now ready for the restore step. We'll fully restore the database using the `restore database` command. Remember, this will restore all of our current datafiles with those that existed during the backup; this process can take some time.

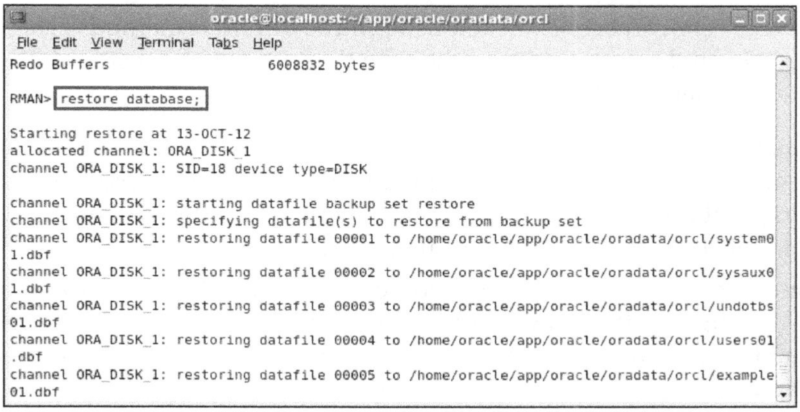
oracle@localhost:~/app/oracle/oradata/orcl
File Edit View Terminal Tabs Help
Redo Buffers 6008832 bytes
RMAN> restore database;
Starting restore at 13-OCT-12
allocated channel: ORA_DISK_1
channel ORA_DISK_1: SID=18 device type=DISK
channel ORA_DISK_1: starting datafile backup set restore
channel ORA_DISK_1: specifying datafile(s) to restore from backup set
channel ORA_DISK_1: restoring datafile 00001 to /home/oracle/app/oracle/oradata/orcl/system01.dbf
channel ORA_DISK_1: restoring datafile 00002 to /home/oracle/app/oracle/oradata/orcl/sysaux01.dbf
channel ORA_DISK_1: restoring datafile 00003 to /home/oracle/app/oracle/oradata/orcl/undotbs01.dbf
channel ORA_DISK_1: restoring datafile 00004 to /home/oracle/app/oracle/oradata/orcl/users01.dbf
channel ORA_DISK_1: restoring datafile 00005 to /home/oracle/app/oracle/oradata/orcl/example01.dbf

As in our previous example, the restore operation reads the blocks for each datafile from the existing backup pieces and reconstructs them as complete datafiles. Next, we need to recover the database up to the present time and return the database to an OPEN state.

oracle@localhost:~/app/oracle/oradata/orcl
File Edit View Terminal Tabs Help
channel ORA_DISK_1: restore complete, elapsed time: 00:02:05
Finished restore at 13-OCT-12
RMAN> recover database;
Starting recover at 13-OCT-12
using channel ORA_DISK_1
starting media recovery
media recovery complete, elapsed time: 00:00:01
Finished recover at 13-OCT-12
RMAN> alter database open;
database opened
RMAN>

Our database has now been fully restored to its most current state.

Performing incomplete recoveries

As we mentioned previously, an incomplete recovery occurs when the backup is restored and some, but not all, of the changes are applied. However, we need to set a condition, such as a time, in order to establish the point at which recovery will be stopped. In this section, we'll perform an incomplete recovery using one of these conditions as an example.

Understanding incomplete recovery

Incomplete recovery can be performed using three different methods. The method chosen depends on the granularity of the data that needs to be restored. Each method has certain advantages and disadvantages.

- **Sequence-based recovery**: In this method, we use a log sequence number to establish the stopping point of the recovery. For example, if the sequence number of our current redo log is 435, we might only recover our database up to the archivelog with the sequence number 429.
- **Time-based recovery**: In this method, we define a time up to which changes will be applied. If we need to recover the state of the data on Wednesday at 11:42 P.M., during recovery, we can roll forward the changes to that point in time.

- **Change-based recovery**: In this method, we establish the **System Change Number** (**SCN**) that forms the limit for the number of changes that can be applied. This allows us to recover to the exact point before a statement occurred.

For instance, let's say that the `EMPLOYEE` table of our `Companylink` database was accidentally dropped. Our application cannot function without this table, so it is necessary to recover the table even at the risk of losing any data that was changed after the drop. Which method of incomplete recovery should we use? Let's examine our options.

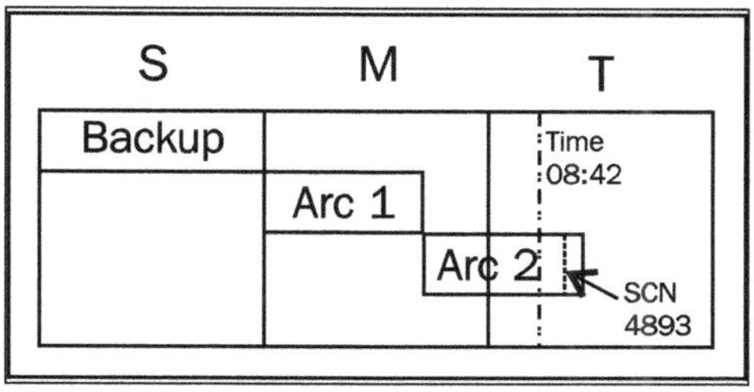
S
M
T
Backup
Arc 1
Arc 2
Time
08:42
SCN
4893

The last backup occurred on Sunday. Because we're operating in ARCHIVELOG mode, we have the sequence of archivelogs, **Arc 1** and **Arc 2**, since the backup. Let's say that our best estimate indicates that the drop occurred near 08:42 A.M. on Tuesday. We could use sequence-based recovery, that is, restore the backup and apply the changes from **Arc 1**. We have rolled forward to a time before the drop, so we have recovered the `EMPLOYEE` table. However, we have also lost all of the transactions in **Arc 2** up to our estimated time. This method is the simplest, but may not achieve a granularity that is fine enough to satisfy our requirements. Instead, we could use time-based recovery and recover the changes up to our estimated time of 08:42 A.M.. This gives us a much finer granularity for recovery, and may solve the problem. However, our time is only an estimate. We may recover to this time only to find that the table was actually dropped a few minutes earlier. Even if it wasn't, there could be transactions after the drop that we could still save if we had a method that could achieve an even finer granularity. Finally, we could use change-based recovery. With this method, we would use an external tool, such as Oracle's **Log Miner**, to find the exact SCN of the offending `DROP TABLE` statement. For the sake of argument, let's say the SCN of the drop is 4893, as indicated in our diagram. We could then restore the database and recover exactly up to the point before the `DROP TABLE` statement occurred—at SCN 4893. This preserves the largest number of transactions while still saving the table. However, finding the exact SCN can take time, and we might not have that luxury during recovery. Thus, the choice of method is based on the level of granularity we require to save the data.

Performing a time-based incomplete recovery

Let's step through a time-based incomplete recovery to show these concepts at work. We'll need to do a little setup to determine whether we're successful or not. Some of the results you see will not reflect your own, so be sure to record the information as indicated. Again, do not attempt this unless a successful backup has already been performed, and your database is running in ARCHIVELOG mode.

Our scenario is that we need to recover our database up to the point before a table was dropped. For safety's sake, we'll create this table now.

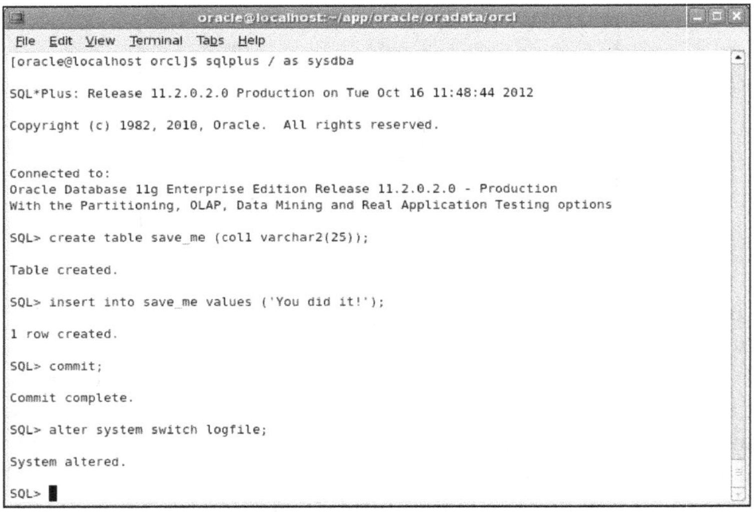
oracle@localhost:~/app/oracle/oradata/orcl
File Edit View Terminal Tabs Help
[oracle@localhost orcl]$ sqlplus / as sysdba
SQL*Plus: Release 11.2.0.2.0 Production on Tue Oct 16 11:48:44 2012
Copyright (c) 1982, 2010, Oracle. All rights reserved.
Connected to:
Oracle Database 11g Enterprise Edition Release 11.2.0.2.0 - Production
With the Partitioning, OLAP, Data Mining and Real Application Testing options
SQL> create table save_me (col1 varchar2(25));
Table created.
SQL> insert into save_me values ('You did it!');
1 row created.
SQL> commit;
Commit complete.
SQL> alter system switch logfile;
System altered.
SQL>

We've done several things here. First, we've created a test table **save_me** and inserted a value into it. This will serve as the reference point to indicate whether we're successful or not. It is very important that we issue a `COMMIT` statement here, so the changes are flushed to the redo logs. As an added precaution, we switch the redo logfile so that it is written out to archivelog. Next, we need to establish the time before we drop the table.

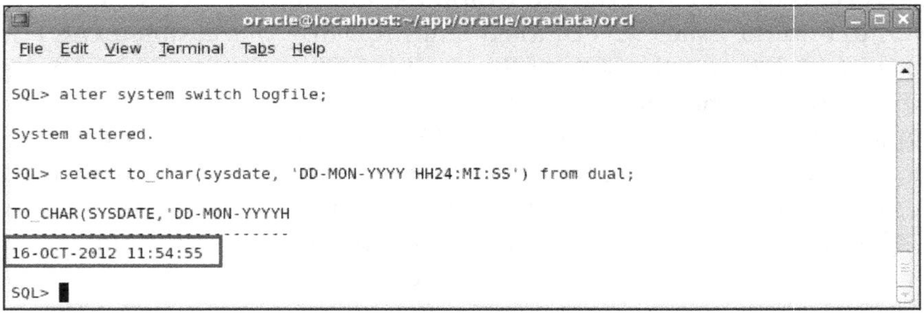
oracle@localhost:~/app/oracle/oradata/orcl
File Edit View Terminal Tabs Help
SQL> alter system switch logfile;
System altered.
SQL> select to_char(sysdate, 'DD-MON-YYYY HH24:MI:SS') from dual;
TO_CHAR(SYSDATE,'DD-MON-YYYYH
16-OCT-2012 11:54:55
SQL>

We issue a SQL statement to determine the current time in a 24-hour time format. At this point in time, the `save_me` table still exists and has not been dropped. This will be our exact target recovery time, so record this time, because yours will differ. We're ready, so now it's time to drop our table.

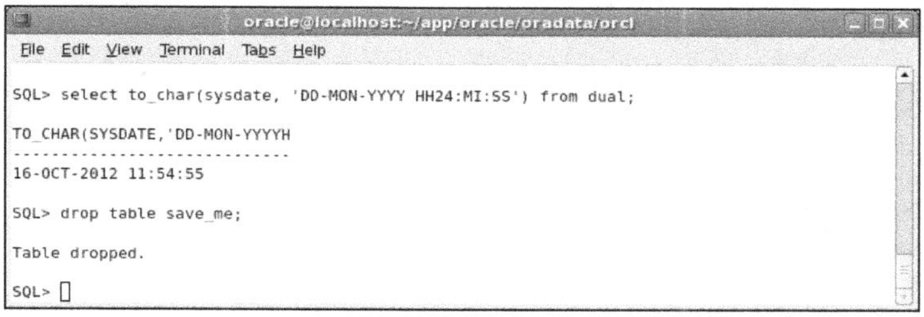

```
oracle@localhost:~/app/oracle/oradata/orcl
File Edit View Terminal Tabs Help
SQL> select to_char(sysdate, 'DD-MON-YYYY HH24:MI:SS') from dual;

TO_CHAR(SYSDATE,'DD-MON-YYYYH
-----------------------------
16-OCT-2012 11:54:55

SQL> drop table save_me;

Table dropped.

SQL>
```

As another added precaution, we'll switch the logfile one more time. This also simulates the passage of time in a real-world environment.

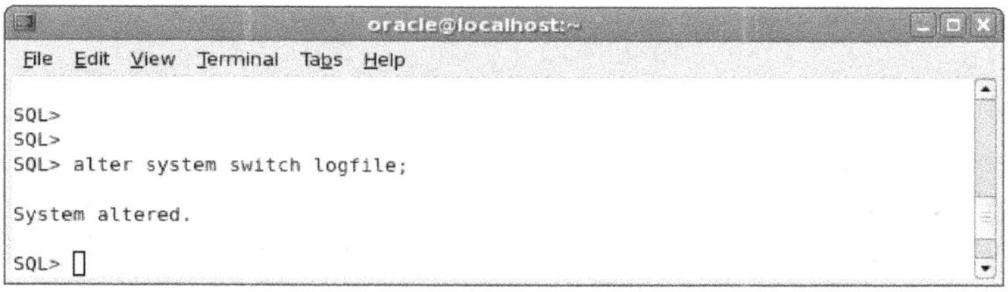

```
oracle@localhost:~
File Edit View Terminal Tabs Help
SQL>
SQL>
SQL> alter system switch logfile;

System altered.

SQL>
```

The table has been dropped. It's time to see if we can recover it. Because recoveries can only occur in a database that is in the MOUNT state, we'll need to do this in our database.

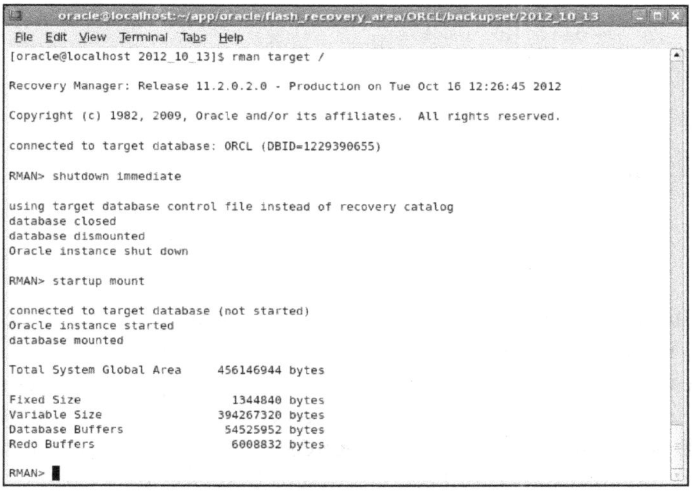

```
oracle@localhost:~/app/oracle/flash_recovery_area/ORCL/backupset/2012_10_13
File Edit View Terminal Tabs Help
[oracle@localhost 2012_10_13]$ rman target /

Recovery Manager: Release 11.2.0.2.0 - Production on Tue Oct 16 12:26:45 2012

Copyright (c) 1982, 2009, Oracle and/or its affiliates.  All rights reserved.

connected to target database: ORCL (DBID=1229390655)

RMAN> shutdown immediate

using target database control file instead of recovery catalog
database closed
database dismounted
Oracle instance shut down

RMAN> startup mount

connected to target database (not started)
Oracle instance started
database mounted

Total System Global Area     456146944 bytes

Fixed Size                     1344840 bytes
Variable Size                394267320 bytes
Database Buffers              54525952 bytes
Redo Buffers                   6008832 bytes

RMAN>
```

Next, while still in RMAN, we'll need to run a command to establish the format that we'll use to set our recovery time frame. We are using the RMAN `sql` command to execute a SQL statement that will not run natively in RMAN. We will carefully denote the same time format that we used to query our recovery time previously. Be cautious of the syntax here, especially the single and double quotes. They must be exactly correct.

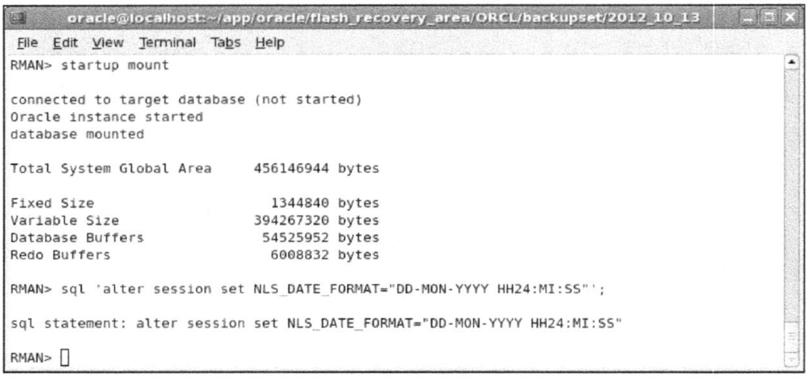
oracle@localhost:~/app/oracle/flash_recovery_area/ORCL/backupset/2012_10_13
File Edit View Terminal Tabs Help
RMAN> startup mount
connected to target database (not started)
Oracle instance started
database mounted
Total System Global Area 456146944 bytes
Fixed Size 1344840 bytes
Variable Size 394267320 bytes
Database Buffers 54525952 bytes
Redo Buffers 6008832 bytes
RMAN> sql 'alter session set NLS_DATE_FORMAT="DD-MON-YYYY HH24:MI:SS"';
sql statement: alter session set NLS_DATE_FORMAT="DD-MON-YYYY HH24:MI:SS"
RMAN>

Next, we'll need to run the remainder of the restore and recover commands in a `RUN` script. Remember that these commands should be exact and that case sensitivity is enforced within quotes. Also remember to use the time you queried earlier rather than the one you see here.

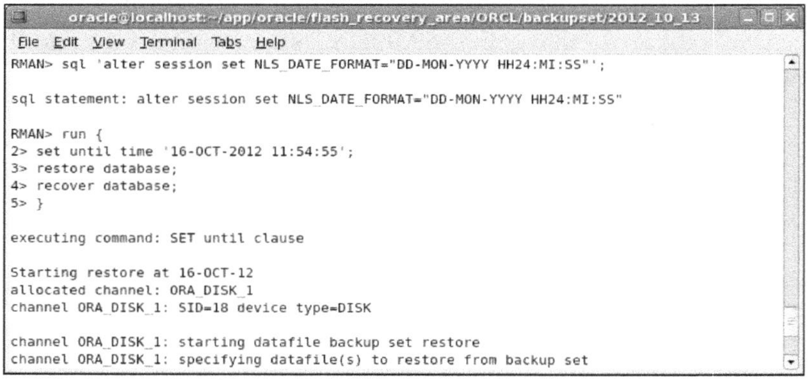
oracle@localhost:~/app/oracle/flash_recovery_area/ORCL/backupset/2012_10_13
File Edit View Terminal Tabs Help
RMAN> sql 'alter session set NLS_DATE_FORMAT="DD-MON-YYYY HH24:MI:SS"';
sql statement: alter session set NLS_DATE_FORMAT="DD-MON-YYYY HH24:MI:SS"
RMAN> run {
2> set until time '16-OCT-2012 11:54:55';
3> restore database;
4> recover database;
5> }
executing command: SET until clause
Starting restore at 16-OCT-12
allocated channel: ORA_DISK_1
channel ORA_DISK_1: SID=18 device type=DISK
channel ORA_DISK_1: starting datafile backup set restore
channel ORA_DISK_1: specifying datafile(s) to restore from backup set

Let's examine this `RUN` script in detail. First, after establishing the `RUN` block, we use the `set until time` command. We do this to establish the exact time up to which we want to recover. Note that this sets the time down to the exact second. Next, we use the `restore database` command to restore from backup. Last, we use the `recover database` command to initiate recovery. We've already set our recovery point in time, so the command will recover up to that point.

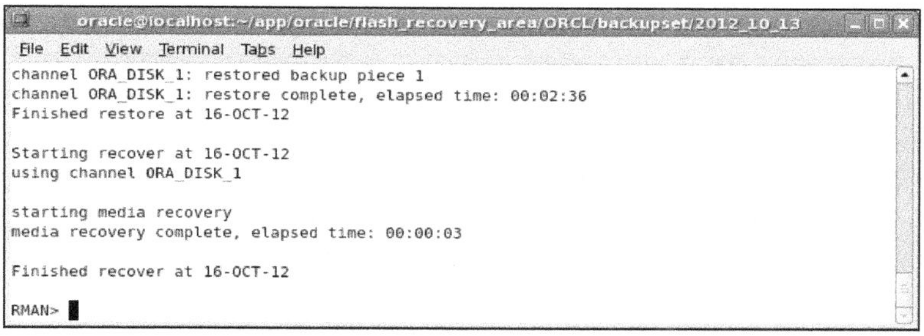
oracle@localhost:~/app/oracle/flash_recovery_area/ORCL/backupset/2012_10_13
File Edit View Terminal Tabs Help
channel ORA_DISK_1: restored backup piece 1
channel ORA_DISK_1: restore complete, elapsed time: 00:02:36
Finished restore at 16-OCT-12
Starting recover at 16-OCT-12
using channel ORA_DISK_1
starting media recovery
media recovery complete, elapsed time: 00:00:03
Finished recover at 16-OCT-12
RMAN>

Our restore and recover operations have completed successfully. However, we must remember that we're currently in a mounted state. We must open the database to check if we've successfully rescued our table. When we perform an incomplete recovery, we must open the database in a special way. During an incomplete recovery, we recover changes up to a point in the past and not all changes. In a sense, our database now exists in the state that it was in several minutes ago. Because of this, the redo logs are no longer valid, because they can contain changes that exist in the future. Thus, we must open the database with a special clause called `RESETLOGS`. This opens our database with a completely new set of redo logs.

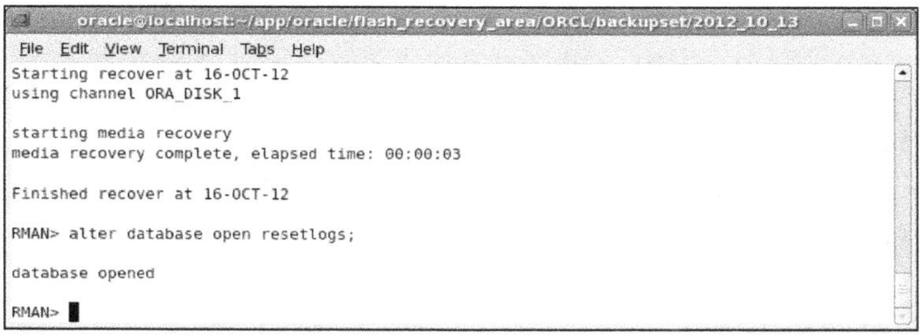
oracle@localhost:~/app/oracle/flash_recovery_area/ORCL/backupset/2012_10_13
File Edit View Terminal Tabs Help
Starting recover at 16-OCT-12
using channel ORA_DISK_1
starting media recovery
media recovery complete, elapsed time: 00:00:03
Finished recover at 16-OCT-12
RMAN> alter database open resetlogs;
database opened
RMAN>

All of our recovery operations are now complete, and the database is open. It's the moment of truth. Let's return to SQL*Plus to see if we were successful. Keep in mind that we dropped the `save_me` table.

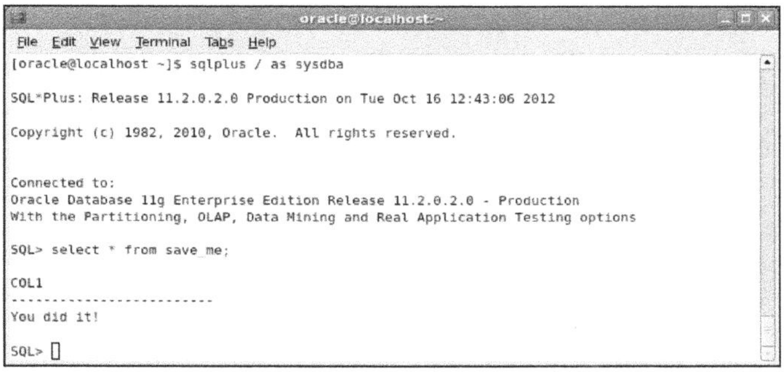
oracle@localhost:~
File Edit View Terminal Tabs Help
[oracle@localhost ~]$ sqlplus / as sysdba
SQL*Plus: Release 11.2.0.2.0 Production on Tue Oct 16 12:43:06 2012
Copyright (c) 1982, 2010, Oracle. All rights reserved.
Connected to:
Oracle Database 11g Enterprise Edition Release 11.2.0.2.0 - Production
With the Partitioning, OLAP, Data Mining and Real Application Testing options
SQL> select * from save_me;
COL1

You did it!
SQL>

Congratulations! We were successful at one of the trickiest operations a DBA will ever have to perform—an incomplete recovery. Although this is a controlled test, it does illustrate the concepts and steps needed to perform a time-based incomplete recovery. The syntax for sequence-based and change-based recoveries is similar, and mainly consists of a different statement for `set until`. Although an incomplete recovery is not something we want to do every day, we want to be prepared to face it if necessary. Again, practice is an extremely important part of this preparation.

Using the Data Recovery Advisor

In an attempt to further simplify recoveries, Oracle introduced the **Data Recovery Advisor** (**DRA**) in Version 11*g*. The DRE is a framework that is integrated into the **Automatic Diagnostic Repository** (**ADR**) that we learned about in *Chapter 6, Managing the Oracle Instance*. The DRA can provide a streamlined interface for database recovery using either a command-line interface or Enterprise Manager. However, there are a few requirements of which we must be aware. They are as follows:

- The DRA can only operate when the database is in the NOMOUNT state or higher. It cannot be used when the database is completely closed. This is not too much of a concern, because it follows that the only aspect of recovery that the DRA cannot perform is the recovery of an initialization parameter file.
- The DRA does not support the use of Real Application Clusters, although it can perform recovery in a single-instance mode.
- The DRA does not support the recovery of Data Guard databases.

Performing recovery using the DRA command-line interface

The DRA uses an advisory approach to perform database recovery. As such, in order to understand the problem, we need only "ask RMAN". As we've mentioned, the DRA is integrated with the ADR, which should be aware of any problems. In this example, we'll create a failure scenario by again dropping the datafile from the USERS tablespace. We'll then attempt to create a database table in the failed tablespace, which will alert the ADR of the problem. Then, we'll use the DRA to advise and repair the failure. We'll begin by dropping the datafile for the USERS tablespace. For safety's sake, do not attempt to do this unless a recent database backup has been taken. If you've followed the examples thus far and performed an incomplete recovery, a new backup is required since a `RESETLOGS` command was executed during the recovery that resets the database.

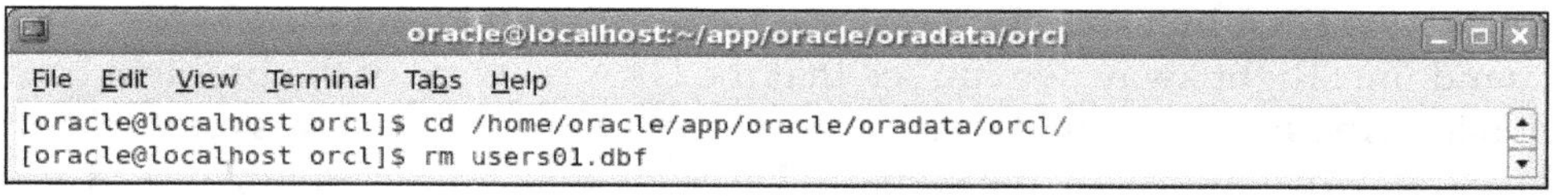
oracle@localhost:~/app/oracle/oradata/orcl
File Edit View Terminal Tabs Help

```
[oracle@localhost orcl]$ cd /home/oracle/app/oracle/oradata/orcl/
[oracle@localhost orcl]$ rm users01.dbf
```

Next, we'll attempt to create a table in the failed tablespace associated with `users01.dbf`.

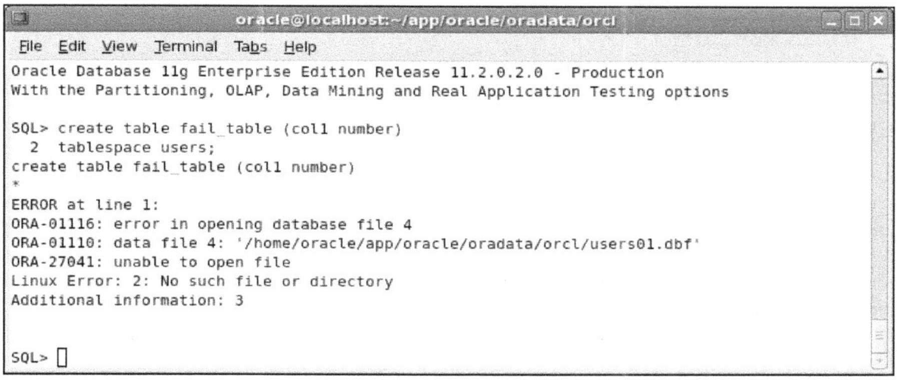
oracle@localhost:~/app/oracle/oradata/orcl
File Edit View Terminal Tabs Help

```
Oracle Database 11g Enterprise Edition Release 11.2.0.2.0 - Production
With the Partitioning, OLAP, Data Mining and Real Application Testing options

SQL> create table fail_table (col1 number)
  2  tablespace users;
create table fail_table (col1 number)
*
ERROR at line 1:
ORA-01116: error in opening database file 4
ORA-01110: data file 4: '/home/oracle/app/oracle/oradata/orcl/users01.dbf'
ORA-27041: unable to open file
Linux Error: 2: No such file or directory
Additional information: 3


SQL>
```

So, we've confirmed that we have a lost datafile. As we've already learned, we could simply perform the steps in RMAN to recover this datafile. However, let's log in to RMAN and see if the DRA can help us.

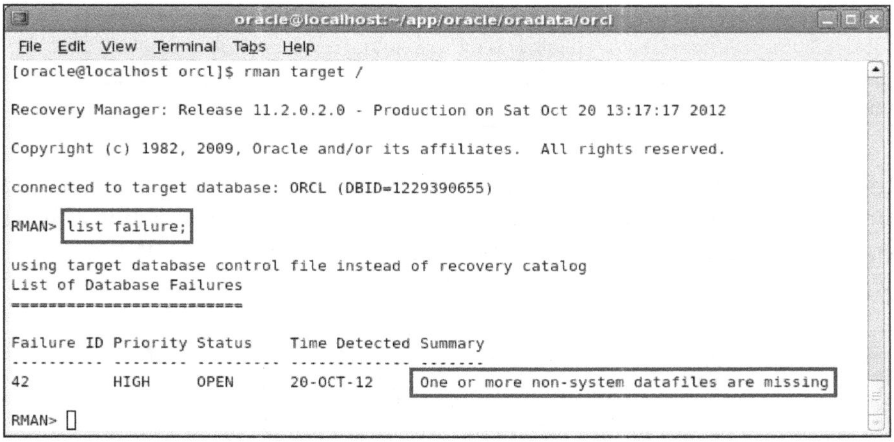
oracle@localhost:~/app/oracle/oradata/orcl
File Edit View Terminal Tabs Help

```
[oracle@localhost orcl]$ rman target /

Recovery Manager: Release 11.2.0.2.0 - Production on Sat Oct 20 13:17:17 2012

Copyright (c) 1982, 2009, Oracle and/or its affiliates.  All rights reserved.

connected to target database: ORCL (DBID=1229390655)

RMAN> list failure;

using target database control file instead of recovery catalog
List of Database Failures
=========================

Failure ID Priority Status    Time Detected Summary
---------- -------- --------- ------------- -------
42         HIGH     OPEN      20-OCT-12     One or more non-system datafiles are missing

RMAN>
```

We invoke the DRA by using the `list failure` command from the RMAN command line. Right away, we can see that the DRA is aware of the problem because it reads information from the ADR. It reports that **One or more non-system datafiles are missing**, which is exactly the scenario we've created. At this point, we can ask the DRA for advice on how we can proceed.

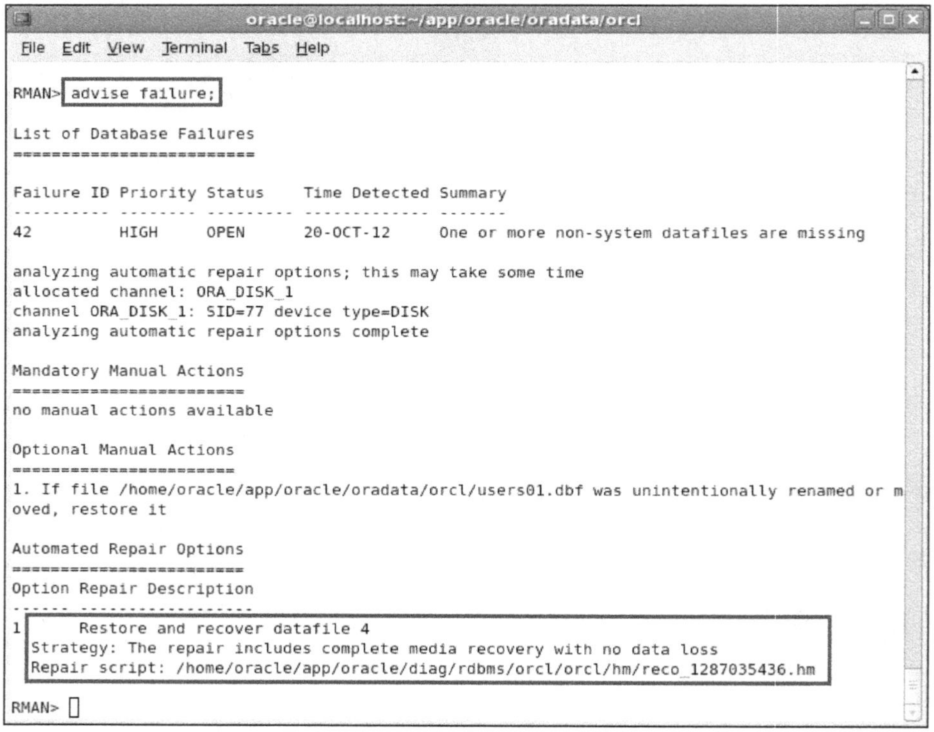
oracle@localhost:~/app/oracle/oradata/orcl
File Edit View Terminal Tabs Help
RMAN> advise failure;
List of Database Failures
=========================
Failure ID Priority Status Time Detected Summary
---------- -------- --------- ------------- -------
42 HIGH OPEN 20-OCT-12 One or more non-system datafiles are missing
analyzing automatic repair options; this may take some time
allocated channel: ORA_DISK_1
channel ORA_DISK_1: SID=77 device type=DISK
analyzing automatic repair options complete
Mandatory Manual Actions
========================
no manual actions available
Optional Manual Actions
=======================
1. If file /home/oracle/app/oracle/oradata/orcl/users01.dbf was unintentionally renamed or m
oved, restore it
Automated Repair Options
========================
Option Repair Description
------ ------------------
1 Restore and recover datafile 4
Strategy: The repair includes complete media recovery with no data loss
Repair script: /home/oracle/app/oracle/diag/rdbms/orcl/orcl/hm/reco_1287035436.hm
RMAN>

Using the `advise failure` command, we're given a wealth of information about our approach to recovery. The DRA indicates that the basic approach is to **Restore and recover datafile 4**. However, it's gone a step further than that. We see that it has actually generated a repair script for our use. Let's take a look at it.

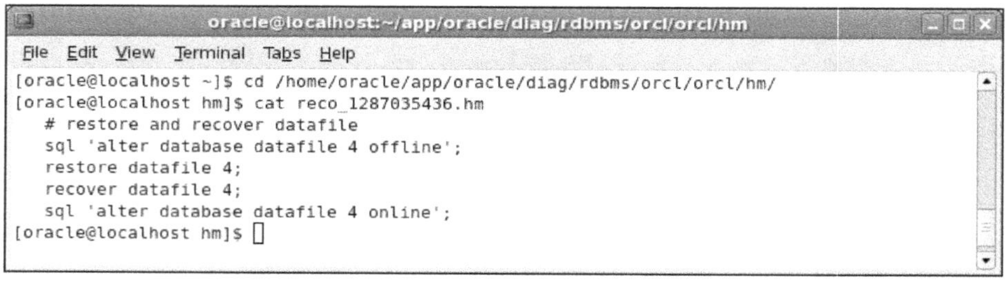
oracle@localhost:~/app/oracle/diag/rdbms/orcl/orcl/hm
File Edit View Terminal Tabs Help
[oracle@localhost ~]$ cd /home/oracle/app/oracle/diag/rdbms/orcl/orcl/hm/
[oracle@localhost hm]$ cat reco_1287035436.hm
restore and recover datafile
sql 'alter database datafile 4 offline';
restore datafile 4;
recover datafile 4;
sql 'alter database datafile 4 online';
[oracle@localhost hm]$

As we can see from the script (the repair script that you generated will likely be named differently), it performs the same steps that we have learned for complete recovery. It takes the failed datafile offline, performs a restore and recover, and then brings the datafile back online. We can easily cut and paste this script into RMAN and perform the recovery. However, we can also use the DRA to repair the failure without these extra steps.

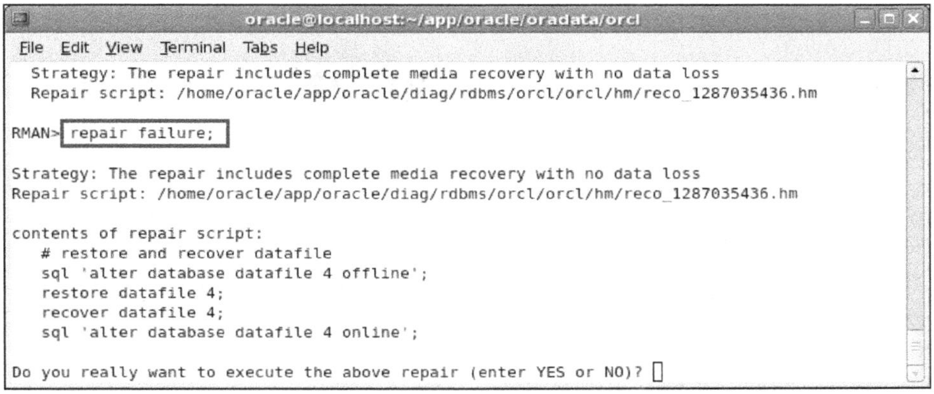
oracle@localhost:~/app/oracle/oradata/orcl
File Edit View Terminal Tabs Help
Strategy: The repair includes complete media recovery with no data loss
Repair script: /home/oracle/app/oracle/diag/rdbms/orcl/orcl/hm/reco_1287035436.hm
RMAN> repair failure;
Strategy: The repair includes complete media recovery with no data loss
Repair script: /home/oracle/app/oracle/diag/rdbms/orcl/orcl/hm/reco_1287035436.hm
contents of repair script:
restore and recover datafile
sql 'alter database datafile 4 offline';
restore datafile 4;
recover datafile 4;
sql 'alter database datafile 4 online';
Do you really want to execute the above repair (enter YES or NO)?

By using the `repair failure` command, we invoke the DRA to read the script generated by it and perform the recovery. It is crucial to understand that the `advise failure` command must be executed before the `repair failure` command, because the `advise failure` command creates the necessary scripts for repair. The DRA presents us with the steps that it will perform, and then asks us if we wish to proceed. We respond by typing `YES`.

oracle@localhost:~/app/oracle/oradata/orcl
File Edit View Terminal Tabs Help
channel ORA_DISK_1: reading from backup piece /home/oracle/app/oracle/flash_recovery_area/ORCL/backupset/2012_10_20/o1_mf_nnndf_TAG20121020T124856_886018dh_.bkp
channel ORA_DISK_1: piece handle=/home/oracle/app/oracle/flash_recovery_area/ORCL/backupset/2012_10_20/o1_mf_nnndf_TAG20121020T124856_886018dh_.bkp tag=TAG20121020T124856
channel ORA_DISK_1: restored backup piece 1
channel ORA_DISK_1: restore complete, elapsed time: 00:00:25
Finished restore at 20-OCT-12
Starting recover at 20-OCT-12
using channel ORA_DISK_1
starting media recovery
media recovery complete, elapsed time: 00:00:00
Finished recover at 20-OCT-12
sql statement: alter database datafile 4 online
repair failure complete
RMAN>

After confirming that we wish to proceed, the DRA invokes the repair script and successfully restores the datafile. Note that we never even needed to shut down the database. The DRA gave us the best possible advice for recovery of the datafile. Thus, we analyzed and repaired a database with a lost datafile using just three commands. While it is important to understand exactly how the DRA is performing the recovery, using its interface can provide a quick way to fix even serious problems that require recovery.

Performing recovery using the DRA with Enterprise Manager

Although using the DRA from the command line is very simple and straightforward, we can further simplify this operation using Enterprise Manager. Just as RMAN interfaces with the DRA, so does Enterprise Manager. In this example, the `users01.dbf` datafile has been deleted again. This time, we'll use the DRA through Enterprise Manager to recover the file. To access this functionality, we'll log in to Database Control from a web browser. Because we're performing recovery operations, we'll log in using the `SYS` user account with the `SYSDBA` role.

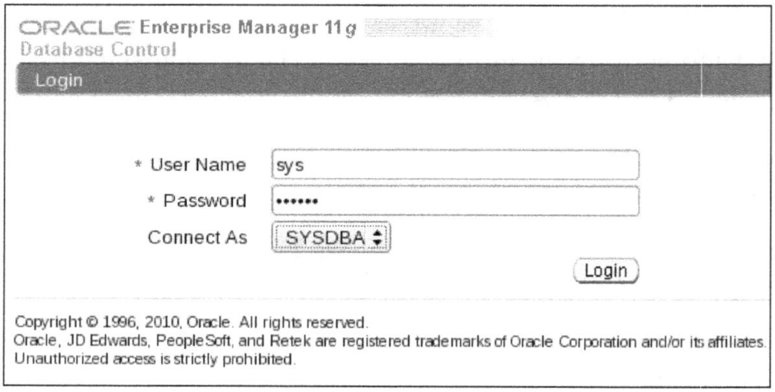
ORACLE Enterprise Manager 11g
Database Control
Login
* User Name
sys
* Password
Connect As
SYSDBA
Login
Copyright © 1996, 2010, Oracle. All rights reserved.
Oracle, JD Edwards, PeopleSoft, and Retek are registered trademarks of Oracle Corporation and/or its affiliates.
Unauthorized access is strictly prohibited.

To enter the **Data Recovery Advisor** page, we scroll to the bottom of the page to the **Related Links** section, and click on the **Advisor Central** link.

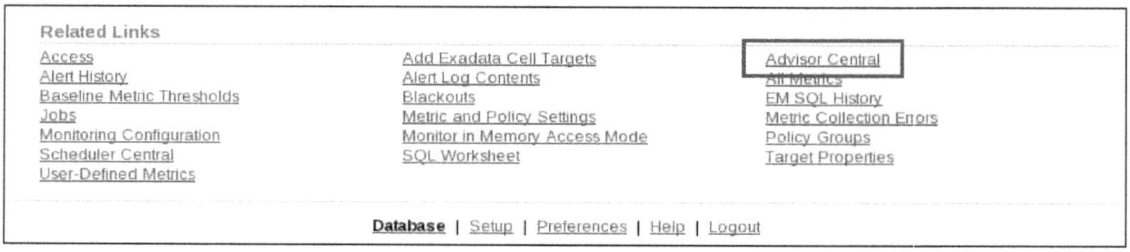
Related Links
Access
Alert History
Baseline Metric Thresholds
Jobs
Monitoring Configuration
Scheduler Central
User-Defined Metrics
Add Exadata Cell Targets
Alert Log Contents
Blackouts
Metric and Policy Settings
Monitor in Memory Access Mode
SQL Worksheet
Advisor Central
All Metrics
EM SQL History
Metric Collection Errors
Policy Groups
Target Properties
Database | Setup | Preferences | Help | Logout

Within **Advisor Central**, we click on the link for **Data Recovery Advisor**.

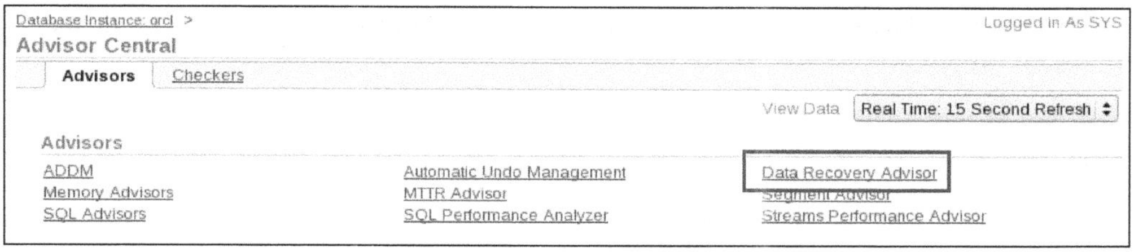
Database Instance: orcl >
Logged in As SYS
Advisor Central
Advisors
Checkers
View Data
Real Time: 15 Second Refresh
Advisors
ADDM
Memory Advisors
SQL Advisors
Automatic Undo Management
MTTR Advisor
SQL Performance Analyzer
Data Recovery Advisor
Streams Performance Advisor

We see the page titled **View and Manage Failures**. From the list of failures, we see that a datafile is missing again, as we would expect. We click on the **Advise** button to invoke the DRA to advise us of the failure. We need to enter our username and password for the database server (OS credentials, not database credentials) under **Host Credentials** in order for the DRA to function.

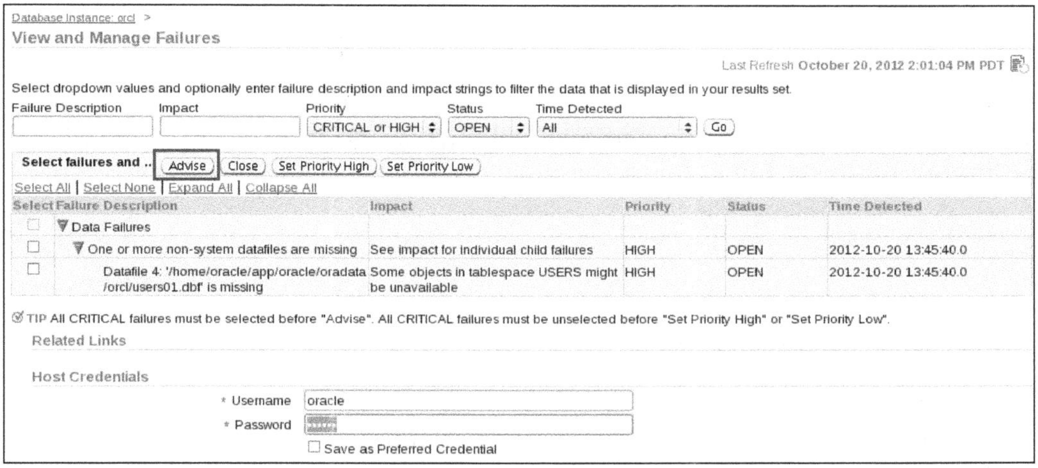
Database Instance: orcl >
View and Manage Failures
Last Refresh October 20, 2012 2:01:04 PM PDT
Select dropdown values and optionally enter failure description and impact strings to filter the data that is displayed in your results set.
Failure Description
Impact
Priority
CRITICAL or HIGH
Status
OPEN
Time Detected
All
Go
Select failures and ..
Advise
Close
Set Priority High
Set Priority Low
Select All | Select None | Expand All | Collapse All
Select Failure Description
Impact
Priority
Status
Time Detected
Data Failures
One or more non-system datafiles are missing
See impact for individual child failures
HIGH
OPEN
2012-10-20 13:45:40.0
Datafile 4: '/home/oracle/app/oracle/oradata/orcl/users01.dbf' is missing
Some objects in tablespace USERS might be unavailable
HIGH
OPEN
2012-10-20 13:45:40.0
TIP All CRITICAL failures must be selected before "Advise". All CRITICAL failures must be unselected before "Set Priority High" or "Set Priority Low".
Related Links
Host Credentials
* Username
oracle
* Password
Save as Preferred Credential

We are then presented with a general assessment of the situation. We click on **Continue with Advise** to continue.

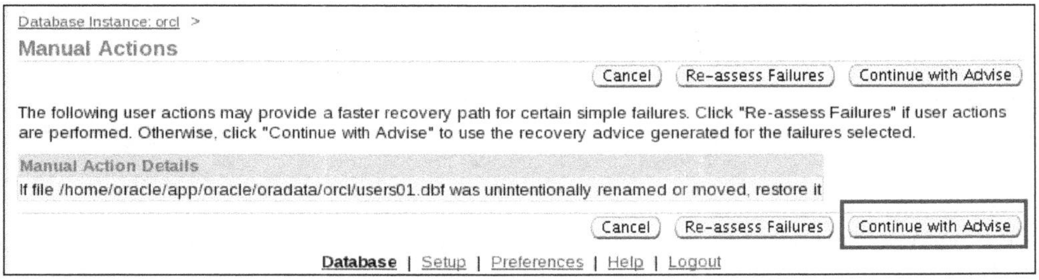
Database Instance: orcl >
Manual Actions
Cancel
Re-assess Failures
Continue with Advise
The following user actions may provide a faster recovery path for certain simple failures. Click "Re-assess Failures" if user actions are performed. Otherwise, click "Continue with Advise" to use the recovery advice generated for the failures selected.
Manual Action Details
If file /home/oracle/app/oracle/oradata/orcl/users01.dbf was unintentionally renamed or moved, restore it
Cancel
Re-assess Failures
Continue with Advise
Database | Setup | Preferences | Help | Logout

After continuing, we're presented with a repair script to recover from the failure. At this point, we could cut and paste this script output into RMAN and repair the failure manually. However, we'll click on **Continue** to repair the failure from within Database Control.

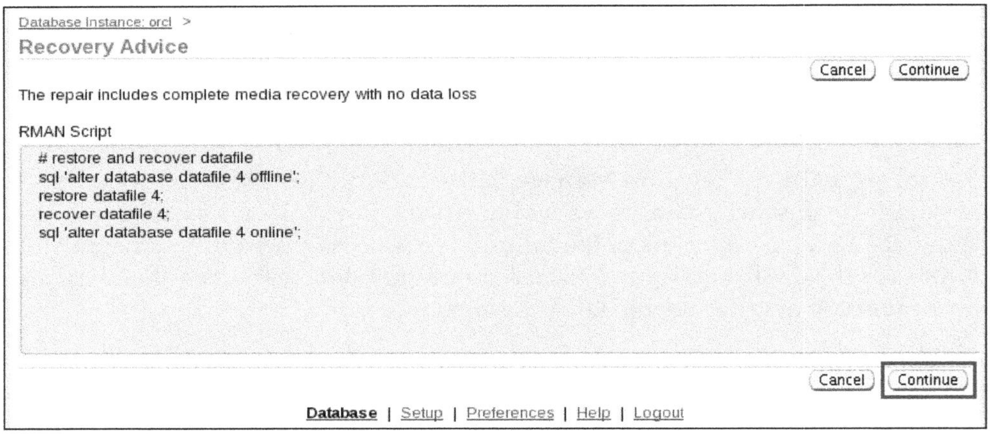
Database Instance: orcl >
Recovery Advice
Cancel
Continue
The repair includes complete media recovery with no data loss
RMAN Script
restore and recover datafile
sql 'alter database datafile 4 offline';
restore datafile 4;
recover datafile 4;
sql 'alter database datafile 4 online';
Cancel
Continue
Database | Setup | Preferences | Help | Logout

The DRA presents us with a final review of the actions that will be taken. We click on the **Submit Recovery Job** button to continue.

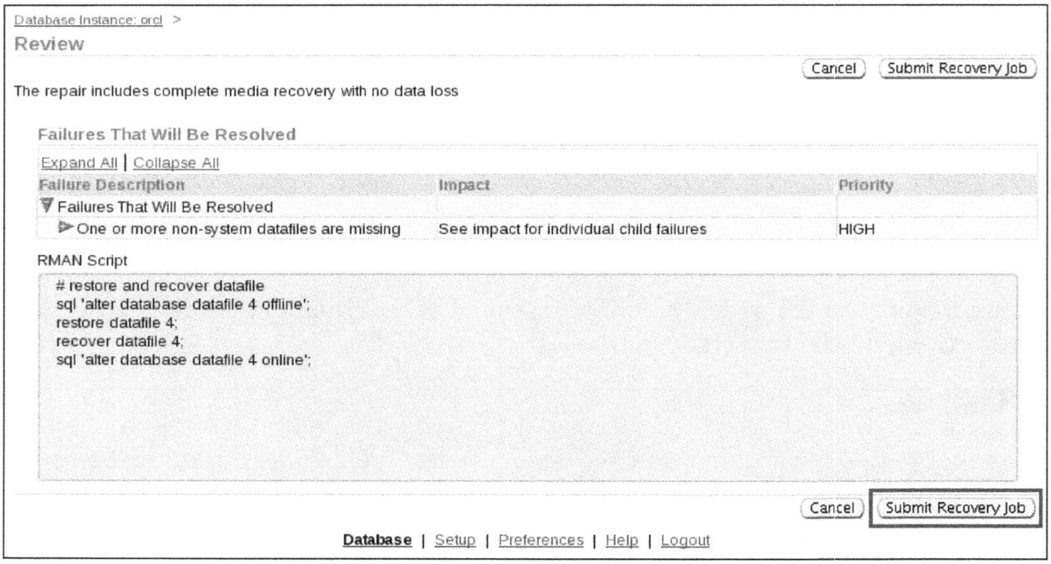
Database Instance: orcl >
Review
Cancel
Submit Recovery Job
The repair includes complete media recovery with no data loss
Failures That Will Be Resolved
Expand All | Collapse All
Failure Description
Impact
Priority
Failures That Will Be Resolved
One or more non-system datafiles are missing
See impact for individual child failures
HIGH
RMAN Script
restore and recover datafile
sql 'alter database datafile 4 offline';
restore datafile 4;
recover datafile 4;
sql 'alter database datafile 4 online';
Cancel
Submit Recovery Job
Database | Setup | Preferences | Help | Logout

The recovery job is created and run automatically. After a few seconds, we can refresh the window to see that the job has run successfully.

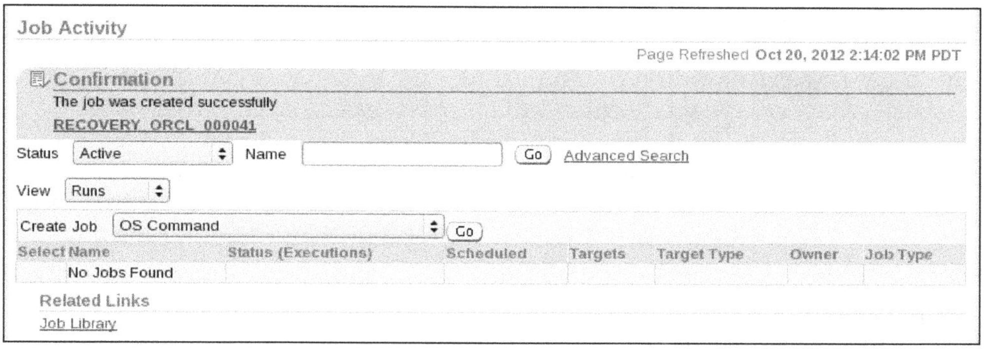
Job Activity
Page Refreshed Oct 20, 2012 2:14:02 PM PDT
Confirmation
The job was created successfully
RECOVERY_ORCL_000041
Status Active Name Go Advanced Search
View Runs
Create Job OS Command Go
Select Name Status (Executions) Scheduled Targets Target Type Owner Job Type
No Jobs Found
Related Links
Job Library

As a final check, we can confirm that the recovery has taken place by querying the data dictionary. As we can see, all datafiles, including `users01.dbf`, are up and available.

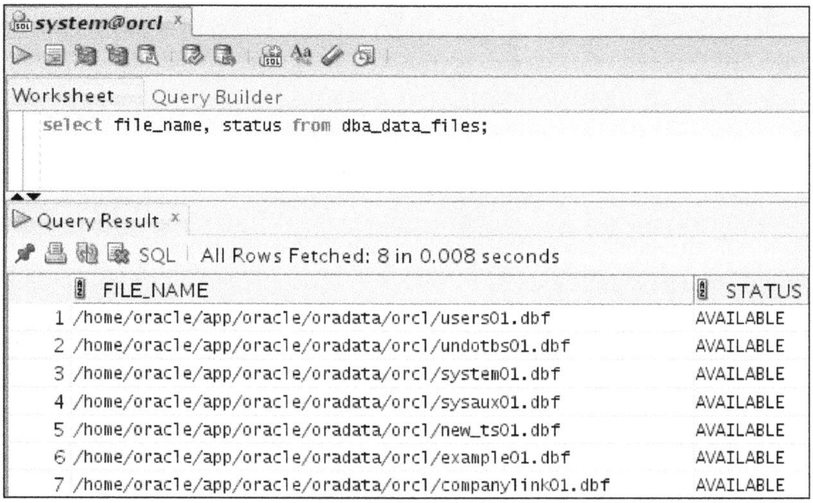
system@orcl
Worksheet Query Builder
select file_name, status from dba_data_files;
Query Result
SQL All Rows Fetched: 8 in 0.008 seconds
FILE_NAME STATUS
1 /home/oracle/app/oracle/oradata/orcl/users01.dbf AVAILABLE
2 /home/oracle/app/oracle/oradata/orcl/undotbs01.dbf AVAILABLE
3 /home/oracle/app/oracle/oradata/orcl/system01.dbf AVAILABLE
4 /home/oracle/app/oracle/oradata/orcl/sysaux01.dbf AVAILABLE
5 /home/oracle/app/oracle/oradata/orcl/new_ts01.dbf AVAILABLE
6 /home/oracle/app/oracle/oradata/orcl/example01.dbf AVAILABLE
7 /home/oracle/app/oracle/oradata/orcl/companylink01.dbf AVAILABLE

Certification objectives covered

- Overview of Data Recovery Advisor
- Using Data Recovery Advisor to perform recovery

Summary

In this chapter, we've explored the important and sometimes complex subject of database recovery. We've discussed the importance of database recovery as it relates to the strategy we use for backup. We've learned how to perform recoveries from both cold and hot backups. We've explored incomplete recoveries and performed an incomplete recovery using the point-in-time recovery method. Finally, we've explored the Data Recovery Advisor and saw how it can be used to simplify recovery using both command line and Enterprise Manager. In our next chapter, we'll explore the techniques used in Oracle to migrate data, including Oracle's Data Pump tool.

Test your knowledge

Q 1. Which of the following is the least important consideration when performing a database recovery?

a. Whether the database is in ARCHIVELOG or NOARCHIVELOG mode
b. The practiced skill level of the DBA performing the recovery
c. Whether complete or incomplete recovery is required
d. The number of redo logs in the database

Q 2. Which two options of the following best describe operations that are involved in performing a database recovery?

a. Restore
b. Rename
c. Recover
d. Undo

Q 3. Which of the following is *not* required to perform a complete recovery of a database?

a. A database backup
b. A flash recovery area
c. Archived logfiles
d. Redo logfiles

Q 4. Up to what level of granularity does a complete recovery recover data?

a. Up to the point of the last redo log switch
b. Up to the point of the last written archivelog
c. Up to the last time SMON performed instance recovery
d. Up to the last committed transaction

Q 5. What distinguishes an incomplete recovery from a complete recovery?

a. An incomplete recovery is only possible with incremental backups
b. An incomplete recovery is only possible if the backup is done with RMAN
c. An incomplete recovery is only possible if the backup was done to an FRA
d. An incomplete recovery does not recover all of the available transactions

Q 6. We attempt to open our database from a closed state. The database reaches MOUNT state and then displays an error indicating that datafile number 6 is missing. We need to perform database recovery, but we want to open the rest of the database while this recovery is occurring. Choose the correct statements to do this and place them in the correct numbered order.

1. `alter database datafile 6 online;`
2. `alter database datafile 6 offline;`
3. `startup`
4. `shutdown immediate`
5. `recover datafile 6;`
6. `restore datafile 6;`
7. `alter database open;`

a. 2, 7, 6, 5, 1
b. 4, 5, 6, 3
c. 6, 5, 4, 3
d. 4, 2, 6, 5, 1, 7

Q 7. Which of the following *cannot* be used as a condition for an incomplete recovery?

a. The SCN of an `UPDATE` statement that incorrectly changed a table
b. The point in time when a `DROP TABLE` statement occurred incorrectly
c. The commit point when a `DELETE` statement incorrectly deleted rows
d. The log sequence number of the last archivelog before a subsequent missing archivelog

Q 8. We are currently running our `Companylink` database, which was backed up six days ago, in NOARCHIVELOG mode. We open the database and observe that datafile number 8 is missing. What are our options for recovery?

a. Restore the database and perform an incomplete recovery up to the point before datafile number 8 was dropped.
b. Restore the database and perform a complete recovery that will recover datafile number 8.
c. Restore the database, losing all the transactions since the last backup was completed.
d. No type of recovery is possible. All data is lost.

Q 9. During the creation of a table in the COMPANYLINK tablespace, it is found that a datafile for that tablespace is missing. You enter RMAN and issue the command `repair failure`. What is the outcome of this command?

a. A failure is listed indicating that a datafile is missing.
b. A script is generated that can be used to perform recovery of the datafile
c. A script is generated and automatically run that successfully recovers the datafile
d. An error occurs, since the command was run before a repair script was created using `advise failure`.

14
Migrating Data

The most important aspect of any database is the data it contains. However, the data within a database doesn't always stay there—it often needs to be migrated in some way. **Data migration** involves the movement of a database's data to another location—out to the filesystem, in from the filesystem, or between databases. Let's consider an example. Data warehouses often take large amounts of data from mainframe systems as input to serve in a mid-tier data store. The process of reading that data, perhaps stored in an external flat file and inserting it into another database is data migration. The Oracle database includes a number of methods and tools for migrating data. In this chapter, we'll examine the process of data migration and the native tools we can use to accomplish it.

In this chapter, we shall:

- Examine external loading methodologies
- Use SQL*Loader to input data
- Understand the Data Pump architecture
- Use Data Pump to migrate data

Understanding external data access

Many types of programs that access databases are also required to reach out into the operating system for external data. A typical example of this is a PL/SQL program that loads data into a table from an external flat file. This program reads and processes each line in the file, then inserts that data into the table. In this section, we will examine Oracle's recommended method for accessing external files from a database—the directory object.

Creating directory objects

For many years, the primary method of performing operations that require operating system access was to use the Oracle-supplied `UTL_FILE` PL/SQL package. `UTL_FILE` could be used to read from and write to files. Access to the various OS directories was specified using the parameter, `UTL_FILE_DIR`. Thus if `UTL_FILE_DIR` was set to `/home/oracle` or `E:\app\oracle`, a program with the "execute" permission on `UTL_FILE` could read and write files in that directory. Thus, assigning directory values to the `UTL_FILE_DIR` parameter required a certain amount of care, since they represented a way for an attacker to access the operating system, provided they could take control of a database account. For instance, the `UTL_FILE_DIR` parameter could be set to `*`. This would allow `UTL_FILE_DIR` to read from and write to any directory in the operating system to which the `oracle` privileged account had access. The result could be disastrous if a database account was breached.

While the use of `UTL_FILE` is still very common today, Oracle has provided a new standardized way to access external data—through the use of directory objects. A **directory object** is a type of referential database object that simply refers to an operating system directory. We can think of it as a "doorway" in the database to an OS directory. Accessing data with directory objects is often much simpler and more direct than using `UTL_FILE` and doesn't require any special initialization parameters to be configured. Access to use directory objects is controlled by standard Oracle security methods. In order to make use of a directory object, the `READ` and `WRITE` privileges must be granted. The permissions necessary to create directory objects are governed by the `CREATE ANY DIRECTORY` system privilege. Thus, a user without that privilege cannot create directory objects. This is exactly as it should be—this privilege should not be given out lightly, since it allows direct access to the operating system. Let's create a directory object that we'll use in future examples. We'll begin by creating a folder (in Windows) or a directory (in Unix-based systems). This will serve as the directory that is utilized by the directory object.

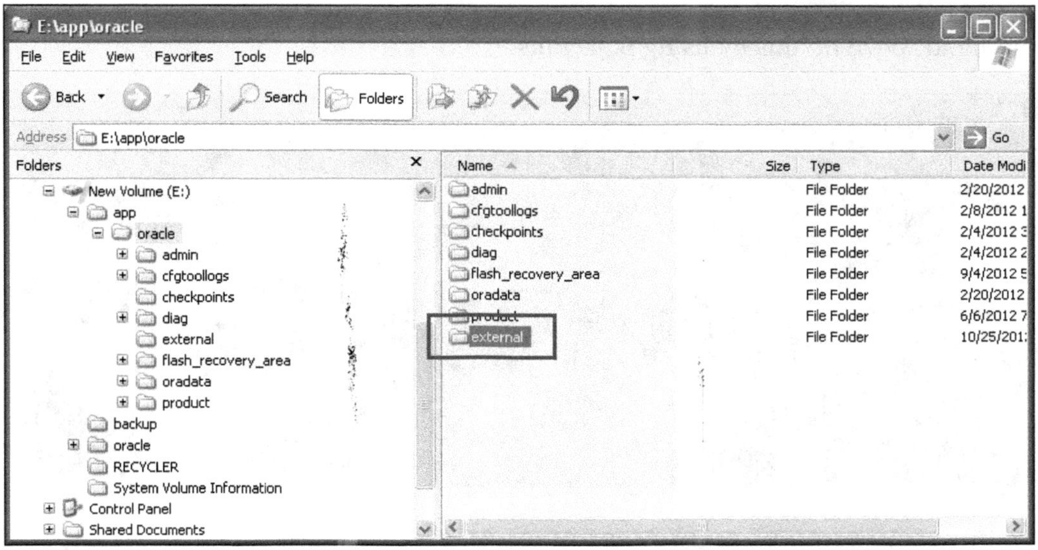
E:\app\oracle
File Edit View Favorites Tools Help
Back Search Folders
Address E:\app\oracle
Go
Folders
New Volume (E:)
app
oracle
admin
cfgtoollogs
checkpoints
diag
external
flash_recovery_area
oradata
product
backup
oracle
RECYCLER
System Volume Information
Control Panel
Shared Documents
Name
Size
Type
Date Modi
admin
cfgtoollogs
checkpoints
diag
flash_recovery_area
oradata
product
external
File Folder
2/20/2012
2/8/2012
2/4/2012
9/4/2012
6/6/2012
10/25/201

Here we've created a folder called `external` in the `E:\app\oracle` directory. We'll execute some of these examples in a Linux environment, so we could also use commands shown in the following screenshot to create a similar directory:

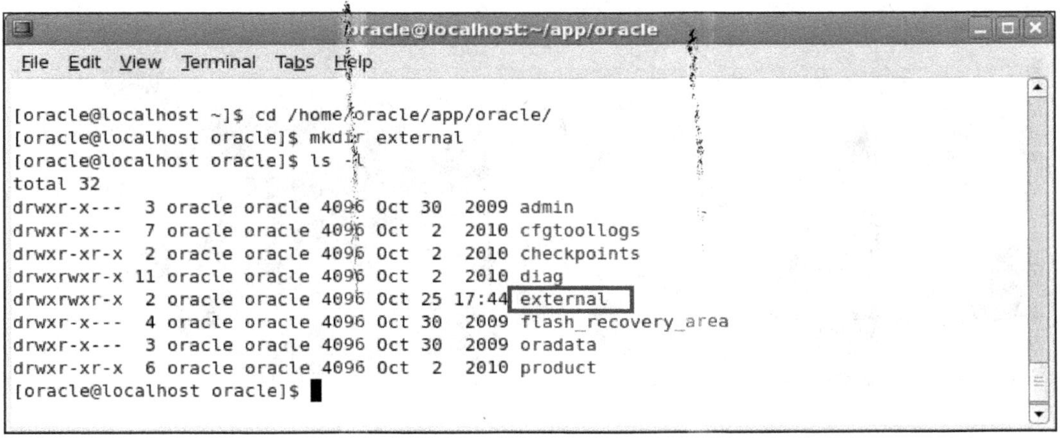
oracle@localhost:~/app/oracle
File Edit View Terminal Tabs Help
[oracle@localhost ~]$ cd /home/oracle/app/oracle/
[oracle@localhost oracle]$ mkdir external
[oracle@localhost oracle]$ ls -l
total 32
drwxr-x--- 3 oracle oracle 4096 Oct 30 2009 admin
drwxr-x--- 7 oracle oracle 4096 Oct 2 2010 cfgtoollogs
drwxr-xr-x 2 oracle oracle 4096 Oct 2 2010 checkpoints
drwxrwxr-x 11 oracle oracle 4096 Oct 2 2010 diag
drwxrwxr-x 2 oracle oracle 4096 Oct 25 17:44 external
drwxr-x--- 4 oracle oracle 4096 Oct 30 2009 flash_recovery_area
drwxr-x--- 3 oracle oracle 4096 Oct 30 2009 oradata
drwxr-xr-x 6 oracle oracle 4096 Oct 2 2010 product
[oracle@localhost oracle]$

Once the directory exists, we create a directory object using the `CREATE DIRECTORY` command. We'll do this by using SQL*Plus.

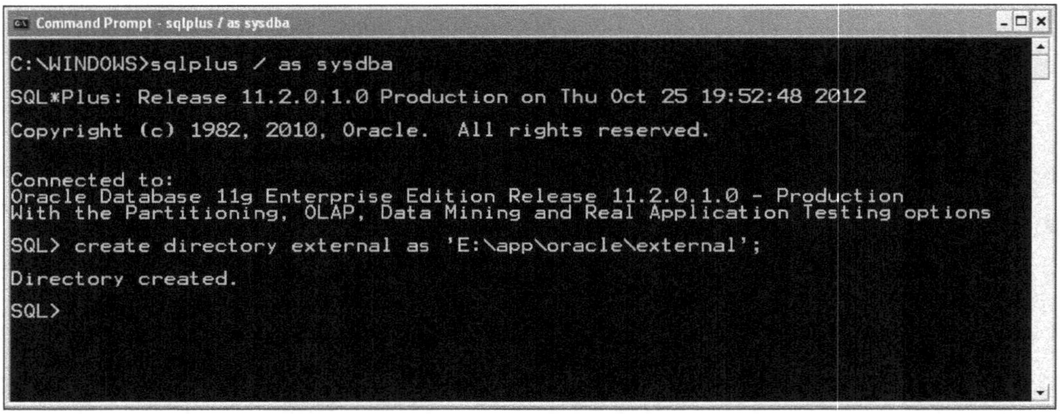
Command Prompt - sqlplus / as sysdba
C:\WINDOWS>sqlplus / as sysdba
SQL*Plus: Release 11.2.0.1.0 Production on Thu Oct 25 19:52:48 2012
Copyright (c) 1982, 2010, Oracle. All rights reserved.
Connected to:
Oracle Database 11g Enterprise Edition Release 11.2.0.1.0 - Production
With the Partitioning, OLAP, Data Mining and Real Application Testing options
SQL> create directory external as 'E:\app\oracle\external';
Directory created.
SQL>

Once a directory object is created, the owner, in this case `SYS`, has privileges to it. We need to grant access to any other users who will work with it as well. We do this using a standard `GRANT` statement with the `READ` and `WRITE` privileges, along with the `ON DIRECTORY` clause.

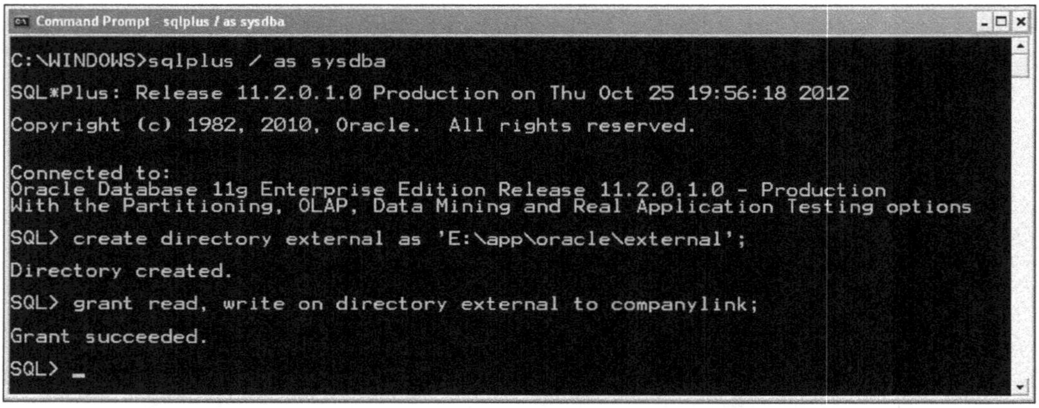
Command Prompt - sqlplus / as sysdba
C:\WINDOWS>sqlplus / as sysdba
SQL*Plus: Release 11.2.0.1.0 Production on Thu Oct 25 19:56:18 2012
Copyright (c) 1982, 2010, Oracle. All rights reserved.
Connected to:
Oracle Database 11g Enterprise Edition Release 11.2.0.1.0 - Production
With the Partitioning, OLAP, Data Mining and Real Application Testing options
SQL> create directory external as 'E:\app\oracle\external';
Directory created.
SQL> grant read, write on directory external to companylink;
Grant succeeded.
SQL> _

Now that we have a directory object in place and the `COMPANYLINK` user has the necessary permissions, we can use it for our next external access method—external tables.

Creating external tables

The types of tables with which we're familiar store their data within the appropriate tablespace as a table segment. Thus, their storage resides solely within the datafiles of the database. However, we can also make use of another type of table that stores its data outside of the database entirely. This type of table, called an **external table**, uses a directory object to access files stored at the operating system level to instantiate any query made against it. Thus we query an external table just as we would do with any other table and see in the results in a manner we would expect. However, the data returned is actually stored in a file outside the database, rather than a table segment. We cannot create indexes or execute DML statements, such as `INSERT`, `UPDATE` or `DELETE`, against external tables.

Why would such an object be useful? One common operation that must be performed in databases is called ETL—extraction, transformation, and loading. **ETL** is the process of extracting data from an outside source, transforming it to fit the needs of our database, and loading it into its end state. Let's use an example to illustrate this. Say that our Companylink application uses city, state, and zip code information for mailing lists. Each month we receive an updated file with this information in the form of a **Comma-separated Values** (**CSV**) file. This file contains a list of all the cities and towns in the United States with their zip codes. Since this information can change from time to time due to rezoning, we receive the most updated list each month. Each month, because our database applications cannot read the file natively, we must run a database job that reads the CSV file, loads the raw data into a staging table, and then uses application logic to alter it and load it into other tables. If we could eliminate the step of loading the file into the staging table, we could significantly reduce the time and effort in keeping our zip codes up to date. Using an external table is an excellent way to do this.

The first step in creating an external table is to create a file, stored in the OS destination directory of our directory object. We create the following CSV file, called `external.dat`, and place it in our `E:\app\oracle\external` directory. This is a small subset of data from our `EMPLOYEE` table. The individual column values are delimited by commas. Take note of the third row. It contains two commas together without any values in between. This is intentional—it represents a NULL value.

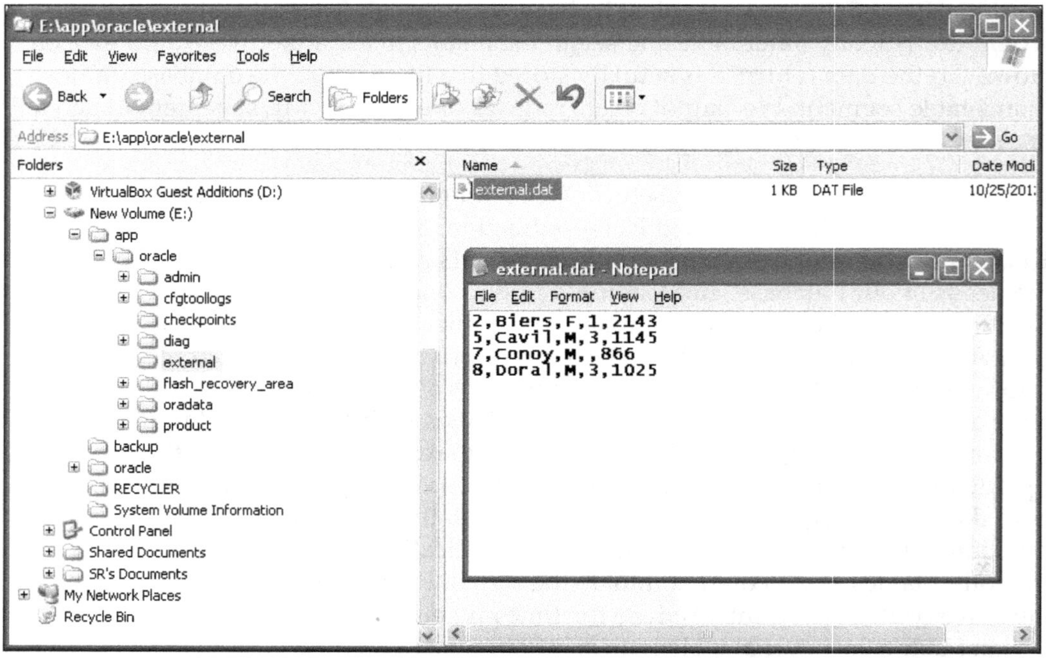
E:\app\oracle\external
File Edit View Favorites Tools Help
Back
Search
Folders
Address E:\app\oracle\external
Go
Folders
VirtualBox Guest Additions (D:)
New Volume (E:)
app
oracle
admin
cfgtoollogs
checkpoints
diag
external
flash_recovery_area
oradata
product
backup
oracle
RECYCLER
System Volume Information
Control Panel
Shared Documents
SR's Documents
My Network Places
Recycle Bin
Name
Size
Type
Date Modi
external.dat
1 KB
DAT File
external.dat - Notepad
File Edit Format View Help
2,Biers,F,1,2143
5,Cavil,M,3,1145
7,Conoy,M,,866
8,Doral,M,3,1025

In order to create an external table, we must use an existing directory object. Although we use the `CREATE TABLE` DDL command with which we're familiar, we'll use a new clause, `ORGANIZATION EXTERNAL`, to distinguish it as an external table. This is shown in the following screenshot of SQL Developer. We'll connect as the `COMPANYLINK` user by clicking on the `companylink@orcl` connection and creating our external table.

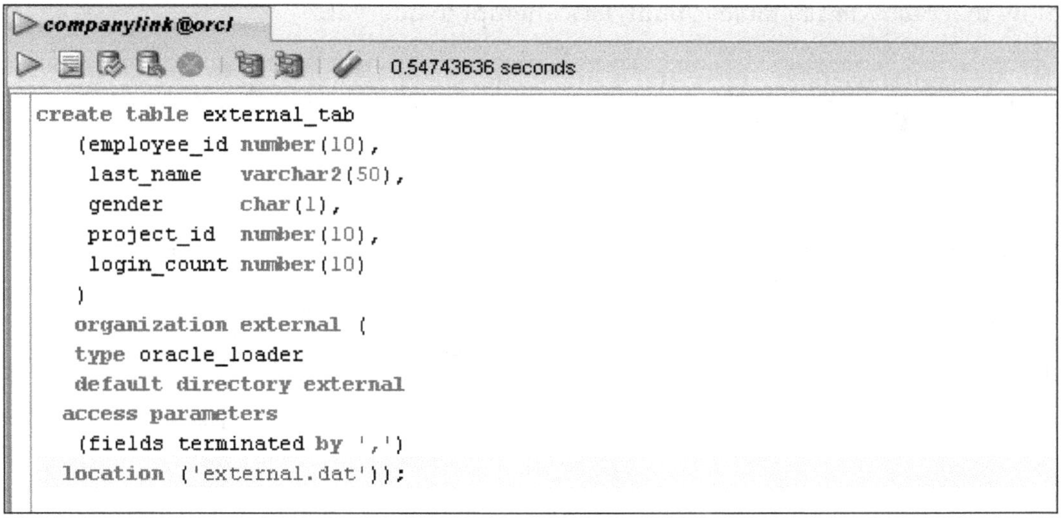
companylink@orcl
0.54743636 seconds
create table external_tab
(employee_id number(10),
last_name varchar2(50),
gender char(1),
project_id number(10),
login_count number(10)
)
organization external (
type oracle_loader
default directory external
access parameters
(fields terminated by ',')
location ('external.dat'));

Let's examine the syntax we've used to create our `external_tab` table. The first section is merely the standard definition of a table, with column names and datatypes. However, we should note that each of these columns and their datatypes correspond directly to the data in our `external.dat` file. There are five fields in this file, one for each column in our external table, and the datatypes must match. In the next section, we will use various clauses to define the location and data structure of our external file. These clauses are listed as follows:

- `organization external`: This distinguishes our table as an external table.
- `type`: For this, we use the `oracle_loader` keyword to instruct Oracle to implicitly use the SQL*Loader tool to extract the data from the file into our table. We will examine explicit use of the SQL*Loader tool in the next section of the chapter.
- `default directory`: This specifies the name of our directory object, `external`.
- `access parameters`: For this, we use the `fields terminated by` clause to indicate that our source file is comma-delimited.
- `location`: This specifies the name of the source file, `external.dat`, within our directory object.

Now that our external table is built, let's attempt to query it.

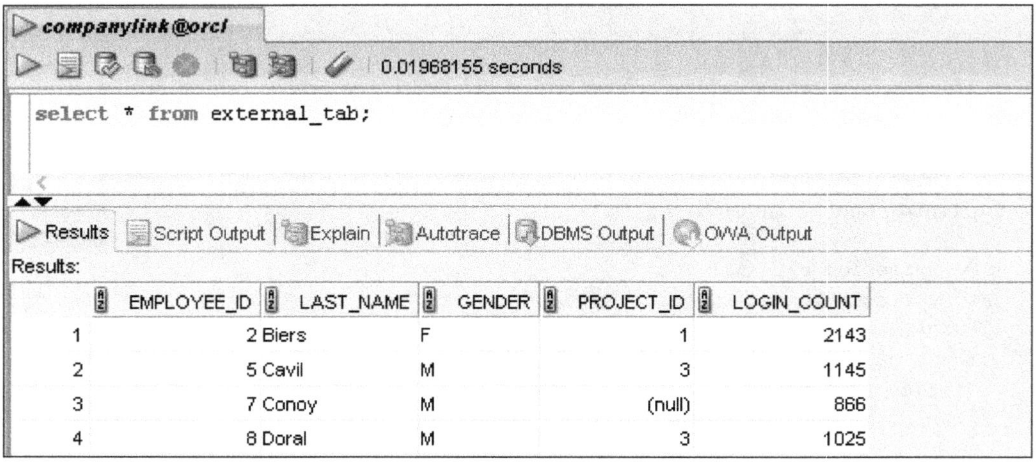
companylink@orcl
0.01968155 seconds
select * from external_tab;
Results
Script Output
Explain
Autotrace
DBMS Output
OWA Output
Results:
EMPLOYEE_ID
LAST_NAME
GENDER
PROJECT_ID
LOGIN_COUNT
1 2 Biers F 1 2143
2 5 Cavil M 3 1145
3 7 Conoy M (null) 866
4 8 Doral M 3 1025

We see the same data displayed, in the same order, as it exists in our source file. Notice the row where `employee_id` equals `7`. The `project_id` column shows a `(null)` value. This corresponds directly to the row in the source file with two commas placed together with no values in between. This is interpreted as a `NULL` value. In order to test our new external table, let's change a value directly within the source file and see if it is reflected in our resulting data. In `external.dat`, we'll change the value for `EMPLOYEE_ID` in the first row from `2` to `3` and `PROJECT_ID` from `1` to `4`.

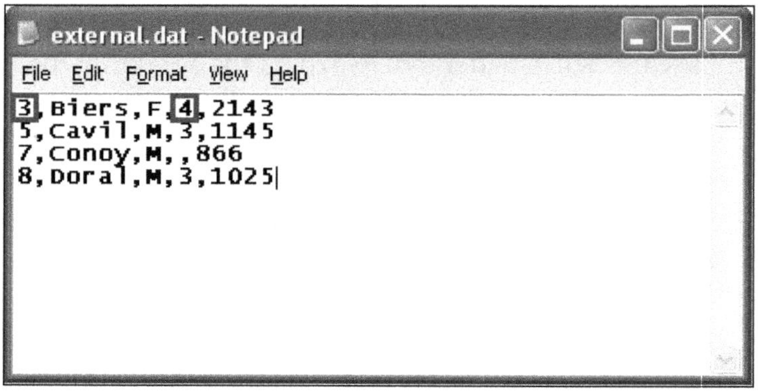
external.dat - Notepad
File Edit Format View Help
3,Biers,F,4,2143
5,Cavil,M,3,1145
7,Conoy,M,,866
8,Doral,M,3,1025

Now we'll execute our query again. Notice that the new data automatically reflects the changes made in the source file.

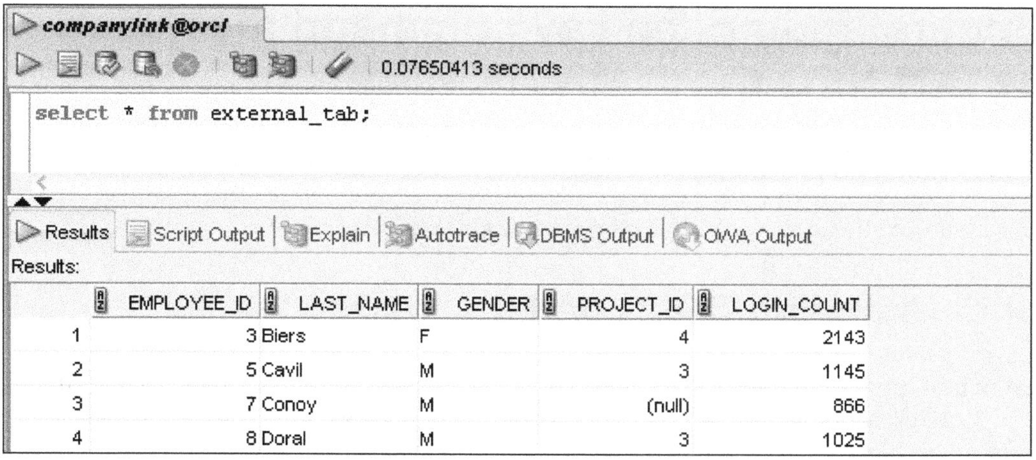
companylink@orcl
0.07650413 seconds
select * from external_tab;
Results
Script Output
Explain
Autotrace
DBMS Output
OWA Output
Results:
EMPLOYEE_ID
LAST_NAME
GENDER
PROJECT_ID
LOGIN_COUNT
1 3 Biers F 4 2143
2 5 Cavil M 3 1145
3 7 Conoy M (null) 866
4 8 Doral M 3 1025

The syntax of the creation of external tables can also be extended to include a number of other features, including the ability to save rejected rows and generate a named logfile. These aspects are normally associated with SQL*Loader, so we'll examine them in the next section.

Loading data with SQL*Loader

Using an external table can be an extremely useful way to load data into tables, but there are other methods as well. As we mentioned, the `type oracle_loader` clause in our `CREATE TABLE` statement for an external table implicitly uses Oracle's SQL*Loader tool to load data on the fly. This utility can also be used explicitly from the command line. **SQL*Loader** is Oracle's de facto tool for loading large amounts of data into database tables. A common use of SQL*Loader occurs when flat file data is extracted from mainframe systems and migrated to mid-tier Oracle systems that function as operational data stores. In such cases, it is crucial that the data is loaded quickly and accurately. It is also important that SQL*Loader is flexible enough to accommodate many types and structures of data. Not every flat file extract is comma-delimited—the data may be extracted with a different delimiter that separates data or the data may not be delimited at all. Data is often extracted by position and width under certain rules, such as the first 25 characters from the first field, the next 12 characters from the second field, and so on. Fortunately for us, SQL*Loader can handle all of these challenges. In this section, we'll construct the component parameter files that allow us to load data with SQL*Loader and explore its features.

Understanding the key command files used by SQL*Loader

We can invoke SQL*Loader's functionality by using the `sqlldr` command-line program. However, there are a number of different component files that specify how the program is run and tell us what occurred during the load. In this example, we will assemble these files and load data into the table.

Understanding SQL*Loader's load paths

As we construct the necessary files for our data load, we must first answer an important question about the method used to actually move the data into the table. SQL*Loader supports two different load paths that specify how data is migrated from an architectural perspective. Our choice can greatly affect the performance of a large load, so we must understand both. A **conventional path** insert takes the data in the source file and constructs basic `INSERT` statements using the individual source data values as bind variables. These statements are then run against the table and data is inserted in the conventional way that `INSERT` statements operate. The data is read into the buffer cache, and redo and undo are generated in the same way as a typical `INSERT` statement. This process tends to lessen the impact of the load on the overall performance from the user's perspective. SQL*Loader also supports a second methodology. A **direct path** insert loads data, but does so by bypassing the normal processing of the buffer cache. Instead, the source data values are read and constructed into data blocks that are read into the PGA and then written directly to database datafiles. No undo is generated for these types of load, which can result in dramatically faster load times. However, as we might expect, this performance comes with a cost. Direct path loads can only be used when certain conditions are true. Firstly, the table being loaded will not be locked against other DML changes, so a certain amount of isolation is needed to ensure the table is not modified during the loading process. Secondly, any foreign keys on the table being loaded must be disabled prior to the load, although primary keys have no such requirements. In real-world production environments, it is not uncommon to disable many different types of constraints during a data load, including the primary key, so this requirement is not always a concern. Thirdly, any triggers on the table that fire on `INSERT` statements will not operate. Also, direct path loads are not supported against certain objects, such as clustered tables. Although these requirements exist for direct path loading, they are not so stringent that it is unreasonable to conform to them. For this reason, direct path is the method of choice in many situations where performance of the load is crucial.

Understanding the input data file

The source data file itself is generally the file over which we as DBAs have the least amount of control. These data files are extracted from an external data source and are structured in a standard format to facilitate loading into a table. These formats can utilize various delimiters to distinguish various fields, as well as positional formatting. One of the most common formats is the one we used as the source data file for our external table—a CSV file with comma-separated values. Let's examine this file with an emphasis placed on the comma separation.

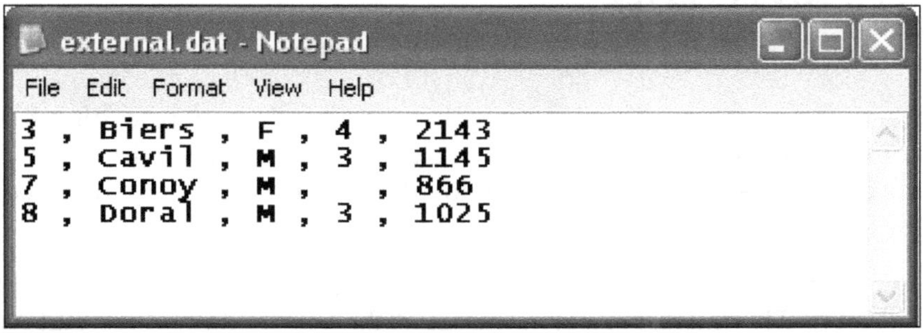
external.dat - Notepad
File Edit Format View Help
3 , Biers , F , 4 , 2143
5 , Cavil , M , 3 , 1145
7 , Conoy , M , , 866
8 , Doral , M , 3 , 1025

The commas delimit the "breaks" between data fields and indicate that a new field has begun. The third line in this file has two commas with no intervening value, so that the value will be processed as `NULL`.

> **The real-world DBA**
>
> SQL*Loader can use any number of delimiters, but the delimiter chosen must take the existing data into account. If our source file contains commas within the data, this must be considered, else we will find our fields delimited in the wrong place. We must often use quotes in conjunction with delimiters to handle these situations.

Source data for SQL*Loader can also be formatted by position. Here, we've altered our source file and added a few rows to see this effect.

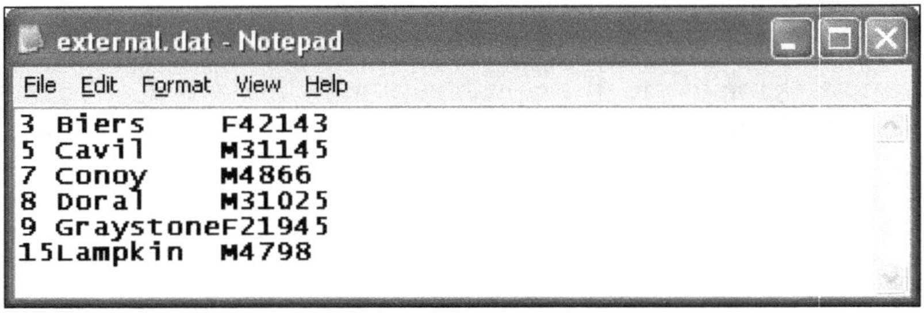
external.dat - Notepad

File Edit Format View Help

```
3 Biers    F42143
5 Cavil    M31145
7 Conoy    M4866
8 Doral    M31025
9 GraystoneF21945
15Lampkin  M4798
```

Here, in the absence of delimiter characters, we use the character position to define the limits of the fields in the file. The first two characters form the first field, the second nine characters form the second field, and so on. Special care must be taken when using `NULL` values in this format.

For our purposes, we'll use the same comma-delimited file that we utilized in our external table. The most important aspect of the source data file is that we understand how the data is structured within the file.

Constructing a parameter file

The SQL*Loader **parameter** (**PAR**) file is an optional command file that can be used to establish a number of the overall parameters that will be used during the loading process. This file contains the location of other command files, as well as the location of various output files generated during the loading process. This information can be entered from the command line, so the parameter file is not always used. However, it is generally considered proper coding standard to do so. Let's construct a parameter file for our load and examine what it contains. We will create this file in our `external` directory.

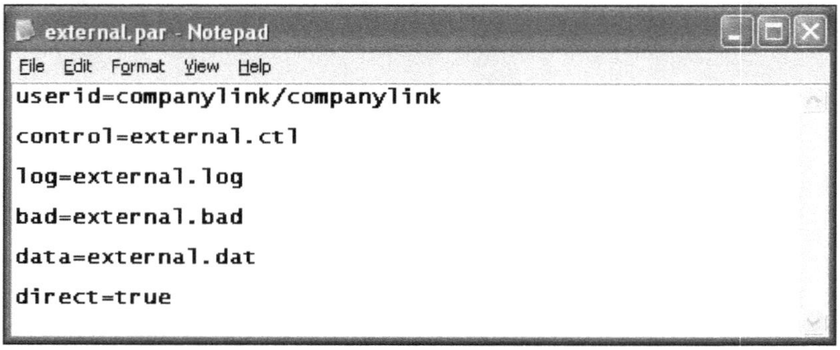
external.par - Notepad

File Edit Format View Help

```
userid=companylink/companylink

control=external.ctl

log=external.log

bad=external.bad

data=external.dat

direct=true
```

The `userid` option specifies our username and password. The `control` option indicates the name of our control file. This file is used to establish the various characteristics of our load, and will be discussed in detail in the next section. `Log` specifies a named logfile for our job. The `bad` option indicates the name of the file that will contain "bad" rows—rows that do not fit within the specifications provided in the control file. The `data` option defines the name of the source datafile that will be read. Finally, specifying `direct=true` instructs SQL*Loader to use a direct path load. The parameter file can contain many other types of instructions as well.

Constructing a control file

The real heart of a SQL*Loader job is the control file. A SQL*Loader **control file** (not to be confused with a database control file) is used to define the specific parameters that control how a load operates, such as the delimiter of the data and whether data will be appended or inserted. Let's build one that we'll call `external.ctl`, which will load our source data into a table.

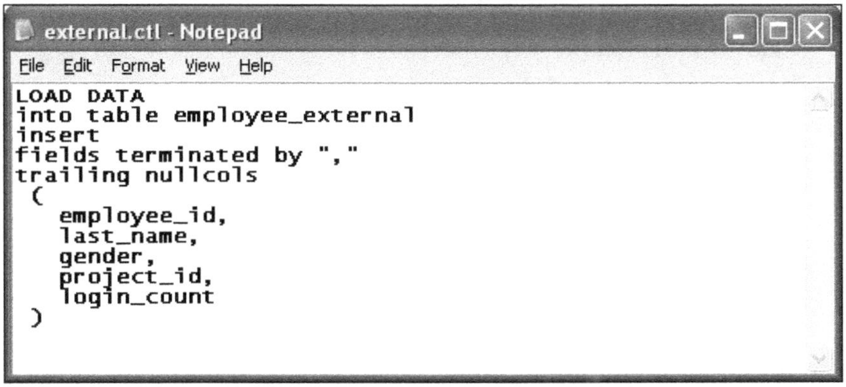
external.ctl - Notepad
File Edit Format View Help

```
LOAD DATA
into table employee_external
insert
fields terminated by ","
trailing nullcols
 (
   employee_id,
   last_name,
   gender,
   project_id,
   login_count
 )
```

The control file begins with `LOAD DATA` and then specifies the target table for data insertion, `employee_external`, which we will create shortly. The next keyword, `insert`, indicates that we are performing a "data insert". SQL*Loader supports a number of different load operations, including the following.

- `INSERT`: This is the default method. This only works with a table that has no rows.
- `TRUNCATE`: This method truncates all rows from the target table before inserting values from the source datafile.
- `APPEND`: This method adds rows constructed from the source data to any existing rows in the table.
- `REPLACE`: This method removes rows from the target table and then inserts the source data.

The next option, `fields terminated by ","`, defines the delimiter for our source data as a comma. Next, the phrase `trailing nullcols` indicates that any fields with trailing whitespace, such as space characters, will have that whitespace removed. The last section defines the order of the table columns into which we're loading. As with the parameter file, there are many other types of keywords that can be used to further define our load job.

Running a SQL*Loader job

Before we actually run the SQL*Loader job, we must first create the target table for our load. We create this table to specifically coincide with the structure of our source data file.

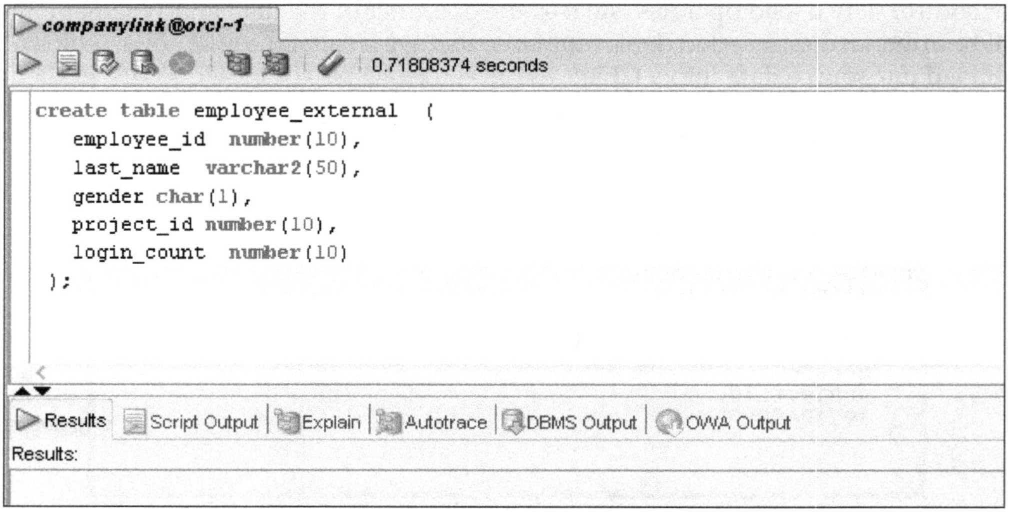
companylink@orcl~1
0.71808374 seconds
create table employee_external (
employee_id number(10),
last_name varchar2(50),
gender char(1),
project_id number(10),
login_count number(10)
);
Results
Script Output
Explain
Autotrace
DBMS Output
OWA Output
Results:

With our target table created, we're ready to run our load job. The majority of the work in preparing this job is the work we've already done in creating our SQL*Loader files. Now that this is complete, we simply invoke SQL*Loader from the command line using the `sqlldr` command. We must ensure that we've navigated to our `external` directory so that the files in question can be read without specifying their full directory paths.

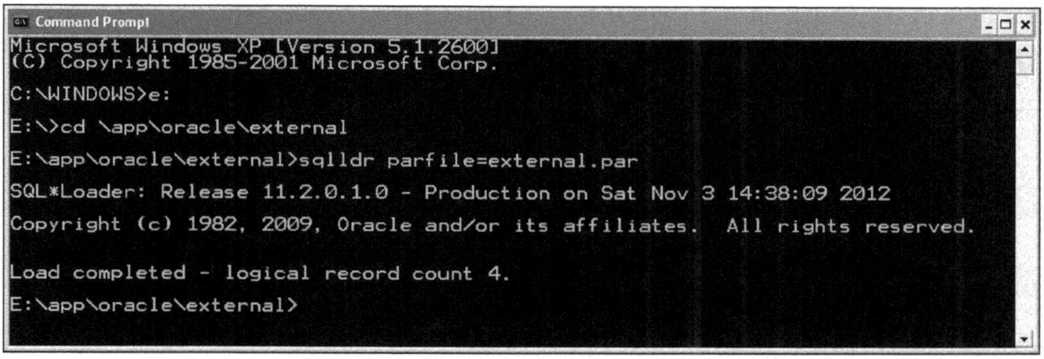
Command Prompt
Microsoft Windows XP [Version 5.1.2600]
(C) Copyright 1985-2001 Microsoft Corp.
C:\WINDOWS>e:
E:\>cd \app\oracle\external
E:\app\oracle\external>sqlldr parfile=external.par
SQL*Loader: Release 11.2.0.1.0 - Production on Sat Nov 3 14:38:09 2012
Copyright (c) 1982, 2009, Oracle and/or its affiliates. All rights reserved.
Load completed - logical record count 4.
E:\app\oracle\external>

Issue the `sqlldr parfile=external.par` command and the loading begins. If there are any errors, they will be reported at this point. Instead, we see that we have successfully processed four records of data in the source file. We will confirm that the data was inserted into our target table with the following query from SQL Developer:

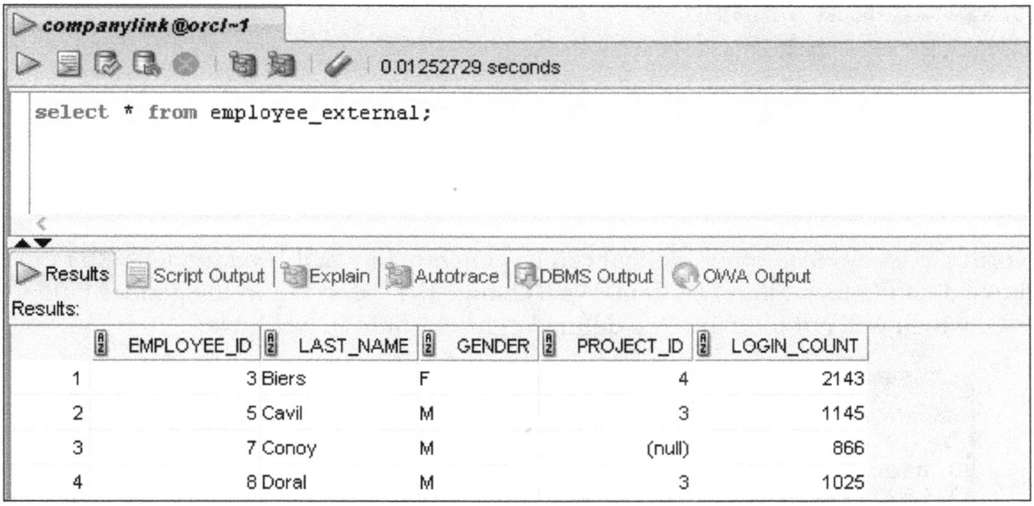
companylink@orcl~1
0.01252729 seconds
select * from employee_external;
Results
Script Output
Explain
Autotrace
DBMS Output
OWA Output
Results:
EMPLOYEE_ID LAST_NAME GENDER PROJECT_ID LOGIN_COUNT
1 3 Biers F 4 2143
2 5 Cavil M 3 1145
3 7 Conoy M (null) 866
4 8 Doral M 3 1025

Our data is verified. Notice that SQL*Loader handles our `NULL` value in row 3 just as expected. In the same directory from which the `sqlldr` command was executed, we also have an `external.log` file, containing the log of the SQL*Loader operation. A portion of this log is shown in the following screenshot:

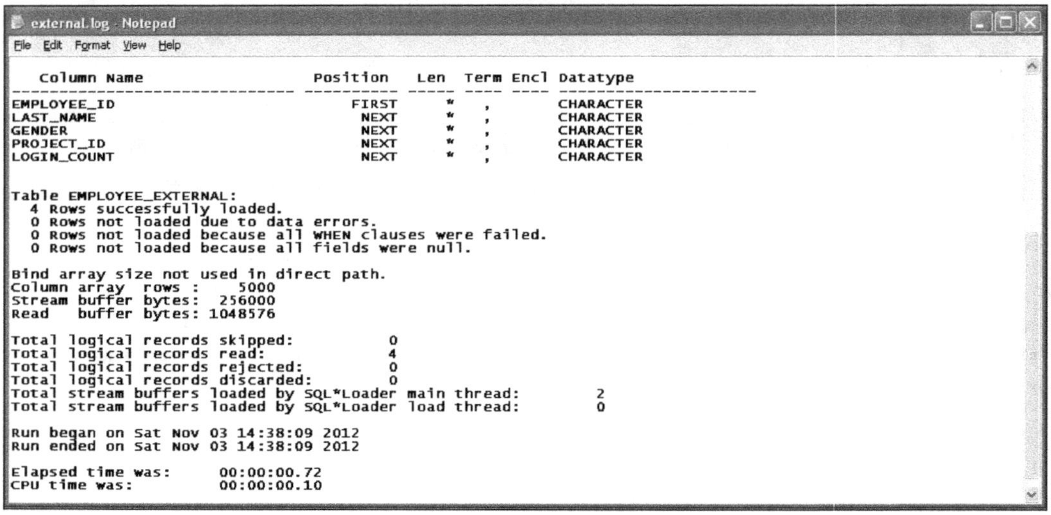

```
external.log - Notepad
File  Edit  Format  View  Help

   Column Name                  Position   Len  Term Encl Datatype
------------------------------ ---------- ----- ---- ---- ---------------------
EMPLOYEE_ID                         FIRST     *   ,       CHARACTER
LAST_NAME                            NEXT     *   ,       CHARACTER
GENDER                               NEXT     *   ,       CHARACTER
PROJECT_ID                           NEXT     *   ,       CHARACTER
LOGIN_COUNT                          NEXT     *   ,       CHARACTER


Table EMPLOYEE_EXTERNAL:
  4 Rows successfully loaded.
  0 Rows not loaded due to data errors.
  0 Rows not loaded because all WHEN clauses were failed.
  0 Rows not loaded because all fields were null.

Bind array size not used in direct path.
Column array  rows :    5000
Stream buffer bytes:  256000
Read   buffer bytes: 1048576

Total logical records skipped:          0
Total logical records read:             4
Total logical records rejected:         0
Total logical records discarded:        0
Total stream buffers loaded by SQL*Loader main thread:        2
Total stream buffers loaded by SQL*Loader load thread:        0

Run began on Sat Nov 03 14:38:09 2012
Run ended on Sat Nov 03 14:38:09 2012

Elapsed time was:     00:00:00.72
CPU time was:         00:00:00.10
```

The log specifies the characteristics of our load job in detail including the list of table columns, the begin and end times, and the number of rows loaded. If errors had occurred during the loading process, we would use this log to debug them.

In order to examine another file that can be generated by SQL*Loader, let's alter our source data file to contain bad data. We'll change the value `'F'` in the gender field to `'FF'`, which will not load into the defined `CHAR(1)` field in our table.

```
external.dat - Notepad
File  Edit  Format  View  Help
3,Biers,FF,4,2143
5,Cavil,M,3,1145
7,Conoy,M,,866
8,Doral,M,3,1025
```

We also need to change the options in our control file, `external.ctl`, to append the data instead of inserting.

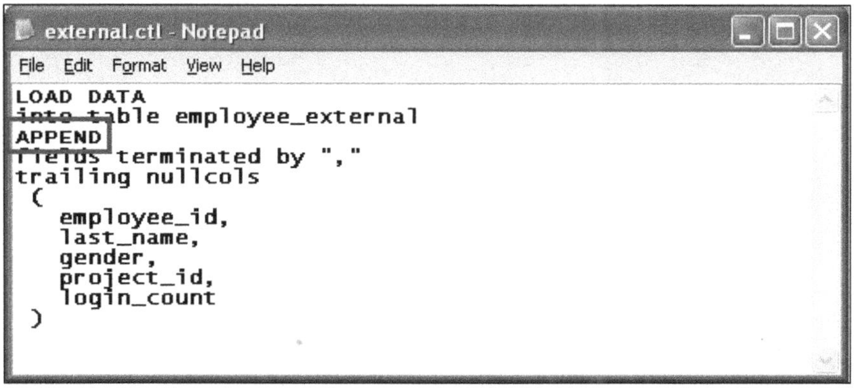
external.ctl - Notepad
File Edit Format View Help
LOAD DATA
into table employee_external
APPEND
fields terminated by ","
trailing nullcols
(
employee_id,
last_name,
gender,
project_id,
login_count
)

Now, we run our job just as we have done before, using the `sqlldr` command.

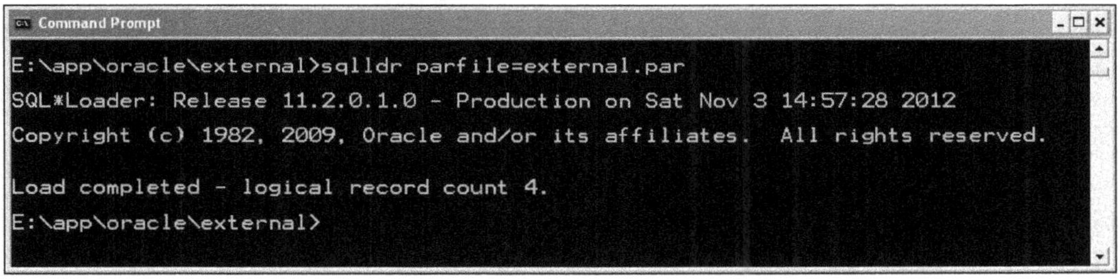
Command Prompt
E:\app\oracle\external>sqlldr parfile=external.par
SQL*Loader: Release 11.2.0.1.0 - Production on Sat Nov 3 14:57:28 2012
Copyright (c) 1982, 2009, Oracle and/or its affiliates. All rights reserved.
Load completed - logical record count 4.
E:\app\oracle\external>

Again, we process four logical records from the source data. But did these records insert successfully? We can now see a new file, `external.bad`, in our working directory. This is the `bad` file we defined in our parameter file. It contains the rows that were rejected due to errors.

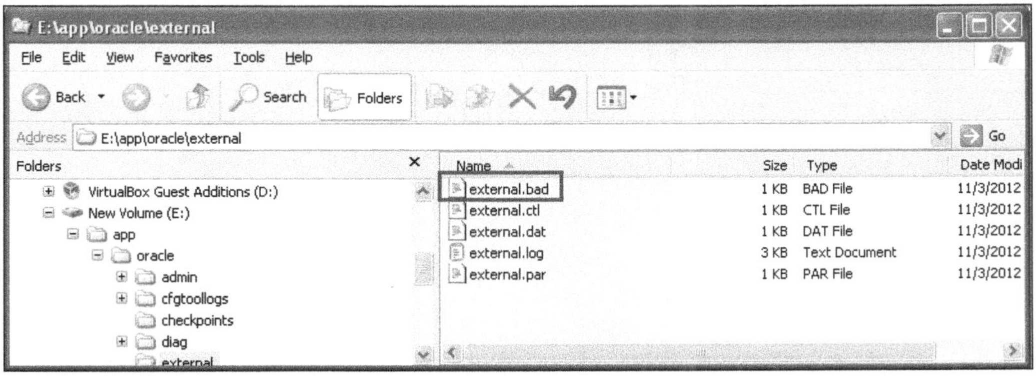
E:\app\oracle\external
File Edit View Favorites Tools Help
Back Search Folders
Address E:\app\oracle\external Go
Folders
VirtualBox Guest Additions (D:)
New Volume (E:)
app
oracle
admin
cfgtoollogs
checkpoints
diag
Name Size Type Date Modi
external.bad 1 KB BAD File 11/3/2012
external.ctl 1 KB CTL File 11/3/2012
external.dat 1 KB DAT File 11/3/2012
external.log 3 KB Text Document 11/3/2012
external.par 1 KB PAR File 11/3/2012

An examination of this file reveals what we have predicted–the first row with `'FF'` for the `GENDER` field is rejected.

external.bad - Notepad
File Edit Format View Help
3,Biers,FF,4,2143

Our newest logfile (which overwrites the previous one) can give us further information on the nature of why the row was rejected.

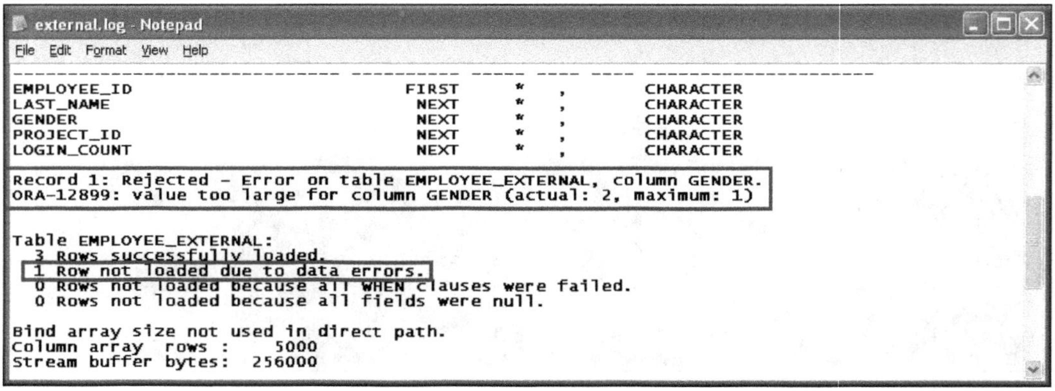
external.log - Notepad
File Edit Format View Help
EMPLOYEE_ID FIRST * , CHARACTER
LAST_NAME NEXT * , CHARACTER
GENDER NEXT * , CHARACTER
PROJECT_ID NEXT * , CHARACTER
LOGIN_COUNT NEXT * , CHARACTER
Record 1: Rejected - Error on table EMPLOYEE_EXTERNAL, column GENDER.
ORA-12899: value too large for column GENDER (actual: 2, maximum: 1)
Table EMPLOYEE_EXTERNAL:
3 Rows successfully loaded.
1 Row not loaded due to data errors.
0 Rows not loaded because all WHEN clauses were failed.
0 Rows not loaded because all fields were null.
Bind array size not used in direct path.
Column array rows : 5000
Stream buffer bytes: 256000

An `ORA-12899` error was generated, indicating a value in the `GENDER` field that was too large. Armed with this information, we can now address the problem and re-run the job.

Migrating data with Oracle Data Pump

While SQL*Loader is an excellent tool to load data from an external file, it lacks the ability to offload data for the purposes of populating another database. Historically, standard tools such as Export (`exp`) and Import (`imp`) were used for such a purpose. However, as time went on and the needs for transporting data evolved, these tools began to show their age. So, in Version 10*g*, Oracle introduced a new tool to replace Export and Import - Oracle Data Pump.

Understanding the architecture of Data Pump

Oracle **Data Pump** is the primary tool used to transport data from one Oracle database to another. It is an extremely effective tool for this purpose, but it is also important to understand its limitations. It is not a replacement for SQL*Loader and cannot load delimited data or data from another RDBMS into an Oracle database. It cannot be used to present flatfile data to a user in the way that an external table can. Nor is it a backup and recovery tool in the way that RMAN functions. With these limitations being taken into consideration, Data Pump is an extremely useful tool in its own right to transport data between databases. It is superior to Export and Import tools in every way and, although architecturally different, uses much of the same style of command syntax. Those who are familiar with Export and Import tools will have little trouble adapting to the new functionalities provided by Data Pump.

Unlike Export and Import, Data Pump is not a client-side tool. It functions on the server side and thus tends to be used by DBAs. The data dump files generated by the two sets of tools are not interchangeable—Data Pump cannot read Export and Import files and vice versa. From this, it follows that environments that host Version 9*i* databases cannot rely on Data Pump alone for a data transport method. However, Export and Import both still exist in 10*g* and 11*g* for backward compatibility.

We invoke two different clients in order to utilize Data Pump—Data Pump Export (`expdp`) and Data Pump Import (`impdp`). As we might expect, data exported using `expdp` can then be imported using `impdp`. In Windows environments, these two tools are `expdp.exe` and `impdp.exe`. The data output for `expdp` can be in the form of Data Pump dump files, which structure the data using XML or in SQL files that contain only the DDL needed to create the objects in question. Additionally, Data Pump writes a logfile out that describes the actions that were taken. Data Pump is not backward-compatible with the older Export and Import tools and cannot read dump files generated by them.

When either of these tools is launched, a server process is spawned that does the reading and writing of data. A control table is then created in the database that stores information about the Data Pump job. This table makes possible one of the unique features of Data Pump that is unavailable in traditional Export and Import. After launching a Data Pump job, it is possible to attach a session to the job with another session to monitor the progress of the job. This is extremely useful when executing long running jobs that run in the background. Data Pump runs using the `DBMS_DATAPUMP` system-supplied package. In truth, we don't actually need to use the `expdp` and `impdp` clients, but it is generally much easier to do so than to invoke the package itself. Data Pump primarily operates using the direct path read and write methods that we described for SQL*Loader, although it can also operate in an external table path mode, which is analogous to conventional path. Unlike SQL*Loader, however, Data Pump itself decides the method that will be used. Data Pump features an impressive array of functionalities using certain job keywords.

- `COMPRESSION`: Data Pump output files can be compressed to reduce space usage.
- `CONTENT`: Data can be exported/imported with only the structure, only the data, or both.
- `ENCRYPTION` : All or part of the dump files can be encrypted using the AES128, AES192, or AES256 encryption algorithms.
- `ESTIMATE_ONLY`: Jobs can be run to estimate approximate run times.
- `EXCLUDE` and `INCLUDE`: Data Pump can export and import data while excluding or including only certain object types.
- `NETWORK_LINK`: Data Pump can make a direct network connection to another database via database links and transport the data directly without dumping the data to disk.
- `PARALLEL`: Jobs can make use of parallelism in order to perform more efficiently.
- `QUERY`: Exports and imports that only extract or load a portion of table data can occur based on a `WHERE` clause condition.
- `REMAP_TABLE`: Imported table names can be mapped to a new table name.
- `REMAP_SCHEMA`: Imported tables can be mapped to a new schema.
- `REMAP_TABLESPACE`: Imported tables can be mapped to a different tablespace than the one from which the data was exported.
- `TABLE_EXISTS_ACTION`: Certain actions such as `APPEND`, `REPLACE`, `SKIP`, and `TRUNCATE` can take place if the imported table already exists.

Additionally, a number of job control actions can be taken by attaching the session to an existing job. These include stopping or restarting the job, displaying the status of the job, and adjusting the level of parallelism.

All of these functions provide us with an extremely flexible and powerful tool to migrate data between Oracle databases.

Exporting data Using Data Pump

Both `expdp` and `impdp` are invoked from the command line. If we so choose, we can execute either type of job using the executable followed by a set of **keyword** options like the ones above that define how the job will run. Let's run a very basic Data Pump export using this method.

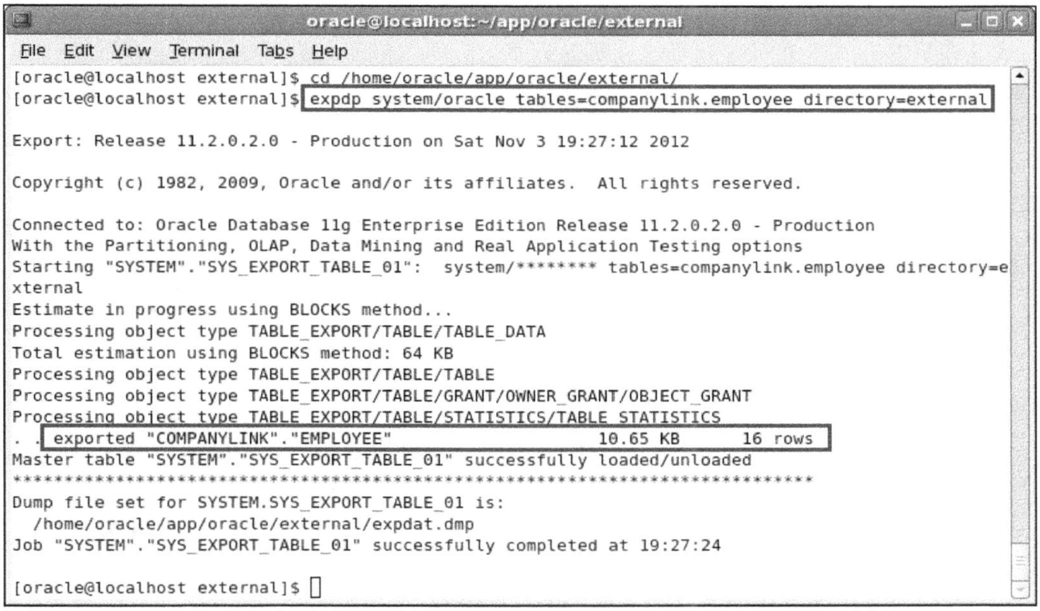
oracle@localhost:~/app/oracle/external
File Edit View Terminal Tabs Help
[oracle@localhost external]$ cd /home/oracle/app/oracle/external/
[oracle@localhost external]$ expdp system/oracle tables=companylink.employee directory=external
Export: Release 11.2.0.2.0 - Production on Sat Nov 3 19:27:12 2012
Copyright (c) 1982, 2009, Oracle and/or its affiliates. All rights reserved.
Connected to: Oracle Database 11g Enterprise Edition Release 11.2.0.2.0 - Production
With the Partitioning, OLAP, Data Mining and Real Application Testing options
Starting "SYSTEM"."SYS_EXPORT_TABLE_01": system/******** tables=companylink.employee directory=e
xternal
Estimate in progress using BLOCKS method...
Processing object type TABLE_EXPORT/TABLE/TABLE_DATA
Total estimation using BLOCKS method: 64 KB
Processing object type TABLE_EXPORT/TABLE/TABLE
Processing object type TABLE_EXPORT/TABLE/GRANT/OWNER_GRANT/OBJECT_GRANT
Processing object type TABLE_EXPORT/TABLE/STATISTICS/TABLE_STATISTICS
. . exported "COMPANYLINK"."EMPLOYEE" 10.65 KB 16 rows
Master table "SYSTEM"."SYS_EXPORT_TABLE_01" successfully loaded/unloaded
****
Dump file set for SYSTEM.SYS_EXPORT_TABLE_01 is:
/home/oracle/app/oracle/external/expdat.dmp
Job "SYSTEM"."SYS_EXPORT_TABLE_01" successfully completed at 19:27:24
[oracle@localhost external]$

Here we invoke Data Pump export using `expdp` followed by the username and password of the user performing the export and two keywords, `tables` and `directory`. The `tables` keyword specifies the name of the table to be exported, while `directory` indicates the name of the directory object that points to the destination directory for the output dump file. This directory now contains two files from the export, `expdat.dmp`, the default name of the dump file, and `export.log`, the log of the Data Pump session.

Although we can take the approach of specifying all the keywords on the command line when using Data Pump, as with SQL*Loader, it is generally clearer to use a **parameter file**. We can specify each keyword in this file, allowing for better organization. Let's create a parameter file and explore a few more keywords for our export.

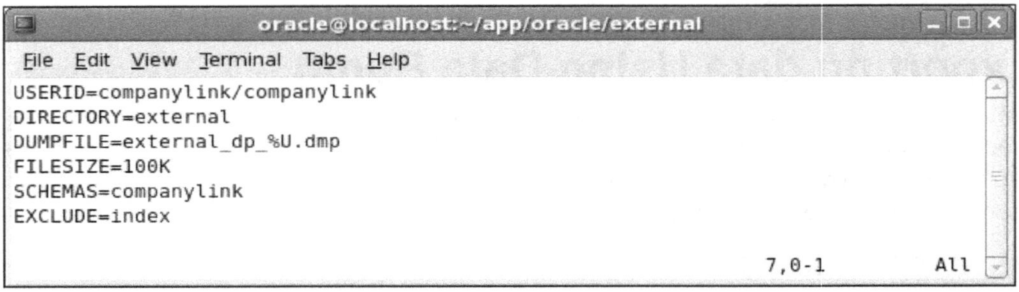
oracle@localhost:~/app/oracle/external
File Edit View Terminal Tabs Help
USERID=companylink/companylink
DIRECTORY=external
DUMPFILE=external_dp_%U.dmp
FILESIZE=100K
SCHEMAS=companylink
EXCLUDE=index
7,0-1 All

Here we create a parameter file, `external_dp.par`, which contains several keywords that control the export job. Let's examine them.

- `USERID`: This is the username and password that will run the job.
- `DIRECTORY`: This is the name of the directory object used.
- `DUMPFILE`: This is the name of the dump file that will be output. We use the %U qualifier (for unique) to guarantee a uniquely numbered file will be output in the case of multiple files.
- `FILESIZE`: This is the max size of a dump file. When that size is reached, another will be created.
- `SCHEMAS`: This is the name of the schema that will be exported. In this case, all of the tables in the `companylink` schema will be exported.
- `EXCLUDE`: This specifies the exclusion of indexes from being exported.

So, in summary, the parameter file indicates that we will export the entire `companylink` schema to the `external` directory in dump files with a max size of 100K, excluding any indexes. Let's run this now.

```
oracle@localhost:~/app/oracle/external
File  Edit  View  Terminal  Tabs  Help
[oracle@localhost external]$ expdp parfile=external_dp.par

Export: Release 11.2.0.2.0 - Production on Sat Nov 10 13:32:35 2012

Copyright (c) 1982, 2009, Oracle and/or its affiliates.  All rights reserved.

Connected to: Oracle Database 11g Enterprise Edition Release 11.2.0.2.0 - Produc
tion
With the Partitioning, OLAP, Data Mining and Real Application Testing options
Starting "COMPANYLINK"."SYS_EXPORT_SCHEMA_01":  companylink/******** parfile=ext
ernal_dp.par
Estimate in progress using BLOCKS method...
Processing object type SCHEMA_EXPORT/TABLE/TABLE_DATA
Total estimation using BLOCKS method: 1.062 MB
```

We will invoke Data Pump export using the `parfile=external_dp.par` command-line syntax to direct export to take the parameter file as input for all keywords. The export completes successfully.

```
oracle@localhost:~/app/oracle/external
File  Edit  View  Terminal  Tabs  Help
. . exported "COMPANYLINK"."MESSAGE"                     6.710 KB       9 rows
. . exported "COMPANYLINK"."PROJECT"                     6.695 KB       5 rows
. . exported "COMPANYLINK"."TEST_TAB"                    5.421 KB       1 rows
. . exported "COMPANYLINK"."WEBSITE"                     7.781 KB       8 rows
. . exported "COMPANYLINK"."AUDIT_TEST"                      0 KB       0 rows
. . exported "COMPANYLINK"."EMAIL_COPY"                      0 KB       0 rows
. . exported "COMPANYLINK"."EXAMPLE_TABLE"                   0 KB       0 rows
Master table "COMPANYLINK"."SYS_EXPORT_SCHEMA_01" successfully loaded/unloaded
******************************************************************************
Dump file set for COMPANYLINK.SYS_EXPORT_SCHEMA_01 is:
  /home/oracle/app/oracle/external/external_dp_01.dmp
  /home/oracle/app/oracle/external/external_dp_02.dmp
  /home/oracle/app/oracle/external/external_dp_03.dmp
  /home/oracle/app/oracle/external/external_dp_04.dmp
  /home/oracle/app/oracle/external/external_dp_05.dmp
Job "COMPANYLINK"."SYS_EXPORT_SCHEMA_01" successfully completed at 13:33:22

[oracle@localhost external]$ 
```

The output indicates that five dump files have been generated, each limited to 100K. We can confirm this by examining our `external` directory.

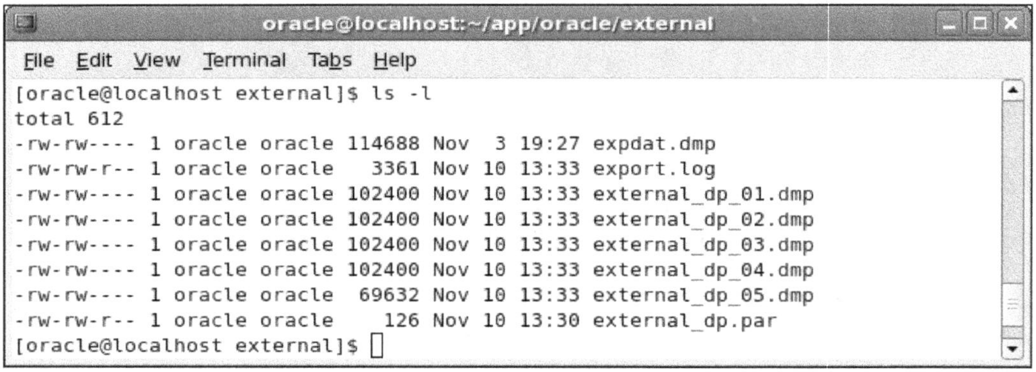
oracle@localhost:~/app/oracle/external
File Edit View Terminal Tabs Help
[oracle@localhost external]$ ls -l
total 612
-rw-rw---- 1 oracle oracle 114688 Nov 3 19:27 expdat.dmp
-rw-rw-r-- 1 oracle oracle   3361 Nov 10 13:33 export.log
-rw-rw---- 1 oracle oracle 102400 Nov 10 13:33 external_dp_01.dmp
-rw-rw---- 1 oracle oracle 102400 Nov 10 13:33 external_dp_02.dmp
-rw-rw---- 1 oracle oracle 102400 Nov 10 13:33 external_dp_03.dmp
-rw-rw---- 1 oracle oracle 102400 Nov 10 13:33 external_dp_04.dmp
-rw-rw---- 1 oracle oracle 69632 Nov 10 13:33 external_dp_05.dmp
-rw-rw-r-- 1 oracle oracle   126 Nov 10 13:30 external_dp.par
[oracle@localhost external]$

Importing data using Data Pump

Data is generally exported for one of two reasons. Exports might be done to preserve an existing snapshot of any number of tables or schemas — a process we might refer to as a **logical backup**. Thus, if data is lost or mishandled through DML statements, we can return the table to the state it was in when the export was taken. However, often data is exported so that it can be migrated into another database. This process involves importing the data with Data Pump import, which is invoked using the `impdp` utility from the command line. In addition to simply importing the data into the database in the same way that it was exported, Data Pump import can also do a certain amount of data transformation. During import, we can direct the source table names to be changed, remap one schema or tablespace to another, or even restrict imported data using a `WHERE` clause.

> **The real-world DBA**
>
> Even though we might use the term "logical backup" for exports, we should never confuse them with an actual database backup. While exports can store table data, they cannot be used to restore the infrastructure of a database the way an RMAN backup can. Exports are also point-in-time snapshots of table data, so there is no way to use them in conjunction with archivelogs to recover them up to the point of failure. Although it is recommended practice to use both, exports are not a substitute for true database level backups.

Let's perform a simple Data Pump import to familiarize ourselves with the concepts. We'll use an existing export from a previous example as the source. We must remember that, when a table is exported, it is exported by its name. If we were to directly run an import without specifying the name of our new table, Data Pump would attempt to place the data in the existing source table. Thus, we'll use `REMAP_TABLE` to change the name of the destination table.

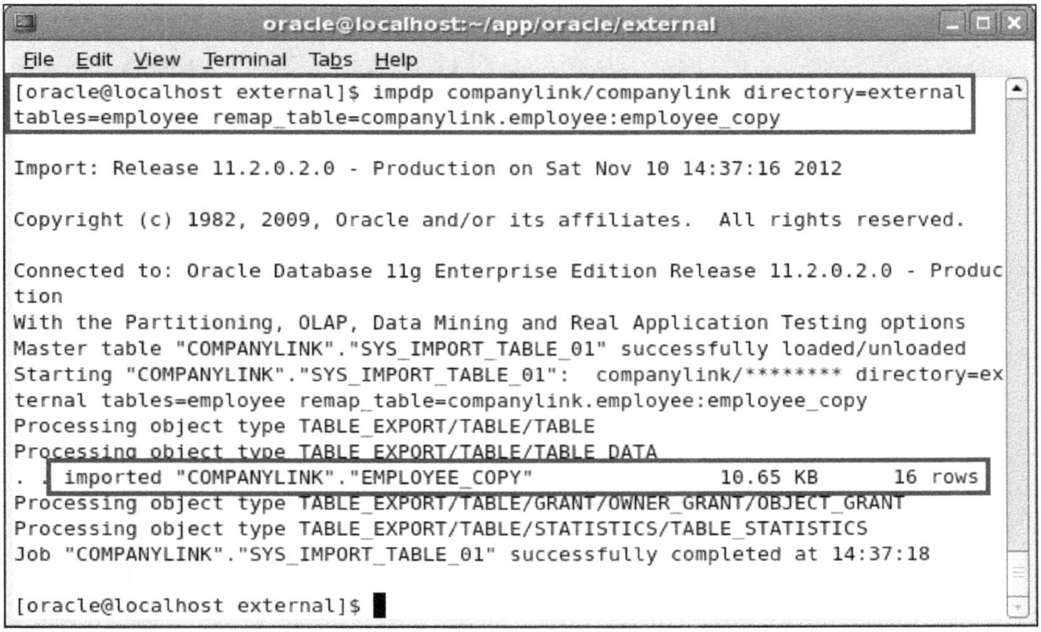

```
oracle@localhost:~/app/oracle/external
File Edit View Terminal Tabs Help
[oracle@localhost external]$ impdp companylink/companylink directory=external
tables=employee remap_table=companylink.employee:employee_copy

Import: Release 11.2.0.2.0 - Production on Sat Nov 10 14:37:16 2012

Copyright (c) 1982, 2009, Oracle and/or its affiliates.  All rights reserved.

Connected to: Oracle Database 11g Enterprise Edition Release 11.2.0.2.0 - Produc
tion
With the Partitioning, OLAP, Data Mining and Real Application Testing options
Master table "COMPANYLINK"."SYS_IMPORT_TABLE_01" successfully loaded/unloaded
Starting "COMPANYLINK"."SYS_IMPORT_TABLE_01":  companylink/******** directory=ex
ternal tables=employee remap_table=companylink.employee:employee_copy
Processing object type TABLE_EXPORT/TABLE/TABLE
Processing object type TABLE_EXPORT/TABLE/TABLE_DATA
. . imported "COMPANYLINK"."EMPLOYEE_COPY"                   10.65 KB      16 rows
Processing object type TABLE_EXPORT/TABLE/GRANT/OWNER_GRANT/OBJECT_GRANT
Processing object type TABLE_EXPORT/TABLE/STATISTICS/TABLE_STATISTICS
Job "COMPANYLINK"."SYS_IMPORT_TABLE_01" successfully completed at 14:37:18

[oracle@localhost external]$
```

We will invoke Data Pump import using the `impdp` command and specify several keywords. We indicate that `external` is the name of the directory object that contains our source dump file. It is interesting to note here that, since we have not specified the name of the dump file, Data Pump will choose the default name, `expdat.dmp`, as the source file. Thus, our first export of the employee table alone is used, rather than the schema-level export we performed. We'll use that export as a source for a more advanced import shortly. We specify the table to import using the `tables` keyword and `remap_table` to supply the new table name. We can query from the `employee_copy` table to see and verify our results.

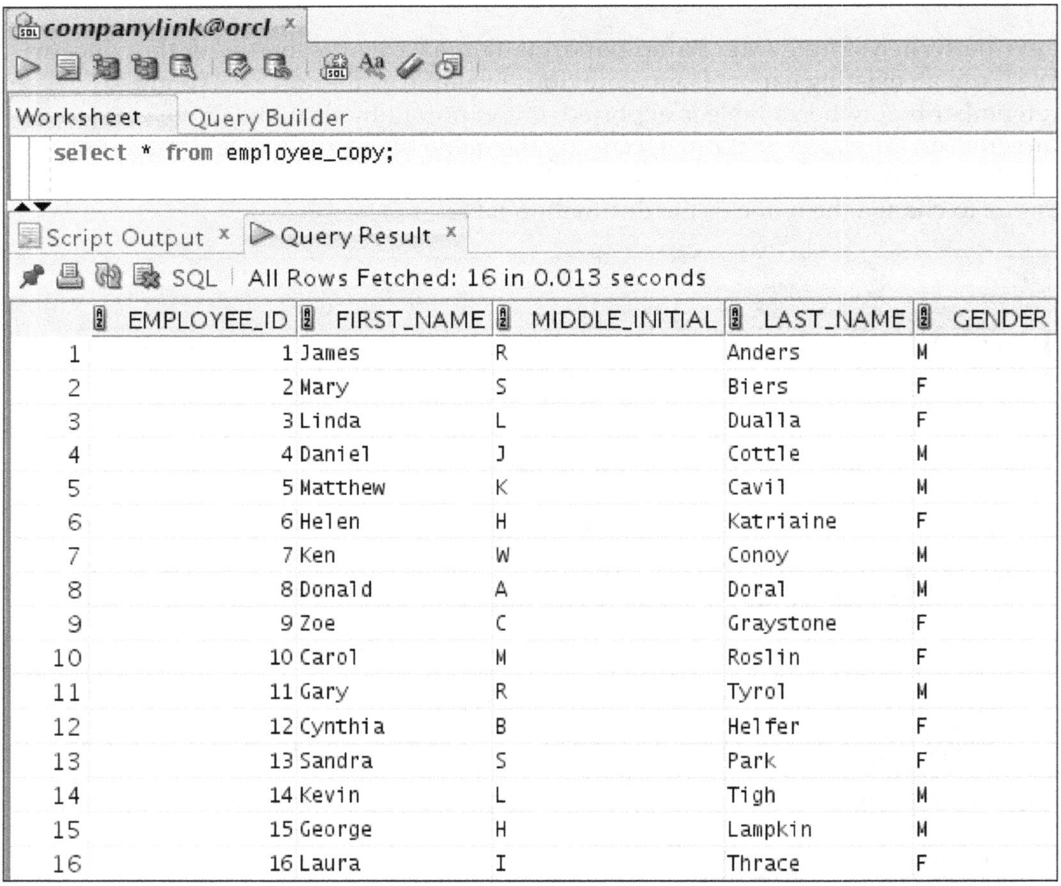
companylink@orcl
Worksheet
Query Builder
select * from employee_copy;
Script Output
Query Result
SQL
All Rows Fetched: 16 in 0.013 seconds

	EMPLOYEE_ID	FIRST_NAME	MIDDLE_INITIAL	LAST_NAME	GENDER
1	1	James	R	Anders	M
2	2	Mary	S	Biers	F
3	3	Linda	L	Dualla	F
4	4	Daniel	J	Cottle	M
5	5	Matthew	K	Cavil	M
6	6	Helen	H	Katriaine	F
7	7	Ken	W	Conoy	M
8	8	Donald	A	Doral	M
9	9	Zoe	C	Graystone	F
10	10	Carol	M	Roslin	F
11	11	Gary	R	Tyrol	M
12	12	Cynthia	B	Helfer	F
13	13	Sandra	S	Park	F
14	14	Kevin	L	Tigh	M
15	15	George	H	Lampkin	M
16	16	Laura	I	Thrace	F

As with Data Pump export, it is a good practice to use a parameter file with more complex imports. The names of export and import parameters are very consistent, making them easier to remember. Let's prepare an import parameter file, named `external_impdp.par`.

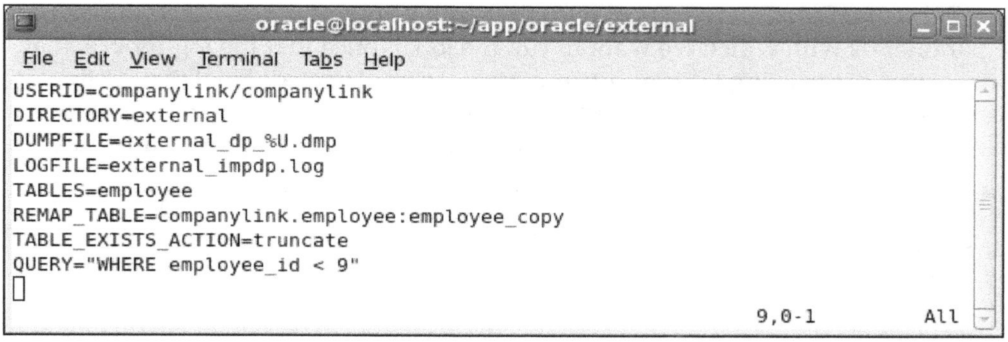
oracle@localhost:~/app/oracle/external
File Edit View Terminal Tabs Help
USERID=companylink/companylink
DIRECTORY=external
DUMPFILE=external_dp_%U.dmp
LOGFILE=external_impdp.log
TABLES=employee
REMAP_TABLE=companylink.employee:employee_copy
TABLE_EXISTS_ACTION=truncate
QUERY="WHERE employee_id < 9"
9,0-1 All

This import uses a number of keywords to control the nature of the job, several of which we've seen before. The `TABLE_EXISTS_ACTION` keyword indicates the action that will be taken if the destination table, `employee_copy`, exists, which it does. In our job, we specify a value of `truncate` that directs Data Pump to issue a `TRUNCATE TABLE` command before importing the data. We also use the `QUERY` keyword to specify that only those rows that meet the query condition we've specified will be imported. In short, we will import the `employee` table from our schema-level export into the `employee_copy` table, truncating the table before import and only importing rows with an `employee_id` less than 9. Let's run this import now and see if we get the expected results.

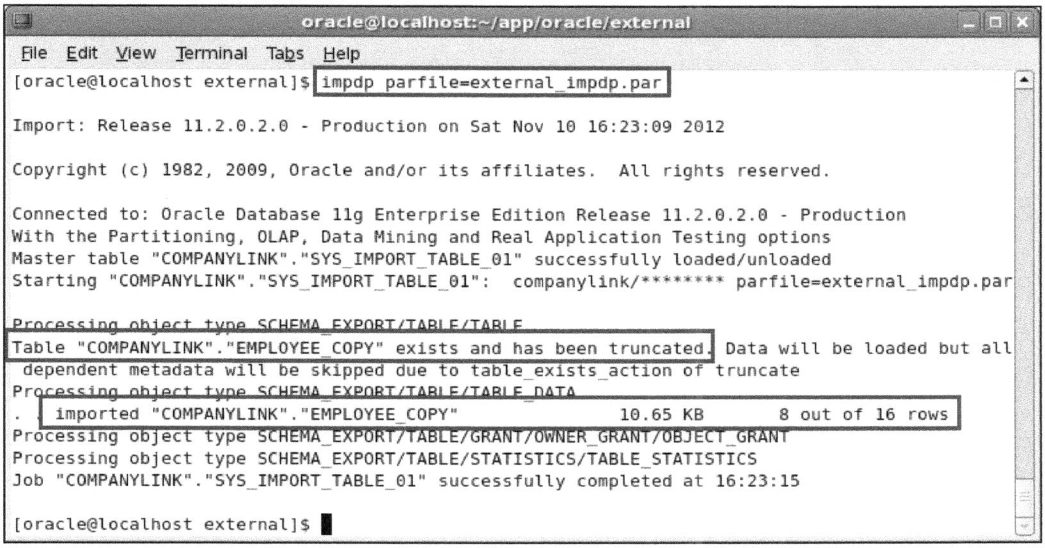
oracle@localhost:~/app/oracle/external
File Edit View Terminal Tabs Help
[oracle@localhost external]$ impdp parfile=external_impdp.par
Import: Release 11.2.0.2.0 - Production on Sat Nov 10 16:23:09 2012
Copyright (c) 1982, 2009, Oracle and/or its affiliates. All rights reserved.
Connected to: Oracle Database 11g Enterprise Edition Release 11.2.0.2.0 - Production
With the Partitioning, OLAP, Data Mining and Real Application Testing options
Master table "COMPANYLINK"."SYS_IMPORT_TABLE_01" successfully loaded/unloaded
Starting "COMPANYLINK"."SYS_IMPORT_TABLE_01": companylink/******** parfile=external_impdp.par
Processing object type SCHEMA_EXPORT/TABLE/TABLE
Table "COMPANYLINK"."EMPLOYEE_COPY" exists and has been truncated. Data will be loaded but all
dependent metadata will be skipped due to table_exists_action of truncate
Processing object type SCHEMA_EXPORT/TABLE/TABLE_DATA
. . imported "COMPANYLINK"."EMPLOYEE_COPY" 10.65 KB 8 out of 16 rows
Processing object type SCHEMA_EXPORT/TABLE/GRANT/OWNER_GRANT/OBJECT_GRANT
Processing object type SCHEMA_EXPORT/TABLE/STATISTICS/TABLE_STATISTICS
Job "COMPANYLINK"."SYS_IMPORT_TABLE_01" successfully completed at 16:23:15
[oracle@localhost external]$

We will invoke Data Pump import with the same keyword, `parfile`, to indicate the parameters with which we want to run the job. Notice that the log reports that it recognizes the existing table and truncates it, as we directed. Finally, note that because we specified an import condition with the `QUERY` keyword, only 8 of the table's 16 rows are imported. We can verify this by querying our destination table.

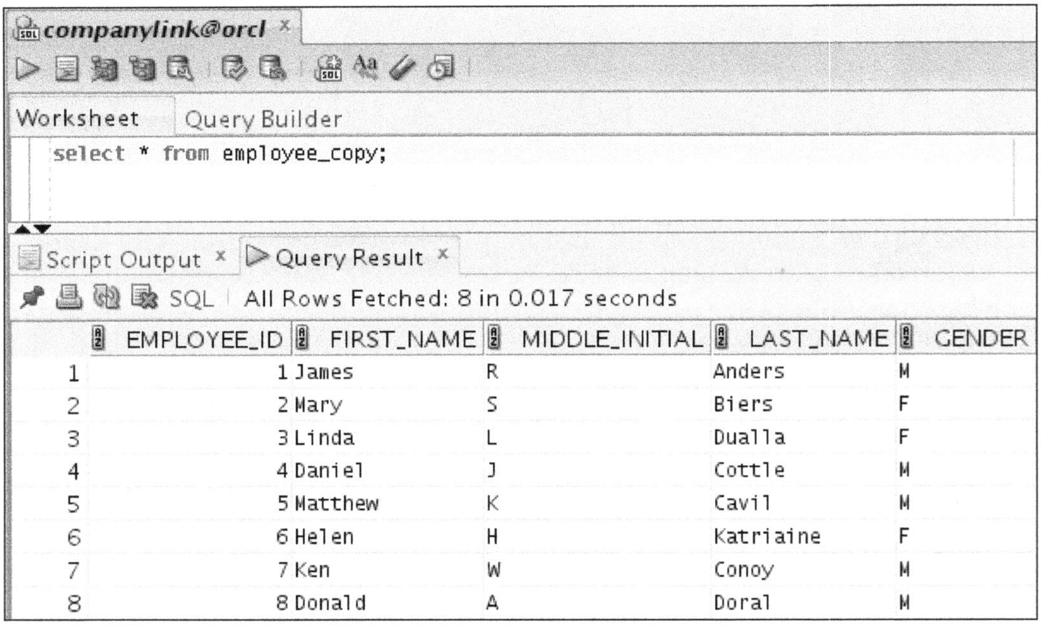
companylink@orcl
Worksheet
Query Builder
select * from employee_copy;
Script Output
Query Result
SQL
All Rows Fetched: 8 in 0.017 seconds
EMPLOYEE_ID FIRST_NAME MIDDLE_INITIAL LAST_NAME GENDER
1 1 James R Anders M
2 2 Mary S Biers F
3 3 Linda L Dualla F
4 4 Daniel J Cottle M
5 5 Matthew K Cavil M
6 6 Helen H Katriaine F
7 7 Ken W Conoy M
8 8 Donald A Doral M

Using Data Pump with NETWORK_LINK

To complete our look at Data Pump, we point out one interesting feature that can greatly improve the efficiency with which we migrate data. Provided that the source database and the target database for migration can communicate over a network, we can use the `NETWORK_LINK` keyword to transfer data directly over the network, without the need to create dump files. This can substantially decrease both the time and disk space required for data migration. It can decrease time since the number of operations required is cut from two to one—we only need to import the data from the source directly into the destination. Disk space is not required at all since no dump files are generated. In order for this operation to execute, a database link to the source database is required. For example, let's imagine we're logged into a database other than our `Companylink` database, called `EXTRN_DB`. This database stores a database link object, called `C_LINK`, that points to the `Companylink` database. We want to execute an import on `EXTRN_DB` that imports the data from the `companylink` schema. We could export the data from the `Companylink` database, move the dump files across the network, and then import them into `EXTRN_DB`. Or we could use the `NETWORK_LINK` feature. A parameter file for such an operation might look like this:

```
oracle@localhost:~/app/oracle/external
File  Edit  View  Terminal  Tabs  Help
USERID=companylink/companylink
DIRECTORY=external
LOGFILE=migrate_data_nl.log
SCHEMAS=companylink
NETWORK_LINK=c_link
                                                   6,0-1          All
```

Certification objectives covered

- Describe and use methods to move data
- Explain the general architecture of Oracle Data Pump
- Use Data Pump Export and Import tools to move data between Oracle databases

Summary

In this chapter, we've examined the many ways we can migrate database data in Oracle. We've explored how external tables can be created to read data directly from an external file. We've examined the SQL*Loader tool and used it to read data from an external file and load it into the database. Finally, we've used Oracle's Data Pump to export data from and import data into database tables, as well as examining a number of Data Pump's transformational features.

Test your knowledge

Q. 1. Which of the following types of database objects is required in order to utilize an external table?

a. An index
b. A PL/SQL package
c. A directory object
d. A partitioned table

Q. 2. Your applications make use of an external table. Which of the following types of statements could be executed against it?

a. `SELECT`
b. `DELETE`
c. `CREATE INDEX`
d. `UPDATE`

Q. 3. In which type of scenario would you be best served using an external table?

a. The source data resides in a Data Pump dump file.
b. The source data resides on a remote database.
c. The source data resides in a CSV and is too large to load directly into the database.
d. The source data contains a number of anomalies and poor structure.

Q. 4. Which of the following is correct regarding the load paths available with SQL*Loader?

a. A direct path load generates redo and undo data in the same way as DML statements.
b. Foreign keys must first be disabled when using a conventional path load.
c. A direct path load affects user performance less negatively than a conventional path load.
d. A conventional path load constructs `INSERT` statements using bind variables.

Q. 5. What is the purpose of the `CONTROL` keyword in a SQL*Loader parameter file?

a. It defines the name of the control file for the SQL*Loader job.
b. It specifies the location of the database control files.
c. It indicates the name of the SQL*Loader job.
d. It defines the load path which will be used.

Q. 6. Which type of load operation is not supported by SQL*Loader?

a. `INSERT`
b. `TRUNCATE`
c. `DELETE`
d. `APPEND`

Q. 7. Which of the following statements is true regarding Data Pump?

a. It can be used to load flatfile data.
b. The use of Data Pump requires the use of `expdp` and `impdp` to run.
c. Its choice of load path, either external table or direct, is user-selectable.
d. It is possible to monitor a Data Pump job from a separate session.

Q. 8. We want to load the objects in the `companylink` schema into a new schema called `new_app` in a separate database. Which Data Pump keyword option would be useful for completing this task?

a. `REMAP_TABLE`
b. `REMAP_SCHEMA`
c. `REMAP_TABLESPACE`
d. `TABLE_EXISTS_ACTION`

Q. 9. Which of these is not a feature supported by Data Pump?

a. The ability to read the dump files generated by traditional Export and Import tools.
b. The ability to compress dump files.
c. The ability to encrypt dump files.
d. The ability to export and import only table structure without data.

Q. 10. You need to migrate data from one database to another. However, neither the source nor the destination hosts have enough space to store the dump files required. Which of the following options can aid you in migrating the data?

a. Export the data using `DIRECT=TRUE`.
b. Import the data using a remote username and password.
c. Export the data using `REMAP_DATABASE`.
d. Import the data using `NETWORK_LINK`.

Preparing for the Certification Exam

In this book, we've laid out the subjects needed to take the Oracle Database 11*g*: Administration I exam. In order to pass this exam, you'll need to achieve a high level of competence in these areas. However, there are some helpful hints that are mentioned here to help you on your way.

About the exam

This exam is listed as exam code 1Z0-052 on the Oracle Certification website at `http://certification.oracle.com`.

This is given as a proctored exam at a participating Pearson VUE exam site. A candidate is given 90 minutes to answer 70 questions and must achieve a passing score of 66 percent. The 70 test questions are taken randomly from a larger bank of questions by the testing software. The test itself is in multiple choice format; however, the number of choices can vary greatly between questions. Some questions have as many as six possible choices for the answer. Additionally, some questions have multiple correct answers; the candidate must respond with all the correct answers in order to achieve full credit on the question. The exam costs $195 to take. In the event the candidate fails the exam, they must wait 14 days before retaking the exam. The 1Z0-52 exam is the second test required to achieve the **Oracle Certified Association (OCA)** certification. The first test required is 1Z0-051—Oracle Database 11*g*: SQL Fundamentals I. For assistance on that exam, refer to the first book of this series.

Helpful exam hints

Some of the hints that might prove helpful are as follows:

- **Understand the subject matter**: Exam 1Z0-052 requires an extensive knowledge of the subject matter. In reality, it is one of the most comprehensive tests given in the entire Oracle Database Certification series. Each subject area must be thoroughly understood before taking the test.
- **Don't cut corners**: Passing the test is all about preparation. Where possible, don't drag out your preparation over a long period of time. Try to set aside a period of time that you will spend in dedicated preparation, and then take the test. Do not skip subjects. Your exam will be 70 questions generated from a larger bank of questions. While it is likely that not every subject will be on your exam, any subject is possible. Don't risk skipping any particular subject.
- **Know your terms**: This exam is heavily oriented toward terminology. Being familiar with the terms involved is crucial to passing the exam. In this book, we have focused on using the terms that are present on the test to help facilitate this. However, the terms used on the test are not always those used by real-world DBAs. When you see terms in this book with which you are unfamiliar, keep this in mind.
- **Learn by doing**: Most people learn a subject more thoroughly by actually doing it. In this book, we began by taking the reader through the process of installing Oracle and building a database to facilitate the "learn by doing" process Take advantage of the sample database and examples used in this book.
- **Supplement your learning**: This book covers all the necessary subjects to pass the exam, but don't hesitate to supplement your knowledge from other sources. Take advantage of practice exams and sample questions where possible. Search the Internet—some sites have forums visited by people who have taken the test. Their comments may give you some insight into whether you're ready to take the exam. However, beware of the "braindump" type of practice exams. Many have inaccurate questions and answers.
- **Don't sweat it**: Be mentally and physically prepared on the day of the exam. Eat properly and get plenty of rest. Prepare well, and be confident. Many candidates like to schedule the exam in the earlier part of the day so they're mentally fresh. Choose a test site with which you're familiar to minimize the risk of being late. Stress is a candidate's worst enemy.
- **Watch the wording**: Certification tests in general can be notorious for the wording of their questions, and Oracle's are no exceptions. Read each question carefully. Test candidates generally do not have trouble completing the exam within the time allotted provided they are properly prepared.

- **Watch out for poorly worded questions and double negatives**: The exam is multiple choice, and some questions have many correct answers. You must get every one of the answers correct for full credit on a question; only partial credit is awarded for each correct choice.
- **Use the questions to your advantage**: There is no penalty for guessing in the exam, so make sure you answer all the questions. Also, you have the ability to skip questions and return to them later. The answer for one question may help jog your memory on another. When you read a question, try to deduce the solution without immediately referring to the possible answers. If you think you're right, don't let the answers sway you. Some candidates like to skim the test and complete the "easier" questions first. This can give you some momentum for the remainder of the test.

A recommended strategy for preparation

While passing the certification test is certainly the goal, earning a certification without understanding the subject matter is useless. Many "braindumps" and "exam crams" attempt to push a candidate through the certification process, mostly on memorization. Even if a candidate does pass the exam, they are left without the requisite knowledge to function in their certified field. This book attempts to actually teach you proficiency in the subjects you need, and includes many examples to prepare you for becoming a real-world DBA. To that end, we recommend that you take a real-world approach in preparing for the test. It may take longer than simply cramming for the exam, but when you're finished, you'll be much better prepared.

After you've finished this book, take a "dry run" at the test. Without reviewing, go back and answer the questions in this book as well as any sample questions you may have from other sources. When you check your answers, make a note of the questions you've missed, as well as their subject areas. From this, you have a list of subjects on which you need to focus. This prevents you from spending an inordinate amount of time on the subjects you already know. Using your list of review subjects, go back through the book and re-read the sections that cover these areas. Work through the examples again and write your own variations of these examples. For instance, say that, after completing your dry run, you find that you have a good grasp of **Automatic Memory Management** (**AMM**), but are still unsure as to which parameters are used in **Automatic Shared Memory Management** (**ASMM**). Read through that section in *Chapter 10, Managing Database Performance*, and try out the examples. Then, see if you can configure each type of memory management in your example database. Once you are done with your review of the subject areas, take the test questions again. Repeat the process of studying and working with the remaining subject areas. Use this iterative process to fully prepare for every subject. Once you feel you're ready, take the test. Good luck!

Test Your Knowledge – Answers

Chapter 1, Introducing the Oracle Relational Database System

Q1	c
Q2	b
Q3	d
Q4	c
Q5	a

Chapter 2, Installing the Oracle Database Software

Q1	b
Q2	d
Q3	c
Q4	b
Q5	c
Q6	d
Q7	b

Q 8	a
Q 9	b
Q 10	d
Q 11	b
Q 12	c
Q 13	d

Chapter 3, Creating the Oracle Database

Q 1	c
Q 2	c
Q 3	d
Q 4	c
Q 5	c
Q 6	d
Q 7	a
Q 8	b
Q 9	a
Q 10	d
Q 11	c
Q 12	b
Q 13	c
Q 14	a
Q 15	c

Chapter 4, Examining the Oracle Architecture

Q 1	b
Q 2	d
Q 3	c
Q 4	d
Q 5	b

Q 6	a
Q 7	d
Q 8	c
Q 9	c
Q 10	b
Q 11	d
Q 12	b
Q 13	a
Q 14	b

Chapter 5, Managing Oracle Storage Structures

Q 1	a
Q 2	d
Q 3	d
Q 4	c
Q 5	c
Q 6	b
Q 7	c
Q 8	a
Q 9	b
Q 10	d
Q 11	b
Q 12	d

Chapter 6, Managing the Oracle Instance

Q 1	b
Q 2	b
Q 3	c
Q 4	b
Q 5	a

Q 6	c
Q 7	a
Q 8	a
Q 9	d
Q 10	d
Q 11	d
Q 12	b
Q 13	c
Q 14	c
Q 15	a
Q 16	d
Q 17	a

Chapter 7, Managing Security

Q 1	c
Q 2	d
Q 3	d
Q 4	b
Q 5	d
Q 6	c
Q 7	a
Q 8	d
Q 9	d
Q 10	c
Q 11	b
Q 12	c
Q 13	c
Q 14	d

Chapter 8, Managing Concurrency

Q 1	b
Q 2	c
Q 3	a
Q 4	c
Q 5	b
Q 6	c
Q 7	a, d
Q 8	d
Q 9	c
Q 10	a
Q 11	b
Q 12	a, b
Q 13	c
Q 14	c
Q 15	c, d

Chapter 9, Configuring an Oracle Network

Q 1	b
Q 2	c
Q 3	a
Q 4	d
Q 5	b
Q 6	d
Q 7	d
Q 8	a
Q 9	b

Chapter 10, Managing Database Performance

Q 1	b
Q 2	c
Q 3	c
Q 4	c
Q 5	b
Q 6	a
Q 7	a
Q 8	b
Q 9	d
Q 10	c
Q 11	d
Q 12	b
Q 13	b
Q 14	c
Q 15	d

Chapter 11, Understanding Backup and Recovery Concepts

Q 1	c
Q 2	a
Q 3	d
Q 4	c
Q 5	a
Q 6	d
Q 7	b
Q 8	c
Q 9	d
Q 10	a
Q 11	d

Q 12	a
Q 13	b

Chapter 12, Performing Database Backups

Q 1	c
Q 2	a
Q 3	c
Q 4	d
Q 5	a, c
Q 6	b
Q 7	b
Q 8	b
Q 9	d
Q 10	c
Q 11	a
Q 12	b
Q 13	a

Chapter 13, Performing Database Recovery

Q 1	d
Q 2	a, c
Q 3	b
Q 4	d
Q 5	d
Q 6	a
Q 7	c
Q 8	c
Q 9	d

Chapter 14, Migrating Data

Q 1	c
Q 2	a
Q 3	c
Q 4	d
Q 5	a
Q 6	c
Q 7	d
Q 8	b
Q 9	a
Q 10	d

Online chapter 1, Managing Oracle Tables

Q 1	d
Q 2	c
Q 3	a
Q 4	a
Q 5	a
Q 6	d
Q 7	d
Q 8	b
Q 9	a
Q 10	d
Q 11	b
Q 12	c

Online chapter 2, Managing Other Database Objects

Q 1	b
Q 2	c
Q 3	b
Q 4	a
Q 5	c
Q 6	a
Q 7	b
Q 8	a
Q 9	d
Q 10	d
Q 11	b
Q 12	c
Q 13	b
Q 14	a

Index

Symbols

A

B

C

D

E

F

G

H

I

J

K

L

M

N

O

Q

R

T

U

V

W

[PACKT] enterprise
professional expertise distilled
PUBLISHING

Thank you for buying
OCA Oracle Database 11*g*: Database Administration I: A Real-World Certification Guide

About Packt Publishing

Packt, pronounced 'packed', published its first book "Mastering phpMyAdmin for Effective MySQL Management" in April 2004 and subsequently continued to specialize in publishing highly focused books on specific technologies and solutions.

Our books and publications share the experiences of your fellow IT professionals in adapting and customizing today's systems, applications, and frameworks. Our solution based books give you the knowledge and power to customize the software and technologies you're using to get the job done. Packt books are more specific and less general than the IT books you have seen in the past. Our unique business model allows us to bring you more focused information, giving you more of what you need to know, and less of what you don't.

Packt is a modern, yet unique publishing company, which focuses on producing quality, cutting-edge books for communities of developers, administrators, and newbies alike. For more information, please visit our website: `www.packtpub.com`.

About Packt Enterprise

In 2010, Packt launched two new brands, Packt Enterprise and Packt Open Source, in order to continue its focus on specialization. This book is part of the Packt Enterprise brand, home to books published on enterprise software - software created by major vendors, including (but not limited to) IBM, Microsoft and Oracle, often for use in other corporations. Its titles will offer information relevant to a range of users of this software, including administrators, developers, architects, and end users.

Writing for Packt

We welcome all inquiries from people who are interested in authoring. Book proposals should be sent to author@packtpub.com. If your book idea is still at an early stage and you would like to discuss it first before writing a formal book proposal, contact us; one of our commissioning editors will get in touch with you.

We're not just looking for published authors; if you have strong technical skills but no writing experience, our experienced editors can help you develop a writing career, or simply get some additional reward for your expertise.

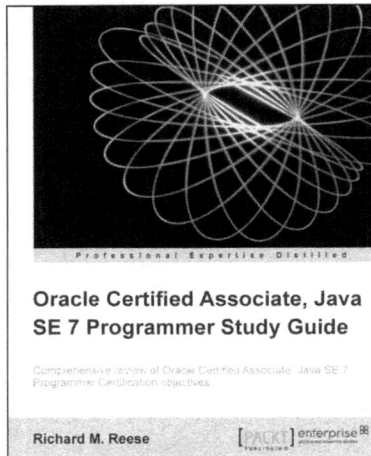

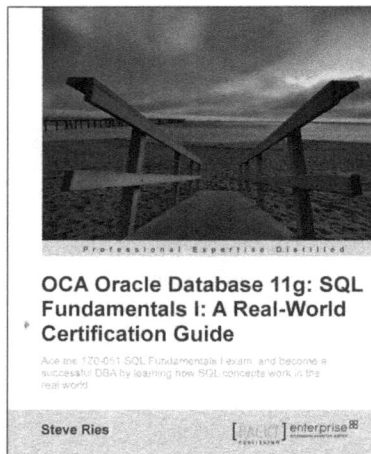

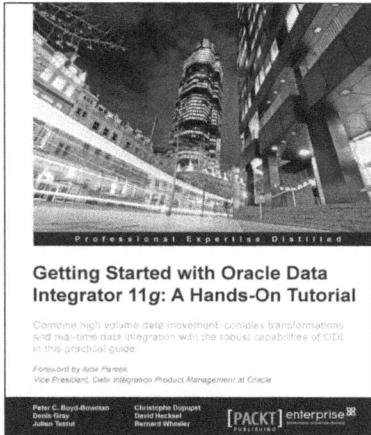

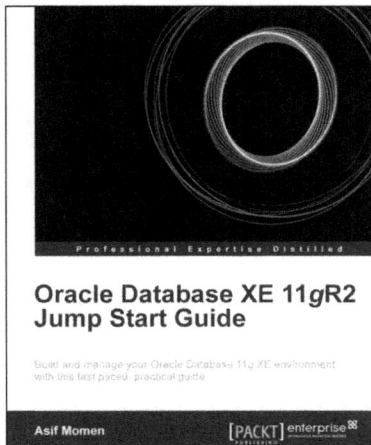

www.ingramcontent.com/pod-product-compliance
Lightning Source LLC
Chambersburg PA
CBHW060946210326
41598CB00031B/4729
9781849687300